Third Edition

CRISIS ASSESSMENT, INTERVENTION, AND PREVENTION

Lisa R. Jackson-Cherry
Marymount University

Bradley T. Erford
Loyola University Maryland

330 Hudson Street, NY, NY 10013

Director, Teacher Education & the Helping Professions: Kevin M. Davis
Portfolio Manager: Rebecca Fox-Gieg
Content Producer: Janelle Rogers
Content Project Manager: Pamela D. Bennett
Media Project Manager: Lauren Carlson
Portfolio Management Assistant: Anne McAlpine
Executive Field Marketing Manager: Krista Clark
Executive Product Marketing Manager: Christopher Barry
Procurement Specialist: Deidra Smith
Cover Designer: Melissa Welch
Cover Photo: Getty Images/Feng Wei Photography
Full-Service Project Management: Garima Khosla, iEnergizer Aptara®, Ltd
Composition: iEnergizer Aptara®, Ltd
Printer/Binder: LSC/Crawfordsville
Cover Printer: LSC/Crawfordsville
Text Font: 10/12, Palatino LT Pro

Library of Congress Cataloging-in-Publication Data available upon request

ISBN 10:   0-13-452271-0
ISBN 13: 978-0-13-452271-5

To all crisis workers who give selflessly to alleviate the pain of others. This work is also dedicated to my family, who has sacrificed and continues to be my source of support: my husband, Jim; my daughters, Gabrielle and Alexandra; and my parents, Barbara Jackson and Francisco Japzon, M.D. I am ever-mindful that all my fortunes and blessings are gifts from God.

LRJC

This effort is dedicated to The One: the Giver of energy, passion, and understanding; Who makes life worth living and endeavors worth pursuing and accomplishing; the Teacher of love and forgiveness.

BTE

PREFACE

The purpose for writing this text was to convey the practical implications of and applications for dealing with crisis situations. Prior to September 11, 2001, crisis counselors' and university faculty members' conceptualization of crisis was generally limited to individual clients, primarily addressing suicidal client needs. But recent events (e.g., terrorism, school shootings, natural disasters), coupled with renewed societal concerns over continuing violence (e.g., homicide, intimate partner violence, rape, sexual abuse), have expanded our conceptualization of crisis and the needs of the new generation of counselors. This text addresses this expanded concept of crisis in today's world and includes the practical applications that will help crisis counselors to be able to serve diverse clients immediately in a changing world. Crisis intervention and crisis roles differ from traditional counseling. Understanding these differences is imperative to assisting individuals in a variety of crises. Crisis counselors, when able to assess and intervene effectively, may also assist individuals in responding to future crises—a preventive approach.

Preservice students and mental health professionals in the field need crisis intervention training to effectively intervene in the various crisis situations they will encounter in their roles as counselors with diverse populations and across settings. This short text provides vital information on assessing and reacting to various crises involving suicide, homicide, intimate partner violence, sexual assault/abuse, bereavement/grief, substance use, natural disasters, war, and terrorism. The text provides practical applications for various crisis situations experienced by crisis workers. The text allows students to become familiar with various crisis issues and situations and to practice necessary skills before encountering the problem for the first time in the field. The text features numerous crisis situations not found in other crisis texts and is of benefit to various counseling specialties (e.g., school counseling, university counseling, mental health counseling, and pastoral clinical mental health counseling). Students see the process as a whole and are exposed to crucial information, clinical considerations, and practical experiences on every crisis topic.

NEW TO THIS EDITION

The third edition of *Crisis Assessment, Intervention, and Prevention* has been purposefully revised with new and expanded content to address the needs of a diverse group of counselors in the field and counselors in training. The following features are new to this edition:

- Introduction of a new Task Model for Assessment and Intervention developed and integrated throughout the book.
- A new chapter addresses counselor safety issues.
- A new chapter addresses counselor self-care and wellness issues.
- A new chapter addresses needs and interventions with first responders in crisis situations.
- New and expanded chapters address crisis counseling in the community and schools/universities.
- Updated references and citations connect practitioners with the latest information.
- Standardized chapter features including case studies, Voices from the Field, Activities, Think About It features, and resource lists.

ORGANIZATION OF THIS TEXT

The text is divided into two parts. Part I: *Elements of Crisis Intervention,* which includes Chapters 1 through 5, reviews the fundamental information related to crises and crisis intervention.

In Chapter 1: *Basic Concepts of Crisis Intervention,* Lisa R. Jackson-Cherry, Jason M. McGlothlin, and Bradley T. Erford acknowledge that crises occur in a variety of settings for a variety of reasons. Responses to crises are equally variable. Chapter 1 also provides basic frameworks for assessing and conceptualizing crises, along with a discussion of how crisis intervention may differ from traditional counseling. A new task model of crisis assessment and intervention is introduced in Chapter 1 and integrated into all of the chapters. The model is a more comprehensive approach to assessing the whole person for a more accurate intervention.

Chapter 2: *Safety Concerns in Crisis Situations,* was written by Charlotte Daughhetee, James Jackson, and Latofia Parker. When responding to a crisis, counselors need to be able to act promptly, meaning that crisis preparedness is essential to best practice during emergency situations. A brief overview of crisis planning guidelines and crisis counselor safety procedures is presented.

In Chapter 3: *Ethical and Legal Considerations in Crisis Counseling,* Paul F. Hard, Laura L. Talbott-Forbes, and Mary L. Bartlett propose that crisis counselors well versed in crisis procedures and processes will be able to provide ethical, skilled help in all types of crisis conditions. The goal of this chapter is to provide information on ethical and legal considerations related to preventive measures, federal legislations, sentinel court findings, and best practices regarding privacy matters in crisis counseling.

Chapter 4: *Essential Crisis Intervention Skills,* by Bradley T. Erford and Lisa R. Jackson-Cherry, provides an overview of the fundamental skills needed to engage in effective crisis intervention work. The skills covered in this chapter focus on Ivey, Ivey and Zalaquett's (2012) microskills hierarchy. At the heart of this hierarchy is the basic listening sequence, an interrelated set of skills that will not only foster the development of rapport with clients but also aid in the identification of interventions to help achieve a successful resolution to the client's crisis state. Examples of the skills in use, as well as practice exercises to foster individual skill development, are provided.

Part I concludes with Chapter 5: *Loss Grief, and Bereavement,* by Lisa R. Jackson-Cherry and Bradley T. Erford, which covers approaches to crisis counseling with mourners, theories of grieving, and the variables that affect how a bereaved person mourns. A common element in most crisis events is the experience of grief, loss, and bereavement. The loss and grief can be connected to a person, things, role, occupations, sense of purpose, and meaning, etc. The chapter also addresses how timing, cause of death, and the role the relationship played in a person's life all mediate the mourning process, followed by an attempt to distinguish between "normal" grief and complicated bereavement. Chapter 5 concludes with an outline of the components that should be implemented when preparing for and providing effective death notifications. A death notification given with empathy, calmness, and accuracy of information can assist loved ones gain a sense of control. The information in this chapter has been included to assist crisis counselors in being prepared and equipped when called upon to either give or assist with a death notification. Effective death notifications decrease the need for intense debriefings and a complicated grief process, reduce counselor burnout, and may open the door for individuals to seek counseling when they are ready.

Part II: *Special Issues in Crisis Intervention* comprises the remaining chapters of the text.

Chapter 6: *Risk Assessment and Intervention: Suicide and Homicide,* by Judith Harrington and Charlotte Daughhetee, recognizes that suicide and homicide continue to play increasingly important roles in American society and on the world stage and that they affect us personally as we, family members, friends, and those in extended social networks struggle with the ever-increasing challenges of modern life. As personal liberty has increased, the chance for violent responses to stressful situations has increased. The effectiveness of the care given by professional emergency first responders, as well as the effectiveness of ordinary people in responding to their own crises and the crises of those about whom they care, is improved by background knowledge involving current trends in and treatments for suicide and homicide impulses.

Chapter 7: *Understanding and Treating Substance Use Disorders with Clients in Crisis*, by William R. Sterner, reviews substance use disorders and the disease of addiction, including causes, manifestations, and treatment. There are numerous models and theories about the causes of alcoholism and drug addiction, and this chapter introduces the medical and moral/legal models as well as important genetic, sociocultural, and psychological theories.

Chapter 8: *Intimate Partner Violence* is by Amy L. McLeod, John Muldoon, and Lisa R. Jackson-Cherry. Intimate partner violence (IPV) involves the infliction of physical, sexual, and/or emotional harm to a person by a current or former partner or spouse with the intent of establishing power and control over the abused partner. IPV is a major public health concern, and it is imperative that crisis counselors be able to recognize and respond to IPV survivors competently. This chapter provides an overview of the facts and figures associated with IPV, discusses the cycle of violence commonly experienced in abusive relationships, and explores various perspectives on survivors who stay in relationships with abusive partners. Common crisis issues experienced by IPV survivors, including dealing with physical injury, establishing immediate safety, and reporting IPV to the police, are also highlighted. In addition, this chapter explores special considerations regarding IPV in lesbian, gay, bisexual, and transgender (LGBT) relationships, relationships characterized by female-to-male violence, abusive relationships in racial and ethnic minority populations, and abusive dating relationships among adolescents and young adults. Guidelines for crisis counselors who are conducting IPV assessments, responding to IPV disclosure, planning for client safety, and addressing the emotional impact of IPV are provided. Finally, the goals, theories, and challenges associated with IPV offender intervention are discussed.

Chapter 9: *Sexual Violence*, by Robin Lee, Jennifer Jordan, and Elizabeth Schuler, reveals that sexual violence is one of the most underreported crimes, with survivors facing a number of potential physical, psychological, cognitive, behavioral, and emotional consequences. Crisis counselors who work with survivors of sexual violence need to be aware of the multitude of challenges these individuals face, best practices for treatment, and support services available in the local community.

In Chapter 10: *Child Sexual Abuse*, by Carrie Wachter Morris and Elizabeth Graves, child sexual abuse is defined, signs and symptoms described, treatment interventions discussed, and guidelines for working with law enforcement and child protective services personnel provided. In addition, this chapter addresses sexual offenders, their patterns of behavior, and common treatment options.

Chapter 11: *Military and First Responders*, by Seth C. W. Hayden and Lisa R. Jackson-Cherry, acknowledges that serving the needs of military personnel and families presents unique challenges for counselors working in a variety of settings. Military families are a significant part of our communities, with more than two-thirds residing in the larger civilian community and the remainder on military bases. While this population has long benefited from the work of skilled counselors, the current and anticipated needs of military and their family members requires an understanding of military culture in addition to effective methods to support this population. This chapter provides an in-depth discussion of the military experience and offers various approaches to assist military service members and their families. A new section to this chapter addresses the unique issues encountered by first responders. Law enforcement officers, emergency medical service professionals, and firefighters respond to various crisis situations daily and are exposed to various traumatic events that could impact their lives and their families. First responders are the first to arrive at a scene and to intervene in horrific and traumatic situations. Occupational stressors, medical emergencies, threats to personal safety, acts of violence, deaths, and crimes are common daily occurrences. Understanding the roles of first responders, their limitations based on departmental policies, and how to work as a team with first responders is important for crisis counselors. Common intervention programs with first responders are discussed to meet their unique needs.

In Chapter 12: *Emergency Preparedness and Response in the Community and Workplace*, by Jason M. McGlothlin, the information and interventions from the preceding chapters are integrated into an overview of the various disasters and crises that crisis counselors may need to address. Crisis intervention models and clinical implications for disasters and terrorist situations are explored.

In Chapter 13: *Emergency Preparedness and Response in Schools and Universities*, by Bradley T. Erford, crisis management in the school and university is explored, including the components of a crisis plan and the role of counselors and other officials. Mitigation and prevention strategies are emphasized as critical elements in the educational environment. Crisis preparedness, response, recovery, and debriefing procedures are applied to school and university settings. Special emphasis is given to strategies for how to help students and parents during and after a crisis event. Like Chapter 12, the content of this chapter infuses information found in previous chapters to allow readers to synthesize what they have previously read.

Finally, Chapter 14: *Counselor Self-Care in Crisis Situations*, written by James Jackson, Latofia Parker, and Judith Harrington, provides a brief overview of counselor self-care concerns and wellness.

ACKNOWLEDGMENTS

We thank all of the contributing authors for lending their expertise in the various topical areas. As always, Kevin Davis and Rebecca Fox-Gieg our editors at Pearson, have been wonderfully responsive and supportive. Thanks to Linda Clark and Garima Khosla for shepherding this book through production with great care. Thanks also to Claudia Forgas for copyediting to Karen Jones for proofreading. Their attention to detail was greatly appreciated. Special thanks go to the outside reviewers whose comments helped to provide substantive improvement to the third edition: Nicole M. Cavanagh, University of South Carolina; Perry C. Francis, Eastern Michigan University; Melanie Iarussi, Auburn University; Jason McGlothlin, Kent State University; Tiffany Schiffner, Rollins College; and Carol M. Smith, Marshall University.

BRIEF CONTENTS

CONTENTS

Part II   Special Issues in Crisis Intervention

Chapter 9   Sexual Violence   275

Robin Lee, Jennifer Jordan, and Elizabeth Schuler

ABOUT THE EDITORS

Lisa R. Jackson-Cherry, Ph.D., LCPC, NCC, ACS, NCSC, PCE, is a professor in the Department of Counseling at Marymount University. She is the coordinator of program accreditation and assessment and program director for pastoral clinical mental health counseling. She received her Ph.D. in Counselor Education and Supervision, an Ed.S. in Counseling, a Masters of Criminal Justice from the University of South Carolina, and her B.A. in Psychology and Sociology from the University of Notre Dame of Maryland. She is the recipient of the American Counseling Association's (ACA) Carl Perkins Government Relations Award for her initiatives in psychological testing; the recipient of the Outstanding Service Award, Leadership Award, and Meritorious Service Award given by the Association for Spiritual, Ethical, and Religious Values in Counseling (ASERVIC); Outstanding Leadership recipient of the European Branch of the American Counseling Association; and Outstanding Service and Leadership Awards from the Licensed Clinical Professional Counselors of Maryland. Dr. Jackson-Cherry is a licensed clinical professional counselor in Maryland, National Certified Counselor, approved clinical supervisor, and national certified school counselor. She is approved as a pastoral counselor educator by the American Association of Pastoral Counselors and is certified as a disaster mental health counselor by the American Red Cross. She is a Fellow with the American Counseling Association and is currently serving her second elected term on the Governing Council for ACA. She served on the Executive Board of the American Association of State Counseling Boards and is past-president of ASERVIC. She is the past membership co-chair and southern regional representative for the Counseling Association for Humanistic Education and Development and has served as past Secretary and Legislative Representative for the Licensed Clinical Professional Counselors of Maryland. She was appointed as a board member of the Board of Professional Counselors and Therapists in Maryland (BOPCT), serving as chairperson for 4 years, chair of the Ethics Committee, and Legislative/Regulations Committee. She was presented with citations from the Governor and Secretary of Maryland for her service and leadership on the BOPCT. Her research focuses mainly on the areas of ethical and legal issues in counseling and supervision, issues in military and first responders, risk assessment, and religious and spiritual integration. She teaches courses primarily in the areas of crisis assessment and intervention, pastoral counseling integration, and clinical mental health counseling internship. She is currently in private practice in Maryland, where she works with children, adults, and families focusing on anxiety, depression, substance use, autism, and behavioral issues. She served for many years as lead counselor with COPS-Kids (Concerns of Police Survivors-Kids) during National Law Enforcement Officers Week, providing group counseling to children who experienced the death of a law enforcement officer-parent in the line of duty. Prior to her faculty appointment in 2000, her previous clinical experiences consisted of clinical director for a mobile crisis team in Baltimore City, behavioral specialist (Grades K–5), conflict resolution coordinator/counselor (Grades 9–12), group co-facilitator for a women's maximum security correctional facility, dual diagnosed population, police department youth counseling services division, and crisis intervention training facilitator for law enforcement basic trainees and hostage negotiators. She has written numerous articles, book reviews, book chapters, and participated extensively at state, national, and international conferences over the past 20 years.

    Bradley T. Erford, Ph.D., LCPC, NCC, LPC, LP, LSP, is the 2012–2013 president of the American Counseling Association (ACA) and a professor in the school counseling program of the Education Specialties Department in the School of Education at Loyola University Maryland. He is the recipient of the American Counseling Association (ACA) Research Award, ACA Extended Research Award, Thomas J. Sweeney Award for Visionary Leadership and Advocacy, ACA Arthur A. Hitchcock Distinguished Professional Service Award, ACA Professional Development Award, and ACA Carl D. Perkins Government Relations Award. He was also inducted as an ACA Fellow. In addition, he has received the Association for Assessment and Research in Counseling (AARC) AARC/MECD Research Award; AARC Exemplary Practices Award; AARC President's Merit Award; the Association for Counselor Education and Supervision (ACES) Robert O. Stripling Award for Excellence in Standards; Maryland Association for Counseling and Development (MACD) Counselor of the Year; MACD Counselor Advocacy Award; MACD Professional Development Award; and MACD Counselor Visibility Award. He is the editor/coeditor of numerous texts, including *Orientation to the Counseling Profession* (Pearson Merrill, 2010, 2011, 2018), *Group Work in the Schools* (Pearson Merrill, 2010), *Group Work in the Schools* (2nd ed., Routledge, 2016), *Transforming the School Counseling Profession* (Pearson Merrill, 2003, 2007, 2011, 2015), *Group Work: Processes and Applications* (Pearson Merrill, 2010), *Developing Multicultural Counseling Competence* (Pearson Merrill, 2010, 2014, 2018), *Crisis Assessment, Intervention and Prevention* (Pearson Merrill, 2010, 2014, 2018), *Professional School Counseling: A Handbook of Principles, Programs and Practices* (pro-ed, 2004, 2010, 2016), and *The Counselor's Guide to Clinical, Personality and Behavioral Assessment* (Cengage, 2006). He is also an author/coauthor of *Forty Techniques Every Counselor Should Know* (Merrill/Prentice-Hall, 2010, 2015); *Assessment for Counselors* (Cengage, 2007, 2013), *Research and Evaluation in Counseling* (Cengage, 2008, 2014); *Educational Applications of the WISC-IV* (Western Psychological Services, 2006); and *Group Activities: Firing Up for Performance* (Pearson/Merrill/Prentice-Hall, 2007). He is the general editor of *The American Counseling Association Encyclopedia of Counseling* (ACA, 2009). His research specialization falls primarily in development and technical analysis of psychoeducational tests and has resulted in the publication of more than 70 refereed journal articles, 130 book chapters, and a dozen published tests. He was a member of the ACA Governing Council and the 20/20 Committee: A Vision for the Future of Counseling. He is past president of AARC, past chair and parliamentarian of the American Counseling Association–Southern (US) Region; past-chair of ACA's Task Force on High Stakes Testing; past chair of ACA's Standards for Test Users Task Force; past chair of ACA's Interprofessional Committee; past chair of the ACA Public Awareness and Support Committee (co-chair of the National Awards Sub-committee); chair of the Convention and past-chair of the Screening Assessment Instruments Committees for AARC; past president of the Maryland Association for Counseling and Development (MACD); past-president of Maryland Association for Measurement and Evaluation (MAME); past-president of the Maryland Association for Counselor Education and Supervision (MACES); and past-president of the Maryland Association for Mental Health Counselors (MAMHC). He was also a senior associate editor and board member of the *Journal of Counseling & Development*. Dr. Erford has been a faculty member at Loyola since 1993 and is a licensed clinical professional counselor, licensed professional counselor, nationally certified counselor, licensed psychologist, and licensed school psychologist. Prior to arriving at Loyola, Dr. Erford was a school psychologist/counselor in the Chesterfield County (VA) Public Schools. He maintains a private practice specializing in assessment and treatment of children and adolescents. A graduate of the University of Virginia (Ph.D.), Bucknell University (MA), and Grove City College (BS), he has taught courses in testing and measurement, psychoeducational assessment, life-span development, research and evaluation in counseling, school counseling, counseling techniques, practicum and internship student supervision, and stress management (not that he needs it, of course).

ABOUT THE CONTRIBUTING AUTHORS

Mary L. Bartlett, Ph.D., LPC-CS, NCC, CFLE, is a licensed professional counselor, a national board certified counselor, a certified family life educator and mental health consultant, a researcher, and a trainer. She earned her doctorate in counselor education from Auburn University and holds the position of Professor of Leadership and Ethics with the United States Air Force at Air University in Montgomery, Alabama. Dr. Bartlett is an experienced clinical counselor, and her primary areas of research are suicide and resilience. She is a master trainer for the Suicide Prevention Resource Center, an Army National Guard-qualified Master Resilience Trainer, has completed the Air Force Resilience Training program, and is well published in the field of suicide prevention, intervention, and postvention. She speaks internationally and trains leadership and mental health professionals on suicide- and resilience-related matters.

Charlotte Daughhetee, Ph.D., NCC, LPC, LMFT NCC, LPC, LMFT, is a professor in the graduate program in counseling at the University of Montevallo with counseling experience in K–12, university, and private practice settings. She earned her M.Ed. in school counseling and Ph.D. in counselor education from the University of South Carolina. She has experience in crisis intervention in school and university settings and has presented and published on crisis intervention and counselor trainee evaluation. She also serves as the chair of the Department of Counseling, Family & Consumer Sciences and Kinesiology.

Elizabeth Graves, Ph.D., LPCS, NCC, is an assistant professor in the Human Development and Psychological Counseling Department in the College of Education at Appalachian State University in Boone, North Carolina, where she serves as the program director for the Professional School Counseling Program. Her research focus is the study of resilience development in survivors of child sexual abuse, a passion sparked from her decade's work in both the professions of school counseling and clinical mental health counseling. As a result of her work in the counseling field, she earned MINT (Motivational Interviewing Network of Trainers) membership and a certificate in Spiritual Guidance and Formation; she leads trainings and groups in both.

Paul F. Hard, Ph.D., LPC-S, NCC, is an associate professor of counselor education at Auburn University at Montgomery. He has provided individual and group counseling in both private practice and community agency settings, focusing on addictions, relationship counseling, sexual minorities, and trauma. His research interests have been in the areas of ethics, counselor/professional impairment and wellness, complicated grieving in prenatal and postnatal loss, professional credentialing and advocacy, sexual minority issues in counseling, and ministerial termination.

Judith Harrington, Ph.D., LPC, LMFT, is a counselor educator at the University of Montevallo, and is an approved trainer for the *Assessing and Managing Suicidal Risk* curriculum for mental health professionals on behalf of the Suicide Prevention Resource Center. She designed and has taught an annual three-credit hour graduate counseling course in suicide prevention, intervention, and postvention for two universities for 9 years and frequently trains mental health professionals via workshops and seminars. In addition, she served on the Standards, Training, & Practices Committee for the National Suicide Prevention Lifeline for 5 years. She facilitated a Survivors of Suicide loss bereavement group for 14 years, and was the first- and twice-elected president of the Alabama Suicide Prevention and Resources Coalition (ASPARC). With assistance from the federal Garrett Lee Smith Youth Suicide Prevention grant, she developed the Comprehensive Suicide Prevention and Resources Directory, found at www.legacy.montevallo.edu/asparc.

Seth C. W. Hayden, Ph.D., NCC, is an assistant professor of counseling at Wake Forest University. Dr. Hayden has provided career and personal counseling in community agencies and secondary school and university settings. Dr. Hayden's research focuses on the career and personal development of military service members, veterans, and their families. In addition, he explores the connection between career and mental health issues and integrated models of clinical supervision designed to facilitate growth in counselors' ability to formulate interventions. Dr. Hayden is a licensed professional counselor in North Carolina and Virginia as well as a national certified counselor, a certified clinical mental health counselor, and an approved clinical supervisor.

James Jackson, Ph.D., LPC-S, NCC, is an assistant professor and graduate counseling program coordinator at the University of Montevallo. He has experience as a school counselor, outpatient therapist, and group and foster home therapist, and he continues to provide services through his private practice in Montevallo, Alabama. James's interests include diversity, identity development, social justice, and self-care. Moreover, as a former professional touring musician, James enjoys integrating creative activities in his work with those he serves in clinical and educational settings.

Jennifer Jordan, Ph.D., is an associate professor and director of the counseling and development program at Winthrop University. She is also the director of the Winthrop Community Counseling Clinic. She serves as executive director of the South Carolina Counseling Association and is vice president of the South Carolina Board of Examiners for Licensure of Professional Counselors, a marriage and family therapist, and a psycho-educational specialist.

Robin Lee, Ph.D., is a professor in the professional counseling program of the Womack Educational Leadership Department at Middle Tennessee State University, specializing in mental health counseling. Dr. Lee earned a Ph.D. in counselor education and supervision from Mississippi State University, and an M.Ed. in community counseling and B.A. in psychology from Delta State University in Cleveland, Mississippi. Dr. Lee is a licensed professional counselor with Mental Health Service Provider status in Tennessee, a national certified counselor, and an approved clinical supervisor.

Jason M. McGlothlin, Ph.D., PCC-S, is an associate professor in the counselor education and supervision program at Kent State University (KSU). He earned his doctorate in counselor education from Ohio University and is currently a Professional Clinical Counselor with Supervisory endorsement (PCC-S) in Ohio. Prior to joining the KSU faculty, he practiced in community mental health, private practice, and suicide prevention/hostage negotiation facilities. His areas of teaching, service, publication, and research include the assessment, prevention, and treatment of suicide. He is the author of *Developing Clinical Skills in Suicide Assessment, Prevention and Treatment* (American Counseling Association, 2008) and the founder of the SIMPLE STEPS model for suicide assessment.

Amy L. McLeod, Ph.D., is the Counseling Department chair and an associate professor at Argosy University Atlanta. Dr. McLeod's research interests include counselor education and supervision, multicultural issues, women's issues, assessment, and crisis intervention.

John Muldoon, Ph.D., LPC, CAAP, is a specialist professor at Monmouth University. Dr. Muldoon has a doctorate in counselor education from the University of South Carolina. He is also a co-occurring and substance abuse counselor. Previously, Dr. Muldoon was the director of a batterer intervention program for domestic violence and worked at multiple levels of care with people who had substance abuse issues. Dr. Muldoon is licensed as a professional counselor in New Jersey, South Carolina, and Pennsylvania. He is also a Certified Addictions Professional in Florida. Dr. Muldoon's teaching interests include substance abuse treatment, group counseling, and counseling theory and techniques. His major areas of research are in domestic violence, substance use, aging issues, and trauma.

Latofia Parker, Ph.D., NCC, CRC, is an assistant professor in the graduate program in counseling at the University of Montevallo. She has counseling experience working with individuals and families in rehabilitation counseling. She earned her M.S. in rehabilitation counseling from Troy University and her Ph.D. in counselor education from the University of Alabama. She has experience in helping individuals and families deal with the onset of disability and other health-related crises. As a professor, she integrates concepts of self-awareness, counselor's wellness, and crisis prevention/intervention throughout all her courses.

Elizabeth Schuler is a master's level graduate student in clinical mental health counseling at Middle Tennessee State University. She received her B.Sc. at Middle Tennessee State University. Her interests include relationship dynamics, adolescence, and family issues.

William R. Sterner, Ph.D., LCPC, ACS, NCC, is an associate professor in the Department of Counseling at Marymount University. He worked for a number of years as a clinical mental health counselor and drug and alcohol counselor in various community counseling settings. He is in private practice in Maryland and is an approved clinical supervisor. He also has experience in conducting drug and alcohol assessments, case management, and treatment placement with clients in the criminal justice system. His research interests include supervision, quantitative methodology, spirituality issues in counseling, substance abuse, incivility issues in higher education, and counselor competencies in assessing and managing suicidality.

Laura L. Talbott-Forbes, Ph.D., MCHES, is an associate professor in the Department of Human Studies at the University of Alabama at Birmingham. She has served as a prevention specialist with general college student health issues and director of substance abuse prevention programs at a large university. Her research interests include the prevention of substance abuse, education and early intervention with potentially suicidal persons, and other public health issues that impact young adult health.

Carrie Wachter Morris, Ph.D., NCC, ACS, is an associate professor of Counseling and Educational Development at the University of North Carolina at Greensboro, where she coordinates the school counseling track. She served as president (2015–2016) of the Association for Assessment and Research in Counseling (AARC). She has nearly two dozen articles in national peer-refereed journals, one book, and an additional 10 chapters in different works. She presents regularly at state, regional, and national conferences on topics related to the scholarship of teaching and learning in counselor education, crisis, and school counselor education.

Basic Concepts of Crisis Intervention

Lisa R. Jackson-Cherry, Jason M. McGlothlin, and Bradley T. Erford*

PREVIEW

Crises occur in a variety of settings for a variety of reasons. Responses to crises can come in various forms and can include multiple levels of complexities. In this chapter, basic frameworks for assessing and conceptualizing crises are presented, along with a discussion of how crisis intervention may differ from traditional counseling.

A BRIEF INTRODUCTION TO CRISIS INTERVENTION

If asked to think about a crisis, what comes to mind? Natural disasters? School shootings? Suicide? Domestic violence? How do some people survive crisis events adaptively and with resilience, while others endure mental health issues for months, years, or a lifetime? To begin, situations such as tornadoes, earthquakes, acts of terror, and suicide do not in and of themselves constitute crises. A crisis is an event that may or may not be perceived as a disruption in life. A crisis does not necessarily lead to trauma. Typically, a crisis is described using a trilogy definition; that is, there are three essential elements that must be present for an event to be considered a crisis: (1) a precipitating event, (2) a perception of the event that leads to subjective distress, and (3) diminished functioning when the distress is not alleviated by customary coping mechanisms or other resources.

When terrorists bombed the World Trade Center in New York City in 1993, the crisis was experienced by many individuals and families. Six families lost loved ones, approximately 1,000 individuals were injured, and the jobs, careers, and work of countless people were interrupted. Using the trilogy definition, it is obvious that all of those who experienced diminished functioning following the crisis event experienced trauma. People throughout the rest of the world, however horrified, continued to function as normal. For these individuals, the crisis event was not perceived as traumatic and it did not disrupt their everyday lives.

James and Gilliland (2017) reviewed a number of definitions of crisis that exist in the literature and summarized crisis as "a perception or experiencing of an event or situation as an intolerable difficulty that exceeds the person's current resources and coping mechanisms" (p. 3). When a crisis is perceived as disruptive to one's life, the

*The authors wish to acknowledge Dr. Stephanie Puleo for her outstanding contributions to the first two editions of this chapter.

crisis may be experienced as a traumatic event. Fortunately, most individuals can work through crisis events. For many who experience a crisis, the experience can assist in preventing or working through future crises, therefore decreasing trauma in the future. No formula exists that explains why some individuals can work through a crisis, while others who experience the same crisis find it traumatic and disruptive to daily functioning. Therefore, the idea that an individual's perception of an event determines whether the event will become traumatic is paramount to understanding an individual and making a plan of action for him or her. However, an individual's perception of an event can be influenced by various determinants, such as the individual's level of resilience, resources, coping mechanisms, and support system.

Often a crisis can lead to additional crises that can be debilitating and impact not only the person affected but also the entire family or community system. When a person encounters multiple crises, or when past crises the person was exposed to were not resolved effectively, the person or system could experience trauma. When a person experiences trauma, he or she may need assistance from a crisis counselor to assess the situation, evaluate options for adjusting to the crisis, explore resources currently available to the client, work through the current crisis, and connect with new resources and referrals. As a first exposure to the potential characteristics of a crisis, see Case Study 1.1 and answer the discussion questions that follow. Also read Voices from the Field 1.1.

CASE STUDY 1.1

The Nguyens: A Natural Disaster Affects a Family System

Vin and Li Nguyen are recent immigrants to the United States. They reside in a small town along the Gulf Coast of Mississippi, where a number of other Vietnamese immigrants have settled. Like many new members of the community, the Nguyens are learning to speak, read, and write English and are hoping to become naturalized citizens of the United States someday. After arriving in the United States, the Nguyens invested all of their money in an old shrimp boat in order to support themselves by selling their daily catch to local seafood processing facilities.

Recently, the shrimp boat was heavily damaged, and the seafood processing facilities were destroyed by a hurricane. Subsequently, the Nguyens had no income for quite a while. With limited income and no health insurance, they relied on the county department of public health for prenatal care when Li became pregnant. Li's pregnancy progressed normally; however, her daughter was born with spina bifida. As you read this chapter, try to conceptualize the Nguyens' situation according to the crisis models presented.

Discussion Questions

1. What incidents have occurred in the Nguyens' lives that could be considered provoking stressor events?
2. Beyond the provoking stressor events, are there additional stressors that the Nguyens must address?
3. What resources are the Nguyens using?
4. What additional information do you need to determine whether the Nguyens are in crisis?
5. What factors will predict the outcome for this family?

VOICES FROM THE FIELD 1.1
My First Day

Beth Graney

I spent the summer planning all the classroom lessons and groups I would offer students in my first position as the only school counselor in a K–12 school in rural Iowa. After the principal shared with me that the previous counselor never really connected with many of the kids, I knew I needed to be especially creative to win their trust. The principal told me the town had a saying, "If you aren't born here, you're not from here!" How would a big city girl from Chicago ever fit in?

All of these thoughts raced through my head, drowning out the din of my radio as I drove the 20 miles to school. The newscaster's report that a couple died in a motorcycle accident the previous night barely registered. When I arrived early that morning, the principal greeted me at the door and pulled me into her office. "The parents of two of our students died last night, and other students have arrived at school crying. You have to do something," she blurted as she hurried off to take care of notifying the rest of the staff. My mouth went dry and my thoughts started to race. What should I say? What should I do? What strategies would be most effective? More importantly, I thought, I don't know a single student in this building!

As I entered the large classroom that was now my office, I saw 20 kids ranging in age from early elementary to high school. As I put down my bag on the desk, I looked at all of the crying kids, pulled up a chair, and said, "Who wants to start?" Someone began with, "They are my friends, my neighbors, and our classmates!" I listened. Soon another child said,

"My grandma is sick," and then another said, "My dad lost his job," and "My parents are getting divorced." I listened. As the morning progressed, some kids went on to class, others went home, and more came from class or home to share their grief and fears with the group. I listened some more. When the long day finally ended, I didn't know everyone's name that I had written on the sign-in sheet by memory, but I had a growing sense of community.

Two days later, after listening to many students and teachers explain how this tragedy had affected them, the principal told me the funeral service would be held in the gym because the gathering would be so large. She thought it would be important for me to be there to support the kids in case anyone needed immediate assistance. I listened as the minister and other family members eulogized the parents. After the service, I met many of the parents and community members, and again I listened to their grief and pain. When a person dies, the family and friends grieve. But in a small town, when someone dies, the whole town grieves.

As I drove home that day, I felt drained and wondered whether I had been helpful because I had no great insights or strategies to offer the students or parents as to why something so difficult and tragic had happened. All I really did was listen. It was then that it struck me that it was the first skill ever taught in my graduate counseling program: Listen! And so began one of my most memorable years in counseling. My phone didn't stop ringing and my sign-up sheet was never empty. I made the transition from big city girl to rural school counselor simply by listening.

CRISIS INTERVENTION THEORY

The study of crisis intervention began and has been documented in earnest since the 1940s in response to several stressor events. During World War II, numerous families experienced disorganization and changes in functioning after individual family members left home to participate in the war effort. In most cases, disorganization was only temporary and families found ways to adjust. Families that had the most difficulty reorganizing and adapting to the absence of their loved ones seemed to experience the greatest degree of distress. Studies of families in crisis following war separation led Reuben Hill (1949) to propose a model through which family stress and crisis could be conceptualized by taking into account the family's resources, perception, and previous experience with crises. Additional research on families and crisis events was launched following a more acute stressor event, the Cocoanut Grove nightclub fire that claimed nearly 500 lives in Boston, Massachusetts. Studies of the responses of the survivors of the fire, family members of those who died, and the community illuminated some common reactions to such a traumatic event and led Gerald Caplan and Erich Lindemann to propose recommendations for responding to community crises. In the decades following the 1940s, the original models proposed by Hill, Caplan, and Lindemann were expanded, with more attention to contextual variables and outcomes.

Caplan and Lindemann are often credited as pioneers in the field of crisis intervention. Their work began after the Cocoanut Grove nightclub fire, in which so many people died in Boston in 1942. Lindemann, a professor of psychiatry at Harvard Medical School and Massachusetts General Hospital, worked with patients dealing with grief following traumatic loss. Although many people died as a result of the fire, hundreds who were at the nightclub on that fateful night survived. The survivors and the grieving relatives of those who perished provided Lindemann with an opportunity to study psychological and emotional reactions to disaster. Based on his interviews with those who survived the fire as well as relatives of the deceased, Lindemann (1944) outlined a number of common clinical features, including somatic distress, feelings of guilt, hostility, disorganization, behavioral changes, and preoccupation with images of the deceased. Lindemann referred to these symptoms as "acute grief," which was not a psychiatric diagnosis but was a call for intervention nonetheless. Today, many of the symptoms of acute stress disorder identified in the *Diagnostic and Statistical Manual of Mental Disorders* (DSM-5; American Psychiatric Association [APA], 2013) seem to parallel Lindemann's description of acute grief.

In addition to describing clinical features of acute grief, Lindemann outlined intervention strategies for dealing with the symptoms. Because acute grief was not considered a psychiatric diagnosis per se, Lindemann suggested that helpers other than psychiatrists could be of assistance. This idea was further fueled by the large number of people in need of intervention following the Cocoanut Grove fire, and became a cornerstone in the conceptualization of community mental health.

In response to the needs of the number of people experiencing acute grief following the nightclub fire, Lindemann worked with his colleague Gerald Caplan to establish a community-wide mental health program in Cambridge, Massachusetts, known as the Wellesley Project. By studying and working with individuals who had experienced loss through the fire or similar traumatic events, Caplan developed the concept of "preventive psychiatry" (Caplan, 1964), which proposed that early intervention following a disaster or traumatic event can promote positive growth and well-being. Lindemann's "basic crisis theory" introduced the field to focus on crisis intervention as a distinct area in the helping field requiring specific interventions. His theory allowed others to build upon and develop alternative perspectives. Crisis intervention is not the same as brief therapy. Brief therapy attempts to decrease symptoms associated with ongoing mental health problems. Crisis intervention attempts to assist individuals who are experiencing temporary affective, behavioral, and/or cognitive symptoms associated with a crisis event.

Building on Caplan's model, Beverley Raphael (2000) coined the term "psychological first aid." Following a train accident in Australia in 1977 in which many people died, Raphael worked with bereaved families and injured survivors of the train disaster. She advocated for attention that included comfort and consolation, immediate physical assistance, reunification with loved ones, an opportunity to express feelings, and support during the initial period of time following a traumatic event. In particular, she described the need to consider Maslow's hierarchy of needs, and the importance of attending first to basic survival needs before attempting more traditional forms of counseling (James & Gilliland, 2017). In describing crisis reactions, Raphael noted that the full impact of trauma may be experienced a considerable time following the initial crisis event, thereby leading an individual to undergo a period of "disillusionment." Much of her work subsequent to the 1977 train accident focused on the prevention of post-traumatic stress disorder (PTSD).

In his classic work, Caplan (1961) offered this explanation:

> People are in a state of crisis when they face an obstacle to important life goals—an obstacle that is, for a time, insurmountable by the use of customary methods of problem-solving. A period of disorganization ensues, a period of upset, during which many abortive attempts at solution are made. (p. 18)

What is important to note in Caplan's description is that the concept of crisis refers to an outcome of a precipitating event, not to the precipitating event itself. Similar to more recent definitions of *crisis*, Caplan described the outcome, or the crisis, as the state of disequilibrium that is experienced.

There are several schools of thought pertaining to crisis theory, and the concept of disequilibrium following a stressful event seems to be common to all of them. Some theories focus on the disequilibrium experiences of individuals, while others take a more contextual, systemic stance. Many researchers and theorists take the point of view that the disequilibrium that constitutes a crisis can be understood by examining an individual's past experiences, cognitive structures, behaviors, and competencies. In their studies on hysteria, Freud and Breuer (2004) concluded that many of the neurotic symptoms that contributed to clients' states of equilibrium were repressed memories of past traumatic events. Their disequilibrium was sustained by destructive defense mechanisms.

Other crisis theorists contend that the disequilibrium is the result of ineffective psychological tools, such as negative or faulty thinking, poor self-esteem, and maladaptive behavior. According to "adaptational" theory (James & Gilliland, 2017), individuals who become incapacitated or dysfunctional following stressful events are those who perceive and interpret stressful events negatively. Negative thoughts, irrational beliefs, and defeating self-talk lead to paralyzing rather than helpful behaviors. From a cognitive-behavioral perspective, crises may be ameliorated when individuals replace their faulty thinking and ineffective behaviors with more positive thoughts and adaptive behaviors. From an interpersonal perspective, self-confidence and self-esteem also counter the disequilibrium of crises as individuals become more focused and reliant on their own abilities.

Applied crisis theory comprises four crisis domains: developmental, situational, existential, and ecosystemic crises (James & Gilliland, 2017). *Developmental crises* are events that are expected to be experienced by the majority of individuals during normal development. However, for some, the developmental crisis event could cause considerable trauma. Examples of developmental crises include pregnancy, graduation, retirement, career transition, and aging. *Situational crises* are events that are often unexpected and involve some degree of a catastrophic, shocking, or random act. Examples of situational crises include a terrorist attack, a sexual assault, job loss, an accident, and a sudden illness. *Existential crises* may or may not involve religious faith or spirituality but are events that affect one's sense of meaning, purpose, freedom, independence, forgiveness, shame, or other core beliefs. *Ecosystemic crises*, which include natural or human-caused events, impact not only the individual but also any of the systems (families, schools, communities) connected with the crisis event.

It is important for the crisis counselor to understand the individual's perception of a crisis before categorizing the crisis into one or more of the four crisis domains. The reason is that the crisis domain acts as a framework for understanding the individual's perception of the event and its effect on his or her life. For example, consider the case of a woman who enters a crisis center pregnant. Initial observation may lead a crisis counselor to assume that the woman is experiencing a developmental crisis. However, upon learning that the pregnancy is the result of a rape, the crisis counselor may categorize the pregnancy as a situational crisis. It is also possible that the woman is thinking of terminating the pregnancy, which may have forced her into an existential crisis because following through would conflict with her religious beliefs. As this example indicates, a crisis must be understood by how it is perceived by the individual affected by it.

Regardless of the theory adopted, crisis intervention requires that a crisis counselor undertake a series of tasks to understand the client's circumstances, ameliorate the most harmful aspects of the crisis, and help return the client to precrisis or baseline functioning as safely, quickly, and efficiently as possible. Theories are assumptions about *why* an individual may experience a crisis and perceive it as traumatic. Theories provide a rationale or explanation that informs a crisis counselor's guiding practice, or *how* a crisis counselor works through the crisis with a client. This guiding practice is one's model of practicing in crisis intervention.

THE TASK MODEL OF CRISIS ASSESSMENT AND INTERVENTION

The task model of crisis assessment and intervention, developed by Jackson-Cherry (2018) for this third edition (see Table 1.1), focuses on four important areas of crisis assessment that lead to an effective four-task intervention plan for individuals in virtually every type of crisis, regardless of setting. Assessment of safety and stabilization; bio-psycho-social-spiritual elements; clarification of the problem(s); and coping skills, resources, and supports are essential first steps toward more accurately defining the actual crisis situation. Only when a thorough assessment is completed can an effective crisis plan be developed to address the actual problem(s). In traditional counseling, the definition of the problem may be very clear and the plan may follow a prescribed sequence. However, due to the complex nature of individuals in crisis, a reliable and valid definition of the problem can only be clarified after appropriate and comprehensive assessment tasks are completed and followed by an appropriate crisis plan.

Four Essential Crisis Assessment Tasks

ASSESSMENT TASK 1: ADDRESS SAFETY, STABILIZATION, AND RISK   A crisis counselor should always maintain a sense of safety for self and others (see Chapter 2). Safety should be the main priority for the client, community, and counselor. Therefore, a thorough risk

---

TABLE 1.1 The Task Model of Crisis Assessment and Intervention (Jackson-Cherry, 2018)

Level I: Four Essential Crisis Assessment Tasks

Assessment Task 1: Address Safety, Stabilization, and Risk

Assessment Task 2: Follow a Holistic Bio-Psycho-Social-Spiritual Approach

Assessment Task 3: Clarify the Problem(s)

Assessment Task 4: Explore Coping Skills, Resources, and Supports

Level II: Four Essential Crisis Intervention Tasks

Intervention Task 1: Normalize and Educate

Intervention Task 2: Explore Options

Intervention Task 3: Develop a Plan and Obtain a Commitment

Intervention Task 4: Prepare Documentation, Follow Up, and Provide Referrals

---

assessment should be the first step in the assessment and the main goal for the counselor. Due to the nature of a crisis, risk should be assessed at varying times throughout crisis intervention. A client may be referred (or self-referred) for a perceived presenting problem that is not the primary problem causing the difficulties, and the client could present with varying degrees of lethality (i.e., none, low, moderate, or high) and types of risk (i.e., homicidal, suicidal). Lethality must always be assessed at the beginning of the relationship. If any degree of lethality is present, a comprehensive plan must be discussed with the client and documented. Not assessing for risk in a crisis situation, or waiting until the end of a session to conduct such an assessment that is not thorough, is negligent. If a person were to leave a session and follow through with suicidal or homicidal ideation or behavior that was not thoroughly assessed, the standard of care could be questioned. Adhering to the standard of care is a primary focus of Assessment Task 1, and if lethality is present, it should continue to be a focus in subsequent steps.

Often a person who is at risk may not initially report ideation or intentions of suicidal or homicidal behavior. Clients need to know that the crisis counselor is willing to explore the delicate issues that are leading to thoughts or behaviors of suicide or homicide, can provide an emotionally safe environment, and is competent to assist with an appropriate plan. Allowing for an open and thorough assessment helps clients understand that the counselor is fully present, cares, and is competent to assist with lethal thoughts. An assessment of safety and lethality actually enhances the rapport between the client and counselor. Importantly, if a client is experiencing intense crisis circumstances that affect the client's baseline functioning, then it is unlikely that the counselor and client can collaboratively progress through the essential intervention tasks that follow. A client has to be stabilized enough to progress through the intervention tasks of this model and collaborate in the intervention plan. Thus, client stabilization is the main focus before moving forward with additional tasks. If the client is unable to work collaboratively toward the additional tasks and unable to implement life-saving plans, the main goal for the counselor should be for the immediate safety of the client or others, and options for intensive care, including hospitalization, should be pursued.

ASSESSMENT TASK 2: FOLLOW A HOLISTIC BIO-PSYCHO-SOCIAL-SPIRITUAL APPROACH

Next, crisis counselors should thoroughly assess a client for physical, medical, substance, psychological, social, spiritual, and other concerns. Often, individuals experience a crisis because of medical issues such as pain associated with a physical condition or noncompliance with medical practices (including medication noncompliance); religious/spiritual and/or other existential conflicts; and other reasons. These medical issues often present with symptoms consistent with mental health issues during a crisis. If medical and other issues the client faces are not assessed, the diagnosis of the client may be incorrect, leading to an ineffective and inappropriate treatment plan or referral. Without this kind of assessment, the root problem will never be addressed and symptoms may actually increase over time, making the situation worse for the client. A comprehensive assessment of all of these considerations must be conducted in order to determine the cause of or connection to the perceived or actual crisis event.

A medical assessment may include questions such as the following:

- When was your last medical examination?
- Have you presented to the emergency room or another physician with an acute or chronic medical complaint? How often? When was the last visit?
- Have you been diagnosed with any medical condition(s)? Have you been prescribed any medications for the medical condition(s)? Have you been compliant with the recommended medication regimen? If not, what has prevented you from continuing to take the medications as prescribed? Has the medication affected your thoughts, mood, or behaviors? What was your life like prior to the medical condition(s)?
- Have you had medical complaints that are not being addressed by a medical doctor?
- Have you had any recent injuries? When was the injury? Did you receive medical attention? What was the treatment plan set by the physician? Have you been compliant with the treatment plan? Has there been a follow-up? Have you felt your mood change since the injury? If so, in what ways? What was life like prior to the medical condition(s)?

These questions begin the process of the ABCDE assessment and a described baseline.

It is essential to assess the baseline functioning of the client during the present crisis situation and prior to the crisis. Later, the goal may be to formulate a plan that moves the person back to precrisis functioning or to develop a new baseline. Most crisis models follows an ABC (affect, behaviors, cognitions) assessment approach. However, this task model follows an ABCDE assessment approach (*Affect, Behaviors, Cognitions, Development,* and *Environment*). Keep in mind that while some assessment measures may fall into more than one category, all impact the overall assessment.

Affect consists of how a person presents during the assessment and may include nonverbal communication. Is the client withdrawn, distant, restrictive in speech or space, agitated, incongruent in presentation, and so on?

Behaviors are assessed to determine a person's response to and potential to move through the crisis. For example, since the precipitating crisis, what has the client done (or not done) in response to the crisis event? What resources has the person accessed or not accessed? How have the person's eating habits, sleep, work, and normal activities and behaviors changed from before the crisis? What is preventing the person from moving toward the behaviors that were evident in precrisis daily living?

Cognitions, or thoughts, include thinking patterns, distortions, and deficiencies. In most situations, cognitions affect behaviors and how a person presents emotionally (i.e., affect). Are cognitive distortions present that are preventing the person from moving personal behaviors toward the precrisis or new baseline functioning? Are cognitions restrictive? For example, does the client believe no actions will improve the situation? For risk assessment, does a person believe that there is only one way to "fix" the problem (e.g., suicide, homicide), and is the person not willing to evaluate other options in the development of a plan?

In addition to the ABC assessment commonly used as the main criteria in the field, crisis counselors should understand the appropriate development and environment factors that may affect a person's response to a crisis. A person's response and functioning should be assessed based on normal levels of *development*, and plans should be made based on the developmental functioning level of a client. How does a client's current functioning abilities affect how he or she perceives the crisis? Are there limitations in the cognitive processing domain (e.g., how clients frame and perceive problems)? How do physical or emotional limitations affect the client's ability to use resources or follow through with a plan? For example, a young adult with autism spectrum disorder may need a plan established with goals appropriate for his functional level and ability to process the situation, which may be far different from a person not diagnosed with autism spectrum disorder. A person with a lower intellectual ability attempting to process the impact of the death of a parent will need to be given information in a very different way, with more concrete and simplified information than a person of normal intellectual ability.

The *environment*, which includes common multicultural components (e.g., socioeconomic status, religious or spiritual influences, racial and ethnic identification with groups, sex, resilience, physical disabilities, sexual orientation, educational level), must also be assessed and considered. In addition, personality characteristics formed by these components may promote or hinder moving past the crisis. For example, if a client is experiencing a spiritual crisis and in the past relied on a religious or spiritual leader to cope, a referral to the person's religious or spiritual leader may be crucial for intervention. However, this client, feeling guilty and intimidated by the perceptions and judgment of others, may not act (behavior) on this past coping skill in contacting a spiritual leader if the person believes (irrational cognitions) that a Higher Power will never forgive the action that is causing such emotional and spiritual pain.

A thorough ABCDE assessment allows the counselor to obtain information that is useful in developing a plan to get the person back to precrisis baseline functioning or to develop a plan to create a more stable new baseline.

ASSESSMENT TASK 3: CLARIFY THE PROBLEM(S)   Although a client may present initially with a particular problem (which should be taken into consideration), the actual problem may not be known until a complete history is taken. For example, a person may have lost a life partner 5 years ago, but the death of the partner's pet may be the actual crisis due to the meaning placed both on the pet and the significant other relationship. Counselors should be aware that a client may be facing multiple crises, since an event may affect many parts of the client's life and cause multiple traumas or retraumatization.

They should also realize, when working with several individuals in the same family, that each person may have a different presenting problem.

During this task, active listening, offering unconditional positive regard, and being nonjudgmental are essential. Likewise, empathically phrased yet challenging questions may be required to understand the actual crisis so that an effective action plan can be developed. These steps are important for the client to gain control over the problem and begin the healing process. Providing a client with the space to share personal stories in his or her own words will allow the client to gain some control over the crisis. Identifying any attached meaning the client has to the perceived crisis can lead to an in-depth understanding of the actual crisis and a more effective intervention plan.

ASSESSMENT TASK 4: EXPLORE COPING SKILLS, RESOURCES, AND SUPPORTS   After clarification of the problem(s), crisis counselors explore the coping skills, resources, and supports that were available to the client when he or she dealt with past crises and adjustments. They also explore which coping skills, resources, and supports were effective and ineffective, as well as which are available and unavailable for the current crisis. The client and counselor also discuss potential new resources, coping skills, and supports that the client may not be aware of or may not have used in the past. Counselors assess these resources using a variety of research-based approaches, including resilience-based, positive psychology, hope-based, and wellness models. The motivation of the client is also assessed.

Four Essential Crisis Intervention Tasks

INTERVENTION TASK 1: NORMALIZE AND EDUCATE   In most situations, a vital aspect of crisis intervention is to normalize a person's response to the crisis. Unless the person has acted out of malicious intent to harm another person, a person in crisis may behave in a variety of ways. It is always easy to look back and think that one should have acted differently, but in a crisis situation, most people try to make the best decision during a situation that is often out of their control at the time. Often, clients experience normal reactions (e.g., fear, abandonment, hopelessness, loss of control) to an abnormal event. Because clients in crisis are feeling and thinking that things are out of control, they may be unable to control their feelings and thoughts as they do in other situations or do not like the feelings and thoughts they are experiencing. Clients can become overwhelmed, and the crisis can be even more debilitating due to these new feelings and thoughts. Counselors should understand the normal responses to crisis events and teach clients that many of their feelings and thoughts are normal. This normalizing can actually release much of the power the perceived crisis may have over a person.

INTERVENTION TASK 2: EXPLORE OPTIONS   Using the information collected during assessment tasks 1–4, the crisis counselor and client should collaboratively explore and evaluate all the options known to the client, as well as those developed by the counselor. Even when there is evidence of lethality to self or others, the intent is to work collaboratively in developing a plan for the safety of the person or others. In some situations, when the client is not able to commit to any plan involving safety, the counselor may have to move into a directive approach. The safety of the crisis counselor is as important as the safety of the client in crisis; therefore, if there is any sense of potential harm by the client, the crisis counselor should make his or her personal safety a priority. For example, if the crisis counselor believes the client should be hospitalized due to high suicide lethality, but through the discussion of this option the client becomes agitated and there is a fear of personal safety, then collaborating is no longer the mode of interaction and the counselor arranges to have the client hospitalized.

INTERVENTION TASK 3: DEVELOP A PLAN AND OBTAIN A COMMITMENT The resulting intervention plan is individualized and based on the comprehensive assessment of the client. The counselor must take into account the risk factors, bio-psycho-social-spiritual elements; medical information; and coping skills, supports, and resources. The plan should be documented as part of the discharge summary when referring the client to another mental health professional and used as a plan for follow-up. Client commitment is essential for ownership and responsibility. Plans should have attainable and measurable goals to demonstrate progress.

INTERVENTION TASK 4: PREPARE DOCUMENTATION, FOLLOW UP, AND PROVIDE REFERRALS In a typical crisis situation, a client may be referred to another mental health professional in the community for continued or long-term care to meet client needs as specified in the intervention plan. In this case, proper documentation should be completed to terminate the case with detailed information on the referral and the intervention plan. If the crisis occurred during a long-term case, documentation and follow-up must be made in a manner outlined in the plan. See Case Study 1.2, which incorporates the task model of crisis assessment and intervention. Also read Voices from the Field 1.2.

CASE STUDY 1.2

Integration of the Task Model of Crisis Assessment and Intervention

Mary, a mental health counselor who is in private practice, frequently receives referrals to her practice for at-risk students from schools and the community. The parents of 4-year-old Lilly contacted the practice because their daughter is at risk for being expelled from her third preschool for severe behavioral issues (biting and hitting other children).

Before meeting Lilly in the office, Mary conducts an observation at the preschool. There, she witnesses Lilly punch another girl in the face over a firetruck. In response, the teacher takes the firetruck from Lilly and comforts the child who was punched by Lilly. Throughout the preschool observation, Lilly does not appear to engage in any normal developmental child-play interaction with other children. At lunch, Lilly sits with the other children and does not interact except to try to take food from a few of them using threatening gestures. In response, the other children give Lilly their food. At the end of this observation, it seems clear that Lilly demonstrates several defiant behaviors and appears to show no remorse for her actions.

A week later, Lilly and her parents arrive for their first in-office visit with Mary. After meeting with the parents and Lilly together and then spending some time with Lilly alone, Mary decides to have the parents join them again. On her way out to get the parents, Mary stops behind Lilly as she colors and tells Lilly that she is going to get her parents. Lilly does not respond, nor does she display any body movements in reaction to Mary's voice. Curious, Mary gives several other commands that are ignored by Lilly, who simply keeps her head lowered and continues to color. Mary keeps these observations in mind as she proceeds with the assessment.

Assessment Task 1: Address Safety, Stabilization, and Risk

Because Mary often works with at-risk clients, she knows that she needs to assess and be mindful that any person, no matter the age, could exert harm to self or others. Children, depending on their ability to express appropriate emotions and control their actions, could become violent (and Mary already witnessed Lilly engage in violent behavior during the observation). With safety for self and others in mind, Mary starts an in-depth assessment of Lilly. Lilly's parents provide most of the information because Lilly appears to be content coloring and does not respond to basic initial questions. Mary asks Lilly's parents: Has Lilly demonstrated threatening behaviors or actions to family members, friends, animals, or toys? In what environment does Lilly show more anger or violence? Does Lilly behave violently toward herself (e.g., scratching, biting, cutting, hitting her head or other body parts against a wall or object)? Has Lilly made any verbal threats to others? The task of addressing safety, stabilization, and risk would continue during other assessment tasks.

Assessment Task 2: Follow a Holistic Bio-Psycho-Social-Spiritual Assessment Approach

Mary continues her assessment to obtain a more holistic understanding of Lilly, her family, and her social life. Mary asks Lilly's parents: Has Lilly witnessed any violence on television or with family members? Does Lilly play with friends or other family members her age? How would you describe her play? How would you describe your parenting style (e.g., how do you provide encouragement, reinforcement, rewards, consequences, and punishment)? What seems to calm Lilly when she becomes frustrated? What activities does Lilly enjoy? Did she reach her developmental milestones on time? When did she learn to walk and talk? Does she have any chronic or acute medical conditions (e.g., ear infections, urinary infections)? Is she on any medications? Has there been a history of domestic violence or sexual violence in the family or with Lilly?

Mary asks about Lilly's most recent child well visit with a pediatrician. Lilly's parents indicate that, aside from her vaccinations, Lilly has not been seen by a doctor regularly, with the exception of the local urgent care center, where her chronic ear infections are treated. Mary asks the parents whether they followed up after the ear infections. They say they assumed that the medicine healed the ear infections.

Noticing that Lilly still does not respond, Mary initiates a conversation with Lilly and begins to color with her. Lilly grabs the crayons and throws them across the room and then goes to stand in the corner. Lilly's parents indicate that this behavior is normal for Lilly, in that when she becomes violent, she knows that she must go to stand in the corner. Mary asks if there was ever any discussion between the parents and Lilly when this happened. They say, "No, she learned this in preschool." Mary quietly walks behind Lilly and snaps her fingers. No response. Mary asks Lilly to turn around. No response.

At this point, Mary is highly suspicious that something more is happening with Lilly than solely behavioral issues (the original presenting problem). Mary moves in front of Lilly and motions for her to come and sit down. Lilly proceeds to sit back on the floor. Mary (while covering her own mouth), starts talking to Lilly. Lilly reaches up and tries to lower Mary's hand from her mouth and stares at her lips. Mary then says, "Do you want to color or use the blocks?" Lilly nods and says, "Color."

During this assessment, Mary noted the ABCDE observations. Lilly's *affect* was observed when receiving directives (e.g., behaviors ranged from being withdrawn to being interested in activities to anger). Lilly displayed a range of *behaviors* when she did not get her way or became frustrated (e.g., throwing the crayons and putting herself in a time out). Lilly's *cognitive* functioning appeared to be intact when she could focus on Mary's face. Mary inquired about *development* milestones such as talking, walking, and play activities to compare Lilly's development to typical or normal developmental functioning, although it seemed her speech development was limited compared with other normal 4-year-old children. Finally, Mary assessed for *environment* factors such as peer interactions, socioeconomic status, medical illnesses, living arrangements, social interactions, exposure to violence, and parenting styles.

Assessment Task 3: Clarify the Problem(s)

Mary shares her observations with the parents and states that she thinks another problem may need to be evaluated prior to addressing the behavioral issues. While Lilly's aggressive behaviors need attention, Mary indicates that she wants to rule out any medical issues. Mary wants Lilly's parents to make an appointment for Lilly to see a pediatrician and have a hearing test conducted to rule out any hearing issues before addressing the behavioral issues.

Assessment Task 4: Explore Coping Skills, Resources, and Supports

Mary speaks with the parents about several referrals of pediatricians since Lilly has not had a well visit recently. Lilly's parents indicate that they are living with the maternal grandparents and rely on friends for transportation and on Medical Assistance. Together, they look into pediatricians who are providers with their plan. Mary explores how the parents currently react to Lilly's hostile behaviors and offers possible new responses to integrate, such as looking at Lilly so she can see their facial expressions.

Intervention Task 1: Normalize and Educate

At appropriate times, Mary normalizes how the parents must be feeling during their discussions with her (e.g., frustration, not feeling like good parents, being scared of a possible medical condition, worry about finances). Mary also provides some education into what happens at a wellness visit to the pediatrician and insight into age-appropriate developmental tasks of 4-year-olds.

Intervention Task 2: Explore Options, and Intervention Task 3: Develop a Plan and Obtain a Commitment

Mary informs the parents that the well visit and hearing test need to be completed in order to rule out any medical issues before proceeding with behavioral intervention. Together, the parents and Mary develop a time frame to make contact with a pediatrician, evaluate health care options, and schedule a follow-up appointment after the medical appointment is completed.

Intervention Task 4: Prepare Documentation, Follow Up, and Provide Referrals

Mary documents the assessment and plan as agreed upon, including the hearing and pediatric referral, and schedules a follow-up visit with Lilly and her parents.

In the end, Lilly was medically assessed at having a 90% hearing loss in both ears. Her behavioral symptoms were the reason for the mental health referral but, after the holistic assessment and intervention, it was determined that the priority for crisis assessment was medical intervention. Mary could not have addressed the behavioral issues effectively if the medical issue (i.e., hearing loss) was not addressed first.

Discussion Questions

1. What other environment variables could have been explored to develop a holistic plan of action for Lilly?
2. What educational information could also be provided to the parents?
3. What could Mary do if the parents refused to have Lilly's hearing evaluated?
4. Aside from this case study, what other medical conditions could have symptoms that could be misdiagnosed for mental health issues?
5. Are there other referrals that could be made to assist the family?

VOICES FROM THE FIELD 1.2
Treating the Whole Person: The Need for Medical and Mental Health Collaborations

Lisa R. Jackson-Cherry

During the early part of my clinical career, I fought the medical model. I worked in agencies where the medical model was the foundation and often little attention was given to clinical psycho-social, let alone spiritual and religious, issues. I soon became frustrated that all of my training and my focus on mental health concerns were secondary, at best. As coordinator of a mobile crisis team in the City of Baltimore, we worked as a team with psychiatrists, case workers, psychiatric nurses, and mental health counselors. I started becoming aware that many medical issues mimic mental health symptoms, but I continued to be frustrated with the lack of understanding for addressing mental health issues in crisis situations.

I have learned over the years not to fight the medical model because, while professing to treat the whole person, I might miss an important aspect of the treatment for the client. I learned the importance of collaborating in order to treat the whole person. Over the years, I observed medical issues often resembling mental health symptoms and came to realize that if the medical issues are not ruled out, the mental health

treatment plan could be totally inaccurate. I grew more aware of this in my private practice, where I am referred individuals who are currently in crisis but may continue on my caseload for long-term counseling.

My practice over the last decade, although independent, has been with a family practitioner in a rural area. One case stands out as a good example of the need for collaboration with other professionals to provide treatment for the whole person. I was referred a young man about 10 years ago after a recent discharge from the hospital for attempting to kill a family member. At the time, he was 12 years old. He had been diagnosed with a psychosis–not otherwise specified (NOS); had been hospitalized multiple times per year for suicidal or homicidal behaviors; had been with multiple mental health counselors; and had a list of medical issues, including type 1 diabetes and unassessed "cognitive abilities." These issues did not allow him to monitor his diabetes without assistance from others. In addition, he lived many years being severely abused and neglected by his biological parents and siblings, and his charts indicated that his biological mother was a heavy substance user during her pregnancy.

(continued)

He was eventually adopted into a loving family but only after many years of maltreatment in foster homes. Early on, I spoke to his family and asked if he ever had been evaluated for fetal alcohol syndrome (FAS). My observation of his interactions, facial features, and processing, as well as the history of his early upbringing made me wonder whether FAS had anything to do with his cognitive abilities and presentation. At the same time, I could tell he was a very insightful child; more insightful than kids his own age and even some adults. I referred him to Children's Hospital, where he received a positive diagnosis of FAS. The need to integrate the development and environmental factors in his treatment plan were crucial.

Ten years later, he currently lives in a residential community. I see him not only for stabilization of his psychosis but also for PTSD, relationship issues, meaning-related issues, and to assist his team in the goal for him to become more independent. It is imperative for his team and me to work together on all of these issues. Often, he presents with sluggish, withdrawn affect and behaviors. His cognitive abilities during these times seem more disorganized and incoherent than his normal baseline. My first thought, if I did not know his medical issues, would be that he is depressed and possibly having current racing thoughts—a mental health focus. However, my first question is not about mental health. In knowing his medical issues and his inability to monitor his diabetes (developmental assessment), my first question is, "When was the last time you checked your sugar?" followed by, "What was the reading?" Then, we usually take a few minutes to check his sugar and, in most instances, his observed "depressed mood" is the result of a blood sugar reading in the range of 40–50. The next step is not to continue with mental health discussions but to contact his residential counselor, who waits for him in the waiting room, and follow the treatment plan outlined by the facility to raise his blood sugar to an acceptable level before any mental health counseling can occur. The medical concerns must be addressed prior to any mental health counseling. At the end of each session, I complete a form for the agency that includes any medical issues addressed during the session, my consultation with team members, and actions I have taken.

I have learned the importance of collaboration and the need to address medical issues. Of course, some professionals believe they are more knowledgeable about the human condition than others. That is OK. My goal is to help the client. However, over the years, in collaborating with other medical professionals, often on my initiating contact, I have witnessed them reach out more and include mental health updates in their treatment plans. Perhaps we are all seeing that treating the whole person involves many professionals.

The ABC-X and Double ABC-X Models of Crisis

The ABC-X and Double ABC-X models of crises were developed through research with families, but the concepts outlined in the models may be generalized to individuals or to larger groups or communities. From his studies of families experiencing separation and reunion as a result of World War II, Reuben Hill (1949, 1958) postulated the ABC-X model of family crisis (Figure 1.1). According to this theory, there is an interaction among a provoking stressor event (A), the family's resources (B), and the meaning that the family attaches to the stressor event (C). The crisis (X), a state of acute disequilibrium and immobilization of the family system, is an outcome of this interaction.

Hill's original ABC-X model continues to provide a framework for much research in the area of stress and crisis; however, a few scholars (Boss, 2002; McCubbin & Patterson, 1982) have expanded the model. Among the better-known variations of Hill's work is the double ABC-X model of crisis proposed by McCubbin and Patterson (1982). Writing from a systems orientation, which assumes that systems naturally evolve and become more complex over time, McCubbin and Patterson considered recovery and growth following crisis. The concept of adaptation was introduced to describe lasting functional changes that occur in order to meet the demands of a crisis or stressful event.

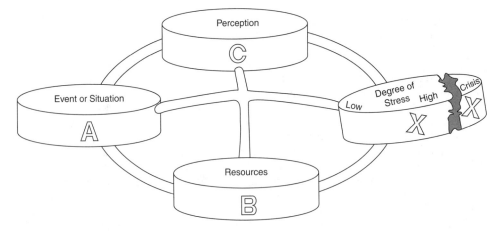

FIGURE 1.1   The ABC-X model of family crisis.

According to these scholars, Hill's original model was somewhat incomplete in that it outlined only those factors that contributed to a crisis or breakdown in functioning. Following a state of disequilibrium or incapacitation, additional stressors may accrue, and additional resources may be identified and acquired. Subsequently, new perceptions that take into account the original event and related hardships or stressors are formulated, along with the application of resources and coping strategies to meet the needs of those stressors.

According to McCubbin and Patterson (1982), there is a "double A" factor that includes Hill's original concept of a provoking stressor plus the buildup of further stressors that must be addressed. These stressors may include unresolved issues related to the crisis-provoking event, changes that occur unrelated to the event, and any consequences of attempts to cope (McKenry & Price, 2005). The "double B" factor refers to resources available at the time of the provoking stressor along with tangible and intangible resources that have been acquired or strengthened. Fortified coping resources would be included in this concept. The "double C" factor refers not only to perceptions and meanings assigned to the original provoking stressor but also to accumulated stressors, resources, coping, and the entire situation. Perceptions are influenced by religious beliefs, family and cultural values, and how the situation may have been reframed. In the model proposed by McCubbin and Patterson, the original crisis (Hill's X factor) constitutes a beginning point, while adaptation ("double X") occurs later in time. Adaptation is an outcome variable involving changes in functioning and perception. More than the simple reduction of stress, adaptation is the degree to which long-term change has occurred in response to the demands of stressor and crisis events.

McCubbin and Patterson (1982) referred to positive long-term changes that occur in response to crises as *bonadaptation*. It was their contention that following crises, some individuals and families do not merely return to their previous states of equilibrium; instead, they are better able to function and handle stress and crisis events. While McCubbin and Patterson referred to positive adaptation as bonadaptation, others have labeled this concept *stress-related growth* (Park, Cohen, & Murch, 1996) or post-traumatic growth (Tedeschi & Calhoun, 2004).

Elements of Stress and Crisis Theory

PROVOKING STRESSOR EVENTS   Boss (2002) categorized stressor events and situations by source, type, and severity. Sources are either internal (i.e., originating within the family) or external (i.e., attributable to someone or something outside the family). Examples of internal stressors include partner violence and chemical dependency. These stressors begin within the family and are accompanied by changes in the way the family functions. Partners and family members often adopt various roles, behaviors, and communication styles in their attempt to cope with and survive the actions of the abusive or addicted person. As familiar coping strategies become increasingly inadequate, families cease to function effectively and healthily. "Crises" in these families are rarely a one-time occurrence.

Another example of an internal stressor is infertility. Within the context of the family life cycle, most couples expect to be able to conceive and carry a pregnancy to term. Infertility is considered an internal stressor because the inability to achieve a successful pregnancy originates with one (sometimes both) of the partners as opposed to something outside of the family. It can become a crisis situation because the partners face psychological and relationship changes that affect the way they function. Each menses is encountered as a crisis situation. In response to this crisis situation, many couples are able to redefine their relationships and reframe their meanings of pregnancy and parenting; unfortunately, however, many couples do not respond well and ultimately separate.

External stressors originate outside the family but affect functioning nonetheless. Examples of external stressors include natural disasters, terrorism, financial decline due to the stock market, and the rising costs of goods and services. Some external stressors are attributable to forces of nature (e.g., hurricanes, tornadoes, earthquakes), some to humans (e.g., violent crimes, job termination), and some to a combination of the two. Individuals and families typically have less control over external stressors than they do over internal stressors. For example, families have little control over the stock market. However, the ramifications of a declining stock market could have a substantial influence on a family's future.

As with internal stressors, however, the degree to which crises caused by external stressors are experienced is contingent on available resources and the meaning attached to the stressor event. In the United States, the spring 2011 tornado outbreak (an external stressor) interrupted normal functioning and triggered crises for hundreds of families in Alabama, Missouri, and 13 other states. Families who seemed to be the most resilient and to have the least difficulty recovering from this crisis were those with available resources such as social support, housing, and financial assets.

Beyond classifying stressors by their source and type, Boss (2002) described stressor situations according to their duration and severity. Some stressors are onetime events, happen suddenly, and resolve quickly; these are considered acute stressors. An automobile accident, for example, might disrupt a family's equilibrium as broken bones heal and alternate transportation is used, but ultimately, the family's balance is restored. Other stressors, such as lifelong illnesses, infertility, and poverty, persist over long periods of time and are considered chronic. Families caring for aging family members may experience chronic stress and may face disequilibrium and crisis each time the elderly family member's health takes a turn for the worse. The crisis is triggered by changes in health but is the result of additional demands for financial, social, and other resources as well as the perception and meaning the family attaches to the elderly person's decline. Finally, it is important to consider whether a stressor situation is an isolated event or part of an accumulation of stressor events. It is often the case that any one stressor event may not be enough to trigger a crisis, but the cumulative effect of the pileup of stressors taxes resources, disrupts equilibrium and functioning, and results in crisis.

RESOURCES Resources may be defined as traits, characteristics, or abilities that can be used to meet the demands of a stressor event and that can be available at the individual, family, or community level. They may be tangible (e.g., food, clothing, shelter) or intangible (e.g., social support, self-esteem). When resources are adequate to meet the demands created by a stressor situation, the crisis situation is less likely to be perceived as problematic—and less likely to lead to trauma. Two types of resources are important: those that are available and used to mediate the initial stressor and those that are acquired, developed, or strengthened subsequent to a crisis situation (McCubbin & Patterson, 1982). Individual resources may include finances, education, health, and psychological qualities. Family resources include the internal, systemic attributes of cohesion and adaptability, along with resources such as financial management, communication skills, compatibility, and shared interests. Community resources include external supports, such as social networks, on which the individual or family can draw.

MEANING OR PERCEPTION Whether a stressor event results in crisis depends not only on available resources but also on the meaning attached to the event. One's meaning and perception of the event is the main determination of whether an event becomes a crisis. The meaning attributed to a stressor event is subjective and comes from the way it is appraised through both cognitive and affective processes. Factors contributing to this qualitative variable include the ambiguity associated with the stressor situation, denial, and the belief and value orientation of the individual or family. Ambiguity occurs when facts cannot be obtained. It is often the case that specific information about the onset, development, duration, and conclusion of an unpredictable stressor event is unavailable. When information is unavailable, individuals may be uncertain in their perception of who is included in their families or social support systems. With limited understanding about who is in and who is out, it becomes difficult to ascertain how various roles, rules, and functions will be carried out. Whereas sometimes stressors themselves are ambiguous because data are not available, at other times facts are available but are ignored or distorted. The resulting denial may be a useful coping strategy in the short term but may be damaging if it prevents further action during a crisis situation (McKenry & Price, 2005).

COPING In his original ABC-X model, Hill (1949, 1958) considered coping behaviors as part of the family's resources (represented by "B") to be used in response to demands of a stressor event ("A"). While many researchers agree that coping behaviors are a subset of available resources, coping itself is a separate construct, often interacting with both resources ("B") and perception ("C"). Any effort taken to deal with stress may be considered coping. Thus, coping is a process that requires cognitive as well as behavioral activities (McKenry & Price, 2005). Cognitively, people experiencing stressor events must appraise what is happening and assess any potential for harm. They must also evaluate the consequences of possible response actions. Following appraisal, there are three types of coping responses that may be used: direct actions, intrapsychic mechanisms, and efforts to manage emotions.

Direct actions are those behaviors that typically are thought of as "fight, flee, or freeze" responses. Examples include acquiring resources, asking for help, and learning new skills (McKenry & Price, 2005). These actions are used in relation to the environment in order to master stressors and are thought of as problem-focused coping strategies. Emotion-focused coping strategies, conversely, involve mechanisms used to change feelings or perceptions when there is little that can be done to change a stressor. Intrapsychic responses are those responses that are often thought of as defense mechanisms (e.g., denial, detachment) and allow people to alter their interpretations of the stress-provoking situation (Boss, 2002; McKenry & Price, 2005). Additional emotion-focused strategies are used to manage emotions generated by the stressor. Examples include the use of resources such as social support or of alcohol and drugs. Obviously, specific coping responses are neither adaptive nor maladaptive; they are simply efforts to manage.

Ecological and Contextual Considerations

Boss (2002) and Collins and Collins (2005) suggested that stress and crisis are affected by contextual factors. Collins and Collins advocated a "developmental–ecological" perspective to conceptualizing crises. Some crises are triggered by stressor events that are developmental in nature; that is, these developmental crises are expected events in the life span of the individual or family. However, regardless of whether the stressor event is developmental or situational, life span variables must be considered to determine their meaning and impact on the stress or crisis situation. In addition to considering developmental factors, Collins and Collins maintained that the context provided by environmental factors such as interpersonal relationships, community resources, and society at large must be recognized. This approach suggests that each crisis is unique, since the ecological determinants for each person will be unique. Therefore, crisis counselors need to be aware that even though many of the clinical considerations and approaches may be similar for a specific crisis and for many individuals experiencing that crisis (e.g., sexual assault), the person in crisis will experience the crisis differently than someone else due to the unique and personal ecological determinants. In essence, do not simply generalize and implement a generic approach to a particular crisis without first assessing the client's unique ecological factors. Complete Think About It 1.1.

Boss (2002) proposed a similar contextual approach to the study of stress and crisis, stating that "factors in addition to the stressful event influence family vulnerability or breakdown" (p. 28). According to Boss, stress is mediated by contextual dimensions, which may be either internal or external. The internal context comprises three dimensions that may be controlled or changed: the structure of the family, psychological

---

THINK ABOUT IT 1.1

Think about the things in your life that have created stress. Were they developmental or ecological? How did these stressors affect you?

elements such as perception and assessment, and philosophical elements such as values and beliefs. The external context comprises environmental or ecosystemic dimensions over which there is no control. External influences on stress and crisis include historical, economic, developmental, hereditary, and cultural contexts. Now analyze the stressor events experienced by the Nguyen family as Case Study 1.1 continues and concludes.

CASE STUDY 1.1 (continued)

The Nguyens: A Natural Disaster Affects a Family System

Stressor events are those occurrences—positive or negative, predictable or unforeseen—that provoke change in the functioning of a system. They may be categorized as normative or nonnormative. The Nguyen family has experienced a number of provoking stressors, some of which they chose, others that they did not.

Stressors may be categorized by source, type, and severity, and they should be considered within the external context. The external context includes variables such as culture, history, education, and heredity over which the Nguyen family has no control. Crisis counselors who work with the Nguyens need to explore the family's Vietnamese culture as well as possible additional cultural issues related to being part of an immigrant community along the Gulf Coast of the United States. Imbedded in these considerations is the fact that the Nguyens chose to leave Vietnam for the United States some 30 years after the Vietnam War. What kinds of social prejudices and biases does this couple face simply by being Vietnamese? Are there additional biases that they endure by virtue of being immigrants in a post-9/11 U.S. society?

The Nguyens's situation is complicated by their economic status, another component of their external context. Prior to the hurricane, they were making a living in the shrimp industry. They had few bills and no debt; however, they had no medical insurance. On those rare occasions when they required medical attention, they were able to use community public health resources. In the aftermath of the hurricane and the tough economic times that followed, numerous public, nonprofit health agencies were forced to close their doors, making it difficult for the Nguyens to access prenatal care. When their daughter was born with a birth defect, they found it necessary to travel to a larger city to receive care for her needs. Thus, they incurred transportation and lodging expenses, further affecting their delicate economic status.

Having lost their livelihood as shrimpers to the hurricane, the Nguyens were forced to look for work elsewhere. They were fortunate to have a rather large social support network as well as acquaintances who helped them find employment once retail outlets began to reopen in the months after the hurricane. Unfortunately, the retail jobs they found paid little more than minimum wage and did not include medical insurance. The Nguyens' educational background and minimal fluency in English made it difficult for them to pursue higher-paying jobs.

The Nguyens were also influenced by internal contextual factors—those factors that originate within the family and are accompanied by changes in the way the family functions. When they chose to leave their family and friends in Vietnam in order to move to the United States, the structure and definition of their family became less clear, particularly given the limited opportunities they had to return for visits. They also were forced to wrestle with issues related to caring for their aging parents. Once the Nguyens were living in the United States, their family structure changed further when they became parents themselves.

For the Nguyens, a relatively young couple, becoming parents could be considered a "normative" stressor—something normal, predictable, and developmental in nature. The stressor of becoming parents could also be considered volitional, as a degree of choice was involved. Conversely, nonnormative stressors are those that are unexpected. A catastrophic event such as the hurricane and all of its ramifications should certainly be classified as nonnormative. For the Nguyens, having a child with spina bifida is also a nonnormative and nonvolitional stressor, and its lasting implications make its presence chronic.

To ameliorate their situation, the Nguyens have several resources, derived from both internal and external contexts, on which they may rely. Although they left friends and family behind in order to move to the United States, they are members of a fairly large immigrant community. From this community, they receive a tremendous amount of social support. In addition, the Nguyens were able to use public community resources for health care and for other basic survival needs in the weeks and months after the hurricane. The Nguyens possess strengths such as initiative, resourcefulness, and a strong work ethic that have helped them to be resilient in the face of their stressors.

Discussion Questions

1. Apply the task model of crisis assessment and intervention to the case of the Nguyens and develop a treatment plan for intervention.
2. What sources of resilience and support can the Nguyens harness to cope with their circumstances?
3. What additional developmental or situational crises are likely to occur in this family in the years ahead? How can you help prepare or inoculate them to better adjust to those circumstances?

KEY CONCEPTS RELATED TO CRISIS

To help plan effective crisis response strategies, it is important to keep a number of key concepts in mind but to be aware that many of the terms used in the stress and crisis literature are used inconsistently, interchangeably, or without specificity. For example, in Western culture, the word *stress* is widely used to describe emotional phenomena ranging from feeling mild irritation and frustration to being frozen with fear. As the word relates to crises, however, it applies more to the ability to function than it does to affect. While the definitions of many terms seem intuitively obvious, some have unique connotations within the context of crisis intervention. In this section, key phrases and concepts used to describe crisis intervention theories and models are defined.

Stress

The term *stress* was introduced into medical literature by Hans Selye (1956), to describe nonspecific responses of the human body to demands that are placed on it. Stress activates what Selye called the "general adaptation syndrome," which is associated with biological responses. Changes in hormonal patterns, such as increased production of adrenaline and cortisol, over time, may deplete the body's energy resources, impair the immune system, and lead to illness. Selye distinguished between two types of stress: (1) distress (i.e., changes that are perceived negatively) and (2) eustress (i.e., changes that are perceived positively). He noted that distress tends to cause more biological damage than eustress, the latter seeming to contribute to well-being. Thus, how stress is perceived has an effect on adaptation.

The terms *stress* and *crisis* often have been used interchangeably in the literature, thus creating a bit of confusion. Boss (2002) has attempted to distinguish between the two concepts, stating that stress is a continuous variable (i.e., stress may be measured by degree), whereas crisis is a dichotomous variable (i.e., there either is or is not a crisis). Stress may be thought of as a process that exists over time, such as the stress of having a loved one serving in the military in a hostile environment. In contrast, crisis may be thought of as a temporary period of time during which typical coping ceases and there is intense disorganization and disequilibrium. A family accustomed to coping with the stress of having a loved one serving in the military and stationed in a combat zone may experience crisis when that individual returns home. The family's boundaries, structure, and coping mechanisms may have changed during the loved one's absence, leaving the family inadequately equipped to function with that loved one's homecoming.

Stress is the pressure or tension on an individual or family system. It is a response to demands brought about by a stressor event and represents a change in the equilibrium or steady state of an individual or family system (Boss, 2002; McKenry & Price, 2005). The degree of stress experienced hinges on perceptions of, and meanings attributed to, the stressor event. While anything with the potential to change some aspect of the individual or family (e.g., boundaries, roles, beliefs) might produce stress, increased stress levels do not necessarily always lead to crises. Often, stress can be managed, and the family or individual can arrive at a new steady state.

Trauma

Stressor events that involve trauma are powerful and overwhelming, and they threaten perceptions of safety and security. Some may be single incidents of relatively short-term duration, whereas others may occur over longer periods of time, resulting in prolonged exposure to the threatening stressor. Just as the terms *stress* and *crisis* have been incorrectly used interchangeably, so too have the terms *crisis* and *trauma*. A crisis is the event which, by itself, cannot result in trauma. The crisis event cannot be controlled. If a person perceives the crisis event in a way that affects daily functioning, the crisis event may become a traumatic experience. Likewise, stress may or may not be experienced as a result of an event. Rather, it depends on the individual's perception of the crisis. According to the DSM-5 (APA, 2013), a traumatic event involves threatened or actual death or serious injury, or a threat to the well-being of oneself or to another person. Traumatic events may be human-caused accidents or catastrophes, such as the 2003 ferry disaster in New York City. The ferry reportedly had not been running a straight course and struck a concrete pier while attempting to dock at the Staten Island end of its run. The crash killed 11 people and injured dozens of others. Other traumatic events include acts of deliberate cruelty. The multiple terrorist attacks on September 11, 2001, in New York City, Washington, DC, and Pennsylvania; and school shootings such as those at Virginia Tech in Blacksburg, Virginia; and Chardon High School in Chardon, Ohio, are all examples of acts of deliberate human cruelty, as are the numerous homicides and sexual assaults that occur in the United States each year. Additional traumatic events include natural disasters—events such as Hurricane Floyd, which struck the Carolina coast in 1999 and resulted in 56 deaths; the F-5 tornado that left a trail of death and destruction in Oak Grove, Alabama, in 1998; the flood that occurred in Cedar Rapids, Iowa, in 2008; and the earthquake that resulted in tens of thousands of deaths in China in 2008.

Responses to Trauma

In general, people experiencing traumatic events respond with intense feelings of fear and helplessness (APA, 2013). Most people respond to trauma within a normal range of reactions to abnormal events, whereby the individual's baseline is not disrupted to the point that causes impairment or dysfunction. Others become significantly distressed and impaired, and a few develop illnesses such as acute stress disorder (ASD) and PTSD. The risk for psychological disturbance tends to increase with the magnitude or intensity of the traumatic stressor and with the degree to which the event was human caused and intended to harm.

Following the Cocoanut Grove fire in 1942, practitioners became more aware of "common reactions to abnormal events" that do not necessarily constitute psychiatric illnesses. Reactions to traumatic events typically include physical, behavioral, cognitive, emotional, and spiritual responses, which tend to occur in stages, but ultimately are temporary. These transient reactions are often referred to as reactions to posttraumatic stress. Physical responses involve the autonomic nervous system as the person prepares to "fight, flee, or freeze" and may be experienced through symptoms such as palpitations, shortness of breath, nausea, muscle tension, headaches, and fatigue. Behaviorally, individuals may experience sleep and dietary changes, social withdrawal, purposeful avoidance of or attention to reminders of the trauma, changes in relationships, and increased use of alcohol or other mood-altering substances. Cognitive responses include rumination, preoccupation, forgetfulness, and difficulty concentrating. Emotional responses include distress, anxiety, impatience, irritability, anger, and symptoms of depression. Finally, spiritual responses are centered on existential questions and attempts to find meaning in the traumatic event. These reactions may transpire over a period as long as 2 years, but they are not considered pathological.

While most people return to a level of equilibrium and healthy functioning following a reaction to traumatic stress, some may experience consequences that impair their ability to function. Many of these peoples experience one or two of the trauma- and stressor-related disorders described in the DSM-5 (APA, 2013): ASD or PTSD. These two disorders are similar in their symptomology and differ mainly in their temporal association with exposure to the traumatic event. According to the DSM-5, the diagnostic criteria for ASD and PTSD include hyperarousal (e.g., hypervigilance, difficulty concentrating, exaggerated startle responses, sleep disturbance), reexperiencing (e.g., flashbacks, nightmares, intrusive thoughts), negative cognitions and mood (e.g., memory lapse, exaggerated negative beliefs, distorted cognitions, lessened interest in activities), and avoidance (e.g., attempts to avoid reminders of the traumatic event, inability to recall components of the event, detachment, dissociation, restricted affect)—symptoms that lead to distress and impairment in key areas of functioning such as work and interpersonal relationships. If these symptoms appear within 1 month of exposure to the trauma, ASD is diagnosed. If exposure to the traumatic event occurred more than a month prior to the development of these symptoms, PTSD is diagnosed. If symptoms persist for more than 3 months, PTSD is considered chronic.

Coping

A crisis event may be perceived as traumatic due to a lack of resources or failed coping strategies. *Coping* is defined as any behavioral or cognitive action that is taken in an effort to manage stress. In general, coping is considered a process (Erford, 2018). The process begins with an appraisal of a stressor and its potential for harm. If the situation is perceived as challenging or threatening (as opposed to irrelevant), further assessment takes place to determine what responses are possible and what their potential outcomes might be. Responses to stress fall into three broad categories: problem-focused coping, emotion-focused coping, and avoidance-focused coping (Linley & Joseph, 2004).

Problem-focused coping involves taking direct behavioral actions to change or modify aspects of the environment that are thought to be the causes of stress. When this type of coping strategy is employed, efforts are made to define the problem, generate possible solutions, weigh alternatives in terms of their costs and benefits, choose an alternative plan, and act. Emotion-focused coping, on the other hand, is more likely to be used in situations deemed unlikely to change. The aim of such coping is to reduce affective arousal so that the stressful situation may be tolerated, and it generally involves cognitive processes that change the meaning of a stressor or create emotional distance from it. Avoidance-focused coping, the third type of response to stress, may be viewed as a subset of emotion-focused coping, in which responses such as distraction or diversion are employed to avoid the stressor and the emotions that would be associated with it.

Coping may lead to successful or unsuccessful, adaptive or maladaptive outcomes. Following the experience of a traumatic stress event, for example, some individuals may choose to increase their alcohol consumption. While this behavior does little to address the needs brought about by the stressor, it may be an effective (albeit unhealthy) way to keep unwanted emotions at bay (McKenry & Price, 2005). Whether coping averts crisis and leads to adaptation depends on the particular person who is experiencing stress, the specific type of stress being encountered, and the features of the stressful encounter that the person attempts to manage. Although problem-focused, emotion-focused, and avoidance-focused coping have all been linked to adaptation or post-traumatic growth (Linley & Joseph, 2004), none of these approaches to coping guarantees a positive outcome. Problem-focused coping seems to be most valued in Western culture (Hays & Erford, 2018), yet it can be counterproductive if the situation that is causing stress is unalterable. If the stressor is unalterable, problem-focused efforts fail and distress is likely to persist. In such times, emotion-focused coping might be the better option. Avoidance-focused coping is least likely to result in adaptation or growth and most likely to lead to impaired well-being (Linley & Joseph, 2004). Complete Think About It 1.2.

THINK ABOUT IT 1.2

Think about the ways in which you cope with stress (and possibly trauma). What material factors and cognitions help you cope? What people help you cope? How could these material factors, cognitions, and people be considered protective factors in your life?

Adaptation

Adaptation—an outcome of stress or crisis—is the degree to which functioning has changed over an extended period of time and may be measured by the fit between the individual or family system and the environment. Some individuals and families benefit from the challenges of adversity. Successfully dealing with adversity often results in an outcome that is better than one that might have been reached without the adversity. Many individuals and families change to the point where they have the resources to meet the demands of stressors while continuing to grow. Quite often, changes have occurred in functional behaviors such as rules, roles, boundaries, and interpersonal communication patterns, resulting in families being better equipped to meet the challenges of future stressors. Conversely, for some individuals and families, an imbalance continues between stress demands and the capability to meet those demands. Many families may adopt unhealthy and unproductive responses to stress. Unhealthy coping behaviors, such as addictions or domestic violence, result in additional stress. Furthermore, it is often the case that coping behaviors that appear to be healthy contribute to stress. A parent, for example, might take a second job in order to increase the family's financial resources. Working extra hours, however, removes that parent from the home and may contribute to strained family relationships and a decrease in other nontangible resources.

Resilience

Individuals or families that bounce back from adversity are considered to have resilience. There are three distinct types of phenomena that are included in discussions of resilience: better than expected outcomes in at-risk groups of people, effective functioning that is sustained even under highly adverse conditions, and effective functioning that is regained or recovered after trauma (Masten & Obradovic, 2008). Numerous studies have attempted to identify factors that determine these outcomes. Although there has been some confusion in the literature about whether to conceptualize resilience as a personal trait or as a dynamic process (Luthar, 2006), the prevailing viewpoint favors process. Thus, resilience may be defined as the dynamics that contribute to positive adaptation following exposure to experiences that have the potential to disrupt functioning (Masten & Obradovic, 2008).

Early studies of resilience focused on individuals with schizophrenia and factors that would predict the course of the illness for them, but most research through which the concept has been studied and developed has focused on children experiencing adversity. Among the multiple adverse conditions studied have been parental mental illness, chronic illness, poverty, community violence, abuse, and catastrophic events (Luthar, 2006). Through these studies, a variety of concepts have been identified as protective factors that operate to ensure resilience. For the most part, these factors involve relationships.

Masten and Obradovic (2008) summarized several fundamental adaptive systems that seem to make a difference in human resilience. Beginning in early childhood, adaptation and the likelihood of resilience seem to depend on the quality of relationships with attachment figures. Attachments that are described as "secure" seem to moderate anxiety by allowing children to feel confident, connected, and reassured. As secure, confident children mature, they develop competence, self-efficacy, and mastery. Mastery develops as individuals learn they can interact successfully with their environments. In times of adversity, those with mastery motivation are likely to persist in their efforts to manage the environment.

Related to mastery is the ability to apply cognitive skills to solve problems. People who are resilient seem to be better at applying cognitive skills during times of adversity than those who are less well adapted. During times of high stress or threat of harm, it is important to be able to continue to think and plan effective responses. Thinking and problem solving during stressful situations are enhanced when emotions, arousal, and attention are self-regulated (Masten & Obradovic, 2008).

Being a part of larger social systems also seems to play a role in resilience. Social groups and networks provide resources such as information and support that are important in dealing with adversity. For children, attending school provides opportunities to acquire knowledge, develop social skills, and practice self-regulation, all resources that might be called for in times of stress. For older children, adolescents, and adults, being part of friendship networks, clubs, work groups, or civic organizations also has the potential to contribute to resilience. Among the larger systems most studied are religion and spirituality. Religious and spiritual connections provide attachment-like relationships and social support, as well as opportunities to practice self-regulation through prayer and meditation (Masten & Obradovic, 2008). In addition, religious and spiritual beliefs influence the way people attribute meaning to stressful situations and events and contribute to post-traumatic growth (Gerber, Boals, & Schuettler, 2011).

Whether individuals experiencing adverse conditions demonstrate resilience depends on the operation of protective systems that have evolved through biology and culture (Masten & Obradovic, 2008). If the systems are operating normally, the capacity for resilience is optimal; if they are damaged, the potential for resilience is compromised. Read Voices from the Field 1.3.

VOICES FROM THE FIELD 1.3
Human Resilience in the Aftermath of Katrina

Beth Graney

We landed in the New Orleans airport 6 weeks after Hurricane Katrina devastated the coastal areas and encountered the first of many eerie and unsettling sites we would experience over the next 2 weeks. Six school counselors from our county were given permission to volunteer with the Red Cross Disaster effort to provide counseling to victims of the hurricane. Our mission, or so we thought, was to offer assistance to school-aged children. However, upon arriving, we quickly found that the Red Cross had different ideas. Due to the devastation caused by the hurricane, most children were still with parents in shelters throughout Louisiana and other states.

(continued)

As a licensed professional counselor (LPC), I was able to function as a counselor/therapist; however, "my office" was outside, at a drive-through Red Cross site handing out food and cleaning supplies to folks who had lost their homes or were beginning the clean-up process. As cars came through, we offered people advice on safety issues for cleaning up mold, pamphlets on medical concerns typical after a devastating event, and warning signs of depression and other mental health concerns. The days were long and hot with a steady stream of cars from 7 a.m. to 6 p.m. or later. From the beginning, I was talking and listening to people, listening to their experiences, sharing their pain, but at first I wasn't clear about how I was offering counseling or mental health assistance.

Yet as the days passed, I noticed that many people came again and again, and each time I heard a little more of their story. Some days a person seemed pretty upbeat only to come back later in the day with tears, anger, or frustration at the bureaucracy involved in getting anything meaningful accomplished. I heard stories of amazing escapes from the hurricane or the flooding from the levees bursting. People told me how they witnessed great acts of selflessness and heroism—stories that never made the papers. Others talked of all they lost: "I don't even have one picture of my three kids," "I not only lost my house, my possessions, my car, but my job too," "All of my important medical papers are gone as well as all of my insurance information." Most heartbreaking were the loss of friends and relatives: "I still can't reach my daughter," "My mother died because she wouldn't leave her house." One woman was trying to find a place to continue her chemotherapy treatment from breast cancer, while another talked about leaving with her son who was a quadriplegic and trying to replace important medical equipment she could not bring when she left.

Yet, each day, there was laughter and happiness in spite of the hurricane, because people had survived and so they could begin again. At times, people pulled their car out of the line so we could talk in-depth about their situation—not for answers necessarily, just for a few brief moments to allow themselves to grieve before they got back in line to pick up yet another bottle of bleach and a new mop to continue their clean-up.

I learned many things about people and how they come to terms with hardship, loss, and devastation. First hand, I learned that Maslow was right: people's primary needs such as food, clothing, shelter, and safety must first be met before they can deal with higher level emotional needs. I learned that people can and do survive against overwhelming odds and the most difficult of circumstances. Often they do so with great resolve, courage, and even optimism. Quickly I noted that most people were able to deal with the loss of their possessions because they realized they could have lost the important people in their lives. Humor, along with revisiting past success, was the most commonly used strategy to deal with the hardship people were experiencing. I learned that normalizing sadness, fear, grief, and many other emotions comforted people more than I would have expected and that even in the most difficult times, most people see humor and joy in life.

On the trip home, my colleagues and I, after lots of tears and discussion, individually and collectively came to the conclusion that people really are resilient and go on to become stronger through difficult times. As for me, I learned that I can sleep on a cot with 80 other people snoring and coughing in the same room. I can go a day without a shower; I can eat a meal from the ERVE (Red Cross Emergency Response Vehicle); and I can stand on my feet for 12 hours a day in hot weather! I learned that, just like the people who survived the storm, you bond with those who have responded to the same disaster because no one else fully understands what you have experienced. Most of all, I learned that I am more resilient than I knew and sometimes the best, most helpful counseling does not take place in a nice, quiet office!

CRISIS INTERVENTION AS A UNIQUE FORM OF COUNSELING

Crisis intervention is a unique form of counseling, distinguished from other forms of counseling by its purpose, setting, time, and intervention plan. The American Counseling Association (2011) defines *counseling* as a "professional relationship that empowers diverse individuals, families, and groups to accomplish mental health, wellness, education, and career goals." While crisis intervention does not stray from this definition, the ways in which relationships are formed, clients are empowered, or goals are accomplished often seem divergent from other forms of counseling. It is sometimes the case that crisis intervention occurs within counseling relationships that are ongoing. For example, a client who already has an established relationship with a counselor in a school or an agency may reveal suicidal ideation, making it necessary for the counselor to adjust to a crisis intervention strategy. At other times, crisis intervention occurs between counselors and clients who do not already know each other. Disaster mental health counselors respond by going to sites where catastrophes have occurred and meeting new clients in these environments. Typically, there is only one meeting, which may be as brief as a few minutes and likely occurs in a chaotic setting with minimal privacy. Whether working in an office or in the field, within established counseling relationships or new ones, the crisis counselor's goal is the safety and stability of clients—that is, working toward restoring equilibrium. Once the client is safe and stable, other forms of counseling may be initiated or resumed. Consider, as an analogy, a car accident in which an individual may have experienced a severe medical trauma. It is essential for the emergency medical technician (EMT) to stabilize the patient to prevent further injuries prior to transferring (referring) the patient to a surgeon at the hospital.

Traditional counseling is typically a scheduled event that lasts for a specific period of time (e.g., a 45- to 50-minute session), and it is expected to consist of more than one such session over a period of time. Traditional counseling sessions take place in mental health agencies, private practices, hospitals, correctional facilities, schools, residential facilities, and other locations related to mental health services (Gladding, 2010).

Because a crisis is not a scheduled event, crisis intervention thus happens at the spur of the moment. While crisis intervention can take place in nearly any counseling setting, it has much broader borders—taking place in one's home (e.g., after a child is reported missing), a makeshift shelter (e.g., after a hurricane), an emergency room (e.g., after a rape), or any one of numerous other contexts.

Crisis intervention may also be conceptualized differently by different types of counselors. For example, clinical mental health counselors and couples and family counselors typically have scheduled clients that meet on a regular basis and a plan to help guide treatment. For these types of counselors, crisis intervention is seen as a part of counseling and could (in some ways) be anticipated if the counselor knows the client well enough. By contrast, school counselors often see students on an unscheduled basis and as a result of crises. Thus, for school counselors, crisis intervention is a model used more frequently and without much foresight into the crisis.

ROLES OF AND COLLABORATION BETWEEN MENTAL HEALTH WORKERS DURING A CRISIS

Most individuals who work in mental health professions are familiar with basic counseling skills that can help clients adapt during crises or stressful situations. The brief descriptions that follow illustrate how different mental health professionals—including professional counselors, psychiatrists, psychologists, social workers, paraprofessionals, and hotline workers—can be helpful in crisis situations.

Professional Counselors

In practice, professional counselors differ from psychiatrists and psychologists in that they work from prevention, developmental, and wellness perspectives.

Counselors often work through advocacy and collaboration and play a vital role in a comprehensive crisis leadership team (Kerr, 2009). Professional counselors can provide short-term or long-term counseling and therapy and may work with individuals or groups. Similar to psychologists, most licensed professional counselors may diagnose and treat mental and emotional disorders. Overall, these mental health professionals need a minimum of a master's degree to become licensed to practice (Newsome & Gladding, 2013). Professional counselors can assist individuals in crisis situations by doing the following:

- helping them to gain insight into the ways crisis affects their lives in a cognitive, behavioral, and emotional manner over a lengthy period of time
- providing specific treatment goals and objectives related to crisis
- monitoring and assessing the magnitude of severity of a crisis situation
- providing insight into co-occurring mental and emotional disorders and crisis (e.g., showing a client diagnosed with bipolar disorder how to cope with and monitor crisis)
- providing specific crisis intervention strategies during a crisis and over a period of time
- providing clients in crisis with resources and preventive measures
- assisting in alleviating symptoms associated with the crisis
- preparing clients to handle future crises

Some professional counselors bring various types of expertise in crisis intervention to their work, as these examples illustrate:

- Marriage and family counselors work from a systemic perspective. They provide support for couples and families and may involve the family in the resolution of the crisis on a short- and long-term basis.
- Pastoral counselors provide religious or spiritual integration in times of a crisis. Often, a crisis involves a spiritual or religious disconnect or dimension that must be explored. It is also important to understand any religious or spiritual coping mechanisms that were effective in the past that could be applied to the present crisis. Certainly the notion of incorporating spirituality into crisis intervention has an abundance of benefits and is not the sole property of pastoral counselors. All counselors would want to explore how one's religious and spiritual beliefs can provide solace in times of crises.
- Chemical dependency counselors specifically address the use of drugs and alcohol as a coping mechanism during crisis.
- Professional counselors who specialize in treating children, adolescents, adults, or geriatric populations bring a developmental perspective to the conceptualization and treatment of crisis.
- Rehabilitation counselors assist people diagnosed with acute or chronic disabilities in the personal, social, or psychological effects of those disabilities on employment or independent living (U.S. Bureau of Labor Statistics, 2015).
- School counselors work to maximize student achievement and to "promote equity and access to opportunities and rigorous educational experiences for all students" as well as helping to facilitate "a safe learning environment and work[ing] to safeguard the human rights of all members of the school community" (American School Counselor Association, 2008, p. 2). School counselors can be helpful in

school crisis situations by using individual counseling, group counseling, and classroom guidance activities and by collaborating with key stakeholders. Individual counseling can be helpful to those who are directly affected by crisis (e.g., by working with a student on expressing feelings after his or her house caught on fire). Providing group counseling to those who have been exposed to crisis (e.g., by establishing a support group for students who have divorced parents) could ease the pain of the initial impact of the crisis and create a support network among the group members. School counselors may provide primary or secondary preventive programs via classroom guidance activities on crisis, suicide, handling stress, self-regulation, and communication skills. Lastly, school counselors may collaborate with school system personnel as well as with parents, families, and members of the community on preventing and responding to crisis (e.g., by providing school staff with materials and training on recognizing suicidal behavior).

Psychiatrists

As noted earlier in this chapter, much of the early work in the field of crisis intervention was done by two psychiatrists working in the Boston area in the 1940s. According to the APA (2016), psychiatrists are physicians who have obtained specific training and experience in treating mental and emotional disorders. The key difference between the scope of practice of psychiatrists and that of other mental health practitioners is that psychiatrists are medical doctors and can prescribe medication to clients.

> Psychiatrists are especially suited to triaging direct and indirect victims in various settings, such as on consultation in hospitals' emergency rooms, intensive care and burn units, general medical floors or inpatient psychiatry units. Or psychiatrists may volunteer for agencies such as the American Red Cross, where they may be part of a mental health team providing grief support, notification of death to family members, or crisis intervention. (APA, 2004, p. 21)

Psychologists

Clinical and counseling psychologists are mental health practitioners who engage in the assessment, diagnosis, and treatment of mental and emotional disorders. To be licensed to practice, state licensure boards require completion of a doctoral degree. In a few areas of the United States, including New Mexico and Louisiana, and in the Indian Health Service and the military, where access to psychiatrists is often limited, psychologists with specific training may prescribe medication. With regard to their participation in crisis intervention, much of their work is identical to that of professional counselors.

Social Workers

Social workers engaged in crisis intervention also function in a manner similar to professional counselors. Depending on the scope and focus of practice, some social workers may be employed after earning a bachelor's degree, while other, more specialized clinical practice settings may require a master's degree. Although performing many of the same duties as counselors, social workers are well equipped to concentrate on the resource needs of their clients.

Paraprofessionals

Some individuals within the mental health community have limited formal education and training in the professional mental health field, but they perform essential tasks (e.g., case management duties, residential care) for individuals in crisis. Paraprofessionals can do the following:

- Manage resources that help facilitate stabilization (e.g., make sure clients keep all medical, financial, emotional, environmental, and social service appointments).
- Ensure clients are aware of appropriate resources that could be seen as preventive actions to crisis (e.g., make sure that a client has appropriate resources to pay a natural gas bill to have heat in the winter).
- Provide an outlet for clients to decrease isolation and talk to others (e.g., talk with individuals in crisis and provide assurance that someone cares for them and their situation).
- Participate in executing the modality and frequency aspects of the treatment plan—in other words, make the connections set out in the treatment plan. For example, the professional counselor may develop a treatment plan for someone in a residential program that involves attending Alcoholics Anonymous groups daily, attending a group on a specified psychosocial issue three times per week, and addressing a medical issue. The paraprofessional case worker may be responsible for following through with the treatment plan by assisting the client in making the appointments and setting up transportation to the appointments or groups.

To be effective, a crisis worker, whether a professional or a paraprofessional, must be able to (1) rely on life experiences and emotional maturity to remain stable and consistent, (2) remain calm and poised in order to de-escalate the situation, (3) use creativity and flexibility to adapt to rapidly changing situations, (4) maintain energy and resilience to keep up with the rigor of working in a crisis situation, and (5) use effective clinical skills in a timely fashion in order to create a trusting and safe environment and suspend one's values just for the crisis time in order to stabilize the client and refer him or her on to another professional (James & Gilliland, 2017). Keep these characteristics in mind as you complete Activity 1.1.

ACTIVITY 1.1

In the crisis situations that follow, what might be some activities, interventions, responsibilities, and considerations for each of the mental health professionals discussed earlier?

Crisis Situation 1

Alan and Mary have been married for 3 years. Alan has been cheating on Mary for the past 6 months, and Mary has been cheating on Alan for the past year. Each is unaware of the other's infidelity, but the stress in their house is severe. They yell constantly, and Mary throws objects during arguments. In the past month, Alan has begun to slap Mary during these arguments. Last night Alan hit her so hard that he knocked her unconscious. Mary is now in the hospital talking to a social worker: "I'm afraid of my husband," Mary says, "but I don't have anywhere else to go. I feel so alone."

(continued)

Crisis Situation 2

John F. Kennedy High School, located in a primarily low- to middle-class rural community, comprises approximately 1,000 students, most of whom know one another. Within the past 4 months, the school has been evacuated five times as a result of a call indicating that there is a bomb in the building and that "everyone should get out." As a result of these threats and evacuations, students are scared, parents do not want to send their children to school, and teachers and other school personnel are frightened to go to work. Students also have begun to accuse each other of calling in the bomb threats, and several students have been ostracized and bullied. The Parent Teacher Organization has called a meeting tonight to address this issue.

Crisis Situation 3

Walter Taylor is a 74-year-old African American male who has worked all of his life as a plumber. He has been married to his wife, Martha, for 52 years and has four children and six grandchildren. Due to intense flash floods within the past week from melting snow, the Taylor household is 7 feet under water. When the water came, Walter, his 40-year-old daughter June, and his 13-year-old granddaughter Beverly had to be rescued from their house by boat. Walter's house is destroyed, Beverly is having nightmares and does not want to leave her family, and June is recovering from a head trauma caused while being evacuated.

Hotline Workers

Hotline workers are often the first point of contact for many individuals experiencing a crisis and may handle any number of crises resulting from suicidal and homicidal ideation, domestic violence, substance abuse, and sexual assault. There are hotlines that specialize in these and other specific types of crisis situations. There are even crisis hotlines for specific age groups (e.g., a hotline dedicated to teen callers). Typically, hotline workers are not mental health professionals but volunteers who have undergone specific training in responding to crises. No matter what their focus, crisis hotlines play a vital role in assessing, intervening in, and preventing the occurrence of crises. Crisis hotline workers perform essential tasks during a crisis situation:

- They assess the severity of the crisis situation and the lethality of the caller.
- They provide immediate crisis intervention to the caller in an attempt to de-escalate the crisis. This is critical in a crisis situation because the caller does not have to make an appointment with a professional or wait to get help. Most hotlines are 24-hour services open 365 days a year.
- They provide resources to the caller that may help resolve the crisis.

Table 1.2 presents a selection of toll-free hotlines that serve those in crisis.

Collaboration Among Crisis Workers

Professional counselors, psychiatrists, psychologists, social workers, various paraprofessionals, and hotline workers can all play vital roles in the mental health of people in crisis. Collaboration among these crisis workers works best when the client's treatment goals are clearly communicated, the responsibilities of different crisis workers are known and respected, and an open dialogue in which all differing views of treatment are heard and considered. When crisis workers collaborate in a professional and respectful fashion, a broader scope of treatment that addresses multiple facets of a client's recovery can take place.

TABLE 1.2 Toll-Free Hotlines

General Crisis Intervention Hotlines for Youth (dealing with conflicts, family stressors, suicide, runaway youth, drugs and alcohol, homelessness, and so on)

- Boys Town Suicide and Crisis Line: 1-800-448-3000 (voice)/1-800-448-1833 (TDD)
- Covenant House Hotline: 1-800-999-9999
- National Youth Crisis Hotline: 1-800-442-HOPE

Child Abuse Hotlines

- ChildHelp USA National Child Abuse Hotline: 1-800-4-A-CHILD (voice)/1-800-2-A-CHILD (TDD)
- National Child Abuse Hotline: 1-800-25-ABUSE

Domestic Violence Hotlines

- National Domestic Violence/Child Abuse/Sexual Abuse Hotline: 1-800-799-SAFE (voice)/ 1-800-787-3224 (TDD)/1-800-942-6908 (Spanish speaking)
- Domestic Violence Hotline: 1-800-829-1122

Substance Abuse/Alcoholism Hotlines

- Alateen: 1-800-352-9996
- National Cocaine Hotline: 1-800-COCAINE
- National Drug Information Treatment and Referral Hotline: 1-800-662-HELP

Poison Control Hotline

- Poison Control: 1-800-362-9922

Rape Hotline

- National Rape Crisis Hotline: 1-800-656-4673

Suicide Prevention Hotlines

- National Suicide Hotline: 1-800-SUICIDE (voice)/1-800-799-4TTY (TDD)
- National Suicide Prevention Lifeline: 1-800-273-TALK/1-888-628-9454 (Spanish speaking)

Collaboration with Other Professionals

More than any other mental health professionals, crisis workers tend to collaborate with other types of professionals in the community for the well-being of clients. For example, crisis workers may need to collaborate with religious and spiritual leaders, medical professionals, and law enforcement professionals in crisis situations. Each of these professionals has a different scope of practice that governs their actions with clients. For example, religious and spiritual leaders provide assistance in line with their religious and spiritual values, beliefs, and traditions. Traditional medical professionals tend to practice from a pure medical model and intervene with medical practices that may counter mental health practices. Law enforcement officers protect and safeguard the public by enforcing laws; their intervention may be quite different from crisis workers, because it is based on training and protocols to protect the community and themselves.

FUNDAMENTALS OF WORKING WITH CLIENTS IN CRISIS

The procedures for working with clients in crisis begin with determining, based on assessment efforts, how best to approach such individuals to de-escalate the crisis (see Table 1.1). In other words, there is a need to assess whether the situation calls for counselors to be directive, nondirective, or collaborative.

Directive approaches call for counselors to "direct" or lead the person in crisis in a specific direction. Clients in crisis are typically scattered and unable to plan beyond their current situation. Therefore, providing some form of direction may help. For example, if someone is highly uncertain, spontaneous, or ambiguous and, at the same time, unable to get out of a crisis state, providing direction could provide immediate, though temporary, relief to feelings surrounding the crisis situation. Another example is a person who presents with highly suicidal behaviors and for whom the crisis counselor must (directive approach) initiate an emergency involuntary hospitalization for the safety of the client.

Nondirective approaches allow the person in crisis to come up with the directives while the crisis counselor facilitates that process. If the client can make rational decisions, even though a state of crisis exists, a nondirective approach may empower the client to make progress toward de-escalation. For example, asking clients who are recent flood victims "What might be of most help to you now?" allows them to respond with specifics, rather than having the counselor guess what is needed. The thought process and response of such clients may also empower them and allow them to feel they are regaining some control over their own lives.

A collaborative approach focuses on showing the person in crisis that the counselor is a participant in the journey toward stabilization and normalcy, and that others can provide help, decrease isolation, and allocate resources to them. A collaborative approach is a blend of directive and nondirective approaches—but with a flavor of togetherness. In other words, a collaborative approach provides support and a sense of working together toward a common goal. Collaboration can be particularly beneficial to clients who feel that they have too many options to respond to the crisis, are aware of only options that have been ineffective in the past, or may need some assistance in generating new options.

Complete Activity 1.2 to gain practice identifying these various approaches. Also read Voices from the Field 1.4.

ACTIVITY 1.2

Examples of directive, nondirective, and collaborative approaches in crisis situations follow. Discuss how each could be an appropriate statement in specific circumstances.

EXAMPLE 1

- Please put the gun down. (*directive*)
- What would help you feel more comfortable about putting the gun down? (*nondirective*)
- I want to help, but knowing you have that gun in your hand scares me. Can you put the gun down for me so I can help you more? (*collaborative*)

EXAMPLE 2

- It sounds like you are thinking about killing yourself during most of the day and every day and have decided nothing else can take away your pain. You tell me that you will not follow through with whatever we plan and that you will kill yourself. I am concerned for your safety and want you to be here, alive. I really think some time to focus on just you is the best option. I want to help you stay alive, and the only option I see to do that is for you to be admitted to the hospital (*directive*)
- You have generated some ideas on how you can stay safe and they seem like good options. (*nondirective*)
- I am happy to hear that you do not want to follow through on killing yourself. I also hear you saying that the pain at times is unbearable. You have been able to generate many options for staying alive. Can we continue to work together to see what resources are the best options and make a list so that when you start to have thoughts of wanting to kill yourself you can act on the best options first? (*collaborative*)

EXAMPLE 3

- I'm going to call the police. (*directive*)
- Do you think calling the police will help? (*nondirective*)
- If I bring you the phone, would you call the police? (*collaborative*)

VOICES FROM THE FIELD 1.4
Chardon High School

Jason M. McGlothlin

The day after the shooting at Chardon High School in February 2012, I volunteered to work with the students who witnessed the shooting as well as the students' families. I met with two students for about an hour and a half each and a family for about 2 hours. I listened to their graphic and detailed reports of what happened and saw the tears they shed. I heard the worries they had about returning to the school and the condolences for their classmates who were injured and dead. I heard the countless statements of reaching out to others and of "I hope _____ is okay" and "I need to call _____'s family." I share this story not to discuss what I did but the effect it had on me. Listening and seeing such tragedy, such raw emotion and devastation, had a great impact on me not only as a professional but also as a person. I remember coming home that day and giving my 6-year-old an extra-long hug and listening to him explain the shooting because his teachers talked about it at his school.

However, seeing these students reach out to others and care for their community instilled in me a sense of hope. The notion of self-care, burnout prevention, and taking care of self is critical. However, crisis intervention is a roller coaster of emotions for counselors. Counselors quickly become immersed in the emotional state of the crisis, and then leave. We all need to find the unique way we can take care of ourselves.

CRISIS INTERVENTION IN A TECHNOLOGICAL WORLD

Technology has had an influence on crisis intervention. In an age where many adolescents and adults have smartphones in hand at all times, crises are reported immediately to authorities, help is often obtained quickly and in some instances in real time (e.g., via Skype), and crisis intervention information and resources can be accessed quickly on one's smartphone. Social media such as Facebook and Twitter provide opportunities to share experiences of a crisis in real time. Also, a client in crisis can have easier access to his or her counselor or other mental health providers via text messages, e-mail, and other modes of electronic messaging.

Furber, Jones, Healey, and Bidargaddi (2014) found that both text messaging and phone-based psychotherapy were beneficial resources for clients in crisis. According to Almond and Budden (2012), text messaging is seen as a positive tool during hostage negotiation, suicide prevention, and general crisis intervention. Sude (2013) found that text messaging used in mental health practice increases the responsiveness of counselors to clients, allows clients to be more candid in their communication, is helpful to clients who prefer this method of communication, and may create a more connected feeling between client and counselor. The limitations of texting in practice include ethical concerns such as boundary issues, maintaining confidentiality, and not being able to establish a therapeutic relationship based on feelings because the client and the counselor are not face to face.

Another area in which technology has influenced crisis intervention is online crisis counseling services. Gary (2010) reported that online crisis counseling services is a valuable resource for clients who are in crisis and geographically isolated, are self-sequestered, or have limitations to getting face-to-face counseling (e.g., transportation problems, work release time). In a meta-analysis of the literature regarding online counseling, Richards and Vigano (2013) found a positive perception by clients of online counseling with benefits in the areas of client anonymity, convenience of services, and client disinhibition, to name a few. Counselors must stay attentive to new technological tools that can help them support clients in times of crisis.

Summary

A crisis is a situation that is the precipitating stressor event. If the crisis is perceived as leading to distress, and diminished functioning when the distress is not relieved by familiar coping resources, a person may experience trauma. Many individuals and families are resilient and benefit from having met the challenges of a previous or current crisis situation. How well an individual or family adapts following a crisis is often determined not only by the nature of the crisis event itself but also by the presence or absence of other stressors, the availability of tangible and intangible resources, and how the entire situation is perceived. Crises may occur during normal, developmental transitions during the lives of individuals and families, by situational events that often are sudden and unexpected, or by existential issues that are related to purpose and meaning. It is not uncommon for a crisis event to be perceived as fitting into more than one of these categories.

A task model of crisis assessment and intervention was presented in Table 1.1 and comprises four essential crisis assessment tasks: (1) Address Safety, Stabilization, and Risk; (2) Follow a Holistic Bio-Psycho-Social-Spiritual Assessment Approach; (3) Clarify the Problem(s); and (4) Explore Coping Skills, Resources, and Supports.

These tasks are followed by four essential crisis intervention tasks: (1) Normalize and Educate; (2) Explore Options; (3) Develop a Plan and Obtain a Commitment; and (4) Prepare Documentation, Follow Up, and Provide Referrals.

Crisis intervention begins with an assessment of the provoking event, responses to the provoking event, and the contextual variables that influence the situation. While there are times when a crisis counselor's response to a crisis appears indistinguishable from traditional counseling, crisis intervention generally is thought to be different from traditional counseling because of the occurrence of a crisis event. Paraprofessionals and other mental health professionals provide crisis intervention services, often working in teams where each professional may focus on a particular area of expertise.

Complications of working in crisis situations and with clients in crisis can take a physical, emotional, spiritual, and professional toll on crisis counselors. Each crisis has its own complications.

Whether it is miscommunication with resources and agencies, waiting for follow-up from other parties, dealing with the realities of a lack of resources, or seeing clients "take a step back" in dealing with the crisis, counselors need to remain professional and be patient. Counselors need to rely on their training, skill, and knowledge to focus on the basic skills in building a therapeutic relationship with people.

It is important when reading the remainder of this text to consider the various options for self-care while helping others manage a crisis—proactive ways to avoid burnout and vicarious trauma; manage personal emotions during highly emotional crisis situations (e.g., when working with suicidal clients); and ensure optimal physical, cognitive, and psychological presence when working with clients in crisis. Working with others in a state of crisis is not easy, but it is immeasurably rewarding. Counselors need to stay abreast of their own well-being in order to help others effectively.

2

Safety Concerns in Crisis Situations

Charlotte Daughhetee, James Jackson, and Latofia Parker

PREVIEW

When responding to a crisis, counselors need to be able to act promptly and safely; thus, preparedness is essential to best practice prior to a crisis occurring as well as during emergency situations. A vital part of crisis preparedness is attention to counselor safety and security. This chapter presents an overview of safety and security procedures and other issues of concern during crisis intervention.

SAFETY CONCERNS AND PRECAUTIONS

In addition to an emotional and psychological toll, a crisis event can produce safety and security concerns. Basic safety precautions by the crisis counselor when working with high-risk or dangerous clients can reduce the chances of harm to the counselor, client, crisis workers, and others. The ultimate success of crisis intervention depends on planning, training, and the preparedness of team members. A proactive and safety-conscious plan should be in place prior to the actual crisis. Even though most plans will need to be flexible because every crisis is unique, a preliminary plan is better than no plan.

Proactive Approaches

Although some professional counselors are naturally inclined toward preparedness and plan for every reasonable contingency, many counselors have good intentions about developing an emergency plan but most never seem to follow through with preparations to completion. Indeed, most crisis plans are developed in response to a crisis. However, it is essential for agencies, schools, universities, institutions, and communities to have a crisis plan in place prior to a crisis occurring. When a crisis event occurs, particularly a large-scale disaster that affects many people, crisis teams must be ready, with well-defined roles, resources, and training. Unfortunately, while crises have huge impacts on systems and communities, they are usually low-priority items with respect to planning and resources. The Federal Emergency Management Agency (FEMA, 2014) stresses that crisis planning is an ongoing cycle of planning, organizing, training, evaluating, and improving. Chen, Chen, Vertinsky, Yumangulov, and Park (2013) found that communities that facilitated collaborative partnerships between private and public organizations were the most resilient when faced with a crisis or disaster event. An essential characteristic of these cooperative relationships was the existence of a sense of trust that resulted from common goals, preparation, and joint training of the community crisis team. Just as a community jointly experiences the trauma of a large-scale disaster or crisis, so too must the community mutually work toward recovery and healing.

Crisis teams are also essential in educational settings and comprise personnel within the school or university who have appropriate expertise (Brock, 2013; see Chapter 13). School and university crises can involve events such as the death of a student or faculty member, violent occurrences within the community, or large-scale disasters as well as a crisis experienced by a single student. Schools and universities are often at the center of a community or neighborhood, so a crisis that affects a school or university has a ripple effect within the larger community and vice versa. As recent events show us, schools and universities must be prepared for a wide range of crisis events, including threats and actions of violence. Threat assessment teams on campuses are essential and should incorporate input from all pertinent stakeholders (see Chapter 6).

An effective crisis team coordinates and collaborates throughout both planning and crisis response and has clear, well-defined roles for all the individuals on the team. The team should be committed to ongoing training and evaluation of plans. FEMA (2014) provides helpful information about crisis planning, and Chapters 12 and 13 have additional information on emergency preparedness and response teams.

Safety Issues

As part of a crisis team, counselors contribute to the success of crisis intervention through collaboration with other crisis workers. Ultimately, this collaborative spirit enhances public safety. Even as they are working to achieve public safety, crisis counselors must also be aware of their own safety and take proactive steps to ensure a secure and effective counseling environment.

INTERACTION WITH LOCAL AUTHORITIES   A crisis team comprises workers from across the community or organization who come together in response to a crisis event. Mental health providers are an essential component of any crisis team, and all members of a crisis response team should work together toward the same goal, which is to advance the recovery process following a disaster. Survivors of crises need access to medical care, food and water, shelter, mental health services, basic safety, and sometimes religious/spiritual connections; the realization of recovery is possible only when there is interagency cooperation.

It is important to remember that each crisis worker has a unique role. In the event of large-scale emergency situations (e.g., natural disasters, terrorism, civil unrest), the safety and security of the area will be maintained by law enforcement, in some cases with the assistance of National Guard troops or federal agencies. Law enforcement is responsible for the physical safety of the community. Firefighters and medical personnel provide rescue and first-aid assistance. These first responders will collaborate with crisis counselors by referring clients in need of immediate mental health evaluation services.

Crisis counselors must understand that during the initial impact of a large-scale crisis, the most critical needs correspond to the physiological and safety needs in Maslow's hierarchy of needs: shelter, food, water, and safety as well as the need to be connected with family and loved ones. Mental health professionals are brought in at this early stage to assess clients and provide psychological first aid in order to prevent further personal crises stemming from the disaster; however, some clients may not need the services of mental health professionals until weeks or months after the onset of the crisis. Therefore, follow-up is crucial to make certain that crisis counseling needs are met. Complete Activity 2.1, which asks you to consider disaster preparedness needs.

In addition to collaboration as team members during a large-scale disaster or major crisis, counselors may also collaborate with law enforcement officials regarding a crisis with an individual client. For example, law enforcement may be involved in welfare and well-being checks in situations where a client has become an immediate threat to self and to others. Wilcox (2015) states that it is important for those in law enforcement to receive training in the assessment and management of individuals diagnosed with mental disorders. At the heart of this training should be a partnership and an ongoing relationship with local mental health providers through a collaborative crisis intervention team training model. Police intervention is sometimes the first step in a process that results in treatment for individuals in acute mental health crisis. However, in the event of an arrest, the incarcerated person is often barred from immediate treatment options, which could exacerbate the illness.

Franz and Borum (2011) note that the involvement of law enforcement in crisis intervention teams could help lower the arrest rate of citizens with mental illness and increase access to mental health resources. Clearly, awareness of mental health issues is essential in the assessment and treatment of these citizens, and a cooperative effort to address such encounters is beneficial to the community. At the same time, it is important for counselors to understand that if a crime has been committed, a law enforcement officer must protect the community and uphold the law. Therefore, in order to prevent further harm to the community, the individual may be arrested in the interest of protecting the public.

Counselors may be involved during the initial stage of crisis intervention in a variety of ways, and part of their role at this stage is providing disaster relief that helps meet the basic needs of the community. For example, during the initial stage, counselors might assist with food and water distribution or with temporary relocation and housing

---

ACTIVITY 2.1

In small groups, discuss the following questions.

- If a natural disaster such as a tornado or earthquake hits your area today, would you be prepared?
- Would you have enough food and water for at least three days, a battery-operated radio, flashlights, candles, extra batteries, and so on?
- Do you have cash and gas in the car in case you must evacuate? Why or why not?

- What other aspects need to be taken into account in preparing for this type of disaster?
- In general, do you think the citizens in your community are prepared for such a disaster?
- How does the level of community preparedness affect crisis intervention?

needs to help meet the immediate physiological needs of affected people, while simultaneously assessing people's functioning and possibly intervening in a critical moment. As part of the crisis team, counselors may also be involved in providing support to first responders such as firefighters, law enforcement, and other crisis team members who may experience mental exhaustion or other unmet basic needs, but who may be reluctant to reach out for assistance. First responders need a place to find respite and a listening ear to continue to be effective.

SAFETY CONCERNS IN CRISIS COUNSELING   When clients are a danger to themselves and others, crisis counselors may work alone or in partnership with local authorities to ensure everyone's safety. Law enforcement is usually involved when a client presents a threat to public safety, as with high-threat homicidal and violent clients. Clients who pose a danger to themselves and others may need to be hospitalized (see Chapter 6 for information on voluntary and involuntary hospitalization). Counselors should not transport such clients to the hospital, and should instead enlist the client's family or friends if the client is low or moderate risk and is voluntarily entering an inpatient unit. The only exception is when a crisis counselor is part of a specialized crisis team for which this is the expectation.

Even as part of a crisis response team, at no time should a counselor accompany a high-risk client without another team member. In these situations, several common sense procedures should be followed. The counselor should make sure the car does not have any objects that could be used as weapons, car keys should remain in the possession of the counselor at all times, the client's belongings should be packed in plain view of the crisis team member, and the client's bag should be placed in the trunk of the car. The client should be seated where the counselor can see him or her and should wear a seat belt. If a client decides to leave the car, the counselor should not physically prevent the client from doing so. However, if the client leaves and poses a risk to self or others, it is crucial for the counselor to contact law enforcement or the community service board who can make involuntary hospitalization assessments and/or execute an emergency petition.

A high-risk client who is being hospitalized involuntarily will likely need to be transported to the hospital by ambulance or by police. If a high-risk client suddenly leaves a counselor's office, the counselor should not attempt to physically stop the client and should notify law enforcement for assistance. The counselor should note what the client was wearing, the direction the client was heading, and the brand, model, color, and license plate of the vehicle the client used (if appropriate). Because counselors work closely with hospitals and medical personnel during intervention and treatment of suicidal and homicidal clients, a strong working relationship between mental health providers and local authorities is essential for effective crisis intervention. It is the policy of most police departments, during the transport of a person who is high risk, to restrain that person for the safety of the person, the public, and the police officer. Police officers are not counselors; they are sworn to protect the public. Chapter 6 provides important information regarding assessment of suicidal and homicidal ideation. Read Voices from the Field 2.1.

PHYSICAL SAFETY   Given the likelihood that crisis counseling often takes place in the field, counselors are likely to find themselves in hazardous surroundings and therefore must be aware of safety procedures for their own security and the well-being of their clients. According to FEMA (2014), first responders (e.g., firefighters, police, paramedics)

VOICES FROM THE FIELD 2.1
Dealing with an Aggressive, Hostile Woman in a Prison Setting

Matthew J. Paylo

As the mental health director at a female maximum-security prison, I was familiar with managing aggressive behaviors. It seemed like a daily occurrence that my staff was asked by prison personnel to aid in the de-escalation of an individual who was managing a specific stressor or rebelling against the restrictiveness of the prison setting in general. As a director, I often used professional development training to aid new mental health staff deal with various crisis situations specific to the prison setting. Later, I would realize I still had a few things to learn about managing crises.

One Saturday in November, I found myself trying to get ahead on evaluations and paperwork, and I was the only mental health staff member in the prison. A correctional officer contacted me regarding Delia, a woman who initiated a dispute with another woman on her wing. The correctional officer had managed to lead Delia off the wing and into a holding cell. He reported that she was screaming and clearly agitated by the situation. Delia had been involved in our anger management program, and I recalled that she had recently head-butted a sergeant. The staff had limited tolerance for her actions and behavior.

When I got to the scene, I evaluated the environment and deemed it was safe to enter and engage the woman. Another correctional staff member asked if I wanted to enter the cell; having worked with the prisoner for over 6 months, I did not hesitate. Assessing on the continuum of escalation, I had surmised that she was not just anxious or defensive but was

acting out and using intimidation and posturing to relay her level of frustration. I spoke her name softly, and respectfully inquired about the precipitating event. Using my already existent relationship with her, I transitioned her to focus on communicating verbally instead of acting out physically. Trying not to overreact to her language and threats, I attempted to show her empathy on how difficult this situation must have been for her. Avoiding a power struggle with her was another aim of mine and she seemed to be slowly de-escalating (i.e., she was no longer pacing in the cell and her fists were no longer clenched).

Yet on reflection, I remembered that I was standing not off to the side but directly in front of Delia. This face-to-face posture was an obvious point that I had missed at that moment. Her eyes gazed at the floor and when she raised them toward me she reacted to my stance in a less than positive way. She immediately stated, "Who the f*** do you think you are trying to control me? You can't stop me from leaving. I'll take you out." At that moment I realized my posture was intimidating, and I moved two quick steps to my left. Delia immediately threw a right-handed hook as I moved just out of her reach. The correctional staff flooded the cell.

The point of this story—the same point I have relayed to my staff and students—is that even if you are saying all the right things in the right way, nonverbal communication (posture, positioning, affect, facial reactions, etc.) is often more important and can set the tone for the entire interaction.

---

are on the front lines of disaster and crisis, and face danger from numerous threats, including damaged infrastructure; secondary collapse; unfamiliar surroundings; unstable structures; falling or tripping hazards; falling material or flying objects; exposure to hazardous materials; decontamination; and exposure to smoke, dust, fire, noise, electrical hazards, contaminated air and water, and dangerous equipment.

Crisis counselors are not likely to be on the front lines of disaster initially, but may still be in dangerous areas and should be aware of potential hazards. After the primary response, counselors may be out in the field and should be careful around damaged structures and other hazards. It is imperative that mental health field workers obey all field safety guidelines established by the emergency management team. Crisis counselors should follow the recommendations for medical evaluations and screenings established by federal or local response agencies after exposure to hazardous materials.

All counselors must be knowledgeable about basic safety precautions before entering disaster areas. Survivors are sometimes reluctant to leave their property, which may put their own lives and the lives of others at risk. In these situations, counselors may only be able to offer information about disaster relief services and basic safety. Counselors must be aware of their surroundings and the context of interactions with survivors. It is easy for counselors to become complacent with misguided ideas such as "I'm a helping professional—who would hurt a person trying to help someone else?" The reality is that individuals who perceive they or someone they care for is being threatened (e.g., physically, mentally, spiritually) may go into "fight or flight" mode, thereby creating a precarious situation for counselors and other crisis workers.

Individual clients in crisis can present an increased risk for the counselor, particularly the sole practitioner in private practice. One of the most dangerous settings for a counselor is an isolated private practice. Despenser (2007) notes that sole private practitioners are vulnerable because their practices are secluded from others and there may not be an adequate prescreening process to identify clients who may pose a safety risk to them. The most dangerous setting is a counselor practicing alone in his or her home due to the isolation from others. Even counselors who have solo practices in multipurpose buildings with other people nearby are at risk, as the other occupants in the building may not be aware of calls for help. Often, such multipurpose office buildings provide a false sense of security. The counselor may feel safe because of people and activity next door; however, the workers in the real estate or law office in the adjoining suite are focused on their tasks and are not attuned to the needs and potential risks of the private practitioner next door. Having other people in the building does little to help if a counselor decides to see clients in the evening after the other offices have closed and the workers have gone home. Counselors should always have a clear escape route that cannot be blocked by chairs or coffee tables, remove objects from the office that could be used in an attack, install panic alarms, and consider carrying pepper spray. If a client becomes threatening, the counselor should remain calm and attempt to redirect the client, thereby defusing the threatening situation.

Although private practitioners rely upon referrals for much of their livelihood, it is prudent to consider where the referral is coming from and to obtain as much information as possible from professional referral sources. New clients should be screened carefully. Despenser (2007) identifies three referral mechanisms: (1) referrals from other professionals; (2) nonprofessional referrals (former clients or friends); and (3) self-referred clients who find the counselor's name listed online, for example. When another mental health professional, a doctor, or a lawyer makes a referral, it is vital that the counselor discuss with the referral source the reasons for the referral and other pertinent information. Generally, with nonprofessional referrals, the counselor will not be able to learn much about the client's medical or mental health history. While a counselor may have some sense of security in these cases, depending upon the nature of the counselor's relationship with the nonprofessional referral source, it is still essential that the client be screened via phone before the counselor agrees to provide services. Self-referred clients should always be screened. Today, a number of counselors have their own websites and list themselves on online professional resource websites. These online resources provide potential clients with comprehensive information about the counselor and serve as excellent marketing tools. At the same time, counselors should keep in mind that sharing too much personal information online or in other public forums can be dangerous for them.

A potential client can screen the counselor through various sources, but the counselor has no information about a self-referred client and, therefore, should screen such clients through a screening phone call. Screening phone calls are critical to counselor safety, particularly with clients referred by nonprofessionals or with self-referred clients. During screening phone calls, it is crucial that counselors pay attention to their intuition and not ignore subtle warning signs. According to Despenser (2007), ignoring red flags and gut feelings may be due to a need to be needed, not wanting to appear unhelpful, or countertransference issues. Your intuition is an indispensable screening tool. Listen to it. If there is a decision to not take a client, a counselor should still make a referral to other known resources.

During a screening phone call, ask the client for medical and psychological history including medications (Despenser, 2007), and legal history. Ask why the client is seeking counseling now to determine whether there is a recent crisis event in the client's life. Be alert for information regarding past incidents of self-harm or violence. Pay attention to the client's tone of voice and any verbal cues that the potential client might express, such as "You must get lonely by yourself in that office." Safety procedures for new clients could include having another person present in the office when seeing a new client. Some factors can indicate a greater risk for dangerous behavior from a client seeking private practice counseling services. Signs for concern in a client include a history of violent behavior, a psychiatric or forensic history, intoxication, erratic speech and behavior, and sexual posturing and insinuation. Additionally, Despenser (2007) identifies warning signs such as a history of self-harm and abuse, vengeful or paranoid statements, and recent changes in the client's situation or support system.

Whenever possible, counselors should get a thorough history, preferably from the referral source, before seeing a client. Once again, the dangers of self-referred clients and those referred by nonprofessionals are evident because it is not possible to get such a history. Prescreening is often a luxury. With many crisis situations, the amount of information gathered prior to making the first appointment varies and may be rather limited. Thus, having a safety plan in place prior to seeing clients is strongly advised. See Case Study 2.1, which considers safety precautions for counselors. Also complete Think About It 2.1.

CASE STUDY 2.1

Safety Precautions for Counselors

Cathy Jones is a part-time sole practitioner, a professional counselor who sees clients in the evenings from 5:00 p.m. until 9:00 p.m. at an office building. On most nights, she is the only person in the building. She is trying to build her practice and has been networking and promoting her practice any way she can. She receives a voice mail from someone named Mr. Smith, who explains that he is looking for a counselor. She returns his call, and the following conversation takes place.

CATHY:	Hello, is this Mr. Smith?
MR. SMITH:	Yes, that's me.
CATHY:	This is Cathy Jones. I'm returning your call.
MR. SMITH:	Oh yeah, the counselor.

CATHY:	You left a message saying you want to set up a counseling appointment? I'm calling to see if you are still looking for a counselor and what you are seeking a counselor for to determine if I am able to assist you.
MR. SMITH:	Great, yes, I found your name and picture on that site about counselors and I thought you looked like a nice lady. So I decided to call you.
CATHY:	Can you give me an idea of why you're interested in counseling?
MR. SMITH:	Well, my girlfriend just broke up with me and I'm pretty upset about that. I can't believe she would do this to me after all we've been through. I guess I shouldn't be surprised, women always let me down. I've been in counseling before and I know how it works. I've got plenty of money, so you don't have to worry about me being able to pay your fees.
CATHY:	So, you want to seek counseling to discuss the recent loss of this relationship.
MR. SMITH:	Yeah, I know I've got to get a handle on this before I spiral out of control. My last girlfriend called the cops on me when I confronted her new boyfriend, and I don't want that to happen again. I really want to handle things differently this time. I know I have to change how I react to things like this.

Discussion Questions

1. Should Cathy Jones take on Mr. Smith as a client? Explain.
2. If yes, what safety precautions should she take?
3. How might Cathy's desire to increase her practice get in the way of screening?

Workplace Safety and the Professional Counselor

According to the Occupational Safety and Health Administration (OSHA, 2015), 20% of workplace injuries take place in health care and social service settings; 50% of these injuries are due to assaults and violent incidents from patients and clients. The actual rate may be much higher, since research shows that assaults of this type are often unreported (OSHA, 2015). The reason health care and social service workers are at a higher risk for workplace violence is due to multiple factors, including working with a client population

THINK ABOUT IT 2.1

Think about why a counselor might be reluctant to terminate a counseling relationship with a dangerous client. What other ethical considerations should be implemented if a counselor chooses to terminate a counseling relationship with a dangerous client? What safety precautions should a counselor put in his or her personal safety plan?

that has a history of violence and/or substance abuse, facility design that impedes visual contact with other workers, poor lighting, and a lack of means to communicate for help during an emergency. The following factors can increase a client's risk for violence to self and others: long waits in emergency rooms, the feeling that one has limited control over their current situation, a lack of support from family and friends, a sense of hopelessness, and a pattern of impulsivity. Additionally, budget considerations may leave facilities understaffed and the staff overworked. Combined with a high turnover rate among workers, these factors create a dangerous work environment and a high risk for assault.

What effect does workplace violence have on mental health workers? According to OSHA, workers who have experienced a violent incident may have

- short and long-term psychological trauma;
- fear of returning to work;
- changes in relationships with coworkers and family;
- feelings of incompetence, guilt, powerlessness; and
- fear of criticism by supervisors or managers. (OSHA, 2015, p. 22)

Mental health workers who have been assaulted should have access to debriefing and counseling to address trauma and stress concerns. It is very important that workers who have experienced a violent incident find support and care as soon as possible to mitigate the shock and distress that may result from such an episode.

Hughes and Gilmour (2010) researched the concept of work safety and climate. Community mental health workers, particularly those who work with clients who are at high risk for violent behavior, would benefit from increased safety training and general attention to safety issues in the workplace to create an atmosphere where safety is attended to and valued. Hughes and Gilmour reported that the majority of workers who attended voluntary training on managing violent clients felt better prepared and safer as a result of such training. Flannery, LeVitre, Rego, and Walker (2011) stress that safety training for new professionals is an important priority. Ongoing training should be provided that addresses the use of self-defense, appropriate restraint practices, and restraint-free procedures. Additionally, they recommend communication skills training, supervision, and mentoring. The integration of trauma-informed practices in the workplace is recommended.

Trauma-informed treatment has emerged in recent decades due to an increasing awareness of the long-term effects of traumatic events on individuals. According to the Substance Abuse and Mental Health Services Administration (SAMHSA, 2015), trauma from past events can arise when a client does not feel safe or supported in a therapeutic environment. A trauma-informed therapeutic environment is one where the client is a respected participant in a collective approach to treatment. Resilience and hope are fundamental elements of this approach. Substance abuse, eating disorders, depression, and anxiety can be current symptoms that are connected to previous trauma; however, most clients who seek counseling for such issues may not realize that these presenting problems are connected to earlier trauma in their lives. Trauma-informed treatment calls for mental health practitioners to work in a collaborative manner to empower clients and families and promote resilience. SAMHSA puts forth six key principles for working from a trauma-informed perspective:

- safety
- trustworthiness and transparency

- peer support
- collaboration and mutuality
- empowerment, voice, and choice
- cultural, historical, and gender issues

With an understanding of the possible long-term effects that can emerge from a previous trauma, counselors can work with clients from a more perceptive, informed, and strengths-based perspective. The SAMHSA website has many resources on creating trauma-informed therapeutic environments and provides useful information on trauma-informed treatment (www.samhsa.gov/nctic/trauma-interventions).

Complete Think About It 2.2.

COUNSELORS MOST AT RISK   Flannery et al. (2011) indicated that inpatient settings and residential house counselors are most at risk for assault from clients. Counselors in training who are young and with less experience are also at increased risk. Female counselors are just as likely as males to be assaulted. Violent incidents increase because inpatient and residential clients are likely to be diagnosed with severe psychopathology and because staff members spend more time with clients. Counselor education programs should directly address the concept of safety and security, especially prior to internship placement.

Violent clients pose a real threat to counselors, and some form of aggressive client behavior is likely to occur during every mental health provider's career. Kivisto, Berman, Watson, Gruber, and Paul (2015) found that three out of four psychologists surveyed had experienced harassment from clients, one in five had been threatened, and one in seven had been stalked.

According to the American Mental Health Foundation (AMHF, 2015), data on worker assaults in recent years indicate that clients most at risk for assaulting mental health workers include those with a history of violence, a history of substance abuse, and a diagnosis of schizophrenia. Counselors should also take note of any loss of reality testing, such as delusional thinking or hallucinations. Impulse control issues (e.g., mania, intoxication) are also risk factors for violence. Every counselor, regardless of setting, should institute safety rules and abide by them. To assume that violent client behavior "couldn't happen here" is to put oneself in peril.

STALKING   Another danger faced by mental health providers is the threat of being stalked by a client. Purcell, Powell, and Mullen (2005) surveyed 1,750 psychologists and found that 19.5% reported being stalked by a client. The majority of stalking incidents involved male outpatient clients with a female psychologist victim. Most of

---

THINK ABOUT IT 2.2

Think about the ways in which a counselor's previous trauma might impede his or her work with clients. How might this previous trauma manifest itself in the session? What should a counselor do if he or she experiences emerging trauma while working with a client? What should you do if you become aware that a counseling colleague is becoming impaired due to a previous trauma?

the stalkers had a diagnosis of a personality disorder or psychotic disorder; however, some of the stalkers were diagnosed with substance use, major depressive, or anxiety disorders, or had no previous clinical diagnosis. Purcell et al. found that clients who stalk were motivated by a need for intimacy, infatuation, resentment or revenge, or a misinterpretation of the therapeutic relationship as a friendship or romance. They stress that mental health providers must be very clear about the nature of the therapeutic relationship and set firm boundaries, preferably in writing. Setting boundaries should include not allowing contact between sessions, not extending session length, keeping personal information private, not friending clients on social media, and not placing personal objects (e.g., family photographs) in the office, which may give the client too much personal information or may create an atmosphere of familiarity. When clients cannot respect the nature of the therapeutic relationship and continually violate boundaries, the counseling relationship should be terminated and the client referred for a psychiatric evaluation. In extreme cases, the counselor may have to obtain a restraining order for self-protection. As always, counselors should seek supervision and consultation and should clearly document all events, actions, and decisions. Cyber stalking has become a major threat as well. Personal information about practitioners is readily available on various websites, and harassing clients can use social media and online forums to stalk and verbally attack practitioners.

IN-HOME COUNSELING   Some agencies offer in-home counseling, especially to low-income, homebound, or senior clients who may have difficulty finding transportation to counseling centers. In-home counseling is a highly effective service delivery method, but it brings with it increased safety concerns. In-home services should never be conducted alone; counselors should be accompanied by co-counselors or behavioral aides. In-home counseling agencies should make it a practice for counselors to check in by phone prior to each session and after leaving the client's home. When conducting in-home counseling, counselors should familiarize themselves with the community and the environment prior to the actual session. Where are the building exits? Is there adequate lighting? What time of day is the session scheduled? Who will be home when a session is scheduled? If the counselor feels uneasy about the environment, he or she should leave the premises. See Case Study 2.2, which addresses in-home counseling safety issues. Read Voices from the Field 2.2.

CASE STUDY 2.2

Ensuring the Safety of Young Clients

For the past three months, you have been seeing an 11-year-old male client referred for behavioral concerns by the special education teacher at an elementary school located in a small, rural community. Your client has demonstrated several temper outbursts with his teachers and has also been in fights with boys in his class who he claims were "making fun" of him. The client is large for his age and has cognitive and other developmental delays, and the principal and the special education teacher want him to learn strategies for emotional regulation and anger management. He lives on a small farm with his father and grandfather, both of whom are in agreement that he would benefit from interventions focused on his behavior; consequently, these counseling goals are stated in his Individualized Education Plan (IEP). Because his father and grandfather have expressed concerns about his behavior at home, you have been seeing the client at home as well as at school. These sessions have gone well; he has readily engaged in the therapy process, rapport is clearly in evidence, and you, his father and grandfather, and the school are pleased with his progress.

Sitting outside on the back porch during today's home session, however, a different concern arises. The client tells you that his father and grandfather sometimes beat him with a belt when he is "bad." He lifts his shirt to show you "where it hurts," and you see his back and stomach covered with dark bruises, many of which clearly show the outline of a belt buckle. You realize your client needs you to take action to protect his safety; at the same time, you are aware that the father and grandfather, both large men, are inside the house.

Discussion Questions

1. How will you act to ensure the safety of your client, while at the same time maintaining your own personal safety?
2. What is your responsibility as a mandated reporter?
3. What will you do next?

VOICES FROM THE FIELD 2.2
Reflections on Personal Safety During In-Home Counseling

James Jackson

"Mom, it's the insurance salesman" is the typical reaction from children answering the door when I make an initial home visit with a client family. This reaction is not surprising since my outward appearance in terms of physical features (i.e., a middle-aged White male), my business casual attire, and my briefcase mark me as an outsider who appears different from most who call upon this home. Over the years of providing in-home counseling services to children and families as part of my contract work with the Department of Human Resources, I have grown accustomed to this reaction. Scheduling changes for client sessions are an expected aspect of this work as clients' lives are impacted by systemic forces outside their control; minimum-wage employment doesn't often offer much flexibility in terms of work schedule, and unreliable—or absent—transportation is a common challenge faced by many.

Many of my clients are masters at effectively coping with limited resources and thrive while focusing on taking life day-by-day, adapting as needed. So, when a regularly scheduled weekly session is changed due to a work schedule conflict, I appreciate that the client still wants to have the session, although at a time much later in the day after the client gets home from work. Safety never enters my mind. I have been to this client family's apartment several times in the past. It is located in an older subsidized housing complex made up of regimented brick buildings that appear almost identical in the daylight; strange how different it looks . . . and feels . . . by night. "Why did I have to park so far away?" I wonder to myself as I walk alone on the dark, cracked sidewalk past the silent windows of the buildings, streetlights broken or dimly buzzing. Suddenly, I am aware. I clutch my briefcase a little tighter, realizing my reaction offers no real security. I am aware that I do not feel entirely safe, and even as the realization strikes me, I begin thinking about my client's family members who live and sleep here each night. How safe do they feel? What steps are they taking to minimize risk? I resolve to invite them to discuss safety planning as part of our work together . . . and to engage in intentional planning for my own safety as well.

FORENSIC INPATIENT UNITS   Mental health providers working in forensic inpatient units have an increased risk of harm from violent clients. Such clients may require physical restraints, and staff at inpatient units must be trained in proper restraint methods. Staff training should focus on using therapeutic methods to de-escalate a violent client and on empowering the client to take ownership of his or her treatment so that the need for restraint can be reduced (see Chapter 4) (Simon, 2011). Inpatient mental health workers should be cognizant of the fact that federal policy requires that alternatives be attempted before restraints are used and that restraints be used only when absolutely necessary. In addition, a client can remain in restraints for a defined amount of time, and a restrained client must be assessed in a timely manner. Freeman and Sugai (2013) point out that recent advocacy efforts have encouraged many states to reexamine state laws regarding restraints and to use restraint and seclusion as a last resort.

RESEARCH AND RECOMMENDATIONS ON CLIENT VIOLENCE   Jussab and Murphy (2015) state that client violence is not uncommon and may be underreported; therefore, the significance of the violent incidents may not be appropriately acknowledged and tracked. Counselors who have suffered a violent incident with a client must often continue to work with the client, or at least work in the same facility. The long-term effects of close proximity to a source of trauma and the inability to distance oneself from an attacker can contribute to increased burnout and stress. Mueller and Tschan (2011) report that fears and anxiety around the attack often linger, and that mental health workers who have suffered an assault are prone to lower levels of job satisfaction and may begin to question their professional competency.

Jussab and Murphy (2015) examined the aftereffects of client violence on counselors. They identified three main themes with six subthemes that may emerge after an experience of client violence. The first main theme is "processing the moment to moment experience of client violence" (p. 290). Embedded within this main theme are the subthemes of experiencing fear and having an inner dialogue about what to do to contain the incident. One of the counselors who participated in the research commented:

> Relying on therapeutic skills to deal with the violent incident brought a sense of foolishness and the inner dialogue highlighted frustrated failure as she registers her disappointment with the usefulness of her clinical engagement skills in the midst of the incident. (p. 291)

The second main theme is "professional vulnerabilities and needs as a result of client violence" (p. 290). The questioning of one's competency as a practitioner and the need to get appropriate support from supervisors and coworkers are the subthemes for this theme. Finally, the third main theme is "the ruptured therapeutic relationship" (p. 290). Within this theme, the subthemes include rejection of the client or accepting the client through formulation. Client acceptance could be regained through empathy and a process of examining the reasons for the client outburst. The resultant emotional and psychological harm experienced by a counselor in this situation would often go unnoticed by supervisors. Thus, it is imperative for supervisors and organizations to be mindful of the inner turmoil experienced by counselors who have suffered a violent attack from a client.

Jussab and Murphy (2015) make the following recommendations for managing the aftereffects of a violent incident committed by a client: (1) practitioners should be aware that client violence happens infrequently, sporadically, and usually is perpetrated by a lone client; (2) practitioners should engage in intentional self-care; (3) practitioners should examine and accept emotional and psychological distress; (4) practitioners should be alert to coworker distress and provide support; and (5) workplaces should examine safety policies and procedures. In particular, Jussab and Murphy note that low levels of violence in a facility should not be tolerated. Their research indicates that practitioners need to process the experience of a violent client incident within a context of safety and support. Jussab and Murphy also assert that each incident be reported so that a clear picture and accurate statistics can emerge regarding this workplace safety threat. Failure to do so leads to a state of passive acceptance of violence and an increased risk of burnout and workplace violence within the profession. This concept of passive acceptance of violence was also noted by OSHA (2015) as a factor in the high risk for violence to health care and social service workers. If clients perceive that acting out and being aggressive are tolerated and will not be reported, they are more likely to engage in such behavior. Passive acceptance of low-level violence fosters an undercurrent of threat and undermines safety for workers as well as the therapeutic process of clients. See Case Study 2.3, which provides an example of workplace safety considerations for counselors.

Read Voices from the Field 2.3.

CASE STUDY 2.3

Counselor Safety

Carol works as a college counselor at a small university counseling center that has one other counselor on staff. The counseling center is located in the basement of a campus office building that is vacant each day by 6:00 p.m. Carol and her colleague have an unwritten safety rule that they will not schedule appointments later than 4:30 p.m. Carol occasionally breaks this rule when she knows the client well. One day a married female student named Victoria calls to inquire about marriage counseling; she states that she and her husband, Robert, are disagreeing about many issues and they want couples counseling to improve communication. Carol suggests several possible appointment times, but Victoria works and cannot possibly come in until 6:30 or 7:00 p.m. Since the case seems straightforward, Carol agrees to meet the couple at 7:00 p.m. for an initial session.

When Carol unlocks the counseling center door and admits the couple, she immediately feels anxious. The husband's appearance seems unkempt, and he does not make eye contact with Carol. Carol and the couple proceed to her office, fill out intake forms, and go over informed consent. Although Robert is quiet, he appears to be amenable to treatment, signing all documentation. Carol feels increasingly uneasy, and for the first time, she realizes that her office is arranged with the clients between her and the only door. Robert stares at the floor while Victoria explains to Carol that she and her husband have been disagreeing because he has a diagnosis of schizophrenia and he refuses to take his medication. Victoria hopes that through couples counseling Robert will become more compliant with his medication and they can learn to communicate and interact more positively. Carol maintains an appearance of calm and listens to Victoria while Robert remains silent.

When Carol finds out from Victoria that Robert is under the care of a psychiatrist, she explains to the couple that before any relationship work can be effective, it is necessary that all medical issues be addressed. She further explains that it would be inappropriate for her to work with the couple unless she was working collaboratively with the psychiatrist. The couple agrees to make an appointment with the psychiatrist the next day, and Carol has them both sign releases in case the psychiatrist wishes to speak with her. Carol escorts the couple from the counseling center and breathes a sigh of relief as she locks the door behind them.

Discussion Questions

1. What was Carol's initial mistake?
2. How could she have handled the situation differently?
3. What factors might have caused Carol's complacency with regard to safety?
4. What safety plan changes should Carol and her colleague institute?

VOICES FROM THE FIELD 2.3
Knowing Your Client's History and Avoiding Retraumatization

James Jackson

After hearing various accounts of an 8-year-old client's explosive behavior that was occurring in multiple settings, I was determined to assess first-hand the troubling pattern of outbursts. My consultation with client treatment team members and caregivers confirmed that a behavioral assessment was indicated, so I made arrangements to conduct the assessment in the group room of the care facility where most of the outbursts had been reported. Upon my arrival, I received further information from the direct care facility staff, who indicated the client was required almost daily to be placed in the "time-out room," and that after her daily visit to the room, the client was able to maintain appropriate behavior the remainder of the day. This was my first time visiting this particular care facility, and I was pleased that video surveillance cameras located in the group rooms made it possible for me to conduct the assessment from a monitoring room without interfering with the client's normal routine. I used a structured behavioral observation template for recording client behaviors, and noted the time each behavior occurred.

I began my observation as the client entered the group room with her aid. The client appeared appropriately engaged with the other group members and was completing her assigned task, which included a coloring activity, with minimal redirection. After an hour of observing, I was beginning to wonder if this might be one of those rare reported days in which the

client was able to consistently maintain appropriate behavior. However, just as the group was transitioning to a new activity, the client threw her crayon to the floor and said, "No. I wanna keep doing this." Her aid picked up the crayon and tried to hand it back to the client, but the client refused and proceeded to crumple the paper she had been working on. The aid informed the client that she would now have to go to the "time-out room," took the client by the hand, and calmly led her from the group room into the next room with the designated time-out area; I watched with interest, as the care staff had indicated that this intervention was used almost daily.

I saw the aid lead the client (who seemed rather complacent) to a corner of the room to what appeared to be a lit storage area with a windowed door. Although the client now began to resist, the aid was able to force the client into the storage area and quickly shut the door, holding the doorknob tight so the client could not open the door. The client became visibly upset and began beating the plywood and cinderblock walls with her bare fists, yelling epithets at the aid while demanding to be released. "Not until you calm down," replied the aid, keeping both hands on the doorknob. Watching in shocked disbelief as this scene began to unfold on the video monitor, I recalled the client's history of repeated traumatic experiences, as well as seizures of unknown origin. Immediate safety concerns for my client flooded my mind, followed closely by liability concerns.

While the focus of this chapter has been the safety of the counselor, clients who initiate violent incidents are also at risk. They are, of course, at risk for harm to themselves while in the act of lashing out violently. Moreover, once a client has engaged in violence, the client will then be labeled violent, which may set off a self-fulfilling prophecy effect that will influence the client's behavior and treatment in the years to come. Now complete Activity 2.2 to practice thinking about safety precautions in various counseling settings.

ACTIVITY 2.2

In this chapter, we have reviewed a variety of safety concerns for counselors and have pointed out that, while some settings may have a higher potential for danger, counselors in all settings should be aware of safety issues and have safety policies and plans. In small groups, identify potential dangerous situations in the following settings. Also, for each setting, identify some security policies and procedures that would improve safety.

- K–12 school counselor's office
- university counseling center
- inpatient psychiatric hospital
- sole practitioner private practice
- for-profit counseling agency
- in-home counseling program

Summary

Working in crisis situations, counselors are at an increased risk for their personal safety and well-being. Proactive, preventive crisis planning and awareness of crisis safety protocols are vital. Collaboration, planning, and training with first responders and other crisis workers increases safety and improves crisis intervention services.

Counselors in solo practices are at a high risk for potential physical assault by violent clients. Private practitioners are cautioned to screen new clients carefully, particularly if these potential clients have been referred by nonprofessional sources or if the clients have self-referred. In addition to screening, counselors should design their offices for safety: they should install panic alarms, remove objects from the office that could be used in an attack,

and have an exit strategy in the event of a violent incident. Counselors who work in inpatient and residential treatment facilities are at the greatest risk for assault from a client, and new professionals and young trainees in such facilities are more likely to be assaulted. The effect of these attacks can result in trauma, doubts about one's effectiveness as a practitioner, complacency, and burnout. Research indicates that therapeutic support for counselors who have been assaulted is essential for the psychological well-being of the counselor and organization. Administrators should review safety procedures, should not tolerate even low levels of violent behavior from clients, provide debriefings when safety issues occur, and revise safety plans as needed with staff input.

3 Ethical and Legal Considerations in Crisis Counseling

Paul F. Hard, Laura L. Talbott-Forbes, and Mary L. Bartlett

PREVIEW

While crisis planning can never be perfect, it does provide a framework for appropriate response and decision making in crisis situations needing immediate responses. Prepared counselors well versed in crisis procedures and processes will be able to provide ethical and effective interventions in all types of crisis conditions. This chapter will examine the ethical and legal considerations related to preventive measures, federal legislations, sentinel court findings, and relevant applications of best practice regarding privacy matters in crisis counseling. Crisis counselors need to be particularly aware of state and federal laws and professional ethics that govern and advise clinical practice in crisis situations. The discussion will focus on prevention considerations; the Health Insurance Portability and Accountability Act (HIPAA); the Family Educational Rights and Privacy Act (FERPA); application of the *Tarasoff* decision; negligence and malpractice; documentation and record keeping; informed consent; confidentiality; termination in crisis intervention; and spiritual and multicultural considerations.

PREVENTION CONSIDERATIONS

It has often been observed that it is far more effective and economical to prevent a problem rather than to correct it. Primary prevention of ethical and legal issues in counseling is a far more effective strategy than the costly and distressing efforts to address an ethical or legal lapse after it has occurred. Counselors can focus on five areas to foster core prevention: (1) wellness, (2) continuing education, (3) peer supervision and consultation, (4) ethical decision-making models, and (5) an understanding of federal laws (discussed later in this chapter) and state laws applicable to crisis intervention. While there is no panacea to prevent ethical or legal violations, when these five areas are synthesized into the counselor's professional worldview, best practices follow and act as a shield for both client and counselor.

Wellness

The American Counseling Association (ACA) 2003 Task Force on Impaired Counselors (Lawson & Venart, 2005) observed that counselors working in disaster or crisis circumstances are particularly vulnerable to secondary trauma, vicarious trauma, and compassion fatigue. Because such a compromised condition may leave the counselor vulnerable to ethical or legal lapses, attention to the well-being of the counselor is vital as a preventive measure. In their seminal work, Pearlman and MacIan (1995) noted 10 helpful strategies for crisis counselors to use to promote and maintain wellness: (1) discussing cases with colleagues, (2) attending workshops, (3) spending time with family or friends, (4) travel, vacations, hobbies, and movies, (5) talking with colleagues between sessions, (6) socializing, (7) exercising, (8) limiting caseload, (9) developing one's spiritual life, and (10) receiving supervision. These strategies are important to maintaining ethical practice. Moreover, Lawson and Venart (2005) noted that wellness and self-care are vital to counselors, since the care that they provide to others is only as effective as the care they give themselves.

Continuing Education

Continuing education is required by certifying and licensing bodies as a means of ensuring that a counselor's practice remains both competent and current. Many such entities also require that a portion of the continuing education be related to ethics in order to ensure that counselors continue to be versed in current ethical issues as well as current ethical decision-making models. Counselors should participate in continuing education to effectively compare their professional behavior with the standard of care, and routinely review professional codes of ethics a part of their ongoing personal education.

Peer Supervision and Consultation

Peer supervision and consultation are essential to ethical instruction and practice (Corey, Corey, Corey, & Callanan, 2014; Remley & Herlihy, 2014). Engaging in peer consultation when confronted with ethical concerns exposes those concerns to colleague input and enhances protection for both the counselor and client. Avoiding conversations related to ethical dilemmas out of shame or fear often results in negative outcomes. By contrast, pursuing open and honest dialogue about client challenges reduces the likelihood of negative outcomes that may occur when one works in isolation.

Ethical Decision-Making Models

The *ACA Code of Ethics* (American Counseling Association [ACA], 2014) provides guidelines on key areas in which counselors make decisions. However, the code provides little direction on the process counselors should follow when making ethical decisions. One way that counselors practice soundly is by rooting their ethical decisions in a theoretical model. In fact, section I.1.b of the code recommends that counselors "use and document as appropriate an ethical decision making model" (p. 19). The code also outlines some components of an effective decision-making model.

There are a variety of ethical decision-making models a counselor can use. The counselor should determine which model to use consistently based on his or her personality, values, expectations, the treatment setting, client base, and available time (Corey et al., 2014; Remley & Herlihy, 2014). Regardless of the model chosen, counselors should apply the core principles of autonomy, nonmaleficence, beneficence, justice, and fidelity when making ethical decisions.

Sentinel work by Forester-Miller & Davis (1996), entitled *A Practitioner's Guide to Ethical Decision Making*, is the basis for *ACA Code of Ethics'* ethical decision-making standards (ACA, 2014, section I.1.b). The practitioner's guide outlines a seven-step decision-making model: (1) identify the problem, (2) implement the *ACA Code of Ethics*, (3) establish the parameters of the dilemma, (4) generate all possible courses of action, (5) consider the consequences of all options and select a course of action, (6) evaluate the course of action selected, and (7) implement the course of action.

A sampling of models are provided by Corey et al. (2014), Remley & Herlihy (2014), and Sheperis & Sheperis (2015), and include

- *Beneficence model:* It uses an A-B-C-D-E worksheet that includes the steps of assessment, benefit, consequences and consultation, duty, and education.
- *Feminist model:* The core of this model is to create a gender-equal ethic that is based on nonsexist moral principles such as holistic, intuitive, emotional, compassionate, personal, and contextual processing styles. The model calls for involvement of the client at every stage of the decision-making process.
- *Social constructionist model:* It uses an interactive process that places the decision in the social context and involves negotiating, conceptualizing, and possibly arbitrating.
- *Transcultural integrative model:* It includes cultural factors counselors can use in a variety of settings with client populations. It emphasizes principles that link all cultures, such as altruism, responsibility, justice, and caring.

Any of these ethical decision-making models can support counselors in making effective decisions.

While no two models are the same, all include some form of the following constructs: (1) identify the problem, (2) check your feelings, (3) identify potential issues (e.g., cultural, spiritual, familial), (4) review relevant professional codes, (5) know laws and regulations, (6) involve the client in the process, (7) obtain peer or supervisor consultation, (8) consider courses of action, (9) consider the implications of decisions, (10) choose a course of action, and (11) follow up with a supervisor, legal counsel, and the client.

It is important to understand that a counselor's decisions must also always abide by the parameters set forth by state and federal legislation that govern mental health practice.

HEALTH INSURANCE PORTABILITY AND ACCOUNTABILITY ACT

The Health Insurance Portability and Accountability Act (HIPAA) of 1996, also known as the *Kennedy-Kassebaum Bill*, is federal legislation that was implemented to address a number of perceived shortcomings in the management of information in the health care industry. It was the first federal legislation to protect automated client records, and it mandated that all electronic transactions include only HIPAA-compliant codes, provide security provisions, and require national provider identification numbers. The current version of the legislation covers a wide range of areas that impact both the health care industry and patients (Hebda & Czar, 2013; HIPAA, 2011).

What Is HIPAA?

In the 1970s and 1980s, the American public perceived that health care information was not controlled and protected by the health care industry to the degree that it should be, in view of the increasing ability during those years for data to be compiled, manipulated, and used to negatively affect individuals and families. As a result of several high-profile security breech and misuse cases and the resulting pressure on Congress, the legislative branch created health care information handling and protection standards of their own and communicated to the health care industry that these rather restrictive standards would be implemented if the health care industry did not solve the problem on its own.

The health care industry subsequently promulgated standards for information handling, management, and control that met congressional approval. Congress enacted these standards and HIPAA (Public Law 104-191) went into effect on August 21, 1996, and included four areas of legislation: (1) privacy requirements, (2) electronic transactions, (3) security requirements, and (4) national identifier requirements (Corey et al., 2014; Hebda & Czar, 2013; Pozgar, 2016b; Remley & Herlihy, 2014; U.S. Department of Health and Human Services [HHS], 2002). However, the version of HIPAA that became law in 1996 did not include privacy rules. Congress instructed the U.S. Department of Health and Human Services (HHS) to dictate privacy rules for the health care industry within 3 years. The 3-year period was provided in order to give the health care industry a chance to develop privacy rules for their own profession, submit the privacy rules to Congress, and obtain congressional approval. This did not occur, and in the absence of such legislation, HHS followed the requirement of the 1996 act and implemented standards for privacy of individually identifiable health information, referred to as the *Privacy Rule*, which became effective in 2003. A few of the privacy provisions are as follows: (1) patients must be able to access their records, (2) patients have the right to request and/or make corrections to their records, (3) patients must be informed of how their personal information will be used, (4) patient information may not be used for marketing purposes without prior consent, and (5) health insurers or providers must designate a privacy officer and train employees (Pozgar, 2016). The Privacy Rule is still in effect and can be located at the HIPAA website of the HHS Office for Civil Rights (Corey et al., 2014; Hebda & Czar, 2013; Remley & Herlihy, 2014).

The Privacy Rule seeks to balance the concept of individual privacy against the need for medical professionals to have access to information in order to best do their jobs. It establishes that the right to privacy with regard to medical information is not absolute and therefore puts the onus on designated health care providers to protect the information they collect, use, and transmit. The Privacy Rule and other aspects of HIPAA govern information that contains personal identification categorized as protected health information. The protected health information must be treated according to the standards and procedures established by HIPAA whenever it is created, transmitted, or received in any form whatsoever: electronic, paper-based, or by means of oral transmission. In short, if information contains individually identifiable material, it is considered protected health information and is fully impacted by HIPAA (Pozgar, 2016b; Remley & Herlihy, 2014).

Those who collect, use, or transmit protected health information and who are covered under the requirements of HIPAA are referred to as *covered entities*. HIPAA defines *covered entities* as health plans, health clearinghouses, and health care providers. *Health care provider* is sometimes used to refer to covered entities. *Health care provider* refers to a wide variety of health professionals (including counselors) in private and public practice who provide medical care and public health services—such as primary care, disease diagnosis, and public education—and are paid by a third party (Teitelbaum & Wilensky, 2013). HIPAA defines a number of terms that relate to the health care arena and establishes standards through the Privacy Rule that define how individuals and organizations in health care are to collect, use, transmit, and handle protected health information.

Counselors also need to be familiar with the HIPAA Security Rule, which took effect in April 2005. The Security Rule requires that covered entities maintain three safeguards—administrative, physical, and technical—so that electronic protected health information remains confidential, secure, and integral. An example of an administrative safeguard is the clear identification by an organization of which employees or classes of employees can have access to protected health information. An example of a physical safeguard is the placement of workstations of those who have access to protected information away from high-traffic areas, with computer monitors shielded from direct view of the public. This safeguard has affected the way in which counseling settings are architecturally designed and how workstations are set up. An example of a technical safeguard is ensuring that information systems housing protected health information are secured against intrusion (Pozgar, 2016). See Case Study 3.1, which considers a situation where protected information was accessed and misused. Also read Voices from the Field 3.1.

CASE STUDY 3.1

The Misuse of Protected Information

Betty had to pick up her 14-year-old daughter, Traci, early from school due to a plumbing problem that closed the school early. Since Betty, the custodian of client records for an outpatient mental health center, was scheduled to work for several more hours, she allowed her daughter to complete her homework at the work desk near her. Since Betty had to run charts to clinicians at various times, her daughter was left unsupervised. Bored, Traci began browsing through patient charts that had been left on the desk and through client records on her mother's computer (she gained access with the password she saw her mother use, posted inside her mother's desk drawer). Traci even went as far as prank calling clients who had been tested for HIV, pretending to be with the clinic and reporting false results. One client died by suicide after receiving Traci's call that she was HIV positive.

Discussion Questions

1. List the HIPAA violations committed in this case study (based on an actual 2003 incident).
2. Who is liable in this case? Why?

Gina Palmer

HIPAA and social media do not mix. With the popularity and pervasiveness of social media in our everyday lives, it is easy to see how patient privacy can be breached without even realizing it. My rule is to never post messages or comment about work in any way; never post pictures from work and never "friend" any current or past patients via social networking sites. The rest is common sense.

How HIPAA Affects Crisis Counseling

Crisis counseling differs from the kinds of services that are typically provided by health care workers. Crises such as hurricanes, tornadoes, and homicides typically occur quickly and often in unanticipated ways, so counselors must respond immediately to stabilize the situation and provide a way for people to move forward. There may be limited time to obtain HIPAA-required releases when critical care is needed, or it may be impossible to obtain such releases as a result of severe injury, unavailability of family members, or other unforeseen consequences of the disaster. According to the HHS (HHS, 2005), HIPAA is not intended to interfere with the provision of emergency medical care associated with declared emergencies such as hurricanes, and covered health care providers may exercise their professional judgment and act as long as such actions are in the best interests of the patient.

Actions permitted by health care providers may include disclosure of individually identifiable medical information to government officials at the local, state, or federal level; police; first responders; public health officials; or anyone whom the health care providers deem necessary to best serve the patient. In any case, the federal government has the authority to waive sanctions and penalties associated with violations of the Privacy Rule, even in cases where a public health emergency is not declared (HHS, 2017). At the same time, it is important for crisis counselors to work under the direction of the point agency (e.g., Red Cross, Green Cross, FEMA) during a crisis. Well-intentioned counselors who make decisions that counter the point agency may do more harm in some circumstances.

For work with clients who are a serious threat to safety, the HIPAA Privacy Rule allows disclosure of protected health information under the "Serious Threat to Health or Safety" provision. Release of information to anyone whom the health care provider reasonably believes may lessen the threat to health or safety (including the target of the threat) is allowed; however, in the case of a threat to health and safety, release of protected health information to law enforcement is allowed only when the information is needed to identify or apprehend an escapee or a violent criminal (HHS, 2006).

In cases where a crime has occurred or where law enforcement officials are investigating a suspected crime, covered entities are allowed to disclose protected health information under the "Law Enforcement Purposes" provision of HIPAA. This provision sets out conditions in which disclosure of protected health information may—and, in some circumstances, must—be made (HHS, 2005a). Disclosure of protected health information to law enforcement is allowed in the following circumstances:

- in response to a court-ordered warrant, subpoena, or summons
- in response to an administrative or investigative demand by law enforcement

- when a request for protected health information is limited to information required to locate a suspect, fugitive, material witness, or missing person
- to apprehend a perpetrator of a crime against the member of a covered entity's workforce
- to apprehend a violent criminal
- to report child abuse or neglect (no consent required)
- to report adult abuse, neglect, or domestic violence (if the individual agrees or it is required by law)
- to report the death of an individual when death is suspected to be a result of criminal conduct
- to report a medical emergency
- to comply with federal security activities associated with national security
- when a request is made by a correctional institution or official having lawful custody of an individual

Professional counselors should distinguish *permissive* aspects of the Privacy Rule (i.e. "may" be released) when other statutes such as state privilege laws may be more restrictive. That is, while the Privacy Rule may indicate conditions in which protected health information can be disclosed, other statutes, such as state privilege laws and organizational policies, do not allow disclosure. In such cases, the client's private health information should be protected. See Case Study 3.2, which considers how the HIPAA Privacy Rule applies to the sharing of protected health information. Also see Case Study 3.3, which examines a protection of privacy issue.

CASE STUDY 3.2

HIPAA and Protected Health Information

Allen is a licensed professional counselor at a Community Mental Health Center (CMHC). A physician at a local hospital requested a substance abuse evaluation on a current patient. No cooperative agreement exists between the hospital and the CMHC. When Allen arrives at the hospital, the charge nurse gives him the patient's chart and invites him to sit in the records area to review the patient information prior to seeing the patient. Allen sees the patient, performs the evaluation, obtains all the necessary releases, and leaves documentation with the physician. While he is there, the physician asks Allen to see another client, and the charge nurse provides him with the client's chart.

Discussion Questions

1. What, if any, violations of the HIPAA Privacy Rule have occurred here?
2. If violations were committed, who is liable?

CASE STUDY 3.3

Protection of Privacy

Rose is a person transitioning from male to female. Rose is living in a shelter after her home was destroyed in coastal flooding. Formerly known as Robert, Rose disclosed her transgender status to the shelter counselor and requested special accommodations for privacy. The counselor left Rose's documentation visible on the desk while tending to other clients. A shelter worker inadvertently saw the note, and attempting to be of help to the counselor (and to Rose), mentioned the special needs request to other shelter workers. Rose's circumstances were then made known to other shelter residents, resulting in objections from the community and embarrassment to Rose.

Discussion Questions

1. How are privacy regulations for client privacy to be observed in disaster shelter circumstances?
2. What minimum expectations for privacy should a client expect in a disaster shelter?
3. In circumstances of a breach of information, what steps should be taken to sanction these actions?
4. Who should be sanctioned and how?
5. What can be done to minimize the damage of a breach of privacy?

FAMILY EDUCATION RIGHTS AND PRIVACY ACT

In 1974, Congress passed the Family Educational Rights and Privacy Act (FERPA), also known as the *Buckley Amendment*, prompted by concerns about privacy violations and the inclusion of immaterial comments and personal opinions in educational records (Kaplan & Lee, 2013; Wise, King, Miller, & Pearce, 2011). All private and public schools, colleges, and universities are subject to FERPA if they receive funding from the U.S. Department of Education. Confusion regarding HIPAA and FERPA continues to be of concern as institutions of higher education and governmental partners struggle to strike a balance between the two federal laws. This is of particular concern for counselors who work in an educational environment and are providing direct mental health services. Counselors who work in an educational environment should remain current in their understanding of federal privacy regulations, the content to be disclosed in the educational record, and the need to document student mental health needs (Barboza, Epps, Byington, & Keene, 2010; HHS, 2008; U.S. Department of Education, 2008; Wise et al., 2011).

What Is FERPA?

Essentially, FERPA (20 U.S.C. § 1232g; 34 CFR Part 99) gives parents certain rights to their child's educational records until the child is 18 years of age (an "eligible student"). After this point, the right to privacy regarding the contents of the educational records is provided to the eligible student, thus denying parental access without consent (U.S. Department of Education, 2008). All schools, public or private, that receive federal funding must follow FERPA or face the loss of federal funds (Remley & Herlihy, 2014). According to the HHS and the U.S. Department of Education (2008), a parent or an eligible student has the right to inspect and review the student's educational records. Additionally, the parent or eligible student who believes an educational record to be inaccurate may ask the school to amend the record. If a school refuses to amend an educational record, the parent or eligible student can request a formal hearing and may place in the record a statement about the information being contested.

Schools must obtain written permission to release information; however, FERPA allows the release of information in certain situations—for example, when a student transfers to another school and there is a legitimate educational interest; or when financial aid is being requested, a judicial order has been issued, or there is an emergency. Parents are to be notified when records are transferred to other schools and may receive copies of those records upon request (Remley & Herlihy, 2014). Under FERPA, colleges may release educational records, such as grades and financial records, to parents of college students claimed as dependents on parental tax forms. The release of student records to parents occurs either when the parent shows tax record proof that the student is a dependent or when the student signs a waiver allowing the release of records to parents (Elliott, Fatomi, & Wasan, 2014). See Case Study 3.4, which focuses on the statutes that apply to a student's counseling records.

Prior to FERPA, educational institutions could be quite lax about how they communicated student information. In fact, Senator James L. Buckley of New York was motivated, in part, to introduce this legislation due to such abuses of confidential material (von Feigenblat, Dominguez, & Valles, 2015). Schools were known to reveal contents of student records to parties who had no educational interest or need to know. FERPA has served to advance professionalism in educational institutions, while at the same time securing students' rights to privacy and confidentiality. Read Voices from the Field 3.2 and 3.3.

FERPA contains a provision that exempts certain personal records. Records that are exclusively in the possession of the counselor and are not revealed to others are excluded from FERPA (Elliott et al., 2014). These records include those made by school personnel, such as counselors, who keep such records in their "sole possession." Due to this exemption, counseling case notes are not considered part of the educational record and do not have to be revealed (Remley & Herlihy, 2014).

CASE STUDY 3.4

Student Counseling Records

Adam, a student in a clinical mental health counseling program, is completing his internship in a mental health center. The center has an outreach program at the local high school, and its counselors have been given space to work in the school's counseling office. Adam has been working with Ben, a grade 10 student who was referred for trouble concentrating and declining grades. Ben's teacher and parents are very interested in his progress in counseling and check in with Adam frequently. After three sessions, Ben reports that he has been depressed since his older brother died by suicide 4 months ago at college. Ben's teacher is heading Adam's way for an update.

Discussion Questions

1. Are Ben's counseling records covered by HIPAA? By FERPA? Or both?
2. Do any factors complicate this case regarding access to counseling records by parents, Ben, or school faculty?

VOICES FROM THE FIELD 3.2
Protecting Confidentiality During a Crisis

Cindy Wiley

Your first priority as a counselor is to protect your client—in this case a school-aged student Julie has come to you in crisis, trusting in you to alleviate pain while guarding and maintaining confidence. When a student presents in such a state, it is hard to remind that student, and yourself, that while what you talk about is confidential, there are exceptions to that confidentiality. I think most counselors are afraid that the counselor–student relationship, which is paramount, will be ruined even if confidence is appropriately breached for the safety of the student. If worded in a manner that adequately portrays your concern and need to involve other resources, most students will understand. What students will ultimately remember is that you genuinely care for them and their well-being. In a state of crisis, most students are truly asking for help. Your job is to make sure that you "circle the wagons" to support them.

Counselors in any setting have the responsibility to convey to clients the limits of confidentiality in the beginning of any counseling relationship rather than when an emergency is experienced where the limits

may be broken. Providing this information at the beginning of the relationship allows counselors to establish boundaries and shared responsibility for information relayed in sessions. The *ACA Code of Ethics* (ACA, 2014, A.2.a, Informed Consent) states:

> Clients have the freedom to choose whether to enter into or remain in a counseling relationship and need adequate information about the counseling process and the counselor. Counselors have an obligation to review in writing and verbally with clients the rights and responsibilities of both counselors and clients. Informed consent is an ongoing part of the counseling process, and counselors appropriately document discussions of informed consent throughout the counseling relationship.

Therefore, even in circumstances where a client is unable to give consent (e.g., due to detox, resistance), the information should be addressed. In the event of a refusal or inability to sign, a counselor can indicate "client refused to sign" or "client was unable to sign." This shows you still met your professional responsibility.

VOICES FROM THE FIELD 3.3
The Importance of Crisis Training for University and College Staff

Yulanda Tyre

Accidental death is one of the leading causes of mortality among college students. These occurrences can have a devastating ripple effect on a college campus. During my first year at a small campus, the university experienced the loss of a popular athlete, which led to a crisis for a large number of students. The incident happened on a summer night and prompted students

to come out onto the university quad and cry and grieve together. I can't stress the importance of training staff outside of the college counseling center in effective collaboration with community resources including churches, the Red Cross, and other organizations. This training is crucial to helping those affected in a college community to heal after a crisis.

How FERPA Affects Crisis Counseling

According to the U.S. Department of Education (2007), an emergency situation creates an exception, and schools may release information from general, medical, or mental health records in order to protect the health and safety of others. It is important to note that this exception is only for the time of the emergency and is not blanket consent to release student information. The information may be released to appropriate individuals who are tasked with protecting health and safety such as law enforcement officials, medical personnel, and public officials. Law enforcement officials hired by schools are considered school officials and therefore have an "educational interest" and are permitted to view records. Threatening remarks made by a student and overheard by school personnel can be reported to appropriate officials because such remarks are not considered part of the educational record.

The aforementioned policies apply to higher education settings as well, with the following additions. Regarding disciplinary actions and rule violations, the final results of a disciplinary proceeding may be released to an alleged victim even if the perpetrator has not been found guilty of violating rules or policies (U.S. Department of Education, 2007). If a perpetrator has been found guilty of violating rules or policies, the institution may disclose the final results of a disciplinary hearing to anyone. Most colleges and universities have their own campus police; investigative records of campus law enforcement are not subject to FERPA and may be released to outside law enforcement without student consent. See Case Study 3.5, which considers whether HIPAA or FERPA were violated when student information was released by a university.

In situations concerning health and safety, higher education institutions may disclose educational records to a parent if the student is involved in a health or safety issue or is under 21 years of age and has violated the school's drug and alcohol policies. Also, according to the U.S. Department of Education (2008), "a school official may

CASE STUDY 3.5

FERPA Violation or Not?

A female student attending a public university in Oregon accused three players from the university basketball team of raping her in March 2015. One of her attackers had been suspended from a previous college team over similar allegations. The female student received counseling at the university's counseling clinic. Nothing was done to the three athletes until May 2015 (well after basketball season), when university administration kicked them off the basketball team and expelled them from the university. When the female student learned that the coach had recruited one of the athletes despite his history of sexual assault, she filed a suit against the university for negligence and emotional distress. The university accessed the female student's counseling records and sent them to its attorney. University officials contended that since the female student went to the health clinic, the records belonged to the university and further held that the claim of emotional distress (a medical condition) entitled the school to her medical records under FERPA.

Discussion Questions

1. Did the university violate FERPA or HIPAA?
2. What facets of this real-life case are operative in the decision of whether a violation has occurred?

generally share information with parents that is based on that official's personal knowledge or observation of the student." Therefore, in situations where a student's behavior involves the health and safety of self and others, school officials can communicate with parents. In fact, a school official may report concerns about student behavior to anyone, although it is wise to make such reports only to campus personnel, such as administrators, counselors, or campus police, who can intervene appropriately with the student (Ells & Rockland-Miller, 2010).

The Application of HIPAA and FERPA to College and University Student Records

In higher education institutions, the interaction between HIPAA and FERPA can be very confusing and frustrating to parents, staff, and faculty members. Wise et al. (2011) explain that HIPAA contains an exemption that excludes FERPA-covered records from HIPAA regulations. However, treatment records such as university student counseling case files are exempt from FERPA but may be covered by HIPAA. The interplay between HIPAA and FERPA has yet to be fully understood, and higher education institutions currently interpret HIPAA and FERPA in different ways. Figure 3.1 summarizes information from Wise et al. (2011) on when HIPAA and FERPA are invoked, overlap, and do not apply in university training clinics, specifically. FERPA was never intended to block the information flow between higher education institutions and others concerned about student health and safety. Therefore, faculty, staff, and administrators who are troubled about the welfare of a student may contact the student's family or other entities and express general observations about health and psychological concerns, while protecting the privacy of the student's medical or mental health records (Wise et al., 2011).

College and university settings focus on providing prevention services to students, and, as a result, students are a captive audience for counseling services as colleges and universities strive to provide easy and quality mental health access (Wilcox et al., 2010).

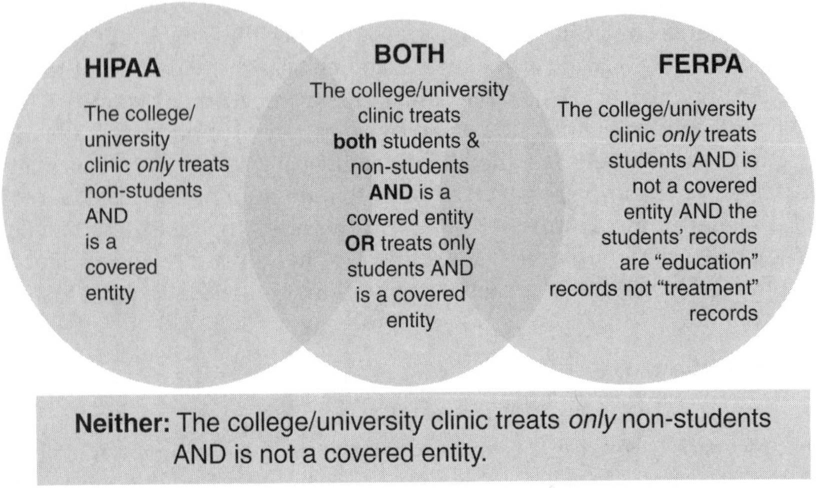

HIPAA

The college/ university clinic *only* treats non-students AND is a covered entity

BOTH

The college/university clinic treats **both** students & non-students **AND** is a covered entity **OR** treats only students AND is a covered entity

FERPA

The college/university clinic *only* treats students AND is not a covered entity AND the students' records are "education" records not "treatment" records

Neither: The college/university clinic treats *only* non-students AND is not a covered entity.

FIGURE 3.1 When does HIPAA, FERPA, both, or neither apply to college/university training clinics?

Many college and university students needing mental health services often do not seek assistance for a variety of reasons (Eisenberg, Hunt, & Spear, 2015). This finding is problematic, as suicide is the second-leading cause of death among college-age students (American Association of Suicidology, 2012; Eisenberg et al., 2015).

The convergence of HIPAA and FERPA makes it difficult to determine when these statutes apply to student clients, how they affect student client rights, and how they impact counselors and their supervisors. It is important for university clinics to follow all HIPAA requirements. Doing so is particularly confusing at university counseling training facilities and requires even more diligence because clients are also students at the university (Wise et al., 2011). If a counselor were to inadvertently transfer a client's mental health record (e.g., clinical treatment notes) to an educational record or file, this action may constitute a failure to maintain the confidentiality of the mental health record (if it takes place without the client's consent) and increase who can access the record. Therefore, this unfortunate transfer could mean that the counselor and his or her supervisor violated federal law and caused significant harm to the client. Confidentiality and record keeping are covered in more detail later in this chapter. Complete Activity 3.1, which asks you to apply FERPA as a school counselor. Also complete Think About It 3.1.

ACTIVITY 3.1

It is not uncommon for school counselors to make contact with a parent once it is determined that a child is a potential threat to himself or herself. Consider the following example:

COUNSELOR: Hello, Mrs. Smith. This is Ms. Collins. I'm your daughter Jill's school counselor. Today your daughter's teacher, Mrs. Potter, found a note Jill had written that suggests she is feeling suicidal and may have a plan to kill herself. I met with Jill and believe she is having passing thoughts of suicide but do not believe she has a current plan. It is school policy for me to contact a parent to pick up the child and make a referral for further assessment.

PARENT: I can't come right now. I'm in the middle of a meeting. Jill has been talking about suicide for several weeks since her father left us. I think she is just seeking attention.

COUNSELOR: Yes, Jill mentioned she is feeling very sad about her father leaving, and this is why she is considering suicide as an option. We take all reports of potential suicide seriously to ensure student safety, and require that the student be seen for follow-up before returning to school. I realize this is inconvenient, but I truly believe your daughter is in emotional distress.

PARENT: Thanks for your concern, but I really don't think it's that serious and I simply can't leave work right now, especially since my husband left. I can't risk losing my job.

Break into small groups and discuss how the conversation in this scenario will continue from this point. Consider who you might also need to speak with if the parent continues to resist. Reflect on the limitations and latitude FERPA allows and how to proceed.

THINK ABOUT IT 3.1

Think about the *ACA Code of Ethics*, HIPAA, and FERPA. What potential conflicts immediately come to mind when you consider working in a crisis or disaster situation? How might these conflicts change as the crisis becomes less acute? How might you address these conflicts?

THE *TARASOFF V. REGENTS* DECISION

In the *ACA Code of Ethics* (ACA, 2014), counselors are charged with recognizing trust as an important component of the counseling relationship, and counselors are obligated to facilitate a trusting relationship through the maintenance of client confidentiality. However, disclosure is required "to protect clients or identified others from serious and foreseeable harm or when legal requirements demand confidential information must be revealed" (section B.2.a). This standard was adopted as part of the counseling practice after the landmark California Supreme Court case of *Tarasoff v. Regents of the University of California* (1976).

As context for the *Tarasoff* case, in 1969 Prosenjit Poddar was seen by a psychologist on a voluntary outpatient basis at the University of California, Berkeley. Poddar confided his intent to kill a woman he claimed to be his girlfriend, a woman the psychologist surmised to be Tatiana Tarasoff, when she returned from Brazil. Alarmed by the disclosure, the psychologist contacted the campus police and then began proceedings to have Poddar committed for a psychiatric evaluation. In the interim, police picked Poddar up and questioned him. The police found Poddar to be rational, and he did not demonstrate risk in their presence. He promised not to have contact with Tarasoff, so the police released him. The psychologist followed up on his concerns with a letter to the campus police chief in which he again expressed his concern; however, the supervisor of the psychologist requested that the letter be returned, ordered all case notes destroyed, and ordered that no further action be taken. Poddar did not return to see the psychologist, nor was he committed or evaluated by any additional mental health professionals. Furthermore, no one contacted Tarasoff or her family to alert them that a threat had been made. Two months later Tarasoff was stabbed to death by Poddar, and her parents brought suit against the *University of California Board of Regents* (Corey et al., 2014; Remley & Herlihy, 2014). Initially, a trial court ruled that the university was not liable because Tarasoff was not the patient in this case, and therefore it had no duty of care toward her. Upon appeal, however, the California Supreme Court ruled there are some circumstances in which a therapist should break confidentiality, specifically when such a disclosure is necessary to avert danger to the client or others. This act of breaking confidentiality when disclosure is necessary to avert danger is known as the *duty to warn*.

What Was the Effect of Tarasoff v. Regents?

Part of what makes this case and the duty to warn/protect complicated is that there have been many interpretations of this case ruling. An examination of the various state laws demonstrates that how and when a counselor should break confidentiality differs depending on the circumstances; and since many states depend on court rulings rather than statutes to guide the actions of a counselor, this issue is not clear across all jurisdictions (National Conference of State Legislatures, 2015). Additionally, many legal experts are unable to give specific guidance as to when counselors should alert the police or identified victim regarding a threat to a person's life. While some courts have limited the application of the duty to warn to situations in which victims are identifiable, subsequent decisions have indicated that the duty to warn extends to unknown victims, which further complicates the matter. Another confusing part of this ruling involves the terms *duty to warn* and *duty to protect*, which are often used interchangeably by professionals.

Legal definitions of the terms *duty to warn* and *duty to protect* are established by state legislation and state court rulings, so these definitions will vary from state to state. Counselors must be aware of the laws applicable to the states in which they are licensed and in which they intend to practice. Generally speaking, the duty to warn and the duty to protect represent degrees of what is essentially the same duty: first, the duty to inform someone of a danger or hazard with the idea that he or she will take action to protect himself or herself (this is the duty to warn); second, the duty to protect someone by taking an action that reduces the danger or hazard to that person directly (this is the duty to protect). For example, when a counselor makes a telephone call to a family member whom a client has threatened, the counselor does so under the concept of duty to warn. If, on the other hand, the counselor arranges to have a client hospitalized who has threatened to harm himself, that action is taken under the concept of duty to protect, since it consists of a direct action (hospitalization) that makes it less likely that the client will execute the threat. In the *Tarasoff* case, the victim was not protected, and the appellate court ruled that the health care provider should have taken steps to protect the victim. In addition, in *Gross v. Allen*, a 1994 California appellate court case, the court ruled that the *Tarasoff* concept applied not only to cases in which clients threaten homicide but also to cases in which clients threaten suicide, so reasonable measures are expected to be taken in cases of threatened suicide (Erford, 2018).

The *Tarasoff* ruling, in fact, establishes a duty to protect and not just a duty to warn. The ruling and interpretation of the *Tarasoff* principle for counseling professionals involves the awareness of the protective measure as a legal obligation to warn an intended victim of potential harm. For example, case outcomes have indicated that the duty to warn is extended to those who are foreseeably endangered by a client's conduct, including people who are unintentionally injured by the client, whole classes of students that have been threatened by the client, bystanders who may be injured by the client's act, and individuals whose property is threatened by the client (Corey et al., 2014; Remley & Herlihy, 2014). Furthermore, in *Ewing v. Goldstein* (2004) the court ruled that in California a therapist could be held liable for failure to warn when the information regarding the client's potential to harm another person is obtained from family members who may be participating in counseling with the client. The precedent established from this case requires a counselor to weigh the credibility of the person offering the information. Additionally, Remley and Herlihy (2014) point out that the *Tarasoff* principle is not applied in every jurisdiction of the United States; specifically, Texas has rejected it.

When a decision is made that a client is a danger to another person or persons, the counselor must then determine what the necessary steps are to prevent the harm from occurring. After notifying the potential victim or contacting appropriate authorities as needed to ensure the intended victim's safety, the counselor must take other steps to prevent harm, which can include continuing to work with the client on an outpatient basis. This option is considered less restrictive, whereas the option to pursue an involuntary commitment would be considered very restrictive. These decisions are challenging for most counselors. Therefore, it is highly recommended that counselors seek peer supervision and consultation on a regular basis—but particularly whenever the issue of breaking confidentiality becomes a factor in practice. This principle is known as the *duty to consult principle* and can assist crisis counselors in decreasing liability issues in similar cases. Counselors should not practice in isolation, should practice according to reasonable standards, and should maintain accurate documentation to be able to verify when and why a decision to break confidentiality was made, particularly as it relates to the duty to warn (Knapp & VandeCreek, 2012).

Another consideration regarding confidentiality and the issue of duty to warn is how multicultural factors come into play. Perhaps the best way to preserve the counseling relationship, should the need arise to break confidentiality or to follow through on the duty to warn, is to assess how clients' cultural needs may influence your practice. This assessment should occur not only at the onset of the counseling relationship but also, as indicated in sections B.1 and B.2 of the *ACA Code of Ethics* (ACA, 2014), periodically throughout your work together. This is essential, regardless of cultural context.

How Tarasoff v. Regents Affects Crisis Counseling

Collins and Collins's (2005) seminal work on the *Developmental-Ecological Model of Crisis Intervention* identifies three goals for a crisis worker dealing with a potentially violent individual: (1) ensure that the client remains safe, reduce lethality, and stabilize the environment, (2) help the client to regain short-term control, and (3) connect the client with appropriate resources. The course of accomplishing these three goals, however, is balanced against the counselor's decision that a duty to warn exists and confidentiality must be broken in part to accomplish those very goals. Counselors working with people in crisis often encounter unique circumstances when a duty to warn or protect prevails; one particularly challenging circumstance is dealing with clients who are HIV and AIDS positive.

The *Tarasoff* case and deliberations surrounding a counselor's duty to warn have become a routine aspect of counselor education and are an expected consideration in the standard of care. Counselors, however, should be cautious when broadly applying the duty to warn since various states may apply this principle differently and others have enacted no law similar to the *Tarasoff* decision. Johnson, Persad, and Sisti (2014) reported that, while 34 states have an actual duty to warn in statute or common law, 11 states give permission to warn (which may not shield the counselor from liability), and 6 states have no such statute or common law guidance. Further, in those states that have some form of *Tarasoff* law, the health care providers to whom it may apply (counselor, physician, etc.) may vary widely, and these providers are often poorly informed of their state's law on the matter. For example, Pabian, Welfel, and Beebe (2009) queried psychologists representing four states regarding their knowledge of legal and ethical obligations to clients in imminent danger, which resulted in alarming findings: (1) the majority were incorrectly informed about their state's law and believed that they had a legal duty to warn when they did not, or (2) they assumed that warning was the only available legal option when there actually were other options available that did not impinge on client privacy. While the principles of duty to warn and duty to protect are useful, counselors should not assume that *Tarasoff* applies without explicitly researching their state law. Counselors should be aware of the changing nature of legislation and of the pertinent regulations for their own state.

Interestingly, Houser and Thoma (2012) noted that, even though counselors in Texas may not break confidentiality to warn or protect a person whose life has been threatened by another, counselors are mandated to report suspected child abuse and have the option of reporting positive HIV results to various entities. Likewise, the *ACA Code of Ethics* (ACA, 2014) indicates that counselors are "justified in disclosing information to identifiable third parties, if the parties are known to be at serious and foreseeable risk of contracting the disease" (section B.2.c). The *ACA Code of Ethics* further stipulates, however, that counselors must confirm the diagnosis and assess the client's intent to inform the third party about his or her disease or to participate in any behavior that may be harmful to an identifiable third party. The word *justified*, as compared with *required*, warrants consideration; in addition, counselors are encouraged to evaluate their own thoughts about whether they will agree to work with, and how they will effectively work with, clients who are HIV positive. It is also important to keep in mind that not every exposure to HIV results in harm, thus making the process of determining how to proceed a gray area that a counselor must navigate carefully. When dealing with this and other precarious issues of this sort, counselors are wise to stay informed about specific statutes in their jurisdiction that have been passed regarding the duty to warn and third-party conversations and, of course, to review the guidelines of confidentiality periodically with clients, and seek supervision and consultation as needed (Corey et al., 2014; Remley & Herlihy, 2014). See Case Study 3.6, which takes a closer look at the duty to warn.

CASE STUDY 3.6

Assessing When to Implement a Duty to Warn

Stan, a retail employee, escaped harm from a building during an active shooter incident by a pair of ethnic minority males. A few months later, Stan began experiencing symptoms of post-traumatic stress disorder and was sent to counseling through his employee assistance program (EAP) when his supervisor noticed an increase in conflicts with coworkers. In the most recent session, Stan became agitated and shouted to the counselor, "I hate those people. I'm going to kill them all," after which he abruptly left the session.

Discussion Questions

1. Does this incident indicate a duty to warn?
2. What *Tarasoff* criteria are met or not met?
3. How should the counselor proceed?

NEGLIGENCE AND MALPRACTICE

Once a counselor and a client have entered into a professional relationship, the counselor has assumed a duty of care toward the client. Providing the best care is an issue of competence, and counselors are responsible to ensure their decision-making process is sound and driven by evidence-based practices. Generally, when poor treatment interventions are selected, a counselor's competence may be called into question (Remley & Herlihy, 2014).

A breach of duty owed to another is considered negligence; negligence that occurs in a professional setting is malpractice. Professional negligence results when a counselor departs from the usual standard of practice that is expected of professionals in a similar situation (Corey et al., 2014). References to legal and ethical issues that can arise during practice are discussed throughout the *ACA Code of Ethics* (ACA, 2014), particularly in section I. In section I, matters related to standards and the law, ethical decision making, and conflicts between ethics and laws are addressed.

Malpractice is established if the court finds that a counselor has breached his or her professional duty, failed to take appropriate action (omission), or did something that should not have been done (commission) relative to the standard of care (Remley & Herlihy, 2014; Scott & Resnick, 2012). A standard of care is clinical treatment that does not depart from what a reasonable and prudent counselor with similar training and in a similar situation would carry out (Corey et al., 2014; Zhang & Parsons, 2016). The challenge of a standard of care is that the "standard" may vary by court rulings. To prove malpractice, four factors (the four Ds) must be present: "a dereliction of duty that directly results in damages" (Scott & Resnick, 2012, p. 540). In the event of a lawsuit, a counselor's only defense is documentation in the case file that proves that the counselor conformed to the standard of care. A means of protection is to never practice without having professional liability insurance.

Common reasons for counseling-related malpractice suits include issues around documentation, informed consent, client abandonment, premature termination, sexual misconduct, and failure to control a dangerous client (Corey et al., 2014). While the primary cause of litigation for counselors continues to be inappropriate relation with clients, the inappropriate handling of suicide crisis is a close second (Bartlett & Forbes, 2015; Remley & Herlihy, 2014). According to the Healthcare Providers Service Organization (HPSO, 2014, 2015, 2016), proper documentation is crucial in legal action and is often the only source of evidence in a case; in fact, good documentation can keep a counselor out of court. Specifically, in crisis situations, risk management concerns will focus on documentation, record keeping, informed consent, confidentiality, and termination. It is prudent for counselors to be familiar with risk management strategies, regardless of the client's situation (Zhang & Parsons, 2016). Basic elements of risk management include being client centered, being clinically appropriate, being supportive of treatment and the therapeutic alliance, having a working knowledge of legal regulations and issues, and remembering to do no harm (Simon, 2012). For example, Bartlett & Forbes (2015) state that "suicide litigation has resulted in many of the largest settlements awarded to plaintiffs; the act of suicide is deemed preventable by law, and as a result lawsuits brought against practitioners are pervasive" (p. 27). Read Voices from the Field 3.4 and complete Think About It 3.2.

VOICES FROM THE FIELD 3.4
Avoiding Litigation When Providing Crisis Counseling

Emmett Poundstone

When providing crisis counseling, two major elements are necessary to avoid litigation. First, the counselor must have the necessary education/training, experience, and credentials to provide crisis counseling. If there are any doubts, the counselor should consult with some individual who has more credentials or the state regulatory board. Second, the counselor must provide adequate documentation regarding the counseling services. If a counselor has any doubts about his or her activities, it is advisable to consult with an attorney who has mental health experience.

THINK ABOUT IT 3.2

Think about the following article on boundary violations. Read the ACA legal case *Failure to Properly Monitor and Supervise Services Treating Counselor Who Continually Failed to Establish Professional Boundaries and Who Developed a Personal Relationship with the Client* found at www.hpso.com/risk-education/individuals/legal-case-study/Failure-to-properly-monitor-and-supervise. After a review of this case, discuss the following questions: What errors did the counseling supervisor make? How should the counseling supervisor have initially intervened? What are your thoughts on having supervision of supervision? What errors did the treating counselor make? What are your thoughts on the resolution of this case? Should there be a risk management recommendation for university-employed counselors?

DOCUMENTATION AND RECORD KEEPING

There is a useful old saying in the helping professions, "If it's not written down, it didn't happen." A counselor may have done everything right with a client, but failure to document means that no evidence exists of the counselor's actions and decisions. Documentation is an essential part of the standard of care of the counseling relationship, as discussed in the *ACA Code of Ethics* (ACA, 2014, section A). Appropriate professional documentation and record keeping display diligence and also promote client welfare (Bond & Mitchels, 2014; Luepker, 2012). While client welfare is a counselor's main purpose, there is no denying that documentation can either help or hurt a counselor in legal cases (HPSO, 2016; Welfel, 2016). For improvements in charting, see *Good Documentation Brings Peace of Mind* by HPSO (2016), which lists a number of effective documentation practices. Good documentation is particularly crucial in crisis situations such as suicide, homicide, mandated reporting (e.g., child, elderly, and vulnerable persons), and disaster relief where the risk of litigation increases. Complete Activity 3.2, which asks you to rewrite case note entries.

ACTIVITY 3.2

Examine the following case note entries. Rewrite these entries to improve them.

1. Client says she is doing better today.
2. Client's appearance is good.
3. Client went to doctor as requested.
4. Client began new medication last week.

Zhang and Parsons (2016) suggest that client records should include identifying data, background/historical data, diagnosis and prognosis, treatment plans, informed consent, progress notes, and a termination summary. Diagnoses are seldom provided in a true crisis situation. It would be inappropriate to diagnose prematurely. Incorrect diagnoses lead to inappropriate treatment plans. Outside of a true crisis situation, counselors document a client's diagnosis and whether it was reported by the client or received with the referral (e.g., if the client was discharged from a hospital). It is important to indicate by whom and when the diagnosis was provided so that no confusion exists that the diagnosis was given by a party other than the counselor. It is crucial that a risk assessment be conducted on every client, regardless of the stated presenting problem. If the assessment produces any degree of lethality (either stated or observed) it is equally important to justify the actions taken and to follow up in subsequent case notes on the status of the risk. In addition, inappropriate information should not be included in client records. Inappropriate information is anything that is not treatment-related and that could be problematic if viewed by others. Such information includes personal opinions, discussions of a third party, sensitive information, and any past criminal behavior. However, in cases of threats to self or others, documentation of follow-up assessments should be included in the client's records (Corey et al., 2014; Remley & Herlihy, 2014; Zhang & Parsons, 2016). The requirement to maintain and secure client records is not limited to ACA; it is also endorsed by organizations such as the American Mental Health Counselors Association, American School Counseling Association, American Association for Marriage and Family and Therapy, American Psychological Association, and the National Association for Social Workers.

Counselors must keep documentation of their interventions with clients. Admittedly, crisis conditions (e.g., a disaster site) are not always conducive to writing case notes, but counselors working with clients in crisis need to clearly document exact dates, pertinent details, assessments, and treatment decisions. It is important to remember that although case notes must be succinct, they should never be vague. Case notes must be specific enough to demonstrate that the treatment reflected prevailing standards of care. The documentation must clearly illustrate the session with details that capture the essence of what occurred and validate treatment decisions. The need for client files to be in a locked and secured location applies during crisis events, and providing for confidential file storage in crisis situations must be addressed in crisis planning (American Red Cross, 2013; Jongsma, 2014). Complete Think About It 3.3.

Another consideration is that crisis responders are transitioning to the use of on-site and cost-effective electronic health records (EHRs) to meet the real-time data capture needs of vulnerable clients. Portable EHR systems employed in a crisis must be

THINK ABOUT IT 3.3

Think about being in a mass disaster situation. How would you keep records when in the field after a flood, tornado, or house fire? You are given the choice of documenting client information with an EHR system or on paper-based forms. Which option would you choose, and why? What would the advantages and disadvantages be of each documentation approach for you as the crisis counselor? What legal and ethical issues might you need to consider when comparing both approaches?

adaptable to situational changes and available to the provider in multiple languages (Glasgow, Kaplan, Ockene, Fisher, & Emmons, 2012), because disasters do not discriminate by geography. The ability of the EHR to document mental health data is an efficient and patient-centered approach in the field. The use of EHR is not limited to community-based disaster relief settings but has the potential for daily use in hospital emergency departments, where mental health emergencies are likely to present (Furukawa, 2011). This evolution in medical record keeping produces new legal and ethical considerations for counselors responding to crisis situations.

See Case Study 3.7, which looks at a client's privacy rights in relation to documentation.

CASE STUDY 3.7

Privacy Rights Records

When Jeff was 16 years old, he saw a counselor for conduct issues. During one of those sessions, Jeff volunteered that he had tried on his sister's undergarments. Ten years later, Jeff is experiencing a life crisis. His estranged wife is suing for custody of their children, and Jeff is concerned that his childhood counseling record may be discoverable by the court.

Discussion Questions

1. If you were Jeff's adolescent counselor, how might you have best documented the issue he described?
2. What information should and should not be entered into the clinical record?
3. Can you offer any reassurances regarding the retention and availability of his older record?
4. If you were his current counselor, how would you record this disclosure about his previous counseling?
5. What information should Jeff's attorney be aware of regarding his rights of confidentiality?

INFORMED CONSENT

Clients enter counseling without much information about what will take place. They may in fact often have many misconceptions about the process of counseling and the nature of the counseling relationship. Clients must enter counseling freely and be fully informed of what is to be expected in the counseling relationship. Informed consent occurs when clients understand all the possible risks, benefits, and potential outcomes of counseling (Remley & Herlihy, 2014). The *ACA Code of Ethics* (ACA, 2014) states that "counselors have an obligation to review in writing and verbally with clients the rights and responsibilities of both counselors and clients" (section A.2.a). The *ACA Code of Ethics* further specifies that the counselor must explain to the client "the purposes, goals, techniques, procedures, limitations, potential risks, and benefits of services; the counselor's qualifications, credentials, relevant experience, and approach to counseling; continuation of services upon the incapacitation or death of the counselor; the role of technology . . ." (section A.2.b). Informed-consent forms should also include an explanation of office policies, fees, billing arrangements, record keeping, the right to refuse treatment, and the potential effect of refusal. Both client and counselor must sign the informed-consent form in order for it to become part of the counseling record.

In a crisis or large-scale disaster, obtaining informed consent will rarely involve papers and a clipboard (American Red Cross, 2013). Documented consent in such circumstances may be impossible, impractical, or delayed at a minimum. For example, a counselor may be called upon to provide support to someone wrapped in a thermal blanket at the scene of a disaster standing in front of the ruins of their home. Counselors should introduce themselves, explain their role, describe the general limitations of confidentiality, and ask permission to speak with the client. The counselor may ask a few practical questions:

- "What are you not comfortable with me disclosing when I contact those you have asked me to?"
- "How do you want me to identify myself and my association with you when I call?"
- "If I contact a person, and he or she is not there, may I leave a message and identify myself?"

If a crisis victim refuses intervention, the counselor should withdraw, offering to be available in the event that future service is wanted. If the client agrees to speak with the counselor, consent needs to be reassessed throughout the exchange and may be withdrawn at any point should the survivor elect to discontinue (American Red Cross, 2013). The privacy of the client should be protected as much as the circumstances of the disaster allow. Protecting privacy may involve moving the survivor from more trafficked areas or moderating one's voice to minimize the likelihood of being overheard. Often the counselor may be asked to contact others on the survivor's behalf, such as community resources or loved ones. The counselor should clarify with the survivor that they give consent for the contact, who they wish to have contacted, and what specific information to share, being mindful to share only the minimal amount necessary. If a client is unable to sign, the crisis counselor should note why there was no written consent.

CONFIDENTIALITY

Gladding (2010) defines confidentiality as "the professional, ethical, and legal obligation of counselors that they not disclose client information revealed during counseling without the client's written consent" (p. 34). The *ACA Code of Ethics* (ACA, 2014) states that "counselors disclose information only with appropriate consent or with sound legal or ethical justification" (section B.1.c). In situations where a client is a danger to self or others or where the professional counselor is mandated by law to report abuse or is required by a court of law to disclose information, confidentiality can be legally breached (HPSO, 2017). In situations other than these, a client must give consent for the release of information. Client records are confidential, and they must be kept in a secure and locked location for a specified time in accordance with professional ethical standards and the legal requirements of the state and HIPAA regulations (Zhang & Parsons, 2016).

In crisis and disaster circumstances, provisions for confidentiality are certainly more challenging; however, the ethical standards and requirements of the profession still apply. Counselors should be aware of the latitude that may be allowed for confidentiality in difficult circumstances, yet strive to ensure the protection of client information. For example, it may be difficult for a university to conceal the names of students who were victims of a sexual assault as the media may acquire the names and report details of the incident before a university spokesperson has the ability to make an official statement. While university law enforcement officers generally work in conjunction with other local and state authorities, it is not always possible for the details to remain sealed. Further, it is also impossible to prevent media sources from listening to police and hospital scanners and reporting information that is potentially false ahead of the justified facts (Y. Tyre, personal communication, October 11, 2015). Complete Activity 3.3, which focuses on client confidentiality. Also complete Think About It 3.4 and read Voices from the Field 3.5.

ACTIVITY 3.3

You have just determined that your client is a potential suicide threat and you must therefore break confidentiality and notify someone to discuss a plan of safety. Decide whom you will contact and exactly what you will discuss. Write a narrative of the conversation you will have with both the client and the person(s) to whom you will be disclosing. Consider how much you may disclose, what guidelines you are given by the *ACA Code of Ethics* to handle this scenario, and what other sources you might consult to determine how to guide your conversations.

THINK ABOUT IT 3.4

Think about potential breaches of confidentiality. Read the ACA legal case *Alleged Breach of Confidentiality* found at www.hpso.com/risk-education/individuals/legal-case-study/Alleged-Breach-of-Confidentiality. After reviewing this case, discuss the following questions: What would you have done differently? How would supervision have helped? How would peer consultation have assisted this counselor? When would a conversation with an attorney have been appropriate?

VOICES FROM THE FIELD 3.5
Confidentiality during Chaotic Circumstances in the Field

Erin Martz

When providing counseling services in a disaster mental health capacity, you may find yourself facing a variety of ethical challenges. One issue to consider is the feasibility of ensuring confidentiality in potentially chaotic situations. Bear in mind that many first responders with whom you will be working may request access to information to maintain the welfare of those being helped collaboratively. Approach these requests from a treatment team perspective to ensure clients feel informed and empowered at a potentially disempowering and confusing time in their lives.

TERMINATION IN CRISIS INTERVENTION

Because crisis intervention is generally brief and focused on immediate needs, crisis counselors must use appropriate termination skills with clients. Appropriate termination should not only bring closure for the crisis counseling relationship but also bolster the goals and plans laid out in the crisis counseling process. A distinction should be made between termination and abandonment. Appropriate termination may decrease the allegations of perceived abandonment by a client.

Termination occurs when a counselor or a client decides to end the counseling relationship. According to section A.11.c of the *ACA Code of Ethics* (ACA, 2014), professional counselors terminate cases when the treatment goals have been reached and the client no longer needs counseling, when the client is not being helped by further counseling or might be harmed by further counseling, when the client or someone associated with the client poses harm to the counselor, or when the client does not pay counseling fees. In those circumstances where clients need further counseling services after termination, the counselor provides the client with referral information for other appropriate mental health providers. Unfortunately, lack of attention to termination documentation can lead to lawsuits based on abandonment (Corey et al., 2014). A final termination summary should be added to the client file. Bond and Mitchels (2014) recommend that this summary include the reason for termination, a summary of progress, the final diagnostic impression, a follow-up plan, and other pertinent information. Complete Think About It 3.5.

When a client is neglected, deserted, or negligently terminated, the counselor has committed abandonment of the client. The *ACA Code of Ethics* (ACA, 2014) prohibits abandonment; section A.12 states, "Counselors do not abandon or neglect clients in counseling. Counselors assist in making appropriate arrangements for the continuation of treatment, when necessary, during interruptions such as vacations, illness, and following termination." Special considerations for termination at university counseling clinics would include times when a student drops out of school, leaves school for medical purposes, is placed on academic probation or conduct suspension, or graduates from the institution.

A counselor must think about myriad factors when considering or faced with terminating a therapeutic relationship. It is highly recommended that a counselor discuss the process of termination with the client during the first appointment and have clinical documentation of this discussion. While a discussion about termination at the outset of the therapeutic relationship does not prevent unforeseen circumstances for termination,

---

THINK ABOUT IT 3.5

Think about termination documentation. How would the termination summary for a client in a disaster response setting differ from the termination summary for a student graduating from a university? How would the termination summary for a client in a disaster response setting differ from the termination note for a client being discharged from a clinical mental health center? When a client has a suicide crisis and does not return to the clinical mental health center following hospital discharge, how would the final client contact be documented?

it better prepares the client and goes far in the preservation of the counseling relationship. The following list highlights a few of the many circumstances that increase a counselor's risk of malpractice due to abandonment:

- The counselor is no longer receiving compensation from the client for professional services.
- The counselor recognizes that a referral might be in order.
- Therapeutic goals are no longer being achieved.
- The counselor is abruptly unavailable.
- The counselor fails to follow up after a client's hospital discharge.
- The counselor does not respond to a client's request for crisis treatment.
- The counselor allows managed care to dictate termination.
- The counselor lacks clinical coverage during planned absences (i.e., vacation time).
- Records do not verify outreach efforts to a client who breaks or misses appointments.
- A high-risk client drops out of treatment.
- A client is "fired" or refused treatment.
- A client is not notified in writing that a case is being closed.
- The client's record indicates a failure to review/consult/refer.
- Another treatment team member or staff member's notes do not verify that a treatment plan is being followed.

For further information on abandonment, see ACA, 2014, Corey et al., 2014, and Remley and Herlihey, 2014.

Corey et al. (2014) recommend that clients be given written information about the closure plan, including contact information for other counselors or resources. In the event that a client misses appointments and stops coming to counseling, the counselor should send a follow-up letter expressing interest in the client's welfare and asking the client to contact the counselor within a set period of time if the client wants to resume counseling. If a termination letter is to be sent to the home of the client, written consent to send any information to that address should have been obtained during the informed-consent process. Similarly, written consent to leave any information on a client's phone should have been obtained during intake. The written consent should state the specific address or phone number for which the client has granted permission. The counselor should document all attempts to contact a client. See Case Study 3.8, which focuses on the factors a counselor must take into consideration when terminating a therapeutic relationship.

CASE STUDY 3.8

Termination Considerations

Sarah lost her home and two family members in a series of tornadoes that recently swept across her state. She began to experience symptoms of acute trauma and approached you for care as a disaster relief counselor. You began seeing Sarah regularly since arriving at the disaster site. Sarah has engaged well therapeutically, and appears to be making progress. You were notified by the Red Cross that your term of service will be up in a week and need to terminate with each of your assigned cases at the location. When you mention discontinuing services with Sarah, she becomes distressed.

Discussion Questions

1. What obligations do you have to Sarah?
2. How will you ensure her continued recovery?
3. To what resources can you refer her?
4. Which ACA ethical code is applicable in this case?

As mentioned previously, termination in a mass crisis or disaster circumstance should be understood from a special perspective. Formal assessment, admission, and ongoing counseling normally are not possible under such circumstances. According to the American Red Cross (2013), ongoing care and provision of counseling services should be referred to local counseling services, case managers, and area providers in order to avoid therapeutic abandonment. An example of how such a conversation would occur follows:

COUNSELOR:	I'm glad we had the chance to work together these past few weeks since your home was destroyed. I understand this has been a very surreal and overwhelming time for you.
CLIENT:	I don't know what I would have done without you.
COUNSELOR:	Well, actually you did a lot of the work to move forward under difficult circumstances and have a lot to feel proud of. You have devised a plan of recovery for yourself, are in the process of securing more permanent housing, and have been able to return to work with transportation assistance. All of this means our work together has reached the right conclusion. At this time, I'd like to suggest community resources you may access for longer-term recovery support.

The severity of responses to mass crisis may have long-lasting effects for some. Psychological distress may remain high long after crisis counseling support services have been provided to those affected. This begs the question: What ethical responsibility do counselors have to ensure a healthy transition from crisis counseling to appropriate community-based treatment services once the additional support has been removed? There is some uncertainty about this limit of responsibility; therefore, many counseling training programs include crisis intervention course work. For those who are already in practice, it is recommended they seek some training in crisis response counseling to explore whether they want to work with crisis populations, or how they will work with a person who has survived a mass disaster and is referred to them for support (Norris & Rosen, 2009).

SPIRITUAL AND MULTICULTURAL CONSIDERATIONS

To dismiss discussions surrounding a client's religious or spiritual views related to a crisis is to devalue the client's worldview and not treat the entire person. Often, clients may entertain ideas that tragedy has come about as a result of God's wrath or disfavor.

Counselors should be prepared to safely explore these concerns. This requires that counselors examine their own religious or spiritual biases and understand that many survivors have symptoms of secondary trauma of a spiritual nature (Zalaquett, Carrión, & Exum, 2009). Disaster workers might hear clients question whether their sin had brought the disaster upon them. Further, disaster counselors may have to contend with remarks from volunteers working the crisis who may express such concepts of judgment to clients (Hard, 2012).

If the disaster occurs in a school system where the common separation of church and state is stressed, counselors must take that into consideration. Keep in mind that according to the Supreme Court, the First Amendment as applied to public schools was intended for public schools to not sanction or support a specific religion or faith over others. Counselors must find a balance between honoring the guidelines of the state and recognizing (and honoring) the needs of clients, regardless of where the tragedy took place (Remley & Herlihy, 2014).

In the case of a counselor responding to a person's life crisis, perhaps related to suicide, an examination of personal religious beliefs is essential to ensure maintaining a value-neutral assessment. Failure to take a nonjudgmental stance may result in further risk to the client; by assuming that the client has the same moral or religious beliefs, counselors may foster shame and anger in the client who then may withhold pertinent information needed to assess his or her level of lethality (Granello & Granello, 2007a). Even secular counselors should exercise sufficient latitude to explore these questions with clients; doing less results in a failure to meet the needs of the client.

Research indicates that marginalized populations may find that predisaster norms set the tone for the postdisaster reality. Therefore, contrary to popular belief, disaster is not a social leveler, and minorities may find that their circumstances have declined (Hard, 2012). Lesbian, gay, bisexual, and transgender (LGBT) persons may find themselves further marginalized following a disaster. As Hard observed, while national service organizations (e.g., American Red Cross) may have LGBT-affirming policies, individual volunteers may be from less accepting backgrounds, thus requiring counselors to act as diversity advocates on behalf of LGBT victims. Therefore, counselors should be versed in multicultural sensitivity and make efforts to indicate their sensitivity to multicultural issues. The counselor's respect for cultural diversity should not vary according to setting, whether in a school, private practice, or university setting, which is often a multicultural microcosm. For example, Asian Americans are primarily focused on time orientation that is either past or present. In contrast, Native Americans tend to be present-oriented when exposed to traumatic circumstances. These variances require that counselors be aware how time orientation, and similar factors, influence the crisis response of clients in order to accurately assess current mental status and needs (Remley & Herlihy, 2014). At the same time, it is important to not place all persons from a perceived culture into the same template, but to assess individuals in their unique cultural perception. Having an understanding of differences is important, but making decisions based on assumptions may not be helpful.

In addition, some cultures are more socially focused rather than individually focused. Responses from people of these cultures will be directed toward what is most beneficial to the community's best interest. People from different cultures will vary in terms of eye contact, body language, affect, willingness to discuss personal matters, and in their response to authority figures. Ethical practice requires the development of multicultural competence among counselors; therefore, counselors are responsible for being well versed in multicultural competencies when serving others (ACA, 2014; Remley & Herlihy, 2014).

Summary

Legal and ethical matters can be confounding for counselors in the best of circumstances. In times of crisis, it is all the more imperative that counselors be well acquainted with legal and ethical obligations. Crisis counselors may often find their normal coping mechanisms overwhelmed in the midst of disaster or crisis interventions. When the counselor's normal coping is impaired, fertile conditions develop that can lead to a lapse in professional judgment. The prevention of ethical and legal entanglements is far more preferred than the remediation of problems following a lapse in behavior or judgment. This chapter discusses preventive considerations for crisis counselors, including wellness recommendations, continuing education, supervision and peer consultation, and ethical decision-making models.

HIPAA was enacted to address a number of perceived failings in the management of information in the health care industry. FERPA was enacted to address concerns about privacy violations and the inclusion of immaterial comments and personal opinions in student educational records. HIPAA and FERPA have not only added additional layers of protection to client records but also increased the complexity of counselor responsibility in protecting both the client's and their own interests. HIPAA and FERPA have provisions for crisis situations, but confidentiality is still central to ethical practice, even during times of crisis. Crisis counselors must be familiar with the particulars of HIPAA and FERPA, including when they apply and overlap, as well as other legal requirements in their state. Furthermore, they should consult with an attorney to remain current on the legal aspects of care in crisis as well as standard practice circumstances.

Other areas of ethical and legal concern for counselors include the duty to warn, negligence, and malpractice. The 1976 case of *Tarasoff v. Regents of the University of California* is the impetus behind many duty to warn laws. This chapter discusses the impact of this case on crisis counseling, when such duty may exist, and its implications. A breach of duty owed to another is considered *negligence*; negligence that occurs in a professional setting is *malpractice*. In the often chaotic circumstances of crisis and disaster counseling, counselors should be careful to avoid these pitfalls.

The matters of documentation, informed consent, confidentiality, referral, and termination may be considered commonplace in normal, more structured practice settings. However, such matters of ethical concern or legality must be attended to whether the counselor is working one-on-one with a client in a life crisis or intervening with clients in a large-scale disaster.

Counselors must examine their own religious or spiritual biases and understand that often survivors may show symptoms of secondary trauma of a spiritual nature. They should also be aware that marginalized populations may find that predisaster norms set the tone for postdisaster reality and that their circumstances have declined following a disaster.

Planning, preparedness, and a commitment to legal and ethical practices in all situations will ensure that counselors maintain standards of care, whatever the situation.

4

Essential Crisis Intervention Skills

Bradley T. Erford and Lisa R. Jackson-Cherry*

PREVIEW

This chapter provides an overview of the fundamental skills for the provision of effective crisis intervention work. The skills discussed here will focus on Ivey, Ivey, and Zalaquett's (2014) microskills hierarchy. At the heart of this hierarchy is the basic listening sequence, an interrelated set of skills that will not only foster the development of rapport with clients but also aid in the identification of interventions to help achieve a successful resolution to the client's crisis state. Examples of the skills in use as well as practice exercises to foster individual skill development are provided.

ESSENTIAL CRISIS INTERVENTION MICROSKILLS

A reasonable question at this point is, "What is the difference between basic counseling skills and crisis counseling skills?" Simply put, the difference is less about what the counselor does or the techniques and strategies he or she employs and more about contextual application, or where and in what situation skills are applied. The essential foundational skills necessary for effective crisis intervention work are indeed the basic tools on which the success of interventions may depend. It is important to stress that these skills will help create the counselor–client relational conditions necessary for positive change (i.e., therapeutic alliance). The skills covered in this chapter are *basic* counseling skills applied to crisis situations, and these basic skills form the foundation for the use of more advanced counseling skills. When working with clients in crisis, it is essential to listen, be empathic, and respond skillfully.

These skills will provide the client with alliance-building constructs such as empathic understanding, genuineness, and acceptance, and will greatly facilitate the development of a safe therapeutic environment. They will also aid in establishing rapport and developing an effective therapeutic alliance with the client. Rapport can be understood as a harmonious or sympathetic relationship. In crisis intervention work, the development of rapport starts with the initial contact and continues throughout the process. The crisis counselor's primary concern should be fostering this rapport in order to develop a cohesive and supportive relationship with the client. How the crisis

---

* Special thanks to Joseph Cooper for his outstanding contributions to the first two editions of this chapter.

counselor conducts himself or herself is crucial, as this may be the client's first encounter with a counselor and this interaction may either encourage or discourage the client from seeking counseling in the future or from following up when a proposed crisis plan is developed. The crisis counselor's ability to gain a client's trust is paramount in a crisis intervention since the counselor must ask the client sensitive questions to gather information for referrals or crisis planning.

The skills covered in this chapter focus on Ivey et al.'s (2014) microskills hierarchy—a set of verbal and behavioral responses that facilitate the process of counseling and alliance formation, regardless of the crisis counselor's theoretical orientation. For some, this chapter may be a review of the basic skills taught in a previous skills course, while for others it may be the first consideration of these skills. Either way, it is always important to continuously be aware of and apply effective skills, since doing so is the hallmark of effective crisis counseling. Ivey et al. present these skills as a hierarchy that is organized in a systematic framework. At the bottom of the hierarchy are the basic attending skills, such as patterns of eye contact, body position, vocal tone, and silence. A bit farther up the skills hierarchy is the basic listening sequence, which includes asking open and closed questions, using reflecting skills, and summarizing. In this chapter, each of these basic skills is reviewed, along with practical examples of the skills in use.

ATTENDING SKILLS

Good communication involves more than just verbal content; crisis counselors communicate with more than just words. Most meaningful communication takes place nonverbally. The next time you are engaged in conversation with someone, take a moment to pay attention to all of the nonverbal cues your partner is giving you. What does his facial expression say to you? What is conveyed by the look in his eyes? Does he have a closed or open body stance? Although important in social relationships, these attending skills are even more important in the counseling relationship. Bedi (2006) surveyed clients who had received counseling and asked them to identify the specific counselor behaviors that most helped to form a working alliance. Following validation and education, clients ranked nonverbal gestures, presentation, and body language as the next most important alliance-building factors. These nonverbal attending behaviors communicate a counselor's interest, warmth, and understanding to the client; they include eye contact, body position, tone of voice, and silence.

Eye Contact

Maintaining good eye contact is how a crisis counselor conveys interest, confidence, and involvement in the client's story (Egan, 2013). Through eye contact, clients know a counselor is focusing on them and fully committed to the helping process. Moreover, for those clients who have difficulty with closeness, making eye contact can be an important vehicle of change. However, good eye contact is not the same as staring your client down. There should be natural breaks in eye contact; eye contact should be more of an "ebb and flow" as you collect your thoughts and listen to the client's story. Also, it is essential to be sensitive to differences in how eye contact is expressed across cultures. For example, whereas direct eye contact is usually interpreted as a sign of interest in the European-American culture, some Asian and Native American groups believe direct eye contact is

ACTIVITY 4.1

Form pairs. One person takes the role of listener, while the other takes the role of speaker and is to talk about anything of interest for about 5 minutes. During this time, the listener should maintain eye contact with the speaker as he or she normally would in everyday conversation. After 5 minutes, each pair should process the experience. What feedback does the speaker have regarding the listener's level of eye contact? Was it too much? Darting? Too little? Empathic? What was most comfortable? Based on the feedback, do the exercise again, but this time have the listener try to incorporate some of the feedback received about his or her level of eye contact. Process the activity again, and then switch roles.

a sign of disrespect (Hays & Erford, 2018). Some African Americans may maintain greater eye contact when talking and less eye contact when listening, and many African American men will not look directly into the eyes of an authority figure because in the Black cultural context avoiding eye contact shows recognition of an authority–subordinate relationship. Also, for clients who are overly fragile or under much stress and pressure, direct eye contact may increase their level of anxiety. For example, imagine you are seeing a client in crisis, a 20-year-old female college student who states she was raped last night. As she tells you what happened, you notice she stares down at the floor and often avoids your eye contact. Should you confront her on her lack of eye contact and ask her to look at you directly when she speaks? Of course not. Her lack of eye contact is probably due to her feelings of shame and anxiety and is serving an emotion-regulating function. In a crisis situation, especially if a client is feeling overwhelmed or ashamed or is experiencing paranoia, be aware that a client who avoids your eyes is probably doing so as a protective mechanism. This reaction is normal in a crisis.

So how do you determine how much eye contact to maintain with a client? Unfortunately, no universal rule or criterion exists for what is considered either appropriate or inappropriate eye contact. As already noted, eye contact varies among cultures and is influenced by the intensity of emotions involved in the crisis situation. A good rule of thumb to follow is to maintain a moderate amount of eye contact while monitoring your client's level of comfort and to adjust your eye contact accordingly (Young, 2013). Also, it is helpful for you to become aware of your own attending behavior so you can understand how this behavior may affect the counseling relationship. Professional counselors must be particularly aware of their use of eye contact during crisis counseling sessions. It is important to use eye contact and other nonverbal attending behaviors to reduce anxiety and de-escalate anger and agitation. Complete Activities 4.1 and 4.2 to gain a deeper understanding of your own attending behaviors.

Body Position

As with eye contact, your body position should convey to the client your interest and involvement. Face the client and adopt an open, relaxed, and attentive body posture, as this will assist in putting your client at ease. Counselors should not cross arms and legs and should not sit behind a desk or other barrier. In addition, Egan (2013) recommends that the counselor lean slightly toward the client, as this communicates that the counselor is listening to the client and interested in what the client has to say. Slouching in a

ACTIVITY 4.2

This activity will help you become aware of how your clients might perceive your overall pattern of nonverbal communication. Begin by forming pairs. One person will be the communicator and will face the other person, who will serve as the mirror. For the next 5 minutes, the communicator can talk about anything he or she wants, and throughout this time, the mirror is to nonverbally mirror each gesture, facial expression, eye contact, and movement of the communicator. It is important that the mirror not attempt to "interpret" the message that is being sent by the communicator but just to mirror the perceived nonverbal communication. At the end of 5 minutes, each pair should process the experience. What was it like to see your nonverbal communication mirrored back to you? Did you learn anything about how you come across to others? Is there anything you would want to change or do more of? Switch roles and process the activity again.

chair or leaning away from the client may be perceived by the client as lack of interest or boredom. The physical distance between counselor and client should also be taken into consideration; getting too close can be overwhelming and uncomfortable, whereas being too distant can make the counselor appear aloof and may be awkward for the client. Although in Western cultures the average physical distance for conversation is typically 2 to 4 feet, this "comfort zone" will vary from client to client (Young, 2013). When in doubt, you could let the client arrange the chairs at a distance that meets his or her individual comfort level. However, keep in mind that there are instances when this option is not desirable. For example, in a crisis setting, you may be faced with a client who is paranoid or experiencing homicidal or suicidal ideation. Would you want to be within hitting or kicking distance of this client? Also, it would not be a good idea to have this client sitting between you and the door. Use your best judgment. By taking into account body position, you can create a safe environment for both you and your client. Your safety should always be a priority. You should never do anything that makes you feel uncomfortable or jeopardizes your physical safety. Use your body posture and physical space to comfort clients and de-escalate the anxiety, anger, or agitation a client in crisis might feel.

Vocal Tone

Have you ever had the experience where you are engaged in conversation with someone and you find yourself becoming increasingly anxious and tense, regardless of the topic? The next time this happens, pay attention to your partner's tone of voice, for you may be unconsciously responding to the emotional tone conveyed in your partner's voice. Emotions are frequently conveyed via tone of voice. The pitch, pacing, and volume can all have an effect on how a client responds emotionally to a crisis counselor. There is much to be said for a calm and soothing voice in times of distress, especially when the client is in a crisis situation. Do not underestimate the power of this attribute; your control and calmness may be among the greatest benefits to your client in crisis. Your voice can do much to help create a soothing and anxiety-regulating atmosphere for the client. Learn to use your voice as a therapeutic tool. For example, if your client is overly agitated, it is often helpful to speak more slowly and in a soothing tone, as this will help your client to slow things down and begin to focus.

ACTIVITY 4.3

In small groups, assign one person to be the speaker. Instruct the speaker to talk in a normal tone of voice for a few minutes about anything of interest. Have the other group members close their eyes as they listen to the speaker, paying close attention to the tone of voice, pacing, volume, and so on. After 2 or 3 minutes, stop and have the listeners give the speaker feedback on his or her voice. What was their reaction to the tone, volume, accent, rate of speech, and other char- acteristics? After this processing, repeat the activity, but this time have the speaker make changes in voice tone, volume, or pacing to deliberately create different reactions. How did the listeners respond to the changes in vocal qualities? What were the listeners' emotional responses to the various vocal qualities? Finally, have the listeners imagine themselves as a cli- ent in crisis. What types of vocal qualities would they prefer to hear?

Also be aware of your own internal process and how your tone of voice is convey- ing your *own* emotional state when working with a client in crisis. It is not uncommon for your own rate of speech to increase when you hear something that causes you to feel anxious, such as a client who discloses homicidal ideation to you. If your client is agi- tated and using pressured speech, and your speech also begins to race, your rate of speech could exacerbate your client's state.

To convey a sense of empathic understanding, it can be helpful to emphasize spe- cific words used by your client. This technique of giving increased vocal emphasis to certain words or short phrases is called *verbal underlining* (Ivey et al., 2014). For exam- ple, consider the difference between "You were very hurt by your husband's actions" and "You were *very* hurt by your husband's actions." In the latter comment, the counse- lor places the emphasis on the word *very* to help reflect the intensity of the client's expe- rience. Again, modulate your voice tone to comfort clients and de-escalate the anxiety, anger, or agitation clients in crisis might feel. Complete Activity 4.3, which considers the vocal subtleties in the spoken word.

Silence

Beginning crisis counselors often have difficulty using silence with their clients. They want to keep talking to fill in any lapses or void in the session, usually as a way to mol- lify their own anxiety and discomfort with a client in crisis. Or worse, they will engage in a monologue or resort to lecturing or teaching the client. However, constantly inter- vening or throwing a barrage of questions at a client in crisis can feel overwhelming and intrusive to a client who is already feeling overwhelmed. Clients in crisis need space to think, to sort out their thoughts, and to process what is happening. The coun- selor needs that time as well. This point cannot be over accentuated: silence is impor- tant for both clients and professional counselors. It is essential for crisis counselors to develop a comfort with silence pauses.

Many beginning counselors are afraid to use silence, because they believe the silence conveys their incompetence as a counselor. However, the opposite is true. Silence, if used appropriately and at the right time, can convey acceptance and empathic understanding. In essence, the message of silence is "I am here for you if you need me, yet I respect your need to take your time with this." See Case Study 4.1, which looks at the use of silence in a crisis interview.

CASE STUDY 4.1

Using Silence in Counseling

The following exchange between Carol and her counselor illustrates how important silence can be in a crisis. Carol is an adult female who presented to counseling with severe symptoms of depression, suicidal ideation, and an attempt to kill herself yesterday with an overdose of sleeping pills.

CAROL: I just want to die. All of the emotional pain, sadness, and humiliation. I just had another miscarriage, my third one, and I'm almost certain I'll never have children. (*Pauses for 15 seconds to think.*) On top of that, my husband is growing more distant too, and I worry he might leave me for someone who he can have a family with.

COUNSELOR: So you're also feeling worried about how this is going to impact your marriage, and whether or not your husband will want to be with you.

CAROL: (*Silence for 30 seconds as she looks down and to the right.*) Yes, but I realize that if he truly cared for me, he wouldn't leave. I think maybe he is just as hurt and in as much pain as I am. It's my own insecurities, really. (*Pauses for 15 more seconds.*) And if he did want to leave, then he is not the right person for me to be with. Maybe I deserve better than that.

COUNSELOR: (*Silence for 20 seconds as the counselor gathers her thoughts.*) So there are a couple of things at work here. First, your husband's behavior could represent how he is grieving, and your insecurities may have distorted how you have been making sense of his behavior. And second, you realize that what is important for you is to be with someone who truly and genuinely cares for you and is committed to the marriage.

Discussion Questions

1. How effective was the counselor's use of silence?
2. What alternative responses may have also been helpful?
3. Put yourself in the position of the client. What would you have been thinking to yourself during the periods of silence?

Egan (2013) developed a conceptual framework for active listening using nonverbal communication. He used the acronym *SOLER* to help counselors remember key nonverbal techniques to use to convey that they are physically and psychologically present with clients. These techniques also help convey a counselor's genuineness and respect toward the client, and put the client at ease. When applying SOLER, reflect on the extent to which your posture communicates availability and openness to your client, and adjust accordingly. Observe yourself on video during counseling role plays. Remember to relax!

SOLER

S: ➔ *Squarely* face the client. Sitting facing the client gives the impression of attentiveness and engagement.

O: ➔ Adopt an *open* posture. An open posture can show that you are available to listen, while crossed hands or legs can convey unavailability. Sitting with your hands either by your side or resting on your lap if you are writing things down is appropriate.

L: ➔ *Lean* (slightly) toward your client to convey your interest in and engagement with them.

E: ➔ Make *eye* contact. Maintain appropriate and culturally sensitive eye contact to convey your interest and engagement.

R: ➔ Stay *relaxed*. Try to be relaxed and natural with your client. This helps put them at ease. Fidgeting or maintaining a ridged stance can convey the impression you are not comfortable with your client.

THE BASIC LISTENING SEQUENCE

The basic listening sequence represents a set of interrelated skills used to achieve three overarching goals: (1) to obtain an overall summary and understanding of the client's presenting issue; (2) to identify the key facts of the client's situation; and (3) to identify the core emotions and feelings the client is experiencing (Ivey et al., 2014). In short, these skills allow you to understand the structure of your client's story. Through the use of these skills, you will not only convey empathy, respect, warmth, and congruence to your client, but also lay the foundation for your understanding of the client's issues and the development of subsequent interventions to help achieve a successful resolution to his or her crisis state. The basic listening sequence involves the ability to ask open and closed questions as well as the reflecting skills—paraphrasing, reflecting feelings, and summarizing. An explanation and overview of these skills, examples of each skill in use, and some brief exercises to help you practice these basic listening skills follow. Also read Voices from the Field 4.1.

VOICES FROM THE FIELD 4.1
Reflective and Active Interventions

Joseph Cooper

Crisis intervention requires us to be both reflective *and* active in our interventions, and it is important to know when to use each. Here is an example of the need to be active: I once had a client in crisis who set her shirt on fire while sitting in the waiting room as I was getting her file and preparing for the session. This was not a time to reflect and listen! We put out the fire; made sure she was not injured; and then actively assessed suicidal/homicidal intent, safety issues, and developed a plan of action, which called for her to be hospitalized. I had to take an active and directive role in ensuring her safety. Crisis counseling often requires us to be quick on our feet and to have the ability to explore alternatives and to actively assist our clients in dealing with their problems.

Asking Open and Closed Questions

Questioning is a primary skill that allows crisis counselors to gather important and specific information about clients. Questions allow counselors to make an accurate assessment of their clients' issues and to guide and focus clients so they can make the most effective use of the counseling session. However, the use of questioning can be a double-edged sword. Used inappropriately, questioning can impede communication and block client disclosure. Drilling clients with questions can give too much control to the crisis counselor. Moreover, bombarding clients with questions could confuse and frustrate clients as well as increase their level of anxiety. Crisis counselors definitely do not want counseling sessions to sound like an interrogation, although many of the initial intake questions are used to gather information and are therefore necessary in crisis intervention. Counselors must be careful to appropriately pace the questions to guard against increasing clients' stress levels. Thus, crisis counselors need to be aware of how to use questions appropriately and pay close attention to the types of questions used to gather information. The two types of questions, open and closed questions, are examined next.

OPEN QUESTIONS   Open questions usually elicit fuller and more meaningful responses by encouraging the client to talk at greater length. Open questions typically begin with *what, how, could, would,* or *why* and are useful to help begin an interview, to help elaborate the client's story, and to help bring out specific details (Ivey et al., 2014). With open questions, the client can choose the content and direction of the session and take more control. The following guidelines illustrate the use of open questions for crisis workers:

1. *To begin the interview:*   "What would you like to talk about today?" "How can I be of help to you today?" "Tell me why you've come in today."
2. *To elicit details:*   "Give me an example." "What do you mean by 'just give up'?" "What do you usually do when you're feeling down?"
3. *To enrich and deepen:*   "Tell me more." "What were your feelings when that happened?" "What else is important for me to know?" "In what ways does that help?"
4. *Focus on plans:*   "What are some things you can do to stay safe?" "Who are some people you can call when you feel this way again?" "How will you make that happen?"

Finally, be careful when using *why* questions and questions that are leading in nature. Questions that begin with "Why" often cause the client to intellectualize and can lead to a discussion of reasons. In addition, *why* questions can cause the client to become defensive or criticized, to feel "put on the spot." When this happens, it is not uncommon for the client to become more guarded and to shut down. For example, think back to a time when you were younger and your parents asked the question "Why did you do that?" How did you feel and what was your reaction? Take a moment to consider the following: "Why do you hate yourself?" versus "You say you hate yourself. Help me understand that." Which of these approaches would you prefer your counselor to use? In addition to making clients become more defensive, *why* questions can also lead clients to feel more hopeless and despondent, as in this example:

COUNSELOR: Why do you continue to go back to a man who abuses you?

SUSAN: I know, I know. It sounds pathetic.

THINK ABOUT IT 4.1

Think about your questioning skills. How can you use open and closed questions effectively in your work with clients during and outside of a crisis? Self-monitor conversations with friends, colleagues, students, and clients. Do you use good questioning techniques? Explain.

Another roadblock to the use of effective questions involves questions that are leading in nature. Leading questions often contain a hidden agenda because the answer or expectation is already imbedded within the question. Although well intentioned, these types of questions place too much power in the hands of the crisis counselor and tend to push the client in a preconceived direction. Here are a couple of examples of leading questions: "You didn't really want to kill yourself, did you?" or "Don't you think you will feel better if you stop drinking?" Try to guard against the use of these types of questions. Crisis counselors want to hear a client's story as he or she understands and experiences it. Open questions allow the counselor the opportunity to achieve this end without imposing values and expectations on the client. Complete Think About It 4.1.

CLOSED QUESTIONS   Closed questions can be used when crisis counselors need to obtain very specific, concrete information and get all the facts straight. Such questions typically either elicit a "yes/no" response or provide specific factual information, such as the number of drinks a client consumes in a week or the age at which he or she began experiencing symptoms. In contrast to longer-term counseling, where information is gathered more slowly and the treatment plan develops over many weeks, crisis counseling often requires quick and focused responses. Thus, closed questions are very useful and in fact necessary in crisis counseling because the counselor must gather specific information to aid in the prompt assessment of the problem and development of a plan of action (James & Gilliland, 2017). Here are some examples of closed questions:

"Are you thinking of killing yourself?"

"When did these symptoms begin?"

"Do you have a family member or friend to call on when you are feeling overwhelmed?"

"How old were you when your parents divorced?"

As can be seen from the above examples, closed questions are good for obtaining the necessary details to aid in assessment and intervention when a client is in crisis. It is not unusual for crisis sessions to integrate many closed questions for gathering pertinent information related to the crisis. It is important to obtain the details needed for an assessment before opening up the session for more open ended answers since a counselor is never sure how much time one will have with a client. At the same time, crisis counselors should still guard against the overuse of closed questions, which can cause clients to shut down and simply wait for the next question to answer.

Many agencies require the completion of a crisis intake form that includes questions that a client is required to answer. One way to approach such questions and concurrently get more information from the client on his or her issue is to use a "question-tree format." This format ensures that a crisis counselor asks the (surface) questions required for the crisis intake as well as follow-up questions that may provide insight into the client's issue that would contribute to a more effective crisis plan. Using this format, the counselor asks the client a required closed question first, then proceeds with specific "follow-up" questions that are dependent on the unique situation of the client and allow for more detail. For example:

COUNSELOR (INITIAL QUESTION):	When did you first start using cocaine?
CLIENT:	When I was 15 years old.
COUNSELOR (FOLLOW-UP QUESTION):	Tell me what was happening when you were 15, when you first started using.

There is a category of closed questions that is similar in nature to leading questions and should not be used. Referred to as *negative-interrogatives* (James & Gilliland, 2017), they are closed questions that are used in a subtle way to coerce the client into agreeing with you. Questions that begin with *don't, doesn't, isn't, shouldn't, aren't,* and *wouldn't* often suggest a command for the client to do something. For example, "Shouldn't you stay away from her?" or "Isn't it a good idea to stop drinking?" imply the client should agree with the crisis counselor and do something different. For counselors who want to work collaboratively with clients, a better way to ask this question would be as follows: "You stated earlier that one of the problems that brought you in today is your drinking. Would you like some information on how I can be of help to you with that?" See Case Study 4.2, which shows how open and closed questions can be fluently integrated.

CASE STUDY 4.2

Effective Use of Open and Closed Questions during an Interview

The following dialogue provides a brief example of how the crisis counselor uses a blend of open and closed questions to obtain important information about Susan, who just discovered her husband is having an affair and is planning on leaving her. Susan presented with substantial suicidal ideation.

SUSAN:	I've gotten to where I can't even sleep at night. My mind just races, and I can't stop thinking about everything.
COUNSELOR:	Tell me more about some of the thoughts you have been having as you lay in bed unable to sleep. (*Open question to facilitate exploration and information gathering*)
SUSAN:	That I will never be in a happy relationship again. That my husband never really cared about me and just used me. That this pain will never stop. I wonder how I can get my life back together without him.
COUNSELOR:	You wonder if you will find peace again without him and want so much for this pain to go away. (*Empathic paraphrase*) What are some of the feelings you have been experiencing? (*Open question*)

SUSAN:	Mainly down—angry and depressed. Like I said, I've been thinking of checking out—ending it all. I feel this tremendous pain inside my chest, very hurt and sad I guess. I feel like he never really cared about me. He is so selfish.
COUNSELOR:	You're feeling very hurt and betrayed. Susan, tell me when you began experiencing these symptoms? (*Closed question to identify timeline of symptoms*)
SUSAN:	I would say about three months ago, when I found out about his affair, but they have gotten much worse over the last month.
COUNSELOR:	You say they have gotten worse over the last month. What do you make of that? (*Open question to identify client's understanding of her progressing symptoms*)
SUSAN:	Well, when I first found out about the affair, I would talk a lot with my friends and family, but I felt like they were getting sick of hearing me complain all the time. So lately I have just been trying to tough it out and deal with it on my own.
COUNSELOR:	And is this the first time you've sought counseling for this?
SUSAN:	Yes.

Discussion Questions

1. How effective was the counselor's use of open and closed questions?
2. What alternative responses by the counselor might also have been helpful?
3. Put yourself in the position of the client. What counselor responses would have elicited even better or more informative responses by the client?

As Case Study 4.2 demonstrates, the crisis counselor began with open questions to encourage exploration and to help identify the client's thoughts (e.g., "I will never be in a happy relationship again") and feelings (e.g., anger, grief, and hurt) associated with the breakup of her marriage. The crisis counselor then moved to closed questions to obtain more specific information regarding the duration of her symptoms and her experience in counseling.

OPEN VERSUS CLOSED QUESTIONS   As mentioned earlier, in crisis intervention work crisis counselors often need to use closed questions to quickly identify and bring out specific details in order to seek the resolution of the crisis state. However, they can often obtain the same information by asking open questions, so counselors should try to refrain from moving too quickly into a closed questioning approach unless they are unable to obtain the information otherwise. Consider the examples of closed questions and their open question counterparts in Table 4.1.

Notice in the examples in Table 4.1 that you can probably get all you need to know, and much more, by a subtle change in the wording of your questions to make them more open in nature. Complete Activity 4.4 for some additional practice.

TABLE 4.1 Open versus Closed Questions

Closed	Open
Were you afraid?	What feelings did you experience?
Are you concerned about what you'll do if your husband returns?	How do you think you may react if your husband returns?
Do you see your drinking as a problem?	What concerns do you have about your drinking?

Reflecting Skills

Reflecting skills are a set of interventions used to help stimulate clients' exploration of their thoughts and feelings related to the presenting problems. Such skills serve a number of important purposes. At the most basic level, reflecting skills are a form of active listening that conveys to the client your interest in and understanding of what the client may be struggling with. Thus, reflecting skills allow counselors to convey empathy, genuineness, and acceptance to clients, which in turn facilitates the creation of a sense of safety. Moreover, reflecting skills will stimulate a deeper exploration and understanding of the problem so that the client can examine the issues more objectively. The reflecting skills covered here are paraphrasing, reflecting feelings, and summarizing.

PARAPHRASING   A paraphrase is how a counselor feeds back to the client the essence of what has just been spoken. By paraphrasing, the counselor reflects the content and thoughts of the client's message. In other words, the crisis counselor is mirroring back to the client, in a nonjudgmental way, an accurate understanding of the client's communication and the implied meaning of that communication. Thus, paraphrasing is a reflecting skill used to convey empathic understanding and to facilitate the exploration and clarification of the client's problems (Ivey et al., 2014). It is important for counselors to be sure the paraphrased information is accurate by checking with the client. Some clients in crisis may not feel they can refute what is being said, or their crisis state may impede their ability to completely follow the session. However, paraphrasing gives these clients permission to approve or disapprove of the accuracy of the paraphrase and its implied meaning, thereby increasing their control. When the counselor paraphrases the client's information inaccurately and does not seek affirmation by the client, the counselor may then define the actual primary presenting problem inaccurately, which in turn may change the direction of the session and/or interfere with the development of the most appropriate

ACTIVITY 4.4

Take a moment to practice changing these questions from closed to open questions.

1. Why did you quit your job?
2. Do you think you should stop using drugs?
3. Do you get 8 hours of sleep a night?
4. Did you feel angry with him?
5. Don't you think there are other ways for you to cope with your anger?

treatment plan for the client. The importance of checking is compounded when the client needs the counselor to use a more directive approach due to the severity of the crisis. Young (2013) proposed that reflecting skills are important because they provide the counselor with a way to do the following:

1. Communicate empathy.
2. Give feedback that enables the client to confirm or reject the impression he or she has been giving.
3. Stimulate further exploration of what the client has been experiencing.
4. Capture important aspects of the client's story that may have been overlooked or covert. (pp. 123–124)

Paraphrasing, if used appropriately, is a powerful therapeutic tool. Appropriate use means crisis counselors must develop the ability to take the essence of the client's statement and reflect back those thoughts and facts in *their own words*. When the counselor uses paraphrasing accurately, the client will continue to explore and elaborate. On the other hand, the counselor should not "parrot" back to the client what has been said. Parroting back would be a simple word-for-word restatement, not a paraphrase. Consider this example:

SUSAN: I feel so put down and disrespected by my husband. He is just like my father in a lot of ways. He was verbally abusive and full of anger. I never really felt important to him. Why do I let men treat me this way?

COUNSELOR: You feel put down and disrespected by him. Is that correct?

As you can see from the above paraphrase, the crisis worker simply parrots back what the client has said, which adds little and keeps the focus superficial. A better response might be as follows:

COUNSELOR: Although you're trying to understand this pattern of hurt and disappointment that you've experienced from the important men in your life, it sounds like you're blaming yourself for this. Am I hearing that correctly?

To develop your paraphrasing skills, you may find it helpful to first identify the key words or content that captures the essence of your client's concern. Once you have the key content in mind, try to translate it into your own words. Examples of a client's statements, the possible key themes or words, and the resulting paraphrase follow.

EXAMPLE 1

Client: I'm so fed up with him. I try and try to get through to him, and he just shuts me out.

Possible key themes or words: *fed up, being shut out, failed efforts to connect.*

Paraphrase: You're at your wit's end with this. In spite of your efforts to connect, you come up against a closed door. Is that correct?

EXAMPLE 2

Client: Exactly, and that's why I've been thinking about leaving him. I know I deserve much better, but I just keep going back to him. I can't seem to make that first move.

Possible key themes or words: *leaving her husband, being stuck, hesitation, self-worth.*

Paraphrase: Although a part of you knows this is not the way you want to live your life, it's still difficult to break out of this cycle. Is that right?

As you can see from these examples, identifying the key words or themes can really aid in your ability to develop accurate paraphrases that convey the essence of your client's meaning without coming across as superficial. Complete Activity 4.5 to practice your paraphrasing skills.

REFLECTING FEELINGS   A wealth of research attests to the usefulness of accessing and working with feelings and emotions in counseling (Greenberg & Pascual-Leone, 2006). Naming and identifying a client's feelings can serve a number of important functions (Young, 2013). By reflecting feelings, a crisis counselor can help the client to become aware of the emotions experienced in relation to the issue at hand. This awareness can then increase the client's overall level of self-awareness and deepen his or her self-disclosure. In addition, reflecting feelings can have a positive impact on the therapeutic relationship, and a convincing amount of research has shown the quality of the therapeutic relationship to be one of the strongest predictors of counseling outcomes (Horvath, Del Re, Fluckiger, & Symonds, 2012). Moreover, it is not necessarily the specific theoretical approach of the helper but the strength of the therapeutic relationship that is associated with the successful achievement of a client's counseling goals. The therapeutic relationship should be characterized by an experience of mutual liking, trust, and respect between the client and the helper. In addition, helper qualities such as accurate empathy, unconditional positive regard, and genuineness greatly contribute to the development of the helping relationship. Thus, the reflecting skills play an important role in the development of this vital working alliance by conveying these "relationship enhancers" to a client (Young, 2013). As with paraphrasing, reflecting feelings can promote the development of accurate empathy and help to create a safe environment for the client. Read Voices from the Field 4.2.

ACTIVITY 4.5

Think about the following client statements and try to identify the key themes or words. Then, based on these key themes or words, develop a paraphrase of your client's statement.

1. "I don't know what to do with my life. I hate my job and everything seems so meaningless. I can barely muster the energy to get out of bed in the morning. Sometimes I just want to sleep for days."

2. "I'm still in shock that my husband is having an affair. I really can't believe it. I thought we had the perfect marriage. How could I have been so stupid to not see this was happening? I feel like such a fool."

3. "I can't tell if I am coming or going. I can't sleep, I have nightmares, and I feel like a zombie throughout the day. I am so tense my body aches. No matter what I do, it just keeps getting worse."

VOICES FROM THE FIELD 4.2

Reflecting Your Way through a Crisis

Joseph Cooper

Clients often come to counseling in crisis. They may be feeling overwhelmed, confused, think they are going "crazy," or in more serious cases, feeling suicidal or homicidal. In these situations, our own anxiety might lead us to become overly directive, give unwanted advice, or drill clients with questions. However, I have found doing the opposite is the key. In other words, using reflecting skills in these situations can go a long way to help a client become more emotionally regulated. Simple paraphrases, reflecting feelings, and even silence can help the client to feel understood, accepted, and safe. And clients are more likely to take the risk of changing and developing a healthy plan of action when they feel safe.

To reflect feelings, a crisis counselor must be able to recognize and put words to those feeling states observed in the client. And what is the best way to practice reflecting feelings? One way is to work on becoming more aware of your own feelings and being able to accurately name these feelings. Doing so will help you accurately recognize and name the feelings clients may be experiencing. For example, when people are asked, "How are you feeling *right now*?" the most common responses are "fine," "good," and "ok." Notice, however, that these responses do not reflect feelings and do not provide any understanding of what a person may be really feeling. It is important to be able to not only correctly identify and name the core feelings we all experience as humans (e.g., anger, sadness, fear, surprise, joy, love, disgust) but also accurately recognize and name our moment-to-moment feeling states that represent the finer shadings of those core emotions. For example, some of the finer shadings of the word *anger* are *irritated, bitter, enraged, frustrated,* and *sore*. By increasing your feelings awareness and feelings word vocabulary, you will be able to more easily and correctly identify and respond to a client's feelings. Again, due to the nature of individuals in crises, it is important to confirm the accuracy of your reflections.

How does a counselor identify a client's feelings, especially if these feelings are not explicitly stated? When clients do not state their feelings directly, counselors may still be able to infer these feelings either from the context of a client's communication or from the client's nonverbal behaviors (e.g., facial expression, posture). Thus, it is important to attend to not only what is being said but also how it is being communicated. The following practical tips will aid you in reflecting a client's feelings (Evans, Hearn, Uhlemann, & Ivey, 2011; Ivey et al., 2014):

1. To aid in identifying a client's feelings:
   a. Pay attention to the affective component of the client's communication.
   b. Pay attention to the client's behavior (e.g., posture, tone of voice, facial expression).
   c. Use a broad range of words to correctly identify the client's emotions.
   d. Silently name the client's feeling(s) to yourself.

2. To aid in reflecting feelings to a client:
   a. Use an appropriate introductory phrase: "Sounds like . . ." "Looks like . . ." "You feel . . ." "It seems . . . ."

b. Add a feeling word or emotional label to the stem: "Sounds like you're angry."
c. Add a context or brief paraphrase to help anchor or broaden the reflection. This context should add the link or meaning for the perceived feeling: "Sounds like you're angry at your father's refusal to put you in his will."
d. Pay attention to the tense. Present tense reflections can often be more powerful than past tense reflections: "You *feel* angry versus you *felt* angry."
e. Do not repeat the client's exact words (parroting).
f. Reflect mixed emotions: "You're feeling both angry and hurt about your father's behavior toward you."
g. Check out the accuracy of the reflection of feeling with the client: "Am I hearing you correctly? Is that close? Have I got that right?"

Consider the following example:

Susan:	I just sit around the house wondering what to do. We used to spend time with my husband's friends, but they know that we're no longer together. So there is no one for me to really spend time with. I really miss them, and my own friends seem so busy. I would hate to burden them with all of my problems.
Counselor:	You're feeling both sad and lonely right now, and you're concerned you may be just another burden on your own friends. Is that about right? (*Reflection of feeling with check for accuracy*)
Susan:	Yes, I don't want to bring everyone down with all my problems.

There is one last point to consider when reflecting feelings. Whereas in traditional psychotherapy the focus is often on uncovering feeling after feeling by attempting to unearth the "core" issue, in crisis intervention work the task is quite different. Thus, guard against going too far with uncovering feelings, as this could exacerbate the client's crisis state by overwhelming him or her with emotion. Strive for a balance of skills to build rapport, and when you do reflect feelings, be sure to keep the focus directly related to the client's presenting concerns (James & Gilliland, 2017). Complete Activity 4.6, which gives you an opportunity to practice identifying feelings so you can develop accurate reflections of feelings. Also complete Think About It 4.2.

ACTIVITY 4.6

Take a moment to read each of the following vignettes and identify the feelings embedded within the client's communications. Once you have identified the feelings, come up with your own reflection of feelings.

1. "I don't know what to do. My husband keeps working late into the night, and I feel like I never get to see him. When we do get some time together, he is moody and reserved. To make matters worse, I saw a charge on our credit card statement to a local hotel. I think he is having an affair."

2. "Ever since I was mugged, I've been having a hard time. Because of the nightmares, I can't sleep at night, and I'm exhausted all during the day. On top of that, I'm panicky and nervous all the time. I worry I might be losing my mind."

3. "I can't believe what my father did. He stole all the money from the trust fund grandmother had willed to my brother and me. I've been calling him day and night, and he won't return my calls. I might have to get a lawyer, but I don't know how I'm going to afford it. Why would he do this to us?"

THINK ABOUT IT 4.2

Think about your skills in identifying and reflecting feelings. How skilled are you at identifying your feelings and the feelings of friends, colleagues, and clients? How skilled are you at reflecting those feelings? Self-monitor conversations you have over the next week and practice identifying and reflecting the feelings of others.

SUMMARIZING   The final skill in the basic listening sequence is summarizing, a process through which a crisis counselor can begin to put together the key themes, feelings, and issues that the client has presented. By distilling the key issues and themes and reflecting this back to the client, counselors can begin to help clients make sense of what may have originally seemed to be an overwhelming and confusing experience. In addition, when clients are feeling overwhelmed and are flooded with anxiety, they will often go on tangents in many directions, making it difficult for the crisis counselor to keep up. When this occurs, brief summaries are often a useful tool to help refocus the client and reintroduce some structure into the session, which will help modulate the client's (and the counselor's) anxiety. Thus, a summary not only is used to end a session or to begin a new session by recapping the previous session but also can be used periodically throughout the session, helping to keep a focus and put together the pertinent issues at hand for the client.

So when should a crisis counselor summarize? Although much will depend on the client and the content being discussed, Evans et al. (2011) offered a number of useful suggestions to help determine when a summary is in order: (1) when your client is rambling, confused, or overly lengthy in his or her comments; (2) when your client presents a number of unrelated ideas; (3) when you need to provide direction to the interview; (4) when you are ready to move the client from one phase of the interview to the next; (5) when you want to end the interview; and (6) when a summary of the prior interview will provide you an opening to the current interview.

When summarizing, you do not have to report back to the client every single detail he or she has disclosed. This would, of course, require a prodigious memory. The key is to capture the important elements, content, feelings, and issues and to reflect these back to the client in a concise manner. The following three types of summaries are particularly relevant to crisis intervention counseling:

1. *Focusing summaries:*   These summaries are often used at the beginning of the session to pull together prior information the client has given and to provide a focus to the session. "Last time we met you were having trouble sleeping, and you were having nightmares and feeling panicky throughout the day. We identified some coping skills and relaxation exercises for you to use. Tell me how these have worked out for you so far."

2. *Signal summaries:*   These summaries are used to "signal" to the client that you have captured the essence of his or her topic and that the session can move on to the next area of concern. Signal summaries help to provide both structure and direction to the session. "So before we move on, let me make sure I understand things correctly. You discovered your husband is having an affair. . . ."

3. *Planning summaries:*   These summaries help provide closure and are used to recap the progress, plans, and any recommendations/agreements made. Such

summaries are good for ending the session on a positive note and for providing a sense of direction for the client. "Let's take a look at what we've covered today. Ever since you were mugged, you've been having panic attacks and nightmares. We covered some coping techniques and relaxation exercises for you to practice between now and the next time we meet . . . ." (Young, 2013, pp. 161–163)

So, to put it all together, here is one more example of a summary statement: "Let me see if I understand you correctly. Yesterday you found out your son has been using cocaine for the last 6 months and has stolen money from you on a number of occasions. You're experiencing a mixture of feelings, especially shock and anger, and you're worried he might turn out to be an addict like your father was. However, you're determined to do all you can to not let that happen to him. How about discussing some possible directions we can go in from here." Note that this summary captures the key issues and feelings without being too wordy and offers a transition for the counselor and client to begin identifying some action steps to take. Case Study 4.3 provides an example of reflecting skills in practice.

CASE STUDY 4.3

Integrating Paraphrasing, Reflected Feelings, and Summarizing

The following dialogue between Susan and her crisis counselor demonstrates the skills of paraphrasing, reflecting feelings, and summarizing:

SUSAN:	I really thought things were going well with my husband, so it came as a complete shock when I found out about the affair.
COUNSELOR:	You were really blindsided by this. (*Paraphrase*)
SUSAN:	Exactly! And I've been trying to push away the pain, but I can't seem to stop thinking about it. Sometimes I just want to strangle him for putting me through this. Other times I want to die!
COUNSELOR:	Even though you want so much for the pain to go away, it's still there, especially your hurt and anger toward him. Is that right? (*Paraphrase with a reflection of feeling*)
SUSAN:	Yes, and sometimes I can't tell which is worse, my anger or just the hurt I'm going through. I sometimes lie in bed at night and wish something terrible would happen to him. I'm not saying I want to kill him or anything, but I just want him to suffer like I'm suffering.
COUNSELOR:	And this reflects the intensity of your grief right now, wanting to see him suffer, too. (*Reflection of feeling*)
SUSAN:	Very true.
COUNSELOR:	So, in essence, you never expected something like this to happen to you, and it has been difficult for you to tough it out and to push away the pain, grief, and anger that you've been feeling. Is that about right? (*Summary with check for accuracy*)

Discussion Questions

1. How effective was the counselor's use of paraphrasing, reflecting feelings, and summarizing?
2. What alternative responses may also have been helpful?
3. Put yourself in the position of the client. What counselor responses would have elicited even better or more informative responses by the client?

DE-ESCALATING CLIENT EMOTIONS

There are four primary objectives when counseling agitated clients: safety, client emotion management to regain control, avoidance of physical restraint, and avoidance of escalating coercive interventions. Richmond et al. (2012) reviewed the literature on verbal de-escalation of agitated patients and suggested the following guidelines for environment, people, and preparedness:

*   Physical space should be designed for safety.
*   Staff should be appropriate for the job.
*   Staff must be adequately trained.
*   An adequate number of trained staff must be available.
*   Objective scales should be used to assess agitation (pp. 18–20).

Richmond et al. (2012) also determined that 10 domains of de-escalation exist that help practitioners in their care of agitated clients. These domains and the key recommendations associated with them appear in Table 4.2.

It is important to remember that the association between agitation and aggression is not fully understood in causal terms (Nordstrom & Allen, 2007). Richmond et al. (2012) summarized four different types of aggression and suggested that each type required a different style of intervention.

Instrumental aggression is generally used by people who have learned that they can get their way through threats or actual violence. So, if a client makes an overt threat, unspecified counter offers should be used. For example:

CLIENT:	If I don't get what I want, I'm gonna hurt someone bad.
	(*Might be countered with . . .*)
COUNSELOR:	That's not a good idea.
CLIENT:	Why not?
COUNSELOR:	Let's not find out. Now, you were saying that . . .

In fear-driven aggression, the client is on the defensive and may behave aggressively in order to protect against being hurt. In such situations, a professional counselor should give the client plenty of personal space, three to four times the normal space, and match the client's pace and rhythm until the client is fully focusing on the content of the discussion rather than the internal state of fear. For example:

CLIENT:	I'm so angry! I'm so angry!!
COUNSELOR:	I can help you calm down and fix things. I can help you calm down and fix things.

TABLE 4.2   The Domains of De-escalation and Associated Recommendations

Domain	Recommendations
Domain 1: Respect personal space.	Respect the patient's and your personal space.
Domain 2: Do not be provocative.	Avoid iatrogenic (body language) escalation.
Domain 3: Establish verbal contact.	Have only one person verbally interact with the patient. Introduce yourself to the patient and provide orientation and reassurance.
Domain 4: Be concise.	Be concise and keep it simple. Repetition is essential to de-escalation.
Domain 5: Identify wants and feelings.	Use free information to identify wants and feelings.
Domain 6: Listen closely to what the patient is saying.	Use active listening.
Domain 7: Agree or agree to disagree.	
Domain 8: Lay down the law and set clear limits.	Establish basic working conditions. Limit setting must be reasonable and done in a respectful manner. Coach the patient in how to stay in control.
Domain 9: Offer choices and optimism.	Offer choices. Broach the subject of medications. Be optimistic and provide hope.
Domain 10: Debrief the patient and staff.	Debrief the client. Debrief the staff.

Source: Based on Richmond, J. S., Berlin, J. S., Fishkind, A. B., Holloman, Jr., G. H., Zeller, S. L., Wilson, M. P., Rifai, M. A., & Ng, A. T. (2012). Verbal de-escalation of the agitated patient: Consensus statement of the American Association for Emergency Psychiatry Project BETA De-escalation Workgroup. *Western Journal of Emergency Medicine, 13*, 17–25. doi:10.5811/westjem.2011.9.6864, pp. 20–23.

Irritable aggression stems from two causes: boundary violations and chronic anger. Irritable aggression based on boundary violations is usually displayed by individuals who have experienced some humiliation or interpersonal violation and are trying to put their world back into some semblance of order. For example, a partner may have cheated on the client and the client is struggling to regain self-integrity and self-esteem while perceiving that life and other individuals are unfair. Usually, the best approach in this instance is to agree with the client that anger is a justifiable emotion, in principle, but that the resolution to the problem cannot occur while enraged. For example, "I want to know more about your situation and help you, but I can't until you get control over your emotions so we can talk about it and figure out what to do and what not to do."

Finally, irritable aggression based on chronic anger is displayed by clients who are angry at the world and seem to be looking for ready excuses to "lose it." Their behavior is characterized by erratic and unrealistic demands aimed at relieving the pressure they allow to build up. They create fear and confusion through feigned or real attacks. When interacting with an escalated, chronically aggressive client, it is essential not to appear defensive or startled, but to respond in an emotionless manner, repetitively offering choices and options for resolving or de-escalating the situation. Let the client know that as soon as he is willing to cooperate, you are more than willing to work with him. Set firm limits, but be prepared to engage in physical restraint if required. Unfortunately, chronically aggressive patients often push the limits by doing the opposite of what you have asked.

The National Association of Social Workers (NASW, 2017) notes that reasoning with angry, out-of-control people is not likely possible. In such cases, de-escalation becomes the primary goal. Reasoning and problem solving are possible only after de-escalation occurs. De-escalation requires the counselor to remain calm, even when one is frightened and angry. Professional counselors are well advised to practice de-escalation interventions repeatedly until they become automatic. NASW provides recommendations on a practitioner's physical stance and verbal interventions when faced with an aggressive client.

Regarding physical stance:

1. Never turn your back . . .
2. Always be at the same eye level . . .
3. Allow extra physical space . . .
4. Do not stand full front to client. Stand at an angle so you can sidestep away if needed.
5. Do not maintain constant eye contact.
6. Do not point or shake your finger.
7. DO NOT smile. This could look like mockery or anxiety.
8. Do not touch . . . physical contact [is easily misinterpreted] as hostile or threatening.
9. Keep hands out of your pockets, up and available to protect yourself . . .
10. Don't be defensive, judgmental . . . or parental . . . . (NASW, 2017, pp. 1–2)

Regarding verbal de-escalation interventions:

1. . . . [C]almly bring the level of arousal down . . .
2. Do not get loud or . . . yell . . . Wait until he/she takes a breath; then talk. Speak calmly at an average volume.
3. Respond selectively; answer all informational questions [but] . . . DO NOT answer abusive questions.
4. Explain limits and rules in an authoritative, firm, but always respectful tone. Give choices . . .
5. Empathize with feelings but not with the behavior . . .
6. Suggest alternative behaviors where appropriate . . .
7. Give the consequences of inappropriate behavior without threats or anger.
8. Represent external controls as institutional rather than personal.
9. If you assess that de-escalation is not working, STOP! You will know within 2 or 3 minutes . . . Tell the person to leave, escort him/her to the door, call for help, or leave yourself and call the police. (NASW, 2017, p. 2)

Finally, at a more basic level, when reflecting feelings, a useful way to help defuse a client in an emotional crisis state is to also reflect the client's stated, or unstated, need or goal that is implied within the context of their narrative. Because of the interpretive aspects, checking for accuracy is also important with this skill. The formula for this would be: "You feel _____ because _____ and you want (or need) _____."
For example:

MIKE:	Every time I do something for her, it's not good enough and she puts me down. (*Yelling.*) It's all I can do to keep from killing her.
COUNSELOR:	You're *feeling* so angry and hurt right now *because* she puts you down, and you really *want* to be more respected and valued in your relationship. Is that correct?

Here is another example:

COURTNEY:	(*Sobbing, holding herself, and rocking and shaking.*) I can't take it anymore. After my husband and daughter were killed in the car accident, everything just fell apart for me. I just think maybe I should be dead too.
COUNSELOR:	You're *feeling* so much pain and grief *because* of the loss of your family, and you want so much to find your own *peace* now. Is that how you feel?

De-escalation is about transferring calmness to the client and showing the client genuine interest in what he or she has to say. Be respectful, set clear limits, and trust that you have supplied the conditions that allow the client to want to respond positively. If the client possesses a weapon, do not be a hero and try to de-escalate the person; simply comply (NASW, 2017). In a crisis situation, the above interventions can go a long way to helping your client feel safe with you, to diffuse overwhelming emotions, and to set the groundwork to begin working on a plan of action.

Summary

In this chapter, the basic counseling skills used in crisis intervention work were reviewed. The use of these skills will aid in the development of the counseling relationship with the client and will greatly facilitate the creation of a safe therapeutic environment. The nonverbal attending behaviors such as eye contact, body position, and tone of voice communicate interest, warmth, and understanding to the client. Be sure to face the client and adopt an open, relaxed, and attentive body posture, while maintaining culturally appropriate eye contact with the client. Tone of voice should be steady and clear and should be used to convey a sense of safety, warmth, and security for the client.

The skills covered in the basic listening sequence include asking open and closed questions, paraphrasing, reflecting feelings, and summarizing. The basic listening sequence allows the gathering of important information about the client's issues and the development of

trust and rapport. Finally, the basic listening sequence allows the crisis counselor to pull together the key issues to begin the collaborative process of determining a plan of action for the client. Open and closed questions are used to gather information, to aid in assessment, and to provide focus and direction to the session. Paraphrasing is a reflective skill used to mirror back to the client, in a nonjudgmental way and in one's own words, an accurate understanding of the client's communication and the implied meaning of that communication. Like paraphrasing, reflecting feelings is a reflective skill used to convey to the client an understanding of the client's emotional experience. In crisis situations, the use of these skills should be checked out for accuracy. This is an additional step from the original use of the skill. Through this awareness, the client can reach a higher level of overall self-awareness and deepen self-disclosure. Summarizing puts together the pieces, helping the client make sense of what may have originally seemed to be an overwhelming and confusing experience. Summarizing can also be used to keep the session focused, to provide direction to the interview, and to provide closure to the session by reviewing the progress, plans, and any recommendations/agreements made. By using these skills appropriately, you create the necessary conditions for positive change. Four primary objectives when counseling agitated clients were reviewed: safety, client emotion management to regain control, avoidance of physical restraint, and avoidance of escalating coercive interventions.

5

Loss, Grief, and Bereavement

Lisa R. Jackson-Cherry and Bradley T. Erford*

PREVIEW

This chapter covers crisis counseling with individuals who are grieving the loss of someone or something, models and theories of grieving, and assessment components in determining when the loss affects an individual to the point where daily functioning is interrupted. The chapter addresses how timing, the cause of death, and the role the relationship played in a person's life all mediate the mourning process, followed by a discussion that distinguishes between "normal grief" and "complicated grief." Further, the concepts of grief and loss are not limited to loss due to death but include other aspects in life where losses occur and can impact the lives of individuals. Grief and loss can be a component of any crisis experience. This chapter focuses on how the mourner's belief system (e.g., faith, spirituality, religion) and cultural influences are integral to coping, preventing dysfunction, and finding meaning in life after a loss.

This chapter also includes the appropriate process to follow when providing a death notification. Death notification involves notifying someone of a loved one's death, which can be difficult for both the person receiving the news and the one providing it. The information in this chapter will help crisis counselors be prepared and equipped when called upon to either provide or assist with a death notification in a variety of settings. Effective death notifications decrease the need for intense debriefings, complicated grief processes, and burnout. Although agencies and schools may have a protocol for issuing a death notification, which should be followed, the steps outlined in this chapter can be infused into any environment, professional or personal, as a "best practice" in giving a notification of death.

HISTORICAL PERSPECTIVES AND MODELS OF GRIEF WORK

Nearly 2.5 million Americans die each year (Centers for Disease Control and Prevention, 2014a), leaving behind millions of husbands, wives, mothers, fathers, sisters, brothers, children, friends, coworkers, uncles, and aunts to mourn their losses. Factors that determine whether the death will cause a significant crisis event that impairs daily functioning are as follows: how the person died (e.g., whether it was sudden and unexpected or the

---

* Our gratitude to Lourie Reichenberg for her outstanding contributions to the first two editions of this chapter.

result of a prolonged or chronic illness); cultural and spiritual influences of the bereaved; individual temperament; life circumstances; unresolved issues connected with the death; previous experiences with death and loss; and the order of death (e.g., whether it is a grandparent at the end of a long life or a young person just starting out in life).

Of course, grief and loss reactions are not solely related to issues of death and dying. Feelings of loss may occur after many developmental or situation-related changes. This chapter focuses on many of the different types of losses people encounter but does not address every type of loss specifically. Although there has been an increased deployment of crisis counselors to respond to natural disasters, acts of terrorism (e.g., New York, Pennsylvania, and the Pentagon on September 11, 2001), hostage situations, and school shootings, it is more likely that a counselor will intervene with a client or family experiencing a recent death or a situational or developmental loss that affects the individual or family, such as divorce, job/career loss, ability/health loss, and elderly issues around loss.

Each person responds differently to a loss. This chapter does not define major and minor losses, as it is truly the perception of the loss for the individual that will determine whether the loss becomes a crisis. More importantly, crisis counselors should attempt to understand how a loss can impact and cause other losses and how these multiple losses should be perceived when developing a crisis plan or offering a referral. For example, the loss of a spouse of 40 years may not be the main crisis event for the survivor, although it may be the presenting issue that brought the client into crisis counseling. Rather, multiple losses may have occurred in relation to the death that may cause even more dysfunction for the client. Perhaps the couple cared for an adult child with special needs in the home and now the remaining spouse will not be able to do so alone; perhaps the loss of the spouse who was the main income earner now puts the family in financial crisis; or perhaps the loss of the spouse now creates an existential crisis for the survivor as to what meaning or purpose exists without the other person. It is important to understand how a presenting loss may influence other parts of life for the bereaved in order to determine how to best intervene.

Working with grieving clients is an important part of both crisis counseling and traditional counseling. Many people seek counseling specifically to help them cope with a recent loss. But far more frequently the client has been in counseling for a while for issues unrelated to death and then experiences the death of a family member or has memories of a previous death triggered by the counseling. At such points, what was previously career counseling or couples counseling may become crisis intervention as the counselor helps the client through the initial impact of the death. For some clients, that will be all that is needed, and they will return to their previous treatment plan. However, for other clients, more extensive counseling may be necessary to help them make sense of the loss and find meaning in life once again. Grief counseling has become so prominent in the practice of professional counselors that the *Diagnostic and Statistical Manual of Mental Disorders* (DSM-5) now has a section dedicated to grief diagnoses, including complicated grief (American Psychiatric Association, 2013).

In his work *Mourning and Melancholia* (1917), Freud proposed what was probably the first psychoanalytic theory of grieving. Mourning occurs when the libido psyche stubbornly hangs on to a lost object, refusing to give it up. Grieving ends, according to Freud, when the client lets go of attachment to the lost object and becomes free to devote his or her libido to another love object. Although drive theory is not as accepted today as it once was, Freud's writings on mourning provided the basis from which grief work later evolved.

Lindemann's Approach

In what is perhaps the first research conducted on sudden death, Lindemann (1944) studied the 1942 Cocoanut Grove nightclub fire in Boston and intervened with many of those who lost someone in the fire. Lindemann identified three tasks of mourners: (1) emancipation from the bond to the deceased, (2) readjustment to a life in which the deceased is missing, and (3) formation of new relationships (Berzoff & Silverman, 2010). Like Viktor Frankl's (1959) later work with concentration camp survivors, Lindemann observed feelings of intense guilt in many people who survived the fire. Adjustment required letting go of the deceased. Lindemann believed that grief was resolved when the mourner severed the relationship with the deceased and moved on to form new attachments. For many years, Lindemann's work remained the main resource on bereavement.

The Death Awareness Movement: Kübler-Ross

Beginning in the 1960s, Elizabeth Kübler-Ross was credited with creating the death awareness movement. Her works, including *On Death and Dying* (1969) and *Death: The Final Stage of Growth* (1975), affected a core change in attitudes toward and education about the dying process and helped to reduce the taboo surrounding the discussion of death in the United States. Kübler-Ross was famous for her work with terminally ill patients, which led to her development of the five stages of dying: (1) denial, (2) rage and anger, (3) bargaining, (4) depression, and (5) acceptance. Kübler-Ross later applied the stages of dying to grief.

Although the model was originally presented as a sequential stage model, the stages of death and dying have since been adapted as more of a spiral, moving forward, and then circling back over time. Kübler-Ross (1969) also warned that what people experience is far more than mere stages. It is not enough to identify the stages, she wrote, "It is not just about the life lost but also the life lived" (p. 216).

The five stages of death and dying developed by Kübler-Ross have given countless caregivers a framework in which to understand dying patients. Many counselors base grief counseling on these early works on death and dying. They are presented here with the following caveats. Kübler-Ross's work does not apply to catastrophic or sudden death because there is no time to say good-bye and the dying person is not able to go through the stages of grieving. Nor did Kübler-Ross, in her historic writings, consider the stages to be concrete or contiguous; rather, her writings were based on observations of common emotions experienced by people in the midst of the dying process (1969, 1972, 1975).

- *Stage I: Denial.* "Not me." "I am not dying." "A miracle will happen." Such comments are typical reactions to being told of a terminal illness. According to Kübler-Ross, denial serves a protective function in the initial stages by cushioning the blow that death is inevitable.
- *Stage II: Rage and anger.* "Why me?" The seemingly arbitrary nature of the news of one's impending death almost always causes one to erupt into anger and rage. Such anger is often targeted at those who are living and will survive, as well as at

God for handing down the death sentence. Kübler-Ross believed such feelings were not only acceptable but also inevitable.

- *Stage III: Bargaining.* "Yes, me, but . . ." In the bargaining stage, one begins to accept the inevitability of death. But one bargains for more time, often by offering to do good deeds or change in a specific way.
- *Stage IV: Depression.* "Yes, me." The depression stage is the beginning of acceptance. Initially, the person mourns previous regrets and losses, but this turns into an acceptance of the impending death and what is referred to as "preparatory grief." During this time, the dying person begins to face any unfinished business and prepares to "let go" peacefully.
- *Stage V: Acceptance.* "Death is very close now, and it's all right." Some people are able to cope with the news of a terminal illness and work through the anger and sadness to reach an emotional equilibrium that allows them to live out their final weeks and months with inner peace.

Research shows that a person's ability to cope with major life stressors in the past is predictive of the manner in which the person is likely to cope with chronic illness and face death. Other factors that facilitate the process of death acceptance include having lived a full life, harboring few regrets about the way in which one lived, being able to talk frankly about the terminal illness with family and medical personnel, holding hope for a life after death, having a close relationship with a significant other, and being concerned for one's children and close friends. Fear at the end of life seems to be mostly related to how people view the actual process of their dying: anxiety surrounding their pain and being able to cope with it, their desire not to become a burden to their family, existential issues connected with their death (meaning, purpose, unresolved issues), and their uncertainty about how loved ones will survive after they are gone.

Kübler-Ross did not believe that everyone reached the stage of acceptance of his or her own death, but she firmly believed in open communication, with supportive physicians and family members telling the person about the impending death and facilitating the process of emotional adjustment as much as possible. With terminally ill patients, adequate pain management can be the most frequent predictor of emotional adjustment at the end of life.

Multiple parallels exist between the stages of death and dying and the ways in which people adapt to other losses in life (e.g., ending a relationship, leaving a job, experiencing any other sudden crisis). In *On Grief and Grieving* (Kübler-Ross & Kessler, 2005), published after Kübler-Ross's death, the authors wrote specifically about the internal and external world of grief.

Kübler-Ross (1975) wrote that the stages of dying "apply equally to any significant change (e.g., retirement, moving to a new city, changing jobs, divorce) in a person's life" (p. 145); these changes are commonly referred to as developmental or situational changes. Further, Kübler-Ross believed that if people could accept the ultimate knowledge of their own death and integrate this knowledge into their lives, they could learn to face the challenges and losses that come their way productively and face death with peace and joy as the final stage of growth.

Over the years, a broader approach to death education has focused on the unique needs and perspectives of the individual. Workshops, support groups, and end-of-life planning all serve to educate the individual about transitions at the end of life. Berzoff and Silverman (2010) categorized death education as prevention (i.e., preparing for the inevitable), intervention (i.e., dealing with the immediate), and postvention (i.e., understanding the crisis or experience). A good example of effective death education was an event sponsored by a local church that offered a 5-week workshop that examined the music of Brahms's *Requiem* along with Kübler-Ross's five stages of death and dying. Such workshops often help reduce death anxiety. Assess your reaction to Kübler-Ross's perspectives on grief and loss by completing Activity 5.1 Also read Voices from the Field 5.1.

ACTIVITY 5.1

Draw a circle and divide it into slices like a pie, based on your feelings about death (e.g., grief, regret, hope, sadness). The size of each slice should accurately depict the amount of the emotion you are feeling. How do the sizes of your slices differ from those of other counselors or from clients? What implications might your findings have for the counseling process?

VOICES FROM THE FIELD 5.1
Impact of Death on the Living

Monica Band

As a community mental health professional, I am used to expecting the unexpected. Sometimes I meet clients at the office, but most of the time I travel into the community, visiting or searching for clients who may not have a permanent residence. The only thing consistent about my day is checking the schedule in the morning. On this particular day, I was scheduled to see a client whom I had met several times before. My initial purpose for meeting with him was to discuss his medication compliance and assess for risk, due to his history of suicidal ideation and medication-hoarding behavior.

I arrived at the client's apartment, and we sat down at the kitchen table. The client looked as if he had not slept and avoided eye contact, which differed from the baseline I was used to experiencing. I picked up on the client's nonverbal behavior and asked him immediately if something was upsetting him. "He's gone and I didn't get to say good-bye . . ." the client tearfully said as he used both hands to cover his face. The client slumped over in the chair and began to hyperventilate. In a calm voice, I asked him for more information. He was silent and stared at the wall with his eyes darting back and forth, as if he was searching for answers. I repeated his name, which seemed to snap him back again into reality. He fixed his gaze on me. I will never forget how he looked at me. The client touched his chest and grasped his shirt, as if he was in physical pain.

The client's close friend died from a fatal shooting. The police and medical services arrived on scene, but it was too late. He later found out from the police officer what happened. The death was unexpected. The way in which the client's friend died also enraged and concerned the client. As the client shared details of his experience, he presented with denial and anger. The client's anger was directed toward whomever shot his friend. The client shared some memories of his friend and explained that his friend was "funny" and "gentle." He smiled as he shared these memories, but the smile was quickly wiped away by sadness. I gave the client time to express his thoughts and feelings. I consulted with my supervisor. I conducted a risk assessment of the client due to his recent loss, his history of suicidal attempts during depressive episodes, and his living alone with minimal supports. The client required more stabilization, and he agreed to a further assessment by Emergency Services. He was hospitalized, then discharged to outpatient mental health.

When I returned to the office, I debriefed and processed with my supervisor. That day made me think of my own mortality and the fragility of life. When I got home, I made sure I let people in my life know that I love them and gave my parents a hug. I think I had to do that for my own self-care.

Worden's Task Model of Grieving

In a significant move away from stage theories, Worden (2009) proposed a task model of grieving that empowers the bereaved to accomplish the following four tasks:

- *Accept the loss:* After a period of disbelief, the person must begin to accept that the death is real. A pervasive sense of shock, numbness, or unreality may be felt for a long time. A sudden death, or a death far away, makes it particularly difficult to grasp that death has occurred. As people begin to work through this task, they start to accept the reality of the facts surrounding the death of their loved one and the meaning behind the loss, and to accept that the person is not coming back. People who remove pictures or otherwise avoid any reminders of their loss are hindering themselves from the task of accepting the loss.
- *Experience the pain:* Working through the pain of grief is the second task Worden believes people must undertake. Some people may dissociate from the pain, immersing themselves in work, cleaning, and any other methods of keeping busy. Still others may feel overwhelmed by their sorrow. Recognizing and labeling the pain rather than avoiding it helps them to grieve and to move forward through the pain and grieve successfully.
- *Adjust to an environment without the person:* To accomplish this task, people must learn to continue on despite the loss of a love object in their world. While it is impossible to clearly delineate precisely what has been lost, the void of grief is often deep. Coming home to an empty house, missing the communication and companionship of a loved one, and celebrating special holidays, birthdays, and milestones in other people's lives can all serve to increase the pain associated with loss. To successfully work through this task, mourners must learn to cope and adjust to the many different voids left after the loss of a loved one.
- *Reinvest emotional energy in other relationships:* Grieving persons are called on to emotionally relocate the lost person and to move on with life, while still honoring their loved one. Worden (2009) considers it a "benchmark of a completed grief reaction" when the person is "able to think of the deceased without pain" (p. 46).

Like a physical illness or wound, grief takes time to heal. Therefore, Worden does not assign time periods to grief. Parkes and Prigerson (2009) indicate that widows may take three or four years to move through the grief process and achieve stability in their lives. During that time, they are working to return to a level of equilibrium. Grieving requires effort, and those who do not take the time to work through the tasks of mourning will delay the grief process (Worden, 2009). Worden's task model has also been extended to losses other than death.

Attachment and Loss

Past and current research indicate that most people in mourning do not believe that the relationship ends with the death of their loved one. This belief is contrary to the medical view of grief, in which mourning is a phase from which people should recover. The distinction between normal grief and clinical depression is important and will be discussed in depth later in this chapter. For most people, grief is an accepted and normal part of the life cycle, from which they eventually return to their previous level of equilibrium.

Drawing on the classic works of Ainsworth, Parkes, Winicott, Seligman, and others, Bowlby produced a three-volume series that became the seminal work on attachment and loss (1960, 1973, 1980). Bowlby (1980) noted four phases of the mourning process: (1) numbing, which lasts from a few hours to a week; (2) yearning or searching for the lost figure, lasting for months or even years; (3) disorganization or despair; and (4) some degree of reorganization.

The numbing phase is often expressed as being stunned or shocked at the news of a death. The yearning phase is seen by Bowlby (1971) as normal and may result in efforts by the bereaved to locate the lost person. Such searching may include motor restlessness—the inability to slow down or to control continuous movement—or scanning the environment. The bereaved may develop a sense that the person is present with them or may construe sights or sounds to be an indication that their loved one is near.

Cultural background affects the expression of grief. For example, a 50-year-old Iranian woman who lived with her adult son and his family sought treatment 10 years after the death of her husband. She continued to be sad and expressed the desire to return to his grave "and dig him up" with her hands. Her son and his wife only wanted her to be happy and live out her years with them and her grandchildren. Culturally sensitive counselors must be aware of any cultural traditions or family expectations that affect the grieving process.

Disorganization or despair often takes the form of irritability or bitterness. In most cases in which there is a target of the anger, it may be clergy, doctors, or surviving family members. Self-reproach is also common and can be intense and unrelenting. Anger associated with grief must be discussed. Anger falls along a continuum from anger to rage to violence. Anger that is externalized, spoken, and processed is less likely to manifest itself in negative behaviors, which can mask the underlying feelings of grief and loss.

Bowlby (1971) noted that in most instances of disordered mourning the loss was almost always of an immediate family member—most notably, a parent, child, or spouse. In other words, the strength of the attachment bond and the closeness of the relationship are important variables that profoundly affect the grieving process. Bowlby saw mourning as a time of transition during which mourners adapt to the loss, reorganize their lives, and find new roles for themselves. During this period, it is necessary for the bereaved to experience sadness and despair, and so much work must be done by the bereaved. Where one previously defined oneself as part of a couple, he or she is now single. Those once connected to a mother as a child now see themselves as orphans. Bowlby noted that this redefinition of self is a painful but necessary process. The bereaved can reestablish themselves and develop plans for the future only when they have recognized that their loved one will not return.

Pathology tends to result when people do not take the time to grieve or do not grieve properly, resulting in devolution of the natural process of mourning into clinical depression. Loss can be a provoking agent that increases the risk of an emotional disorder developing, or the person may have a preexisting vulnerability that increases his or her sensitivity to loss. Either can result in a pattern of disorganized mourning. Bowlby (1971) noted that depression-prone individuals deal with death differently than do those who do not become depressed. Numbness, for example, is common to all mourners. After an initial few days or a week of numbness, however, the healthy mourner may begin to talk about the pain and suffering of the deceased and express frustration at not having been able to do more to help. In contrast, depression-prone mourners may experience numbness that lasts indefinitely and may dissociate themselves from feelings of grief.

UNDERSTANDING GRIEF

In the DSM-5 (American Psychiatric Association, 2013), *bereavement* has been narrowly defined as the loss of a loved one with whom one has had a close relationship, as opposed to the more broad term, *grief*, which applies to any loss circumstance. Even though there are many similarities, every grief experience is different. In Western culture, grief is an intensely personal experience that affects not only the individual but also the entire family system and in some situations (e.g., 9/11, natural disasters, school shootings) entire communities. Grief reactions vary by culture, individual, and relationship to the deceased. Spiritual and religious beliefs may affect the grieving process as well. All of these factors should be considered as mediators of the mourning process and will be discussed in greater detail.

Cultural Similarities in Grieving

Cross-cultural research has found similarities in intrapersonal experiences of grief. In a classic study of 78 different cultures, Rosenblatt, Walsh, and Jackson (1976) found that people in all cultures express grief through tears, depressed affect, anger, disorganization, and difficulty performing normal activities. Every culture has "rules" for acceptable grieving that prescribe the behavior that is expected and allowed but does not address the internal emotions that are felt. For instance, widowed women in some Middle Eastern cultures are expected to become incapacitated by their demonstrations of grief, whereas widows in Bali are strongly discouraged from crying. In many Hispanic cultures, it is believed that the deceased wants something from the living.

An awareness of cultural variations in mourning should lead a culturally competent crisis counselor to ask clients about their cultural traditions, rituals related to death, spiritual and religious beliefs and practices, grief responses that are culturally proscribed or prohibited, and what the clients expects their continued relationship with the deceased to be like.

Helping people to find meaning in the lives of their loved ones, individually and in what they meant for society, can be an important part of coming to terms with the loss. In collectivist societies, death affects the entire village or community. For example, bereavement, known as "sorry business," is a very important part of Australian Aboriginal culture. Funerals can involve entire communities, and the expression of grief can include self-injury. The grieving relatives may live in a specially designated area, called the sorry camp, for a period of time. The relatives may also cut off their hair or wear white pigment on their faces (Australian Academy of Medicine, 2016).

Guilt is not always a part of loss but is more common in suicide, sudden death, or other situations in which people have not been able to say good-bye, have left something unsaid, or feel that they somehow could have done something to change the outcome (Hooyman & Kramer, 2008). Recent and ongoing research distinguishes between normal (or uncomplicated) grief and complicated mourning, which may require additional grief work or additional steps before the grief work can begin.

Delayed or masked grief reactions can complicate the mourning process. According to Worden (2009), grief that is repressed or denied can result in aberrant behavior or can cause physical symptoms. He notes that pain can be a symptom of repressed grief and that many people who are treated for somatoform disorders are really experiencing the pain of loss. This is particularly noticeable if the physical symptoms are similar to those experienced by the deceased. Similarly, unexplained depression, acting-out behavior on the part of adolescents, and overly intense grief reactions that occur after seemingly minor losses can all be indications of repressed grief. Thorough assessment and clinical skills are required to identify the problem. Complicated grief will be discussed later in this chapter. Complete Think About It 5.1.

Ambiguous Loss and Disenfranchised Grief

Boss (2006) expanded the concept of grief to include loss that is ambiguous or disenfranchised. Included in this definition are relationships that are not always recognized (e.g., gay and lesbian relationships, lovers, friends, coworkers), loss that is not recognized (e.g., perinatal loss, abortion, pet loss), grievers who are not recognized (e.g., the very old, the very young, persons with developmental disabilities), and disenfranchised death (e.g., murder, suicide, AIDS). Coping with a loss that is an experience rather than the actual death of a person (e.g., children who are kidnapped, family members who disappear, or soldiers who are missing in action) can also be considered an ambiguous loss. As Boss noted, one of the primary tasks of a family is to come together to grieve the loss of a family member. Not knowing whether the person is dead or alive prevents any type of grieving from beginning. The person is physically gone from their lives, but little support is available, and in many instances, friends and family do not understand the depth of the loss or know what to say.

In such situations the primary mission of the crisis counselor is to understand the stress of the situation, the ambiguity surrounding decision-making processes, and the manner in which this stress and ambiguity affect the family relationships, and then to help the family develop resilience (Boss, 2006). Long-term effects of living with ambiguous loss can include depression, anxiety, guilt, ambivalence, and interpersonal conflicts. Each client heals at his or her own pace. After an ambiguous loss, the client may take years, even decades, to develop the perspective necessary to become centered again and to create a healthy and fulfilling life. During that time within a couple's relationship, the partnership is at risk. It is not uncommon for couples to initially reach out to each other in their pain, but since each person is apt to grieve differently and at a different pace, the couple may begin to find fault and blame each other. During infertility treatments, after a miscarriage, or after the loss of a child, couples should be referred to couples counseling. An example of an ambiguous

---

THINK ABOUT IT 5.1

Think about your own religious, cultural, and ethnic background in relation to death and dying. Is there a tradition, ritual, or attitude that is different from others who do not share your background? What is different about it? What do you say to explain the tradition or ritual to others who are unfamiliar with your custom?

loss through miscarriage and infertility is provided in Case Study 5.1, which poignantly reflects the experience of a young woman who desperately wanted to have a baby and was told she never would be able to conceive or carry to term.

CASE STUDY 5.1

Miscarriage and Infertility: Ambiguous Losses

What followed for Aisha was a self-described "week of hell"—the emergency room trip, a stomach pump, the nurse who rebuked her, saying, "You tried to kill yourself. You don't deserve sympathy." This humiliation preceded commitment in a private mental hospital, a court hearing to determine her sanity, and the requirement that, before leaving the hospital, Aisha schedule an appointment with a counselor.

Aisha and her husband of three years were facing not only the reality of never giving birth to their own children but also the possibility of a diagnosis of cancer. It was too much to bear, and after a day spent drinking with her husband and friends to calm down, Aisha went home and "tore the kitchen apart," broke her arm against the wall, swallowed a bottle of antianxiety medication the doctor had given her, and then called her mother, who finally assisted Aisha in getting help. She sat down to wait for the emotional help she so desperately needed. No one was listening to Aisha. No one had grasped the totality of her pain. "I just want someone who can understand what I am going through," she cried. From the moment she learned she could never bear a child, Aisha was grieving the loss of future plans that would never be realized. She would never be a mother, never hold her infant, and never have a family. All of those holidays, birthdays, years stretching out ahead of her, alone and barren.

She feared that her husband would leave her for someone younger who could give him children, and that she could never look at children again without being reminded of her loss. All she had ever wanted was to be married and raise a family. Now that dream was shattered.

How to go on? Why go on? The existential questions stretched like open fields for miles in front of her—questions that were not easily answered by the meaningless mantra of well-meaning friends and relatives: "You can adopt," or "Relax, you'll get pregnant."

More than losing her footing, Aisha had her future plans yanked right out from under her in one horrible afternoon. She needed time just to accept the reality of her loss before she could even start to think about the future. It was months before she was able to accept the diagnosis. It was even longer before Aisha could start to dream again about the color, the texture, and the design she would weave into the rug of her new life.

Discussion Questions

1. What are some losses experienced by the couple and by the individuals in the couple?
2. What makes Aisha's loss ambiguous?
3. What are the primary and secondary considerations a professional counselor would need to address?
4. How can you better help Aisha to grieve and move on to a healthier, more vital life?
5. With a peer as a client in this situation, role-play implementation of the task model of crisis assessment and intervention presented in Table 1.1.

When working with women who have recently miscarried or are coping with infertility, hollow reassurances and suggestions about the future are ineffective. Empathy, being with the person as they experience the pain, and being a witness to their grief will help them cope with the loss and move the grieving process forward. The loss of the ability to have children is similar to the loss of the future. In Aisha's case, discussed in Case Study 5.1, the professionals failed her. A nurse shamed her suicide attempt. Later, a psychiatrist and a counselor gave her platitudes instead of helping her come to terms with and process her loss. Even the physician who gave Aisha the bad news failed to ensure she received adequate counseling. He focused on saving her body but ignored how she felt about the prospect of living life without children. Once Aisha was able to define the loss she was feeling—the need to nurture a baby—she was able to find an appropriate outlet by volunteering to rock babies in the hospital nursery. Years later, she was able to see that there were actually benefits of not having children of her own. She and her husband were able to take trips their friends could only dream of. Her husband was able to fill his parenting need by coaching a basketball team. The couple ruled out adoption but was able to build a fulfilling life that included friends and nurturing other people's children.

When helping clients adjust to an ambiguous loss, the first step is to acknowledge the depth of the loss, not to minimize the pain. In Case Study 5.1, Aisha felt isolated because none of her friends knew what to say. There are no greeting cards expressing sorrow for infertility. None of the men in her life were comfortable talking about reproduction. In addition to her grief over the loss of the future she had envisioned and over her inability to provide a child for her husband, Aisha felt depressed and hopeless about her future. When hope is gone, the risk of suicide increases.

Whether childless by choice or happenstance, at midlife, women who lead a lifestyle of childlessness may feel a resurgence of ambivalence surrounding not having had children. While friends are discussing the "empty nest," those without children have difficulty relating. As one woman said, "How can you discuss the empty nest when your nest was never feathered?" As others take pleasure at the birth of grandchildren, those without children may feel further isolated and begin to doubt their place in life: "It didn't occur to me that they live on through their children and their children's children, for generations. But my life stops with me."

Coping with this type of loss involves helping people clarify the missing role and then find other outlets and activities that provide a meaningful substitute. Those who feel isolated could be referred to Resolve, the national infertility association (www.resolve.org), to find information, research, and support groups for people working through infertility. Online support is also available for women who experience loss through a miscarriage. BellaOnline (bellaonline.com) provides a clearinghouse of information and online blogs.

Someone who feels isolated and alone, for example, may benefit from adopting or rescuing a dog. Those who feel they have much to give to children may find meaning by volunteering at an elementary school, becoming a foster grandparent, or tutoring children after school. Younger men or women who are missing children in their lives can be encouraged to become a special aunt or uncle to a niece or nephew, become a Big Brother or Big Sister, become foster parents, or house an exchange student from another country. Complete Activity 5.2, which focuses on

ACTIVITY 5.2
Looking for Death

In American culture, grief is frequently hidden. Look for personal and cultural images of grief and coping with grief in the media and your immediate environment. Discuss your findings with the class or a peer.

helping you become more sensitized to the way grief and coping with grief are hidden in American culture.

MEDIATORS OF THE MOURNING PROCESS

In his classic research, Bowlby (1980) notes five conditions that affect the course of grieving and should be used in a crisis intervention assessment: (1) the role of the person who died; (2) the age and gender of the bereaved person; (3) the cause and circumstances surrounding the death; (4) the social and psychological circumstances affecting the bereaved at that time of loss; and (5) the personality of the bereaved, especially as it relates to one's capacity for making attachments and for coping with stressful situations. Applying these five conditions in a crisis intervention assessment can also help determine whether a client is experiencing complicated grief, which to some extent mirrors the new DSM-5 category of persistent and complex bereavement. The role of the person who died and the circumstances surrounding the death are examined in the sections that follow. Readers are also encouraged to take into consideration other conditions noted here that may affect the bereaved.

Relationship: The Role of the Person Who Died

Just as every relationship in a person's life is unique, so, too, is every death. The closeness of the relationship, whether the person who died was a spouse of 30 years or a distant uncle, is a key ingredient in how the death is perceived and mourned and what the length of the grieving process will be. It is important to define the unique attachment or loss associated with the death so that if a referral is needed, this information can be transferred as well.

Some of the most difficult deaths to accept are those of people we are the closest to: our children, our parents (especially if the death is experienced by a child), and our spouses or life partners. The death of a sibling, too, can have a tremendous effect on a family. Each of these relationships is discussed in more detail below. Crisis counselors are encouraged to consider other deaths that may be particularly difficult to accept.

DEATH OF A CHILD   The death of a child reverses the natural generational order of death and can have a devastating influence on the entire family. Children play multiple roles in their parents' lives—socially, psychologically, and genetically. So the death of a child disrupts the parents' attachment not only to the child in the moment but also to their dreams and expectations for the future, as well as to the child's place in the generational structure of the family. Epidemiological studies have found that the death of a child leaves parents more susceptible to depression, illness, and premature death due to changes in the immune system.

Many authors write of the differences in grief responses between men and women, with a focus on the impact of grief on a woman's continuing relationship with her surviving children (Walsh & McGoldrick, 2004; Wang, 2007). Unfortunately, little research is available that is specific to fathers. In general, men are less likely to express their grief by verbalizing or expressing their emotions; rather, they tend to stay busy and become task oriented.

When there is a death in the family, parents are not the only grievers. Siblings, too, may be distraught by the loss and experience survivor guilt. Often, a parent's coping response may be functional for him or her but may have a negative influence on his or her partner or surviving children. Sometimes a parent's behavior toward surviving children may change. The research indicates that the grieving process is determined to a large extent by the quality of the parents' relationship. Maternal depression, marital discord, and separation are likely to result in additional psychological fallout for the remaining children. Previously well-adjusted siblings often develop symptoms of anxiety, school refusal, depression, and severe separation anxiety. Some parents may withdraw from their surviving children, while others may turn to another child as a stand-in for the deceased. Both coping styles are fraught with problems. A stable, secure environment in which both parents nurture each other as they go from one stage of mourning to the next, while also helping their surviving children to express and cope with their own feelings, seems likely to foster the best outcome.

Losing an adult child is rare. Only 10% of adults over 60 years of age experience the death of an adult child. Parents who lose a child in their later years are at a significant disadvantage; since it is rare, very few other people can empathize with their loss. In addition, these parents experience a sense of failure; it does not seem natural to them to bury their own children (Bryant, 2003).

DEATH OF A PARENT   Children mourn differently than adults. The way in which children mourn depends on their age, level of cognition, emotional development, relationship to the deceased, and the quality of the support network available to them. Clinicians working with children need to take these factors into account when developing individualized treatment programs for bereaved children or adolescents. Five- to seven-year-olds are especially vulnerable due to their lack of cognitive ability to understand fully the concept and permanence of death. Complications may result, and these children may develop a fear of losing the other parent. Preadolescents and adolescents are strongly influenced by their peers and the need to belong. They may feel isolated and different from their friends who have not experienced the death of a parent. Particularly vulnerable are teenage daughters who lose their mothers.

SIBLING LOSS   Losing a sibling at any age or stage of life is difficult. But often the loss of a brother or sister is a silent loss. When a sibling dies, parents or children are often viewed as the primary mourners, and sibling grief is often forgotten. In fact, when a sibling dies, one loses more than the relationship; one loses a part of oneself. A 60-year-old client whose brother had recently died said, "It was like losing my hard drive," because no one else shared her childhood memories and experiences, nor was there anyone she could talk to about her parents, family history, and other childhood recollections.

The effect of sibling loss is complicated by factors such as the age of the child, the inability to accept death, and the inability to discuss emotions. Eighty-three percent of children who die leave behind at least one sibling (Doka, 2002). The death of a child can disrupt the entire family system. Ultimately, it is the manner in which the parents cope with the death that is the most relevant to the surviving children's ability to cope. Whenever there is a question of whether a child should be referred for counseling or not, err on the side of caution and seek professional help with someone experienced in child psychology and grief.

Charles and Charles (2006) note the importance of working with families who have lost a child to help them develop coping skills that allow them to facilitate the grieving process in their other children. Even young adolescents and teens who appear on the surface to be coping well may really be presenting a facade. This failure to grieve can have a deleterious effect on normal childhood and adolescent development and may even affect future generations. "Without intervention, unresolved trauma tends to be passed along from generation to generation" (Charles & Charles, 2006, p. 86). Somatic symptoms are particularly common in children experiencing grief and loss. Stomachaches, headaches, and loss of appetite are common. It is also common for young children to regress to an earlier form of behavior during this time. Sleep disturbances, nightmares, and enuresis may occur, as might a drop in school performance, lack of concentration, and school refusal. Adolescents may begin using alcohol or drugs as a way of self-medicating to cope with their feelings. Professional help should be sought for substance abuse problems as well as for any grief that turns into severe depression or is accompanied by hopelessness or suicidal ideation.

LOSS OF A SPOUSE   The loss of a spouse can be devastating. The effect is compounded when the person is elderly. More than 75% of deaths occur in the over-65-years age bracket (Erford, 2016). Therefore, the death of a spouse frequently occurs at a time when losses associated with health, retirement, and decreased independence and mobility have a cumulative effect.

Guilt over "what could have been" in the relationship, as well as guilt about surviving when one's loved one died, is a normal part of the grieving process. When we consider that four out of every five survivors are women and that the average age of women who lose their husbands is 53 years, we can see that many women are living alone long after the death of their spouses (Rock & Rock, 2006). For most of these women, making meaning of the rest of their lives becomes a primary focus.

The need to make sense of the death of a loved one has been considered one of the necessary conditions for adjustment or recovery. However, studies have shown that a widow who lost a spouse and had not found meaning in the death by 5 months was not likely to have found meaning at 18 months (Carnelley, Wortman, Bolger, & Burke, 2006). Especially at the end of life when losses are frequent, a bereaved person may not have enough time to work through the death of a loved one before another loss occurs. Such back-to-back losses are called *grief overload*.

THE LOSS OF ANIMAL COMPANIONS   Pets can play important roles in people's lives by reducing loneliness and isolation for the elderly, providing a purpose in life, and even replacing the loss of human social contact. For some people, losing a pet can be as difficult as losing a family member. For these reasons, pet loss is included in this discussion of grief and loss.

More than 62% of American households and 70% of families with children live with pets. Pets have become so common in the United States that more people now live with a pet than live with children (American Pet Products Association, 2016). Toray (2004) notes that some people—particularly those who live by themselves, have no children in the household, and are socially isolated—may be at higher risk for prolonged or intense grief. Grief over the loss of a pet can be magnified due to lack of support by society for the loss of a pet.

For children, however, the loss of a pet is frequently their first experience with death. If handled sensitively, the loss of a pet can provide a valuable opportunity to learn about death and to be involved in the grieving process. Children may express anger at their parents or the veterinarian for not being able to save their pet. They may also express fear and concern that others may be taken from them as well. Burial or other rituals are particularly important for children and help them feel involved in the grieving process.

Elderly people who live alone may become especially distraught after the death of a pet. Companion animals provide unconditional love and help owners maintain a daily schedule. It is critical to take such losses seriously and to help seniors cope with their loss and begin to find a new sense of purpose.

According to Toray (2004), the optimal pet loss counselor is one who recognizes the human–animal attachment and is skilled in bereavement and grief counseling. As with other types of loss, the primary goal of counseling is to validate the person's loss; reduce the pain, regret, guilt, and sadness that follow the death of a pet; and help the person resume a healthy level of functioning. Some people may decide to get another pet, while others may take the time to reassess the commitment necessary to raise another pet.

Cause of Death

It seems to be human nature to scan the obituaries looking for causes of death. An immediate flurry of questions results when someone dies. How did he die? When? How long did he know? What did he do to prevent it? What happened? By gathering the details associated with the cause of death, questioners are distancing themselves from death and assessing the potential likelihood of the same type of death happening to them. Such distancing does nothing to help the bereaved and often leaves them feeling alienated and alone. By blaming the victim for his or her own demise (e.g., "He smoked cigarettes," "She didn't wear a seat belt," "He had a family history of heart disease") or projecting blame onto others, people are actually reassuring themselves: "This will never happen to me." The effect of this reaction is to leave the bereaved feeling alone in their grief. To be supportive, crisis counselors should acknowledge that the death could have happened to any one of us.

TERMINAL ILLNESS When the dying process has been prolonged by treatment for a chronic, long-term illness, families may have to grapple with difficult financial, legal, religious, and ethical decisions about treatment. Questions about who makes the final decision, what the patient would want, how long to continue life support, and other ethical issues may arise. An extended illness can deplete a family's financial and emotional resources.

Helping families shift from the fighting spirit so necessary to battle an illness and adopt an attitude of acceptance or "letting go" can provide a valuable opportunity to create the sacred space in which the dying person can approach life's end on his or her own terms. When the focus shifts from curative efforts to end-of-life care, dying persons should have the following four needs met: (1) freedom from pain: physically, the focus should be on comfort care and reducing fear; (2) legal and ethical issues: they should have the opportunity to put affairs in order, to allow a natural death, and to experience a more humane transition; (3) emotional support: they deserve to have a sacred space in which acceptance of the coming separation from their loved ones is acknowledged, they are given the opportunity to grieve, to make amends, and to say good-bye to loved ones; and (4) social support: they deserve to have people around them, to have family support for themselves and for the other members of their family (Corr, Nabe, & Corr, 2012).

In their work with dying people and their families, crisis counselors can be instrumental in creating the space necessary to allow families to experience appropriate end-of-life care. Over the past few decades, the hospice movement has provided many new resources and opportunities to facilitate end-of-life decisions, provide quality care, and help people experience a good death. In his book *Dying Well*, Ira Byock (1997), a physician and former president of the American Academy of Hospice and Palliative Medicine, tells the story of his own father's death from pancreatic cancer. The family gathered at his father's bedside, providing comfort care and medication for pain, sometimes laughing and sometimes crying as they recounted stories from their childhood. As his father drew his last breath, the family held his hands, complete in the knowledge that these were precious moments and that they were honored to be sharing this final experience with their beloved father. They remained in his room for an hour, crying and holding each other, before calling the mortuary. As Byock reported, "It was real, and yet so unreal. Dad was dead. The world had forever changed, yet it still turned; the sun still came up. The next day Mom and I boarded a plane and took Sy home" (p. 24).

As more and more people forgo heroic efforts at life's end and elect instead to allow a natural death, social workers and crisis counselors will be called upon to help families through the transition from medical interventions to palliative care and, eventually, death. Crisis counselors can help families share their feelings about the complicated situation, consider different options, and accept the ambivalence that can result from the conflicting emotions, including relief that the person is no longer suffering. Crisis counselors may be instrumental in helping family members deal with any guilt or regrets over their actions and eventually come to peace with the loss.

SUDDEN DEATH   Sudden death creates special problems for survivors. Unlike a death following a prolonged illness, sudden death denies family members the opportunity to come to terms with unfinished business, to prepare for the loss, and to say good-bye. Sudden loss often leads to intensified grief. The world as the survivor knew it has been shattered. Concurrent crises and secondary losses such as lost income, a lost home, or even the loss of spiritual beliefs may also occur. Several factors should be taken into consideration when working with survivors of sudden loss: (1) natural versus human-made losses (e.g., heart attacks and tsunamis are examples of natural causes; hostile actions and bombings are human made); (2) the degree of intentionality (e.g., accident versus drunk driving); and (3) how preventable the death was.

SUICIDE, HOMICIDE, AND COMMUNITY LOSSES: SCHOOL SHOOTINGS, TERRORIST ATTACKS, AND NATURAL DISASTERS   Losses connected with suicide, homicide, and various types of community-wide disasters pose unique grief issues. These issues are discussed in more detail in other chapters of this text.

Normal versus Complicated Bereavement and the DSM-5

Bereavement, which most people experience several times over the course of a lifetime, is considered a normal response to the death of a loved one. Prolonged or complicated bereavement occurs when symptoms are of unusual duration or severity and interfere with life activities. Both of these conditions are defined and addressed below. The DSM-5 (American Psychiatric Association, 2013) recognizes persistent complex bereavement disorder as a condition for further study.

NORMAL BEREAVEMENT   According to the DSM-5 (American Psychiatric Association, 2013), bereavement occurs after losing through death someone with whom a close relationship existed. The state or grieving encompasses a range of reactions. Normal reactions to the death of a loved one can include some symptoms that may mimic a major depressive episode such as sadness or somatic symptoms, although the symptoms and duration can be expected to vary across cultures. In general, bereaved individuals experience symptoms of depression, but the experience of the symptoms do not persist or cause significant clinical disruption to normal life. Classic somatic symptoms that a mourner may experience include interrupted sleep, lack of energy, and appetite disturbances. These symptoms are also found in depression, and yet clinical depression differs from the sadness of grief in several important ways. Any guilt associated with grief tends to be very specific to the loss and does not permeate all areas of life, as depression does. Neither does grieving generally lower the self-esteem of the bereaved.

The American Psychiatric Association (2013) has cautioned against attaching a diagnosis of major depressive disorder to an individual who is experiencing bereavement even if the symptoms mirror the criteria, since in most cases the individual is exhibiting a normal grieving response. Indeed, even the diagnosis of other specified depressive disorder is cautioned for symptoms related to bereavement. Rather, a diagnosis of other specified trauma- and stressor-related disorder (e.g., persistent complex bereavement disorder) should be considered for complicated grief or bereavement.

Depression may co-occur with bereavement, particularly if the person has a previous history or diagnosis of clinical depression. Only in those cases of risk to self or others should a referral for medication be suggested. Antidepressants will decrease the emotions experienced in grief by numbing the pain, but they will not help the person come to terms with the attachment loss (Seligman & Reichenberg, 2011). Referral for medical treatment should be made only when the loss affects the normal functioning of the individual and the loss is perceived as exceeding current coping skills or resources. Crisis counselors are crucial when assessing and referring individuals in their immediate grief. The grief process is a normal process, and often individuals do not want to feel the normal reaction to their loss. However, in order to move forward in the healing process, it is important to experience the feelings associated with the loss and not to deaden the feelings through medication. Doing so will only prolong or delay the grief process.

COMPLICATED BEREAVEMENT   Although most bereavement reactions fall into the "normal" category, will quickly resolve, and will soon return the bereaved to previous levels of functioning, 10 to 15% of people will go on to experience more enduring grief reactions (American Psychiatric Association, 2013; Bonanno et al., 2007). Individuals displaying symptoms of normal bereavement may subsequently be diagnosed as having complicated bereavement. Prior to the DSM-5, complicated bereavement was categorized by the severity and duration (exceeding 2 months) of symptoms and was often (inappropriately) diagnosed as major depressive disorder.

To help differentiate between normal and abnormal grieving as well as describe how bereavement can significantly affect life, the American Psychiatric Association (2013) has introduced a new category of disorder to the DSM-5: "other specified trauma- and stressor-related disorder" (309.89). The diagnosis of other specified trauma- and stressor-related disorder can be applied to individuals who have experienced a death that causes significant distress and clinical impairment and whose symptoms align with severe and persistent grief and mourning; the specifier "persistent complex bereavement disorder" would be applied in such instances. Other specified trauma- and stressor-related disorder (specified by "persistent complex bereavement disorder") is applied most often to individuals who meet the following diagnostic criteria (American Psychiatric Association, 2013):

1. "The individual experienced the death of someone with whom there was a close relationship." (p. 789)
2. At least one of these symptoms has persisted more often than not, with clinical impairment, in an adult for at least 12 months following the death (at least 6 months for a child): persistent yearning of the deceased; intense sorrow in response to the death; preoccupation with the deceased; preoccupation with the circumstances of the death.
3. At least six of these symptoms have persisted more often than not, with clinical impairment, in an adult for at least 12 months following the death (at least 6 months for a child): difficulty accepting the death; experiencing emotional numbness; difficulty in positive reminiscing; bitterness or anger related to the loss; self-blame; desire to die; difficulty trusting others; feeling detached; feeling life is meaningless; confusion about one's role in life; reluctance in pursuing life goals.
4. The individual is experiencing significant occupational, social, or other impairment.
5. The bereavement reaction conforms to cultural, religious, or age-appropriate norms.

By administering the Beck Depression Inventory (Beck, Steer, & Brown, 1996) along with an additional single-item question ("Even while my relative was dying, I felt a sense of purpose in my life") asked at 8 weeks after the loss of a loved one, Guldin, O'Connor, Sokolowski, Jensen, and Vedsted (2011) were able to predict those who were at risk for developing complicated grief.

According to the literature, clients with symptoms of complicated grief may benefit from earlier intervention, as these symptoms portend a less favorable outcome and may result in increased medication, job-related problems, the development of psychopathology, and even death (Guldin et al., 2011). As mentioned, perception of the relationships, different causes of death, personality of the bereaved, roles associated with the death, and other mediators can increase the length of time for and complicate the bereavement process. For example, a married woman who loses her spouse of 50 years can be expected to experience bereavement for years just as a father who lost his only son in a tragic school shooting may experience grief over a longer period of time.

Other losses in life can result in symptoms similar to both "normal" bereavement and complicated grief. A survey of survivors of Hurricane Katrina found that 58% had severe hurricane-related loss, and only 3.7% had lost a loved one. The bulk of the loss was related to tangible losses that resulted from the hurricane, such as jobs, homes, and support networks. Researchers found that predictors of later development of compli-cated grief included predisaster issues such as lack of social support, ethnic-minority status, and preexisting psychopathology (Shear et al., 2011).

Other losses such as separation or divorce, being fired from a job after 20 years, or even retirement can lead to loss of meaning in life. Horwitz and Wakefield (2012) sug-gested that as many as 25% of people who are diagnosed as having a major depressive disorder could actually be experiencing "normal" sadness reactions as the result of a major loss. Until additional research is conducted and better definitions of bereavement and complicated bereavement are established, clinicians must carefully assess the symptoms of their bereaved patients to distinguish between the normal depressive reactions to death and other losses, and the more prolonged symptoms of grief associ-ated with persistent and complex bereavement, major depressive disorder, or post-traumatic stress disorder (PTSD).

INTERVENTIONS FOR GRIEF AND LOSS

In the past decade, growing controversy over the effectiveness of grief work has necessitated taking a closer look at the empirical evidence related to such work. Sev-eral articles published in notable journals have suggested that grief work, especially with normal bereavement, could actually do more harm than good. Larson and Hoyt (2007) investigated such claims and found no evidence to support a harmful effect of bereavement counseling. Rather, they noted that previous claims of harm were actu-ally based on misrepresentations of several meta-analyses and subsequent republica-tion of erroneous results.

Despite limited research on effective interventions for the grieving process, it has become fairly common practice to help clients "work through" their grief. This is not to suggest that there is a linear, preferred method or manner in which to do this; rather, as memories and thoughts come up, the bereaved client addresses the feelings, accepts them, and moves on.

Worden (2009) notes that one of the most important benefits of grief counseling is educating the client about the dynamics of the grieving process. Crisis counselors should help clients understand that there is no set period of time for the mourning process, that sadness and grief are normal, and that the process is not linear but rather comes and goes like waves, in particular with developmental milestones where the loved one is no longer around to share in the experiences. Specifically, holidays, birthdays, and the first-year anniversary may be particularly difficult. Holidays may be extremely difficult on the first anniversary but may reoccur each year. Some people may also experience increased sadness during the change of the seasons and may not feel appreciably better until an entire year has gone by and anniversary dates begin to include new memories of life after the loss of their loved one. An effective intervention is to help the person realize that such times may be difficult and encourage them to plan ahead for additional support during holidays, birthdays, and anniversaries of the death. This in itself can normalize the resurgence of grief symptoms and normalize the reactions.

When working with bereaved clients, Wang (2007) underscores the need for the crisis counselor to join with the client empathically and genuinely. By practicing the necessary conditions of unconditional positive regard, genuineness, and empathy, the client feels heard and no longer alone, and the crisis counselor, who cannot do anything to solve the client's grief or bring the loved one back, *can* do the one thing available—be there in an empathic, genuine, respectful, and honest way.

Restoring Life's Meaning

Helping people focus on recreating a meaningful existence is the most important function of the grieving process. Hope gives us the courage to live, even in conditions of despair. Hope is an orientation of the spirit. The biggest job of the crisis counselor when working with bereaved clients is to help them make sense of the loss, accept the changes that they did not wish for or create, and restore meaning to their lives. Working on meaning and purpose often becomes the goal of long-term counseling after the crisis is stabilized.

Spirituality, religion, and faith-based practices are also an important part of a person's coping strategies and help to give life meaning. Having a spiritual connection or influence can often help people transcend suffering and adapt to life's difficulties when they occur. Crisis counselors, who may or may not be grounded in a religious tradition of their own, must approach clients with respect and dignity, without proselytizing about their own faith, and with recognition of the boundary between crisis counseling and spiritual counseling. By following a theoretical model that addresses issues of spirituality and religion, crisis counselors can improve client rapport and more accurately assess and work with people in all stages of development and with diverse types of crises. Acknowledging a person's belief system can also provide a source of strength and support and shed light on areas in which matters of faith may be contributing to suffering. Some examples in which adherence to religious doctrines may actually add to the pain mourners experience might occur surrounding issues of suicide, gay or lesbian relationships, and married interracial couples.

Many individuals have a faith story that illustrates (or narrates) their spiritual beliefs, and these stories are often brought up in the counseling session. Understanding the influence of faith or spirituality is integral to the crisis planning or referral process. This understanding starts with the counselor asking the client how faith or spirituality has influenced his or her life, how it has or has not been helpful, and whether the client has relied on his or her faith or spirituality in a past crisis. Clients need to know that it is okay to address their spiritual, philosophical, and moral dilemmas in the counselor's office. Unfortunately, counselors might avoid the discussion of faith and spirituality with clients for fear that clients will perceive such questions as an attempt by counselors to impose their beliefs.

Spiritually competent crisis counselors who have effectively incorporated spirituality into their counseling practices can appreciate a richer assessment of the whole person (mind, body, and spirit), a deeper rapport, and a fuller understanding of the person's beliefs, goals, and life's purpose (Borneman, Ferrell, & Pulchaski, 2010). People who identify with a particular religious belief system and those who may be skeptical about counseling in the first place are frequently reassured and more comfortable with the process if the clinician incorporates spirituality and meaning making into the assessment process.

Much has been written about the importance of incorporating spirituality into the counseling process (Cashwell & Young, 2011; Pargament, 2011; Parker, 2011; Sperry & Shafranske, 2005), but less has been written about how to do it. In general, crisis counselors should be familiar with the stages of faith development as well as cognizant of ethical boundaries related to discussing spiritual issues with clients. Being aware of one's own spiritual attitude, and keeping that attitude out of the counseling process, is crucial. People want and need to be able to discuss aspects of their faith with clinicians. In recognition of that need, Christine Pulchaski, a physician, developed the FICA spiritual assessment, a four-step process that includes questions clinicians can ask to quickly assess a patient's spiritual attitude:

1. *Faith, Belief, Meaning:*   Do you consider yourself a spiritual or religious person? Where do you find meaning in life?
2. *Importance and Influence:*   How important is your faith to your life? How do your beliefs help you to cope in times of stress?
3. *Church and Community.*   Are you a part of a faith-based or religious community? If so, what type of support does this community provide?
4. *Apply and Address:*   How would you like me to address or apply this information in our work together? (Borneman et al., 2010)

Using the FICA spiritual assessment is just one way in which the importance of spirituality can be assessed and seamlessly incorporated into the therapeutic process to provide a richer, more integrated, and more positive experience for the client. Crisis counselors should also have an understanding of the developmental stages of faith.

Faith development theory (FDT) is a cognitive–structural model of spiritual and religious development that counselors can use to assess the client's stage of spiritual growth and development and to identify any developmental crisis that may be occurring. FDT is nonsectarian and allows clinicians to "work with the client's faith structures without having to endorse or challenge specific religious beliefs" (Parker, 2011, p. 112). Like Kohlberg's (1976) stages of moral development, Fowler's (1981) model of faith development views faith as a universal human activity that manifests differently over the course of a lifetime. The stages range from childhood to later life, with most people growing through the stages developmentally, although not all will achieve the final stage in which faith is universalized. According to Fowler, FDT incorporates the following six stages:

- *Stage 1—Intuitive–Projective Stage:* An egocentric stage that is most often seen in childhood (ages 3 to 7 years), where fantasy and reality are intertwined. The imagination is powerful and images can be either positive and enforcing of values or destructive and terrorize the child (e.g., monsters in the closet at night). The emergence of concrete operational thinking and the child's desire to know how things work and to distinguish between what is real and what is imagined often marks the transition to Stage 2.
- *Stage 2—Mythic–Literal Stage:* A narrative is used to give meaning to life at this stage, where logic, cause and effect relationships, and a sense of justice begin to emerge as well as the seeds of taking another's perspective. The child begins to take on the beliefs, stories, and symbols of his or her community or family. Story making becomes a way of making sense of the world. In this stage, a person may become too literal, and goodness and evil may be seen as a black and white duality.
- *Stage 3—Synthetic–Conventional Stage:* Personal identity is formed at this stage, and worth tends to be determined by the approval of others. Generally, the development of personal identity occurs in adolescence, but for many it

may provide the faith balance they hold for the rest of their lives. Fowler (1981) refers to this stage as a conformist stage in which faith and values mesh nicely with the expectations and judgments of others. When the emergence of autonomy gives rise to critical reflection on how one's beliefs and values were formed, or how one loses faith in leaders or the establishment, the transition to Stage 4 may begin. Leaving home, establishing one's own identity, and other experiences that result in self-examination of values are also likely precursors to transitioning to Stage 4.

- *Stage 4—Individuative–Reflective Stage:* The recognition at this stage of the worldviews and experiences of others leads to critical reflection on one's own beliefs and outlook. For some, this critical reflection occurs in young adulthood, with the rise of responsibility for personal beliefs, attitudes, commitments, and lifestyle. For others, it occurs later in life (late 30s to 40s) if at all. Highlights of Stage 4 include tension between individuality and group membership; a recognition of injustice (sexism, racism, nationalism); demythologization of symbols; and a broadening of one's worldview.
- *Stage 5—Conjunctive Stage:* This stage moves beyond the logic of prior stages. In it, one begins to view truth as multidimensional and relative. The exceptions lead one to search for deeper spiritual meanings and a justice worldview that extends beyond family, state, or religious denomination. There is a danger that people in this stage may become cynical or passive, firmly planted in the physical world and unable to transcend or to act upon their newfound beliefs. Those who are able to act are likely to put their efforts toward creating a better world.
- *Stage 6—Universalizing Faith Stage:* Although Fowler (1981) believed this stage is rarely achieved, those who do reach this level of faith development believe in the inclusiveness of all beings. They may rise above religious boundaries and social or political structures, and they may become radicalized in their attempts to help humanity. People in this stage recognize the impermanence of everything, are free of ideological bonds, and are sometimes honored and revered for their beliefs.

By understanding the stages of faith development, the crisis counselor is better able to assess the effects of the crisis on the client and to help the client identify and work through any faith stage transition that coincides with the ongoing crisis. Identifying the client's stage of faith development can lead to an identification of transitions between stages in contrast to stable periods, and it can help determine how current life crises may be intersecting with faith stages in a beneficial or disharmonious way.

Crises, both physical and spiritual, can happen in life at any time. Helping clients recognize and distinguish a faith stage transition from a life crisis can help normalize the experience, provide a manner of looking at the two crises separately, and help the client understand the effect one has on the other. For example, a client who is proceeding with a divorce and then finds he is being excommunicated from the religious institution he has belonged to for 20 years must come to terms with the loss of not only his marriage but also his supportive faith-based community. Helping him separate the two types of grief and acknowledge and work through the loss of each, can help this client move forward and perhaps find others who are struggling with similar issues. Walsh (2012) believes counselors have an ethical obligation to rise above their own sectarian religious or spiritual beliefs to provide safe places in

ACTIVITY 5.3

Consider Fowler's stages of faith development. What stage best fits your spiritual development? Are you currently in a stable period or in a period of transition? How has your faith affected other areas of your life (e.g., work, relationships, decision making)? How might your stage of religious or spiritual development positively affect your role as a crisis counselor? What might be some limitations?

which clients can explore their opinions, feelings, and beliefs. Having a faith development perspective can increase counselor competency in working with spiritual and religious issues and can help assess the role of spirituality or religion in a client's life, regardless of religion or denomination (Parker, 2011). Complete Activity 5.3 to gain further insight into how you can integrate spirituality into grief work with clients. Also complete Think About It 5.2

Interventions

Grief is an individual, subjective experience with many different facets There is no single model of grief counseling because grief work must consider the importance of culture, background, religious and spiritual issues, and family history as well as the individual qualities, circumstances, and personality of the mourner. Helping people focus on recreating a meaningful existence or moving toward a new meaning becomes the most important function of the grieving process.

By taking into account individual grieving styles, crisis counselors can tailor appropriate interventions. Doka (2005) identified a continuum of grieving styles ranging from intuitive to instrumental. People who are intuitive respond to grief affectively, while instrumental grievers are more likely to react cognitively or behaviorally.

Doka (2005) suggested that *recovery* from a loss may not be possible or desirable and instead described *amelioration* of grief, a return to similar (or better) levels of functioning with diminished pain. The bereaved maintain connections to the deceased through memory, biography, legacy, and spirituality. Crisis counselors face the challenge of helping the bereaved celebrate connections, while avoiding potential problems such as an inability to grow or move forward.

The emotional impact of the loss of a family member, especially the death of a spouse, can linger for years, even decades, depending on circumstances, age, cause of death, social support, and other mediators. Because loss of a family member can have detrimental effects on the health and mental health of survivors, a thorough assessment that includes the physical, psychological, cognitive, and spiritual effects of the loss should be conducted with these clients.

THINK ABOUT IT 5.2

Think about how you might use the FICA spiritual assessment tool and Fowler's stages of faith development. Would you be comfortable incorporating these tools in your clinical work? Do you consider meeting the client's spiritual needs as part of your responsibility as a clinician? Are you prepared to listen for clues to spiritual suffering and to approach clients about spiritual issues? How do your own religious and spiritual issues affect your work with patients in the area of death and dying?

Crisis counselors should routinely ask how their clients found out about the death. Especially in sudden loss, including suicide, the survivors should be encouraged to talk about what happened as often as possible, to have their reactions validated and believed, and to be with others who have been through similar experiences. It is not helpful to tell clients that they need medication or should not think about the death. Nor is it helpful to refer clients to support groups prematurely. Grassroots organizations such as Compassionate Friends, Parents of Murdered Children, and Mothers Against Drunk Driving can offer support and information for survivors.

For the treatment of complicated grief, cognitive behavior therapy has been found to be effective. Mindfulness-based cognitive therapy has also shown promise in helping people to accept what has happened to them and stay focused in the moment without dwelling on the past or worrying about the future. Mindfulness-based practices such as meditation, focused breathing, and body scans can also help people in crisis reduce their distress and can promote long-term well-being (Humphrey, 2009).

Boelen, de Keijser, van den Hout, and van den Bout (2007) found that cognitive distortions and maladaptive behaviors not only are common in complicated grieving but also contribute to its creation. In one study, they compared cognitive behavior therapy with supportive counseling. The results indicated that six sessions of pure cognitive restructuring combined with six sessions of exposure therapy were more effective than supportive counseling. Since avoidance and negative thinking are central to the creation of complicated grief, Boelen et al. (2007) concluded that "encouraging patients to confront and work through the loss is important to treating complicated grief and more helpful than targeting thinking patterns" (p. 283).

Writing a life history or creating a personal narrative as one approaches the final stage of life can help give life meaning and can provide a valuable integration of the totality of one's life. Butler (1963) was the first to describe the universal occurrence of life review in older people. Butler noted that the "looking-back process" was set in motion by the nearness of death, coupled with the additional time available for self-reflection that is a by-product of retirement. Dreams and thoughts of death and of the past are reported to increase in the seventh and eighth decades of life.

Congruent with Erikson's (1997) psychosocial crisis of stage 8 (i.e., integrity versus despair), depending on the environment and the individual's character, life review can increase reminiscences and mild nostalgia, which can result in adaptive and positive integration of one's life, or it can result in increased anxiety, depression, and despair. Those who cannot integrate, comprehend, and realistically accept their lives as adequate run the risk of inner turmoil, increased rumination, depression, and possibly suicide. Erikson suggested that it is not the process of life review but the achievement of integrity that promotes successful aging.

Other classic interventions such as logotherapy (Frankl, 1959); narrative therapy (Neimeyer, 2001); expressive therapy through art, music, or journaling; mindfulness meditation (Davidson et al., 2003); and other types of counseling that address spiritual needs can all contribute to meaning making and can be effective tools for working with people in crisis. As in all therapy, the role of the crisis counselor is to provide empathy, detect suffering and address it, normalize the grief reactions, gather enough information to determine the type of grief experiences and other issues that complicate the grieving process, and provide psychoeducation about what lies ahead in the next stage of development. Counselors who are able to do this in a culturally and spiritually competent manner can help relieve a client's distress and improve that person's quality of life, no matter what the crisis or which stage of faith development the person is experiencing. In general, the mourning process concludes when the person feels more hopeful, experiences a renewed interest in life, is able to discuss the loss without extreme emotion, and responds to condolences with gratitude rather than avoidance. Read Voices from the Field 5.2.

VOICES FROM THE FIELD 5.2
Working with Clients Experiencing Loss and Grief

Randall M. Moate

One of the primary tenets of Buddhist philosophy is the idea that suffering is a part of the human condition. While at first glance this idea may sound bleak, it is not intended in that way. Simply put, this idea refers to the notion that whatever brings us pleasure or happiness also has the capacity to bring us pain. Another way to understand this idea is to consider the things that fill up our lives with meaning or happiness, such as careers, personal interests, family, children, friendships, romantic relationships, possessions, good health, goals, and personal values. While the presence of these things gives our lives meaning, purpose, and pleasure, loss of any of them can create a void that causes fear, confusion, and sadness. How we experience loss and grief is personal to each of us, yet experiencing loss and grief is something that is common to all humans. This is something that binds us together as part of the human experience.

As a counselor, something that I have had to overcome is a natural reaction to want to dive in and pull my clients out of their grief. When someone has experienced a loss and is submerged in grief, my initial reaction is, "How can I help my client feel better as soon as possible?" In other words, I want to help my client move out of the sad or painful place, and bring my client toward a happier place in the present. What I have come to learn is that this is precisely the wrong thing to do. Clients experiencing acute grief, or a vacuum of meaning after a major loss, need space and time to grieve and to settle into this painful space. I have found that clients will move forward from their grief and loss on their own time, when they are ready to do so. Attempting to move clients from this place before they are ready is almost guaranteed to turn out badly. It has been my experience that clients resent, or take poorly to, feeling ushered out of their state of grief by their counselors.

When working with clients who have experienced loss and grief, I have found that these individuals want several things. They want me to deeply listen to their story, experience a compassionate and human connection with me, and sense that I have understanding and empathy for their experience. But how does one achieve these things? To counter my knee-jerk reaction to want to dive in and save my clients, I have developed a personal maxim I use in counseling that I call "*less* is more"—which refers to *less* questioning, *less* intervention, *less* technique, and *less* direction on my behalf. This results in my coming across to my client as being *more* helpful, *more* compassionate, and *more* understanding. Clients in deep grief are not looking for a magic solution from me. In truth, even if they were, I possess no magic solutions or answers that could fill the void from their loss. What I can do, however, is carefully listen to my clients, help them sit with their grief, and through my body language and presence communicate a sense of compassion and respect.

Perhaps the most valuable thing I do when working with a client who is experiencing grief, or coping with loss, is share hope. Sometimes after major losses and when grief is at its apex, a client may experience a loss of hope. From the perspective of the place that they are in, it seems as if things will never get better. I have witnessed some of my clients make profound changes in their lives and overcome huge obstacles. I hold onto these memories in a special place within me, as they remind me that people are resilient and have the capacity to change. Amidst the despair, confusion, and sadness my client may present during session, these memories act as a lighthouse for me and orient me toward a sense of hope and optimism. I then, in turn, try to act as a lighthouse for my clients and help orient them toward the hope and optimism I feel for their situation. While I rarely find it appropriate to verbalize this during a session, I believe that my clients can sense it nonetheless.

Group Support

Short-term bereavement support groups can sometimes provide positive adjunctive support to individual grief work, especially when the type of loss results in feelings of isolation (e.g., suicide, homicide, HIV, miscarriage, infertility). As with all therapeutic groups, clients should be screened prior to participation to ensure that they are appropriate for the group. Parents who have lost a child should not be put in groups with those who have miscarried. People who have lost a grandparent should not be grouped with people who have lost a spouse or a child. As much as possible, the makeup of support groups should be homogeneous. Looking ahead to Case Study 5.3, which follows later in the chapter, Shayna felt comfortable in a support group for young adults (aged 23–29 years) who had lost a spouse, fiancé, sibling, or parent. During each week of the 6-week group, clients were asked to process a different aspect of their loss. In week 1, clients were asked to talk about the person they lost. In week 2, they were asked what surprised them most about the grieving process. In week 3, they had a type of "show and tell," with each person bringing in an object and explaining its relationship to the person they had lost. Week 4 was devoted to rituals, and each person in turn lit a candle as he or she spoke of rituals that had proved helpful. During the final two sessions, the group members processed their feelings toward one another and the connections they had made, vowing to continue meeting outside of the group environment. As with all other groups, it is important to screen clients beforehand for readiness for the group experience. In general, most people will not be ready to join a support group in the first month after a loss.

Support groups for suicide loss survivors should help members focus on the unique elements of their loss. Many survivors are eager to know why their loved one ended his or her life, so reconstructing the final days, looking for clues, and talking about their last telephone call may be integral to the grieving process. It is important to indicate that there may never be an answer to the survivor's "why" questions. It is more important to be able to understand why the loss is keeping the survivor from healing and moving forward without the loved one. Common questions to help achieve this understanding could focus on the survivor's perception of role: "What does it mean to you that your oldest son is not alive?" or "What does it mean to you that he committed suicide?" Absolving guilt is another important aspect. Processing these feelings together as a group helps normalize the feelings so that the guilt frequently begins to dissipate. Another distinctive goal of survivor support groups is to prevent future suicides. Family members and friends of a person who has completed a suicide are more likely to attempt suicide themselves. The reason is unclear, but it may be that once the taboo of suicide has been breached, it becomes an acceptable alternative to life. Another possibility is that the survivor empathizes with the other's despair. Whatever the reason, individual and group interventions with survivors of suicide loss should have a goal to prevent future suicides.

Working with Children

According to Worden (2009), "the same tasks of grieving that apply to the adult obviously apply to the child" (p. 235). But such tasks have to be modified to meet the social, cognitive, emotional, and developmental stages of the child. Preparing children, first-time funeralgoers, or people from cultures not familiar with the concept of viewings and funerals in traditional American society for what to expect can help decrease additional crisis or anxiety. A child attending a funeral for the first time may have extreme reactions to specific funeral customs (e.g., open caskets, touching the dead body, graveside burial), but if explained appropriately, these customs can help the healing process.

Following the death of a parent, children need support, continuity, and nurturance. In a two-year study of 125 schoolchildren who experienced the loss of a parent, Worden (2001) found that 80% were coping well by the first or second anniversary of their parent's death. The stability of the remaining parent was the greatest predictor of the level of a child's adjustment to a parent's death. Based on the study, the following needs of bereaved children were identified:

1. Bereaved children need to have their questions answered in an age-appropriate way. They need to know that they were not responsible in any way for their parent's death. Frequently asked questions on children's minds include the circumstances surrounding the death: "How did my mother [or father] die?" "Where is my dad [or mom] now?" If the parent died from disease or cancer, the concept of contagion may need to be explained to children who think they might contract their parent's illness: "Will it happen to me?"
2. Children need to feel involved. Developing a ritual, allowing children to be involved in the funeral, and including them in decision making are important. For example, having a child place a memento in the casket, light a candle, or decide which dress mommy will wear allows a child of any age to be included in the rituals of mourning.
3. Children's routines should be kept as consistent as possible. This can be difficult for the grieving parent, but research has shown that children do better when they know what to expect, can rely on the remaining parent for support and nurturance, and have families that exhibit an active rather than a passive coping style. Families in which the surviving parent is not coping well, is young, is the father, becomes depressed, or begins dating within one year of the spouse's death are likely to have children who have more anxiety, lower self-esteem, and less self-efficacy and who exhibit more acting-out behavior.
4. Children need a way to remember the deceased. Photographs, scrapbooks, and memory books filled with stories or pictures of the deceased can all help children remember. Such books may be referred to again and again as they grow older.

Due to their limited life experiences and coping skills, children may have more difficulty mourning than adults. Children's reality is often formed through fantasy and play. They are likely to fill in the blanks with assumptions or partial truths suited to their developmental age. They have a limited understanding of the world around them; therefore, they need playtime to act out their feelings of anger, anxiety, or fear. If a child regresses or participates in acting-out behavior, a thorough assessment may be in order. A screening instrument for identifying bereaved children who are at increased risk can be found in Worden's book *Children and Grief: When a Parent Dies* (2001). Interventions that have been found to be especially useful in helping children of all ages come to terms with their grief include play therapy, expressive art therapies, peer support groups, camps, and bibliotherapy with books such as *Tear Soup* (Corr & Balk, 2011) or *Waterbugs and Dragonflies* (Stickney & Nordstrom, 2010).

Mourning may be a lifelong process for children who lose a parent. Feelings may be reactivated during adulthood when life events (e.g., weddings, other deaths or losses, reaching the same age as the parent who died) trigger the memory of loss. Recognition of these potentially vulnerable times allows people to actively plan their grief work.

Psychoeducation may mean simply explaining that the bereaved may reexperience the intensity of the grief at various milestones or developmental achievements. This knowledge may assist the individual in knowing this to be a normal possibility and potentially decrease future crises related to the original loss. See Table 5.1 for suggestions and techniques on counseling grieving children and adolescents. Also read Voices from the Field 5.3.

TABLE 5.1 Counseling Grieving Children and Adolescents

General Developmental Considerations

- Children typically do not perceive death as reality until approximately age 7.
- Before age 2, the child's concept of death is primarily "out of sight, out of mind." Some theorists would argue that if a child is capable of love, then that child is capable of experiencing some sort of grieving.
- Children aged 2 to 7 (Piaget's preoperational stage) experience death as magical, egocentric, and causal. They see death as temporary, see a possibility of reviving the dead, see the dead person as living in a box underground, think their own thoughts or actions caused the death, think death is like sleep, and have an inaccurate estimate of life span (e.g., they may think people live over 150 years).
- Children aged 7 to 12 (Piaget's concrete operations stage) have a concept of death that is curious and realistic. Children are interested in details of death; begin to internalize the universality and permanence of death; conceptualize that all bodily functions stop; can comprehend thoughts of an afterlife; and can estimate accurately how long people live. They think of death's occurrence in specific observable, concrete terms, and they believe that very old, severely handicapped, and extremely awkward people are those who die.
- Adolescents aged 13 and older (Piaget's formal operations stage) have a concept of death that is self-absorbed. They understand mortality and death as a natural process. Coming to terms with death is a primary task of adolescence. Denial of one's own death is strong; they feel omnipotent. They are more comfortable talking about death with peers than with adults.
- Some children may experience guilt about the death (they may have wished the person dead), so it is important to convey the following:
  - Thoughts don't kill.
  - No one is perfect. (Give them permission to be imperfect.)
  - All people die at some point.

  Also help children who experience guilt remember the following:
  - the good times with the deceased
  - meaningful relationships with the deceased

  Guilt may be displayed in many ways, including forgetting, inattention, and aggression.

Dos and Don'ts When Counseling Grieving Children and Adolescents

Do

- Tell the truth (e.g., "I don't know" is an OK answer to "why" questions).
- Maintain structure, rules, and limits to provide security.
- Hug.
- Have adult caretakers save special items from the deceased person to give the client later (e.g., a collection, a Bible, a sweatshirt).

Table 5.1 Counseling Grieving Children and Adolescents (*Continued*)

- Be a good role model (e.g., Do not be afraid to cry in front of the client. It lets him or her know that you care and that it is OK to cry).
- Talk about loss and death before a significant death occurs, if possible.
- Help the client make decisions about attending the funeral (if the death is recent).
- Tell the client he or she did not cause the death by angry thoughts or words.
- Reinforce that the client will be taken care of, and remind him or her of available resources.
- Recognize that children and adolescents express grief physically. They flush out the wound by beating, pounding, or running it out.
- Allow younger clients to select the play activities needed to work through their grief.
- Be prepared to listen to the client's beliefs on religion and spirituality.
- Let the client talk about feelings through drawings.
- Give the client something to do to help combat helplessness, such as plant a tree to remember the person or write a story about the person.
- Suggest bibliotherapy.
- Use third person when talking to a child or adolescent—doing so is less threatening (e.g., say "Many children/adolescents feel . . ." instead of "Do you feel?")
- Look through photo albums with the client.
- Allow the client to share precious moments.
- Talk about the loss whenever the client brings it up.
- Answer only what is asked. Let the client be in charge of what he or she is ready to hear.
- Expect children to regress somewhat: clinging, fear of the dark, etc.
- Talk about the cause of death to children in understandable terms (e.g., He died because his heart could not work anymore.).

Don't

- Underestimate the client's grief.
- Try to protect the client from feeling pain.
- Assume that the client will respond to the loss as you would.
- Worry about saying the "right words."
- Try to find something good about the death: "Aren't you glad mommy isn't in pain anymore?"
- Associate tears with grief. Some children and adolescents do not cry, which does not mean they are not equally affected.
- Push the client to talk about the loss.
- Worry about crying in front of the child. Tears give the child permission to be real too.
- Shut the client out by excluding him or her from conversations about the deceased, death-related discussions, and grief-promoting rituals.
- Be overly simplistic about the death, focusing on heaven and not the loss.
- Demand maturity as a substitute for grief, e.g., "Now you are the man of the house."
- Allow the client to be the emotional caregiver to the parents.
- Worry about the client's appetite.

Table 5.1 Counseling Grieving Children and Adolescents (*Continued*)

- Use abstract language to soften the death. Use the words *died* and *dead*. Avoid words like *lost*, *sleeping*, *gone to another place*—these are all contexts that the person could possibly return from.
- Promise you will not die.
- Be afraid of initiating talk about the death. Refer to the deceased by name.
- Assume that the client will always want to talk about the death. Children in particular handle bits and pieces of grief at a time.
- Single out the grieving student (if counseling takes place at school); treat the student the same as other peers.
- Equate death with illness.

Counselors should communicate with young clients using concrete terms they understand, establish a good rapport with young clients, and answer questions factually. They should avoid philosophical interpretations and fantasy stories. Finally, if a counselor does not know the answer to a question, he or she should admit it. Children appreciate honesty.

VOICES FROM THE FIELD 5.3
The Power of Normalizing and Preparing for Future Grief Reactions

Lisa R. Jackson-Cherry

For many years, I have worked with COPS-Kids (Concerns of Police Survivors-Kids) during National Police Week, which is held each year in May in Washington, DC. During this time, COPS-Kids provides group counseling to hundreds of children who lost a parent or parents in the line of duty. It was not uncommon to have a child in a group one year and see the child again a few years later in another group. That was what happened with Macy. I never knew how a simple statement of normalizing a future grief reaction could empower a young person and prevent further crisis until I saw Macy again.

Macy was in my middle school group when I first met her. Her father was killed in the line of duty just a year earlier. She was able to share many fond memories of her father and was experiencing what appeared to be normal grieving around his absence in her life. In the group counseling she attended, we talked about upcoming events where deceased fathers or mothers (or both) would not be present to share in their sporting, academic, religious, or other developmental achievements. I can recall telling all of my groups that often the death of our loved ones can affect us at every life transition and event, even later into our lives. Moreover, I explained that the intense grief reactions we had at the time of the death that we believed we had worked through can come back and we can reexperience those intense feelings we experienced when the death first impacted our lives. I also spoke about other feelings that were not present at the death but that could come up for the first time, like resentment and jealousy, and feelings toward others not connected with the death. I was hoping to prepare the children for events and to normalize any retriggering of feelings in life.

Three years later, Macy was in my high school group. She spoke to the group about her intense feelings of grief and new feelings of resentment toward her peers and God when her father was not with her at her Grade 8 graduation, father–daughter dance, and Confirmation, or when he was not there to help her with her basketball skills when she tried out for the high school team. She said she remembered what I had said 3 years ago, and it was those words that allowed her to understand that what she was reexperiencing was normal grief in response to a new event and to talk it through with her supporters.

Family Interventions

Walsh (2012) recommends that a systems approach be taken with the loss of any family member. This approach views the interactions among relationships, family processes, and the extended family as key to understanding how the death has affected the entire family system. Connectedness, communication, and mutual support and respect among members of the family seem the most likely to engender a balanced response to the loss. Two extremes run the risk of developing dysfunctional patterns: (1) families in which grief is avoided and pain is hidden and (2) families that cannot eventually work together to pick up the pieces and begin to form new attachments. Such patterns can affect the family for generations to come. Finding meaning in the loss can help family members begin to heal.

DIFFICULTIES IN GRIEF COUNSELING

Withdrawal

When the survivor feels that no one understands or when the circumstances of the death or loss are so rare that no one in the survivor's social network has experienced such a loss before, the result can be withdrawal and isolation. This loss of empathy and connection causes the person to withdraw to make sense of the tragedy. The person may be overwhelmed with feelings of loss, guilt, anger, shame, or vulnerability. And yet no one in the person's support network can share in his or her specific form of loss. The person feels alone and, in this aloneness, may lose faith in all he or she believed to be true. An example of withdrawal is presented in Case Study 5.2. Complete Activity 5.4, which asks you to consider your views on end-of-life issues. Also complete Think About It 5.3.

CASE STUDY 5.2

A Case of Bereavement-Related Withdrawal

Shayna, a woman in her mid-20s, presented for counseling several months after the death of her fiancé, Jerod, from a rare viral infection. While hospitalized for the virus, Jerod had a heart attack, lapsed into a coma, and died several days later. He was 25 years old. Shayna was distraught, as was Jerod's family. The death was completely unexpected—and making sense of it was deferred for months as they awaited autopsy results. It was only after the autopsy that they discovered that a rare and fatal virus had crystallized in Jerod's organs, and one by one his organs failed. Even then, the cause of death was not fully comprehensible. It did not make sense.

His mother and father were in their 40s; his younger brothers and sisters still lived at home. His death was out of chronological order. Shayna was sad and could not stop searching for answers. She sought out her minister and a psychic, and she even attended new age healing sessions in her efforts to make sense of the tragedy. She had a large support network of college friends and coworkers of her own age. While initially supportive of her grief, many of her friends had never experienced the death of a loved one, and one by one, they stopped asking about her loss and began to focus instead on their latest career moves, graduate school plans, and other day-to-day activities. Shayna stopped returning their calls. She began to isolate herself from friends and family and, other than going to work, did not leave her house. She reported, "No one can understand what I am going through." She could no longer relate to the trivial matters that made up the drama of her young friends' lives. "Only someone who has experienced death can appreciate the fragility of life," Shayna said.

Shayna's counseling focused on building a bridge back to her life. At first, her days were filled with yearning to have her fiancé back, while at night she dreamed about him but could not communicate with him. Each morning she awoke sad and frustrated. Those first sessions early in counseling were very painful as Shayna recounted the story of her fiancé's death. Nothing could be done to help except to be present, empathic, and bear witness to her pain. This gave her comfort in the knowledge that someone else was accompanying her on this painful journey. She was not alone.

Counseling included discussion of the unconscious needs reflected in Shayna's dreams and the importance of establishing rituals to honor her fiancé. Each night she would light a candle and talk to his picture. This gave her comfort and a newfound way to communicate with him. Shayna also talked about the goals she and her fiancé had for the future. She decided to continue on the same path for a while and to move ahead with one of their goals—to get a dog. The puppy proved to be source of solace and support.

Shayna continued to go to work as an accountant, although she had many physical symptoms including anxiety, waking up in the middle of night, loss of interest in food and daily routines, and poor concentration. Cognitive behavioral therapy helped her identify and rate her anxiety. She learned how to do breathing exercises to regulate her breath and ward off panic attacks, and how to conduct a simple body scan meditation at night to help her relax and get back to sleep.

Gradually, Shayna began to confide in two coworkers who checked in with her regularly. The trust and support she found in these two women helped her begin to integrate the trauma into her life and start to reconnect with the community. When she was ready, she participated in a support group, run by a local hospice specifically for young people who were widowed or had lost siblings or significant others. Finally, she found a group of people of her own age who could relate to her, and she began to tell her story in an empathic, supportive environment. "I no longer feel like I'm a freak," she said. "I looked at the men and women in that room and realized that every person has baggage. Everyone has some trauma or some deep dark secret that they're living with. I'm not alone." Within a year, Shayna was ready to continue on the path she had set for herself prior to the death. She applied to graduate schools, was accepted, and the following year moved to New York.

Discussion Questions

1. What symptoms of grief did Shayna exhibit?
2. What facts surrounding the death of her fiancé made recovery more difficult?
3. What other questions would you ask about Shayna's life to help in your clinical decision making?
4. What type of treatment would you recommend?
5. With a peer as a client in this situation, role-play implementation of the task model of crisis management and intervention presented in Table 1.1.

THINK ABOUT IT 5.3

Think about your own history of loss and grief. Grief counseling is not the place for counselors to work out their own unresolved grief issues, and those who find themselves in acute grief should first seek their own counseling before trying to help others. People who have worked through their own grief successfully can be instrumental in helping others work through their grief. Think back on your earliest experience with death. How old were you? How did you feel? What helped you to cope with the loss? Now think of a more recent loss you experienced. Again, what coping skills did you develop? Look into your future. What do you expect will be the most difficult death for you to accept? How will you cope? What thoughts arise when you think about your own death?

Counseling the Crisis Counselor

Working with grieving clients can raise some of our own issues surrounding grief, loss, and mortality. To avoid secondary (vicarious) traumatization or compassion fatigue, counselors learn to establish healthy boundaries, seek supervision, and recognize transference (Renzenbrink, 2011). Appropriate self-care is particularly important for crisis counselors (see Chapter 14).

When working with grieving clients, Worden (2009) warns against cutting counseling short because of the counselor's own frustration or anger. He offers that nothing is more frustrating for a crisis counselor than not being able to help a client, and yet, in the case of the death of a loved one, there is nothing a counselor can do. Participating in a client's grieving process has a profound effect on crisis counselors, who must make sure that their own issues do not get in the way. Worden is particularly concerned about three areas that might affect a crisis counselor's ability to be helpful: (1) counselors who have had a similar loss that they have not worked through, (2) counselors working with a client's loss when they fear a similar loss of their own (such as the death of a parent or child), and (3) existential fears resulting from the counselor's failure to come to terms with their own mortality. The last issue can be addressed if counselors are willing to explore their own history of loss and fine-tune their death awareness.

Clinicians working with dying patients frequently have difficulty with one or more types of death. Perhaps one of the most important traits for crisis counselors to possess is knowledge of their own limitations and recognition of their own unresolved issues. By recognizing that not every counselor can work with every issue, they are better prepared to help those they can help and provide appropriate referrals for those they cannot. Counselors who do grief work or who work with dying clients should (1) recognize their own limitations and accept these limitations with compassion and

ACTIVITY 5.4

It has been said that we all come into the world in the same way, but the way we die is different for everyone. Think about all that you have read in this chapter related to death and dying. What experiences have you had with grieving families or people who are facing their own deaths? Which of the experiences that you have read about here would be the most difficult for you? Which would be easier? How could you best educate yourself in preparation for addressing future clients' needs surrounding issues of death and dying that might arise in the course of your professional work?

without judgment, (2) work to prevent burnout by practicing mindfulness meditation and active grieving, and (3) know how to ask for help, seeking supervision when necessary (Halifax, 2011; Renzenbrink, 2011; Worden, 2009). Working in pairs, when possible, can help relieve some of the stress.

EFFECTIVE DEATH NOTIFICATIONS

Historically, crisis counselors seldom acted as first responders in the death notification process, although in their personal lives, death notifications were inevitable. Often when the notification is for someone personal, all the counseling skills one has learned and practiced may not be as effective as one would expect. In a professional role, counselors traditionally have become involved with clients after a death notification to assist individuals in dealing with the grieving and healing process. In crisis intervention, it is likely that a crisis counselor will intervene when the death of a loved one causes so much stress to the surviving significant other that it affects the person's normal daily functioning and, in some cases, increases suicide lethality. It is also possible in every crisis situation outlined in this text that a counselor may be called to give a death notification or provide support for someone who is the primary death notifier. As counselor roles and job opportunities in the community become more diverse (e.g., in police departments, fire departments, military settings, religious settings, chaplaincies, crisis centers, hospitals, and other agencies such as Red Cross, Green Cross, and Hospice), the likelihood of participating in a death notification increases. With the increase of counselors working with first responders during recent national crises (e.g., Hurricane Katrina, Hurricane Isabel, terrorist attacks on September 11, 2001), counselors have been placed in the role of giving or being part of giving death notifications more frequently.

Even if a counselor intends to work in a private practice, it is not impossible to be asked to assist with a death notification or to be consulted about how to tell another family member about a death. No two death notifications are ever the same due to the actual event, unique relationships, ecological determinants, and the developmental level of and perception of the death by the survivor. However, the level of preparedness of the crisis counselor in the notification process may affect the initial situation of the notification, how a survivor responds during the crisis state, and whether a person seeks professional counseling in the future.

Although no crisis counselor who provides a death notification can ever be fully prepared for the response of the person receiving the notification, several components form the foundation for an effective death notification. As outlined in the training protocol for the Maryland State Police (Jackson-Cherry, 2009; Kanable, 2010; Page, 2008), but adapted for the training of crisis counselors for this section, death notifications should be provided in person and in pairs, in an appropriate time frame with accurate information, in plain language, and with compassion. In preparation, complete Activity 5.5 and Think About It 5.4.

In Person and in Pairs

Whenever possible, death notifications should be made in person, not by telephone. The human presence during the notification of the death of a loved one is essential. The presence of a crisis counselor can be crucial if the survivor has a reaction that

ACTIVITY 5.5

Take a few minutes and reflect upon a time when you were notified of a death. Who died? Who provided the death notification? What were the circumstances? How was the death relayed to you? What were some of your initial feelings or thoughts? What kind of influence did the actual process of the death notification have on you? What made the notification process helpful? What could have made the death notification process better?

requires assessment of self-risk or the need for immediate medical attention. Crisis counselors can assist clients during the initial shock, which may be devastating and demobilizing and may interrupt intact normal thought processes. Counselors can also help the survivor formulate a plan for informing others close to the deceased. It is helpful to work in pairs in case questions need to be answered, multiple survivors are present with various needs (age and developmental appropriateness), and as a safety precaution for the notifying team members. If possible, when there are children in the same room, take the specified adults into a private area to notify them of the death. It would be helpful for the crisis worker to have information on hand to share with those receiving the notification on the grieving process and developmental grieving of children.

Team members may be a combination of law enforcement officers, chaplains, professional counselors, pastoral counselors, medical staff, clergy, school counselors, case managers, other family members, or friends of the victim. For example, in homicide or suicide cases, the team ordinarily would consist of law enforcement and possibly a clergy member, and/or a professional counselor. Many crisis response teams work in collaboration with law enforcement agencies and in these situations, members of the crisis team may be called on to be present at the notification. In a hospital setting, the team may consist of a medical doctor, nurse, chaplain, professional counselor, and a social worker. In a school setting, the team may consist of the school counselor, administrator, and teachers. In the military, depending on the branch of service, the team would consist of a Casualty Assistance Officer (CAO) and possibly a chaplain. If the family is living on the military installation, a professional from the family support center may also be involved in the notification. Depending on the setting and circumstances of the death in each example, outside professional counselors may be included to assist with any crisis situation or death notification.

In our society, family members do not always live in the same community or even in the same state as one another, which makes the process of the death notification being done "in person" often impossible. Depending on the setting, crisis counselors may not be able to offer an "in person" notification. In these circumstances, contact can

THINK ABOUT IT 5.4

Think about your own personal losses and where you are in the grief process. If you were called on to issue a death notification or act as a support counselor in the death notification process, could you be present for the bereaved and provide the necessary support for his or her loss?

be made with a medical examiner, law enforcement department, religious clergy, or friend or family member in the survivor's home area to deliver the notification in person to the next of kin. In other cases, these persons may be called to act as a physical support while the notification is done by phone.

In Time and with Accurate Information

Timeliness of a death notification is essential so that a person is informed in person by the appropriate individual rather than by hearing it from outside persons. At the same time, it is imperative to first verify the accuracy of the information to be sure that the correct information regarding the correct person is being given to a survivor. This must be done in a short amount of time, given the nature of the event. For example, in law enforcement cases it is important that relatives (next of kin) be notified in a timely manner and with accurate information so that relatives do not see or hear the news of the death on the television or radio. When a death occurs on campus or in a school, it is also important for those closest to the deceased to be notified initially. In these instances, it would be preferable for administrators, crisis counselors, and faculty to receive the information first so as to prioritize who should be notified (e.g., team members, classmates, close friends) and in what manner (e.g., small groups, team players, homerooms, LISTSERVs). This also allows for those giving the notifications to be able to assess whether more intervention is needed for some individuals. Prior to any event, agencies and school settings should designate a contact person or alternate person who will be responsible for collecting and dispensing information. Even if a team is formed to gather information, only one person should be designated as the communicator so that differing accounts or information are not relayed. Inaccurate or differing information from several sources could cause confusion, chaos, or panic.

Accuracy of the information does not necessarily mean a crisis counselor has to have the full details, as this depends on the situation. For example, the sudden and tragic death of one of our graduate students was reported by a student to faculty the morning following the incident. Although essential to provide information in a timely manner, it would have been premature to inform other students without receiving confirmation of the student's death from the family member or another firsthand source. At the same time, it was not as crucial to have the details of the circumstances (e.g., drunk-driving case) as it was to confirm and provide accurate information as to the identity of the student so that we could formulate a response to the students. For other situations, more detailed information may be needed at the time of the death notification.

It is essential to make an accurate notification. Mistaken death notifications may cause undue trauma and in some cases have caused medical complications for the person being informed. Before the notification, move quickly to gather information by contacting family members for confirmation and to issue condolences. Be sure that the victim's identity has been confirmed. (Read Voices from the Field 5.4.) If administrators need to report the death via electronic communications, be sure the entire name of the deceased has been verified (first names alone are not sufficient) so as not to cause any further chaos or generate rumors. For example, in the above situation, all the students could not be contacted individually, although faculty advised

VOICES FROM THE FIELD 5.4
Learning from Mistakes

Lisa R. Jackson-Cherry

In working with a police department counseling center during an internship experience, I was asked to ride along on my first death notification to provide added support. A briefing was conducted with the team as we traveled to a small rural town. When we reached our destination, the team leader knocked on the front door, which was opened by an elderly woman. After the leader introduced us, he asked the woman if she was Mrs. Smith. "Yes," she replied. The leader continued, "I'm sorry to be the one to inform you that there was a car accident and your husband, Bill, was killed. He did not survive his injuries." She appeared visibly shocked and started to sob uncontrollably. As we sat down to continue to talk, another woman came running from the adjacent yard. The leader turned to the woman and said, "Would you be willing to stay with Mrs. Smith until we can contact her family? Her husband, Bill, was in a car accident and died." This woman also began shaking and sobbing and said, "This is my mother-in-law. I'm also Mrs. Smith and Bill is my husband. My husband, Bill, is her son." At this time, we knew we had the correct family but the next of kin we were informing was not the correct person.

In all of our preparation, we did not go over the unique issues that we may encounter in a small rural town. In this case, most of the family members lived on the same street, many sharing the same names. In not asking for the complete name of the woman we were notifying and asking the relation of Bill to her, we not only gave devastating news of her son's death (not her husband's death) but then gave a less than full and compassionate notification to the actual wife of the deceased. Needless to say, we did follow through with debriefing and put into practice necessary procedures to ensure a mistake like this never happened again. This is one reason why I believe counselors should be prepared to assist with death notifications and why it is imperative to include this information in the text. I think of this family often and wonder about the impact of this notification on them, as it still weighs heavy on my mind over 20 years later.

students in their classes. The student LISTSERV needed to be used. When using a LISTSERV to provide follow-up on associated events (e.g., services, memorial services), the one person appointed to communicate information should provide frequent updates and give first and last names in all correspondences. It should not be assumed just because previous e-mails were sent out that all previous messages have been read by the receivers. Messages may seem redundant, but accuracy should be consistent. Correspondences with university administration (Vice President for Academic Affairs, President, Dean, Student Services) should be made to ensure university policies are followed. Contact with the Campus Ministry and Counseling Center should be made, and these services should be relayed and made available to students, faculty, and staff in an appropriate time frame. Evaluating the uniqueness of the situation is imperative in order to provide any other interventions. In the university student case, the student was enrolled in a practicum placement. Contact with the on-site supervisor was necessary not only for notification but also to ensure a plan for the deceased student's clients. Furthermore, the religious beliefs of the family needed to be explored and conveyed to the students before their attendance at the funeral service. In this example, flowers were prohibited, and there were specific expectations due to religious beliefs during the service, including prohibiting any outward expressions of emotions that were believed to prevent the passing of the deceased from this world to the next. In the end, students needed an extra debriefing with faculty after the service to work through their unexpressed grief.

In Plain Language

It is important that the death notification be given to the survivor in a calm, direct, and simple manner by the crisis counselor. Too much or vague information can cause survivors to panic before getting the full, accurate information. A crisis counselor can demonstrate care by stating the notification in clear and concise language. For example, "I have some very bad news to tell you" or a similar statement allows a brief but crucial moment for the survivor to prepare for the shock. The follow-up statement should also be provided in plain language, such as "Your daughter, Jill, was in a car crash and she was killed." It is important to avoid vague statements such as, Jill was "lost," "hurt," or "passed away." It is important to include a definitive conclusion of what occurred such as " . . . and she was killed" or " . . . there were no survivors" to prevent conveying a message of false hope of survival. It is important to refer to the victim by name to provide another level of verification and also to personalize the deceased.

One of the most important gifts a crisis counselor can offer to a survivor is the gift of the crisis counselor's control and calmness during the death notification. Over-emotional crisis counselors can increase the potential for panic or chaos. Survivors often have many questions, and some questions may be asked multiple times. As with a child's experience with a death notification, survivors will often repeat the same question for verification of facts. It is crucial to patiently answer questions about the circumstances regarding the death that a crisis counselor may be privy to, such as the location of the deceased's body, how the deceased's body will be released and transported to a funeral home, and whether an autopsy will be performed. However, the sharing of this information should always take into consideration the developmental stage and clinical assessment of how much can be handled by the survivor at the time of the notification. Oftentimes, crisis counselors may not know the answer to a question, and it is better for them to acknowledge this to survivors than to give false information. It is important for crisis counselors to state that they will attempt to find the answers to the questions they cannot answer. If there are questions they have offered to explore, it is imperative that they follow up directly with the survivor, even if another agency or office will be contacting the survivor to provide the information.

With Compassion

Presence and compassion may be the only resources crisis counselors can provide during the initial death notification process. It is important for them to accept the survivor's reactions and emotions to the death notification, and also important to recognize their own emotions associated with the notification. Although overemotional crisis counselors can increase confusion and possible panic with survivors, it is better for a crisis counselor to express appropriate emotion than to appear cold and unfeeling. It is important to relay to survivors that death is a personal event and that due to the unique situation, they may feel various emotions, including sadness, anger, frustration, relief, and guilt. Normalizing the vast array of emotions survivors may experience during the grief process is important. Print resources that reveal the grieving process, reactions to grief, explaining death to a child (if appropriate), and referrals for mental health counseling or a funeral home may be helpful and can be left with the victim. Imposing personal religious beliefs is not helpful and could be harmful. Statements such as, "This was God's will," "She led a full life," and "I understand what you are going through" do not demonstrate compassion or regard for the person's unique grief experiences associated with loss.

It is essential to take time to provide information, support, and direction to the survivor. Never simply provide a death notification and leave. It is important to offer information about funeral planning, normal grief process, and referrals for counseling. The bereaved may not be ready for counseling at that moment, but may be in need of counseling in the near future. Also, it is not recommended that the crisis team provide the survivor with the victim's personal belongings during the death notification. Survivors often need time before accepting the victim's belongings, but eventually survivors will want to take possession of those belongings. Likewise, crisis counselors should never transport survivors (to the hospital or home or to other agencies) unless law enforcement is a part of the notification team. No one can ever truly predict the emotional reaction to the death of a loved one, and the safety of the crisis counselor is always a priority.

Follow-Up

Crisis counselors should always leave their names and phone numbers with survivors, or information on a referring counselor, and a follow-up contact with the survivor should be scheduled for the following day, since most funeral arrangements must be made soon after the death. Some individuals, depending on their social support system, may request assistance from team members for funeral arrangements. If a crisis counselor is asked by the survivor to help with these plans, it is imperative to assist the survivor based on the customs, traditions, religious beliefs, and personal preferences of the family. Most survivors are confused at the initial notification, and others may feel abandoned after the notification. Many survivors will want clarifications or may need more direction on necessary arrangements.

Following up is an important last step in completing the death notification process and may be a crucial factor enabling a survivor to reach out for continued mental health services. Often, counseling services are necessary for clients to work through the extended or complicated grieving process. A death notification event may be the first exposure a survivor has to a mental health professional, so the interaction could encourage or discourage further connections with crisis counselors. The members of the notification team should be clear with one another on any follow-up assignments.

Debriefing with Team Members

Debriefing with team members should occur immediately after the death notification. This debriefing time should be used to plan for any follow-up with the survivors and to review how the death notification process was implemented and received. Processing what went well and what could be improved upon will be helpful for future death notifications. In addition, death notifications can be stressful and emotionally draining to the individuals involved in the notification process. Team members should share concerns with one another. It is important to discuss feelings or thoughts associated with the death notifications that may have triggered personal unresolved grief issues. Taking care of oneself is essential when taking care of another person's initial grief. The stages of grief and loss can certainly take place among crisis counselors. When debriefing, it is important to take into consideration that crisis counselors experience grief and should be encouraged to process that grief. As a final activity, choose either Case A or Case B in Activity 5.6 and prepare a death notification strategy as an individual, in small groups, or as a class. Substantial modifications are often needed in schools and universities because the losses are more likely to stem from suicide, accidental death, or death of a teacher or other staff. Also read Voices from the Field 5.5.

ACTIVITY 5.6

Case A: Death Notification in a Community Setting

You are part of a crisis team that has been called to give a death notification to the next of kin for a person who was killed during a random shooting. You are not sure how the person was involved in or became a victim of the shooting. Work with your team to plan what needs to be addressed and then role-play a death notification to the family.

Case B: Death Notification in a School Setting

The principal of your high school contacts you in the morning and states that there was a phone message left the night before that a Grade 9 student (John) was killed in an automobile accident. As a school counselor and a member of the crisis response team for the school, work with your team and decide what needs to be addressed in this process and to whom notifications will be made.

VOICES FROM THE FIELD 5.5
A Death Notification in Elementary School

Maegan Vick

It was after school during a faculty meeting when the police showed up. Most of the staff was already in the meeting. I just happened to be in my office, about to head that way, when I got called to the front office. When I walked in, I noticed Eric, one of our Grade 1 students, who had suffered a traumatic brain injury when he was a toddler. Eric was still waiting with his teacher for his father to pick him up in the front office. I said hello to Eric and then noticed a police officer in the corner speaking with the secretary. The police officer introduced himself and walked with me to my office without saying a word. I knew something was terribly amiss. The police officer sat down with me and said Eric's father had been killed in a car accident on the way to pick him up from school that day. This was especially tragic because Eric's mother had been killed in a car accident when Eric was a toddler. Eric was in the car with his mother during that fatal car accident and that was how Eric got traumatic brain injury. Now, with both parents deceased, Eric was all alone.

Eric's teacher, Ms. Smith, waited anxiously in the front office after she saw the police officer walk with me to my office. As we returned, I watched her glistening eyes search my face for any indication of what was happening. When my eyes met hers, it was as if she already knew her fear had come true. While Eric waited in the office with the secretary, I pulled his teacher to the hallway where we could be alone. "I'm sorry to have to tell you this," I said to her, "but Eric's father's was killed in a car accident on the way to pick him up today." Ms. Smith sank to the floor with a muffled scream, "No, no, no! It's just not fair . . . his mother was killed this way . . . I just . . ." There were not any words that could comfort her at this moment. All I could do is tell her we would take care of Eric. During the next couple of hours, we tried to contact Eric's closest relative, his uncle Matt.

The following day Eric's uncle, Matt, came to meet with me. He wasn't sure how to tell Eric about his father. It's hard enough for any first grader to understand that his mother and father are both dead, much less a child with traumatic brain injury. I encouraged

(continued)

Eric's uncle to be as honest and as concrete as possible. He asked me if we could tell Eric together. We did.

"Daddy will not be coming home. He died. His heart stopped beating. His eyes will not open. Daddy loved you, but he will not be back."

"Eric bad?" Eric asked. "Daddy mad?"

"No, you were not bad," I said, "You are a good boy. Daddy died. He cannot come back. He loved you very much. You'll go home with Uncle Matt, Jayne, and Ally."

Only the slightest sign of revelation appeared on Eric's face. "I go home with Jayne and Ally?"

We then read a short children's story about "Elmo remembering his daddy." I gave this book to Eric's uncle so that Eric could read it at their house. Eric's uncle called a few days later asking if Eric should attend the funeral. I encouraged him to make a decision with which he felt comfortable. Some believe that allowing a young child to attend a funeral can help provide closure. Uncle Matt took Eric to the funeral.

In the end, Eric adjusted well to his new home and new school. His uncle grew more confident with his ability to help Eric grieve and understand. Our school learned to cope with a tragedy. I will always remember Eric.

Summary

This chapter on grief, loss, and bereavement reviewed several different psychological theories of grief, including Freud's original drive theory, Kübler-Ross's groundbreaking work on death and dying, and the task model put forth by Worden. The importance of attachment across the life span was discussed in relation to the work of Bowlby on the role of attachment and loss. More recently, Walsh proposed a family systems perspective to understand how a family member's death affects the entire family. Fowler's faith development theory and the FICA spiritual assessment tool were introduced as means to explore the role of spirituality, religion, and faith in the client's life.

We are all born the same way, but each of us dies differently. Death can come peacefully at the end of a life well lived, or it can be untimely, traumatic, or life-changing for the bereaved. As in the case of infertility, Alzheimer's, or missing persons, loss can also be ambiguous. It is not possible in this space to create specific interventions for every possible grief experience. Rather, the goal is to help professionals learn about grief and bereavement, be able to identify the nuances differentiating normal from complicated grief, and understand and address any continuing issues of their own concerning death and dying.

Type of relationship, attachment, cause of death, and timing are unique to each situation and require individually tailored counseling responses. Professionals who work with crisis intervention, and particularly death and dying, would do well to follow basic communication skills: to be fully present and responsive to the needs of the bereaved, to be open to familial and cultural adaptations to loss, to encourage and foster strength and resilience, and to take into account any spiritual or religious values that the client has. The ultimate goal should be to provide appropriate and timely interventions during times of crisis so that people can experience and process their grief in a healthy manner and not become stuck in patterns that lead to depression, complicated bereavement, or result in more serious pathology. If successful, we will have helped our clients forge a path through their grief and once again find meaning in their lives.

Each person responds differently to a loss. This chapter does not define major and minor losses, as it is truly the perception of the loss for the individual that will determine whether it becomes a crisis. More importantly, counselors should attempt to understand how a loss can affect and cause other losses and how these multiple losses are perceived when developing a crisis plan or offering a referral. The DSM-5 task force cautions against attaching a premature diagnosis to individuals who are experiencing bereavement. The new diagnosis of other specified trauma- and stressor-related disorder (specified by "persistent complex bereavement disorder") is discussed as an alternative for complicated grief and bereavement and previous diagnoses.

Death notifications are often viewed as the least-favored duty for any professional. Notifying someone of a loved one's death can be difficult, not only for the person receiving the news but also for the person providing the death notification. It is always important to be sure that the person providing the death notification is not experiencing personal unresolved grief issues and can provide a sense of calmness and compassion in the notification. Death notifications can be unpredictable, since no one knows how another person may react in receiving such news. Individuals may respond with a continuum of responses—from numbness, excessive sadness, and melancholy to anger. Unknown circumstances may lead a person to project their feelings on to the person providing the notification. It is always important to understand that reactions will differ and to keep your personal safety in mind when providing a death notification.

Although the likelihood of a counselor being involved in providing a death notification has increased over the years due to expanded job responsibilities, research suggests that counselors have little preparedness in this area. Indeed, counselors have been involved in death notification more often in their personal lives, but this does not mean the process they used was effective. Counseling programs offer little to no formal training in this area. Knowing that death is a natural part of the life process, it is an appropriate part of clinical training to include information on providing a death notification. The level of preparedness of the professional counselor in the notification process may affect the reaction and the traumatic impact of the delivery experienced by the survivor, reduce professional burnout, affect the bereavement process, and influence whether a person seeks professional counseling (if needed) in the future.

6 Risk Assessment and Intervention: Suicide and Homicide

Judith Harrington and Charlotte Daughhetee

PREVIEW

Suicide and homicide are viewed as preventable public health problems in both the United States and throughout the world. Deaths caused by suicide and homicide are no longer viewed as atypical. Rather, suicides and homicides have the capability to affect us personally as family members, friends, coworkers, neighbors, members of extended social networks, and even the professional community struggle with the implications of these preventable deaths. Whether intervening before suicide or homicide occurs, as it is occurring, or after it has occurred, mental health counselors play a vital role in society's response to helping those in need with violence-free coping strategies, intervention based on sound practices, or if necessary the best and most productive short-term and long-term response to those left in the aftermath of suicide or homicide. While few expect suicide or homicide to happen to someone they care about, the chance of being closely and personally affected by a suicide or homicide over one's lifetime is no longer distant, if it ever was. The effectiveness of the care given by professional emergency first responders and crisis counselors, as well as the effectiveness of ordinary people responding to their own crises and the crises of those they care about, is improved by background knowledge of current trends in and treatments for suicidal and homicidal impulses and their aftermath. This chapter is explicitly for crisis counselors who wish to learn how to be effective in responding to members of their communities touched by suicide and homicide.

SUICIDE INTERVENTION

The Scope of the Problem

Suicide is a public health problem that all crisis counselors, regardless of setting, must learn to assess and treat because of its prevalence in society. In 2013, the United States lost 41,149 lives to suicide, an increase from recent years to a rate of 13 per 100,000, maintaining its ranking as the 10th leading cause of death across all ages (Centers for Disease Control and Prevention [CDC], 2015d; Drapeau & McIntosh, 2015). Suicide as a cause of death is alarmingly high for many age groups. For children in the United States between the ages of 10 and 14 years, it is the 3rd leading cause of death; for youth aged 15 to 24 years, it is the 2nd leading cause of death. Young adults and middle-aged adults die from suicide at high rates: for adults aged 25 to 34, it is the 2nd leading cause of death; for adults aged 35 to 44, it is the 4th leading cause of death; and for adults aged 45 to 54, it is the 5th leading cause of death (CDC, 2015a). In all age groups, there are more suicides than homicides. Homicide is the 6th leading cause of death for 1 to 4 year olds, 15 to 24 year olds, and 25 to 34 year olds; the 4th leading cause of death for 5 to 9 year olds; and the 5th leading cause of death for 10 to 14 year olds and 35 to 44 year olds (CDC, 2015a). In fact, over the past 60 years, suicide rates have quadrupled for males in the 15- to 24-year-old age category, and they have doubled for females overall. It is estimated that each day approximately 12 youth suicides take place, and for every completed suicide there are between 100 and 200 attempts made. These data suggest that at its lowest rate, 1,200 young people attempt suicide each day (American Association of Suicidology [AAS], 2006b).

Fatalities from self-directed violence are not the only worrisome data. Millions either considered suicide, made a plan, or survived a nonfatal suicide attempt in 2012. That year, 11.5 million individuals considered ending their lives, almost 4.8 million people made a plan to end their lives, and 2.5 million actually made an attempt (National Action Alliance for Suicide Prevention, Suicide Attempt Survivors Task Force, 2014). These troublesome figures indicate that mental health emergencies will engage first responders, crisis interventionists, and counselors on more occasions than they might imagine.

From a statistical standpoint, counselors should know what the terms *incidence, rate,* and *cause of death ranking* mean. *Incidence* is a nominal figure that states literally how many lives were lost to suicide (or any other type of malady). For example, the incidence of suicide in County XYZ was 75 persons. *Rate* is a value explaining data that has been interpreted by leveling a playing field statistically; in other words, if all members of a population (or an age group, gender, or ethnic group) were divided into groups of 100,000, the rate would indicate how many people died per 100,000 people. For example, County XYZ, a very urban and populated county, lost 75 persons to suicide, but its rate of suicide was 10.9 per 100,000, or 10.9. By contrast, County RST, a small, rural, unpopulated county, lost 16 persons to suicide (incidence), but its rate of suicide was 19.7 per 100,000, or 19.7.

Epidemiologists study the causes of death, in part, and track very closely the rates of suicide, as rates provide a more uniform view for analysis. Another example to illustrate this point is that the suicide rate for the elderly, age 65 years and older, is approximately 18 in 100,000, but the incidence is lower here than in other groups because the population number (or size of this group) of elderly persons is smaller. A rate of 18 in 100,000 is considered alarming because it is higher than the national overall rate (i.e., all suicide fatalities in the whole population) of 13 in 100,000, and professionals want to learn why persons in this group (among others) are more prone to die by suicide. Youth have a lower rate of death than the elderly; however, as noted earlier, suicide is ranked as the 2nd leading cause of death among youth, which is also alarming.

Cause of death ranking is often illustrated in chart form listing the 10 highest incidences of deaths per cause (e.g., heart disease, malignancies, respiratory disease, liver disease, unintentional injury). Many special groups have a heightened risk for suicide (e.g., Native Americans; the elderly; persons with life-threatening depression and/or bipolar disorder; victims of bullying; youth; lesbian, gay, bisexual, transgender, queer, questioning, and intersex [LGBTQQI] youth), for whom suicide death rates are higher than the average population, or for whom the cause of death ranking is higher than for most. However, individuals in any demographic group are susceptible to suicidal psychiatric emergencies when certain co-occurring and multiple factors arise. In other words, no matter what demographic or risk group a client may inhabit, *anyone* can become suicidal, at any time for any reason. When in the counselor's office, it is important to regard the client as a one-person sample with his or her unique circumstances and risk factors. Further, while there were over 41,000 suicides in 2013, more than 2.5 million suicide attempts occurred in the same year, sometimes resulting in permanent injury or disabling conditions, and sometimes imperiling a concerned person who tried to prevent the suicide from happening (National Action Alliance for Suicide Prevention, Suicide Attempt Survivors Task Force, 2014).

The suicide rate is at an all-time high both within the United States and throughout the world. According to the World Health Organization (2013), over the past 45 years suicide fatalities have increased by 60%, with suicide attempts occurring more than 20 times more frequently than completed suicides among the general population. Worldwide, the prevention of suicide has not been adequately addressed and remains a taboo topic in many countries. Only a few countries have included prevention of suicide among their priorities, and inaccurate and insufficient reporting remains a problem worldwide. Effective suicide prevention requires input from multiple systems and increased involvement from governments; the professions of mental health, public health, medical health; law enforcement; schools; universities and institutions of learning; the media; and community leaders.

The primary victims of suicide are the deceased; they are persons for whom prevention efforts did not work. The secondary victims are the survivors of suicide loss, frequently suffering from complicated or protracted bereavement. Survivors (of suicide loss) are not to be confused with attempters who have had nonfatal outcomes. Persons who experienced nonfatal self-directed violence are referred to as "attempters" and also as persons of the "lived experience." When examining the vast effects of suicidal fatalities, mental health professionals must be prepared to serve the high numbers of secondary victims, those who survive the suicidal death of a loved one. Conservative estimates are that an average of one in six persons is directly affected by this traumatic form of death. According to a study by Bland (1994), mental health service providers in the United States could potentially serve between 247,000 new secondary victims of suicide if all the survivors of loss presented for counseling and up to 1,100,000 newly identified survivors each year. Bland's study revealed that up to 28 persons were directly impacted for every suicide. Survivors of suicide loss can develop an elevated risk for suicide; more protracted depression, anxiety, and trauma reactions; longer and more complicated grief and bereavement; more demands on medical and mental health services; and greater potential for lost time at work and school. Since bereavement from suicide can remain complicated for many years, imagine these figures multiplied while the bereft persons try to accommodate this loss over 5 or 10 years.

Mental health professionals continue to be undertrained in suicide intervention (Farrow, 2002; Granello & Granello, 2007a; Range et al., 2002). Clinicians experience the assessment and treatment of suicidal clients as one of the most common and most challenging of clinical emergencies, regardless of setting. It is consistently rated by counselors as a highly stressful experience, has a significant emotional impact on the treating clinician, and has become a frequent basis for malpractice suits against counselors over the past 15 years. It is imperative for crisis counselors to strengthen their competency

---

ACTIVITY 6.1

Form a group in which participants stand in two lines facing each other. At the direction of a leader, the participants in line 1 ask their partners in line 2, "Are you having thoughts of suicide?" The members of line 1 should then move to the right (or circle to the other end of the line if they are at the far-right end of the line), and ask the next partner the same question. Continue doing this until all line 1 members have asked everyone in line 2 the same question. Then repeat the activity, but this time, every member of line 2 now asks members in line 1, "Are you having thoughts of suicide?" After the exercise, discuss together as a group the following questions:

• Which role did you prefer: being the person asked or being the person doing the asking? Explain.

• Why do you think it is important to practice asking the question, "Are you having thoughts of suicide?"
• How do you feel about using the word *suicide*, or about looking someone in the eye and asking him or her directly about suicide?
• What are some other equally direct and non-judgmental ways that you could ask about someone's intention to self-injure?
• What has been your experience with suicide, both personally and professionally? Consider what you do and do not know about working with a client in a suicidal crisis or emergency. What more do you need to know before you work with a client who is suicidal?

---

prior to serving suicidal clients, since, due to the high incidence of suicide and suicide attempts, there is little way of avoiding this clinical crisis over the course of one's career (Granello & Granello, 2007b). Complete Activity 6.1, which involves practicing asking another person about suicide ideation.

Prevention, Intervention, and Postvention

Mental health professionals, as a part of providing effective intervention, also invariably grapple with prevention, intervention, and postvention—the three intertwined parts of the mental health profession's responsibility to safeguard clients from unnecessary risk for death from suicide and its protracted aftermath. From a systemic perspective, prevention influences intervention, intervention influences postvention, and postvention influences prevention at both the microlevel (i.e., the individual and direct care levels) and the macrolevel (i.e., the knowledge, research, best practices, and multiple system collaboration levels).

Prevention involves suicide-proofing communities, raising the level of public education and appropriate responding, and collaborating with and equipping other stakeholders such as government leaders, educational institutions, community agencies, faith-based organizations, and groups that serve at-risk populations. The National Action Alliance for Suicide Prevention, in collaboration with other prevention advocacy groups, has launched a promising new initiative referred to as Zero Suicide. (See zerosuicide.sprc.org for more information about this initiative and to access its toolkit and resources.) Prevention also influences counselors to be proactive and to set up early detection procedures for suicide risk. Intervention involves direct service to individuals or families with acute or chronic risk (e.g., low-, moderate-, or high-risk clients) with a strong emphasis on assessment and reassessment, treatment planning, safety planning, means restriction, transition management, and follow-up.

Postvention was once thought to mean exclusively ministering to the needs of those immediately bereaved and traumatized by suicide. In current professional discourse, *postvention* is undergoing revision in its meaning and is thought to encompass a wide range of postventive responses to not only those who are bereaved due to suicide loss but also to those who have attempted (but not completed) suicide (personal communication with G. Murphy, September 22, 2010). Postvention also aims to strengthen the collaborative meta-planning of crisis centers, practitioners, and hospital or clinic emergency departments and the clinical networks that safeguard those who have entered and traverse the mental health system at various points (Cerel & Campbell, 2008; Murphy, 2010). Postvention initiatives are informed by the voices of survivors of loss who speak on behalf of their deceased loved ones and the voices of survivors of nonfatal attempts. The powerful stories of survivors influence mental health prevention advocacy efforts including local, regional, national, and international initiatives with suicide prevention allies and organizations as well as the work of legislators and politicians (Andriessen, 2009).

The American Foundation for Suicide Prevention (AFSP) provides services to survivors of suicide loss, raises public awareness about suicide, supports Survivor Day, offers training and consultation with bereavement support group leaders, and provides resources to survivors of loss and the persons who assist them. The American Association of Suicidology (AAS) and the National Action Alliance for Suicide Prevention are organizations that actively include and support persons of the lived experience (National Action Alliance for Suicide Prevention, Suicide Attempt Survivors Task Force, 2014).

Prevention: Public Education, Competency, and Attitudes

PUBLIC EDUCATION   Public and mental health experts believe that the burden for protecting the public is shared by everyone. Many public awareness and mental health programs have been started by citizens who have been impacted by a personal crisis and had a desire to make a difference for others. This belief has been at the core of many successful health initiatives, such as widespread training among citizens for cardiopulmonary resuscitation (CPR); Mothers Against Drunk Driving (MADD); *F*acial drooping, *A*rm weakness, *S*peech difficulties, and *T*ime (FAST) for detection of possible stroke symptoms; hand-washing during flu epidemics; and car seat safety initiatives. Gatekeeper suicide prevention training is considered one of the top three preventive initiatives related to suicide prevention in addition to physician–patient dialogues that serve as openings for immediate response (Mann et al., 2005). The gatekeeper strategy includes the widespread training of family members, friends, neighbors, teachers, coaches, coworkers, and all concerned persons to recognize and assist when suicide warning signs are exhibited. Mental health professionals and crisis prevention counselors play an essential role in gatekeeper training as change agents, trainers, trainers-of-trainers, and message bearers to the public and institutions that suicide is preventable through recognition of warning signs and empowered "ask the question" skills-building. The gatekeeper strategy aims to enhance an enlightened awareness of risk factors, warning signs, and appropriate response, much like CPR training has saved lives through the help of many "ordinary citizens." The functions of crisis counselors in the prevention arena may include mental health advocacy, social justice advocacy, public awareness campaigns through community events, grant writing, research and development of evidence-based practices for intervention, professional service on suicide prevention boards and foundations, and direct clinical and early detection care with individuals who present with risk.

Counselors can access a plethora of resources in the field of suicidology and through best- and evidence-based practices, can consult with and influence employers, agencies, and school and university administrators in their prevention planning and community response to suicide. The Question-Persuade-Refer (QPR) gatekeeper training program, under the direction of Paul Quinnett (2012) and the QPR Institute, lends itself well to training large groups either in class or online. Another reputable gatekeeper training program, Applied Suicide Intervention Skills Training (ASIST), is available through the Living Works organization. These two organizations can be accessed through their websites at www.qprinstitute.com or www.livingworks.net.

Gould (2010) evaluated and summarized school-based prevention programs, citing four types of evidence-based curricula: (1) awareness/education programs, (2) screening programs, (3) gatekeeper training programs, and (4) peer gatekeeper training programs. For more specific tools on planning prevention strategies within schools, a valuable resource for school counselors and administrators is provided by the University of South Florida (theguide.fmhi.usf.edu/). Visitors to this recognized best-practices site will find a wide range of school-based suicide prevention program designs useful to both counselors and administrators for effective response with prevention, intervention, and postvention. These designs may be adapted by counselors in other agency and clinical settings such as colleges and universities, community agencies, and others.

One often untapped resource for prevention outreach is faith-based organizations. Experts assert that a person's connections to a faith-based community and spiritual convictions provide protective factors, but it is unclear whether appropriate prevention, intervention, and postvention sensitivities are happening from within church cultures. For hundreds of years, suicide has been linked to religious beliefs and codifications (Campbell, 2005; Granello & Granello, 2007a), both as a response to religious persecution, but more often in negative, stigmatizing, and attributive ways, with some church leaders and followers communicating that suicide is a sin, that persons who die from suicide will go to hell, that the suicidal person is not or was not "right with God." Bearers of these types of messages may be unenlightened regarding the epidemiology and causative factors of suicide. While religious or faith group community members are more often a part of the protective response to persons at risk for suicide, perhaps unwittingly, some contribute to risk factors (such as hopelessness, disillusionment that help-seeking works, shame, or social isolation) or create obstacles that impede at-risk persons from obtaining qualified help. It is important to assess a person's faith or spirituality base in the context of protective or risk factors. For example, a woman once reported having frequent suicidal thoughts and also asserted that she "could not do it against God for fear of letting God down." Understanding such deeply held beliefs helps counselors be more sensitive and supportive of clients.

In 2008, the Suicide Prevention Resource Center (SPRC, 2009) convened an interfaith summit on suicide prevention with religious leaders from Judaism, Islam, Hinduism, Buddhism, and Christian denominations (African American Christian Church, the Catholic Church, the Evangelical Lutheran Church, the United Methodist Church, and the Church of Jesus Christ of the Latter Day Saints). A monograph of the proceedings and findings of this summit can be found at www.sprc.org. In short, the common themes that emerged were as follows: all faith groups share a reverence for life; the causes of suicide are multifactorial; critical judgment or shaming can be tempered by compassion; God understands suffering and intent; most suicides can be prevented through a sense of responsibility to each other; suicide is tragic; caring alone may not be enough of a protective factor without other methods of intervention; culturally acceptable language for prevention is needed in faith-based communities; and clergy and other faith-based leaders need intervention training.

COMPETENCY AND ATTITUDES   One of the most important preventive measures that a crisis counselor can take is to become adequately trained in effective suicide response. A counselor can seek training in this area through graduate coursework, seminars, consultation and supervision, intensive field experiences, etc. Those who want to provide safer suicide care might seek training through the SPRC's Assessing and Managing Suicide Risk (AMSR) workshop (SPRC, 2012). AMSR is a thorough and expert-designed best-practices curriculum for professionals in clinical, college and university, and Employee Assistance Program settings. As part of the curriculum, counselors are oriented to 24 core competencies for assessing and working effectively with persons at risk for suicide. AMSR emphasizes proficiencies related to professionals' attitudes and approach; knowledge about suicide; assessment and formulation of risk; documentation; formulation of treatment plans; management of care; and legal and regulatory issues related to suicide.

The AMSR core competencies related to attitudes and approach urge mental health professionals to monitor their own reactions to suicide, resolve the tension between the counselor's goal to prevent suicide and the client's goal to end psychological pain, while maintaining a collaborative working alliance, among other recommendations. All too often, counselors are distracted by their own anxiety, beliefs, and attitudes, and by myths associated with having a suicidal client before them, and for various reasons they are unable or unwilling to conduct a comprehensive assessment that best protects the client. Harrington (2007) and Simon (2004) identified obstacles that may interfere with objective and professional care management, including counselor fear or anger, counselor–client dynamics, problems integrating modern knowledge about suicide (contrasted with being influenced by personal attitudes or beliefs), lack of resources, inadequate assessment, poor treatment planning, inappropriate management of care, and failure to document—all conditions that may impede a clinician's effective performance.

When counselors do not complete periodic self-examinations of their own response to suicide, it is not uncommon for them to negatively attribute the expressed thoughts and behaviors of their suicidal clients as attention seeking rather than as help seeking. Table 6.1, summarized from research by Campbell (2005), reviews the risks when mental health professionals fail to accurately recognize suicidal intent. Outcomes can result in death even when the client did not intend seriously to make a lethal attempt. This is especially true with individuals who may not intend to die but who exhibit risky behaviors, self-injury, and a preoccupation with death. Often, self-injurious clients without intent to die are labeled as attention seekers or drama queens or kings, and their risks go untreated, resulting in their being 40 times more likely to become a suicide attempter whose suicidal behaviors may result in death or permanent injury.

Maris, Berman, and Silverman (2000) itemized 10 errors that interventionists may make when treating persons at risk for suicide: (1) superficial reassurance, (2) avoidance of strong feelings, (3) overprofessionalism, (4) inadequate assessment of suicidal intent, (5) failure to identify the precipitating event, (6) passivity, (7) insufficient

TABLE 6.1 Risk Based on Intent to Die and Survival

	Survival: Client Dies	Survival: Client Lives
Intent: Client Wants to Die	**Suicide** Died by suicide. Possibly a previous or multiple attempter. Likely chose more lethal means.	**Suicide Attempt** Intervention is successful. Ambivalence is present and helping works.
Intent: Client Wants to Live	**Accidental Suicide** An attempt gone awry. Client did not mean to die, but rescue or intervention eluded the victim.	**Nonsuicidal self-directed violence*** So-called attention seeker, or a drama queen or king, or a cry for help. Forty times more likely to die by suicide due to warning signs being ignored or minimized.

*The CDC finds the term *parasuicidal* unacceptable, and thus this term has been replaced with *nonsuicidal self-directed violence* (Crosby, Ortega, & Melanson, 2011).
Source: Adapted from F. Campbell, *Intention style and survival outcome.* Baton Rouge, LA: ASIST Trainers.

directiveness, (8) advice-giving, (9) stereotypical responses, and (10) defensiveness. It is clear that when counselors have done the work necessary to understand and manage their own reactions to the suicidal crisis, they are better prepared to respond with empathy, genuine concern, and positive regard and to use a best-practices and competency-grounded approach to comprehensively assess, intervene, manage, and if necessary, refer (Sethi & Uppal, 2006). It is well understood that the client–counselor therapeutic alliance is a protective factor in the ongoing assessment and care management of a suicidal client's safety; a well-established relationship increases the counselor's ability to obtain information from the client in order to increase treatment options as well as to assist the client through a painful period when other sources of emotional support are limited. As part of its checklist when formulating level of suicide risk, the SPRC's AMSR curriculum (in 2016) includes specific items related to quality of the therapeutic alliance and any transitions with providers during care management.

For current and emerging authenticated practices in the field, counselors are directed to the National Registry of Evidence-based Programs and Practices (Substance Abuse and Mental Health Services Administration [SAMHSA], 2017; SPRC, 2012) and resources from the National Suicide Prevention Lifeline's Standards, Training, and Practices Committee.

Intervention

The window of intervention with an actively suicidal person brings many, even seasoned mental health professionals to the question, "OK, now what do I do?" and "Did I do enough?" There are resources available that offer step-by-step guidelines and well-researched rationale for these responses. Books by Rudd, Joiner, and Rajab (2004), Jobes (2016), Jobes and O'Connor (2016), and Chiles and Strosahl (1995) are but four guides counselors can use for in-depth study. *The Harvard Medical School Guide to Suicide Assessment and Intervention* (Jacobs, 1999) and the *Comprehensive Textbook of Suicidology* (Maris et al., 2000) also provide comprehensive information. SAMHSA regularly produces resources for mental health professionals, including free and downloadable products from its Center for Substance Abuse Treatment such as the Treatment Improvement Protocol (TIP) series. TIP 50 is designed for clinicians and administrators in substance abuse treatment settings and can be obtained at www.sprc.org/search/apachesolr_search/TIP%2050?filters= (Center for Substance Abuse Treatment, 2009).

Frequently, "refresher" and special topic courses and webinars are available through continuing education production companies and through host suicide prevention organizations online.

The rest of this section focuses on assisting counselors who intervene with suicidal clients answer the question, "What do I do now?"

ASSESSMENT   There is no single profile of a suicidal person, and there is no cookie cutter method to formulate a person's level of suicide risk. Intervention begins and continues with effective assessment of suicidal risk. Granello and Granello (2007a) asserted that treatment planning includes assessment and reassessment. The AMSR's 24 core competencies for the assessment and management of individuals at risk for suicide include the following recommendations for clinicians:

- Weave risk assessment into sessions on an ongoing basis.
- Discover risk factors and protective factors.
- Identify if the client exhibits suicide ideation, behavior, or plans for self-directed violence.
- Assess for any warning signs of imminent risk.
- Confer with other collateral persons as needed.
- Formulate a definitive profile of the level of risk (AAS, 2006a).

Formulation of risk (AAS, 2006a; SPRC, 2016a) involves forming an appropriate clinical judgment that a client may attempt or die from suicide imminently or later. The clinician should be able to determine acute (immediate, urgent, emergent, or imminent) or chronic suicidal risk as well as prioritize and integrate these impressions or data into a treatment or care management plan including the development of a safety plan, while factoring in important developmental, cultural, and gender-related data relevant to the client. Clinical judgment by definition is not an "all or nothing" binary approach. There cannot be a 100% or 0% assessment, "yes, the client will or no, the client will not attempt suicide." Factors that the counselor assesses to determine the severity of risk include risk factors, warning signs, contextual history past and present, and protective factors or buffers.

There are two important objectives in assessing for suicidal risk. The profession's standards (AAS, 2006a; National Suicide Prevention Lifeline [NSPL], 2007; SPRC, 2016a) assert that the clinician or interventionist assess for the presence of acute versus chronic risk, and determine whether the risk is considered low, moderate, or high with respect to immediate risk for death or injury, based on the specificity of lethality and availability of intended means, presence of intoxication, chance of intervention, degree of ambivalence, and so forth. In its policy and assessment protocol position statement, the NSPL (2007) recommends that crisis counselors assess for the presence of desire to attempt suicide, capability to attempt, and intent to die. Acute and chronic risk, level of risk, and method of assessment are presented in the sections that follow.

A preamble for conceptualizing acute and chronic risk, alongside level of risk (i.e., low, moderate, or high), is to visualize risk as schematic, and not an "all or nothing" decision. Tables 6.2 and 6.3 present two sets of risk considerations to use when evaluating a client: acute risk versus chronic risk and warning signs versus demographic forecasters. Rather than use these tables as a checklist for client assessment, the counselor is urged to highlight the relevant presentations and note clinical impressions of the client's status. The highest risk is considered as emergent (or emergency), imminent, or acute, and it is possible that an individual's risk has arisen swiftly, perhaps as a result of a recent event, setback, disappointment, or perceived failure (with or without a history of chronic risk). The acutely at-risk individual exhibits behavioral warning signs (enactments of suicidal behaviors) and demonstrates little (or less) ambivalence about dying (wants to die to end the pain) than someone with chronic risk; has a specific plan, method, and timeline; and has chosen a more lethal means. The chronically at-risk individual may be considered to be in crisis or heading to a crisis state; may have struggled with risk factors for a long time or is experiencing transcrisis aftereffects; may be ambivalent about dying and living; or may have risk factors in his or her profile but not yet have a specific plan, method, or timeline to launch an attempt. Acute risk and warning signs are deemed more emergent in nature than chronic risk and demographic forecasters.

To summarize, counselors must remember that there is no one differentiated profile of a typical at-risk individual. Warning signs differentiate a client who may likely be in acute risk, and risk factors may be "markers" for chronic risk with the potential for acute risk later if warning signs are exhibited. Protective factors are mediating conditions that reduce the impact of risk factors. Tables 6.2 and 6.3 provide some distinctions

TABLE 6.2 Acute Risk versus Chronic Risk

	Acute Risk	Chronic Risk
	Survival: Client Dies	**Survival: Client Lives**
Descriptors	Emergent, urgent, imminent, behavioral indicators and warning signs, could lessen and possibly become chronic	More long-running risk, grounded in risk factors, Could be precrisis state, in crisis, or transcrisis, may or may not become acute
Time frame for potential attempt	Hours, 24 hours to perhaps a few days	Days, weeks, months, years
Ambivalence	Little to none. Believes death is the answer to ending the pain	Some to considerable ambivalence, e.g., fifty-fifty wants to live as much as seeking death to end pain
Clinical response	Clinician advised to get help for client immediately, arrange heightened vigilance, not let the client remain alone, provide emergency intervention, use directive style	Clinician advised to monitor risk frequently and regularly, be aware that hospitalization may not be required unless risk becomes acute, develop and maintain therapeutic alliance, perhaps meet more frequently, prepare a safety plan, provide support, help the client develop coping skills, problem-solving skills, life skills
Likely trigger or precipitant*	A sudden or recent event, loss, humiliation, defeat, embarrassment, trapped feeling	Likely to be relationship-based. Risk can rise to acute with a sudden or recent event, loss, humiliation, defeat, etc.

* See Jobes (2016).

TABLE 6.3 Warning Signs versus Demographic Forecasters

	Warning Signs (with Accompanying Risk Factors)	**Demographic Forecasters** ("Markers" for Potential Acute Risk, Few or No Acutely Intent or Behavioral Warning Signs Yet Exhibited)
Likely indicators	Recent loss of relationship	Identity in an at-risk group: Native American, LGBTIQQI, living in a rural setting, ethnicity, Caucasian, age
	Recent defeat, humiliation	
	Ideation, planning	
	Current self-harming	History of attempts
	Recent attempt	Prior ideation
	Excessive alcohol, drugs	History of self-harming
	Recent discharge from hospital	Family history of suicidal behavior
	Psychache	Parental history of violence, substance abuse, hospitalization, divorce
	Anger, aggression, rage	
	Withdrawal	History of trauma or abuse
	Anxiety, panic	History of psychiatric hospitalization, violence, frequent mobility, impulsivity, recklessness
	Agitation	
	Insomnia, nightmares	History of mood diagnosis, anxiety, schizophrenia, eating disorder, etc., Cluster B, Traumatic Brain Injury
	Anhedonia	
	Paranoia	
	Confusion	Low self-esteem, self-hate
	Command hallucinations	Accepting attitude of suicide
	Mood changes	Exposure to suicide
	Hopelessness	Lack of family acceptance of sexual orientation
	Cognitive restriction	
	Substance abuse	Smoking
	Hopelessness	Perfectionism
	Helplessness	Mental illness
	Haplessness	Recent loss, loss of a love
	Overwhelming guilt, shame or self-hate	History of family or friend attempted or died from suicide
	Themes of death	
	Recklessness	Lack of support system
	Behavioral changes	Downward economic mobility
	Altered sleep, altered eating	
	Statements: "ending it all"	
	Threats	
	Researching, rehearsing a method, preparatory actions	
	Attending to important papers	
	Feeling trapped	
	Giving possessions away	

Source: American Association of Suicidology. (2006a). *Assessing and managing suicide risk.* Washington, DC: Author.

to assist assessors in determining risk levels; acute risk factors are contrasted with chronic risk factors, and warning signs are contrasted with demographic potential "predictors" to assist in distinguishing emergent risk (requiring more active intervention) from lower risk (which allows for more client/clinician collaboration).

Triangulation and interrater reliability are concepts in assessment that encourage evaluation via multiple methods and/or multiple reviewers of clinical data to form a more robust or sound conclusion. Multiple forms of assessment may include the clinical interview, symptom checklists, "paper and pencil" validated instruments, repeated assessment over time, collateral interviews with family or friends, consultative review, and multiple specialist evaluations (e.g., with a psychiatrist or another clinician). Clinical judgment based on a variety of assessment strategies is always recommended. Because there is no one type of suicidal client or a one-size-fits-all checklist, clinical judgment is essential to ferret out an accurate understanding of risk.

ACUTE RISK VERSUS CHRONIC RISK   If the crisis counselor begins to suspect that risk factors are present, it is important to learn quickly about how acute or chronic the risk may be. Acute risk means that the individual evidences that he or she may hurt himself or herself in 24 hours or less, stating specificity about a plan, intent, means, and method (Kleespies, 1998). In practice, many clinicians allow for a larger window of time for imminent risk than 24 hours based on the client's stated plans. For example, if a client says "Next Saturday is my 40th birthday, and I'm going end it all on Friday night . . ." which is four days from now, then it would be appropriate to consider this as acute risk and to take appropriate measures.

Jobes (2008) concluded that a stronger correlation existed between acute risk and situations, events, personal defeats, embarrassments, and humiliations that may swiftly tip the scale into emergency, imminent risk, or acute status. Examples of these events might include the breakup of a relationship, getting fired from a job, discovering a betrayal, learning of a foreclosure or a decision to declare bankruptcy, or perceiving one of these setbacks as a huge disappointment or burden to one's family. These events can quickly trigger an acute internal response in someone with suicidal risk factors, so counselors with an acutely at-risk client must be prepared to be more decisive, more directive, and armed with appropriate treatment responses. In summary, acute risk suggests the presence of immediate, imminent, or emergency risk indicated by the intent to die (i.e., to end psychological pain) or to attempt suicide. Acute risk is associated with more formulated specificity about how the client intends to carry out an attempt and generally involves more lethal means.

Jobes (2008) also found that chronic risk is more likely associated with long-term patterns of relationship difficulties such as frequently unsatisfying relationships, conflicts, poor decision-making with respect to friends and partners, and repetitive patterns of difficulties. Risk for suicide with the chronically-at-risk may reveal thoughts of suicide with less specificity, less lethal intent, and greater ambivalence about dying, but instead with more long-running, passive suicidal states of mind reflected in statements such as "What's the point?", "I wish I could make all this go away, it will never get better!", and "If something happened to me, I wouldn't mind." Individuals with chronic risk can be described as having "markers" of potential suicide risk that is not currently imminent. In other words, individuals may present with some identifiers of persons who could become acutely suicidal but are not currently in imminent danger. Just as with other medical diagnoses, the client in your office with a family history of cancer (a risk factor) may or may not ever be stricken with cancer. A person who is chronically in suicide risk may thus have "markers" or risk factors for potential suicide. Chronic risk must be watched closely for the possible emergence of active or acute risk. A few of these chronic "markers" might include the following:

- demographic status in line with certain known risk groups,
- diagnoses including but not limited to mood disorders (depression or bipolar disorder), anxiety, eating disorder, thought disorder, substance abuse/dependency, or some personality disorders,
- a history of trauma, abuse, violence, self-injury, previous hospitalizations, low self-esteem, high self-hate, tolerance and acceptance toward suicide, oppression related to sexual orientation, perfectionism, divorced parents, a family history of suicide attempts or fatalities, and other factors.

It is important to note that someone with chronic risk can become acutely suicidal, and acutely suicidal persons could potentially ease into long-term chronic risk status. But Jobes (2008) found that acutely risk-prone persons responded better to intervention, problem-solving skills, and effective techniques for resolution of suicide risk with the prospect of long-term successful risk reduction than did chronically at-risk persons. An excellent resource itemizing acute versus chronic risk factors can be found at the AAS website (www.suicidology.org) or at the Alabama Suicide Prevention and Resources Coalition (ASPARC) Comprehensive Suicide Prevention Resource Directory (www.legacy.montevallo.edu/asparc). Counselors are urged to download the comprehensive checklists available at the website and use them in ongoing direct assessment for the formulation of risk process.

In summary, chronic risk suggests the presence of longer term potential of suicidality, but with less specificity of intent or plans (e.g., means, methods) to carry out an attempt presently. The counselor has more time to help the client mitigate, manage, or resolve his or her psychological pain (and his or her need to end the pain), can be less directive, and may not resort to immediate protection such as hospitalization as a treatment strategy. The counselor will instead reassess suicidality regularly, manage safety, and attempt to stabilize long-term risk with effective counseling.

Read Voices from the Field 6.1.

VOICES FROM THE FIELD 6.1
Lessons Learned with a Suicidal Client

Gerald Juhnke

Early in my career, and before the advent of cell phones, I worked as a counselor at a large community mental health agency. That is how I met Emily, a 22-year-old single female who had a history of severe depression, hallucinations, and two critical suicidal episodes. Her latest attempt resulted in a 3-week psychiatric hospitalization. Upon her hospital release, Emily was assigned to my client caseload.

During my first meeting with Emily, her case manager, and her psychiatrist, I was struck by the severity of her continued depression. The psychiatrist assured Emily that once her medications achieved a greater therapeutic threshold, she would be feeling better. Together the case manager, psychiatrist, and I helped Emily create a thorough safety plan. She agreed to contact the 24-hour crisis number or page me if she experienced suicidal ideation or her auditory or visual hallucinations returned.

(continued)

Although I voiced concerns to the psychiatrist and hospital supervisor regarding Emily's release, I was assured Emily was not deemed an imminent threat to herself and reminded of the hospital's "least restrictive environment" policy. Upon returning to my home agency, I informed my direct supervisor, a man of great compassion and significant clinical experience, of my concerns. Despite existing agency policy that inhibited clients from counseling more than one time per week, he encouraged me to schedule daily sessions with Emily until I felt she was safe. Some 20 years later, I know his decision saved Emily's life.

Our first two sessions were unremarkable. Emily reported that she preferred being home rather than in the hospital, and she denied suicidal ideation or hallucinations. However, during our third session, it was evident Emily had further decompensated. When pressed, Emily reluctantly discussed the inner voices that ceaselessly called her name and demanded she kill others and herself. When I asked a scaling question regarding suicidal intent, Emily quickly stood, opened the counseling room door, and ran out of the building.

When I exited the building, Emily was about a half block ahead of me. I immediately ran after her. When I finally got relatively close, she ran into oncoming traffic. The cars slammed their brakes and tires squealed as they avoided hitting her. She turned and ran down an alley into a neighborhood. As we ran past a man on the front porch of a home, Emily pointed at me and screamed, "Help me! He's trying to kill me." The man yelled back, "Stop chasing her or I'll call the police!" I turned and cried, "Call the police. I need help!" The man grabbed a rake and pursued me. However, he quickly became winded and stopped chasing me. A few minutes later, Emily ran inside an old house. I heard her scream, "Daddy! A man's trying to kill me!" I stood in the driveway of the house near the sidewalk, fearing that Emily's family members would come out with shotguns and shoot me.

I panicked when the door to the house flung open and a woman came running out. The woman looked at me and said, "Some crazy person just broke into my house!"

Minutes later, I heard a police car siren. I stepped onto the street and frantically waved my arms hoping the officer would stop. The police officer saw me and immediately slammed on the car's brakes. I knew the crisis was over. The police could pull my client from the house and restrain her until we could talk to my clinical supervisor and determine what to do.

The next thing I knew, the patrol officer tackled me and handcuffed my hands behind my back. As I attempted to explain the situation, he jammed me in to the back seat of the patrol car. He then spoke to the woman who had been standing next to me, and he disappeared into the house. When he emerged, he had Emily. She resisted arrest and immediately was handcuffed. He then opened the police car's rear door and shoved her into the seat next to me. Once things were sorted out, he drove both Emily and me back to the agency, where she was reevaluated and rehospitalized.

As an inexperienced counselor, I learned much from these events. First, I learned to pay closer attention to my gut feelings and never simply accept the dismissive decisions of mental health professionals. Now when I believe a client should remain hospitalized, I strongly advocate on his or her behalf. Second, I learned the importance of being a compassionate supervisor who truly listens to supervisees. Despite the many cases my supervisor had, he made time to listen. He heard my concerns and responded accordingly. Had he not broken agency policy and ensured Emily receive daily counseling sessions, Emily likely would have committed suicide before our next weekly session. Finally, I learned never to chase a client. I potentially placed my client, others, and myself in danger by chasing her. Instead, I contact police and allow them to use their training and experience.

LEVEL OF RISK: LOW, MODERATE, OR HIGH   Table 6.4 presents a sample risk assessment guide from the Crisis Center, an AAS-accredited crisis center that has been serving clients since 1970. The guide reflects the telephone and distance counseling tools used by many crisis centers to assess the level of suicidal risk of suicidal callers. Variations of this guide are also used by law enforcement "hostage negotiators" or crisis response teams (Texas Association of Hostage Negotiators, 2003).

TABLE 6.4 A Suicide Assessment Form - Checklist for Assessing Emergency Risk for Suicide

Indicators/Risk Levels	Very low risk	Mild/low risk	Moderate risk	Severe/high risk	Extremely high risk
Method(s) Considered	Vague, no plan	Pills, slash wrist	Drugs, alcohol, car wreck, some specifics	Gun, hanging, jumping; some specifics	In progress; gun, hanging, jumping; very specific knows how, when, where
Suicidal Plans	None	None	Some but no clear intent.	Developed plan with considerable detail.	Well thought out, lethal plans.
Availability of Means	No plan; no availability of means	Not available-will have to get	Available but not close by	Available-has close by	Has in hand or in progress
Suicidal Behavior	None	Ideation	Threat	Attempt low lethal	Attempt high lethal
When attempt is planned	No attempt planned	48 hours or more	24 to 48 hours	24 to 18 hours	Presently (In progress) or within 24 hours
Previous suicide attempt(s)	None	None	Yes (One to Five Years ago)	Yes (Three months to one Year ago)	Yes (Three months ago or less)
Feelings of Loneliness	Hardly ever	Sometimes; support system present	Usually; some support system	Always; limited support system	Always; No support system
Hope/Level of Ambivalence	Hopeful; Readily acknowledges desire to live	Some hope, aware of some desire to live	Hope and some desire to live present, but inconsistent or limited.	Little or no hope for future; does acknowledge some ambivalence	No hope. Does not consciously acknowledge any ambivalence
Intoxication (Use of alcohol or drugs)	Has not been drinking or using drugs	Limited use of alcohol	Limited use of alcohol or drugs; past history of substance abuse treatment	Intoxicated; mixing drugs and alcohol	Mixing drugs and alcohol and evidence of intoxication
Chance of Intervention	Others present	Others expected	Others expected or available	Others available	No one nearby; isolated

Source: Permission granted by the Crisis Center, Birmingham, Alabama.

In addition, the NSPL (2007) recommends following a rubric of assessing risk based on the individual's desire, capability to attempt, and intent to die or attempt suicide. Desire, as it relates to suicidal risk, is indicated by desire to harm self or others; psychological pain such as hopelessness, helplessness, or feeling trapped; and perceiving oneself to be a burden on others.

Suicidal capability is evidenced by

- a past history of suicide attempts, exposure to someone else's death by suicide,
- a history of or even current violent behaviors toward oneself or others,
- having the means to hurt oneself or others,
- current intoxication or substance abuse,
- recent dramatic mood changes or loss of orientation to reality, and
- extreme agitation, rage, increased anxiety, decreased sleep, and recent acts or threats of aggression.

Suicidal intent is reflected by

- an attempt in progress,
- a plan with a known method to hurt oneself or others,
- preparatory behaviors (e.g., giving away possessions, finalizing one's business affairs, saying goodbye [perhaps cryptically], counting pills, reading up on how to use the method, loading and reloading the gun, rehearsing the method), and stated intent to die.

The concept of desire to die by suicide is grounded in the original works of Beck, Joiner, and numerous experts (NSPL, 2007) with influences such as no reasons for living, wishing to die, and not caring if death occurred. It is important to credit leading researchers, such as Joiner (2005) and Rudd (2006), whose work figured significantly in the NSPL recommendations for suicide risk assessment (NSPL, 2007).

Suicide desire alone does not fully explain an individual's risk level; the counselor must further examine the client's evidence of "capability" and intent to attempt suicide. Capability, in suicidological terms, is characterized by a sense of fearlessness to attempt, a sense of "competence" or capacity to attempt, and having specificity and means available by which to launch the plan to die or to attempt suicide. Joiner (2005) and Rudd et al. (2004) cited major factors that are contributory or definitive of suicide capability: history of attempt(s) and/or of violence, exposure to a suicidal death, availability of means, current intoxication or tendency toward frequent intoxication, acute or severe symptoms of mental illness (e.g., psychological pain, agitation, insomnia, loss of reality), recent and significant mood changes, extreme rage or increased agitation, and sleep deprivation. Joiner found that both suicidal desire and suicidal capability are of concern, but that suicidal capability is of greater concern.

Within this risk assessment model using the desire, capability, and intent constructs, suicidal intent is considered the most important because those with suicidal intent often engage in suicidal behavior. Neither desire nor capability predicted active behaviors toward seeking death as strongly as intent, as demonstrated through research with actual suicidal callers to crisis centers (Kalafat, Gould, & Munfakh, 2005). Strong intent to die indicates low ambivalence about dying; for example, a high wish for death leads to low reasons for living, which leads to a more lethal method selected. Alternatively, intent to die coupled with higher levels of ambivalence may allow for the exploration of reasons for living, and the client may present with attempt plans or means that are less lethal. The recommendations issued by the NSPL (2007) include the concept of *buffers*, which are similar to protective factors that may modulate risk. These may include (1) immediate supports, (2) social supports, (3) plans for the future, (4) engagement (or therapeutic alliance) with the helper, (5) ambivalence for living (partly wanting to live and partly wanting to die or end the pain of living), (6) core values and beliefs, and (7) a sense of purpose. Counselors who explore indicators of suicidal risk with a client may form clinical impressions based on the NSPL risk assessment recommendations, which urge clinicians to ask, during one session, three questions in this way:

1. Are you thinking of suicide?
2. Have you thought about suicide in the last two months? (This question further explores recent ideation even if current ideation [today] is not present.)
3. Have you ever attempted to kill yourself? (Prior attempts are considered very high as a risk factor and can be considered a reason to seek consultation immediately about the case.)

See Case Study 6.1, which asks you to assess the type and level of risk, risk factors, warning signs, protective factors, and demographically relevant information for clients who are at risk for suicide. Read Voices from the Field 6.2.

CASE STUDY 6.1

Potentially Suicidal Cases

After reading the following brief cases describing potentially suicidal cases, indicate whether you believe the suicidal risk is acute or chronic and low, moderate, or high risk. Also indicate the warning signs, protective factors, and demographically relevant information.

Case A

Kelson is a 22-year-old White male infantryman who has just spent 27 months in the Middle East. He is headed home for an extended furlough, and he does not understand why he is fidgety and agitated on the 18-hour plane trip home. When he arrives home, he learns that his girlfriend from before he went on active duty is now involved with one of his high school buddies, which he found out about from another friend while running an errand. In addition, his dad has remarried a woman whom Kelson has not met before. The marriage occurred nearly two years ago when he had been deployed for just four months. His new stepmother has moved into the house where Kelson used to live before deployment. His younger brother, in the meantime, graduated from high school and is now in college two states away from home. Kelson goes on a drinking binge the first night he is home and gets into a scuffle at the bar. As a soldier, he knows how to use firearms.

     ❏ Acute risk *or* ❏ Chronic risk

     ❏ Low risk ❏ Moderate risk ❏ High risk

     Risk factors: _____

     Warning signs: _____

     Protective factors: _____

     Demographically relevant information: _____

Case B

Devon is an African American college student who has learned to cope by "doing more." If having one part-time job is good, then two part-time jobs are better. She is prone to getting overinvolved in extracurricular activities, as she thinks that by really overachieving she will be selected for her preferred sorority in college. She has been seeing a counselor because she just cannot seem to focus in class and her grades are not quite good enough to meet the requirements of her desired sorority. Her counselor has asked her if perhaps she is depressed. She was bullied as a teenager by others regarding her appearance and being overweight, and she states that her father also treated her gruffly her entire life. She is bright, attractive, and likeable, but she does not view herself that way. She cannot explain why she is crying all the time, as she believes that she is working as hard as anyone can to "keep it together." She feels that she has put a big strain on her mother and her friends for not "having it together." She has daydreamed about taking a bunch of pills.

❑ Acute risk *or* ❑ Chronic risk

❑ Low risk ❑ Moderate risk ❑ High risk

Risk factors: _____

Warning signs: _____

Protective factors: _____

Demographically relevant information: _____

Case C

Charles is a White male, aged 77 years. During his retirement, he has played a lot of tennis and spent time at his hunting cabin with friends. One of his long-time tennis buddies of over 30 years died suddenly from a heart attack on the tennis court only minutes after Charles had left the club. In addition, Charles's wife has been diagnosed with lymphoma and is undergoing treatments. While she is doing well in spite of the fatigue of the treatments, Charles is very worried about the possibility of her imminent death (before his own), and since his adult children have busy lives and reside in another region, he is primarily the sole caregiver for his wife. Together, they have made a decision to not get out and socialize as much as they had formerly, and they seem to be more socially isolated, except for his occasional tennis matches. On a recent visit to his physician, the doctor became worried and asked him if he was thinking of suicide.

❑ Acute risk *or* ❑ Chronic risk

❑ Low risk ❑ Moderate risk ❑ High risk

Risk factors: _____

Warning signs: _____

Protective factors: _____

Demographically relevant information: _____

Case D

Dakota is a Native American, aged 34 years, who has struggled with substance abuse for many years. Because he feels that his drinking is a loyal gesture to his friends, he has had difficulty in abstaining or understanding the risks of chemical dependence. His father committed suicide when Dakota was 16 years old, and as the eldest son, he was urged to become the head of the family, take care of things, and not repeat the mistakes of his father. Last night, Dakota got a second drunk driving charge. He is in a panic about the shame and embarrassment that this will bring on his family. He has told a friend that he is going to the cliffs to fly with the eagles.

❏ Acute risk *or* ❏ Chronic risk

❏ Low risk ❏ Moderate risk ❏ High risk

Risk factors: _____

Warning signs: _____

Protective factors: _____

Demographically relevant information: _____

Case E

Sandra is a White female, aged 47 years. She has just finalized a divorce from her third husband. For most of her life, she has placed a high premium on having a relationship with a partner, yet her commitments and marriages have seemed rushed and not very thought out, according to some friends and relatives. She is devastated when things do not go well, and her pattern of relationships has been somewhat chaotic and often conflicted. Similarly, she has seen a number of counselors over the years. Sandra's current counselor, in talking to her most recent prior counselor, learned that she has never attempted suicide actively but has often talked about wanting to die "if it happened." She is not sure how she would do it because she is afraid. Sandra is an adult survivor of childhood sexual abuse. She is an active member of her church, and she does not think it would be "OK" to actually attempt suicide.

❏ Acute risk *or* ❏ Chronic risk

❏ Low risk ❏ Moderate risk ❏ High risk

Risk factors: _____

Warning signs: _____

Protective factors: _____

Demographically relevant information: _____

VOICES FROM THE FIELD 6.2
Treating Nonsuicidal Self-Injury

Amanda C. La Guardia

After completing my bachelor's degree, I started working in the mental health field as a case manager assigned to a small number of children and adolescents who had been identified as "at risk" for being removed from their homes and placed into foster care or long-term inpatient facilities. My job was to help ensure these youngsters stayed with their families. I was with each

(continued)

family for up to 12 hours per week, which was more than their licensed counselors. Needless to say, I frequently felt that I did not have the training necessary to help in the way that was needed (which is why I decided to pursue my master's in counseling). One of the biggest challenges I faced with many of my clients was treating nonsuicidal self-injurious behavior. I worked with several adolescent females who used self-injury as a way of coping with either the psychological impact of the trauma they had experienced or their emotional turmoil. I also encountered elementary school-aged boys who engaged in self-injurious behaviors for similar reasons. Rather than perceiving these behaviors as a coping strategy, many of the counselors I worked with judged these behaviors to be the result of mental illness. For example, borderline behavior was a fairly consistent assessment for the females, and impulsivity as a result of hyperactivity was a common assessment for the boys. Thus, I noticed clinicians often did not focus on nonsuicidal self-injury as an important treatment concern. I knew better, but I needed training.

In many cases, the clients that engaged in the most frequent self-injurious behaviors were also contemplating suicide. They would injure themselves in order to deal with their overwhelming emotions (or lack of emotional connection) and to prevent acting out on their suicidal thoughts. This combination was tricky. I knew they needed a better way of coping, but I didn't want to take away the method that they felt kept them from walking down a more dangerous path. Formal and informal ways of assessing their suicidal ideations as well as their need for self-injury became equally necessary. Self-injury and suicidal ideation are separate issues, but they are often interconnected.

Together with my clients, we discussed what situations (external and internal) tended to lead to self-injurious behaviors and worked on developing new ways of coping. I didn't ask them to stop, but I did ask them to take care of themselves and encouraged them to find new ways of dealing with their pain because they deserved happiness however they defined it; they were worth it. I let them know I would be with them as they struggled, and then I made sure that I was.

METHODS OF ASSESSMENT: INTERVIEWS AND WRITTEN INSTRUMENTS   In suicide risk assessment, as with concepts related to the assessment of almost any phenomenon, it is wise to draw data from a variety of methods and sources. There is not one prototypical suicidal person, and there is no cookie cutter risk assessment protocol. Suicide risk assessment relies heavily on clinical judgment and interpretation of available facts, indicators, evidence of past behaviors, rating of current mood and symptoms, and consideration of all these data against the backdrop of the field's knowledge of risk factors, protective factors, epidemiology, and causative factors that are known to increase the risk of suicidal death. It is advisable to be prepared with quality in-session (whether in person or by phone) interview techniques, and also with suicide risk assessment instruments that yield reliable and valid results.

Suicide risk assessment should always begin at the first session in traditional counseling, and it should be the main assessment goal in any crisis situation, including putting one or two specific questions on intake forms completed by the client or the client's caregiver, such as "Are you having thoughts of suicide?", "Have you ever attempted suicide?", and "Have you ever lost a loved one to suicide?" If a client indicates *yes* (or does not answer *no*) to any of these questions, a more thorough assessment should begin immediately. If the client or caretaker does not indicate *yes* to any of these questions on the intake forms, then the clinician should still be poised to listen and look for general indicators. These would include in-session affect, self-report, responses to direct questioning, as well as several potential suicide risk factors: (1) current depression or a history of depression (2) alcohol or drug abuse; (3) suicide ideation, talk, planning; (4) prior attempt(s) (5) a plan with a lethal method; (6) social isolation and limited support; (7) hopelessness or cognitive rigidity; (8), being an older, White male; (9) a history of suicide in the family; (10) unemployment and/or vocational problems; (11) relationship and/or sexual problems, or family dysfunction; (12) stress and negative life events; (13) impulsivity, agitation, aggression; (14) physical illness; and (15) evidence of more than one of these 14 factors and comorbidity (Maris, 1992).

The field has produced a variety of mnemonic devices and acronyms (see Table 6.5) to help counselors remember risk factors and warning signs to assess for suicide in a session or on the phone. These mnemonic devices and acronyms are mostly descriptive of warning signs and the behavioral clues of imminent risk, although a few include demographic risk factors as well. They are not suggested as empirically derived test instruments with validity and reliability. Rather, they are checklists clinicians can use when gathering clinical impressions, and counselors are urged to use the ones that are more suited to their needs. Crisis counselors may wish to adapt one or more of these acronyms into a checklist suitable for documenting the client's status.

It would be insensitive of a counselor to simply read the list of elements associated with a mnemonic device or acronym and ask the client to respond "yes" or "no" to each. A counselor who wishes to establish and maintain a strong therapeutic alliance with a client will absorb information from the client and "think and link" it to the list of elements, without communicating shame or amplifying a client's sense of personal burdensomeness.

As a former emergency room doctor, Shawn Shea saw first-hand one of the highest windows of risk for suicide—that is, the hours, days, and weeks following discharge from a psychiatric emergency room visit or a hospitalization. As a result, he became concerned with how emergency room personnel interviewed patients to adequately and accurately identify their level of risk for suicide. Shea (2011) developed a suicide assessment approach called the Chronological Assessment of Suicide Events (CASE) method, which infuses the principles of effective interviewing (Ivey, Ivey, & Zalaquett, 2014). The CASE method pays particular attention to the immediate features of the patient's or client's suicidal risk, the conditions just prior to the psychiatric emergency (i.e., a 6 to 8 week buildup or a pileup of distress), and the influences prior to 6 to 8 weeks of buildup (e.g., long ago exposure to suicide, family history of suicide, traumatic events). It concludes with questions about the "now" of suicidal feelings and impending days ahead. The CASE method emphasizes five skill sets of question asking:

1. Shame attenuation (normalizing feelings).
2. Behavioral incident specificity (e.g., "Where is the gun?"; "Where are the bullets?"; "And then what did you do?"; "And after that, what did you do?"; "How many pills do you have?"; "Who knows about your plans?").
3. Gentle assumption (e.g., a presupposition such as "What ways have you thought of killing yourself?" as contrasted with "Have you ever thought about killing yourself?").
4. Symptom amplification (e.g., "How much time do you spend thinking about suicide . . . in a 24-hour period?" to which the client may respond, "just when my children are at their father's house on the weekends.").
5. Denial of the specific. This technique often shocks counselors in suicide intervention training, as it requires clinicians to ask clients if they have considered many different methods, which is counterintuitive to the myth that if we talk about suicide, we will give clients the idea for how to do it.

TABLE 6.5 Suicide Mnemonic Devices and Acronyms

Assessment Mnemonic Device or Acronym	Source	Elements
IS PATH WARM	(AAS, 2006b)	**I**deation, **S**ubstances, **P**urpose, **A**nxiety, **T**rapped, **H**opelessness, **W**ithdrawal, **A**nger, **R**eckless, **M**ood
SIMPLE STEPS*	(McGothlin, 2008)	Are you **S**uicidal?; **I**deation; **M**eans; **P**erturbation; **L**oss, **E**arlier attempts; **S**ubstance abuse; **T**rouble-shooting the client's problem-solving ability; **E**motion (hopelessness, haplessness, worthlessness, loneliness, depression); **P**arents or family history, exposure; **S**tress and life events
SAD PERSONS	(Patterson, Dohn, Bird, & Patterson, 1983)	**S**ex: male; **A**ge: older person; **D**epression; **P**revious attempt(s); **E**thanol abuse; **R**ational thinking loss; **S**ocial supports lacking; **O**rganizes plan; **N**o spouse; **S**ickness
SUICIDAL	(Streed, 2011)	This 65-point mnemonic template (S-U-I-C-I-D-A-L) can be applied to the assessment of presuicidal individuals and the assessment of undetermined death. See www.investigativesciencesjournal.org/article/view/8273
MAN THIS ISN'T FAIR	(Sankaranarayanan, 2007)	**M**ental status: depression, anxiety, agitation, guilt, shame, delusions; **A**ttempts at self-destruction; **N**o positive support from family, peers; **T**riggering stressors; **H**opelessness; **I**deas and intent; **S**ubstance use; **I**llness, chronic pain; **S**uicide in family history; Suicide **N**ote; **F**inal arrangements, saying goodbye, giving away possessions; **A**ccess to means; **I**solation; **R**ecent psychiatric hospitalization
NO HOPE	(Shea, 2011)	**N**o meaning; **O**vert change in clinical presentation; **H**ostile environment; **O**ut of hospital recently; **P**redisposing personality disorders; **E**xcuse of explanation for dying
PLAID PALS	(Johnson, 2015)	**P**lan, **L**ethality, **A**vailability, **I**llness, **D**epression, **P**revious attempts, **A**lone, **L**oss, **S**ubstance abuse
PLAID	(Granello & Granello, 2007b)	**P**rior attempts, **L**ethality, **A**ccess to means, **I**ntent, **D**rugs/alcohol
PIMP	(Granello & Granello, 2007b)	**P**lan, **I**ntent, **M**eans, **P**rior attempts
DEAD PIMP	(Whitehead, 2012)	**D**isorder, **E**nvironmental Stressors, **A**ccess to firearms, **D**isinhibition, **P**revious attempts, **I**deation, **M**ale, **P**lan

Jobes (2016) developed an assessment method that merges the interview with the written instrument tool. Known as the Collaborative Assessment and Management of Suicidality (CAMS), this method is evidence-based and theory-based, and it includes close collaboration with the client in session to understand the details about his or her suicidal risk. Jobes's assessment findings are then closely wed to safety planning and treatment planning. This approach has now been adapted into a four-hour online training program with award-winning recognition. The CAMS training program is available through Empathos Resources at www.empathosresources.com.

Several published self-report instruments are available for purchase. The Positive and Negative Suicide Ideation Inventory (PANSI) is a 20-item self-report measure of positive and negative thoughts related to suicide. Items include statements such as "I am in control of my life" and "I think about killing myself," to which clients respond on a 1 to 5 point Likert-type scale. This instrument is intended for use with adults and has been used as an informal screening device for high school students. The instrument is a simple and relatively easy assessment for crisis counselors to use.

The Beck Scale for Suicide Ideation is a self-report instrument requiring 10 minutes to administer that evaluates a client's thoughts, plans, and intentions to commit suicide. It is a 19-item interviewer-administered rating scale that includes items such as "I have made plans to commit suicide" and "I have access to lethal means." This instrument is unique in that it asks the client to recall the time when he or she felt most suicidal and answer the questions from that perspective. It includes items such as "I was ___% decided to commit suicide" and "I have only felt that suicidal ___ (number of) times."

No suicide assessment tools have been identified that empirically assess cultural appropriateness for use with various multicultural populations. Effective assessment procedures, regardless of culture, include the following elements:

- phrasing questions effectively to elicit the most information about suicidal thoughts
- specifically sequencing or structuring questions about suicide
- sequencing questions about specific aspects of suicidal thoughts, plans, and behaviors
- collecting information from collateral sources to best determine how to proceed

In addition, how a counselor phrases and sequences assessment questions should be considered in the context of specific cultures (American Psychiatric Association, 2003; International Association for Suicide Prevention, 2000; Shea, 2011).

There are a plethora of authenticated written suicide assessment instruments available in the public domain without charge or for purchase. We are aware of over 70 products that are tailored to measure suicidal thoughts; suicidal behaviors; suicidal intent; depressive states associated with suicidal thoughts or behaviors; suicidal risks among the elderly, adults, youth, and children; suicidal risk with youth in the judicial system; suicidal proclivity organized around reasons for living; and more. One online source that provides a lengthy list of available validated instruments is the Comprehensive Suicide Prevention Resources Directory at www.legacy.montevallo.edu/asparc. Counselors may also want to search the catalogs or websites of specific publication companies, PsychAbstracts library holding services, and the *Mental Measurements Yearbook*. They may also follow a cyber-referencing route and navigate the Internet to find myriad products, original citations, and reviews.

Counselors making decisions about what products to invest in on behalf of their agency or client populations will want to compare goodness of fit based on several variables such as cost to purchase and resupply, ease in scoring, test–retest properties, administration time for clients, administration time for staff, in-session versus out-of-session assessment possibilities, thoroughness of the information yielded, seamlessness of fit with documentation strategies, and youth and/or adult version availability, reliability, validity. Results from written assessments should become permanent artifacts in client file documentation and subsequently compared to determine the improvement or worsening of the condition. Some of the websites (among many) to search for instruments include the following:

- www.healthline.com/galecontent/
- www.tjta.com/products/TST_007.htm
- www.minddisorders.com/Br-Del/
- www.psychassessments.com.au/Category.aspx?grpld=all&cID=172
- www.encyclopedia.com/doc/1G2-3405700081.html
- www.neurotransmitter.net/suicidescales.html

MULTIPLE TYPES OF ASSESSMENT It is advisable that crisis counselors assess clients more than once, and, with clients who are clearly at risk for suicide, preferably often. Assessment can take place across multiple sessions in a counseling or treatment episode, and within the same session by asking about intent in different ways. It is good practice to use more than one means of assessment, including an interview-style assessment and a formal written and published assessment, as mentioned above. Other means of gathering and confirming data may take the form of interrater reliability (e.g., when you collaborate with a colleague or supervisor to verify findings), in-session conjoint assessment with another care team member, consultation with a psychiatrist or another expert, or assessment by a suicide risk assessment consultant. Finally, collateral information from family members or friends is important if the at-risk individual has been open with them about feelings or behaviors that are suicidal in nature.

TREATMENT PLANNING AND CARE MANAGEMENT WITH A SUICIDAL CLIENT After having assessed for a client's acute or chronic risk as well as having determined the level of risk, many mental health professionals might again ask, "Now what do I do?" Assessment is only part of the intervention process. Rudd et al. (2004), Jobes (2016), and Chiles and Strosahl (1995), among others, provide qualified step-by-step recommendations for appropriate treatment planning and responding. Just as all treatment plans for clients seeking counseling for any condition are customized to meet their needs, the same is true for clients at risk for suicide. The assessment process yields valuable information to assist with the design of appropriate treatment interventions. This section will review several ideas for counselors to consider, beginning perhaps with the most important intervention of all, the development of a customized safety plan.

Developing a safety plan with the client is an industry standard and expectation, but many mental health professionals were trained to write a "no-harm contract." Based on research, best-practice thinking, examination of the potential for false security regarding liability, and more evolved legal, ethical, and clinical reasoning about how much a suicidal client might be able to "agree" to such a "contract," the no-harm contract has been replaced with professional and empirical preference for the safety plan. Even seasoned practitioners who are reluctant to do away with the "no-harm contract" should be advised that not only is it ill-advised, it is in contradiction to many more modern insights about safety planning, and they could run the risk of increasing liability if using "no-harm contracts" even in conjunction with safety plans. Liability for knowing what to do in the case of a suicidal crisis pertains to the professional and not the client, who would be potentially considered not competent to direct treatment decisions if incapacitated with life-threatening depression or multiple symptoms of any diagnosis. Many, if not most, acutely at-risk suicidal clients are not in a psychiatrically oriented or lucid condition to shoulder the burden for knowing enough about suicide or safety planning; therefore, the attempt of the clinician to "contract" with the temporarily disabled client is increasing his or her liability, not reducing it, through the use of a "no-harm contract."

While some authors have referred to safety plans by varying nomenclature (such as *crisis response plan* and *self-care plan*), the NSPL's Standards, Training, and Practices Committee recommends the term *safety plan*.

> We would always use the term "safety plan" . . . other terms [crisis response plan or self-care plan] are too vague and do not explicitly reference the fact that keeping the individual safe is the primary goal in developing a plan—vagueness is not good. In addition, we would never reference a "safety plan" without explicitly stating the avoidance of anything that resembles a "no harm contract"—so would attempt to eliminate any confusion at the outset. (*G. Murphy, personal communication, September 22, 2010*)

Barbara Stanley and Gregory Brown (2009) have written extensively about the components of a safety plan and recommend that clients ask the following questions:

1. When should I use the plan?
2. What can I do to calm/comfort myself if I am feeling suicidal?
3. What are my reasons for living?
4. Who can I talk to?
5. Who can I talk to if I need professional assistance?
6. How can I make my environment safe?
7. What should I do if I'm still not feeling safe?

Stanley and Brown addressed not only what should be included in safety planning but also how to talk through its use with clients. They are widely considered the field's experts on safety planning, and practitioners should explore their resources and seek training in their Safety Planning Intervention.

A comprehensive safety plan addresses specific behavioral actions, determined in concert with the client, and would include several key focal points including means restriction, self-soothing options, self-care options, family involvement options, resource development, and crisis response options (M. Gould & D. Jobes, personal communication, November 10, 2010), in addition to the recommendations that Stanley and Brown suggest. One essential component of safety planning is addressing means restriction (Coombs, Harrington, & Talbott, 2010; Mann et al., 2005) since firearms are the most frequently used method to complete suicide in the United States—and the most lethal with the least amount of time for active rescue or intervention. An example of a safety plan is presented in Table 6.6, written with samples of specific behavioral actions.

TABLE 6.6 An Example of a Multinodal Safety Plan with Specific Behaviors

I will . . . *(List specific behaviors such as the examples listed below).* **Customize the plan with your client.**

1. Remove gun and ammunition from house, car, truck, cabin, barn.

(Note to counselor: Means restriction)

2. Fill doctor's prescriptions weekly (not a month at a time).

(Note to counselor: Means restriction)

3. Take my dog to play in the park.

(Note to counselor: Soothing feelings of distress)

4. Call a friend.

(Note to counselor: Soothing feelings of distress)

5. Eat three meals a day.

(Note to counselor: Self-care)

6. Drink nonalcoholic and noncaffeinated beverages.

(Note to counselor: Self-care)

7. Avoid lonely times by going to my sister's.

(Note to counselor: Family support)

8. Spend the night at my cousin's house.

(Note to counselor: Family support)

9. Go to a community support group for persons who have bipolar disorder.

(Note to counselor: Using resources)

10. Call my sponsor or go to a meeting.

(Note to counselor: Using resources)

11. Call the NSPL: 1-800-273-TALK.

(Note to counselor: Crisis or emergency support)

12. Go to my primary care physician, psychiatrist, or the ER.

(Note to counselor: Crisis or emergency support)

List the names and reliable phone numbers of several people that the counselor can call or who can call the counselor in the event of an escalating situation:

Name:_____Phone: _____

Name:_____Phone: _____

Name:_____Phone: _____

Name:_____Phone: _____

Name:_____Phone: _____

Note: Specific behavioral ideas should be written in the affirmative. For example, in Item #6, instead of "Don't drink alcoholic or caffeinated beverages," restate it in the affirmative "Drink nonalcoholic and noncaffeinated beverages."

A well-facilitated assessment will encourage a client to trust the counselor and provide detailed information, which will allow the counselor to understand when, how, and under what conditions the client becomes vulnerable to suicide.

For example, if a client has revealed that she wants to end her life, particularly when her husband and she experience conflict, her treatment plan might recommend couples counseling and conflict-resolution skills building. If an isolated 80-year-old widower reports being desperately vulnerable between the hours of 5 and 8 p.m. each day as he imagines all of his neighbors having dinner with their loved ones, a treatment plan for him should increase social support during the 5 to 8 p.m. period of vulnerability. Safety plans should always involve resources, actions, and coping mechanisms that the client is able and willing to put into place, and they should be unique to his or her situation.

OUTPATIENT AND INPATIENT TREATMENT DECISIONS AND MANAGEMENT In an earlier era, suicidal clients may have been hospitalized for 20 to 30 days. Changes in the health care insurance industry and managed care have severely reduced the amount of hospitalized care that at-risk persons may obtain, even when suicidal risk remains high. Earley (2007) lamented how difficult it was to secure appropriate durations for inpatient treatment because of insurance payment restrictions. He investigated the trend for transinstitutionalization, wherein clients who may be dangerous to themselves or others have difficulty obtaining appropriate medical care except when identified by law enforcement when troubles arise. In addition, Granello and Granello (2007a) described the potential for counselors to generate "false positives" when assessing for risk; that is, determining that suicidal risk is high for clients when it is low, thus unnecessarily referring clients to inpatient hospitalization for suicidal risk. Referring a client to inpatient hospitalization when his or her risk does not warrant it (a false positive evaluation) can be detrimental and may further alienate the client from seeking professional help for fear of hospitalization among other patients whose conditions are more severe. In contrast, a false negative evaluation might occur when the clinician fails to accurately assess the presence of suicidal risk when there is such a risk. It is not uncommon in almost any community for there to be limited mental health care in hospitals due to the unavailability of beds, limited insurance coverage for adequate lengths of stay, and other factors. These conditions have increased the demands on counselors in outpatient settings to treat and manage the care of low or moderately at-risk clients without the benefit of the security that inpatient hospitalization can provide. That said, when clients present with high acute risk, it is likely that swift referral to an emergency room and probable admission is necessitated. Inpatient hospitalization will likely be briefer than the clinician wishes, and possibly for longer than the client is comfortable. Medical stabilization and pharmacological intervention is the goal of hospital mental health administrators, and discharge planning begins at admission. No matter how difficult, uncomfortable, or disruptive a hospitalization is for clients, it does save lives. Discharge planning and collaboration is essential between hospital personnel and outpatient counselors to eradicate the high window of risk for suicide after discharge. Another idea for transition from inpatient to outpatient care might be partial hospitalization or day programs wherein the client spends 5 to 7 days per week in hospital, but sleeps at home.

Recommendations for adjusting to the current realities of changing trends in insurance companies include increasing the frequency of sessions—for example, from one to two sessions per week—or increasing the length of the sessions, perhaps from

50 minutes to 90 minutes. Provisions might also be made for the client to call in for safety checks between sessions at designated times (Newman, 2012). In addition, clinicians should consider inviting trusted family members or supports to a session to be sure that family members are sufficiently aware of suicidal risk and are involved in implemented safety planning provisions. Counselors should also have collaborative relationships established with psychiatrists and emergency departments in their community as referral options. For clients without insurance, it is especially important to know which community agencies, public mental health resources, and mental health initiatives in a community are designed to provide psychiatric care and potentially distribute needed medications for the uninsured. Primary care doctors (internists and general family medicine physicians) are also options when psychiatrists have long waiting lists.

No one person or clinician can be solely responsible for the inpatient or outpatient care of someone who is suicidal. Mental health counselors are advised to think of care management as a team approach. For more acutely suicidal clients, extra vigilance may be necessary to be sure that they are not left alone (24/7) or at vulnerable times. Family members may be the most centrally responsible people to ensure, for example, that means restriction (e.g., removal of guns, ammunition, pills) is conducted. Other team members may include facilitators of community support groups that are well matched to the client's needs. For example, communities often have support groups for divorce recovery, job hunters, persons with bipolar disorder, Alcoholics Anonymous 12-step groups, veterans, bankruptcy, bereavement, etc. Depending on the circumstances of the suicidal client, accessing group support for specific needs or even individual services at these relevant agencies can become a part of the "syllabus" for care. Crisis center phone numbers should be given to the client for between-session support. If the community does not have a nearby crisis center, the phone number for the NSPL—1-800-273-TALK (8255)—is the best number to provide. Helpers at the NSPL will assist callers in accessing the nearest resources.

A "syllabus" for care might be a step-by-step time management plan the client can develop with the counselor for use when particularly vulnerable, alone, or between sessions. Specific times set in writing for when the client might do activities such as exercise, sleep, eat meals, attend support group meetings, go to the bookstore, and run errands can assist clients who have disorienting depression, or are not functioning well. An adage in suicide intervention is that the clients are encouraged to be able to participate in their own rescue to the degree that they are capable. It is often the case and recommended that the clinician, crisis center counselor, or helping professional may become considerably more directive during times the at-risk individual is in acute risk or hindered from functioning normally. As the client resumes functional ability, the client would be entrusted to execute personal choices. However, this trust arrangement should be reevaluated as long as the client is struggling to perform activities of daily living.

Transitions are a particularly vulnerable time for persons at risk for suicide, and counselors who work with clients via inpatient, outpatient, or partial hospitalization should anticipate and plan for transitions. These transitions might include a change in level of care (from more restrictive to less restrictive, or vice versa), provider, circumstances (e.g., a parent who has come to the client's city to assist during the crisis plans to return home to a remote location), medication, or relationship (e.g., a recent breakup).

Extra safeguards may be built into the care management plan (e.g., more frequent short-term phone contacts between sessions or updated safety planning).

If a clinician believes that a client should be hospitalized, both clinician and client should collaborate in such a way that the client will voluntarily elect to seek admission. When there is some client resistance to hospitalization, the involvement of a trusted family member is recommended to facilitate the decision to go voluntarily. Sometimes a primary care physician or psychiatrist can be influential in securing admission to a hospital. As a last resort, a client may need to be involuntarily hospitalized. States differ as to the process for involuntary commitment, and it is essential that clinicians understand the laws and practices in the state and county in which they are practicing before they ever see clients. It is better to know what to do prior to a crisis for both the clinician and the client. Some states require courts to mandate the "commitment" of an individual; others allow licensed professionals to initiate an emergency petition for involuntary hospitalization with law enforcement transportation; some states integrate mobile crisis teams, while others rely on a community service board that would make the final assessment and determination based on the clinicians' observations. The crisis counselors should also establish professional relationships with community service officers in their jurisdiction and become familiar with protocols.

The follow-up with a client who is at risk for suicide is critical practice (Murphy, 2010). The National Action Alliance for Suicide Prevention's Suicide Attempt Survivors Task Force (2014) reported that over 2.5 million persons attempted suicide in 2012; this group is the single largest at-risk group in the nation. Follow-up as a clinical standard is a form of active postvention that is both preventive and interventive. Follow-ups may include regularly scheduled phone calls, letters, or notes, and even texting or e-mailing, or they may include systemic agreements with provider organizations (e.g., between agencies or practices and hospital emergency room departments). Data about follow-up assessments with crisis center callers is very encouraging in that callers who sought out suicide intervention assistance from centers are very positive and motivated to reduce ambivalence about wanting to die. Clinicians may direct family care team members to obtain helpful booklets from agencies such as the Feeling Blue Suicide Prevention Council (www.feelingbluespc@aol.com) to assist family members of an attempter following a suicide attempt. SAMHSA also has several "after an attempt" resource booklets for medical providers, attempters, and family members of attempters that can be obtained at http://store.samhsa.gov/shin/content/SMA08-4355/SMA08-4355.pdf.

Finally, a word is warranted about theoretical orientation and responsiveness to suicidal clients. Many experts prefer to recommend cognitive behavioral therapy or dialectical behavioral therapy. When individuals are acutely suicidal, it is as if they have a "brain condition" with cognitive distortion and perception and proportion difficulties. Much has been written about theoretical application, but ultimately the intrapsychic themes, psychodynamic themes, self-actualization, and other constructs are better explored after the acute risk has been managed and reduced in favor of cognitive behavioral strategies that work well with the suicidal or cognitively restricted client who may experience psychache and narrow views of other life-saving, pain-reducing possibilities.

Read Voices from the Field 6.3.

VOICES FROM THE FIELD 6.3

A Special Plea for Special Needs: Crisis Intervention with Low Cognitive Functioning Clients

Amanda Evans

A common theme that I noticed when working at the inpatient psychiatric unit as a graduate student was helping professionals struggling to assist patients in crisis who performed at lower cognitive functioning. I can specifically remember several clients who were misunderstood by the hospital staff due to their level of cognitive functioning and were subsequently provided more restrictive care. I think it is very important as a counselor to be mindful that just because a client is an adult does not mean that the client can manage the responsibilities or cognitive complexity of adulthood. A patient who appears to be a 50-year-old male may in fact function cognitively as an adolescent, or as a child. This can be challenging in a hospital setting when clients in crisis require immediate, effective, and appropriate medical attention.

Oftentimes, patients who were lower functioning were expected to cope and manage in the same way as their higher-functioning peers. This included maintaining personal hygiene, medication compliance, following the unit's rules, and establishing appropriate boundaries with their peers.

In addition, I noted counselors who provided treatment to these clients struggled with gathering intake information and establishing aftercare goals. This difficulty in serving lower functioning patients was most evident in the staff's attempt to de-escalate crisis situations. In my opinion, clients who are lower functioning are commonly misinterpreted by helping professionals, leading to unnecessary rapid escalation in crisis situations, physical restraints, and possibly medical restraints.

Based on my personal experiences, I want to encourage counselors-in-training to consider alternative methods to communicate with clients in crisis. When low cognitive functioning patients are in crisis, expecting mature, rational decision-making may be unrealistic; however, helping clients to express themselves, calm down, or self-soothe is ideal. In addition to talking through a crisis, working with individuals through the use of pictures, schedules, sign language, silence, or techniques specific to the client's needs can be very helpful in de-escalating a crisis situation. At times, competent care requires stepping outside of the box and using alternative interventions to best assist clients.

Postvention

Given the prevailing incidence of fatal self-directed violence, a conservative estimate of persons who become newly bereaved due to the loss of a loved one by suicide numbers over 246,000 per year. In the span of a decade, that number would be well over 2 million persons (Montgomery County Emergency Service, Inc., 2006). The job of bereavement counselors is an important one, due both to the large number of survivors of suicide loss in the population and also to the misperceptions and myths about suicide both before and after death. Survivors of suicide loss often report feeling misunderstood, stigmatized, and marginalized. They are prone to bereavement and sorrow, complicated mourning, and post-traumatic symptoms (Harrington, 2011). Their bereavement may be punctuated by the complexities of believing that their loved one "rationally chose" death, as contrasted with viewing suicide as a multifactorial process of debilitation and vulnerability (Survivors of Loved Ones' Suicides, 2006). They may have lost a child, a sibling, or a partner within a cloud of unknown circumstances, such as a bad business deal, a negative performance evaluation at work, or an unspoken act of infidelity that they could not work through, to name a few. All people have bad days and bad events, make bad choices, experience loss or defeat, and yet they do not all become suicidal. Thus, it is important to remember the multiple risk factors that individuals who attempt suicide confront.

The circumstances surrounding the immediate scene of a suicide may include the involvement of law enforcement, investigators treating the scene as a murder, potential arrest warrants being issued, and limited or gruff communication with personnel such as coroners or first responders, possibly punctuated with yellow crime tape around the scene. Of course, many survivors report exemplary conduct on the part of these professionals, and so it is not a universal problem. Adults and children alike are often witnesses to the actual suicide, may discover the body, or have to be involved in cleanup. Many family and religious complications can ensue, with conflicts possible between stepfamily members, family-of-origin, or in-law family members who may disagree about stating the cause of death openly to their communities. Sometimes the suicide may be like one domino in a row of dominoes that continue to fall. For example, consider the scenario in which a middle-aged man dies from suicide, leaving financial problems that result in foreclosure or bankruptcy for the surviving family members, leaving college-aged children unable to continue their schooling, and a partner/mother who must reenter the workforce or sell the house. The suicide can become one crisis of many in a sequence of events, not unlike the ABC-X model of crises (Hill, 1948, 1958) or the Double ABC-X model of crises (McCubbin & Patterson, 1982).

Counselors providing postvention grief services to survivors of loss will want to become familiar with complicated bereavement and mourning, to learn about counseling techniques and countenance directly related to working with suicide loss, and especially to be aware of the feelings of helplessness, sense of responsibility, and internalized guilt that the bereaved feel after a suicide. Many family members have knowledge of their loved one's struggles and may have assisted in ways that in fact prolonged the life of their loved one. Yet, the traumatic circumstances, the stigma or belief that it was a rational choice, or the complicated mourning leave survivors clinging to a sense of guilt-framed attribution of responsibility. Even love, appropriate attention, and excellent clinical care cannot fully immunize someone against suicidal thoughts and behaviors (Blauner, 2002).

Counselors should become familiar with how to find suicide bereavement groups that exist in many localities around the country by visiting either the AFSP or the AAS websites for comprehensive listings. While survivors of suicide loss often report that they speak the same language, a language that other bereft persons do not fully understand, not all survivors will think that a group is the best option for them. Jordan (2006) offered suggestions for other therapeutic responses that counselors can recommend, such as bibliotherapy and Internet resources, psycho-education, family guidance, survivor outreach, cyber groups, survivor conferences, and activism, with activism marking a full circle from postvention to prevention.

Finally, some counselors become crisis advisors to employers, agencies, schools, faith-based groups, and communities. These professionals should be familiar with the national resources available for responsible communication with the media following a suicidal death. All of the prominent national associations have such resources available on their websites for distribution to decision makers, spokespersons, and even media representatives in order to use the public news forum responsibly, to prevent suicide contagion, and to avoid glorifying suicide or misrepresenting knowledge about it. Complete Think About It 6.1.

THINK ABOUT IT 6.1

Think about how society sometimes normalizes language that is violent or self-harming. Have you ever heard friends in casual conversation use phrases to describe their exasperation . . . phrases such as "That's enough to make me wanna kill myself" or "I'm just going to shoot myself if he doesn't quit teasing me"? Perhaps you have seen seemingly humorous references to suicide in unexpected places. For example, a restaurant may have a dessert called "Suicide by Chocolate," or a corporate trainer may talk about "career suicide."

Public messaging is a powerful tool in promoting initiatives that are clinically responsible in the interests of public health. In the world of suicide, it is unacceptable to refer to a fatal suicide attempt as "successful." Only prevention can be considered successful.

All of the ways that we unwittingly toss around the words and concepts of suicide say something to the public in earshot. We may unconsciously maintain stigma and even set up barriers for the public to learn and to trust that help is available. They will not have to worry about being crazy, or a quitter, a loser, or a sinner if they understand that health care professionals know that self-directed violence is the result of involuntary and debilitating attempts to end psychological pain. More empowered and enlightened is to use language that is nonjudgmental and also inviting to persons who may be struggling to be help seeking.

What will you do the next time you hear a so-called humorous reference to suicide? How would you entertain the idea that generally people do not often joke about other life-threatening illnesses, such as cancer, cardiac arrest, or diabetes? We do not see "Cancer by Chocolate" on menus. What small individual act of suicide prevention advocacy will you do when you have the opportunity?

HOMICIDE

While most counselors are aware that they are likely to encounter suicidal clients in their counseling practice (Laux, 2002), they may underestimate the need for expertise in assessment and intervention skills with homicidal clients. There is a general assumption that clients with homicidal ideation are found primarily within the domain of forensic mental health and therefore are not a concern for most counselors. Obviously, clients with a history of certain mental disorders and violent offenses do present an elevated risk to the public, and mental health professionals working with violent offenders endeavor to balance public safety and client rights (Carroll, Lyall, & Forrester, 2004; Large, Ryan, Singh, Paton, & Nielssen, 2011). But violent client behavior is documented in both inpatient and outpatient treatment facilities and therefore ought to be of concern for all mental health practitioners (Warren, Mullen, & Ogloff, 2011). Ongoing reports from the media reveal that the potential for violence and homicide exists in families, schools, colleges, the workplace, and across all communities. Accordingly, it is essential that counselors in all practice settings be equipped to assess the lethality of clients with homicidal ideation and be capable of making decisions regarding the referral and treatment of dangerous clients. Van Brunt (2015) states that while mental illness is often a contributing element, "the core of assessment must be based on threat assessment principles, not clinical pathology" (p. viii). Moreover, counselors in all settings may be called on to provide services to homicide survivors. A homicidal crisis is intense and has long-lasting repercussions for individuals and communities who are left struggling to make sense of their traumatic loss and complicated grief (Currier, Holland, & Neimeyer, 2006). Furthermore, counselors working with clients who experience homicidal ideation find the experience very disturbing (Walfish, Barnett, Marlyere, & Zielke, 2010). In this section, we will explore the issue of homicidal ideation and systems of threat level assessment as well as treatment options.

Homicide can be defined as the willful killing of one person by another person. According to the CDC (2015b), in 2012 homicide by firearms ranked 107 as a leading cause of death and homicide by other means ranked 108. Currently, the homicide rate is at its lowest point since 1964. The Federal Bureau of Investigation (FBI, 2013b) reported homicide incidents of 13,782 for 2009, 13,164 for 2010, 12,795 for 2011, 12,765 for 2012, and 12,253 for 2013, indicating that the rate of homicide fell from 2009 to 2013; and preliminary analysis indicates that the downward trend will continue. While these trends are encouraging, the trauma of homicide is all too real for many people, and knowledge about crisis response related to homicide is essential for counselors. It is also important to note that while overall homicide rates have been decreasing, the rate of mass shootings has been on the rise (FBI, 2013c).

Why has there been an overall steady decline in homicide? Oppel (2011) noted that the decline in all violent crimes has baffled the experts. There are many theories, including demographic changes, more people in prison, and an increase in the number of police, but criminologists have been unable to pinpoint the true cause for the decrease.

Even though there has been a decrease in homicide, the reality is that homicide has a huge impact on our society and on the families and communities touched by homicide. On average, 77% of homicide victims and 90% of homicide offenders are male. Of female victims, 38% were murdered by husbands or boyfriends (FBI, 2013b). Thus, although females do commit homicide, males are the primary risk population. Diem and Pizarro (2010) noted that in intimate partner homicide, male offenders are most often motivated by jealousy or dominance issues, while female offenders are usually motivated by fear for their own safety. African Americans are disproportionately represented among both victims and offenders as are young people (Zeoli, Grady, Pizarro, & Melde, 2015). Approximately one third of victims and one half of all offenders are in the 18- to 24-year-old age range.

"I could just kill him!" That is not an uncommon declaration from a client venting anger at a difficult partner, peer, or work colleague, and counselors must be able to ascertain frustration from true risk of violence (Welfel, 2016). Such threats of harm toward another usually transpire when a client is experiencing extreme psychological suffering and is attempting to resolve feelings of distress; they are expressions of emotion without any real intent to carry out a threat (Warren et al., 2011). The counselor is then tasked with determining whether such pronouncements are simply common idiomatic expressions of anger or are legitimate lethal threats. Fortunately, in most instances, clients are merely indulging in hyperbole to give voice to intense anger or frustration; however, counselors must be prepared to recognize and assess potential lethality in cases where resentment and infuriation have escalated into homicidal ideation and possible violent actions.

Working with potentially violent clients presents a challenge to crisis counselors as they attempt to provide treatment, assess possible violent behavior, and protect would-be victims (Meloy, Hoffiman, Guldimann, & James, 2011). When counseling a violent client, the protection of the public is always on the table. The noteworthy case of *Tarasoff v. Regents of the University of California* (1976) clarified that the duty under California law to warn individuals who are in peril is of greater importance than the preservation of client confidentiality (Rothstein, 2014; Welfel, 2016). Thus, counselors (except those in Texas) must assess the threat of lethality toward others and warn possible victims of harm. While all other states mandate the duty to warn, it is a good idea for crisis counselors to become familiar with the particular details of their own state laws regarding the duty to warn, as these issues are constantly being addressed by legislators at the state and national levels. Welfel (2016) noted that while codes of ethics allow breach of confidentiality regarding dangerous clients, there are state laws that require client protection to take place through hospitalization of the threatening individual (e.g., in Ohio) or contacting police rather than directly contacting the intended victim (i.e., in Texas) and breaching confidentiality. Furthermore, Welfel points out that some states clarify that the harm must be imminent before confidentiality can be breached; consultation with other mental health professionals, as well as legal consultation, is strongly urged before confidentiality is breached. Rothstein (2014) calls for a move toward unity of state laws regarding duty to warn and confidentiality to bring clarity to this issue. In addition to protecting others, crisis counselors should be cognizant of their own safety and implement appropriate precautions, as discussed in Chapter 2.

Assessment of Homicide: Homicide Risk Factors

Certain basic indicators and risk factors tend to be associated with homicide and violence. However, a word of caution about risk factors: While they may assist crisis counselors in assessment, it is important to remember that the existence of risk factors does not mean the client will become violent, and, conversely, the absence of risk factors does not indicate a lack of homicidal intention. Remember, each case must be evaluated on its own terms. Just as the existence of a risk factor cannot predict suicidality, risk factors for homicide in clients cannot predict whether or not the client will act in a violent manner (Van Brunt, 2015).

In many instances, homicide appears to be fueled by interpersonal discord. According to the FBI (2013b), in 2013 approximately 43% of victims were killed by someone known to them (such as a family member, a friend, or an acquaintance), and approximately 53% of women victims were killed by their husbands or boyfriends. Most often, homicide motives were relational and included romantic triangles, disputes over money or property, and arguments fueled by substance abuse. The majority of murders were perpetrated by men, and firearms were the most common killing method; 69% of 2013 homicides were carried out using a gun. Obviously, heightened emotions, substance-induced impulsivity, and easy access to firearms cultivate a context for rash, violent actions, sometimes resulting in death.

Klott and Jongsma (2015) noted that, among other behaviors, homicidal males tend to exhibit impulsivity and have a history of mental illness, family violence, job instability, and overall insecurity. They usually have a need to control intimate relationships and may exhibit possessiveness and rage. The need to control others is most clearly demonstrated in domestic violence cases where batterers control their partners through threats, physical violence, isolation from friends and family, and limiting access to money. Emotional reactivity and acting out of jealousy and revenge was found to be a common theme among domestic violence perpetrators (Juodis, Starzomski, Porter, & Woodworth, 2014). Tcherni (2011) found that poverty, poor education, family system disruption (divorce), and minority status were linked to homicide risk. It should be noted that minorities are overrepresented in low socio-economic populations and that low levels of education are associated with poverty as well. Warren et al. (2011) found that substance abuse, a history of violence, low education, and untreated mental illness were associated with threats resulting in violent actions, with substance abuse being the strongest predictor. Threats may be used by individuals lacking life skills as a maladaptive way to get needs met or manage frustration, but "threats that were issued in a manner that created fear and distress were predictors of significant increased risk of violence, though not always to the individual or individuals threatened" (Warren et al., 2011, p. 153). Warren et al. (2011) also noted that providing mental health treatment to threateners of homicide that focuses on the development of skills to manage emotions and relationships could decrease threats and violent behavior.

Research indicates that particular characteristics and risk factors are associated with youth who commit acts of violence and homicide. According to the CDC (2015e), youth who are at risk for violence have the following characteristics: prior history of violence; drug, alcohol, and tobacco use; association with delinquent peers; poor family functioning; academic problems; and low socio-economic community. Darby, Allan, Kashani, Hartke, and Reid (1998) found that male adolescent violent offenders are likely to have the following characteristics: a history of academic difficulties, substance abuse problems, and involvement with the juvenile justice system. Family of origin disruption and violence, parental endorsement of violent and abusive conduct, and the availability of guns were also found to be significant influences on male adolescent homicidal behavior. Loeber and Farrington (2011) studied risk factors in youth homicide and identified long-term risk factors, including a childhood diagnosis of conduct disorder and family poverty as well as contextual factors such as peer delinquency, drug abuse, and access to weapons. According to Roe-Sepowitz (2007), female adolescent murderers tended to have a history of substance abuse, prior involvement with the juvenile justice system, and very little parental supervision. Peers exert a powerful influence on adolescents, and the peers of female adolescent homicide offenders were prone to abuse substances and to have had previous involvement with the juvenile justice system. In addition, adolescent female offenders had symptoms of mood disorders and exhibited difficulty with anger management. These risk factors speak to the need for early intervention with children and adolescents at risk, as well as their families, through school and the juvenile justice system.

School Homicide and Violence

In recent years, it has become tragically evident that K–12 schools and higher education settings are vulnerable to heinous acts of violence. The FBI (2013c) tracked active shooter events from 2000 to 2013 and found a steady increase over that time span. Of those incidents, 24.4% occurred in educational settings. Moreover, the incidents that occurred in educational settings accounted for some of the highest casualty rates. As with violent incidents in other settings, school shootings are precipitated by a complex interplay of personal issues and environmental circumstances. Again, it is important to note that the presence of certain risk factors cannot predict actual violent acts, but since most violent students communicate their intentions, ongoing threat assessment can help school officials prevent violence and provide intervention to troubled students (Cornell, 2007). By using systematic threat assessment and being attuned to warning signs, educational settings can more clearly identify individuals with violent intent. According to Meloy et al. (2011), "warning behaviors are acts which constitute evidence of increasing or accelerating risk . . . acute, dynamic, and particularly toxic changes in patterns of behavior which may aid in structuring a professional's judgment that an individual of concern now poses a threat" (p. 256).

Meloy et al. (2011) developed a typology of eight warning behaviors that can indicate amplified risk of targeted violence and should be utilized when assessing a threat. They state that "threat assessment is concerned almost wholly with the risk of targeted violence by a subject of concern, and has a behavioral and observational policing focus." (p. 257). The eight warning behaviors are as follows:

1. *Pathway warning behavior*—the individual plans an attack
2. *Fixation warning behavior*—the individual becomes obsessed with a person or cause
3. *Identification warning behavior*—the individual identifies with attackers or warriors
4. *Novel aggression warning behavior*—the individual tries out violent behavior as a test
5. *Energy burst behavior*—the individual increases activities related to the intended victim
6. *Leakage warning behavior*—the individual tells another person about his or her plans
7. *Directly communicated threat warning behavior*—the individual makes an explicit threat to the target or police
8. *Last resort warning behavior*—the individual displays an increase in distress and comes to believe that there is no other way but violence toward the target (Meloy & O'Toole, 2011).

It is hoped that this typology of warning behaviors can make threat assessment more systematized and usable.

O'Toole (2000) recommends that evaluation of a potential school shooter's level of threat be approached with a four-pronged assessment model that includes investigation of several factors: (1) the student's personality, behavior, and traits; (2) family dynamics, family violence, and family attitude toward violence; (3) school dynamics, culture, and climate; and (4) social dynamics, peer network, and community culture. The more areas in which a student has difficulty, the more the student's threat should be taken seriously. Serious threats will necessitate the notification of school officials and possibly law enforcement.

According to Meloy and O'Toole (2011), individuals leak their plans for a variety of reasons, such as excitement, attention, anxiety, or fear. Leakage may be unintentional or intentional. If leakage occurs during counseling, the counselor may be in a duty to warn situation. Leakage that occurs with other individuals such as friends, classmates, or other people on a social media site may not be fully understood as a clear threat and, sadly, no action would be taken. O'Toole (2014) states that individuals planning targeted violence are on a mission. They plan their attacks over a long period of time, and it is likely they will leak information to those around them. Greater awareness in the general public of the concept of leakage might lead to higher levels of prevention.

O'Toole (2014) notes that individuals who are withdrawn, detached from others, and think they have been attacked by another person (whether the attack is real or imagined) may begin to plot a revenge attack. Erford, Lee, and Rock (2015) also state that revenge for bullying or social rejection is a specific motivation for many school shootings. Bullying prevention must be considered an important facet of any school violence prevention program (Duplechain & Morris, 2014).

The U.S. Secret Service (2010) offered this insight into the prevalence of leakage:

> School-based attacks are rarely impulsive acts. Rather, they are typically thought out and planned in advance. Almost every attacker had engaged in behavior before the shooting that seriously concerned at least one adult—and for many had concerned three or more adults. In addition, prior to most of the incidents, other students knew the attack was to occur but did not alert an adult.

This information points to the need to educate students, school staff and faculty, and the public about leakage. Violence in school is usually planned, and school staff and faculty need to be particularly attentive to signs and symptoms of violence as well as to school environmental factors that give rise to bullying, rejection, and the promotion of violence (Miller et al., 2000).

Kanan (2010) highlights the following 10 findings on violent incidents in schools:

1. Incidents of violence are rarely impulsive acts.
2. Prior to most incidents, other people knew about the attackers ideas or plans.
3. Most attackers did not threaten their targets directly prior to advancing the attack.
4. There is no active or useful profile of students who engage in targeted school violence.
5. Prior to the attack, most attackers engaged in some behavior that caused concern or indicated a need for help.
6. Most attackers were known to have difficulty coping with significant losses or personal failures.
7. Many attackers felt bullied, persecuted, or injured by others prior to the attack.
8. Most attackers had access to and had used weapons prior to the attack.
9. In many cases, other students were involved in some capacity.
10. Despite prompt law enforcement responses, most shooting incidents were stopped by means other than law enforcement interventions. (p. 32)

A key point to consider in school shootings is the fact that attackers usually indicate their intentions to someone. Most of the time, other students had some hints that a fellow student was ready to lash out. Part of the difficulty that schools face is the fact that students are reluctant to tell an adult their suspicions. Payne and Delbert (2011) noted that the use of an anonymous hotline for students to report threats, mistreatment, or bullying can be an effective deterrent to incidents of school violence.

In general, college campuses are safe environments, and there is a lower rate of crime on college campuses than off campus (Carr, 2005; Cornell, 2007). Horrific shootings on college campuses are more reflective of problems with mental health access and compliance than of problems with campus safety (Cornell, 2007). Colleges and universities can combat violent incidents through training for faculty, staff, and even students. The implementation of threat assessment and prevention programs on campus and campus-wide warning systems could provide the means to thwart future acts of violence and protect student lives (Van Brunt, 2015). See Case Study 6.2, which addresses the importance of risk assessment in schools.

CASE STUDY 6.2

Risk Assessment in Schools

Mark is a Grade 10 student who is very withdrawn and has few friends. Janice, the school counselor, is concerned about Mark. Last year there was a case where some of the other boys were bullying Mark, and he displayed suicidal ideation. Mark has been seeing a counselor for the past year and the bullies were punished; however, Janice has a gut feeling that the bullying continues "under the radar" of school officials. Mark's English teacher recently stopped by to show Janice one of Mark's tests. Mark did not answer a single question, but instead, drew pictures of guns all over the test.

Discussion Questions

1. What should Janice do?
2. What questions should she ask?
3. What process should she follow?
4. Are there any special considerations since they are in a school setting?

Workplace Homicide

According to the National Center for Victims of Crime (2015), 475 workplace homicides occurred in 2012, which represents a slight increase from the 468 workplace homicides that occurred in 2011. However, the number of workplace homicides has decreased overall since 1993, a year in which 1,068 workplace homicides occurred. Even with this decrease over the years, homicide at the workplace is the 4th leading cause of fatality at work and remains a disturbing concept. Most workplace homicides involve robberies, and individuals who work in retail and hospitality establishments are at greater risk, as are customers and bystanders in these settings. Approximately 80% of workplace fatalities result from shootings.

Just as a school can be held liable for not addressing bullying and threats, the workplace can also be liable for failing to address danger and threats (Lies & Simonsen, 2015). Lies and Simonsen (2015) recommend that workplaces have clearly stated policies regarding violence and threats, a way for employees to communicate concerns, a system to promptly investigate concerns, a discipline policy, training for all employees on the signs and symptoms of violent intent, and an Employee Assistance Program that can counsel employees in distress to help prevent acts of violence.

According to the CDC (2011b), the most dangerous workplace risk factors involve the following:

- Contact with the public
- Exchange of money
- Delivery of passengers, goods, or services
- Having a mobile workplace such as a taxicab or a police cruiser
- Working with unstable or volatile persons in health care, social service, or criminal justice settings
- Working alone or in small numbers
- Working late at night or during early morning hours

- Working in high crime areas
- Guarding valuable property or possessions
- Working in community-based settings

The FBI National Center for the Analysis of Violent Crime (FBI NCAVC, 2001) categorizes workplace violence as follows: (1) violence from criminals who have entered the workplace to commit a crime; (2) violence from customers, clients, patients, and the like, directed toward workers who are providing services; (3) violence against supervisors or coworkers from current or former employees; and (4) violence from an outside person who has a personal relationship with an employee. The prevention of violence from an outside person is nearly impossible, although safety measures can be established to improve workplace security.

Violent acts on the part of employees cannot be specifically predicted, but the following indicators can be used for threat assessment in the workplace: personality conflicts on the job; mishandled termination or disciplinary action; family or relationship problems; legal or financial problems; emotional disturbance; increasing belligerence; increasingly ominous threats; heightened sensitivity to criticism; acquisition of and fascination with weapons; obsession with supervisor, coworker, or employee grievance; preoccupation with violent themes; interest in recent publicized violent events; outbursts of anger; extreme disorganization; noticeable changes in behavior; and homicidal/suicidal comments or threats (FBI NCAVC, 2001). As in school settings, an atmosphere must be created where employees can feel free to come forward and report any disturbing behavior.

The risk of workplace violence and homicide increases during times of extreme job stress. Understaffed job sites, overworked employees, and times of downsizing or labor disputes will create a tense and potentially dangerous context for the development of violent behavior. Additionally, poor management, a high number of grievances, and the lack of employee access to counseling can contribute to violence and homicidal threat in the workplace (FBI NCAVC, 2001). It is essential that workplace employers, particularly in high-pressure workplaces or those undergoing turmoil, be mindful of the need for ongoing threat assessment and be proactive by providing support to employees.

Threat Level Assessment

Various models of threat assessment have emerged over the past two decades, and it is beyond the scope of this chapter to outline all of them. Counselors are encouraged to familiarize themselves with a variety of models of threat assessment.

When a client has overtly indicated intent to harm others or has indirectly exhibited predictors or behaviors of violence and harm to others, this constitutes a direct threat and the counselor must assess the level of threat (Warren et al., 2011). Threat level assessment is critically important to ensure the safety of others and to appropriately guide treatment decisions. While most people who make threats are unlikely to carry out a violent action, all threats must be taken seriously and evaluated (O'Toole, 2000). Threat assessment is the evaluation of the lethality of a threat through an examination of motive, risk factors, intent, and the means and ability to enact the threat.

O'Toole (2000) explains that threat assessment should involve exploration of the following questions: What are the details of the threat? Are the victims identified? Are the details logical, plausible, and spelled out in a specific manner (time of day, method)? Does the client have the means to carry out the threat? What is the emotional state of the client? While emotionality does not specifically indicate lethality, knowing the affective condition of the client provides important assessment and diagnostic information. Are there stressors or triggers that might predispose a client to violence? Is the level of threat low, medium, or high? O'Toole (2000) working with the FBI NCAVC, delineates threat levels as follows:

Low Level of Threat: A threat that poses a minimal risk to victim and public safety.

- The threat is vague and indirect.
- Information contained within the threat is inconsistent.
- The threat lacks realism.
- The content of the threat suggests the person is unlikely to carry it out.

Medium Level of Threat: A threat that could be carried out, although it may not appear to be entirely realistic.

- The threat is more direct and more concrete than a low-level threat.
- The wording in the threat suggests that the person issuing the threat has given some thought to how the act will be carried out.
- There may be a general indication of a possible place and time (though these signs still fall well short of a detailed plan).
- There is no strong indication that the person who issued the threat has taken preparatory steps, although there may be a veiled reference or ambiguous or inconclusive evidence pointing to that possibility—an allusion to a book or movie that shows planning of a violent act or a vague general statement seeking to convey that the threat is not empty: "I'm serious!" or "I really mean this!"

High Level of Threat: A threat that appears to pose an imminent and serious danger to the safety of others.

- The threat is direct, specific, and plausible.
- The threat suggests that concrete steps have been taken toward carrying it out—for example, statements indicating that the person who issued the threat has acquired or practiced with a weapon or has had the victim under surveillance. (O'Toole, 2000, pp. 8–9)

The process of threat assessment must be conducted in an environment that will calm the client, facilitate the de-escalation of intense emotions, and assist in the attainment of precise information regarding the level of threat intent. The assessment of violence is similar to the assessment of other symptoms, in that the client's history of violence, family and medical history, mental status, and drug use must all be investigated. Van Brunt (2015) underscores the need for a calm demeanor and the use of basic rapport-building and active listening skills. Through the use of counseling skills, a relationship can be formed and the client will be more willing and able to open up about his or her thoughts and potential plans. Once rapport is established, the counselor can delve into precise questions to obtain detailed information about the intent of the client to harm another, the extent and intrusiveness of the homicidal thoughts, and the ability of the client to acquire the means to implement homicide plans. When dealing with a client expressing homicidal intent, crisis counselors must always keep the ethical obligation of public safety and the duty to warn at the forefront of their minds, even with low-threat clients. Furthermore, while assessing homicidal ideation, the counselor should also assess for suicidal ideation because homicide and suicide may co-occur.

See Case Study 6.3, which presents a situation where a counselor must assess a client's level of threat. Read Voices from the Field 6.4. Also complete Think About It 6.2.

CASE STUDY 6.3

Assessing for Level of Threat: Marcus

MARCUS:	I hate my supervisor at work. My life would be better if that jerk was dead.
COUNSELOR:	You're so angry at your supervisor that you wish he was dead. Have you had thoughts about harming him?
MARCUS:	Sure, I think about killing him.
COUNSELOR:	Have you come up with a plan to kill him?
MARCUS:	A plan? I mean I've got a 45 at home but no, not a plan exactly.
COUNSELOR:	Are there times when you feel you might act on these thoughts?
MARCUS:	Ha, whenever I'm drunk.

Discussion Questions

1. What level of threat is indicated so far?
2. What other information does the counselor need to assess the threat level?
3. If the counselor determines the supervisor is in danger, what steps should the counselor take?

VOICES FROM THE FIELD 6.4
Leaving No Stone Unturned

Cheryl Lewellen

When assessing for homicidal ideation of potential clients to our nonprofit women's residential substance abuse treatment facility, we begin by using a state assessment issued by the Department of Mental Health. I'm sure most states have a similar standardized assessment. It takes more than an hour to perform and assesses for multiple factors, with both suicidal and homicidal ideation included.

Given the nature of clients struggling with addictions, it is important to continue to verbally assess for both suicide and homicide during individual sessions throughout the 90 days they are here. One of the main factors for this is that many of the women come into the program insufficiently detoxed, and it takes a while for them to gain a clear perspective on their lives. As they begin treatment and open up to aspects of their lives that caused them to use drugs and

(continued)

alcohol in the first place, the clients become aware of the multitude of emotions they had attempted to numb. Many of the clients have suffered abuse on multiple levels either before or during their drug use. Therefore, it is always important to monitor their potential ideation of both suicide and homicide.

As with assessment of suicidal ideation, assessment of homicidal ideation involves asking the client questions to establish whether an individual has thoughts about harming or killing another person, whether they have a plan, and to what extent the plan could be enacted.

THINK ABOUT IT 6.2

Think about counseling a client who requires a threat assessment. The literature emphasizes the need for counselors to maintain calm and use facilitative skills to build rapport while conducting an assessment for homicidal ideation. Would you find that difficult? Put yourself in the situation: What concerns you? What do you feel you need in order to master threat assessment?

Referral

Because of the danger to others and the possible existence of mental disorders in homicidal clients, counselors usually refer clients to or work collaboratively with other mental health providers, particularly psychiatrists, when treating clients who pose a threat to others. Violent clients often need the help of specialists in forensic mental health, and it is a good idea for crisis counselors to be familiar with forensic specialists in their local area.

Clinical assessment of low-threat-level clients may reveal the need for psychiatric evaluation and treatment with psychotropic medication; however, it is imperative that clients with homicidal ideation who are assessed at the high and medium threat levels be referred for psychiatric evaluation and possible treatment with medications. Because of imminent danger to others, high-threat-level clients require immediate law enforcement involvement and probable voluntary or involuntary commitment (O'Toole, 2000; Warren et al., 2011). Medium-threat-level clients need to be monitored closely and may need to be hospitalized. In instances with out-of-control and impulsive clients, homicidal and suicidal ideation may coexist and, therefore, such a client poses a threat to both self and others. The procedures for voluntary and involuntary commitment discussed previously in this chapter in relation to suicide should be followed for homicide cases, with the inclusion of law enforcement in high-threat-level situations. Personal safety of the crisis counselor should always be a priority. A counselor should never attempt to physically stop a resistant client from leaving. If the client is intent on leaving, it is best to get as much information as possible about the client and request law enforcement to intervene.

What is the relationship between mental illness and homicide? Individuals with diagnosed mental disorders are at a higher risk than the general population for violent or homicidal behavior (Laajasalo & Hakkanen, 2004), and individuals with untreated mental illness are more likely to threaten to kill (Warren et al., 2011). It should be noted, however, that this risk is not present across the board and that an elevated threat to others is mainly associated with certain diagnoses (Eronen, Angermeyer, & Schulze, 1998). An increased risk of violent behavior has been found with diagnoses of schizophrenia and other psychotic disorders, but the highest risk of violent and homicidal behavior has been found in individuals with a dual diagnosis of antisocial personality disorder and substance use disorder. Substance abuse repeatedly emerges as a major risk factor for violent behavior and homicide; the comorbidity of substance abuse and any mental disorder will increase the likelihood of violence and should be taken into account when assessing and treating violent clients.

Treatment Options

As stated earlier, a therapeutic alliance is particularly imperative with potential homicide offenders, since client investment in treatment compliance is necessary for public safety (Klott & Jongsma, 2015). Tishler, Gordon, and Landry Meyer (2000) note that mental health providers may struggle with achieving empathy and may experience fear when working with homicidal clients. While such reactions are understandable, it is important to remember that homicidal behaviors are symptoms of a client's illness and that open displays of fear and distaste will undermine rapport building and impair treatment outcomes.

Once the immediate homicidal crisis has been dealt with, the safety of others has been assured, and appropriate medical treatment has begun, long-term treatment planning can proceed. Ongoing assessment of the client is crucial to both treatment outcomes and public safety; therefore, assessment must remain foremost in the crisis counselor's mind. One concern in assessment is the tendency for violent offenders to be less than forthright about the facts surrounding violent acts (Carroll et al., 2004). Crisis counselors should thoroughly examine client history and obtain external substantiation of client facts. Suicidal ideation and homicidal ideation often co-occur, and it is important to assess the risk of both suicide and homicide in clients who have thoughts of harm to self or others.

In addition to ongoing assessment, homicidal and violent client treatment plans typically include anger and stress management, medication, substance abuse treatment (when indicated), and limitation of access to weapons (Hillbrand, 2001; Klott & Jongsma, 2015). Treatment should also include the identification of factors that increase and decrease violent ideation. Brems (2000) discussed several aggression-motivating and -mitigating factors that should be assessed and addressed during treatment of violent clients:

- *Habit strength:* Assessment of the degree to which past violence has worked for the client indicates whether this type of behavior has been reinforced. Clients who have gotten their way through aggression and violence in the past are more likely to use these behaviors in the future.
- *Inhibitions:* A client without inhibitions will be more likely to become aggressive; however, inhibitions may act to moderate aggressive acting out. Examples of inhibiting factors include personal morality and values, impulse control, fear of being caught, and fear of negative consequences. By exploring past times when the client did not resort to violence, a crisis counselor can identify inhibiting factors that can be integrated into treatment.
- *Situational factors:* Exploration of context can yield important data for treatment. If a client is more likely to engage in violent action in certain circumstances, the treatment plan can include avoidance of triggering settings.

By understanding how aggression may have been reinforced in the client's past and by exploring any inhibiting factors and situational contexts, crisis counselors and clients can identify thoughts and behaviors that may lessen violent behavior in the future. The client can begin to learn other ways to cope with anger and aggression. See Case Study 6.4, which presents a situation in which a counselor must assess a client's level of threat.

Compliance with treatment—in particular, compliance with medication—must be stressed with homicidal clients. Nordstrom, Dahlgren, and Kullgren (2006) studied convicted homicide offenders who had been diagnosed with schizophrenia. The majority of offenders were found to have been noncompliant with medication and treatment at the time of their crimes, resulting in active hallucinations and delusions during the homicidal crisis. Therefore, it is essential that crisis counselors conduct ongoing evaluations of medication compliance throughout treatment.

CASE STUDY 6.4

Assessing for Level of Threat: Judy

Judy is a 43-year-old single woman who has been placed on 2 weeks' administrative leave from her job as a research and development technician at a chemical company. Over the years, she has had many personality conflicts with other workers, but her expertise is valuable, and these conflicts have always been smoothed over and worked out. Recently, she "lost it" with her boss and flew into a rage when she was denied time off in compensation for working late the previous week; this incident was the basis for her administrative leave. Her family doctor has prescribed antidepressants for her and has referred her to you for counseling.

Judy expresses anger and a sense of hopelessness about her situation. She is distraught and has to drink wine every night just to go to sleep. Judy is convinced that she will be fired and that the boss is using these 2 weeks to build a case against her. She expresses to you how valuable she is to the company and how much knowledge she has, including her knowledge of tasteless but deadly poisons. She states, "Just one minute in the break room is all someone would need; just slip it in the coffee and they wouldn't know what hit them."

Discussion Questions

1. What level of threat is indicated in this case?
2. Are there factors that increase the homicide risk in this client?
3. What actions should you take?

Family involvement in the treatment of homicidal clients is critical as a support for ongoing treatment compliance. Families can communicate to counselors if clients stop taking medication and can also report observed behaviors of concern that might indicate elevated risk (Klott & Jongsma, 2015). Additionally, families provide a social network foundation that can facilitate client coping. In some instances, family members need to be given information to ensure their own safety. Family members and friends, rather than strangers, were the most frequent victims of homicide offenders with a diagnosis of schizophrenia (Laajasalo & Hakkanen, 2004). This fact highlights the need for families to be an active part of collaborative treatment and ongoing evaluation of homicidal clients.

Early environmental factors influence the development of mental disorders and violent behavior; thus, early intervention with children at risk and their families may deter the development of future antisocial behavior, including homicide (Laajasalo & Hakkanen, 2004). Schools provide the first opportunity for intervention with children who are exhibiting behavioral problems and struggling with academics, both of which are associated with violence. Farmer, Farmer, Estell, and Hutchins (2007) recommend a service delivery structure that supports intervention and prevention in order to promote academic achievement and social skills, intervention with at-risk youth, and developmental systemic prevention strategies. It should be noted that such a delivery structure can be achieved by the full implementation of *The ASCA National Model: A Framework for School Counseling Programs* (American School Counselor Association, 2012).

Homicide Survivor Needs

In the aftermath of a homicide, the family, friends, and sometimes even the community of the victim experience impediments to healing as the mourning process is complicated by the brutality and abruptness of their loss (Rynearson, 2012). Hatton (2003) estimates that there are at least 50,000 bereaved homicide survivors every year in the United States. Unfortunately, homicide survivors may underutilize available services and may also have their grief and trauma compounded during subsequent crime investigations and legal proceedings (Horne, 2003). Homicide survivors often find themselves isolated as members of their social network withdraw due to distress and uneasiness over the terrible circumstances surrounding the loss (Currier et al., 2006) or due to stigmatizing circumstances surrounding the death (Hatton, 2003). This lack of community support can be thought of as a secondary victimization that further complicates the grief process. Collins and Collins (2005) point out that the common grief and loss reactions—such as anger, guilt, and self-blame—are amplified in homicide survivor cases.

Homicide is a violent loss, and survivor grief is complicated and multifaceted (Rynearson, 2012). In essence, violent death rocks the foundations of a survivor's worldview and impedes the ability to make sense of the death or to find meaning within the loss. The bereavement experienced after loss to homicide or suicide usually falls within the category of complicated bereavement—a grieving process that can occur when a death is sudden, developmentally unexpected, or violent. According to the Mayo Clinic (2016), several symptoms may accompany complicated bereavement:

- Extreme focus on the loss and reminders of the loved one
- Intense longing or pining for the deceased
- Problems accepting the death
- Preoccupation with one's sorrow
- Bitterness about the loss
- Inability to enjoy life
- Depression or deep sadness
- Difficulty moving on with life
- Trouble carrying out a normal routine
- Withdrawing from social activities
- Feeling that life holds no meaning or purpose
- Irritability or agitation
- Lack of trust in others

Homicide survivors are almost certain to experience complicated bereavement. Asaro (2001) recommends the following treatment interventions for homicide survivors: (1) promote feelings of safety within the counseling relationship, (2) discuss the specifics of the murder and allow the client to review the murder as needed, (3) address any co-occurring conditions (e.g., substance abuse), (4) normalize and reframe the myriad feelings the client is experiencing, and (5) refer the client to support groups or other resources.

To heal from violent loss, survivors need to feel able to openly express what has happened to them and to fight for change in a system where they have felt injustice. It is also important that survivors find meaning in the death of their loved one by working to benefit others experiencing similar circumstances; this gives meaning to the loss as well as purpose to the survivor (Rynearson, 2012). Saindon et al. (2014) examined the use of restorative retelling, a technique where clients deal with internalized trauma and commemorate the life of the lost loved one from a strength based and resilient stance. They found that restorative retelling showed promise as an intervention, particularly in regard to easing depression, lessening avoidance, and decreasing prolonged grief.

The support experienced in group counseling is especially healing for homicide survivors and cannot be underestimated as a treatment modality (Piper, Ogrodniczuk, McCollum, & Rosie, 2002). According to Hatton (2003), homicide survivors find support group counseling to be one of the most helpful interventions in the bereavement process. Support groups give participants an opportunity to express their feelings without the fear of alienation and stigmatization. Participants can openly talk about their experiences with others who have shared similar experiences and can offer informed support. The U.S. Department of Justice's Office for Victims of Crime website includes links to support organizations and resources across the nation; see www.ovc.gov.

Crisis counselors responding to the crisis of homicide should be prepared for complex and varied reactions and symptoms from individual survivors. Individuals and entire communities can be altered by homicide. At college campuses where a homicide has taken place, students may no longer feel safe, and the stress and anxiety may affect their academic achievement. Communities touched by homicide are altered by the brutal reality of murder within their midst; a coordinated community counseling response and activation of resources will serve to facilitate healing. Additionally, crisis counselors should be sensitive to cultural differences in grief expression. Clients from expressive cultures will show more outward signs of grieving. A lack of outward grief expression may be indicative of a more emotionally restrictive culture, and crisis counselors should not underestimate the inner grief state of less expressive clients (Cavaiola & Colford, 2006). See Case Study 6.5, which focuses on grief counseling for parents who have lost a daughter to homicide. Read Voices from the Field 6.5.

CASE STUDY 6.5

Treatment for Families of Homicide

Debbie, a 19-year-old college freshman, did not show up for classes or for her job one day. When she did not answer her cell phone or come home that night, her roommate was worried and contacted Debbie's family, who decided to report her as a missing person. After 3 weeks of searching and televised pleas for her return, Debbie's decomposing body was found in a wooded area 30 miles from her apartment. She had been sexually assaulted and strangled. DNA found on her body was a match with DNA from a man out on parole from a previous rape conviction. He was accused in Debbie's murder. The killer claimed that he had consensual sex with Debbie in his car and that she was fine when he dropped her off at campus. Debbie's parents were appalled when the killer's defense team attempted to portray Debbie as a wild, out-of-control college student who partied too much, had multiple sex partners, and put herself at risk. The trial ended with a hung jury, and there is uncertainty about when there will be a new trial. Debbie's parents have come to you for grief counseling.

Discussion Questions

1. What factors have contributed to the parents' complicated bereavement?
2. What emotions and reactions might you expect from the parents in this case?
3. What treatment goals and interventions are called for in this case?

VOICES FROM THE FIELD 6.5
Reacting in Crisis Situations

Gregory Pollock

The calm of the day was interrupted by the loudspeaker calling a code for violent behavior being exhibited by a client. I quickly dropped what I was doing and responded to the code. As I approached the area, the commotion of the situation became louder and louder, as my adrenaline levels increased quickly with each step closer to the area. I felt my breath become shallower, my stomach drop, and my body become tense. I had to consciously step back and take a breath and attempt to relax prior to entering the room where the client in question was out of control and becoming violent. How many of us as counselors have been faced with similar situations?

I have learned the hard way that approaching situations such as these while hyped up and excited only adds to the tension and worsens the situation. I think back to my early days in this field where I witnessed staff enter crisis situations in a frustrated state and saw how this exacerbated the situation in very negative ways, at times leading to the staff or client becoming injured.

It is imperative to remain calm when reacting in crisis situations so that we do not add to the situation at hand. I frequently hear from counselors-in-training that they do not feel that they could remain calm in a crisis situation and that when faced with a crisis, they seem to "forget" all of their skills. On the contrary,

their skills are not forgotten, but often masked with anxiety, fear, adrenaline, and stress reactions. So how is it possible to remain calm and keep our wits about us when faced with a crisis? Our training programs do a great job of preparing us for a variety of situations through the use of counseling skills and techniques. Not all counselors have equal opportunities to practice in crisis situations, and those working in situations where crises are more common will have a greater comfort level in dealing with crisis incidents.

It is helpful to remain mindful of ourselves and recognize what is going on internally as we enter situations, whether entering a regular counseling session or a crisis situation. How aware are we of our feelings and thoughts when walking into crisis situations? It is important to control our emotions as we enter crisis situations with the best interest of the client at heart, much like a regular counseling session. There are great consequences to not remaining mindful lest we lose sight of what is needed to best remedy the situation we are faced with.

I refer to a yogic phrase, *Ahimsa*, meaning to do no harm. This is a great term to keep in mind as we prepare for and enter into crisis situations. The best way to ensure that we do no harm to ourselves in yoga is by being aware of ourselves and staying in touch with our bodies to make sure that we do not strain

(continued)

ourselves. It may be difficult to understand the amount of influence that we have on situations, and controlling our emotions goes a long way in enabling us to enter stressful situations in a calm manner.

Maintaining awareness on a daily basis becomes very difficult, especially in light of our listening to and taking on the issues and circumstances of our clients, leaving us vulnerable to compassion fatigue, which in turn can lead to a loss of control in crisis situations. Self-care is vitally important to help us deal with underlying frustrations so that we can maintain our emotional stability.

The most important thing to focus on in crisis situations is maintaining safety of self, the client, and other staff. We also need to focus on what the client needs in crisis situations, and we need to be open to empathizing, understanding, and meeting the needs of the client in a respectful, nonharming manner, while approaching these situations with compassion and a calm, even temperament.

DIAGNOSTIC CONSIDERATIONS FOR SUICIDE AND HOMICIDE

Although suicide risk is associated with depression, bipolar disorder, traumatic brain injury, schizophrenia, and other mental health diagnoses, it is important to remember that anyone can become suicidal at any time for any reason, with or without a diagnosis. For centuries, persons who died from suicide were treated as the scourge of society. Modern views of suicide propose illness-based causes, as a fatal result of self-directed violence resulting from extreme psychological pain. The key to merciful intervention may be to ask not "What is wrong with me?" but rather "What is happening to me?"

The fifth edition of the American Psychiatric Association's *Diagnostic and Statistical Manual of Mental Disorders* (DSM-5) does not include suicide as a separate diagnostic entry, but does include "suicidal behavior disorder" as a condition for further study (American Psychiatric Association, 2013). This disorder would apply to individuals who have attempted suicide within the past 24 months. However, the DSM-5 does include suicidal ideation and risk as part of the diagnostic criteria for the disorders mentioned above as well as in anorexia nervosa and post-traumatic stress disorder.

The DSM-5 includes diagnostic changes to the disorders that have some link to homicidal ideation, most markedly to schizophrenia. The subtypes of paranoid, catatonic, disorganized, undifferentiated, and residual have been eliminated due to their lack of stability. Antisocial personality disorder is another diagnosis linked to homicidal ideation. The DSM-5 has expanded the antisocial personality disorder criteria to augment the description of behaviors related to antagonism and disinhibition. As with suicide, homicide is not a separate diagnostic entry, but "homicidal ideation" is included in clinical diagnoses. Care must be taken to not categorize all individuals with mental illness as dangerous because "research documents that the vast majority of persons with mental illness are not violent, and that only 4–5% of violence toward others is associated with mental illness" (Rosenberg, 2014).

CRISIS INTERVENTION SKILLS FOR SUICIDE AND HOMICIDE

The essential skills needed for suicide prevention, intervention, and postvention include the following:

- openness to checking one's attitudes, emotions, and fears about suicide
- openness to ongoing training in evidence-based practices and best practices
- assessment skills

- management of suicidal risk related to safety planning
- nonjudgmental understanding of the client's perspective for how he or she believes suicide will solve problems, while collaborating to generate other options
- the ability to support transitions in care management and in life
- the ability to provide seamless transition planning for clients' mental health care and life transitions
- sensitive and enlightened responsivity to survivors of suicide loss

The essential skills needed for homicide prevention generally mirror those of suicide prevention with the added responsibility of duty to warn and the use of threat assessment criteria.

Table 6.7 provides a number of online resources for suicide and homicide that provide further research and tools in relation to these areas.

TABLE 6.7 Online Resources on Suicide and Homicide

Resources on Suicide

American Association of Suicidology	www.suicidology.org
American Foundation for Suicide Prevention	www.afsp.org
GLSEN (Gay, Lesbian and Straight Education Network)	www.glsen.org
The Jason Foundation	www.jasonfoundation.com
The JED Foundation	www.jedfoundation.org or
National Action Alliance for Suicide Prevention	www.actionallianceforsuicideprevention.org
National Organization for People of Color Against Suicide	www.nopcas.org
National Suicide Prevention Lifeline (1-800-273-TALK [8255])	www.suicidepreventionlifeline.org
Olweus Bulling Prevention Program	www.olweus.org
StopBullying.gov	www.stopbullying.gov
Suicide Prevention Resource Center	www.sprc.org
Suicide.org ("Suicide Prevention in the Military")	www.suicide.org/suicide-prevention-in-the-military.html
The Trevor Project	www.thetrevorproject.org or www.trevorspace.org/
U.S. Department of Veterans Affairs	www.mentalhealth.va.gov
Youth Suicide Prevention Program	www.yspp.org
Zero Suicide	www.zerosuicide.org

Resources on Homicide

Center for Homicide Research	homicidecenter.org
Justice for Homicide Victims	www.justiceforhomicidevictims.net/resources.html
National Organization for Victim Assistance	www.trynova.org

Source: Adapted from Van Brunt, B. V. (2015). *Harm to others: The assessment and treatment of dangerousness.* Alexandria, VA: American Counseling Association.

Summary

Suicide and homicide are both crisis situations that counselors who are emergency first responders and who provide more long-term treatment are almost certain to be called on to address. These are critical incidents across the span of a professional career. Suicide rates are increasing among all segments of our population, and this trend is expected to continue despite the elaborate prevention efforts ongoing at school, local, state, and national levels.

In the treatment of suicide as a crisis, counselors and other response-oriented personnel may find that their own anxiety surrounding this topic affects their approach to helping clients resolve their own situations. Periodic self-examination is therefore necessary to maintain an adequate degree of separation from the client's crisis, to prevent transference of the crisis counselor's anxieties onto the client, and to avoid damaging the potential for a positive counselor–client relationship. No universally recognized standard of care is in place with regard to a response to suicide and suicide attempts and to treatment of those with suicidal ideation, but professional concepts of foreseeability and assessment of risk have been established to guide and protect crisis counselors as they work with this population.

Three primary goals for the crisis responder dealing with a person threatening suicide or homicide are as follows: (1) ensure client safety, (2) assist the client in achieving immediate short-term mastery of self and situation, and (3) connect the client with formal and informal supports. There are a variety of models presented to help the crisis responder achieve these goals.

Knowledge of suicide risk factors, warning signs, and protective factors is essential for the crisis counselor to make a justifiable assessment of suicide risk in clients who are struggling with this issue. Once the client is assessed, the counselor makes a decision regarding level of risk and actively monitors the client as he or she makes progress and when subsequent events affect the client's disposition. Documentation of the entire process is an increasingly important part of the assessment and treatment cycle; documentation is the single most important factor in justifying and defending a particular course of treatment action.

A variety of treatment options are in place to respond to those struggling with the issue of suicide, including inpatient hospitalization, partial hospitalization programs, and outpatient care. As managed care operations become the norm in American mental health treatment protocols, a comprehensive risk management plan becomes an essential part of cost-effective and medically justifiable care. The risk management plan typically consists of six components: (1) ensuring that all professionals involved understand the statutes relevant to suicide treatment, confidentiality, and informed consent; (2) having a detailed risk management policy; (3) ensuring clinical competency of staff members; (4) maintaining adequate documentation of treatment; (5) implementing a tracking system for follow-up actions; and (6) establishing and maintaining relevant information assessment, and intervention resources for use by counselors and clients.

Responding to incidents of homicide presents many of the same kinds of challenges as responding to a suicide incident, although many crisis counselors underestimate the need for readiness to respond to homicide. In fact, since instances where homicide must be responded to in the counseling setting are becoming more frequent, crisis counselors must prepare themselves to engage with this crisis in a professional, defensible way. Crisis counselors may find themselves in a position of potential influence over those who might become capable of homicide, so the *Tarasoff v. Regents of the University of California* case, which clarified the duty to warn individuals who may be in peril, applies to counselors; it is critical that crisis counselors be aware of their legal duties in these situations.

Counselors may be confronted with homicide risk factors, and violence capable of escalating to homicide must be examined in the educational arena and in the workplace. Crisis counselors must use a threat level assessment to gauge the need for treatment and implement an appropriate treatment option that includes ongoing assessment of risk.

Homicide survivors often experience complicated bereavement. They may feel stigmatized, isolated, and retraumatized by the legal system. Treatment of survivors should address their complicated bereavement issues and help them find resolution and meaning. Support groups for homicide survivors have been found to be helpful.

7

Understanding and Treating Substance Use Disorders with Clients in Crisis

William R. Sterner

PREVIEW

This chapter provides an overview of substance use disorders (SUDs) and the counselor's role in working with clients facing crisis situations. The etiological factors of substance use disorders and various models of addiction are reviewed. Sections in the chapter dealing with treatment are arranged to help counselors understand the sequential treatment process in a crisis setting. Special issues such as relapse, support groups, co-occurring disorders and crises, and cultural considerations are discussed. Case studies and activities are provided throughout the chapter to help the reader integrate and apply the material.

SUBSTANCE USE AND SOCIETY

Throughout history, substances, many of which are now considered illegal in a number of countries, have been used as an integral component of social activities, religious ceremonies, spiritual rituals, and cultural practices. Along with intended sociocultural purposes, substances have also been sought out to alter mood and enhance sensory experience and pleasure. Individuals have continually experimented with mood-altering substances, as well as heuristic routes of administration that both maximize the delivery to, and enhance the effects on, the brain. The list of mood-altering substances is as varied as it is long and includes well known substances such as marijuana (the most commonly used illicit drug in the United States), cocaine, heroin, tobacco, and ethyl alcohol (one of the most widely used and easily accessible mood-altering substances).

Data from the 2013 National Survey on Drug Use and Health (Substance Abuse and Mental Health Services Administration [SAMHSA], 2014) revealed that over 52% of Americans age 12 years and older (about 137 million people) are current consumers of alcohol, and over 25% of Americans age 12 years and older (nearly 67 million people) are current users of tobacco products. Survey results revealed that nearly 25 million

Americans reported using an illicit drug in 2013; 20 million reported using marijuana without a prescription. A growing problem is the nonmedical use of prescription-type drugs, specifically pain medications. A majority (53%) of those reporting use of nonmedical prescription-type drugs indicated the source was family and friends. Of the 22.7 million who reported needing treatment for an illicit drug or alcohol problem, only 2.5 million (11%) received treatment (SAMHSA, 2014). In 2007, the most recent year for which data are available, the economic cost of illicit drug use in the United States was over $190 billion (U.S. Department of Justice, 2011), which is an increase of nearly 5% from the estimated $181 billion in 2002 (Office of National Drug Control Policy, 2004).

Based on these data, one may conclude that substance use has evolved beyond sociocultural practices to more self-serving and unhealthy usage. However, what is not clear is the primary intent for use. Reasons for using substances can be varied and complex, as evidenced by the numerous theories developed to explain use and addiction. Prevailing attitudes, however, may not fully acknowledge factors beyond pleasure-seeking motives—factors such as stress, psychopathology, crisis response, and grief and loss responses to traumatic events such as natural and human-generated disasters, emergencies, and tragedies. Unfortunately, aggregate data do not delineate the extent to which substance use may in fact be as much about pleasure-seeking as it is about compensating for psychosocial, psychopathological, and sociocultural problems.

Classification of Drugs

The number of different drugs that exist worldwide is unknown. Anecdotal reports estimate that the number of different drugs worldwide may be as high as 100,000. To gain some perspective, Kinch, Haynesworth, Kinch, and Hoyer (2014), in their meta-analytic study, reported that by the end of 2013, a total of 1,453 drugs had received U.S. Food and Drug Administration (FDA) approval. Rather than attempting to quantify drugs, a more effective methodology is to classify substances based on the specific physiological and psychological effects. Current drug classifications include cannabinoids (e.g., marijuana, hashish, dronabinol), depressants (e.g., alcohol, tranquilizers, barbiturates, sleeping pills, inhalants), stimulants (e.g., cocaine, amphetamines, methamphetamine, caffeine), hallucinogens (e.g., LSD, phencyclidine, ketamine, mescaline, psilocybin), opiates (e.g. heroin, morphine, OxyContin, codeine, methadone), nicotine, and psychotherapeutics (e.g., Prozac, Zoloft, Ativan, Xanax, BuSpar, Cymbalta, Abilify, lithium, Geodon, Zyprexa, Risperdal). Other drugs can have multiple effects and may fall under several classifications. For example, ecstasy (3,4-methylenedioxymethamphetamine or MDMA), a designer drug popular in the club and bar scene during the mid-1990s, has both stimulant and hallucinogenic effects. Dextromethorphan (also known as DX or DXM), a drug found in many over-the-counter cough syrups, can have both depressant and mild hallucinogenic effects if taken in large doses.

The Comprehensive Drug Abuse Prevention and Control Act of 1970 classified controlled drugs into five schedules based on a continuum of potential for abuse, accepted medical use, and potential for dependence. Drugs listed under Schedule I have the highest potential for abuse and dependence and have no current medical application in the United States (e.g., heroin, LSD), whereas drugs listed under Schedule V have the lowest potential for abuse and dependence and have an established medical application (e.g., cough syrups with codeine).

Current Research on Substance Use, Crisis, and Society

Several recent studies have documented the relationship between natural and human-generated disasters and subsequent patterns of substance use. A meta-analysis of over 30 studies investigating substance use following terrorist attacks in the United States found an increased use of substances in the 2 years following terrorist events, and the rates of use were likely higher than estimated (DiMaggio, Galea, & Li, 2009). One month following the September 11, 2001, attacks on the World Trade Center, increased use of marijuana, alcohol, and cigarettes was reported in Manhattan (Vlahov et al., 2002). A random phone study of 1,507 New York City residents 6 months after 9/11 showed that the incidence of alcohol problems for those who did not have drinking problems before 9/11 was 2% (Vlahov et al., 2006). In addition, a workplace cohort study that took place before and after 9/11 showed that women used more alcohol post-9/11 compared with before this event (Richman, Wislar, Flaherty, Fendrich, & Rospenda, 2004).

Understanding how crisis situations affect those with preexisting conditions has important implications for substance abuse counselors. Examining the effects of substance use following the April 19, 1995, Oklahoma City bombing, a majority of survivors did not develop new substance use disorders; however, a majority of those survivors who did use substances excessively had a preexisting substance use disorder (North, 2010). Compared with a control community, alcohol consumption among Oklahoma City bombing survivors in the year following the Oklahoma City bombing was 2.5 times greater than for the control community (Smith, Christiansen, Vincent, & Hann, 1999). For evacuees of Hurricane Katrina in August 2005, treatment for preexisting psychiatric illnesses, not increased substance use issues, was the main concern (North, 2010). Counselors should assess the types and amount of substances used as well as the source(s) or provider(s) of the substances.

NDC Health compiled data on the use of antianxiety medication following 9/11 in the New York City and Washington DC metropolitan areas, revealing that in the 2 weeks post-9/11 prescriptions for Xanax, Ativan, and Valium increased (Okie, 2001). Regarding adolescent patterns of substance use, changes in usage status for adolescents exposed to Hurricane Katrina were noted: 15% shifted from cigarette non-use pre-Katrina to use post-Katrina, 9% shifted from non-use to use of marijuana, and 25% shifted from non-use to use of alcohol (Rowe, La Greca, & Alexandersson, 2010). Adolescents not in close proximity to the events of 9/11 also experienced increased marijuana use (Costello, Erkanli, Keeler, & Angold, 2004).

Substance use can not only result from crisis situations, but also affect crisis situations. Schneider (2009) found a strong correlation between substance use disorders and suicide. In a review of psychological autopsy studies, Schneider reported that substance-related disorders contributed to a high proportion of suicides. Individuals who abuse substances are nearly six times more likely to attempt suicide than those who report no substance abuse problems (Dragisic, Dickov, Dickov, & Milatovic, 2015). Further, Dragisic et al. found that those with substance use disorders who attempted suicide also had family members who had psychiatric disorders.

Darke (2009) estimated that 5% of the deaths of those who are substance dependent are due to homicide. He noted that homicide is a major risk factor for substance-dependent populations since substance use plays a key role in perpetuating this form of violence, with alcohol contributing the most to substance-related homicides. Substance use also contributes to other forms of violence, including intimate partner violence (IPV) and sexual assault, as many perpetrators of IPV against women resulting in homicide or attempted homicide were using alcohol, drugs, or a combination of alcohol and drugs. Juodis, Starzomski, Porter, and Woodworth (2014) reported that 76% and 65% of perpetrators of domestic homicide had alcohol use and drug use problems, respectively. Regarding victim substance abuse, varying data exist as to the relationship between victim substance abuse and IPV. The National Institute of Justice (2009) highlighted findings from several studies that also indicate an association between victim substance abuse and domestic violence victimization.

The relationship between substances and sexual violence may in fact be "reciprocal in that sexual violence may be a precursor to or consequence of substance use, abuse, or addiction" (Dawgert, 2009, p. 21). A history of sexual victimization may in fact lead to substance use and abuse as a way to cope with the pain and trauma, while substance use may increase the risk for victimization. Gidycz et al. (2007) found that for women who reported a history of sexual victimization, alcohol use contributed significantly to revictimization during the 2-month follow-up period. Further, as alcohol use increased, so too did the risk for sexual revictimization during this period; women with the highest risk had a history of rape or attempted rape and were also heavy drinkers. Gidycz et al. (2007) also found that decreasing alcohol use can reduce the risk for sexual assault. According to the National Institute of Justice (2008), sexual assault on campuses is more frequently associated with alcohol than drugs, with less than 1% of women reporting being incapacitated by date-rape drugs. In addition, the National Institute of Justice (2008) reported that while more women experience forced sexual assault before college, once in college the risk of becoming a victim of incapacitated sexual assault increases. Based on the National Crime Victimization Survey, the Bureau of Justice Statistics (Sinozich & Langton, 2014) revealed that 47% of female students believed the offender was under the influence of alcohol or drugs when the sexual assault occurred, compared with 25% who did not believe substance use by the offender factored into the sexual assault. Complete Think About It 7.1.

THE ETIOLOGY AND RISK FACTORS OF SUBSTANCE USE AND DEPENDENCE

The most widely accepted belief is that addiction is biologically (neurobiologically, specifically) based; however, alternative hypotheses continue to be debated. One reason for the diversity of theoretical perspectives likely stems from the fact that while research continues to make inroads linking addiction to neurobiological mechanisms, no conclusive evidence of a specific biological relationship exists (Capuzzi & Stauffer, 2012; Craig, 2004; Hammersly, 2014), even though evidence of strong statistical associations exists between biological factors and alcoholism (Capuzzi & Stauffer, 2012). Given the nature

---

THINK ABOUT IT 7.1

Think about a person with a substance use disorder. What are some of the problems he or she may be facing? What images or biases come to mind when you think of a person who is addicted to a substance?

and complexity of addiction, other theories and models will likely evolve to help explain biological, psychological, and sociological factors. The National Institute on Drug Abuse (1980) published a historic compendium of over 40 models and theories of addiction to create a forum for discussion of diverse theoretical perspectives, as well as a tool to help practitioners compare and contrast the various theoretical approaches. Understanding the etiology of substance abuse and addiction is especially critical for counselors working with clients dealing with crisis situations. Awareness of which theoretical model(s) are highly associated with client crisis and substance use may help minimize or ameliorate the physiological and psychological symptoms as well as provide counselors with a targeted treatment framework. A brief discussion of several key theoretical models follows.

Genetic and Biological Models

Jellinek, in his classic 1960 text, conceptualized alcoholism as a disease and believed that individuals with alcoholism, like those with any other disease, manifest specific symptoms and characteristics. In the case of alcoholism, symptoms and characteristics include lack of control over drinking, primary symptoms directly attributed to alcohol consumption, symptoms that are progressive, and continued use that would result in death. Jellinek viewed alcoholism as a chronic and irreversible condition; the only treatment option is complete abstinence from alcohol use. Genetic and biological models emphasize that addiction is caused by a genetic predisposition or physiological factors (Capuzzi & Stauffer, 2012). These models assume that causality for addiction is rooted within a person's DNA or other inheritable biological condition that influences the metabolism of substances. Relationships between genetic predisposition and family patterns of alcoholism have been demonstrated. The basis of neurobiological models is that many psychoactive drugs have specific effects on neurotransmitter activity specifically on the limbic system, which influences emotions and the medial forebrain bundle where alcohol and drugs activate pleasure and reward centers (Hernandez et al., 2006). As substance use continues, the brain produces less of the targeted neurotransmitter (e.g., dopamine) within the pleasure center as the drug mimics the effects of the neurotransmitter. This homeostatic process results in addiction as the individual must now substitute substances for the depleted neurotransmitter.

Social Learning, Cognitive, Sociocultural, and Psychological Models

Social learning theory asserts that people learn from one another through observation, imitating, and/or modeling behaviors (Bandura, 1977). In order to explain addiction from a general systems perspective, one must examine how an individual's behavior is influenced by and as part of a related system. The behaviors of an individual are best understood in relation to other members of the system. This model also assumes that individual problems are more systems-based rather than individual-based (Capuzzi & Stauffer, 2012).

A cognitive model applies the basic tenets of cognitive learning. Simply stated, a person's beliefs about substance use influence expectations related to its use (Craig, 2004; Miller & Hester, 2003). If individuals believe that alcohol and other drug (AOD) use can result in positive outcomes, then this expectation will motivate them to increase the amount and frequency of the substance use.

A conditioning model is based on the concepts of classical and operant conditioning. This model views substance abuse problems as a learned habit, a response to a specific behavior(s). When an external stimulus produces a reward or positive experience, then the association is reinforced, increasing the likelihood that repeated actions or behaviors will result when the stimulus is presented again (Craig, 2004; Miller & Hester, 2003).

A broader approach to AOD addiction is viewed from a sociocultural perspective. The basic premise of this model is that the more acceptable and available the substance, the more members of the societal or cultural group will consume (Capuzzi & Stauffer, 2012). This model addresses the role that culture, subculture, and society play in how individuals perceive substance use and abuse.

Finally, the psychodynamic model views substance abuse as originating with problems in childhood development. Issues such as attachment disorders, inadequate parenting, ego deficiencies, and developmental adjustment issues are at the source of eventual abuse and addiction problems. Those who view psychodynamic models as a possible cause for addiction believe that (1) basic psychopathology is likely the root cause of substance problems; (2) individuals who use substances may do so because of problems with affect regulation; and (3) problematic object relations may eventually influence the onset of substance problems (Dodgen & Shea, 2000).

Factors That Increase Risk for Substance Use Disorders

Numerous risk factors have been identified as contributing to initial substance use. Since initial use often occurs during adolescence, most of the commonly identified risk factors reflect events and issues relevant to that developmental stage. Some of the more common factors include poor academic performance, AOD availability, peer pressure, living in a dysfunctional family environment, and undiagnosed problems, such as learning disabilities. Even though initial use typically occurs in adolescence, AOD use and abuse can occur at any age and can be triggered by various issues such as trauma, disasters, or other emergencies.

Differentiating between risk factors for initial use and substance use disorder is an important consideration given that a majority of those who report experimenting or engaging in recreational substance use do not develop problematic usage behaviors. If that were the case, AOD data would yield a much bleaker picture. For individuals who develop substance use disorders, counselors need to be aware of other potential risk factors such as self-esteem and self-worth issues, isolation, intimacy and fear of rejection issues, poor coping mechanisms, and impulsivity and compulsivity patterns.

Counselors must also be knowledgeable of the co-occurring patterns of psychopathology and substance use disorders. Key psychiatric disorders that co-occur with substance use disorders include major depressive disorders, anxiety disorders, schizophrenia, bipolar disorder, and certain personality disorders (e.g., borderline and antisocial personality disorders). Other risk factors that can lead to abuse and dependency problems include low socioeconomic status, cultural and subcultural factors/expectations, criminality, history of abuse, and a family history of substance abuse and psychopathology.

SCREENING, ASSESSMENT, AND DIAGNOSIS OF SUBSTANCE USE DISORDERS

A critical step in the treatment process is properly evaluating the degree to which substance use is problematic and the extent to which it has influenced the individual, especially those clients who are dealing with crisis or trauma situations. Careful screening, assessment, and diagnosis not only provide an accurate clinical picture but also help the counselor conceptualize applicable theoretical models, formulate preliminary treatment goals, and implement techniques and approaches that will align with the client's presenting issue(s) and motivation for change. In crisis settings where there is a time limit on the number of sessions, this comprehensive information is essential in order to determine the best treatment options for clients.

Success at this stage of the treatment process is greatly influenced by the therapeutic relationship that has been established. A strong therapeutic working alliance between counselor and client can help create a trusting and safe environment enabling the client to feel more at ease when discussing substance history, especially sensitive, shameful, or embarrassing information. Creating a collaborative counselor–client relationship can reduce client resistance and ambivalence while increasing motivation to change. Counselors who instill a sense of optimism or hope and focus on the client's strengths and successes are more inclined to find clients open to exploring options. Seeing the client as more than his or her addiction is critical to this process.

Screening

The first step in the evaluation process is to rule out AOD problems. Screening clarifies whether there is sufficient evidence of problematic substance use and, if yes, whether this use warrants further investigation (assessment). Screening is brief in nature and often entails simple screening questions or brief measures related to substance usage. Questions are designed to determine patterns of use and often focus on frequency, quantity, and problem areas. Examples of frequency and quantity questions that might be asked during the screening process include "During the past 30 days, how many days per week did you drink alcohol or use drugs?" or "On a day when you did drink alcohol or use drugs, how many drinks did you have (or, what quantity of drugs do you use)?"

Regarding the quantity question, the counselor must also determine the client's interpretation of a drink. The following example underscores the importance of clarification of the quantity question:

COUNSELOR:	Bob, during the past 30 days, how many days per week did you drink alcohol or use drugs?
BOB:	I've never used any drugs in my life but I do enjoy drinking alcohol. During the past 30 days, I would say I drank an average of 2 or 3 days each week, and that was mainly on weekends.
COUNSELOR:	On those days when you do drink, how many drinks do you consume?
BOB:	I only have a couple beers.

COUNSELOR: By a couple do you mean two?

BOB: Actually, three or four.

Note that if the counselor concluded the questioning at this point, the only information he or she would have is the number of drinks per episode and how many episodes occurred in the past 30 days. The counselor may surmise that there is no need for further evaluation. But what if the counselor probed further?

COUNSELOR: So on those days when you drink, it is often three or four beers.

BOB: Yes.

COUNSELOR: Tell me about the number of ounces in a typical beer. (*The counselor notices a defensive shift in client's posture and his nonverbal facial expression is one of frustration. Client responds in an angry tone.*)

BOB: Why do you need to know this? I like a few beers, and that's no one's business! (*A period of silence follows.*) Okay, so I drink three or four 40s. It's not a big deal.

Making assumptions about the size of the drinks may lead to inaccurate information and miss a potential problem. In this example, the assumption may be that the client consumes three or four 12-ounce beers per occurrence, when in reality he is consuming over three times that amount. Using the consumption question may be more telling than using more extensive questioning (Fleming, 2003). From a sample of men and women, Williams and Vinson (2001) found that asking the question "When was the last time you had more than four drinks (women) or five drinks (men)?" led to detection of problem drinking or criteria for abuse or dependence in nearly 9 out of 10 people sampled. Self-administered screening instruments can also provide valuable information about substance use patterns. Given the information presented in the example above, continued evaluation appears warranted.

Commonly Used Assessment Instruments

Counselors should carefully weigh the advantages and disadvantages of using assessment instruments based on the information gathered during the screening phase. If an assessment instrument is deemed necessary to gain additional information from the client on his or her substance use, the counselor must decide which type will be most efficient in maximizing clinical information while minimizing client time and frustration.

The following considerations apply when using an assessment instrument: the client must sign an informed consent form (e.g., a form that addresses the purpose of the assessment, risks, benefits, how the information will be used, the client's right to refuse consent); the counselor should see the client as more than the results (the assessment is only one of many pieces of the clinical picture); the counselor should ensure that the assessment instrument is applicable and appropriate for the population it will be used to measure; the counselor should have training and competency in administering the assessment; and the counselor must be able to interpret the results (Stauffer, Capuzzi, & Tanigoshi, 2008). Four commonly used assessment instruments are the Alcohol Use

Disorders Identification Test (AUDIT), Michigan Alcoholism Screening Test (MAST), Substance Abuse Subtle Screening Inventory-3 (SASSI-3), and the CAGE.

The AUDIT was developed as a collaborative project by the World Health Organization from a six-nation study to identify early detection of problematic drinking patterns and behaviors (Saunders, Aasland, Babor, de la Fuente, & Grant, 1993). The AUDIT comprises 10 items divided into 3 domains: questions 1 to 3 address alcohol consumption patterns; questions 4 to 6 focus on dependency issues; and questions 7 to 10 address problems associated with alcohol use. The AUDIT questions use a 5-point Likert-type scale (0 to 4) and total scores can range from 0 to 40. A total score greater than 8 points indicates a pattern of harmful or hazardous drinking. Of those diagnosed with harmful or hazardous drinking, 92% had scores greater than 8 points. Of those who were not diagnosed with problematic drinking, 94% had scores less than 8 points. Based on total scores, counselors may incorporate certain interventions. The use of education and reduction approaches is suggested for those who score from 8 to 15. Individuals who score from 16 to 19 likely would benefit from brief interventions or counseling and follow-up. Individuals who score over 20 are at high risk and should be assessed for alcohol dependence and more intensive treatment (Babor, Higgins-Biddle, Saunders, Monteiro, & World Health Organization, 2001).

The MAST is a 25-item measure that uses true–false responses (Selzer, 1971). Each question is scored using a weighted response of 0, 1, 2, or 5. The original scoring indicated that individuals who scored greater than or equal to 5 points were alcohol dependent; individuals who scored 4 points were at risk of developing alcoholism; and individuals who scored less than 3 points would not be considered alcoholic. Other scoring systems classify individual scores of greater than 7 points as alcohol dependent, 5 or 6 points as borderline alcohol dependent, and less than 4 points as not currently at risk for alcohol dependence (Hedlund & Vieweg, 1984). The MAST continues to be used extensively, and the scoring and interpretation are easy. Variations of the MAST have been developed. These include the MAST-R, which modified the language, resulting in 22 items; the Short MAST (SMAST; Selzer, Vinokur, & Van Rooijen, 1975), which contains 13 items; and the MAST-G, a geriatric version (Blow et al., 1992).

The Substance Abuse Subtle Screening Inventory-3 (SASSI-3) was developed as an easy-to-use tool for clinical assessment and treatment to help identify those who have a high probability of developing substance use disorder (Miller, 1999). The inventory has 10 subscales. Eight subscales comprise 67 true–false questions on nonsubstance related issues. The other two subscales include 26 items that address AOD use by a self-report format. Scoring is done by using decision rules related to client recognition of abuse or dependence, defensiveness/denial, personality style similar to those with alcohol dependence, and characteristics associated with those who misuse substances. The more decision rules that apply, the greater the probability of substance dependence. Psychometric data support the SASSI-3 as yielding reliable and valid scores for substance use disorder detection. Of the measures available, the SASSI-3 has also been an important and highly valued tool and has been used extensively by addictions counselors (Juhnke, Vacc, Curtis, Coll, & Paredes, 2003).

The CAGE (Ewing, 1984) is a simple four-question screening tool that can be incorporated into a clinical interview. It is used only with adult and adolescent clients, and it is intended to identify behaviors related to alcohol use only. Each letter in the acronym *CAGE* represents one of the four questions: Have you ever felt the need to *Cut* down on your drinking? Have people *A*nnoyed you by criticizing your drinking? Have you ever felt bad or *G*uilty about your drinking? Have you ever had a drink first thing in the morning to steady your nerves or to get rid of a hangover (*E*ye opener)? Each *yes* response to these questions receives a score of 1 point. Scores 0 to 1 do not reflect any apparent problems, and scores greater than or equal to 2 are a possible indication of alcohol dependence. One concern with the CAGE is the wide variability in accurately diagnosing alcohol use disorders.

Assessment

An assessment is conducted for the following purposes: (1) to ascertain the degree and severity of a problem; (2) to determine the presence of co-occurring disorders; (3) to make accurate diagnoses; (4) to assess the scope of the problem (i.e., whether it is specific to the individual or systemic, such as within the family or support system); (5) to guide the treatment planning process; and (6) to provide a mechanism for communication across treatment personnel (Erford, 2013).

The primary focus of substance use assessment is to gather detailed information on substance use patterns, including drug(s) used; progression of use (amount and frequency of use over time); route of administration; reason for periods of increased usage or abstinence; treatment history; and evidence of tolerance, dependence, and withdrawal. During the clinical interview, obtaining clients' history of substances used helps to establish a pattern and context of substance usage. The assessment should compile information and usage patterns on commonly used drugs such as alcohol, marijuana, opiates, hallucinogens, cocaine, amphetamines and related stimulants, inhalants, nicotine, and caffeine. With the growth of synthetic or designer illicit drugs, the assessment should include questions about use of drug variations such as flakka (a synthetic version of the stimulant cathinone), K2 (synthetic cannabinoids), bath salts (synthetic cathinones), wax (marijuana and butane), purple drank (cough syrup with codeine and promethazine mixed in soft drinks or made into candy), and krokodil (desomorphine, a derivative of codeine that is mixed with oil, gasoline, alcohol or paint thinner and injected), to name a few (see Table 7.1, at the end of this chapter, for resources on commonly used designer drugs).

Inquiring about use of any psychotherapeutic medications, prescriptions, and over-the-counter drugs, including herbal supplements, rounds out the comprehensive picture of usage. Including questions about these types of drugs is beneficial since most clients do not consider them to be problematic, especially if they have been prescribed. Gathering information on these substances provides valuable information on potential synergistic effects resulting from drug interactions. Further, having knowledge of different drug interactions can help determine any potential contraindications that may exist. For example, clients with bipolar disorder who are using lithium are advised to avoid certain drugs that are contraindicated including alcohol, nonsteroidal anti-inflammatory medications such as ibuprofen, and illicit drugs such as ecstasy that can result in changes in lithium levels.

Assessment also provides a comprehensive picture of the client across different psychosocial domains (e.g., medical, legal, education, employment history, family history, psychiatric history). Often information gathered on other psychosocial issues is directly connected to substance use. For example, clients with substance use issues may have an unstable employment history or a pattern of legal problems. It is not uncommon for those with a history of substance-related problems to also have conflicts in their relationships with family and friends. Medical concerns may be directly related to substance use, yet clients may not make the connection or resist addressing the problem.

When conducting a substance use assessment, counselors should also evaluate the client's current level of mental functioning, which is often done using the Mental Status Exam (MSE). The purpose of the MSE is to investigate signs and symptoms of impaired affect, behavior, cognition, and intellectual functioning related to one's mental state. The MSE can also be valuable in differentiating between substance and nonsubstance impaired mental symptoms and for ruling out co-occurring disorders (Rudd, 2006). Given that most clients who have co-occurring substance abuse and mental health issues are likely attending counseling due to acute symptom presentation or concerns associated with these disorders, counselors should evaluate whether a crisis assessment is warranted. For example, clients who have a previous history of psychiatric diagnoses (e.g., bipolar disorder, major depressive disorder, schizophrenia) and substance abuse are at greater risk for suicidal behavior.

One of the more commonly used methods for conducting substance abuse assessment is the clinical interview, a process that includes extensive and detailed questions regarding various content domains. When counselors are conducting the clinical assessment, it is inevitable that clients indicate how they define their substance use. Some clients may be inclined to overestimate or underestimate use or information. Clients may indicate that they fit into certain categories (e.g., social drinkers, recreational users) despite information to the contrary. Therefore, counselors may need to ask additional questions or clarify client responses.

Semistructured clinical interviews are often preferred over structured ones because they allow the counselor to ask specific, structured questions in various domains and provide the counselor with the flexibility to expand on or deviate from questions based on client response. Domains that are commonly covered in a clinical interview are as follows:

1. Demographic information (e.g., name, age, race, height, weight)
2. Presenting complaint or reason for attending
3. Medical history (e.g., diagnoses, medications, hospitalizations, surgeries)
4. Substance use history
5. Legal history (e.g., specific charges, incarcerations, any charges that are pending, parole/probation status, any protection from abuse orders)
6. Employment history (e.g., job history, reason for leaving jobs, conflicts with coworkers or supervisors, work performance and evaluations)
7. Education history (e.g., degrees achieved, problems in school and reasons for them, difficulty with reading or writing)
8. Social and family history (e.g., childhood issues, trauma, or abuse; family discord/dysfunction; marital status; current living arrangements; history of relationship problems; family history of mental illness or substance abuse; history of child abuse or neglect for those with children)
9. Recreational history (e.g., activities of interest, activities impacted by substance use, hobbies, memberships in clubs or groups)
10. Religious/spiritual/cultural history (e.g., current and past religious/spiritual beliefs, practices, attendance; spiritual injuries; cultural/heritage values, beliefs, considerations)

11. Psychiatric/psychological history (e.g., any psychiatric or personality diagnoses, hospitalizations, inpatient/outpatient treatment, suicide attempts and history)
12. Sexual history (e.g., sexual identity, sexual disorders, sexually communicable diseases)
13. Mental Status Exam

Scenarios 1 and 2 provide some guidance on clarifying client presenting information.

Scenario 1: Challenging a Client's Definition of Social Drinking

COUNSELOR: John, you mentioned earlier in our session that you drink daily and often drive when you know you shouldn't. Help me understand how you see your drinking.

JOHN: Well, I don't see it as a problem. I never had a DUI and had only minor issues with my wife when I've gotten home late or with my boss when I've missed time at work because I'm hung over. I guess I see myself as a social drinker because I only drink when I go out after work with my friends.

COUNSELOR: So you classify your drinking as social because of the location, and you have not had any significant consequences.

JOHN: That's how I see it.

COUNSELOR: Tell me how you might view this definition if you got arrested for a DUI, the relationship with your wife got much worse, or you got fired from your job because of your drinking. (*This probe helps the client examine his usage knowing that any one of these scenarios is a real possibility even as a "social drinker."*)

Scenario 2: Differentiating Between Recreational Use and Substance Abuse

BILL: I only smoke pot recreationally as a way to relax and have some fun.

COUNSELOR: How would you classify your pot use?

BILL: I share a joint or two with some friends once a month. It's not a big deal.

COUNSELOR: You mentioned that you only use marijuana occasionally, yet when you were discussing your medical and legal history, you alluded to using it more regularly.

BILL: Just 'cause I have breathing problems and had a few run-ins with the law doesn't mean I have a problem!

COUNSELOR: I sense you're upset right now because we're talking about whether you're use is really recreational. My intent is not to judge or be critical of your choices around marijuana.

> Rather, I'm concerned that your use may be causing problems in other areas of your life.

BILL: Sometimes I use it more as a way to have fun.

Diagnosis

A well-conducted, thorough assessment should yield sufficient data to make accurate diagnoses and establish the degree of impairment. With most other mental health diagnoses, providing a full diagnosis during a crisis phase would be premature and inappropriate due to the symptoms and period of time needed to accurately offer a valid diagnosis. Pure substance use disorders, not including induced disorder categories (e.g., substance-induced mood disorders, substance-induced bipolar disorder) rely on self-reports and can aid the treatment planning and referral process. The purpose of diagnosis is to identify the specific condition(s) or disorder(s) that are causing the impairment in order to provide a basis with which treatment interventions can be applied, or to make an appropriate referral for long-term substance treatment. The main diagnostic tool used for substance use disorders is the *Diagnostic and Statistical Manual of Mental Disorders* (DSM-5) (American Psychiatric Association [APA], 2013). In the DSM-5, substance use and addictive disorders are organized into a number of categories. The two categories of primary interest are alcohol use disorder and substance use disorder, the latter covering a variety of addictive substances, such as amphetamines, cocaine, and inhalants.

Prior to the latest edition, the DSM classified substance use disorders as either substance abuse or substance dependence. As a result of the ambiguity and confusion surrounding dependence and addiction, the DSM-5 does not use the terms *substance abuse* and *substance dependence*. Instead, it uses the umbrella term *substance use disorders* in relation to recurrent alcohol and drug use (APA, 2013). *Dependence* and *addiction* were often used interchangeably, and tolerance and withdrawal were criteria central to a dependence diagnosis. However, tolerance and withdrawal are common and expected responses to prescription medications that act on the central nervous system and as such do not imply one is addicted, especially if these are the only symptoms evident. The reclassification to substance use disorders and the use of severity specifiers (mild, moderate, severe) provide counselors with a reference point for the progression of the substance use pattern, as well as a perspective on how best to approach treatment and which interventions may be most applicable.

According to the DSM-5, at least two of the following criteria must be met for an individual to be diagnosed with a substance use disorder: (1) significant problems exist at home, school, or work due to use; (2) physical hazards occur due to repeated episodes of impaired driving or operating machinery while under the influence; (3) substance use results in recurring legal problems (e.g., public intoxication); (4) tolerance increases; (5) withdrawal occurs; (6) increasing amounts of the substance are taken over time; (7) usage levels are not being reduced; (8) a lot of time is spent acquiring the substance; (9) social or work activities are sacrificed due to use or to recover from use; (10) use continues despite interpersonal and physical effects; and (11) there is craving, a strong urge, or desire for the substance. Severity is determined by the number of presenting criteria (i.e., mild: 2 to 3 criteria; moderate: 4 to 5 criteria; severe: 6 or more criteria). Complete Activity 7.1, which focuses on substance use disorder diagnosis.

ACTIVITY 7.1

When assessing a client for a substance use disorder, which issues and factors do you believe should be   considered to make an accurate diagnosis?

Assessing a Client's Readiness to Change

A client's readiness to change is an essential function to consider during the assessment phase. Evaluating resistance to change allows the counselor to match treatment techniques and motivational approaches to the level of client ambivalence. Several change models have appeared since the 1970s (Connors, DiClemente, Velasquez, & Donovan, 2013), but Prochaska and DiClemente's (1992) five-stage change model focuses mainly on change patterns associated with health behavior change and reflects identifiable stages individuals go through as they are attempting to change substance use behaviors.

Prochaska and DiClemente (1992) identified the following five stages of change:

1. *Precontemplation*—characterized by resistance to change or denying that a problem exists;
2. *Contemplation*—evidence of ambivalence exists and the client is contemplating the effects of substance abuse as well as weighing the advantages and disadvantages of continued use;
3. *Preparation*—resistance has waned and the client has made a decision to change but is uncertain how to go about this process
4. *Action*—the client is committed to making a change and has demonstrated specific goals and behaviors toward this end; and
5. *Maintenance*—the client has maintained a period of abstinence and is working on maintaining recovery and addressing relapse issues and triggers.

Transitioning across stages is rarely a smooth, straightforward process. Clients may move from one stage to the next or make movement across several stages only to experience a setback. Moving back to an earlier stage is not unexpected given that change is difficult and clients will likely experience much frustration and discouragement during the process. Motivational support becomes an integral component to assist in the change process. Understanding the importance of instilling motivation as an antidote for ambivalence and resistance, Miller and Rollnick (2013) integrated their motivational interviewing (MI) approach into the stage of change model based on the belief that motivation is not intrinsically driven as part of one's personality or personal traits but rather is developed through interpersonal interactions. They identified MI as a client-centered, directive, transtheoretical approach emphasizing empathic communication to bring about a client's intrinsic motivation to change that aligns with his or her values and beliefs. MI was developed as an alternative to the directive and confrontational approaches that were widely used and accepted in treating addiction for decades. Miller and Rollnick developed four central processes that serve as the basis for MI: (1) *engaging*—establishing a connection between counselor and client that helps to build the working alliance; (2) *focusing*—involves the counselor developing and maintaining a focused direction in the discussion about change;

(3) *evoking*—assisting the client to take ownership for their motivation for change; and (4) *planning*—establishing a commitment to change with a specific course of action where talk shifts from whether and why it happens to when and how to change. Read Voices from the Field 7.1.

Treatment Admission and Placement

Information gathered during the assessment and diagnosis phases assists the counselor in determining not only treatment planning but also the appropriate level of care for clients in crisis. Clients who present with significant substance use issues will likely require an intensive treatment protocol compared with clients who are abusing a sub stance. American Society of Addiction Medicine (ASAM, 2013) provides comprehensive treatment criteria for patient placement, continued stay, and discharge. The latest ASAM criteria put greater emphasis on co-occurring mental health disorders and substance use disorders. ASAM continues to divide the continuum of treatment into increasing levels of care. The five broad levels of care, now designated by numbers instead of Roman numerals, are as follows:

- *Level 0.5* (Early Intervention) involves screening, brief intervention, referral, and treatment; early intervention services were expanded as a way to reach out to the nearly 20 million individuals who are pursuing addiction treatment;
- *Level 1* (Outpatient Services) is considered a gateway for substance use treatment as well as a level of care that can focus on ongoing chronic addiction and abstinence;

VOICES FROM THE FIELD 7.1
Working with Substance Abuse

Rachel M. Hoffman

"Addiction is an issue with which I never want to work! I don't want to work with clients who don't want to change!" That quote, or something very close to it, was uttered by me at some point (or maybe more) during my graduate counselor training experience. Before being exposed to the field of addiction counseling, I mistakenly believed that addiction was a disorder from which people really had to "hit rock bottom" before they could recover. Now, many years and a lot of education later, I have a completely different view of addictions, and I honestly couldn't imagine working with any other population.

Addiction is a complex phenomenon. Many researchers now believe that addiction is a brain disease that results in neurological adaptations with prolonged substance use. After spending the past several years working in an agency that specialized in addiction, I've learned that it is important to use interventions appropriate for a client's stage of change. Assessing a client's stage of change (i.e., precontemplation, contemplation, preparation, action, and maintenance) allows the counselor to develop interventions based on the client's readiness to change a particular behavior or situation.

In my work with clients, I've appreciated the ability to use motivational interviewing techniques to help the client move through the stages of change. I respect my clients' abilities to make changes that align with their stated goals and desired outcomes. Adopting this strengths-based approach to working with clients has helped me avoid frustration, burnout, and anger in my work with this difficult population. Although I did not initially intend to work with this population, I find my daily work with addictions immensely satisfying and rewarding, and I'm thankful that my career path has led me in this direction.

- *Level 2* (Intensive Outpatient/Partial Hospitalization Services);
- *Level 3* (Residential/Inpatient services); and
- *Level 4* (Medically Managed Intensive Inpatient Services).

Each level also has a withdrawal management designation that aligns with what the counselor believes is needed to manage the physiological and psychological symptoms of withdrawal.

ASAM has developed six dimensions that practitioners can use to assess clients at each level and provide a rationale/justification for a particular level of care. The dimensions also serve as standardized assessment language for general health care and mental health practitioners. The six dimensions are as follows:

1. Acute intoxication and/or withdrawal potential—assessing withdrawal management across different levels of care and making preparations for continued addiction services;
2. Biomedical conditions and complications;
3. Emotional, behavioral, or cognitive conditions and complications;
4. Readiness to change;
5. Relapse, continued use, or continued problem potential—greater focus on addressing early stages of change; and
6. Recovery/living environment.

The ASAM assessment dimensions should be incorporated into the continuous evaluation of the client's progress. Based on the outcome of an assessment, the counselor should identify the most appropriate care and adjust the treatment plan accordingly (Mee-Lee, 2013). When assessing all six dimensions, counselors want to select the treatment level that is least intensive but the safest level of care based on the client's presenting issue and assessed dimensions. See Case Study 7.1, which highlights the ASAM assessment process.

CASE STUDY 7.1

A Client Assessment Using the Six ASAM Dimensions

Rick is a 42-year-old White male brought to the city hospital following a DUI accident that resulted in him breaking his collarbone and arm. Rick's blood alcohol level (BAL) was .42 at the time of his arrest, and this was his second DUI in the past 12 months. Rick's BAL for his first DUI was .12, and he was approved for Accelerated Rehabilitative Disposition (ARD), a pretrial intervention program for nonviolent offenders with no prior record. During the trial for the second DUI, the judge requested a substance abuse evaluation and is considering remanding Rick to treatment in lieu of incarceration. The counselor completed an assessment of Rick using the six ASAM dimensions and made a treatment recommendation.

> *Dimension 1: Acute Intoxication and/or Withdrawal Potential* Rick demonstrated increased tolerance. Based on reported usage, he is at elevated risk for physiological withdrawal. Concerns exist given his pattern of continued use, his high BAL, and his inability to stop drinking on his own. He meets criteria for Level 3.2-WM (Clinically Managed Residential Withdrawal Management).

Dimension 2: Biomedical Conditions and Complications With the exception of his current medical complications, Rick did not present any specific health problems or complications due to alcohol. He is not on any medications. He meets criteria for Level 1 (Outpatient Services).

Dimension 3: Emotional, Behavioral, or Cognitive Conditions and Complications Rick has problems managing anger and often fights with his spouse and coworkers, especially when he is drinking. He lacks coping skills and can be quite reactive when confronted about his alcohol use. Interpersonal skills, specifically communication skills, are poor. He does not take responsibility for his actions and tends to blame others for his problems. He lacks self-efficacy, motivation, and cognitive awareness to make the necessary changes at this point. He meets criteria for Level 3.3 (Clinically Managed Population-Specific High-Intensity Residential Services [adult level only]).

Dimension 4: Readiness to Change Rick is at the precontemplative stage of change. He does not see his use as a problem and believes he can control his drinking without any assistance. He feels others are not understanding him and is in denial about his usage and amount. He is defensive and angry when discussing his alcohol use. He meets criteria for Level 3.3.

Dimension 5: Relapse, Continued Use, or Continued Problem Potential Rick's potential for relapse is very high without intensive treatment. He lacks skills and resources to maintain sobriety. He denies having any friends who do not drink or who provide positive support systems. Without intensive treatment and an established supportive network, his prognosis for maintaining sobriety is very poor. He meets criteria for Level 3.3.

Dimension 6: Recovery/Living Environment Rick has alienated his wife and family. He does not have a good relationship with his wife and does not care what she thinks about his drinking. He has refused to attend 12-step meetings and thinks they are a waste of time. His current support system cannot assist in helping him maintain recovery. His social activities revolve around drinking. He meets criteria for Level 3.3.

Recommendation to the Judge Rick meets criteria for Level 3 for five of the six dimensions. Treatment recommendations are as follows: complete inpatient/residential treatment detoxification protocol followed by Level 3.3 residential treatment (adult level only). Length of stay will depend on progress on all six dimensions and should be reevaluated after 4 weeks. Step down to Level 2.1 intensive outpatient treatment following successful discharge from Level 3 care.

Discussion Questions

1. What treatment approaches might you consider using with Rick?
2. As the counselor, what issues would come up for you as you work with Rick?

SUBSTANCE USE TREATMENT AND CRISIS

Treating substance use disorders becomes more complex when the client is also experiencing a crisis. Clients can be in crisis at any point along the substance use continuum and may require different interventions depending on their level of motivation, stage of change, the significance of the crisis event, intensity of the crisis response, coping capacity, resilience, and existence of co-occurring disorders. Before continuing, complete Think About It 7.2 and read Voices from the Field 7.2.

Counselors should be aware of a multitude of treatment options when working with clients identified with substance use disorders. Over the years, numerous treatment modalities have been implemented to address substance use disorders. Sorting out which treatments are effective has been no simple task. Decisions for treatment approaches have often been based on personal interest or counselor familiarity rather than on empirically supported evidence. Efforts to understand which treatments are effective have increased significantly over the past several decades. Traditional approaches such as confrontational approaches, aversion therapies, insight-based psychotherapy, and educational approaches have generally been ineffective (Miller, Wilbourne, & Hettema, 2003). A comprehensive review of various treatment modalities revealed that approaches such as brief interventions, motivational enhancement, GABA agonists and opiate antagonists, various behavioral treatments, community reinforcement, and social skills training were ranked the highest in terms of treatment efficacy.

THINK ABOUT IT 7.2

Think about your personal characteristics and skill levels. What counselor characteristics and counseling skills/techniques do you believe are important when dealing with clients who use substances as a means to manage a crisis response?

VOICES FROM THE FIELD 7.2
Engaging the Client Who Uses Substances

Steve Zappalla

One of the most common traits of substance use clients is their denial system and strong habit to protect their substance of choice, often at any cost. For the counselor, it is important to relate to and understand their desire to use a substance. Using language, descriptions, and techniques they understand is helpful to gain their trust, respect, and confidence quickly. Meeting clients where they are is extremely important.

Listen carefully to the client's resistance and use calm, reflective statements. Determine the main theme that is bothering the client and avoid attacking the drinking or using problem. It helps to hear what they're saying. Try to see things from the client's point of view, no matter how unreasonable or how irrational he or she seems. Your goal is to create a space to help clients see that what they are doing is not working and try to get them to want to do something about it, not to win a confrontation. It could prove more beneficial to acknowledge different viewpoints.

Try to be encouraging and understanding. Clients often become resistant, even hostile, when they feel frustrated or confused. Clients with substance use disorders tend not to have a very mature emotional coping system and will react quickly with what they know best. The most important thing to keep in mind is that there is a good chance the client does not know any other way. While small steps may seem a success early on, it is critically important to help clients feel and see the long-term benefit of this new behavior. It is most important to help clients see that what they are doing is not working and begin to help them take steps to do something about it.

Given that brief interventions and motivational enhancement approaches were two of the highest-ranked effective approaches to address substance use disorders, integrating a crisis model that aligns with these approaches allows the counselor to effectively address both the crisis response and substance use disorder (see the task model of crisis assessment and intervention presented in Table 1.1). See Case Studies 7.2 and 7.3, which provide practice in applying the model of crisis assessment and intervention.

CASE STUDY 7.2

A Single Crisis Session

Lenora is a 23-year-old woman who was transported to the hospital during the early morning hours by her sister, Mary. Lenora presented as visibly upset, very angry, shaking, disheveled, and crying uncontrollably. Mary told the attending nurse that Lenora had been out drinking earlier that night and met a man. Mary explained that he was buying Lenora drinks and at one point must have slipped her a "roofie." Lenora did not recall what took place, but when the drug wore off she found herself alone in a hotel room several blocks from the bar and unclothed. Lenora reported that she was sexually assaulted and raped several times. Mary also shared that Lenora "has been drinking a lot for the past 6 months" following the termination of a long-term relationship. You are a substance abuse counselor working for a local mental health agency that contracts with the hospital for evening and weekend crisis response calls.

Discussion Questions

1. Explore how you could integrate the task model of crisis assessment and intervention (see Table 1.1).
2. What would be the first thing you would do to address this crisis situation?

CASE STUDY 7.3

Crisis Intervention with a Substance Abuse Client

Francis is a 39-year-old married man who recently learned that his wife of 10 years is filing for divorce because of his marijuana and cocaine addiction. He also learned of an ongoing affair she is having with his best friend. Francis has been distraught for several days upon hearing this news and is contemplating suicide. At his mother's insistence, Francis begrudgingly decides to attend the initial appointment she made for him with a counselor who specializes in substance abuse and crisis issues at the local mental health agency. Francis is aware that his drug use was causing some problems at home and has tried several times to stop, but he has been unable to maintain abstinence for more than a day. He reported that he was in counseling 2 years ago when his wife threatened to leave him but was not motivated to change and dropped out after a couple of sessions. He also did not feel the counselor was listening to him and was instead telling him what to do. He acknowledges his drug use has caused some problems and is really upset over his wife's affair with his best friend. He is coming to the realization that it is too late to save his marriage. He states to the counselor that he has no reason to live. Let's examine how the counselor may structure the first six sessions.

Session 1:

The counselor must undertake several tasks simultaneously. Understanding what was helpful and not helpful from the client's previous counseling experience can provide valuable information as to how the client views counseling, approaches that should be avoided or enhanced, a sense of motivation, and ways to conceptualize how best to establish a working alliance. Establishing a working alliance is essential given the client's fragile emotional state. While the counselor is working to establish rapport and create an environment where the client can feel supported, effort must be directed toward the client's message of desperation and suicide ideation. The counselor must assess the severity of the client's statement around self-harm. During this process, the counselor must assess the level of intent and determine both the subjective (client statements) and objective (specific concrete behaviors) messages. Using direct language (direct questions versus reflective responses) is necessary to evaluate intent, means to carry out the intent, and a clearly developed plan. Conveying this information in an empathic manner creates a sense of care and concern that increases the likelihood the client will come back next session. Let's look at the counselor–client dialogue related to examining intent.

COUNSELOR:	Francis, I appreciate your willingness to seek help and for being open with me. I want to ask you a few questions to help me better understand your emotional state.
FRANCIS:	OK.
COUNSELOR:	Tell me about what you mean by not wanting to live anymore.
FRANCIS:	My world has fallen apart. My wife has been upset about my drug use for some time, and I think it drove her to having an affair. I'm really torn up by this and don't see any reason for living. I really screwed up.
COUNSELOR:	You mentioned or alluded to a couple times today that you don't want to live. Before we talk about what is going on right now for you, let's discuss any previous suicidal thoughts or attempts. Have you made any suicide attempts previously?
FRANCIS:	No, never, but I've thought about it from time to time, especially after my wife and I got into fights about my drug use.
COUNSELOR:	At that time, did you have a plan to hurt yourself and, if you did, did you have the means to carry it out? (*Give examples of methods.*)
FRANCIS:	No, I didn't have a plan. It was just thoughts running around my head that I couldn't let go of. I got really scared of my

thoughts because I didn't feel I had any reason to live. I felt that I'm no good to her or anyone. I felt overwhelmed and the pain was unbearable.

COUNSELOR: You felt so distraught and worthless because nothing seemed to matter anymore. The only solution in your mind was to commit suicide. Describe your intention to hurt yourself at that point.

FRANCIS: I thought a lot in those moments about killing myself, but I didn't because I would have hurt more knowing my children and my mom would have to live with this.

COUNSELOR: Francis, you were aware of the painful outcomes killing yourself would have on loved ones. Help me understand more about your state of mind during that time. Did you think of or have a plan in place and if so did you have a means to carry out that plan?

FRANCIS: No plan. I just wanted the pain to go away. I started to use more drugs to numb out.

COUNSELOR: Did you plan to use more drugs with the hope of killing yourself? (*Exploring drug use as a possible means to carry out suicide is important to assess as it can be easily overlooked with the focus on more acute means of lethality.*)

FRANCIS: No. I never planned or intended to overdose or use drugs to kill myself. Only to take away the pain.

COUNSELOR: So you had no specific plan or means?

FRANCIS: That's right. I guess I chickened out.

COUNSELOR: Choosing to live when you were facing incredible pain takes a lot of courage and strength. (*The counselor continues to use empathy to build support, rapport, and trust.*)

FRANCIS: I guess, but I'm not feeling a lot of courage right now.

COUNSELOR: Describe your current thoughts about wanting to kill yourself. (*The counselor may use a 1 to 10 scale to help assess, with 1 being no intent, plan, or means to kill myself and 10 being a definite plan and means to kill myself.*)

FRANCIS: Kind of like what we talked about before. Feeling really overwhelmed. Maybe a 3 or 4.

COUNSELOR: So a 3 or 4 would indicate feeling overwhelmed like what you felt before or is it more than before?

FRANCIS: Pretty much the same.

COUNSELOR: Thank you for helping me understand. Francis, given these recent painful experiences, do you have a plan or means to kill yourself right now?

FRANCIS: No. I just feel really awful. I just wish the pain would go away.

COUNSELOR: The pain feels really unbearable, so much so that you think that the only way to reconcile it is by not existing anymore. (*If the client mentioned a plan and intent, the counselor would explore in detail the plan and means. The counselor would ask about specific sources to carry out suicide and continue to examine multiple methods until the client states that no other methods have been considered.*)

FRANCIS: Yes. (*Francis cries for several minutes.*) And I don't know what to do next 'cause nothing has worked out and my wife is leaving and screwing around with my best friend because of my drug use.

COUNSELOR: It sounds like you don't want to die, you just want your life to make sense. Right now you are uncertain what direction to go in to alleviate the pain. You know that drugs have not helped the situation, but they have been the only thing that has helped to numb the pain.

FRANCIS: Exactly! I know this is no way to live my life. I'm tired of feeling this way, but it's the only thing I know that works and I'm not sure I want to let go of using drugs at this point. (*The client's affect brightens a little and seems a little hopeful that he is being listened to. Something he complained his wife never did.*)

COUNSELOR: It sounds like the relationship with drugs is causing a lot of pain and problems, but you're not ready to let it go. Maybe we can work together to examine this relationship and the costs/benefits of using versus not using.

FRANCIS: It's something I've been thinking about. I've been trying to figure out why I keep doing this when it causes so many other problems, but I need it and I'm not sure I can give it up right now 'cause it hurts too much when I don't use drugs.

COUNSELOR: Let's not focus on all or nothing options related to use. Would you instead be open to examining your use and understanding what purpose it's serving for you?

FRANCIS: I'd be open to talking about this.

COUNSELOR: To help start that conversation, I have some materials that others have found helpful as they attempted to understand similar issues you've been facing. Would you be interested in looking these over between now and our next session?

FRANCIS: Yes, I'd be interested.

The counselor established that there was no chronic suicidality or previous attempts. Client responses indicate mild risk and the counselor should evaluate and monitor risk on an ongoing basis. The client has difficulty when facing challenging situations, feels overwhelmed, often uses substances impulsively to manage emotional instability, and has a history of fleeting thoughts of suicide but no established intent, plan, or means. During the remainder of the session, the counselor will assess the client's drug use and motivation to change. The counselor is still concerned about the client's strained emotional state and will work to establish a plan in the event that the client's condition worsens before the next session. The counselor may consider using the commitment to treatment statement (CTS), an agreement to commit to the treatment process and to living, and a crisis response plan that outlines specific behaviors the client will engage in if the crisis escalates (see Rudd, 2006).

The counselor and client also work together to examine a realistic plan for substance use. It is evident the client is in the contemplative stage, and the counselor wants to continue to enhance client understanding and awareness. The counselor also commits time in session to discussing the marital issues and explores the dynamics that have triggered this recent crisis situation. The client is feeling better at the end of the session and they agree to meet again in 4 days. At the end of this session the counselor must thoroughly document the session and provide specific content related to the suicidal ideation, established patterns, and current condition. The use of direct client quotes strengthens the record.

Session 2:

The counselor continues to build rapport and establish the therapeutic working alliance using basic reflective skills and advanced skills such as clarification and immediacy as needed while helping the client color in the details related to the presenting problem, including the implications of the affair. In this session, the counselor assesses the client's emotional state and explores behaviors and activity during the past several days and evaluates whether different interventions are necessary. Motivational enhancement approaches continue to serve as a building block for exploration of the client's substance use and assist in shifting the client's ambivalence toward change. The exploration and implementation of treatment options will align with the client's stage of change. Assessing cultural factors and their role in understanding a client's motivation level is important during the second session. Also, the counselor discusses the bibliotherapy assignment and specific reactions, thoughts, insights, and how the client has integrated this information and any newly acquired knowledge into his situation. The counselor and client discuss additional options, including continued bibliotherapy options, and the possibility of listing advantages and disadvantages of current substance use for the next session. At the end of the session, the counselor and client both summarize salient issues, and the counselor reminds the client of the behavioral plan in the event the crisis reemerges.

Sessions 3 to 6:

Evidence of a stronger therapeutic alliance is emerging with ease of rapport and signs that the client is trusting the counselor. The exploration of presenting problems continues. The counselor notices that the client has chosen options to help explore ambivalence, including a handwritten list of the advantages and disadvantages of drug use. The client reported that he knew his substance use was a problem but did not understand the magnitude until he made this list. He reported that he wants to make changes and wants to end this relationship with drugs. He also realized how much he alienated his wife and, while still very hurt and upset over her affair, understands how his drug use contributed to this process. He reported that he wants to change but does not know where to begin. He also reported that he has not used drugs for the past 12 hours and has been feeling a little rough, but indicated he would like to be drug-free in the next month.

The client's attitude has shifted from the first session, and his behaviors indicate that he is preparing to move toward making a change. The counselor recognizes this shift and works with the client to develop a plan to change and specific treatment options that align with the preparation. During this stage, the client's motivation aligns with specific behavioral approaches and the opportunity for the counselor to use other advanced skills such as challenging, advanced empathy, and immediacy. During these sessions, working with the client to establish a support system will be critical.

At this point, the counselor would have a discussion about various types of supports and assess the client's willingness to explore each. It is important that the counselor be knowledgeable of different support options and help the client navigate this process. For example, integrating 12-step support groups is quite common, yet many counselors may not take the time to process the client's apprehensions or fears. Explaining what 12-step groups are about, the types of meetings available, expectations, and what a typical meeting entails can do much to allay client fears. The counselor may suggest to Francis that to help ease into this process, it may be beneficial to see whether a friend would be willing to accompany him the first time. Support is an essential step in enhancing motivation and creating an alternative to relying on drugs as a means of coping.

Discussion Questions

1. What other issues warrant consideration in this case?
2. What other considerations would you integrate into the session 1 dialogue?
3. What counselor responses would you change or revise and why in the session 1 dialogue?

Relapse and Crisis

One of the more critical aspects of substance use treatment is addressing relapse. Relapse is often inevitable, especially for clients who have a chronic, long-term history of substance dependence. Despite efforts to address relapse as part of treatment goals, relapse continues to be problematic for many clients. Estimates on rates of relapse for alcohol dependence range from 50 to 90% within 3 months postdischarge from treatment (Polivy & Herman, 2002). Dennis, Foss, and Scott (2007) found that 36% of respondents with less than one year of abstinence (any substance) were able to maintain it at year 8. For those with 1 to 3 years of abstinence, rates improved to 66%, and they increased to 86% for those with 3 or more years of abstinence. The authors concluded that the first 3 years of abstinence yield the highest risk for relapse. Numerous factors may contribute to this wide variance in relapse rates, such as treatment not addressing relapse issues, clients not following through with treatment goals, and clients dropping out of treatment. Those with substance use disorders may be at a higher risk for relapsing when facing crisis situations. During treatment, counselors need to prepare for relapse by helping clients explore triggers and learn new cognitive and behavioral strategies. Even in short-term crisis centers, these triggers can be identified, explored, and documented when clients are referred for treatment. Examining the client's high-risk behaviors, self-monitoring activities, and coping skills (Moss & Cook, 2012) as well as supporting the client in progressive relaxation techniques can help counselors address relapse concerns (Lewis, Dana, & Blevins, 2002).

Counselors need to help clients differentiate when use is viewed as a "lapse" or a "relapse." A *lapse* is a single episode of using a substance following a period of abstinence. The individual often takes responsibility for this lapse and examines the specific experience or trigger(s) that resulted to build on recovery. A *relapse* is a return to sustained use of the same substance or another mood-altering substance following a defined period of abstinence. Counselors need to be extravigilant to potential warning signs, including client rationalization or denial (or using other defense mechanisms); the client not showing up for treatment; the client not attending 12-step meetings or working with his or her sponsor; the client demonstrating changes in attitudes, behaviors, or thoughts around substance use; and the client reconnecting with unhealthy people or environments. An established support system is an essential piece in addressing relapse during a period of crisis. Clients should be encouraged to seek support from 12-step groups, be aware of the need to commit more time to meetings, and work closely with sponsors. Complete Think About It 7.3.

Harm Reduction

For those with substance use disorders, the main goal of treatment is to establish and maintain abstinence, while incorporating strategies for harm reduction. Getting to a place of abstinence is often a complex and difficult process. Counselors using various approaches may also find using harm reduction approaches is a valuable tool within the treatment protocol. Harm reduction is often misunderstood, and some believe it may encourage continued use. In reality, the ultimate goal of harm reduction is to achieve abstinence and prevent future crisis situations. Harm reduction is a component of treatment that is often used during the early stages of change when clients are expressing resistance. Harm reduction approaches are simply tools to help the client reduce the negative consequences associated with use, regardless of one's usage pattern. Clients in early stages of change are not going to be open to hearing about severing their relationship with their drug. Harm reduction can be helpful to find a common ground and meet clients where they are.

Marlatt (1998) identified five underlying principles of harm reduction: (1) strive for abstinence while considering alternative options to help minimize harm; (2) view prevention as a way to reduce the negative consequences or harmful outcomes associated with use but not focusing specifically on usage; (3) focus approaches on where the client is at that point in their use or addiction and develop approaches accordingly;

THINK ABOUT IT 7.3

Think about relapse. What are your thoughts, attitudes, and beliefs about relapse? What approach would you take if a client reported a lapse?

(4) view harm reduction as a community-oriented process where action is taken at the grass-roots level to advocate for change specific to the needs within that community; and (5) focus on minimizing harmful consequences and not about judging or criticizing client behavior. Using harm reduction approaches helps establish rapport because the counselor is working with client resistance and not targeting complete abstinence, but rather focusing on ways to reduce the harm associated with use. Clients are also more likely to buy into alternatives to reducing harm that can lead to lowered resistance. Harm reduction approaches may lead to an increased motivation for change while examining usage patterns. The dialogue that follows illustrates how a counselor can use harm reduction with a resistant client.

COUNSELOR: Rick, you mentioned that you like to drink and you have no intention of stopping. Spending time out with your friends at the bar is an important part of your social life.

RICK: Yes, so it's not really a good use of your time or mine if these sessions are going to be about you preaching to me about the ills of drinking. I don't have a problem and see nothing wrong with how I spend my time.

COUNSELOR: I appreciate your honesty. My intention is not to preach to you about your alcohol use. Rather, I was wondering if we might examine transportation options so that when you are out drinking you can avoid getting another DUI.

RICK: Well, now that I got my license back, I really don't want to risk losing it again. I need my license so I can get to work. I'm willing to discuss this, but I don't have an alcohol problem.

COUNSELOR: Fair enough. Let's brainstorm some possible transportation options together for the next time you go out with your friends. (*The counselor is not focusing on alcohol reduction at this point. The emphasis is on reducing the negative consequences associated with drinking and driving. By working together, the counselor is not only establishing the therapeutic alliance and working to reduce harm but also helping the client feel comfortable and laying a foundation for later trust and change.*)

Support Groups

Support groups serve a valuable function within the treatment process. Clients with substance use disorders often find that as the condition progresses, they become alienated and isolated from family, friends, and coworkers as they spend more time in relationships with their substances and those who enable the behavior. When clients enter treatment, some are often faced with the hard and painful reality that life is empty and too much damage has been done to repair some relationships. Another obvious issue is that clients often have poor social and coping skills, so engaging in social contact can be difficult. A common treatment goal is to learn to establish social and coping skills, which are critical components in developing and maintaining abstinence. Support groups play an instrumental role in facilitating and practicing these skills. The most common and best known support groups are Alcoholics Anonymous (AA) and Narcotics Anonymous (NA), which are both based on a philosophy that addiction is a disease and individuals are powerless over its effects. In order to recover, they come to understand that they are powerless over the effects of the substance and cannot recover under their own volition and must turn their will over to a higher power.

The underlying mechanism of AA and NA are the 12 steps, a series of sequential action steps that help individuals acknowledge their powerlessness over alcohol or other drugs and move toward accepting responsibility for their recovery. Several common misconceptions exist with respect to 12-step meetings, including the belief that AA and NA are religious-based and that these meetings serve as treatment for a person's addiction. Counselors encouraging clients to attend 12-step meetings should educate clients on the purpose and mission of 12-step meetings, as well as the variety of group options, meeting formats, and meeting structures. Encouraging support group attendance should align with the client's stage of change. Clients may also report feeling discouraged or frustrated after attending a meeting and should be encouraged to try out different meetings to find out which best match client needs. Clients may find other groups like SMART (a four-point program that emphasizes self-reliance and empowerment), Double Trouble (for those dealing with mental health and substance use disorders), Al-ANON (for families of those with substance addiction), Overeaters Anonymous, Sex and Love Addicts Anonymous, and Gamblers Anonymous as options. Complete Activity 7.2, which focuses on enhancing your knowledge of 12-step meetings.

Marital and Family Treatment

Marital and family treatment (MFT) has been an integral part of substance abuse treatment for decades. During this period, research findings have demonstrated a reciprocal relationship between problem drinking and family and marital discord (O'Farrell & Fals-Stewart, 2003). Research has supported that "MFT generally is effective and that behavioral marital therapy, specifically, is among the top 10 most effective treatments for alcoholism" (O'Farrell & Fals-Stewart, 2003, p. 205).

Stress and problems within the marriage and family can contribute to the development and continuation of problematic alcohol use. In cases where abstinence has been achieved, those individuals who continue to deal with unresolved marital and family conflicts may be at a higher risk for relapse. O'Farrell and Fals-Stewart (2003) cited numerous studies highlighting client characteristics that contribute to successful completion of MFT, including being older, entering counseling following a crisis, being

---

ACTIVITY 7.2

Clients unfamiliar with 12-step meetings are often reluctant or resistant to attend because they have misconceptions and fears about what to expect. Counselors can help allay client concerns by educating them about these meetings. For this activity, attend an open meeting of the 12-step group of your choice. Note the sequence of events, format, and structure of the meeting, and other pertinent information. How would you explain these meetings to a client?

employed, having a history of serious alcohol problems, having graduated from high school, and living together with one's family.

Counselor attributes that tend to lead to successful outcomes include addressing client and family members simultaneously; focusing on alcohol problems first; using empathetic listening and dealing effectively with intense anger during the initial stages of counseling; developing a structured, directive approach that includes establishing rules, boundaries, and consequences; and viewing the change process as long term. Treatment goals for MFT include eliminating substance use and addressing marital and family dysfunctional patterns. Initial sessions address negative interactions and feelings, and later sessions focus on increasing positive interactions and communications, developing healthy coping skills, implementing behavior change contracts, and integrating problem-solving skills.

Co-occurring Disorders and Crisis

Substance abuse is the most common co-occurring disorder with severe mental illness. SAMHSA (2016) defines a *co-occurring disorder* as the concomitant occurrence of a substance use and mental health disorder. Co-occurring disorders were first identified in the early 1980s, and treatment outcomes often had poor results, as traditional approaches for treating substance abuse were integrated into existing mental health services (Drake, Mueser, Brunette, & McHugo, 2004). Clients who are diagnosed with a co-occurring disorder may find that crisis situations not only present challenges to maintain abstinence from substances but also trigger symptoms associated with a mental health diagnosis. Counselors working with clients with co-occurring disorders have to be competent in understanding each disorder as well as how to integrate treatment so as to ensure that the disorders are addressed simultaneously. Unfortunately, integrated treatment options within many communities may not be widely available (National Alliance of Mental Illness, 2016).

Counselors need to understand how substance use can present symptoms that mimic mental illness and other medical conditions. As discussed, effective treatment requires counselors to make an accurate diagnosis, but doing so is often unrealistic in crisis settings with short-term exposure to the client. Careful consideration should be given to conducting differential diagnosis, especially if there is evidence that mental health disorders or medical conditions may be present. For example, clients who abuse alcohol may also present with symptoms of depression. If alcohol is the reason for the depression yet the counselor fails to connect this information to a substance use disorder diagnosis, the counselor may incorrectly diagnose the primary cause as a depressive disorder. Similar scenarios may present themselves for clients who use stimulants such as amphetamines or cocaine with symptom presentation manifesting as manic episodes or, depending on the amount of usage, psychotic episodes. If there is no co-occurring psychotic disorder, stimulant-induced psychosis will be temporary and subside as the individual comes off the high. When assessing individuals who present with psychosis, counselors should be aware that while symptom presentation for certain substances may mimic certain psychotic disorders, some differences exist. For example, clients with amphetamine-induced psychosis may present symptoms similar to those of clients with paranoid schizophrenia. However, clients with amphetamine-induced psychosis tend to present with visual hallucinations, whereas clients with paranoid schizophrenia

ACTIVITY 7.3

What type of clients, characteristics of clients, or specific cultural differences would you feel most uncomfortable or fearful working with? Discuss the reason(s) for your concern with classmates.

---

tend to report auditory hallucinations. More time is needed to make most other mental health diagnoses that are not substance use disorders. A client who presents with possible co-occurring mental health disorders while in a crisis center or with a crisis counselor can be documented as follows: "client [demonstrates, presents, or reports] with symptoms consistent with an anxiety-related disorder." This documentation allows the next treatment provider to be aware of possible differential or co-occurring disorders.

Withdrawing from a substance can also create a crisis situation. For clients who establish tolerance and dependence on alcohol and benzodiazepines, withdrawal can have potentially life-threatening consequences. Complications from withdrawal of alcohol can result in serious medical conditions, such as seizures, stroke, tachycardia, and death. Counselors also need to be aware that overdose or sudden death due to substance use (e.g., alcohol poisoning, inhalant use, heroin overdose) can also result in acute crisis situations and trauma for family and friends. Educating clients and their families about drug actions, interactions, and synergistic effects, as well as symptoms of withdrawal, is an important treatment consideration. Complete Activity 7.3, which asks you to consider the clients you would feel uncomfortable or fearful working with.

MULTICULTURAL PERSPECTIVES, SUBSTANCE USE, AND CRISIS

One of the many issues a counselor must consider is the significance of culture in shaping a client's identity. *Culture* refers to the values and beliefs that shape a person's worldview. Pedersen (1991) emphasized the importance of cultural diversity within the counseling relationship and the recognition that all counseling is multicultural counseling. Counselors working with clients with substance use disorders and in crisis need to understand how the culture of substance use influences each client's worldview. Historically, treatment has focused on reduction or abstinence goals, often with little consideration for understanding the role that culture plays in etiology or maintenance of use. Relapse considerations often emphasize exploring both intrapersonal and interpersonal factors yet may not fully explore the implications of culture on substance use behavior.

Counselors must be knowledgeable about and implement multicultural counseling competencies in their practice. Ratts, Singh, Nassar-McMillan, Butler, and McCullough (2015) outlined four multicultural counseling competencies—counselor self-awareness, client worldview, counseling relationship, and counseling and advocacy interventions—that each comprise three dimensions—attitudes and beliefs, knowledge, and skills. Substance abuse counselors should develop self-awareness of attitudes and beliefs that may interfere with their work with clients, including any attitudes or beliefs associated with specific substances and substance usage patterns or behaviors. For example, if a counselor has specific attitudes or beliefs regarding clients exchanging sex for drugs, which may be a common practice within some drug-using subcultures, judgment and biases may spill over into counseling. Counselors should also be aware of the client's cultural worldview and the role substances play as part of that identity. For example, the counselor working with adolescent males should understand whether certain substance use coincides with cultural expectations or rites of passage. Integrating cultural awareness into substance use treatment better aligns the treatment with the client's particular cultural worldview and context.

Counselors should also consider the significance of the client's cultural worldview during the assessment phase, when evaluating motivation and ambivalence. Motivation for continued substance use involves a complex and varied set of factors and circumstances that often manifest as client ambivalence and resistance. In some instances, ambivalence may be less about mood altering and getting high and more about maintaining a client's beliefs, customs, or rituals associated with substance use as it relates to cultural identity or tradition. Assessing cultural meaning as it relates to substance use provides a broader understanding of the cultural dynamics that may help explain ambivalence. Counselors should maintain a cultural focus when working with clients through the five stages of change. Moreover, triggers for relapse behavior should be examined from a cultural perspective. See Case Study 7.4, which explores multicultural considerations when working with a client who abuses substances.

CASE STUDY 7.4

Multicultural Considerations with a Substance Abuse Client

Van is a 26-year-old multiheritage male. Over the past 6 months, Van's use of alcohol and marijuana has increased significantly. His usage has coincided with his disclosure to his parents that he is gay, which conflicts with their beliefs and values. He thinks he has let his parents down and feels depressed and isolated. Van has been attending counseling for the past month. In this session, the discussion focused on understanding substance use and cultural expectations.

COUNSELOR:	Van, we've been talking the last several sessions about your coming out process and how this has devastated your parents. You knew telling your parents that you're gay was going to be hard, but you didn't think it was going to be this painful. They are very angry and disappointed.
VAN:	I didn't want to disappoint them, but I couldn't keep living this lie. They were pressuring me to settle down, get married, and have a family. They believe I'm making a choice to be gay as an act of defying them. The weight of their anger and disappointment sits heavy in my heart.
COUNSELOR:	I'm sensing your pain as we talk and the heavy toll it's taking on you. Tell me more about your parents' cultural beliefs about being gay.
VAN:	In my culture, being gay has always been viewed as some sort of defect and has been looked down on. My parents don't support this lifestyle and believe it's sinful. They made it clear that they would never accept this lifestyle in any of their children. I

was always fearful because I knew I was gay for a long time.

COUNSELOR: You knew deep down that identifying as gay meant you'd never be accepted by your parents so you turned to alcohol and drugs as a way to numb the pain.

VAN: Well, it's a lot easier to drink and get high to take away the pain than to feel it. Yet I still feel it and sometimes it only magnifies the feelings. Maybe I should just give them what they want because I see how much it is hurting them and me. It's so confusing and I don't know what to do.

COUNSELOR: You're questioning yourself and thinking giving them what they want will make everything better. (*Van looks dejected, like he is feeling lost and confused. It is clear he is struggling with his truth versus family and cultural expectations.*)

VAN: Yeah.

COUNSELOR: (*Using an advanced empathic statement to make the implicit message explicit.*) Van, as we've been talking today and over the last several sessions, might it be that you can't accept yourself as a gay man unless your parents can also accept you in that way? That you have struggled for a long time with the realization that being true to who you are means alienating your family? Knowing that you're disappointing them has led to alcohol and drugs as a way to numb the pain. Yet the pain never goes away.

VAN: (*Van sits for several minutes in silence reflecting on the counselor's response.*) I just wanted the pain to stop, but how can it as long as I keep denying who I am. I can't control how they see me, but I can control how I see myself and how I want to live my life. I'm really tired of feeling like I have to be something I'm not. I need to find other ways of dealing with this problem, and I realize using alcohol and drugs is not solving this problem.

COUNSELOR: You want to be true to yourself and find healthier ways of dealing with the pain. We can use our time together to explore what cultural expectations and messages you want to embrace while finding healthier ways to deal with painful emotions.

A multiculturally competent counselor examines any value conflicts and biases that arise as the client is telling his story and addresses them. The counselor also attempts to see the presenting problem from the client's worldview. Strategies for change will likely require exploration and resolution of conflicting cultural messages and healthier ways of coping as the client moves toward embracing his identity.

Discussion Questions

1. What other strategies for change should be integrated into the work with Van?
2. How should the counselor go about dealing with the substance abuse concerns?
3. What other cultural issues do you believe should be considered and why?

OVERVIEW OF THE ELEMENTS OF CRISIS INTERVENTION RELATED TO SUBSTANCE USE

Safety and Self-Care

Clients with substance use disorders can be particularly vulnerable to the effects of crises. Crises can result in greater risk for increased use of substances or lapse/relapse behaviors. Those who engage in substance use tend to be at a higher risk for crisis or trauma while under the influence (Zinzow et al., 2010). When individuals with substance use disorders experience crisis or trauma, the recovery process and the work of the counselor can be challenging (SAMSHA, 2014). Driessen et al. (2008) reported that individuals with substance use disorders who experience trauma tend to have poorer treatment outcomes than those who lack a history of trauma. Clients who increase substance use as a result of crisis or trauma create potentially dangerous outcomes for themselves (e.g. overdose, suicide) and the community (e.g., homicide, DUI-related accidents).

During a crisis, the counselor simultaneously addresses a client's crisis or trauma response and his or her potential risk for or actual substance use. Ensuring that the client is safe is a critical first step in crisis intervention. To effectively address safety concerns in relation to the client, the counselor establishes rapport, trust, and genuineness, and creates a safe environment. Creating an environment where the client is protected and out of harm's way can help de-escalate the crisis situation. The counselor assesses the risk of suicidality or instrumental suicide-related behavior and takes a directive role when the client in crisis presents danger to self or others (read Voices from the Field 7.3). Assessing and placing the client in the appropriate level of care can help reinforce the importance of safety by aligning the client's needs with applicable treatment and interventions. Determining where the client is in the stages of change can be valuable so the counselor can begin to conceptualize appropriate and applicable

---

VOICES FROM THE FIELD 7.3
Substance Use and Crisis Issues

Meghan Brown

Recently, while sitting at my desk, one of the counselors on my team came to my office and noted that a 15-year-old female in her group was "acting out" and refusing to leave the women's restroom. I could hear the young girl yelling at her counselor and to all in the group: "Leave me alone . . . my life is crap!" The counselor returned to her group while I stood outside the restroom, nonchalantly pouring myself a cup of coffee. After a few moments, the young woman came out of the restroom, joined me at the kitchenette, and clearly stated, "No one can understand me . . . no one is me. I'd like to be a butterfly because butterflies are free." I immediately recognized that she was under the influence.

I asked the young woman to enter into an open group room with me. I told her that she did not have to talk to me, but she was more than welcome to talk about anything as I was interested in what had her so upset. During the time she spoke, I was able to conduct an informal Mental Status Exam, explore her judgment, assess her potential for suicide, and observe her behaviors to further assess what substance she had taken. The conversation was very interesting, but frightening due to hearing the girl repeatedly note that she has no reason to live, she wants to die, she will overdose to die, she has a history of psychiatric hospitalizations, she does not like her parents, and she enjoys her relationship with drugs. She remained disorganized in her

(Continued)

thoughts, glared at me, was agitated, and demonstrated trouble regulating her breathing. Every few moments, it appeared as though she was gasping for air. I observed that her trouble breathing was not related to her crying, but potentially more a result of her using a system depressant. I quickly asked her counselor to give the rest of the group a break and to come and sit with her in the open group room while I contacted her parents.

The young woman's parents arrived at the facility within minutes of our phone call. They were concerned and immediately defensive about their daughter's condition. The mother repeatedly noted that she does not think her daughter uses alcohol or other drugs, despite her being involved in chemical dependency treatment and testing positive in her most recent drug screen. I informed the parents that an ambulance had been called for their daughter due to her difficulty breathing and her high risk for suicide. The primary counselor and I worked with the client and the parents to try to keep everyone calm and provide the emergency medical technicians (EMTs) and police officer with the appropriate information.

The young woman repeatedly refused to cooperate with the EMTs and the police officer. As a result of her refusal, the police officer told the young woman's parents that he could not take her to the hospital. Her parents, although initially resistant to the idea that their daughter was under the influence, noted that they were afraid to take her home. They informed me that the police officer refused to "pink slip" their daughter and was going to send her home with them. It was at that point that I reminded the police officer what I had already told the EMTs, that this young woman was clearly under the influence, stated she had no reason to live, and had the means to overdose if she wanted to die. It was only then that the officer agreed to mandate the young woman be taken to the hospital for a 72-hour hold.

The entire length of this event was a total of 45 minutes, but looking back on it all, it seemed more like 3 hours. The situation required legal knowledge, sound ethics, and clinical judgment. I needed to be able to recognize the symptoms of a client under the influence of alcohol and/or other drugs, the risk factors and signs of suicide, and how to keep a client calm in a crisis situation to obtain the information needed to obtain appropriate care for the client. Had I not spent some time with the client to hear the words, "I want to die" and understand the means she had to kill herself, I would not have been able to gain the support of law enforcement to have the young woman mandated to receive care in an emergency room.

interventions. Use of personal support and empathy can be instrumental throughout the crisis situation. Employing harm reduction measures may be valuable for clients who are in the precontemplative or contemplative stages of change. Once the crisis situation has de-escalated, the counselor can enhance safety in a variety of ways, including employing grounding exercises to help clients establish some control when they feel overwhelmed; creating a structured counseling setting with specific routines or rituals; creating opportunities for safe discussion; identifying triggers or behaviors that create feelings of not being safe both in the moment and in general; and developing a safety plan (SAMSHA, 2014).

Counselors also take steps to ensure their own safety when dealing with clients who are in crisis (see Chapter 2). Counselors need to be aware of the dangers of working with clients who pose a threat to public safety or who have a history of violence, especially those who may also be under the influence of a substance (e.g., phencyclidine or other forms of hallucinogens resulting in distortions in one's perception of reality). Counselors should gauge the risk in working with clients who pose safety concerns and can take steps to minimize the risk by screening high-risk clients, avoiding seeing clients when there is a lack of physical security available, recognizing warning signs of violence, avoiding working alone during in-home counseling, and establishing rules prohibiting weapons in session.

Working with clients who have substance use disorders creates unique challenges for counselors. Counselors who constantly face client resistance, ambivalence, motivational concerns, and relapse issues may question their effectiveness in facilitating change. Working with this population requires counselors to integrate self-care techniques into their daily routine to minimize the potential for burnout. Self-care techniques that can be effective when working with clients with substance use disorders include engaging in interests and hobbies; having a strong support network; establishing work boundaries; attending to one's physical, mental, and spiritual needs; learning effective time management; engaging in continued professional development and training; attending counseling to address any maladaptive patterns or interpersonal issues that hinder emotional or psychological well-being; and seeking out supervision.

Diagnostic Considerations during a Crisis

A crisis situation can exacerbate and confound the diagnostic process, especially if the client has co-occurring issues. The first consideration is to differentiate between symptoms that are due to the acute crisis situation and symptoms that present as part of the pathology. Differentiating crisis symptom presentations from pathological symptoms helps the counselor explain to the client that his or her experience is normal by associating those symptoms with the crisis, which can help minimize the client's stress. Explaining to clients how crisis situations can manifest physically and psychologically helps clients better understand the symptom presentation. Further, explaining to clients how crisis situations can magnify affective states and trigger increased substance use may help normalize their experience. As mentioned, the purpose of diagnosis is to determine an appropriate course of treatment. Differentiating between crisis symptoms and other presenting mental health and substance abuse symptoms enables the counselor to properly assess and triage the situation while also identifying appropriate interventions and normalizing the client's experience. Caution is warranted when providing a mental health diagnosis that may require more information than can be obtained in an assessment during crisis intervention.

Essential Substance Use–Specific Crisis Intervention Skills

The intervention skills used for clients with substance use disorders tend to also apply when these clients experience crises. Use of attending behaviors and active listening skills are important in crisis situations. Creating warmth, expressing genuineness, and creating an atmosphere of trust, safety and acceptance not only target the motivational factors inherent with treating substance use disorders but also help clients in crisis de-escalate from the acute stressor and feel more at ease and comfortable with the counselor. Using a directive approach, conducted in a compassionate and empathic manner, allows for clarification and understanding of the crisis threat so that appropriate courses of action can be taken.

Table 7.1 provides a number of online and print resources that will expand your knowledge of the interplay between crises and substance abuse.

TABLE 7.1 Resources on Substance Use and Crisis

Online Resources

Harm Reduction Coalition: harmreduction.org

National Alliance on Mental Illness: www.nami.org

ProjectKnow: www.projectknow.com/research/new-and-designer-drugs/

Substance Abuse and Mental Health Services Administration: www.samhsa.gov

Print Resources

American Society for Addition Medicine. (2013). *The ASAM criteria: Treatment criteria for addictive, substance-related, and co-occurring conditions* (3rd ed.). Chevy Chase, MD: Author.

Hester, R. K., & Miller, W. R. (2003). *Handbook of alcoholism treatment approaches: Effective alternatives* (3rd ed.). Boston, MA: Allyn and Bacon.

Leong, F. T. L., & Leach, M. M. (2008). *Suicide among racial and ethnic minority groups: Theory, research, and practice.* New York, NY: Routledge.

Miller, W. R., & Rollnick, S. (2013). *Motivational interviewing: Helping people change* (3rd ed.). New York, NY: The Guilford Press.

Publishers Group. (2015). *Street drugs: A drug identification guide 2015.* Long Lake, MN: Author.

Rudd, M. D. (2006). *The assessment and management of suicidality.* Sarasota, FL: Professional Resource Press.

Rudd, M. D., Joiner, T., & Rajab, M. H. (2001). *Treating suicidal behavior: An effective, time-limited approach.* New York, NY: The Guilford Press.

Substance Abuse and Mental Health Services Administration. (2014). *Results from the 2013 National Survey on Drug Use and Health: Summary of national findings*, NSDUH Series H-48, HHS Publication No. (SMA) 14-4863. Rockville, MD: Author.

Substance Abuse and Mental Health Services Administration. (2014). *Trauma-informed care in behavioral health services.* Treatment Improvement Protocol (TIP) Series 57. HHS Publication No. (SMA) 13-4801. Rockville, MD: Author.

Summary

Substance use has been an integral part of the human experience and cultural identity throughout time. The reasons that people use drugs vary; however, specific biological, psychological, and sociological circumstances are key factors. Unfortunately, as the data reveal, only a fraction of those needing substance use treatment actually receive care. Failing to address substance use disorder issues can be particularly problematic for clients who are also dealing with crisis issues. Numerous models have been developed in an attempt to explain the complex phenomenon of addiction. Still, there is no consensus on the causality of addic-

tion. Counselors having knowledge of different models and theories of addiction are better equipped to address the array of etiological considerations.

In order to understand and treat clients with substance use disorders, especially those who are dealing with a crisis, counselors must be competent in all aspects of assessment and diagnosis. Proper assessment and diagnosis are instrumental in establishing an effective treatment protocol and resources for the client. Numerous screening and assessment instruments exist, with the clinical interview being one to the most commonly used assessment tools. Treatment must consider both the level of motivation and the nature and severity of the crisis situation. Treatment considerations, especially for clients facing crisis situations, need to factor in admission and placement decisions as outlined by ASAM's level of care criteria.

Understanding the stages of change within the crisis context can assist the counselor in developing both an effective crisis response and a quality therapeutic alliance once the crisis is managed. The implementation of crisis models helps the client return to a precrisis level of functioning and is the first step in the treatment process, especially when a client's crisis response involves an increased use of substances or a relapse. Further, counselors should think about how to structure subsequent sessions based on response to the initial crisis session. Establishing a strong therapeutic working alliance between counselor and client is critical throughout the crisis period. Other considerations include assessing client and counselor safety, client support, risk (on a continued basis), how substance use factors into risk behavior, specific plans once the crisis subsides, and motivation to change. Also, counselors must understand that the risk of relapse is high when dealing with substance use disorders and can become magnified when clients are in crisis. Helping clients identify and address triggers is a key part of treatment, as is helping clients understand the difficulty and inherent challenges and obstacles in maintaining abstinence in both the short and long term. Other matters

that must be considered during counseling include marriage and family concerns, co-occurring disorders, the integration of a harm reduction philosophy and approach into the overall treatment model, and the involvement of support systems such as 12-step groups. Throughout the treatment process, counselors must apply multicultural counseling competencies to ensure that the counselor's cultural attitudes, values, and biases do not interfere with care; the client's worldview is recognized; and culturally appropriate intervention strategies are implemented.

This chapter highlights a number of considerations when working with clients with co-occurring crisis and substance use issues. Substance use can not only lead to crisis situations but also exacerbate them, so counselors need to navigate crisis situations and substance use issues simultaneously. Effectively assessing client motivation to change means counselors understand applicable and appropriate strategies, skills, and approaches that align with the client's current state of change. Further, assessing the stage of change and motivation can have important implications once the crisis has been addressed, especially if substance use precipitated the crisis event. Finally, counselors who can create a therapeutic environment based on genuineness, trust, acceptance, and warmth go a long way toward establishing therapeutic rapport while building a foundation that enhances short- and long-term client change.

8

Intimate Partner Violence

Amy L. McLeod, John Muldoon, and Lisa R. Jackson-Cherry*

PREVIEW

Intimate partner violence (IPV) is a major public health concern, and it is imperative that counselors be able to recognize and respond to IPV victims competently. This chapter provides an overview of the facts and figures associated with IPV, discusses the cycle of violence commonly experienced in abusive relationships, and explores various perspectives on reasons why individuals stay in relationships with abusive partners. Common crisis issues experienced by IPV victims, such as dealing with physical injury, establishing immediate safety, and reporting IPV to the police, are also highlighted. In addition, this chapter explores special considerations regarding IPV in lesbian, gay, bisexual, and transgender (LGBT) relationships; relationships characterized by female-to-male violence; abusive relationships in racial and ethnic minority and elderly populations; and abusive dating relationships among adolescents and young adults. Guidelines for counselors on conducting IPV assessment, responding to IPV disclosure, planning for safety, and addressing the emotional impact of IPV are provided. Finally, the goals, theories, and challenges associated with batterer intervention programs are discussed.

OVERVIEW OF INTIMATE PARTNER VIOLENCE

Intimate partner violence involves "physical violence, sexual violence, stalking and psychological aggression (including coercive tactics) by a current or former intimate partner (i.e., spouse, boyfriend/girlfriend, dating partner, or ongoing sexual partner)" (Breiding, Basile, Smith, Black, & Mahendra, 2015, p. 9). IPV is an inclusive term that can be used to describe violence among opposite- or same-sex couples. The term *intimate* does not imply that the couple is necessarily sexually intimate. IPV can occur in dating as well as marital relationships.

Domestic Violence

Although this chapter focuses on the term IPV as inclusive of a diverse population of victims and perpetrators, this is not the legal term used in federal or state statutes or

*The authors would like to acknowledge Rebecca S. Dempsey, MA, for her assistance in preparing the manuscript. Special thanks go to Danica G. Hays for her outstanding contributions to the first two editions of this chapter.

regulations that outline mandated reporting laws for health care providers or laws that govern law enforcement practices when intervening in domestic violence situations. The legal term used in these contexts is *domestic violence*, a term referred to throughout the chapter. The Bureau of Justice Statistics (2016a) defines *domestic violence* as "violence between spouses, or spousal abuse but can also include cohabitants and non-married intimate partners." States may further narrow this definition, and counselors should be aware of the laws that govern their practice with domestic violence victims and perpetrators in their state. Law enforcement intervention and charges will vary depending on the state's definition of domestic violence or assault, and depending on whether the IPV victim's incident aligns with the definition of domestic violence or assault. See Case Study 8.1, which focuses on an IPV incident.

CASE STUDY 8.1

Physical and Emotional Abuse

For days, Casey had taken extra precautions to make sure that nothing upset Jamie. Casey kept the house extra clean, had Jamie's favorite meals prepared for dinner every night, and tried to seem cheerful and upbeat. Still, Casey couldn't get rid of the uneasy feeling that trouble was brewing with Jamie. It was eight o'clock, and Jamie still wasn't home from work. Casey was concerned. When Jamie walked in the door, Casey smelled whiskey.

"Where have you been? I was so worried!" Casey exclaimed.

Jamie's eyes narrowed. In a low, angry voice, Jamie growled, "I'll go where I damn well please," and knocked Casey into the wall. Casey immediately apologized to Jamie, but it was too late.

"You constantly nag me," Jamie yelled and hit Casey hard across the face. Casey fell to the ground and sobbed.

Jamie walked into the kitchen and said, "I'm hungry."

Not wanting to make matters worse, Casey got up, walked into the kitchen, and started to warm up dinner. Casey's mind was racing, "I can't believe this is happening again. Jamie promised never again after the last time. Jamie promised!"

Discussion Questions

Take out a piece of paper and answer the following questions as quickly as possible:

1. Is Casey a female or male?
2. Is Jamie a female or male?
3. What do Casey and Jamie look like?
4. What is Casey's racial/ethnic background?
5. What is Jamie's racial/ethnic background?
6. Are Casey and Jamie heterosexual, gay, lesbian, or bisexual?
7. Are they married?
8. Does either Casey or Jamie have a disability?
9. Are Casey and Jamie religious?
10. What does Jamie do for a living?
11. What does Casey do for a living?

12. Are Casey and Jamie upper, middle, or lower socioeconomic status (SES)?
13. Whom do you blame for the violence in this relationship?
14. How do your answers to these questions reflect your biases about IPV?
15. How may this influence your work with clients?

Statistics regarding IPV vary due to the range of IPV definitions and methods of data collection used by researchers. It is also important to note that most instances of IPV are never reported, so the available facts and figures are likely a considerable underestimation of the extent of IPV. Regardless of which statistical estimates are consulted, it is clear that IPV is a major public health concern and a common cause of injury that disproportionately affects women. For example, while both women and men are affected by IPV, women are more likely to experience multiple forms of violence (e.g., physical, sexual, emotional) and are more likely to be seriously injured by an intimate partner (Breiding et al., 2014; Catalano, 2013). The most recent data available are from the 2011 National Intimate Partner and Sexual Violence Survey (Breiding et al., 2014) and indicate that approximately 22% of women and 14% of men experienced severe physical violence by an intimate partner in their lifetime. IPV affects women and men in all racial, ethnic, socioeconomic, and religious groups; and some studies suggest that individuals who are members of multiple oppressed groups (e.g., lower-SES women of color) are at increased risk for harm due to IPV because of their multiple oppressed social positions (Walker, 2015; Wong & Mellor, 2014).

The tremendous emotional, social, and physical consequences of IPV for victims are well documented. For example, IPV results in nearly 2 million injuries and 1,300 deaths in the United States each year (Catalano, 2013). Annual health care and lost productivity costs of IPV against women exceed $8.3 billion. Due to IPV victimization, women lose more than 8 million days of paid work annually, which equates to 32,000 full-time jobs. In addition, women are more likely to die at the hands of an intimate partner than an unknown perpetrator. In 2010, 39.3% of all female homicide victims were murdered by a current or former partner or spouse, whereas only 24% of female homicide victims were killed by an unknown offender. The magnitude of the consequences of IPV calls for a greater understanding of the dynamics of IPV and the experiences of victims of abuse. Increased understanding can assist crisis counselors in using more effective and appropriate interventions when working with IPV victims.

CYCLE OF VIOLENCE THEORY

The cycle of violence theory was originally developed by Walker (1979), a psychologist who based her theory on interviews with hundreds of women who experienced domestic violence. Walker noted that the violence described by women in her research typically followed a three-phase pattern: (1) the tension-building phase, (2) the explosion or acute battering incident, and (3) the honeymoon phase of kindness and contrite, loving behavior (see Figure 8.1) Each phase varied in time and intensity during each cycle of violence for the same couple and between different couples.

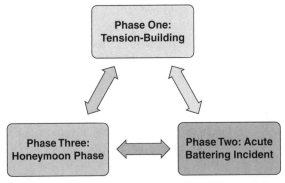

FIGURE 8.1 The cycle of violence.

Phase 1: The Tension-Building Phase

Phase 1, the tension-building phase of the cycle of violence, is characterized by mounting pressure and strain in the relationship. The abused partner "walks on eggshells" around the abusive partner, becoming compliant, nurturing, or whatever it takes to keep the abusive partner's anger from escalating. This phase also involves minor battering incidents (Walker, 1979)—from insults and threats to actions such as throwing a dinner on to the floor and blaming the abused partner for overcooking the food. During the tension-building phase, the abused partner may cope with the minor battering incidents by denying anger about the incident, rationalizing the abuse to himself or herself (e.g., thinking that he or she did something to deserve this), or making excuses for the abuser. Following each minor battering incident, the tension and stress in the relationship build.

Phase 2: The Acute Battering Incident

Phase 2 of the cycle of violence occurs when tensions build to the point of explosion in an acute battering incident that is characterized by unpredictability, uncontrollable rage, brutality, and seriously damaging consequences (Walker, 1979). The acute battering incident is typically triggered by an external event (e.g., stress at work) or the abusive partner's internal state and can last for a number of hours to a number of days. During an acute battering incident, victims have reported dissociative experiences, such as feeling as though they are outside their own bodies and watching themselves being thrown into a wall, choked, or raped. Following an acute battering incident, many victims enter a state of shock and disbelief. Both partners may make attempts to rationalize the violence.

Phase 3: The Honeymoon Phase

Phase 3 in the cycle of violence is characterized by loving and repentant behavior from the abusive partner. The abuser may shower the IPV victim with gifts, beg for forgiveness, and promise never to be violent again. During the honeymoon phase, the abusive partner may also use guilt to attempt to persuade the victim into staying in the relationship, using statements such as "I would be lost without you" and "Don't make our kids grow up without me in their lives." The honeymoon phase results in the IPV victim feeling needed and loved, leading to a renewed commitment to the relationship. The length of the contrite, loving phase varies, although it is typically shorter than the tension-building phase and longer than the acute battering incident (Walker, 1979). After repeated cycles of violence, the honeymoon phase may shorten or eventually be eliminated. The IPV victim who has experienced numerous cycles of violence may experience increased shame and humiliation during the honeymoon phase due to the realization that the abuse will almost certainly reoccur, despite the batterer's promises, which the IPV client now recognizes as empty.

Educating IPV clients about the cycle of violence can help in naming experiences as abusive. For example, some clients may not define their relationships as abusive because violence does not occur frequently. Other clients may see the batterer's apologies and gifts as a unique indication of how special their relationship is until learning that the honeymoon phase is typical during a cycle of violence (McLeod, Hays, & Chang, 2010).

THE DULUTH MODEL

The Duluth model was developed in 1984 by a group of IPV activists and is based on the actual experiences of female IPV survivors. The central component of the Duluth model is the Power and Control Wheel, a visual representation of the most commonly experienced abusive tactics, including economic abuse; using male privilege; using children; minimizing, denying, and blaming; isolation; emotional abuse; intimidation; coercion and threats; and physical and sexual violence (Domestic Abuse Intervention Programs, 2013). The Power and Control Wheel can be used to help female IPV victims normalize and understand their experiences. It can also assist abusive partners in identifying violent behaviors as part of a batterer intervention program. Another component of the Duluth model is the Equality Wheel, which is a visual representation of the changes needed to move from an abusive relationship to a nonviolent relationship.

Although changes in the relationship will be the focus of long-term counseling, counselors seeing clients in crisis should be aware of various resources in the community for referral purposes for clients experiencing IPV, which may be helpful to normalize a victim's experiences while in and after the crisis.

LEARNED HELPLESSNESS THEORY

The concept of learned helplessness originates from the classic research of Seligman (1975), in which dogs were locked in a cage and administered random electric shocks. The dogs quickly learned that none of their responses and attempts to escape were successful in eliminating the unwanted stimulus, and they therefore submitted passively to the shocks. Later the cages were opened, providing the dogs with an opportunity to escape, yet the dogs did not attempt to do so. In other words, the dogs had learned to believe they were not in control of their situation, so even when they actually had the opportunity to control the outcome (i.e., avoid shocks by leaving the cage), the dogs responded with learned helplessness.

Learned helplessness theory has been used to explain why IPV victims remain in abusive relationships. During the tension-building phase of the cycle of violence, the abused partner behaves in an accommodating manner in an attempt to avoid escalating the abusive partner's anger. Eventually, the tension builds to an explosive battering incident, and the victim learns that his or her attempts to control the situation were unsuccessful. An IPV client may reach out for help from family, friends, or the police, yet the battering still continues. Again, the victim receives the message that efforts to control the situation are ineffective. Repeated incidents of uncontrollable violence diminish the victim's motivation to respond, leading to passivity and learned helplessness (Walker, 1979).

Alternatives to Learned Helplessness Theory

Opponents of the application of learned helplessness theory to IPV victims argue that the theory pathologizes the victim, places the responsibility for ending abuse on the victim while ignoring the larger sociocultural context, and implies that leaving the relationship ensures the victim's safety (see Humphreys & Thiara, 2003; Peled, Eisikovits, Enosh, & Winstok, 2000; Werner-Wilson, Zimmerman, & Whalen, 2000). Ecological theory offers an alternative explanation for why the IPV victim stays in a relationship with an abusive partner. According to ecological theory, the sociocultural system (the ideological and institutional patterns of a culture), the institutional–organizational system (the agencies, policies, programs, and professional groups), the interpersonal system (the victim's direct interactions with the abusive partner, children, family, and friends), and the individual system (the victim's perceptions, meanings, and actions) all play roles in the victim's decision (Peled et al., 2000). Complete Activity 8.1, which looks at how the media depicts IPV.

The contextual model of family stress proposed by Boss in Rolling and Brosi (2010) also provides a more comprehensive view of IPV than learned helplessness theory. This model considers the interaction of the stressor event, available resources, an individual's perception of IPV, the external family context (culture, history, economy, development, and heredity), and the internal family context (family boundaries and rules, understanding of a stressor event, and family values, beliefs, and assumptions). This model allows for in-depth understanding of the victim's experiences as well as for intervention in multiple domains.

Constructivist theorists argue that the decision to stay with an abusive partner could result from a rational decision-making process based on weighing the costs and benefits of ending the relationship. The victim who decides to stay in the relationship,

---

ACTIVITY 8.1

Watch and critique a movie that depicts IPV. You may choose a movie from the following list or select a movie of your choice, as long as IPV is a central issue in the film. Movies depicting IPV include *A Streetcar Named Desire* (1951), *Petulia* (1968), *The Burning Bed* (1984), *Crimes of the Heart* (1986), *Sleeping with the Enemy* (1991), *What's Love Got to Do with It* (1993), *Enough* (2002), *Provoked* (2006), and *Private Violence* (2014). How does the movie you chose portray the abusive partner and the IPV victim? Is the cycle of violence evident in the film? What stereotypes or myths are perpetuated by the film? What messages does the film send about staying in an abusive relationship? What positive or awareness-raising messages about IPV, if any, are present in the film? What was your reaction to watching the movie from a personal perspective? What was your reaction to watching the movie from a counseling perspective? Would you be able to work with either the perpetrator or victim in a crisis situation?

instead of being viewed as powerless and helpless, is viewed as choosing to confront violence from within the relationship. In addition, researchers have rejected the notion that the victim who stays in the relationship is helpless and have focused on the inner resources (e.g., resilience, sense of humor, hope, spirituality) and survival strategies of the IPV victim who chooses to stay with an abusive partner (McLeod et al., 2010; Watlington & Murphy, 2006). Counselors are advised to consider how their interventions with victims and perpetrators of IPV may be influenced by their beliefs about IPV and why victims stay in abusive relationships. Since IPV impacts so many individuals and families, counselors must be aware of their beliefs and judgments about perpetrators and victims, since this is a population most likely to be served in a crisis setting. How a counselor views victims and perpetrators in crisis may affect intervention.

COMMON CRISIS ISSUES

The intense emotional and physical stress caused by IPV can often exceed the perceived coping resources of the abused partner. As a counselor responding to an IPV crisis, the overarching goal is the safety of the victim, regardless of whether he or she decides to stay in or leave the violent relationship. Simultaneously, and because in most instances the decision to stay in or leave a violent relationship is in the hands of the victim, counselors should also work to empower clients to solve problems effectively based on the client's unique situation and available resources. Counselors should conduct a triage assessment to determine which aspects of the situation require immediate intervention. In addition, crisis counselors should work with IPV clients in crisis to increase perceived options, mobilize resources, and identify sources of continued support after the crisis is stabilized (Greenstone & Leviton, 2011). Common crisis issues that emerge when working with IPV clients include attending to physical injury, establishing immediate safety, and deciding whether or not to report IPV to the police.

Attending to Physical Injury

Many IPV victims receive treatment in emergency rooms and doctors' offices for injuries inflicted by an intimate partner; yet health care providers often fail to assess the cause of the injuries they are treating (Ramachandran, Covarrubias, Watson, & Decker, 2013; Todahl & Walters, 2011). Just as it is imperative for health care providers to screen for IPV, it is also essential that counselors ask about physical injuries and facilitate medical care when necessary. Physical injury resulting from IPV can range from scrapes and bruises to permanent disfigurement, disability, and death. Emergency medical treatment may be required before any further counseling intervention can occur; therefore, counselors should be prepared to refer clients and arrange transportation to appropriate medical facilities. They should also be aware of free and low-cost medical resources, since victims may not have health insurance. In addition, since IPV can take the form of sexual assault and rape, counselors should be aware of medical facilities that specialize in rape. Advising the client of what to expect during use of a rape kit can help reduce anxiety and allow the client to make an informed decision about consenting to the procedure. Also, when a referral to a medical facility is necessary, crisis counselors should ensure continuity of care by communicating that they are not abandoning the client, checking to make sure that the client arrives at the medical facility safely, and advising the client that counseling is available for continued support once medical needs are addressed.

Establishing Immediate Safety

During an IPV crisis, assessing and planning for physical safety or preventing further harm to the client is paramount. Time is of the essence, and crisis counselors must gain thorough and accurate information quickly by conducting a detailed assessment of the situation, including violence severity, available resources, and barriers to accessing resources (Cronholm, Fogarty, Ambuel, & Harrison, 2011; Kress, Protivnak, & Sadlack, 2008). The counselor must also directly assess the client for suicide and homicide risk and be prepared to take protective measures if needed (e.g., to act on the duty to warn, to arrange for involuntary psychiatric hospitalization of the victim or perpetrator in severe cases). In some situations, the client may not be able to return home safely, so the counselor must arrange for emergency shelter. In the event a client decides to return home, a harm reduction plan should be developed. Provisions for children and pets at risk for harm may also be necessary (Kress et al., 2008). A detailed description of how to construct a safety plan or harm reduction plan is provided later in the chapter.

Reporting Intimate Partner Violence to the Police

The process for reporting an IPV incident to the police is complex and differs from state to state. States outline who is a mandated reporter, what injuries require reporting, and what exceptions are outlined in the law. A counselor should be aware of the mandated state reporting law for domestic violence. The Family Violence Prevention Fund (Durborow, Lizdas, Flaherty, Marjavi, & Family Violence Prevention Fund, 2010) outlines the mandated state reporting laws for "healthcare providers" in all 50 states. In the majority of states, most acts of domestic violence are not reportable without evidence of medical intervention to treat life-threatening injuries (e.g., gunshot wounds, stabbings; see www.acf.hhs.gov/sites/default/files/fysb/state_compendium.pdf).

It is clear that the majority of IPV incidents are not reported to the police (Childress, 2013). A victim may choose not to contact the police due to the belief that the abuse was not serious enough to require police intervention, that the police will not be helpful, or that if the police are called, the relationship with the abusive partner will need to end. In addition, a victim may fear the consequences of contacting the police, such as the loss of housing or the involvement of child protective services. At the same time, many victims do not want to leave the relationship in the hopes that the situation will get better but want the violence to stop.

Children who are exposed to IPV experience a wide range of negative outcomes, including post-traumatic stress disorder (PTSD), decreased self-esteem, academic difficulties, and higher rates of aggressive behavior (Garrido, Culhane, Petrenko, & Taussig, 2011; Goddard & Bedi, 2010). In fact, some forms of exposure to IPV may be a reportable form of child abuse in some states. If it is reported by the victim of domestic violence that a child is also the victim of physical or sexual abuse, a counselor is mandated to report the child abuse. There is no exception to this reporting mandate. However, mandated reporting of child abuse can result in the IPV victim feeling victimized by the counseling agency. In order to minimize the victim's loss of power, counselors

ACTIVITY 8.2

Read the following statements and honestly evaluate whether you agree or disagree with each one and why:

1. IPV is a personal matter. People outside the relationship should not interfere.
2. Women who stay in abusive relationships are partially at fault for the treatment they receive because someone can only treat you as badly as you let them.
3. You cannot be raped by your spouse or partner
4. It is OK to get a divorce if you have been emotionally, physically, or sexually abused by your partner.

5. It is justifiable to resort to physical violence if you find out your significant other has been unfaithful to you.
6. It is OK to be physically violent in self-defense.
7. It is never OK to hit a woman.

What has shaped your responses to these questions (e.g., messages from your family of origin, religious/spiritual teachings, the media)? In addition to the statements listed above, what other messages have you received about IPV? How may your beliefs and values affect your work with clients?

THINK ABOUT IT 8.1

Think about the role of law enforcement in IPV incidents. Some states have laws that require or strongly recommend arrest when police respond to an IPV incident.

What are the pros and cons of mandatory arrest? Do you think mandatory arrest laws are beneficial to IPV victims? Why or why not?

should pay special attention to the informed-consent process regarding limits of confidentiality and encourage the IPV client to report child abuse herself (Todahl & Walters, 2011). Often counselors will need to provide education to clients about domestic violence and the potential impact on or increased risk of violence to other family members.

For members of minority groups (e.g., gay, lesbian, and bisexual individuals; racial and ethnic minorities; immigrants), the decision to call the police may be further complicated by other factors discussed in more detail later in this chapter. Victims may also fear that calling the police will increase the risk for further harm from their abusers (Childress, 2013). Unless suicidality, homicidality, or child abuse is disclosed, or variables meet the outlined mandated reporting for domestic violence as mentioned previously, counselors are not required to report IPV/domestic violence incidents and should support the choice the client makes regarding police notification (Chang et al., 2005; Kress et al., 2008). The counselor should discuss the pros and cons of police intervention with the client and then respect the client's decision. Understanding the laws regarding domestic violence is also helpful for counselors so they can assist their clients in determining what is realistic based on the laws that govern law enforcement officers' actions. State laws differ regarding police intervention, arrest policies, and charges. Complete Activity 8.2 to assess your beliefs about IPV. Then complete Think About It 8.1.

INTIMATE PARTNER VIOLENCE IN SPECIAL POPULATIONS

Culture is important to consider in understanding and treating IPV. Culture guides how clients define, view, experience, and respond to IPV. Counselors responding to IPV should attend to cultural dimensions such as gender, race, ethnicity, socioeconomic status, level of acculturation, language, religiosity, sexual orientation, ability status, and age. With the increased acknowledgment that IPV is a global problem, the social and cultural contexts of IPV are gaining much-needed attention. Unfortunately, the impact of culture on the IPV experience, including the reporting of IPV and help-seeking behaviors, has been largely ignored in the counseling literature. The sections that follow highlight some of the social and cultural considerations relevant to the conceptualization, prevalence, and presentation of IPV, including (1) racial and ethnic minority concerns and the intersection of gender, social class, immigration status, and religiosity; (2) female-to-male violence; (3) LGBT violence; (4) disability status; (5) elder abuse; and (6) dating violence among adolescents and young adults.

Race and Ethnicity

Race and ethnicity are important considerations in understanding and intervening in IPV. Figures 8.2 and 8.3 present lifetime victimization rates for females and males, respectively. Table 8.1 breaks down IPV estimates by race and ethnicity in terms of the prevalence of rape, physical assault, and stalking. While the survey data described in these figures and table provide important information, they do not distinguish rates for IPV specifically or highlight complexities in within-group variation of violence victimization. Complete Activity 8.3 to explore your knowledge of abusive actions against women.

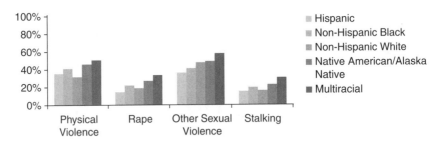

FIGURE 8.2   Lifetime intimate personal violence victimization rates for females by race and ethnicity.
Source: Centers for Disease Control and Prevention (2011). *National Intimate Partner and Sexual Violence Survey.* Retrieved from http://www.cdc.gov/ViolencePrevention/pdf/NISVS_Report2010-a.pdf

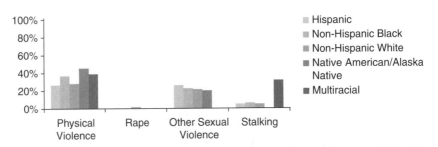

FIGURE 8.3   Lifetime intimate personal violence victimization rates for males by race and ethnicity.
Note: No graphic representation for a particular racial group indicates that data was not reported.
Source: Centers for Disease Control and Prevention (2011). *National Intimate Partner and Sexual Violence Survey.* Retrieved from http://www.cdc.gov/ViolencePrevention/pdf/NISVS_Report2010-a.pdf

TABLE 8.1 Lifetime Intimate Personal Violence Victimization Rates by Race and Ethnicity

		Hispanic	Non-Hispanic			
			Black	White	Native American/Alaska Native	Multiracial
Physical violence	% (F/M)	35.2/26.5	40.9/36.8	31.7/28.1	45.9/45.3	50.4/38.8
	N (F/M)	5.32 m/4.28 m	5.96 m/4.60 m	25.75 m/21.52 m	399,000/365,000	683,000/513,000
Rape	% (F/M)	14.6/*	22.0/*	18.8/1.7	26.9/*	33.5/*
	N (F/M)	2.2 m/*	3.19 m/*	15.23 m/1.29 m	234,000/*	452,000/*
Other sexual violence	% (F/M)	36.1/26.2	41.0/22.6	47.6/21.5	49.0/20.1	58.0/31.6
	N (F/M)	5.44 m/4.26 m	5.97 m/2.82 m	38.6 m/16.51 m	424,000/162,000	786,000/413,000
Stalking	% (F/M)	15.2/5.1	19.6/6.0	16.0/5.1	22.7/*	30.6/*
	N (F/M)	2.30 m/829,000	2.85 m/750,000	12.99 m/3.92 m	197,000/*	414,000/*

Note: N = estimated number of IPV victims in millions (rounded to the nearest 10,000, unless otherwise indicated); *m* = million.
* = not reported; F/M = female/male statistics; race and ethnicity were self-identified in the survey.
Source: Centers for Disease Control and Prevention (2011). *National Intimate Partner and Sexual Violence Survey.* Retrieved from http://www.cdc.gov/ViolencePrevention/pdf/NISVS_Report2010-a.pdf

ACTIVITY 8.3
Identifying Abusive Acts Against Women

Review this list of intentional acts. Circle the acts you would consider abusive toward females, adding more acts to the list as appropriate.

Scratching	Pulling hair	Disrupting sleep
Using physical restraint	Biting	Slapping
Throwing objects	Burning with cigarette	Humiliating in front of others
Pushing	Grabbing	Forcing sex
Calling names	Withholding sex	Committing adultery
Threatening to leave	Threatening to kill self	Threatening to kill others
Poisoning	Kicking	Choking
Destroying property	Using jealousy	Isolating from others
Killing partner	Controlling a schedule	Punishing for no sex
Deciding how a partner dresses	Disrupting meals	Wounding with a knife

Review the list. Would your choices be different if you were considering IPV among racial and ethnic minorities? Toward a male? Toward someone from a more religious background? Toward someone with a disability? Toward someone identifying as LGBT? Discuss how the behaviors you consider abusive may depend on the cultural makeup of the client.

Some studies show lifetime rates for physical and/or sexual abuse as high as 41 to 60%, depending on the amount of time subgroups have resided in the United States (Yoshihama, Dabby, & Asian and Pacific Islander Institute on Domestic Violence, 2015). In contrast, other studies report similar IPV prevalence rates across racial and ethnic groups. For example, the prevalence rates of IPV victimization among Latina and Non-Latina women were 44.6% and 44%, respectively, in one study (Bonomi, Anderson, Cannon, Slesnick, & Rodriguez, 2009). In another study, no significant differences in frequency or severity of IPV incidents were reported between racial minority and White women (Hyman, Frote, DuMont, Romans, & Cohen, 2009). Obviously, the prevalence of IPV can differ depending on the study; hence, reported data may not accurately indicate actual prevalence. Differences may occur for several reasons. First, some of these rates may be underreported due to cultural values or social factors, to be discussed. Second, there are flaws in reporting as individuals get "lumped" into larger racial and ethnic groups, ignoring great variation within each racial or ethnic group. Third, information is self-report data obtained from samples of convenience, samples that vary significantly depending on the setting in which they are obtained. Fourth, many studies gather IPV data from health departments and clinics that serve lower socioeconomic victims of IPV; whereas higher socioeconomic groups may be financially able to obtain counseling services through private practices and therefore may be underreported in many studies.

IPV reporting trends may be associated with community services sought by different racial/ethnic minority groups. For example, African American and Hispanic female

IPV victims were two to three times more likely than White female victims to report IPV to the police in one study (Lipsky, Caetano, & Roy-Byrne, 2009). In another study, 36.2% of racial minority female IPV victims reported IPV to the police, compared with 28.3% of White female IPV victims (Hyman et al., 2009). There are also racial and ethnic disparities with regard to seeking medical and mental health treatment for IPV. Female racial minority IPV victims may be less likely than White female victims to access social services or disclose IPV to family and friends. Hispanic women may be less likely than African American or White women to use hospital treatment services for IPV injury (Lipsky et al., 2009). Finally, Asian American IPV victims may be less likely than African American, White, or Hispanic victims to use mental health services (Cho & Kim, 2012).

Several factors should be considered as we examine cultural variations in IPV. Differences in reporting trends and help-seeking behaviors among racial/ethnic groups may occur for several reasons. Cultural factors may influence the timing, presentation, and sequencing of reporting. They might include cultural solidarity, family structure, gender role socialization, socioeconomic status, and religiosity. Cultural factors such as social isolation, language barriers, economic barriers, dedication to family, shame, and a cultural stigma of divorce also influence IPV reporting. Some immigrants and refugees may also experience fear of deportation or may be familiar only with their home country's cultural mores surrounding IPV. In addition, they may be afraid of police or other legal authorities given their previous experiences with police, military, and government.

Unfortunately, IPV-related resources may be unavailable in certain lower-SES communities of color, affecting reporting and help-seeking trends (Hien & Ruglass, 2009). Various forms of oppression such as racism, heterosexism, classism, and ableism may intersect to further prohibit a sense of safety to report. Alternatively, the degree of cultural solidarity may perpetuate IPV. Strong cultural ties, particularly in smaller communities, may isolate women from outside resources, promote greater acceptance of gender inequities, and result in a stronger tradition of family secrecy. For example, cultural norms, particularly those in non-Western cultures, may restrict victims from seeking legal or medical attention for IPV.

Regardless of the differences in IPV prevalence rates by race and ethnicity, there seem to be similar reasons for remaining in violent relationships. However, there are cultural subtleties in how IPV is recognized and addressed that affect reporting trends across racial and ethnic groups. The interrelated factors include patriarchal family structure, socioeconomic status, immigrant status, and religious and spiritual beliefs.

PATRIARCHAL FAMILY STRUCTURE   Patriarchy denotes clear gender role assignments based on patrilineal descent. Feminists view patriarchy as the most important cause of IPV because it is based on a power imbalance between males and females, and abuse is used as a source of control. In patrilineal societies, where male honor is measured by female chastity and fidelity, IPV could be higher, since any male member of the patriline may be violent toward any female member of the patriline. Patriarchal societies oftentimes create violent environments for women and increased tolerance of IPV.

Traditional gender roles are characteristic of patriarchal family structure, creating cultural pressure to remain in violent relationships. For example, *marianismo* in Latin cultures is the value of having females be economically dependent on males, maintaining the family unit above their own personal needs, and respecting males as decision makers (Villalba, 2018). Patriarchal values may lead Japanese women to view sexual acts with shame and embarrassment and thus lead to underreported sexual abuse (Li, Inman, & Alvarez, 2018). In contrast, many African American households are headed by women. African American women are often stereotypically viewed as the "Black superwoman" (Taft, Bryant-Davis, Woodward, Tillman, & Torres, 2009) who is strong, independent, invulnerable, and stoic. Internalization of this stereotype may make African American women less likely to reach out for support when experiencing IPV. A final example illustrates practices in Arab cultures. The concepts of family honor (*sharaf*) and shame (*ird, ayb*) promote "manliness" of males, sexual purity of females, and fidelity of a wife or mother. The resulting norms and practices shape social and sexual behavior among males and females and in some instances promote IPV without criminal prosecution. In Arab cultures, violence from husbands is often legitimized and accepted by women as occupational or domestic stress, with women tolerating some forms of IPV. For example, approximately 60% of Palestinian women and men support wife beating on "certain occasions" (e.g., when the wife refuses to have sex, disobeys the husband, or challenges the husband's manhood) (Khawaja, Linos, El-Roueiheb, 2008).

SOCIOECONOMIC STATUS   The role of lower SES has been examined in relation to IPV. Poverty is inextricably linked to limited resources, substance use, social isolation, pregnancy, and unemployment. These variables collectively create unhealthy environments that both initiate and perpetuate IPV. Some argue that it may be income or social inequality rather than poverty that is associated with IPV. That is, the wider the gap between the "haves" and "have nots," the greater the violence victimization of those with lower SES. Social disorganization theorists argue that concentrated poverty weakens informal community resources and leads to a lowered sense of self-efficacy in the community for responding to IPV. As a result, violence comes to be viewed as a legitimate means of settling personal disputes, and being viewed in the community as violent or dangerous may boost social status (Taft et al., 2009).

IMMIGRANT STATUS   IPV is common among immigrants and refugees, as migration from one country to another often creates isolation that facilitates IPV. On a global level, approximately 35% of the world's women have been physically assaulted by a partner, with as many as 70% of women in developing countries experiencing IPV (World Health Organization, 2013). For women not highly acculturated to the U.S. culture, there is an overall decrease in the use of social and health care services. Language barriers often prevent women in abusive relationships from seeking assistance. In addition, dissonance with gender roles may perpetuate IPV, as women often become the primary breadwinner in the family due to more restricted employment opportunities for male immigrants (Rizo & Macy, 2011). Lack of knowledge of available resources, distrust of government agencies, and lack of knowledge of the U.S. legal system may also be barriers to help seeking for immigrant women who experience IPV. Undocumented immigrant victims of IPV may be more hesitant to report IPV due to concerns with deportation. With many immigrant and refugee women entering the United States each year, it is imperative that counselors acknowledge the prevalence and consequences of IPV in this population.

RELIGIOUS AND SPIRITUAL BELIEFS   Religiosity, spirituality, and partner violence are linked, in both positive and negative ways. Some individuals who perpetrate partner violence may use (and misuse) religious texts and beliefs to justify or rationalize IPV.

Some IPV victims may stay in abusive relationships due to religious or spiritual beliefs that condemn divorce and promote male domination, superior male morality, the value of suffering, and submission and obedience to husbands.

Some IPV victims may be hesitant to seek help outside of the religious or spiritual community or may be reluctant to disclose IPV in order to preserve the family image. Some religious leaders may be unprepared to respond to issues of IPV. For example, religious leaders may not have formal training in counseling, may be unaware of resources in the secular community for IPV, and may feel torn between promoting traditional values of family unity and the physical, emotional, and spiritual safety of the victim (Nason-Clark, 2009).

Religious or spiritual practices may also serve as protective factors against IPV and as a coping mechanism in recovering from its consequences. For example, in the United States, men and women who frequently attend religious services are less likely to perpetrate and/or experience IPV (Mahoney, 2010). Faith in a higher power can serve as an inner coping resource for religious IPV victims. In the African American community, prayer is used significantly for coping with IPV consequences (Taft et al., 2009). Additionally, religious leaders who are well-trained in responding to IPV may help bridge the gap between religious and community resources for IPV victims (Nason-Clark, 2009).

Female-to-Male Violence

All reviews of IPV statistics reveal that women are significantly more likely to report IPV than are men, no matter the type of abuse (e.g., rape, physical assault, stalking, verbal assault). In addition, there is no doubt that in comparing the groups, women report experiencing more severe forms of abuse than do men. Therefore, female-to-male violence, sometimes referred to as *husband abuse*, has received minimal attention in the counseling literature and is probably underreported.

Why might female-to-male violence be underreported? Gender norms may prevent males who suffer emotional, physical, or sexual abuse from reporting, as disclosure might "emasculate" them. Men may also fail to define their experiences as abusive or may fear being laughed at or ridiculed if they reach out for help. Male victims of IPV may also be reluctant to report abuse from a female partner for fear that they will also be accused of being abusive (Douglas, Hines, & McCarthy, 2012). Additionally, there are fewer IPV resources available for men. Most shelters are designated for women and serve only women and children. Funding and grants are often awarded to clinics and centers that assist women who are victims of IPV. Prevailing myths, discriminative training and education, and biased clinical practices based only on feminist theory or accepted myths that men cannot be the victims of IPV may prevent many in the helping field from intervening or even asking males at intake about being victims of IPV. In order to effectively meet the needs of male IPV victims, counselors should validate their experiences, provide accurate educational information about IPV, and provide gender-appropriate IPV resources.

LGBT Violence

The lifetime prevalence of IPV for LGBT individuals is greater than that in heterosexual couples. The most recent National Intimate Partner and Sexual Violence Survey revealed that approximately 43% of lesbian women and 61% of bisexual women experience IPV, compared with approximately 35% of heterosexual women. Approximately 26% of gay men and 37% of bisexual men experience IPV, compared with approximately 29% of heterosexual men (Walters, Chen, & Breiding, 2013). Prevalence in the transgender community is harder to estimate, yet the problem seems to be more pervasive. While accounting for only 4% of LGBT IPV cases, approximately 50% of rape and physical assault victimization rates involve transgender individuals (National Coalition of Anti-Violence Programs, 2007). In another study on IPV in the transgender community, 35% of transgender individuals reported experiencing physical abuse from a partner (Ard & Makadon, 2011).

Estimating the prevalence of LGBT violence presents difficulties similar to those encountered in estimating violence among racial/ethnic minorities and against males. Among the systems affecting LGBT disclosure of IPV are family and friends, mutual friends of the abused and abuser in the LGBT community, LGBT-affirmative shelters and crisis counselors, the legal system (i.e., attorneys, jurors, judges, laws), public policy, and societal myths based in gender norms, homophobia, transphobia, and heterosexism (Ard & Makadon, 2011; Walker, 2015).

Is IPV a gendered problem, as many feminists assert? Can men be victims and women be batterers? The feminist notion that IPV is caused by traditional gender role socialization in a patriarchal family structure often does not fit LGBT relationships. If IPV is explained as a result of patriarchy, gay and bisexual men cannot be abused, and lesbian and bisexual women cannot be abusive. Feminist theory also fails to account for the experiences of transgender individuals. Thus, feminist theory may leave counselors working with LGBT couples with little information about the causes of IPV (Walker, 2015).

Homophobia and transphobia, or prejudice and discrimination against LGBT individuals and their culture, contribute to the minimization of IPV in the LGBT community and preclude many from seeking help from traditional IPV resources (e.g., shelters, community agencies, the legal system). These attitudes and behaviors are often based in heterosexism, the idea that heterosexuality is normative and thus superior to homosexuality. Stereotypical gender-role misconceptions also negatively impact the transgender community. LGBT couples may internalize heterosexist and transphobic ideas and thus feel responsible for protecting one another due to societal oppression and the resulting social isolation.

An LGBT partner who is being abused may find it difficult to report the abuse for several reasons: (1) the abuser may threaten to "out" the abused if he or she discloses the IPV to anyone; (2) the abused may be fearful of disclosing sexual orientation or transgender identity in the process of disclosing the abuse; (3) the abusive partner may be the only source of support; (4) the abusive partner may share the same friends as the abused partner, and embarrassing the abuser may result in potentially losing the community in which the abused partner feels accepted for his or her sexual orientation and/or gender identity; (5) the process of disclosure may reinforce or strengthen internalized homophobia or transphobia in the abused partner; and (6) the desire to maintain the LGBT community's reputation for offering safety and advocating for equal rights (e.g., marriage, adoption) may outweigh the desire to assert that there is "something wrong" in the community, such as IPV (Ard & Makadon, 2011; Walker, 2015).

Taken together, these factors have contributed to a lack of resources for LGBT individuals who experience IPV. Gay and bisexual men may have fewer resources than do lesbian and bisexual women. Few shelters accept gay and bisexual men due to the propensity toward aggression and homophobia of other male batterers who may be living in the shelter. Transgender IPV victims are rarely welcomed at shelters or other community agencies who define IPV as a problem that impacts women in heterosexual relationships (Walker, 2015). Further, IPV victims seeking services may be revictimized if their relationship is viewed as not being "real" or if they are subjected to other forms of homophobia, transphobia, and heterosexism. Those providing community resources are often placed in a difficult position: since LGBT violence goes against the typical view of the causes and course of IPV, they are left to decide "who to believe" and thus who should receive assistance and who should be reprimanded. This creates many situations where victims are ignored, abusers are unintentionally allowed into similar shelters as those they abuse, and abusers are not prosecuted.

Furthermore, the lack of a uniform definition of LGBT violence leads to the lack of legal protection. For example, LGBT individuals are excluded from domestic violence legislation in some areas (Ard & Makadon, 2011). LGBT individuals may also be reluctant to use law enforcement as a resource for fear of police brutality (Walker, 2015).

Disability Status

Other special populations that have received some attention are individuals with physical, cognitive, or emotional disabilities. Controlling for race, ethnicity, age, and SES, women with disabilities are physically or sexually assaulted at a rate double that of those without a disability (Healey, Humphreys, & Howe, 2013; Smith, 2008). A disability in either the victim or the perpetrator can be a risk factor for IPV, or the disability may be a result of IPV toward the individual.

Vulnerability and powerlessness are prevalent for those in this population, as they often depend on their intimate partners to assist them with activities of daily living, such as providing medication, bathing, dressing, and running errands. Thus, partners could be considered abusive if they remove a battery from a wheelchair, withhold medication, demand a kiss or verbal expression of appreciation before a task, or engage in unwanted sexual touch during bathing or dressing (Smith, 2008). Able-bodied women might not readily consider many of these acts abusive, as they do not experience them. Thus, women with disabilities are concerned not just with typical forms of abuse but also with those specific to disability accommodations.

Unfortunately, women with disabilities experience a higher risk for victimization than do able-bodied women. No information is available for men with disabilities, although elder abuse reports are on the rise in the United States due to legislation protecting this vulnerable class of citizens. The risk for victimization increases if individuals experience multiple oppressions from racism and classism. When women with disabilities seek support, they often find there are inaccessible or insufficient shelters or other community services (Healey et al., 2013). Crisis counselors are strongly encouraged to ensure that the agencies in which they work are prepared adequately for individuals with disabilities; this may include having physical items such as wheelchairs readily available and making referrals for physical health needs. Counselors should be aware of the laws for mandated reporters of abuse of vulnerable persons.

Elder Abuse

With the U.S. population living longer, IPV will increasingly affect those within the elderly population. Elder abuse may occur within intimate relationships as well as extended families. Available data suggest that approximately 3.5 million Americans age 65 years or older experience abuse from someone they are dependent on for care and protection (National Center on Elder Abuse, 2015). Elderly females are more likely than elderly males to experience abuse, and as age increases, so does the likelihood of abuse. In addition to physical, sexual, and emotional abuse, types of elder abuse include neglect (e.g., malnutrition, poor personal hygiene, unsafe or unclean living conditions), abandonment (e.g., desertion of an elder at a facility or public location), financial or material exploitation (e.g., sudden changes in bank account practices, unpaid bills despite availability of resources, forgery), and self-neglect. Vulnerability and power-lessness can be common risk factors for elder abuse, as they are for individuals with disabilities.

Signs of IVP (e.g., bruising, unexplained injuries, confusion) may be overlooked or considered medical issues associated with aging. Mental health service providers may hold ageist beliefs that could negatively impact elderly IPV victims. For example, mental health service providers may be less likely to screen for IPV in the elderly population, less likely to define partner behaviors as abusive in the elderly population, and may be more likely to intervene legally rather than therapeutically when IPV is disclosed by an elderly person (Yechezkel & Ayalon, 2013).

Culturally competent counselors recognize that IPV is a real and salient issue in the elderly population and respond with appropriate screening, interventions, and resources. Counselors should be aware of the laws for mandated reporters of abuse of elder persons.

Dating Violence among Adolescents and Young Adults

IPV begins early for many—sometimes with their first dating experiences. Between the ages of 11 and 17 years, 22% of females and 15% of males experience some form of dating violence (Centers for Disease Control and Prevention [CDC], 2014c). Lesbian, gay, and bisexual youth are particularly vulnerable to dating violence, reporting higher rates of dating violence perpetration and victimization than heterosexual youth (Dank, Lachman, Zweig, & Yahner, 2014). Dating violence, just like other forms of IPV, includes physical, emotional, and sexual abuse, as well as stalking. Adolescents who do not have clear ideas about appropriate boundaries and healthy relationships may characterize abusive behaviors as acceptable or even positive characteristics of a relationship. For example, an adolescent may view possessive, stalking behaviors as a sign that their dating partner cares about them. Many adolescents spend large amounts of time using social media and other forms of technology. It is important to note that dating violence can take place electronically, for example, by sharing sexual pictures of a dating partner without their consent, posting negative comments on a dating partner's social networking page, or using text messages to monitor and control a dating partner's behavior (CDC, 2014c; Draucker & Martsolf, 2010).

Several risk factors are associated with dating violence. For example, adolescents who witness and/or experience some form of domestic violence at home are more likely to harm a dating partner or be harmed by a dating partner than adolescents who do not have this type of IPV exposure (CDC, 2014c). They may have learned from these experiences that violence is a normal and "appropriate" outlet for conflict within intimate relationships, since the abuser seldom gets punished. By the time adolescents enter their first romantic relationship, ideas related to interpersonal skills, expectations, partner selection, pace of intimacy, and sexual behavior are well established. Thus, adolescents and young adults may be simultaneously witnessing IPV within the home and being abused in dating relationships, creating minimal outlets for support and making them less likely to report the victimization to others. Other risk factors associated with dating violence include early sexual activity with multiple partners, poor academic performance, substance use, and mental health issues including depression and anxiety (CDC, 2014c; Dank et al., 2014).

Unfortunately, dating violence in adolescence significantly predicts IPV in young adulthood (Cui, Gordon, Ueno, & Finchman, 2013). Women between the ages of 18 and 24 years experience IPV (including rape and sexual assault) at a higher rate than any other age group (U.S. Department of Justice, 2014). As such, dating violence on college and university campuses is of particular concern. College women who experience IPV possess characteristics that distinguish their IPV experiences from the experiences of IPV victims in other age groups. For example, most college-age women do not live with their partners, do not have children, and are not financially dependent on their partners (Edwards et al., 2012). Thus, when college-age IPV victims make a decision about whether to remain in a relationship with an abusive partner, they may consider other variables. For example, women in one study who decided to remain in the abusive relationship cited envisioning a future with the partner, positive qualities about the partner, and the length of the dating relationship as reasons for staying.

Many IPV victims in this age category do not define their experiences as abusive and minimize their experiences (Edwards et al., 2012). Moreover, less than 20% of college-age women who experience IPV use mental health services or other services designed to assist IPV victims (Prospero & Vohra-Gupta, 2008; U.S. Department of Justice, 2014). Barriers to using formal services include social stigma, expense, and the belief that formal services would not be helpful. Instead, many college-age IPV victims turn to friends or family for support (Prospero & Vohra-Gupta, 2008).

Due to the prevalence of and serious consequences associated with dating violence, multiple prevention programs have been developed for adolescents and young adults. The most effective prevention programs are comprehensive (i.e., they address IPV at the individual, peer, campus, organizational, and community levels), engage participants on multiple occasions, are culturally relevant, and are developed in collaboration with experts on IPV and leaders in the community. For example, since college women frequently turn to friends for support when they experience dating violence (Edwards et al., 2012), some prevention programs train friends and bystanders to recognize signs of dating violence and respond appropriately. In response to the role of technology in the lives of adolescents and young adults, researchers have developed a smartphone app, called the myPlan App, that helps dating violence victims and their friends identify unhealthy and violent relationship characteristics and develop personalized safety plans (Glass et al., 2015). Complete Activity 8.4, which focuses on raising awareness about adolescent dating violence.

ACTIVITY 8.4

Unfortunately, dating violence is a problem that affects many individuals at an early age. When adolescents are first beginning to explore dating relationships, many of them are unaware of what a healthy or unhealthy dating relationship looks like. Work individually or in groups to develop an awareness-raising product that is developmentally appropriate for adolescents. Include information such as facts and figures on dating violence, how to recognize warning signs that a dating relationship may be unhealthy, and how to ask for help if experiencing dating violence. Consider how you could use the brochure or poster you developed in your future counseling practice.

THE COUNSELOR'S RESPONSE TO INTIMATE PARTNER VIOLENCE CLIENTS IN CRISIS

Screening for Intimate Partner Violence

Due to the prevalence of IPV, it is generally agreed that IPV screening should be universal. Just as crisis counselors assess for suicidal and homicidal ideation with every client, they should ask all clients directly about IPV. Most research on IPV screening focuses on assessment in doctors' offices and emergency rooms, since many IPV victims require medical treatment for physical injury inflicted by an intimate partner but may not necessarily seek counseling to address the effects of IPV. Nevertheless, this research provides important information for counselors.

While acknowledging the need for intervention with IPV victims, most health care providers, crisis counselors, health care professionals, clinicians, and health care workers fail to routinely screen for IPV (Todahl & Walters, 2011; L. E. Tower, 2006; M. Tower, 2007). A primary barrier to universal IPV screening is the lack of knowledge of and training on how to ask about IPV, how to recognize symptoms that may indicate an individual is experiencing abuse, and how to respond if IPV is disclosed. Personal variables may also prevent health care professionals and crisis counselors from asking about IPV. For example, clinicians may have negative attitudes toward IPV victims stemming from personal experiences with IPV or have prejudicial attitudes including racism, classism, ageism, and homophobia. Health care workers may also avoid screening for IPV due to fear for their own safety, fear of offending their patients, or perhaps because they do not view intervention in domestic affairs to be part of their health care responsibilities (Todahl & Walters, 2011; M. Tower, 2007). Institutional and professional barriers to IPV screening are the perception of powerlessness to help IPV victims due to insufficient community resources and the fear of marginalization by colleagues (Todahl & Walters, 2011; L. E. Tower, 2006). However, the multitude of reasons for not asking about IPV does not outweigh the argument for IPV screening. Screening can help prevent injury and literally help save the lives of individuals who experience partner abuse.

The first step in screening for IPV is to create a safe environment that is conducive to disclosure. Disclosing IPV can be a very difficult and painful process for victims due to shame, embarrassment, and fear of being judged. Victims may also fear losing their children or being further abused by their partner as a result of IPV disclosure. Crisis counselors can indicate that it is safe to talk about IPV by placing posters and other IPV awareness materials in their office (Chang et al., 2005; Todahl & Walters, 2011). The crisis counselor's interpersonal style can also help create a safe atmosphere. For example,

IPV victims report that counselors who smile, demonstrate care through empowering statements, reduce the power differential by using personal self-disclosure, respect the victim's autonomy, and do not appear to be rushed are more easily accessible and easier to trust and talk to about IPV (Chang et al., 2005; Todahl & Walters, 2011).

There are two absolutes crisis counselors should follow with victims of IPV. First, counselors should never ask about abuse in the presence of the client's partner; doing so may greatly increase the risk for harm to the client. Second, counselors should be careful not to recommend ending the relationship as the only way to establish safety. In fact, the risk for harm to an IPV victim may increase following separation from an abusive partner. Postseparation violence involves the batterer's attempts to regain control over the abused partner and may include physical assault, rape, stalking, harassment, and even homicide (Logan, Walker, & Shannon, 2008). Research on nonlethal postseparation violence among heterosexual married couples indicates that the prevalence of IPV is nine times greater among women who are separated from their abusive husbands than among women who are still living with their husbands; IPV is four times more prevalent among divorced women than among women who are still married (Brownridge et al., 2008).

Once a safe environment and rapport are established, counselors should ask directly about IPV, gathering as many concrete and specific details as possible. When conducting an IPV assessment, counselors should gather information about current violence, the history of violence in the relationship, and symptoms or injuries associated with IPV (Cronholm et al., 2011). Counselors must be comfortable assessing for not only physical abuse but also sexual abuse. Vocal tone and phrasing is especially important during IPV assessment, since counselors do not want to imply judgment or raise the client's level of defensiveness. It may be helpful to begin with more general questions, such as asking the client whether he or she feels safe in the current relationship or whether anyone is hurting him or her. As the assessment progresses, more specific information must be gathered. For example, a counselor may ask who is hurting the client, how arguments usually begin, details of the most recent incident of violence, how long the most recent incident lasted, what specific forms of injuries occurred, and what happened when the incident was over. The client's IPV history is important as well, including childhood exposure to IPV, IPV in previous relationships, the first and worst incidents of violence in the current relationship, past attempts at intervention by others (e.g., family, friends, neighbors, police, the legal system), and the role of mental health and substance use issues in the IPV. Counselors should also inquire whether past or current restraining orders have been issued against the perpetrator or victim and if they are in compliance with the orders.

Counselors should consider conducting a variety of assessments for lethality; suicidal, homicidal (see Chapter 6), and level of threat as perceived by the victim. Often victims have thoughts of suicide or homicide as a means to not endure further abuse. In addition, a threat assessment based on the client's perception of injury should be completed to determine the appropriate crisis response, which may range from developing a safety or harm reduction plan with the victim to seeking immediate police intervention and hospitalization. A lethality assessment includes questions about the severity of violence, other criminal behaviors of the abuser (e.g., assaults or harassment of others, previous criminal charges), failed past interventions (e.g., multiple calls made to 911; abuser ignoring court orders; family, friends, and neighbors have tried to intervene, yet violence continues), obsessive or stalking behaviors, psychological risk factors (e.g., previous homicidal or suicidal threats or attempts, substance use issues, external life stressors, severe depression), perceived threats to the relationship (e.g., victim planning to leave, separation or divorce, infidelity), access to weapons, and behaviors that prevent the victim from accessing emergency resources. Remember that victims may initially deny that they are experiencing abuse. If this occurs, make sure to revisit questions about IPV again in the session or in a subsequent session. The following intake provides an example of how to conduct an initial IPV screening.

COUNSELOR:	Akia, we have talked a lot about your relationship with your boyfriend. I know the two of you have been through a lot and your relationship is really strained right now. I need to ask you if he has ever hurt you in any way.
AKIA:	(*30 seconds of silence while looking down*) Not really.
COUNSELOR:	I know it can be really hard to talk about. Take your time and know that I'm not judging you in any way.
AKIA:	Are you going to call the cops if I talk about this?
COUNSELOR:	As we've discussed before, there are a few situations that would require me to break confidentiality in order to protect you or someone else. I would need to take action if I believed you were going to kill yourself or someone else or in cases where I suspected child abuse. Otherwise, what we talk about is between us. It would be your decision to report to the police.
AKIA:	(*30 seconds of silence, crying*) I feel so embarrassed to say it out loud. (*Crying for 30 seconds*) Last weekend, we both had too much to drink. We started arguing about the same things we always fight about—the bills, his ex-girlfriend, chores around the house. He threw a beer bottle at me and it hit me in the head. I fell over and started crying. He started yelling, "Get up bitch!" He came over and kicked me in the stomach a few times and spat on me. Then he stormed out. He didn't come back home for two nights. When he came back, he had flowers and he cried and he told me he would never hurt me again. I still can't believe it happened. I never thought he would hurt me.
COUNSELOR:	Akia, it took a lot of courage to share that experience with me. I can see how painful it is for you to talk about that night. I need to ask you a few more questions, but let's take it at a pace you feel comfortable with. How are you feeling now?
AKIA:	I actually feel a little better just sharing it with someone else.
COUNSELOR:	I can see that you're relaxing a little. Akia, no one deserves to be hurt. You didn't do anything to bring this violence on yourself.
AKIA:	I don't know what to do. I love him. I know he really does love me, too. I just never imagined this could happen to me.

COUNSELOR:	Let's talk about that. How comfortable do you feel going home today?
AKIA:	I'm not sure.
COUNSELOR:	You know sometimes when someone experiences something as shocking and devastating as what you've gone through, they have thoughts about hurting themselves or hurting the person who hurt them. Have you had those thoughts?
AKIA:	No. I would not ever hurt myself . . . or him. I love him. I would never want to make him feel this awful. The not wanting to go home is more about worrying it could happen again. And just feeling so embarrassed.
COUNSELOR:	OK, we can talk about lots of different options. You're in control of how to handle this situation. I also want to give you some crisis resources in case he does get violent again. First, take me back to that night. Walk me through everything that happened. I know it will be really hard, but really dissecting the details of that night can help us come up with an effective safety plan for you.

Response to Intimate Partner Violence Disclosure

Since nearly all counselors will work with an IPV victim at some point, they must be prepared to respond when a client reports being abused by a partner. Immediately following an IPV disclosure, it is critical for the crisis counselor to validate the victim's experience and communicate that the victim is not to blame for the abuse (Cronholm et al., 2011). Documentation that the client is experiencing IPV is also important. IPV victims indicate that it is helpful for crisis counselors or health care workers to make notes about the disclosure of IPV and to take pictures of physical injuries, which could later be used in court if the victim chooses to take legal action. If some injuries are not visible, using a diagram of a person to indicate where you visually see physical injuries and where the victim reports injuries can also be part of documentation.

Providing the victim with resources and protection is another essential component of responding to an IPV crisis. Counselors should have an extensive list of IPV resources available, including options for emergency shelter, transportation, food, child care, medical needs, mental health care, and legal aid. The National Domestic Violence Hotline can be accessed 24 hours a day, 365 days per year at 1-800-799-SAFE or at www.thehotline.org. Crisis counselors may also consider providing a list of IPV resources to clients whether or not IPV is disclosed. Some agencies place small cards printed with IPV crisis resources in the restroom so that victims may anonymously take the information and hide it if necessary (Cronholm et al., 2011).

While crisis intervention is typically more directive than traditional counseling, counselors should strive to empower IPV victims by giving them as much control over their situations as possible (Todahl & Walters, 2011). Finally, victims indicate that it is helpful to be informed that even if they initially choose not to access IPV resources, they can return to the agency and receive assistance in the future.

Safety Planning and Harm Reduction Planning

It is crucial for a counselor to know whether a client is deciding to stay in the abusive relationship (i.e., will return home) or leave the abusive relationship prior to the client leaving the crisis center or counselor. Depending on the decision of the client, the counselor will want to implement a plan based on the decision, taking into consideration the unique issues of the client and resources available to the client.

SAFETY PLANNING   If a client decided to leave the abuser, the counselor should develop a safety plan with the main goal of keeping the client physically safe. The safety plan is tailored to the unique situation of each IPV victim; therefore, gathering concrete and specific information about the victim's experiences is essential. The counselor and client should determine appropriate supports for the client, locations that provide physical safety (e.g., shelters), and whether law enforcement should be contacted. It is also important to emphasize that a safety plan in no way guarantees the safety of the IPV victim. For example, civil protective orders are designed to prevent an abusive partner from having future contact with an IPV victim and can be tailored to meet the victim's specific needs. A protective order may contribute to an increased sense of safety for many IPV victims. However, approximately half of protective orders are violated by IPV perpetrators, particularly if there is a history of severe violence or stalking in the relationship (Logan et al., 2008). Additionally, some IPV victims may choose not to seek a protective order due to fear of retaliation, negative feelings toward the legal system, or limited financial resources (Hien & Ruglass, 2009).

HARM REDUCTION PLANNING   Harm reduction plans are developed for clients who do not intend to leave the abusive relationship. The goal of the plan is to reduce the amount of harm a victim may encounter by an abuser. Counselors should assess where incidents of violence mainly occur to attempt to avoid those rooms, how to read signs of heightened anger, using code words for children to protect them from danger, using code words to alert neighbors or family members of potential abuse, arranging an escape bag with necessary items (medications, keys, legal documents) in case the victim must leave immediately. All of these things need to be taken into account for the harm reduction plan. It is also important for clients to not demonstrate too many behavioral changes, which may make an abuser suspicious of their leaving. Some harm reduction plans may also integrate strategies to assist in alleviating pain from abuse. Meditation, mindfulness, praying, refocusing, and other self-care techniques may need to be explored with the client as part of the harm reduction plan. Developing a safety plan or a harm reduction plan may allow a client to gain a little control in uncontrollable situations. Read Voices from the Field 8.1.

Intimate Partner Violence Shelters: Opportunities and Challenges

IPV shelters provide a safe haven for many abused women and their children. IPV shelters not only protect victims from additional physical harm but also provide a safe place where emotional healing can begin. Shelter residents are often able to deeply connect with one another around their shared experiences. Shelter staff may provide much needed support and encouragement to victims. Many IPV shelters also offer counseling services and provide victims with comprehensive resources, including legal aid and assistance finding long-term housing and employment.

VOICES FROM THE FIELD 8.1

Safety and Harm Reduction Planning with Intimate Partner Violence Victims

Victoria E. Kress

"My boyfriend hits me. . . . I've lost part of my hearing. . . . I have two missing teeth, and I've had two concussions. . . . I know I need to leave him, but I'm not sure I am ready. . . . He says he'll take the baby from me if I leave. . . . He's threatened to kill me if I leave." When I was in graduate school, I never learned what to say or do when counseling a person making these remarks. The first time I worked with a woman in a violent relationship my first reaction was to tell her to leave, to run to the nearest shelter and to get safe. My client's safety was a priority, of course, but I felt a personal need to protect her as well. As counselors we do have an obligation to encourage client safety, but we also have to balance this with clients' right to autonomy; their right to make their own decisions on their own terms and schedule. So how do we respect a client's autonomy while also facilitating their welfare?

While it may be difficult, I recommend that counselors working with clients in violent relationships should not suggest that clients leave the relationship but should instead encourage their clients to be as safe as possible. People in abusive relationships have typically been told by multiple others to leave, and they themselves have often thought about leaving. Counselors suggesting that clients leave a relationship may indicate an inability to understand the complexity of each client's situation. Maybe more importantly, suggesting that someone leave a relationship indicates that the counselor doesn't believe that the client can make autonomous choices. Finally, at the time a

woman leaves a violent relationship, her risk of being murdered escalates dramatically. So telling a woman to leave a relationship before she is prepared to do so can be dangerous.

Instead of focusing on the client leaving the relationship, I suggest counselors develop a thorough harm reduction plan as a first step. When I develop harm reduction plans, I encourage my clients to do specific things:

- Keep a purse and extra set of car keys in a place that is easy to access for quick escape.
- Identify at least two places where you can go the next time you need to leave the house or go somewhere safe.
- Tell friends or neighbors about the violence and request that they call the police if they get suspicious.
- Identify the safest rooms in your house where you can go if there is fear that an argument will occur.
- Develop and store somewhere safe and accessible an escape kit that includes a copy of a protection order, extra keys, money, checks, important phone numbers, medications, social security card, bank documents, birth certificates, change of clothes, bank and house information, etc.
- Process the safety plan with children when appropriate.
- Practice escape routes and identify rooms that are safe and not close to weapons.

While IPV shelters are invaluable resources for many victims, life in a shelter is certainly not stress-free, and it requires adherence to programmatic rules and regulations that may infringe on a victim's sense of autonomy. In addition, victims may not feel ready to address the emotional impact of their abuse, yet may be required to do so as part of the shelter program. Adjusting to a shared living environment may also present difficulties, particularly for victims from cultural minority groups (Walker, 2015). Finally, as a result of their traumatic experiences, some IPV victims struggle with self-regulation and engage in behaviors such as verbal or physical altercations with shelter staff and residents or with substance use.

Working as a counselor in an IPV shelter can also be stressful. For example, counselors may experience secondary traumatization from exposure to victims' experiences. Counselors must be sure to practice self-care in order to avoid burning out or taking a blaming attitude toward victims. Counselors may also experience the stress of dual roles. For example, a counselor may deeply empathize with a victim during an individual or group session and then later be required to enforce shelter rules (e.g., imposing a penalty for not completing a required chore, dismissing the victim from the shelter for substance abuse). Solidify your knowledge of IPV by completing Activity 8.5.

Addressing the Emotional Impact of Intimate Partner Violence

The emotional consequences of IPV are equally as devastating as the physical consequences. High rates of depression and low self-esteem are common among IPV victims, and IPV is a major predictor of female drug and alcohol use (Langdon, Armour, & Stringer, 2014). Many IPV victims experience symptoms of PTSD, including a re-experiencing of the trauma (e.g., intrusive recollections, nightmares, flashbacks), avoidance/numbing (e.g., restricted range of affect, anhedonia, social withdrawal, inability to recall aspects of the trauma), and increased arousal (e.g., hypervigilance, exaggerated startle response, difficult falling or staying asleep). In addition to the symptoms traditionally associated with PTSD, Walker (2015) argues that IPV victims often experience a cluster of symptoms referred to as *battered woman syndrome*, which includes disrupted interpersonal relationships, difficulties with body image/somatic concerns, and sexual or intimacy problems.

When working with IPV victims, it is essential to consider their trauma history in constructing a treatment plan or making a diagnosis. Unfortunately, many victims are misdiagnosed and prescribed inappropriate medications by mental health care providers who fail to account for the effects of IPV. Medicating a client inappropriately does not address the issue of IPV and can only create another potential problem for the client. Victims may present with depression and anxiety without knowledge of the root of the symptoms. Most victims will not disclose information, which is why counselors should assess for IPV with every client, regardless of the presenting issue. Victims may be empowered by learning that the symptoms they are experiencing are a normal response to a traumatic event (McLeod et al., 2010). See Case Study 8.2, which describes Melinda's experiences as an IPV victim. Then complete Activity 8.6 to address counselor self-care issues in work with IPV.

CASE STUDY 8.2

Counseling an Intimate Partner Violence Victim: Melinda's Journey

Melinda, a 25-year-old, middle-class, African American female, first came to counseling for depression. During the initial intake interview, Melinda reported experiencing difficulty sleeping, frequent crying spells, low self-esteem, and feelings of hopelessness. Melinda's counselor, Candace, screened for suicidal ideation, homicidal ideation, and IPV as a routine part of the initial interview. Melinda denied suicidal and homicidal ideation and said that she had never been abused by her current boyfriend. At the end of the initial session, Candace provided Melinda with a packet of materials that she distributes to all new clients, which included a pamphlet on IPV.

Over the next two sessions, Melinda and Candace developed a strong rapport. During her third session, Melinda tearfully disclosed that her live-in boyfriend sometimes pushes or hits her when he has been drinking. Candace listened empathically to Melinda and let her know that the abuse was not her fault and that she believed her. After Melinda's disclosure, Candace asked for more information about the abuse, including how arguments usually begin, details of the most recent incident of violence, and Melinda's history of experience with IPV. Melinda reported that the last time her boyfriend hit her was a week ago, when he came home drunk from a party. Melinda sustained a split lip but did not require stitches.

Candace also completed a lethality assessment and determined that Melinda's boyfriend had never threatened to kill her, did not have a criminal record, and did not have a gun in the house. Melinda stated that she had never feared for her life when her boyfriend became abusive. She indicated that she did not want to break up with her boyfriend and that she did not think the abuse was serious enough to report to the police. Candace respected Melinda's autonomy and provided her with additional educational materials about IPV and information on 24-hour IPV crisis resources that Melinda could use in case of an emergency. Since Melinda reported that her boyfriend typically drank every weekend, Candace scheduled another appointment with Melinda before the upcoming weekend in order to develop a safety plan. Melinda and Candace collaboratively developed the following safety plan in order to minimize the risk and impact of IPV:

1. Plan to be away from the house when boyfriend comes home drunk.
2. If boyfriend comes home drunk unexpectedly, stay away from the bathroom and kitchen.
3. Pack and hide an emergency bag with clothes, cash, and an extra set of keys in case of the need to flee the house quickly.
4. Program IPV crisis hotline number into cell phone.

Melinda and Candace also discussed ideas for building coping resources, including engaging in self-care activities like reading empowerment books and joining a women's support group at church.

Over the next several months, Candace and Melinda met once a week for counseling. They continued to discuss and evaluate Melinda's safety. Despite her efforts to avoid physical violence from her boyfriend, the incidents of abuse became more frequent over time. Melinda had now sustained several injuries, including a broken arm and a broken rib. A turning point occurred when Melinda learned that she was 8 weeks pregnant with her first child. Melinda decided that she did not want to raise a child in an abusive home. She was ready to leave. Candace and Melinda discussed the risks associated with leaving an abusive partner and tips for ensuring a safe escape. Together, they decided that an IPV shelter was the best option, since Melinda had no trusted family or friends in the area. Candace arranged for transportation to the shelter straight from her office and waited with Melinda until help arrived.

Discussion Questions

1. Are there other considerations that will need to be implemented into Melinda's treatment?
2. What are some short-term and long-term therapeutic considerations?
3. What are some case management issues that must be addressed?
4. What referrals need to be made for Melinda?

BATTERER INTERVENTION

IPV response has two aspects: victim advocacy and batterer intervention. Both are valid attempts to end partner abuse. One model of attending to the needs of both IPV victims and batterers is a Coordinated Community Response (CCR), which involves the collaboration of local councils of service providers in developing a more comprehensive response to IPV incidents. CCR helps victims identify and access multiple available services, of which victims are often not aware. These services focus on advocacy, criminal justice, child services, health care, education, and vocation. Without a network of support, IPV victims face the frustration and fatigue of searching for and navigating through multiple systems and services, thus reducing the likelihood that victims will seek help at all (Shorey, Tirone, & Stuart, 2014). In addition to the efforts of community organizations, over half of the states have laws that make specific reference to batterer intervention programs, and a number of them designate specific entities to certify, license, or establish standards for batterer intervention programs (CDC, 2015c).

Batterer intervention programs have three primary goals: (1) ensuring the safety of IPV victims, (2) stopping future acts of partner violence, and (3) increasing offenders' accountability for their behavior. Batterer intervention programs teach abusive partners to develop empathy for their victims, identify and self-monitor negative thoughts, and identify and interrupt the negative self-talk that often precedes incidents of violence in order to prevent further abuse. Additionally, batterer intervention programs teach gender equality in relationships and typically teach participants to identify various forms of abuse, recognize and detail the type of abuse they have engaged in, take responsibility

ACTIVITY 8.6

Working with victims of IPV can vicariously traumatize counselors; therefore, self-care is essential. Self-care is a preventive process of proactively enhancing health by building resilience against illness and disease. It involves identifying and practicing ways to promote personal well-being. Start practicing self-care now. Make a list of activities that you find personally renewing. Develop a plan to incorporate at least one activity into each day of the upcoming week. Keep a brief journal about your self-care experiences.

for the abuse, and find alternatives to violence, often helping participants learn to develop a nonabusive response to behavior that they might ordinarily respond to in an abusive manner. Although most batterer intervention programs are designed for long-term intervention, counselors should understand the components of these programs and know whether they are available in their community.

Safety

The primary goal of batterer intervention programs is to ensure the safety of the abused partner and any children who may be involved. Steps to ensuring safety include assessment of the resources that are available to IPV victims, assessment of the severity and repetition of violent incidents, and assessment of the effects on children exposed to IPV. Depending on the aforementioned factors, offenders may need to reside separately from the victims. If law enforcement is at the scene and an arrest occurs, incarceration of the offender may provide temporary safety.

Cessation of Violence

The second goal of batterer intervention programs is stopping all forms of violence, including verbal, emotional, physical, and sexual abuses. One of the first steps toward this goal is acknowledgment of one's violent behavior. Such an acknowledgment means discarding denial (e.g., "I didn't do it"), minimizing (e.g., "I only hit her"), and blaming (e.g., "She should have been home on time"). It also means accepting that threats, coercion, and emotional abuses—the types of violence where there is no physical contact—qualify as IPV.

Researchers have investigated the effectiveness of batterer intervention programs in stopping violence and found that the important competencies offenders need to learn are emotion regulation, conflict resolution, adaptive coping skills, and empathy. Bennett and Williams (2011) reviewed four studies of batterer intervention program effectiveness; two studies found no difference in recidivism for men in the batterer program and men in the control condition and the other two had small but significant reductions in recidivism for men in the batterer program. By contrast, research sponsored by the Executive Office of the Department of Health and Human Services in Massachusetts (2015) reports that batterer intervention programs can help batterers make positive changes. Batterers who complete batterer intervention programs are less likely to commit new acts of violence or to violate restraining orders. Batterer intervention programs also tend to be most effective when their central goals of victim safety and batterer accountability have the cooperation of police departments, courts, health care providers, and family members.

Participants in Rosenberg's (2003) study reported that developing supportive relationships with other program participants and the facilitators of the batterer intervention group enabled them to address their violence successfully. In addition, participants reported that learning specific strategies for violence cessation (e.g., taking a time-out, sharing feelings rather than holding feelings inside) was helpful. Research also indicates that participation in a feminist-informed cognitive-behavioral batterer intervention group may lead to a positive change in attitudes toward women and abusive behavior (Schmidt et al., 2007). For example, batterers who participated in this program were less likely to endorse statements in support of IPV (e.g., "Smashing things is not abusive, it's just venting") and more likely to endorse statements in support of nonviolent relationships (e.g., "I cannot be provoked into being violent").

Accountability

The third goal of batterer intervention is increasing individual accountability for acts of IPV in the form of accepting responsibility for one's behavior. Simply saying "I'm sorry," especially if those words have been said on multiple occasions, is not enough. Developing alternatives to battering is an essential component of increasing accountability. One alternative strategy involves understanding and subsequently changing negative self-talk to positive self-talk. Negative self-talk involves destructive comments made when challenged with an uncomfortable or threatening situation. For example, a batterer might say, "I'm so mad that my partner doesn't have dinner ready." The idea is to change this statement to something more constructive, such as "Since dinner isn't ready yet, maybe I can help." A second task in becoming accountable is to learn to recognize triggers or cues leading to violent behavior. Triggers can be words, phrases, or statements that either the individual or partner uses (e.g., profanity, degrading comments); situations that typically create arguments (e.g., payday, drinking/drug use); and physiological changes (e.g., muscle tension, headaches, increased blood pressure/pulse). The identification of triggers enables IPV offenders to be responsible for initiating behaviors that will decrease their level of anxiety, frustration, and anger and thereby prevent any further acts of IPV.

THEORIES/APPROACHES TO BATTERER TREATMENT

Counselors who work with IPV perpetrators may use a wide variety of counseling theories and approaches. Some of the classical theories most commonly applied to batterer intervention are power and control theory (Domestic Abuse Intervention Programs, 2013), moral development theory (Kohlberg, 1984), attachment theory (Bowlby, 1980), and feminist-informed cognitive-behavioral theory. Motivational interviewing and stages of change are approaches to counseling that are showing positive effects in changing batterer behavior.

Power and Control Theory

The predominant model that influences both victim and offender services is power and control theory (Domestic Abuse Intervention Programs, 2013). Essentially, this theory states that IPV occurs when individuals in intimate relationships influence their partner's behavior by controlling them with violence or the use of power. Violence may include verbal taunts or threats, psychologically demeaning statements or actions, physical assaults, and sexual violence.

VIOLENCE IS A LEARNED BEHAVIOR   According to the first principle of power and control theory, violence is a learned behavior. There is no genetic predisposition for violence or existence of a violence gene; instead, people learn violence from many sources, including the media and community dysfunction, but primarily from parents or guardians.

VIOLENCE IS A CHOICE   The second principle of power and control theory is that people choose to be violent. Violence occurs because people are aware of a situation, understand potential rewards and consequences, and then choose to be violent. Sometimes people choose violent behavior because they are not aware of other behavioral options. Similarly, people might be unconsciously aware of behavioral alternatives but are not able to access these behaviors in a crisis situation. To that end, one can choose to "unlearn" violence through training in recognizing pending violence and in replacing violent behaviors with positive coping strategies.

ENDING VIOLENCE IS A PROCESS   The third principle of power and control theory asserts that violence can be stopped when the generational cycle of violence is understood and paired with nonviolent alternative behaviors. People who are seeking to end their violent behavior eventually begin to comprehend that learning to be nonviolent is a process. An individual does not awake one morning and vow to be nonviolent. There are occasional setbacks that require additional learning.

One assumption is that all participants in a batterer intervention program understand that their violence relates to power and control, especially after education about this dynamic. Counselors leading batterer intervention program groups need to be flexible in ensuring that adhering to one theory may distance some participants. If they empower all participants about the use of positive power and control, they may facilitate the identification and naming of abusive behavior and assist batterers to grasp what they have done to harm the physical and emotional well-being of their partner(s) and children. Counselors might ask batterer intervention program participants, "What personal power or personal control do you possess that you can use to change your role in partner violence?" With new self-awareness, batterers can gradually change their thoughts, attitudes, and behaviors and begin to stop blaming counselors, their partner(s), or criminal justice personnel for their current circumstance and consequences (Muldoon & Gary, 2011).

Moral Development Theory

Some batterer intervention programs apply Kohlberg's (1976) classic theory of moral reasoning to individuals who batter. According to Kohlberg, moral development occurs over time and in stages, moving from simple to higher-order moral reasoning. Kohlberg's (1984) moral development model consists of three levels: preconventional, conventional, and postconventional.

PRECONVENTIONAL LEVEL   The majority of children under 9 years of age, some adolescents, and most juvenile and adult criminal offenders operate at the preconventional level that relates to moral decision-making based on being afraid of authority, avoiding punishment, and satisfying personal needs. An IPV offender at the preconventional level of development may attend IPV treatment to avoid going to jail.

CONVENTIONAL LEVEL   At the conventional level (most adolescents and adults), we begin to internalize the moral standards of valued adult role models. Authority is internalized but not questioned and reasoning is based on the norms of the group to which the person belongs (McLeod, 2013). A batterer at the conventional level of moral development may make statements such as "I don't argue with my wife because she'll get upset" (abiding by the conduct of the social order) or "I admit I hit her because she was cheating; I have to accept the penalties just like anyone else" (taking responsibility for a wrongful act).

POSTCONVENTIONAL LEVEL At the postconventional level, individual judgment is about self-principles, and moral reasoning is about individual rights and justice. According to Kohlberg this level of moral reasoning is as far as most people get. Only 10 to 15% are capable of the kind of abstract thinking necessary for stage five or six (postconventional morality). That is to say, most people take their moral views from those around them, and only a minority think through ethical principles for themselves (Kohlberg, 1984). A statement such as "I'm speaking to groups of adolescents about how to treat a partner with respect; I encourage other men to seek help when they're mistreating their partners" would be characteristic of an IPV offender who has reached the postconventional level of moral reasoning.

Empirical evidence suggests that moral development is universal among people of diverse cultural backgrounds (Kohlberg, 1984), and moral education programs are effective in raising levels of moral reasoning (Buttell, 2001), which may result in reduced criminal activity. Batterer intervention programs using a moral education approach do not focus solely on Kohlberg's theory but may educate participants about the levels of moral development, present them with moral dilemmas, and structure discussions that allow them to challenge one another. In a batterer's group, the discussion develops around preconventional reasoning (e.g., "I'm here because my probation officer told me I had to come here" or "I don't want to go to jail"). First, ideas and concepts from this level of moral reasoning are ineffective after deliberation and discarded. Then the discussion should proceed to include conventional-level ideas and concepts (e.g., "What are some ways that you can create a healthier relationship with your partner?" or "How will you ensure your children will not witness more violence, so they don't have to see you get arrested again?").

Attachment Theory

According to attachment theory, excessive interpersonal dependency among abusive men is a consequence of insecure attachment in childhood (Thyer, Dulmus, & Sowers, 2012). In brief, attachment theory historically proposes that the overall quality of the infant–caretaker relationship during infancy and early childhood is both the primary determinant of dependent traits in adulthood (Ainsworth, 1969) and a model for later interpersonal relationships (Bowlby, 1980). The paradox, according to Holtzworth-Monroe, Bates, Smultzer, and Sandin (2007), is that happily married men as well as violent men are dependent on their wives, but dependency is a problem only for the violent men. Relative to the development of excessive interpersonal dependency among batterers, Dutton (Dutton & Sonkin, 2013) argued that battered mothers cannot adequately attend to the demands of the attachment process while simultaneously attempting to negotiate a hostile and dangerous home environment. Consequently, children in this situation become insecurely attached and in adulthood exhibit excessive dependency on their partners. In addition, people with battering issues have difficulty initiating and maintaining an emotionally supportive relationship. As a result, they simultaneously desire closeness with their partners but, given their inability to achieve emotional closeness, engage in violent and controlling behaviors to ensure physical closeness instead.

Similar to incorporating moral development into batterer intervention programs, a batterer program using attachment theory does not focus entirely on attachment issues. A typical batterer intervention program session on attachment initially might include a discussion of healthy and unhealthy relationships, particularly referencing the parental relationships that members observed in their childhood. A description of the types of attachment might follow as members identify the types of attachment they observed as children. The session then might focus on members' current relationships, which may be the relationships within which they had their IPV incident, and they respond to and identify the type of attachment. Members can be asked to discuss the connection between the type of attachment they observed as children and the type they experienced in the relationship within which the IPV event took place. A discussion of the consequences of unhealthy attachment types might follow. The session may then conclude by asking members to identify what they will contract to do to begin progressing toward secure attachments with their partners.

Feminist-Informed Cognitive-Behavioral Theory

Most treatment programs for batterers employ a feminist-informed cognitive-behavioral treatment approach. Feminist theory asserts the primary cause of domestic violence is patriarchal ideology and the implicit or explicit societal sanctioning of men's use of power and control over women (Murphy & Ting, 2010). This ideological stance results in a pattern of behavior including intimidation, male privilege, isolation, and emotional and economic abuse. Many types of cognitive and behavioral therapies—for example, Ellis's (1962) rational emotive behavior therapy and Glasser's (1965) reality therapy—operate under the tenets of feminist theory used in batterer intervention. In batterer intervention program groups, participants would receive psycho-education in conflict resolution, nonthreatening behavior, respect, trust and support, honesty and accountability, responsible parenting, shared responsibilities, and economic partnerships (Domestic Abuse Intervention Programs, 2013).

Motivational Interviewing and Stages of Change

Recent research has shown promising results in the effectiveness of motivational interviewing and stages of change in batterer intervention programs (Murphy & Ting, 2010). Miller and Rollnick (2013) define *motivational interviewing* as a directive, client-centered counseling style for eliciting behavioral change by helping clients explore and resolve ambivalence. The underlying tenet is that readiness to change is a client trait and not imposed by external sources. Motivational interviewing focuses on building a therapeutic alliance that allows the client to explore ambivalence and resistance in a nonthreatening and noncoercive way. The stages of change, or transtheoretical model (TTM), posits that people move through a series of stages when changing a behavior. They will continue until they reach the proper stage in the decision cycle or change will not occur (Norcross, Krebs, & Prochaska, 2011). In this intervention, counselors facilitate movement through the stages of change by using motivational interviewing techniques. Motivational interviewing is often short term, and its techniques could be used in crisis programs with batterers.

CHALLENGES IN BATTERER INTERVENTION

Counselors who work with IPV perpetrators encounter numerous challenges, including the underreporting of IPV incidents, the need to distinguish batterer intervention programs from anger management programs, limited financial resources, and low completion rates. Other issues include IPV and substance use, the duty to protect and the duty to warn, personal safety, and the counselor's comfort working with batterers. Working with victims of IPV is only part of decreasing IPV. The counseling profession needs counselors who are willing to work with batterers in order to assist in ending generations of abuse.

Challenges to Referrals to Batterer Intervention Programs

One of the biggest challenges regarding batterer intervention is that most program participants are court mandated. In order for a judge or probation officer to refer an IPV offender to treatment, someone must first report an IPV incident. Estimates suggest that only 58% of all IPV incidents include a report to the police (U.S. Department of Justice, 2014). The reasons so many cases go unreported are complex and varied: fear of the unknown and of the batterer, existence of children, promises of reform, guilt, lack of self-esteem, love, gender role beliefs, economic dependence, religious beliefs, stigma of a broken home, or denial of a problem. Although many of these reasons are valid, if IPV incidents go unreported, batterer intervention is nearly impossible. Read Voices from the Field 8.2.

Financial Resources

The financial aspect of batterer intervention is also a challenge. A significant number of batterer programs charge fees for services in order to sustain the program's existence. Most federal and state monies for IPV go to battered women's programs—and rightly so. However, if we do not intervene with batterers and re-educate them, IPV will likely never end. Therefore, batterer program staff members have to solicit referrals from judges and probation officers. Unfortunately, potential referral sources often refuse to make appropriate referrals to batterer intervention programs due to their cost.

VOICES FROM THE FIELD 8.2
Working in Batterer Intervention

John Muldoon

I was the director of a batterer intervention program for almost 7 years. While my body sometimes cringed at statements men would make, I also saw the trauma that some male offenders experienced because of growing up with inappropriate or absent male role models and the interconnection of substance use and IPV. My experiences raised my awareness about the lack of equality inherent in batterer intervention. Many of the batterers that chose to attend our program in order to avoid incarceration were either unemployed or working in blue-collar jobs. IPV offenders with higher income levels were often able to hire an attorney to dispute the criminal charges at the time of the incident. I also saw the lack of consistency from one jurisdiction to another and even from one judge or probation officer to another in terms of willingness to understand the general mission of batterer programs and to collaborate with our program. To this end, I know there are pockets of places that are committed to take action to end IPV. Overall, there is work that still needs to happen to educate people about IPV. It continues to be a social crisis that is greatly unknown and misunderstood, except to those who experience it.

Completion Rates

Treatment refusal, overt or passive resistance, and premature termination (i.e., dropout), are common issues confronted by counselors in the typical batterer intervention program (Kistenmacher & Weiss, 2008). Numerous authors have reported treatment noncompliance and client attrition rates ranging between 40 and 70% (Eckhardt, Holtzworth-Munroe, Norlander, Sibley, & Cahill, 2008). Snyder and Anderson (2009) reported that positive treatment outcomes and reduced incidents of violence relate to the frequency and regularity of session attendance. Moreover, Kistenmacher and Weiss (2008) concluded that those batterers who overcome their resistance and complete treatment programs in earnest report the reduction or cessation of violence and the reduction of victim-blaming when compared with resistant batterers or those just beginning treatment.

Coulter and VandeWeerd (2009) concluded that recidivism rates for batterers were substantially lower for those who completed intervention programs when compared with those who stopped attendance prematurely. In addition, re-arrest rates were substantially lower for batterers who completed treatment than are generally found in the literature on batterer recidivism. These findings offer optimism for counselors willing to address the batterer's resistance as a major component of treatment planning.

Assessing Perpetrators of Intimate Partner Violence

Assessment of batterers is important when considering the holistic impact upon victims, victim safety, and changing abusive behaviors. A plethora of surveys exist to assess the severity of batterer behavior. The majority of assessment tools ask questions of victims rather than perpetrators, although both parties can be asked the same set of questions. The more comprehensive assessment tools ask questions that seek to know more about the abusive relationship and invite discussion of how victimization patterns have changed over time and what twists there may have been in the relationship. Typically, an assessment of IPV severity includes a review of the following risk factors: (1) access to/ownership of guns; (2) use of weapon in prior abusive incidents; (3) threats with weapons; (4) serious injury in prior abusive incidents; (5) threats of suicide; (6) drug or alcohol abuse; (7) forced sex of female partner, obsessiveness/extreme jealousy/extreme dominance; and (8) previous victimization or attempts of any violence (National Resource Center on Domestic Violence, 2011). Two of the more common lethality assessment tools are the Danger Assessment (Campbell, 2001) and the Lethality Risk Assessment (National Center for Victims of Crime, 2005). Other questions a counselor must ask include whether the perpetrator has threatened or harmed family pets, has a history of hostage taking, and has threatened to harm or kill children or other family members (National Resource Center on Domestic Violence, 2011).

Based on a review of data on domestic homicide, researchers found that the following factors existed before the killing of an intimate partner: (1) a prior history of domestic violence on the part of the perpetrator; (2) an estrangement, separation, or an attempt at separation by the victim; (3) prior involvement with police by the perpetrator, accompanied by a failure to be deterred by police intervention or other criminal justice initiatives; (4) threats by the perpetrator to kill the victim, with details communicated to the victim, family members, friends, colleagues at work, or others; and (5) a restraining order or an order of protection by the victim against the perpetrator (National Resource Center on Domestic Violence, 2011).

Another significant but often overlooked factor that should be considered when assessing the severity of IPV is stalking. The Stalking Resource Center (2012) of the National Center for Victims of Crime defines *stalking* as a course of conduct directed at a specific person that would cause a reasonable person to feel fear. The center reports that 7.5 million people each year in the United States are victims of stalking; 15% of women and 6% of men have experienced stalking at some point during their lifetime; and 61% of female victims and 44% of male victims of stalking report being stalked by a current or former intimate partner.

When considering co-occurring mental health and substance abuse issues, Thomas, Bennett, and Stoops (2012) found that batterers who abused substances were more violent and were more likely to perpetrate violence that is severe in nature, reported higher levels of anger and trauma, and had a greater proclivity toward a borderline personality orientation. It would then be highly recommended to screen batterers for alcohol and other drug (AOD) problems and substance abusers for IPV. Dual screening serves multiple purposes, including being more vigilant with regard to victim safety, and focusing on anger and trauma issues when working with AOD batterers.

Checklists are another method used to assess perpetrators in a similar manner as those listed above. Several instruments have good psychometric properties, including the Revised Conflict Tactics Scale (CTS2; Straus, Hamby, Boney-McCoy, & Sugarman, 1996); the 24-Item Controlling Behaviors Scale (CBS; Graham-Kevan & Archer, 2003; Ross, 2011); and the 30-Item Abusive Behavior Inventory (Shepard & Campbell, 1992).

Personal Safety

The presumption is that batterers will exert violence only toward their intimate partner. However, counselors should be aware of how they interact with perpetrators and be cognizant of personal safety. Accusations and criticism should be kept at a minimum while balancing skills of challenging and confrontation to assist in empathy building, awareness of violence, and behavioral change. Perpetrators should be held accountable, but they should also be allowed to work in an environment where they can safely explore their behaviors and not feel continuously criticized. Counselors should also be able to identify when clients' emotions become heightened to assist in calming the situation or, if that is not possible, to seek additional means of intervention.

When a situation escalates, Fauteux (2010) advises to not challenge the perpetrator and instead inform him or her of the possible consequences, stay calm, and call for coworkers or a supervisor. Other important suggestions are to know one's environment, what could be used as a weapon, what could be used for protection, and where the nearest exits are located. If an angry perpetrator has not acted on any threats, suggest to him or her that it is not too late to withdraw from the current situation.

Finally, in extreme cases, if violence does occur, Fauteux (2010) notes that violence may not be preempted with a warning and that the individual may or may not express emotion. Assess the best way to maintain personal safety, get out of the violent path, and then follow up for help, which may involve contacting law enforcement. See Chapter 2 for an expanded discussion of safety precautions and Chapter 14 for an expanded discussion of counselor self-care strategies during a crisis. Complete Think About It 8.2 and, as a review, see Case Studies 8.3 to 8.5. For additional resources on IPV, see Table 8.2.

THINK ABOUT IT 8.2

Think about the current state of counselor training in IPV. What level of training and/or experience is needed to counsel IPV victims and perpetrators? Should training in IPV be required in counseling programs? Should experience in IPV intervention be required for licensure? Should all counselors have basic training from IPV programs?

CASE STUDY 8.3

An Ethical Dilemma

You are a counselor leading groups in a batterer intervention program for men. One afternoon a woman whose partner is in the program calls to ask what the program is teaching about violence. During the course of your conversation, the woman discloses that her partner, the program's client, threatened her the night before. Consult the *ACA Code of Ethics* (American Counseling Association, 2014) to inform your discussion of the dilemma.

Discussion Questions

1. What additional questions do you ask?
2. What referrals do you offer?
3. What, if anything, do you do with this information, knowing that confronting your client might cause additional violence to the partner?

CASE STUDY 8.4

Responses to Domestic Violence Crisis Calls

It is about 2:45 on a weekday afternoon. You receive a phone call from a woman who explains that her husband is abusive to her. She also notes that he is not at home, which is why she is making the call now. She further states that she is not sure what he would do if he knew she was talking to someone about the violence. After about 10 minutes on the phone, she becomes erratic and excited, stating that her husband has come home and she cannot talk any longer. She hangs up the phone.

Discussion Questions

1. What do you do?
2. What can you do?

CASE STUDY 8.5

Intervening with an Intimate Partner Violence Solution

It is between 5:45 and 6:00 p.m. on a Tuesday. You are the counselor for this evening's batterer intervention program group. The group starts at 6:00 p.m. and participants have begun checking in and paying their fees. One of the participants has already taken a seat in the group. You are aware that he received a phone call and left the building. A few moments later, you hear yelling outside and go out to see what is happening. Upon walking outside, you notice the member standing in the doorway very calmly. A woman, whom the participant states is his estranged partner, is yelling, screaming, and pointing an accusatory finger at him.

Discussion Questions

1. What do you do with/for the batterer intervention program participant?
2. What do you do with/for the woman?
3. What conclusions can you hypothesize from what you observed?
4. What questions will you/must you ask the batterer intervention program participant?
5. What questions will you/must you ask the woman?

TABLE 8.2 Resources on Intimate Partner Violence

General Intimate Partner Violence Resources

Joyful Heart Foundation: www.joyfulheartfoundation.org

National Coalition Against Domestic Violence (NCADV): www.ncadv.org

National Domestic Violence Hotline: www.thehotline.org

Office on Women's Health, U.S. Department of Health and Human Services: womenshealth.gov/violence-against-women/types-of-violence/domestic-intimate-partner-violence.html

Teen and Young Adult Dating Violence Resources

Break the Cycle: www.breakthecycle.org

Futures Without Violence: www.futureswithoutviolence.org

Know Your IX: knowyourix.org/

Love Is Respect: www.loveisrespect.org

Batterer Intervention Resources

Batterer Intervention Curricula: www.theduluthmodel.org

Batterer Intervention Program Standards: www.stopvaw.org/united_states_standards_for_batterers_intervention_programs

Batterer Intervention Services in Michigan (they sponsor webinars): www.biscmi.org

National Resource Center on Domestic Violence, Harrisburg, PA: www.nrcdv.org

National Online Resource Center on Violence Against Women: www.vawnet.org

Research by Edward Gondolf (www.iup.edu/page.aspx?id=25637), Donald Dutton (drdondutton.com/books/), and Amy Holtzworth-Munroe (psych.indiana.edu/faculty/holtzwor.php)

Summary

IPV is a crisis that is all too common. As a result, counselors must be prepared to respond to the needs of IPV victims. Understanding the cycle of violence is a critical first step for crisis counselors. The cycle of violence consists of the tension-building phase, the acute battering incident, and the honeymoon phase, which is characterized by contrite, loving behavior. It is also important for counselors to examine their beliefs about why IPV victims stay in relationships with abusive partners. In this chapter, various explanations for staying with an abusive partner were offered, including learned helplessness theory and the ecological theory of IPV.

Common crisis issues for IPV victims include attending to physical injury, establishing immediate safety, and deciding whether to report the IPV to the police. When addressing IPV crises, counselors should strive to empower victims to problem solve effectively and respect victims' decisions to stay in or leave an abusive relationship. When addressing IPV in racial, ethnic minority, and LGBT communities, counselors must be aware of the compounded effects of IPV on these populations due to oppression stemming from factors such as racism, classism, transphobia, and homophobia. In addition, issues specific to female-to-male violence, dating violence, and violence against a disabled partner must also be considered.

This chapter discussed barriers to IPV screening and endorsed universal screening of IPV in every crisis situation, regardless of whether the presenting issue is IPV. IPV screening includes gathering concrete and specific details about the client's IPV history and conducting a lethality assessment in order to determine the degree of urgency that is required in responding to the IPV crisis. When IPV is disclosed, the counselor should validate the victim's experience, document that IPV is occurring, and provide resources and continued support to the victim. A specific component of IPV response is safety planning or harm reduction planning, which is based on the victim's decision to stay in or leave the abusive relationship. When responding to IPV, the counselor should consider the emotional consequences of abuse and be careful not to pathologize a normal response to the trauma of IPV. Counselors who work with IPV victims must be mindful of self care in order to avoid vicarious traumatization and burnout.

The chapter concluded with a discussion of the various aspects of batterer intervention. The goals of batterer intervention programs include ensuring the safety of IPV victims, stopping future violence, and increasing the batterers' accountability for their behavior. Batterer intervention programs are based on power and control theory, moral development theory, attachment theory, and feminist-informed cognitive-behavioral theories. Common challenges encountered in batterer intervention include the underreporting of IPV, the confusion surrounding the differences in anger management problems and battering behavior, and limited financial resources.

9

Sexual Violence

Robin Lee, Jennifer Jordan, and Elizabeth Schuler

PREVIEW

Sexual violence is a broad term used to describe an unwanted sexual act that is perpetrated on an individual via force or manipulation without the individual's consent. Forms of sexual violence include sexual assault and rape, unwanted sexual contact and/or touching, sexual harassment, and sexual exploitation. The most common acts of sexual violence are sexual assault and rape. Sexual assault is an underreported crime, with victims facing a number of potential physical, psychological, cognitive, behavioral, and emotional consequences. Counselors who work with survivors of sexual violence need to be aware of the multitude of challenges these individuals face, best practices for treatment, and support services available in the local community. In this chapter, sexual violence is defined, signs and symptoms are described, crisis intervention is addressed, and long-term counseling treatment interventions are discussed. The final section of this chapter addresses sexual offenders, their patterns of behavior, and common treatment options.

SEXUAL VIOLENCE, SEXUAL ASSAULT, AND RAPE

Sexual violence is a crime defined by a wide variety of acts, which include but are not limited to sexual threats, unwanted sexual contact, and rape (Breiding et al., 2014). Sexual violence continues to be an underreported crime. Many of the statistics available differ depending on the definitions used, as well as reporting requirements for various law enforcement groups. Sexual assault is defined under the umbrella of sexual violence.

Historically, the women's movement was responsible for first drawing attention to sexual violence in the late 1960s and early 1970s (Largen, 1985). Women began to gather in communities to discuss problems they were facing, including experiences of sexual assault. In the 1970s, the National Organization for Women (NOW) drew attention to the issue by developing rape task forces, which were designed to investigate and document the problems rape victims experienced in their communities. These task forces began advocating for change in public policies and social institutions, including court systems, public education, and law enforcement agencies.

In the 1970s, the National Organization for Victim Assistance (NOVA) was formed, which led to the development of the National Coalition Against Sexual Assault (NCASA). In 1975, Brownmiller published the classic *Against Our Will*, which brought attention to the issue of rape and sexual assault. Later, in the 1980s, attention was given to acquaintance rape after an article on campus sexual assault was published in *Ms.* magazine (Warshaw, 1988). This article, based on research conducted by Koss (1993), challenged the myth that stranger rape was the most common form of sexual assault. In fact, the Rape, Abuse, and Incest National Network (RAINN, 2015) reports that two thirds of perpetrators are known to the victim. In 1994, the Violence Against Women Act (VAWA) was passed, which was the first federal legislation that focused on violent crimes (including sexual assault) specifically committed against women and children (Roe, 2004). VAWA was reauthorized in 1999, 2005, and 2013. In the most recent reauthorization, VAWA strengthened several aspects of the legislation, such as holding rapists more accountable, providing stricter penalties for repeat sex offenders, creating a federal "rape shield law," providing easier access to services such as rape exams and protection orders, recognizing a broader range of protective orders, assisting communities in training law enforcement, and providing more protective services for women in Indian country.

OVERVIEW OF SEXUAL VIOLENCE

In 1994, VAWA established the Rape Prevention and Education (RPE) program, which is overseen by the Centers for Disease Control and Prevention (CDC, 2015c). In 2001, administration of the RPE moved to the National Center for Injury Prevention and Control (Injury Center). The organization was designed to help with prevention efforts by providing assistance by means of funding, training, and technical support to state agencies and sexual assault coalitions in the United States. This partnership consisted of Injury Center staff, victim advocate groups, prevention programs, survivors of sexual violence, state health department representatives, and others working to eliminate sexual violence. In 2002, the CDC published the first edition of the *Sexual Violence Surveillance* report. The initial report was designed to provide definitions and guidelines for the purposes of collecting data. The most recent report focuses on updating definitions of sexual violence. According to the report, *sexual violence* is "a sexual act that is committed or attempted by another person without freely given consent of the victim or against someone who is unable to consent or refuse" (CDC, 2014b, p. 11) which includes

- Completed or attempted forced penetration of a victim
- Completed or attempted alcohol/drug-facilitated penetration of a victim
- Completed or attempted forced acts in which a victim is made to penetrate a perpetrator or someone else
- Completed or attempted alcohol/drug-facilitated acts in which a victim is made to penetrate a perpetrator or someone else
- Non-physically forced penetration
- Unwanted sexual contact
- Non-contact unwanted sexual experiences (CDC, 2014b, p. 11)

Penetration

A distinction in several of the categories is based on penetration. *Forced penetration* is defined as physical insertion of body parts and/or objects. Examples of force include restraining movement of a person by use of body weight, weapon, or threats.

Alcohol/drug-facilitated penetration is the term used to describe when a person is penetrated by a body part or other object due to the inability to give consent based on intoxication via use of alcohol or drugs. *Nonphysically forced penetration* occurs when the person's ability to give consent is altered due to verbal pressure, intimidation, or abuse of authority. Examples include acquiescing due to pressure, a lie, untrue promises, and rumors.

Noncontact Unwanted Sexual Experiences

Physical contact is not always a part of sexual violence. In fact, some unwanted sexual experiences may occur without the victim's knowledge in various settings such as school or work or through technology. Examples of noncontact unwanted sexual experiences include (1) being forced into sexual situations (e.g., viewing pornography); (2) sexual harassment through verbal comments or behaviors either in person or through technology (e.g., spreading rumors, sending explicit photographs); (3) threats of sexual violence to obtain money or sex; and (4) filming, taking, or disseminating sexual explicit material without someone's knowledge.

Consent

Another key factor of understanding sexual violence is consent. Consent must be freely given in any sexual experience or contact. Consent is defined as words or actions freely given by a person who is competent, both legally (e.g., not a minor, no physical or intellectual disability) and functionally (e.g., not intoxicated, unconscious, sleeping). If a person is not competent based on the previous definitions, he or she is unable to give consent. Another factor is the person's inability to refuse, meaning that a person is unable to disagree with engaging in a sexual experience due to pressure such as use of a weapon, physical violence, intimidation, or misuse of authority.

A recent movement has addressed the idea of consent. This new public awareness campaign—"It's On Us"—is designed to encourage more responsibility on the part of everyone involved instead of focusing only on the crime or perpetrator. In addition, California passed legislation in 2014 to require that any higher education institutions receiving state funds be required to include affirmative consent policies on sexual assault, domestic violence, dating violence, and stalking. In 2015, New York Governor Andrew Cuomo signed similar legislation.

SEXUAL ASSAULT AND RAPE

While the definitions and distinctions regarding sexual violence vary, one form of sexual violence emerges as the most prevalent. According to RAINN (2015), a sexual assault occurs every 107 seconds in the United States. The CDC conducted a national study that provided data regarding rape and sexual assault. According to this report, 1 in 5 women (23 million) and 1 in 71 men (1.9 million) will be raped in the United States (Breiding et al., 2014). The results also found that 44% of women and 23% of men had experienced some type of sexual violence at some point in their lives. Over the years, the rates of sexual violence have either dropped or remained steady. However, it is important to recognize that 68% of sexual assaults will go unreported (RAINN, 2015). Victims of sexual violence may choose not to report due to several factors including fear

ACTIVITY 9.1

Visit the Rape, Abuse and Incest National Network (RAINN) website at www.rainn.org. Explore the website to learn more about how the organization benefits victims of sexual assault.

of retaliation, a lack of confidence that law enforcement will be helpful, and a belief that the crime is a personal matter and should be handled privately.

According to the 2009 National Crime Victimization Survey (U.S. Department of Justice, 2012), 90% of rape victims were female. In addition, women with a history of rape before the age of 18 years were two times as likely to be raped when they were adults. The CDC National Intimate Partner and Sexual Violence Survey results estimate that 19.3% of women have been raped and 49.3% have experienced some type of sexual violence other than rape in their lifetimes. Based on race and ethnicity, 32.3% of multi-racial women, 55% American Indian or Alaska Native; 47% White non-Hispanic; 38% Black non-Hispanic; 35% Hispanic; and 32% Asian or Pacific Islander have been raped during their lifetimes (Breiding et al., 2014). For men, 1.7% of have been raped and 23.4% have experienced some type of sexual violence other than rape in their lifetimes. Based on race and ethnicity, 39.5 of multiracial men, 26% Hispanic; 24% American Indian or Alaska Native; 24% Black non-Hispanic; 22% White non-Hispanic; and 15% Asian or Pacific Islander have experienced some form of sexual violence in their life-times. Complete Activity 9.1 to learn more about RAINN.

Sexual Assault

According to the Bureau of Justice Statistics (2016b), *sexual assault* includes

> a wide range of victimizations, separate from rape or attempted rape. These crimes include attacks or attempted attacks generally involving unwanted sexual contact between victim and offender. Sexual assaults may or may not involve force and include such things as grabbing or fondling. Sexual assault also includes verbal threats.

State laws vary on how degrees of sexual assault are categorized, so it is important for crisis counselors to know the law in their state. While sexual assault is often perceived as being about sex, RAINN describes it as a power and control crime. There are several forms of sexual assault, including (1) rape (penetration of the body); (2) attempted rape; (3) forced performance of sexual acts (e.g., oral sex, penetration of the perpetrator's body); and (4) fondling or unwanted sexual touching (RAINN, 2015).

Rape

The Bureau of Justice Statistics (2016b) defines *rape* as

> forced sexual intercourse including both psychological coercion as well as physical force. Forced sexual intercourse means penetration by the offender(s). This includes attempted rapes, male as well as female victims, and both heterosexual and homosexual rape. Attempted rape includes verbal threats of rape.

This definition allows for same-gender victims as well as the use of drugs and alcohol to perpetrate the act.

A few points are important to remember about rape. First, rape is but one form of sexual assault. Second, physical force is not always used during rape; perpetrators may use other types of force, such as emotional pressure, psychological pressure, or manipulation (RAINN, 2015). Examples of force include threatening harm to family or others close to the victim. Third, there are several types of rape, including acquaintance rape, drug-facilitated sexual assault, intimate partner sexual violence, and statutory rape.

ACQUAINTANCE RAPE   One of the most prevalent acts within the area of sexual assault and rape is acquaintance rape. This term has evolved over the past several decades from what was once described as "date rape." This semantic change helps distinguish sexual assault and/or rape that occurs between people who are in an intimate or dating relationship from sexual assault and/or rape that occurs between people who are not (see Chapter 8, on intimate partner violence).

The term *acquaintance* indicates that while the victim may know the assailant, the victim is not necessarily in an intimate relationship with the perpetrator. According to RAINN (2015), "approximately 4/5 of rapes are committed by someone known to the victim" (para. 1). Females in early adulthood are four times more likely to be sexually assaulted than females in other age groups (RAINN, 2015). Unfortunately, few of these rapes are reported.

Although acquaintance rape occurs within the general population, it is most prevalent on college campuses. According to a report published by the Bureau of Justice Statistics on rape and sexual assault among college-age females, only 20% (students enrolled in postsecondary institutions) and 32% (nonstudents), respectively, of sexual assaults that occurred among college-aged females (ages 18 to 24 years) were reported to law enforcement (Sinozich & Langton, 2014). The Bureau of Justice Statistics report also found that from 1995 to 2013, more than half of sexual assaults and/or rapes of college-age females occurred during the pursuit of leisure activities away from home. Weapons were present in 1 out of 10 incidents of rape and sexual assault. Of those who did not report rape and sexual assault incidents to police, 26% of student and 23% of nonstudent victims felt the assault was a personal matter, and 20% of both student and nonstudent victims were concerned that the perpetrator would retaliate if they did report. Four main factors emerged that increased the risk of college-aged women being a victim of a sexual assault and/or rape: (1) frequent intoxication to the point of incapacitation; (2) single status; (3) previous sexual victimizations; and (4) residing on campus. For detailed guidelines on conducting a campus-wide prevention campaign, see Lee, Caruso, Goins, and Southerland (2003).

Affirmative Consent   An important issue related to acquaintance rape is consent. While consent is not obtained in sexual assaults involving perpetrators not known to the victims, the idea of consent can be unique with acquaintance rape. A new way of thinking about consent is being addressed on college campuses. The term "yes means yes" is being used to describe *affirmative consent*. The message for young people is that consent is mutually agreed upon, is clearly understood, is freely given and not coerced or forced, and is never assumed or implied. While affirmative consent may seem to be a new concept, it is not. In the 1990s, a small college in Ohio, Antioch College, developed a new policy called the *sexual offense prevention policy* (SOPP), which specifically addresses consent.

The policy defines consent, requires that all sexual interactions be consensual, and requires all students and full-time employees sign a statement acknowledging that they understand and agree to the policy. At the time, this policy was considered absurd, mocked, and even parodied by *Saturday Night Live*. But now, 1,400 postsecondary institutions have some type of affirmative consent policy. Voices from the Field 9.1, Think About It 9.1, and Case Study 9.1 address the important societal issue of sexual violence on university campuses.

VOICES FROM THE FIELD 9.1
Advocacy and Working Toward Prevention of Sexual Violence on College Campuses

Michele E. Caruso

The more things change, the more they stay the same. Or so the saying goes. For all of the awareness and prevention efforts, research on effective treatment methodologies, and laws enacted, retracted, and enacted again, in many ways substantial challenges remain in working with sexual violence. This is true when working with the victim directly and with those indirectly affected by it, as well as the countless individuals hiding behind the "it only happens to *those* people" blindfolds or lost in the "ignorance is bliss" places.

I have been involved with this kind of work in some capacity with college students for over 25 years. The fears, anxieties, somatic headaches, depression, and pain are the same. The faces are different. I wouldn't expect, though, the clinical experiences or victim responses to change. We are all human beings, after all, who were not born to be violated in such a manner. What I would have expected to see shift by now is the cultural setup for sexual violence, the cultural response to sexual violence, and the cultural treatment of the victims of sexual violence.

We all know sexual violence does not happen in a vacuum. Nobody wakes up one day and thinks, "Hmmm. I'm bored. I think I'll rape someone today." We allow, condone, and even celebrate behaviors, attitudes, activities, and certainly entertainment that perpetuate sexist, racist, and heterosexist roles that devalue, objectify, silence, and oppress. I would even posit that there has been an escalation in this in the last 20 years. College students are bombarded and saturated with it. We could say there aren't enough conversations to the contrary, but there are. They just aren't getting through the noise. Is it any wonder?

For every college student who "gets it" and is willing to use his or her voice, there are 100 who haven't heard of it, another 100 who don't want to hear of it, and another 100 who have heard of it but are too afraid, confused, or "fill in the blank" to use their voice. These are individuals with great potential to facilitate the needed cultural shift and bring the generations behind them along for the ride. For all of the advocacy, services, and research that take place on college campuses, college students are still vulnerable to the cultural perpetuation of sexual violence. Not only are traditional age college students still the most at risk for being victims of sexual violence, but they are also very vulnerable to the cultural perpetuation of all the factors that contribute to sexual violence.

So, working with college students through prevention efforts or victim services has changed in some ways but has remained the same in many other ways. We might have more dedicated staff on campus to address violence, but the effort is still significantly underfunded. We might have more sexual assault awareness events, but we still have entertainment on the TV in the student unions that contributes to victims being doubted. We might use social networking to spread the word more efficiently than ever about how to assist friends who are victimized, but social networking is also used to spread hateful, disparaging, and damaging sentiments about victims, potential victims, and student advocates just as efficiently. We might have more students looking for a place to find and use their voice to address sexual violence, but we still have boxes we keep people in where voices are not allowed.

I do absolutely remain hopeful and certainly inspired by those on the front lines and behind the scenes in all of the fields that address sexual violence, from counselors and advocates to lawmakers and law enforcement, and everyone in between. However, the challenges in breaking through the cultural noise to access and help victims and to shift the paradigm of the upcoming generations in a way that would actually reduce sexual violence remain.

THINK ABOUT IT 9.1

Think about university responses to campus rapes. On average, 19% of women report being sexually assaulted or threatened with sexual assault on college campuses (Bedera & Nordmeyer, 2015). In response, universities and colleges have started campaigns to prevent sexual assault and rape. Two types of campaigns have emerged, *empowering women* and *empowering men*. Empowering women campaigns focus on targeting risky behavior, self-defense, and empowerment. Empowering men campaigns focus on targeting men to stop abuse and violent behavior. Despite the intent of the campaigns, the most common information provided to women is that women are vulnerable, that there are no safe places, and that women should not trust anyone. In addition, 62% of universities did not provide tips or resources about sexual abuse on campus. What is needed to better address this serious societal problem?

CASE STUDY 9.1

What Is Sexual Assault? Cindy's Story

You have been working as a counselor at a university counseling center. Cindy—an 18-year-old college student—has come to see you because she is failing most of her classes. She recently took her midterm exams and did not pass any of them. In addition, she did not even take two of the exams. She graduated at the top of her high school class, even receiving an academic scholarship covering the majority of her tuition. She reports that she is in jeopardy of losing her scholarship. She is also concerned because her grades will be sent home to her parents in the next few weeks. They have always expected her to excel in school, and she feels they will be very disappointed with her, possibly even insisting she return home to her small rural town, which she was trying to escape.

At your first meeting with Cindy, she also reports that she is having trouble going to her classes because she is sleeping through most of them. She reports wanting to sleep all the time, having a depressed mood, and avoiding her friends, who have convinced her to attend counseling. Cindy's appearance is disheveled, and she is wearing what seem to be dirty clothes.

During the first two sessions, Cindy cries frequently and rarely shares information. Finally, she reveals to you that a couple of weeks ago she went on a date with Dennis, a guy from her sociology class, whom she has been interested in dating since the beginning of the semester. Although Cindy reports that she is not a big drinker, she had a few glasses of wine at dinner. They were having a great time, talking and laughing. She accompanied Dennis back to his dorm room, where they laid on his bed and began kissing. Dennis offered her another drink, after which she became dizzy and thinks she passed out. She is uncertain if she agreed to sex with Dennis, but is convinced her willingness to go to his dorm room indicated to him that she wanted to have sex. She was shocked when she woke up in the hallway outside her dorm room, missing her underwear and feeling sore in her private area. Later that day, she received several text messages from Dennis, who wanted to see her again. When she responded that she was not interested, his next few texts became increasingly hostile. When she asked him to stop and not contact her again, he sent her a video of their sexual encounter. He told her that if she didn't have sex with him again, he would upload the video on social media sites. She is considering meeting him but is terrified he will harm her.

Discussion Questions

1. Does this case meet the legal definition of sexual assault? If yes, what type?
2. What are the issues with consent in this case?
3. In this situation, how would you proceed with Cindy?
4. What are the legal and ethical guidelines that will drive your work with Cindy?
5. With a peer, role-play implementation of the task model for crisis assessment and intervention featured in Chapter 1.

DRUG-FACILITATED SEXUAL ASSAULT   As mentioned earlier, intoxication may increase the risk for sexual assault occurrences. With this knowledge, perpetrators have been known to use drugs, often referred to as "date rape drugs," to prepare for the sexual assault. Drug-facilitated sexual assault typically occurs in one of two ways: (1) the sexual assault occurs after the victim has voluntarily used alcohol and/or drugs; or (2) the perpetrator purposefully uses a drug to incapacitate the person. The three most common drugs used to facilitate sexual assault are (1) alcohol; (2) prescription drugs (e.g., sleep aids, tranquilizers, muscle relaxers); and (3) street drugs (e.g., Rohypnol, Gamma-Hydroxybutyric acid [GHB], Ketamine) (RAINN, 2015; Womenshealth.gov, 2012).

Rohypnol, also known as "roofies," can cause a myriad of effects, including dizziness, loss of muscle control, confusion, lack of consciousness, and, in severe cases, death. Rohypnol's effects can last for more than a few hours (Womenshealth.gov, 2012). GHB is a powerful drug used to treat narcolepsy, yet it is often made on the streets. GHB can cause blackouts, dreamlike feelings, seizures, coma, and possibly death. Ketamine is a legal anesthetic mostly used on animals. Like most anesthetics, it can cause symptoms such as numbness, loss of coordination, memory problems, and depression.

INTIMATE PARTNER SEXUAL VIOLENCE   In intimate partner sexual violence, the perpetrator has an existing relationship with the victim, who may be a partner or spouse. Intimate partner sexual violence was previously referred to as *spousal rape*. This type of violence is rarely reported and most often classified as intimate partner violence or domestic violence (see Chapter 8). However, when it is reported, police officials enforce these cases the same way they would any other reported rape. This type of sexual violence has had an arduous history. In the 1700s, the first legal statement occurred by a chief justice in England, in which he declared a husband could not be guilty of marital rape (Bennice & Resick, 2003). At some point, marital rape was in the context of property, meaning that a man could not "steal" his own property. In the 1970s, advocates worked to modify marital rape exemptions. In the 1990s, marital rape was included as a crime in sexual offense codes in all 50 states.

STATUTORY RAPE   State statutory rape offenses are typically defined based on age of consent, minimum age of the victim, age differential, and the minimum age a defendant can be prosecuted. Age of consent in state statutes ranges from 16 to 18 years of age. The minimum age of the victim ranges from 12 to 18 years of age. Age differential is often dependent on the age of the victim, and ranges from 2 to 10 years (e.g., a 20-year-old perpetrator and a 15-year-old victim).

Within statutory rape laws, many states include an "age gap provision" or "Romeo and Juliet Clause" to protect individuals who are close in age and not causing harm through manipulation or coercion of another individual. The age gap provision and Romeo and Juliet Clause provide courts with the opportunity to use discretion and consider each case individually. Although they are very similar, the provision and clause have minor but important differences. For example:

> [In Georgia, under] the child molestation crime, the law now stipulates that if the victim was at least 14 years of age, the offender 18 years of age or younger and no more than 4 years older than the victim, the same crime will no longer be considered a felony. The offender can be charged with a misdemeanor and will not be subject to the same punishments as those who commit the crime outside of the age gape provision. In other words, with this provision, close-in-age teenage relationships need not have the same consequences as those of older adults seeking to sexually exploit minors. [. . .] Texas is not recognized as having an Age Gap Provision which either reduces the level of the offense or does not consider a crime to have occurred at all. However, Texas does have a Romeo and Juliet Clause. This clause does not stipulate the law. . . . Rather the law remains the same, except that the defendant is given an affirmative defense if certain qualifications are met. [. . .] It is an affirmative defense to the prosecution under Subsection (a)(2) that:
>
> • The actor cannot be more than 3 years older than the victim.
> • The victim was older than 14 years of age at the time the offense occurred.
> • The actor was not at the time registered or required to register for life as a sexual offender.
> • The conduct did not constitute incest.
> • Neither the actor nor the victim would commit bigamy by marrying the other. (Smith & Kercher, 2011, pp. 10–11)

Historically, laws have been enacted to protect minors who are unable to give consent due lack of maturity. Most of the protection was typically for females, to help them avoid becoming victims of sexual violence by older men (James, 2009). However, current statutes tend to be gender neutral.

Rape Myths

One reason sexual assault is one of the most underreported crimes may be the social stigma of being a victim of sexual assault. For many years, myths about sexual assault were commonly accepted, but with continued research and awareness-raising, many of these myths have been dispelled. Some of the more common myths about rape and sexual assault include the following:

• *Myth 1: Rape is about sex.* Rape is typically about the perpetrator's need to exert power and control over another individual, with sex as the weapon of choice.
• *Myth 2: Victims of rape deserve to be raped due to their appearance or their neglect of safety issues.* Although sexual assault and rape awareness have improved over the years, many individuals still believe that victims are to blame for their assault. Some may believe that victims incite a rapist because of provocative dress, appearance, or behavior. Others may blame the victim if they perceive that the victim did not take appropriate safety precautions to guard against an attack. As

discussed later in this chapter, sexual predators will often rape someone with little or no cause to do so—regardless of how a person dresses or behaves.

• *Myth 3: Victims of sexual assault often make false reports based on revenge.* The percentage of sexual assaults that are falsely reported remains low (Lisak, Gardinier, Nicksa, & Cote, 2010; Lonsway, Archambault, & Lisak, 2009). The Uniform Crime Reporting Program of the FBI found that just under 5,000 of the 90,518 forcible rapes reported in the United States in 2006 were determined to be unfounded—either false or baseless complaints. This constitutes 5.4% of forcible rapes reported in 2006.

• *Myth 4: Only strangers lurking in dark alleys commit sexual assaults.* The U.S. Department of Justice (2013) National Crime Victimization Study found that about 80% of rapes were committed by someone with whom the victim was familiar, and 82% of sexual assaults were committed by a nonstranger. Sexual perpetrators are no longer thought of as mentally ill sociopaths who victimize strangers. Those who sexually assault others come from diverse socioeconomic, racial, geographic, and educational backgrounds.

See Case Study 9.2, which asks you to consider the meaning of sexual assault. Then complete Activity 9.2, which looks at the services provided to sexual assault victims in your community.

CASE STUDY 9.2

What Is Sexual Assault? Sherry's Story

You are a counselor in a mental health center. You have a new client named Sherry, a 25-year-old female who made an appointment for depression and anxiety she has been experiencing. During the initial session, Sherry reports that she received an associate's degree at a local technical college in nursing assistance 6 years ago. Since receiving her degree, she has worked primarily as a nursing aide in several rehabilitation centers. She recently quit her job abruptly due to an incident at the rehabilitation center where she was employed for 2 years. Sherry reports experiencing sleeplessness and weight loss. She has difficulty getting out of bed every morning and has not looked for a new job since she left.

Sherry recently ended a 5-year relationship with her boyfriend, although the couple was scheduled to be married in 6 months. She describes several episodes where she has been forced to leave public places after being unable to catch her breath and feeling as if she is being judged by others. After several sessions, she reveals that while working at the rehab center, she was sexual assaulted by a 32-year-old male patient named James, who became a paraplegic after a car accident that left him paralyzed below the waist. Sherry began to spend extra time with James after learning that he had very little to no family support and typically had no visitors. On several occasions, James began to ask questions about Sherry's dating life, and he eventually asked her to date him. James then began asking Sherry to help him deal with his frustrating involuntary erections and ejaculations. When she laughed-off this suggestion, James began to become more suggestive and aggressive with Sherry. He would talk about his previous sexual activities prior to being injured. Eventually,

James's behavior turned to sexual advances, such as groping Sherry and suggesting that they should have sex. After enduring his advances for several weeks, Sherry finally complained to her supervisor and asked to be moved to another wing. Her request was denied due to a shortage of staff. She was encouraged to remain professional and told that James was harmless. One day while Sherry was helping James bathe, James overpowered her and sexually assaulted her with a shampoo bottle. Due to her shock, Sherry left the rehab center that day and never returned. She did not report the incident to her supervisor or the police.

Discussion Questions

1. Does Sherry's experience meet the definition of sexual assault? Why?
2. What are some of the additional problems Sherry might develop resulting from her sexual assault?
3. Keeping these circumstances in mind, how would you proceed to work with Sherry?
4. What are the legal and ethical guidelines that will drive your work with Sherry?
5. With a peer, role-play implementation of the task model for crisis assessment and intervention featured in Chapter 1.

ACTIVITY 9.2

Determine if your community has an agency that specifically deals with victims of sexual assault. Request an interview with an agency official to obtain answers to these questions: What services are provided to victims in the community? Who provides these services? How can victims access these services?

OTHER TYPES OF SEXUAL VIOLENCE

Sexual Harassment

The U.S. Equal Employment Opportunity Commission (EEOC, 2016) defines *sexual harassment* as "unwelcome sexual advances, requests for sexual favors, and other verbal or physical conduct of a sexual nature" that "explicitly or implicitly affect an individual's employment, unreasonably interfere with an individual's work performance, or create an intimidating, hostile, or offensive work environment" (para. 2). Sexual harassment is gender neutral and not always directed at one specific person but at those who are offended by the actions or behaviors. The offense can occur in work or learning environments, various work- or school-related settings (e.g., after-hour meetings, hallways), or any other public location where behaviors such as exposing sexual parts, fondling, or "catcalling" can happen. The federal law that addresses sexual harassment is Title VII of the Civil Rights Act of 1964.

Stalking

According to the Bureau of Justice Statistics (2012), *stalking* is defined as "a course of conduct directed at a specific person that would cause a reasonable person to feel fear"

(p. 1). The Bureau of Justice Statistics estimates that 3.3 million people, ages 18 or older, have been victims of stalking over a period of one year. Specific examples of stalking include (1) making unwanted phone calls; (2) sending unsolicited or unwanted letters or e-mails; (3) following or spying on the victim; (4) showing up at places without a legitimate reason; (5) waiting at places for the victim; (6) leaving unwanted items, presents, or flowers; and (6) posting information or spreading rumors about the victim on the Internet, in a public place, or by word of mouth.

Criminal laws on stalking have been enacted by all 50 states, as well as by the federal government and the District of Columbia. The Bureau of Justice Statistics (2012) reports that 70% of stalking victims knew their offender in some capacity. Technology can be a way for perpetrators to stalk their victims. Cyberstalking can include spying or tracking through a computer, tracking by GPS, posting personal information publicly, sending unwanted electronic communication, and installing video cameras in places that will violate privacy (RAINN, 2015). The effects of stalking can be broad, from causing extreme personal distress to loss of employment to post-traumatic stress disorder (PTSD). RAINN offers several ways to help victims deal with stalking, which include making it clear the communication is unwanted and needs to stop, documenting the incidents, not responding to the stalker, notifying friends and family about the stalking, reporting the stalking to law enforcement, and learning about computer safety.

Sex Trafficking: "Modern Day Slavery"

A growing concern in the area of sexual violence is sex trafficking. Sex trafficking of an individual, at least 18 years of age or older, occurs when the individual

> is coerced, forced, or deceived into prostitution—or maintained in prostitution through one of these means after initially consenting—that person is a victim of trafficking. Under such circumstances, perpetrators involved in recruiting, harboring, transporting, providing, or obtaining a person for that purpose are responsible for trafficking crimes. (U.S. Department of State, 2013, para. 3)

If the individual originally participated in prostitution on his or her own, but was then coerced, forced, or manipulated into soliciting, without consent, he or she is a victim of trafficking (U.S. Department of State, 2013). Evidence of force, fraud, or coercion does not have to be present in order for a minor (an individual under the age of 18 years) to be a victim of sex trafficking when performing any commercial sex act. A *commercial sex act* is defined as "prostitution, pornography, and sexual performance done in exchange for any item of value, such as money, drugs, shelter, food, or clothes" (Shared Hope International, 2015, para. 2).

While exact prevalence rates of sex trafficking are unknown, it is estimated that approximately 4.5 million people are victims of sex trafficking, with approximately 945,000 of them being under the age of 18 (International Labor Organization, 2012). The known victims of sex trafficking are overwhelmingly female, racial and ethnic minorities, and under the age of 18 years (Varma, Gillespie, McCracken, & Greenbaum, 2015).

The Trafficking Victims Protection Act (TVPA), passed in 2000, defines minors under the age of 18 years involved in "commercial sex acts" as victims (Reid & Jones, 2011, p. 207). A multitude of evidence suggests that children who fall into the sex trafficking industry do not possess the ability to make choices and maintain control, thus classifying them as a true victim, not a criminal. However, some governments continue to prosecute these minors on criminal offenses such as prostitution.

In a study conducted by Varma et al. (2015), victims of sex trafficking often exhibited more risk-taking behavior (e.g., using illegal drugs) and were more often victims of childhood sexual abuse. Many victims of sex trafficking also had an extensive history of violent abuse. Homelessness is another area of concern for victims of sex trafficking. Homeless youth often engage in survival sex, meaning that they will trade sexual favors for necessities such as food, shelter, or money. The behavior increases a young person's vulnerability to engaging in sex trafficking. Varma et al. (2015) also found that 39% of the sex trafficking victims interviewed were suffering from untreated mental health disorders, such as bipolar disorder, PTSD, and schizophrenia. Many victims do not disclose their victim status for many of the same reasons that survivors of sexual assault do not (e.g., fear, guilt, distrust of law enforcement). In a 2014 report by the National Center for Missing and Exploited Children, it was estimated that "1 out of 6 runaways were likely child sex trafficking victims. . . . Of those, 68% were in the care of social services or foster care when they ran" (Polaris Project, 2014, para. 5). While the negative effects of engaging in sex trafficking are still widely unknown, a few new findings are coming to light.

Varma et al. (2015) found the following harmful consequences in sex trafficking victims: 70% sustained injuries while "on-the-job," 89% exhibited symptoms of clinical depression, 55% exhibited symptoms of PTSD, 84% reported substance abuse, and 67% reported obtaining a sexually transmitted infection (STI) as a result of their exploitation.

Treatment in this area should focus on support and crisis intervention techniques, as well as services for both mental and physical health (Gibbs, Walters, Lutnick, Miller, & Kluckman, 2015). There is still a lack of research in the area of sex trafficking and the treatment that would be best suited to the victims. However, due to the development or symptoms of PTSD, depression, and anxiety, trauma-focused cognitive behavioral therapy (TF-CBT) is shown to be effective in treating these disorders (Johnson, 2012).

Sexual Violence and School Counseling

Working with an adolescent population, a professional school counselor is highly likely to encounter students who have been exposed to sexual violence. Issues of consent may exist with teen encounters that are sexual in nature. With the broad definitions of sexual violence (e.g., sexual assault, rape, sexual harassment, stalking), it is important for school counselors to be aware of the definitions of sexual violence and the regulations that determine a course of action.

The U.S. Department of Education Office for Civil Rights (OCR, 2011) oversees Title IX, which prohibits discrimination based on sex in educational settings. Educational institutions receiving federal funding are responsible for addressing any form of sexual violence or harassment that creates a hostile environment, which includes taking action to eliminate, prevent, and address sexual violence and its effects.

According to the OCR (2011), a hostile environment occurs when "the conduct is sufficiently serious that it interferes with or limits a student's ability to participate in or benefit from the school's program" (p. 3). Schools are required to investigate any possible sexual violence that occurs either on or off campus. However, the involvement of law enforcement in any criminal investigation does not absolve the school of responsibility. Title IX requires schools to develop and publish a policy against sexual discrimination, identify a Title IX coordinator to maintain compliance and oversee any complaints of sexual discrimination, and develop a comprehensive procedure for students to be able to file complaints, investigate incidents, and impose sanctions on perpetrators.

Based on the school's responsibility to deal with sexual violence, either reported or rumored, a student's right to confidentiality may be a challenge. Victims of sexual violence may request anonymity with reporting and/or responding to an incident. This may be particularly difficult for school counselors who are ethically obligated to maintain confidentiality. School counselors will need to determine if a student's exposure to sexual violence is a limit to confidentiality or not. The OCR (2011) provides the following guidelines for schools dealing with students who request anonymity in the process:

> The school should evaluate that request in the context of its responsibility to provide a safe and nondiscriminatory environment for all students. Thus, the school may weigh the request for confidentiality against the following factors: the seriousness of the alleged harassment; the complainant's age; whether there have been other harassment complaints about the same individual; and the alleged harasser's rights to receive information about the allegations if the information is maintained by the school as an "education record" under the Family Educational Rights and Privacy Act (FERPA), 20 U.S.C. § 1232g; 34 C.F.R. Part 99.15, the school should inform the complainant if it cannot ensure confidentiality. Even if the school cannot take disciplinary action against the alleged harasser because the complainant insists on confidentiality, it should pursue other steps to limit the effects of the alleged harassment and prevent its recurrence. (p. 5)

In addition, the OCR (2011) provides specific guidelines for school counselors:

- designating an individual from the school's counseling center to be "on call" to assist victims of sexual harassment or violence whenever needed; and
- offering counseling, health, mental health, or other holistic and comprehensive victim services to all students affected by sexual harassment or sexual violence, and notifying students of campus and community counseling, health, mental health, and other student services. (p. 17)

See Case Study 9.3, which addresses the dilemma of a school counselor faced with a student who experienced sexual violence. For more information about the OCR guidelines, visit www2.ed.gov/about/offices/list/ocr/letters/colleague-201104.pdf.

CASE STUDY 9.3

A School Counselor's Dilemma

Imagine that you are a school counselor at a local high school. Sara, a 16-year-old student, presents in your office, tearful and distraught. She tells you about a party that happened over the weekend. The party was at her friend Jessi's house after the football game. Jessi's parents were not at home during the party. With no adult supervision, kids were drinking and smoking marijuana. Sara reports that she drank some alcohol but did not do any drugs. She accepted a drink from Michael, who attends the school.

Although she had seen Michael at school, she was not friends with him and had no previous contact. According to Sara, she and Michael chatted as she sipped her drink. She remembers laughing and enjoying talking to him. However, she does not remember anything after that encounter. She woke up in a bedroom, half dressed, and feeling sore in her private area. She found Jessi and learned that Michael had taken Sara upstairs. Jessi reported Sara was laughing as they went up the stairs and seemed OK, so Jessi did not intervene. Sara returned home and began to finish some homework. As she worked, she began to receive text messages from friends about some social media postings about her. Apparently, Michael was describing their sexual encounter at the party on Facebook, bragging to his friends, providing explicit details, and promising to provide pictures he had taken. On Monday after the party, Sara noticed that people were snickering at her. By the end of the day, she had been called "slut" and "whore" by several classmates who are not her friends. Sara is devastated and not sure what she should do. She begs you not to tell anyone. Her father is a local police officer, and she is concerned about what he would do if he learned Michael had assaulted her.

Discussion Questions

1. Does Sara's experience meet the definition of sexual assault? If yes, what type?
2. What are some of the additional problems Sara might develop due to her traumatic encounter?
3. Keeping these circumstances in mind, how would you proceed?
4. What are the legal and ethical guidelines for you? For the school?
5. With a peer, role-play implementation of the task model for crisis assessment and intervention featured in Chapter 1.

EFFECTS OF SEXUAL VIOLENCE

Burgess and Holmstrom (1974) first coined the term *rape trauma syndrome* to describe the cluster of symptoms reported by women who were raped; see Table 9.1 (Burgess, 1985). Burgess, a psychiatric nurse, and Holmstrom, a sociologist, conducted research with women who presented in the emergency room after having experienced a rape. Burgess and Holmstrom described two distinct phases of women's response to sexual assault: (1) the acute phase and (2) the reorganization phase. During the acute phase, the victim experienced a heightened stress level, lasting from several days to multiple weeks. The reorganization phase was a longer-term process of integration, during which the victim regained a sense of control over life. In conceptualizing rape trauma syndrome, Burgess and Holmstrom found commonalities consistent with PTSD, including a significant stressor, intrusive thoughts about the sexual assault, and decreased involvement in their environment (e.g., feeling emotionally numb), as well as various other symptoms such as sleep disturbances, hypervigilance, guilt, impaired memory, and fears about reoccurrence of the sexual assault.

Crisis intervention during the acute phase, and an understanding of the "normal" reactions that victims experience during this phase, can help to decrease the sense of powerless one has over personal reactions. When a victim understands that displayed behaviors are 'normal to the abnormal event' (although different than precrisis functioning), it is possible the reorganization phase can be impacted positively. Normalizing and

TABLE 9.1 Symptoms of Rape Trauma Syndrome

Psychological Symptoms	Behavioral Symptoms
Continuing anxiety	Rage
Severe mood swings	Difficulty sleeping (nightmares, insomnia, etc.)
Sense of helplessness	Eating difficulties (nausea, vomiting, compulsive eating, etc.)
Persistent fear or phobia	Withdrawal from friends, family, activities
Depression	Hypervigilance
Denial	Reluctance to leave house and/or go places that remind the individual of the sexual assault or perpetrator
Difficulty concentrating	Sexual problems
Flashbacks	

Source: Summarized from Rape, Abuse and Incest National Network. (2015). The nation's largest anti-sexual assault organization. Retrieved from https://www.rainn.org

educating victims of common reactions and responses at each stage is crucial. Although the majority of research has focused on females as victims, male victims also can experience these similar responses to rape.

Physical Effects of Sexual Violence

Physical reactions to sexual violence can manifest in varying somatic complaints, including chronic pain, sleep disturbances, hypervigilance, and impaired memory. Sleep disturbances may range from sleeplessness or frequent waking to excessive amounts of sleeping. Victims may deal with other physical issues as a result of the sexual violence, including headaches, pregnancy, STIs contracted during the assault, or permanent physical injuries sustained during the attack. More severe disorders such as gastrointestinal disorders, cervical cancer, and genital injuries may occur. According to the CDC (2015c), more than 32,000 pregnancies per year are the result of a sexual assault.

Cognitive/Behavioral Effects of Sexual Violence

Victims of sexual violence may experience cognitive or behavioral problems and may have impaired memory and/or concentration, including memory loss or the inability to recall certain details in their lives. They may have a marked inability to concentrate on work tasks and other activities of daily living. Victims of sexual violence may change addresses or telephone numbers to try to ensure safety. They may find themselves in a state of hyperalertness, which can manifest as paranoia (e.g., feeling as if they are being followed), compulsive behaviors (e.g., constantly checking the house for intruders), or displaying an imaginary audience (e.g., thinking that others can tell they were sexually assaulted by looking at them).

Emotional/Psychological Effects of Sexual Violence

Emotional and psychological reactions to sexual violence may be either expressed or controlled. Victims who demonstrate more expressed reactions openly show emotions by crying, screaming, yelling, or even laughing. Those who demonstrate more controlled reactions may show little outward emotion or remain completely silent. Victims may experience a wide range of emotions: (1) guilt about surviving the attack, (2) self-blame about not being able to stop the attack, (3) shame if they chose not to report the assault, (4) humiliation with family and friends, (5) anxiety about another attack, and (6) depression that manifests as an inability to return to normal functioning in daily life. Victims may report feeling emotionally numb and being unable to reconnect with the world around them. The violence suffered by victims may affect their emotional and psychological health, which can manifest in different ways including PTSD, acute stress disorder and other anxiety disorders, self-harm, depression, substance abuse, eating disorders, and even suicide.

The *Diagnostic and Statistical Manual of Mental Disorders* (DSM-5) (American Psychiatric Association [APA], 2013) provides criteria for PTSD: (1) exposure to a traumatic event, either directly or to a close friend or relative, witnessing the event, or repeated and/or extreme exposure to details of traumatic events; (2) recurrent distressing memories or dreams related to the traumatic event, dissociative reactions (e.g., flashbacks), or severe physiological reactions; (3) avoidance of thoughts and feelings related to the event, including reminders; (4) negative effects on mood and cognitions; and (5) extreme reactions such as angry outbursts, hypervigilance, sleep disturbances, or difficulty concentrating. The DSM-5 was the first edition of the DSM to include sexual assault as a specific traumatic event, which is defined specifically as "threatened or actual violence (e.g., forced sexual penetration, alcohol/drug-facilitated sexual penetration, abusive sexual contact, noncontact sexual abuse, sexual trafficking)" (p. 274). According to the 2011 National Intimate Partner and Sexual Violence Survey conducted by Breiding et al. (2014), 20% of female respondents and 5.2% of male respondents who have experienced "contact sexual violence" also experienced one or more symptoms of PTSD. These statistics are derived from interviews with 6,879 women and 5,848 men ages 18 and over who completed surveys by phone in the United States.

As discussed above, one of the symptoms of rape trauma syndrome is depression. After experiencing a violent assault, it is reasonable to expect that victims would feel sadness, despair, and hopelessness. The depression victims experience may lead to either a fatal or nonfatal act of self harm. With symptoms of depression, as well as other feelings of loss, guilt, and shame, victims may choose suicide. Statistics correlate in that females make up the majority of victims of sexual violence, depression is more common in females than males (CDC, 2012), and depression is one of the leading causes of suicide. Based on these statistics, the suicide risk of victims increases due to their depression regarding the sexual violence.

While victims of sexual violence may consider suicide, they may also engage in self-harm. The CDC (2011b) defines *self-harm* as an "act of injuring oneself intentionally by various methods such as self-laceration, self-battering, taking overdoses or exhibiting deliberate recklessness but with no intent to die" (p. 90). Examples of self-harm include biting, burning, cutting, hitting the body, pulling out hair, and scratching and picking skin (RAINN, 2015). Many victims of sexual assault may choose self-harm as a way of coping with the distress caused by their traumatic event, albeit not a positive or effective coping mechanism.

Sexual violence may also impact a victim, both physically and emotionally, in the form of an eating disorder. According to RAINN (2015), perceptions of body image may affect victim eating habits. Focusing on food may be an attempt to feel control while dealing with an event for which the victims feels out of control. However, while this focus may provide some relief in the short-term, it can cause long-term physical and emotional damage. The National Eating Disorder Association (NEDA, 2012) speculates that as many as 30% of those suffering from eating disorders have experienced sexual violence.

Those survivors who do not develop symptoms of PTSD may show significant signs of acute stress disorder (ASD) surrounding the event. According to the DSM-5 (APA, 2013), individuals must meet the following ASD diagnostic criteria: (1) exposure to an incident that ended in actual or threatened death, injury, or sexual violation (excluding exposure through media sources; e.g., television, movies); (2) symptoms from categories such as intrusion symptoms (e.g., flashbacks), negative mood, dissociative symptoms, avoidance symptoms or arousal symptoms; (3) disturbance that occurs between 3 and 30 days following the trauma exposure; (4) significant impairment of important areas of functioning (e.g., job performance); and (5) disturbance that cannot be attributed to any medical condition, substance use, or psychiatric disorder. Estimates of ASD in victims of sexual violence range from 20 to 50% (APA, 2013). One of the hallmarks of ASD is an extreme anxiety level that significantly interferes with sleeping patterns, physical energy, and the ability to complete tasks. Avoidance results in withdrawal from situations perceived as threatening. What differentiates ASD from the more severe PTSD is that the symptoms must occur and dissipate within 1 month of the trauma event or exposure (APA, 2013). Intensity, severity, and duration of symptoms must be taken into account when diagnosing ASD and PTSD in survivors of sexual violence.

SEXUAL VIOLENCE AND ADDICTION   The relationship between sexual violence and addiction has been demonstrated and documented both qualitatively and quantitatively. Frequency, duration, and type of abuse are heavily correlated with misuse and abuse of both drugs and alcohol. Victims of sexual violence may turn to substances instead of seeking treatment for a variety of reasons, including (1) feelings of shame and guilt or personal responsibility for the sexual assault incident; (2) lacking access to adequate treatment; (3) lacking resources (e.g., economic, transportation); or (4) feeling fearful. Victims may view substances such as alcohol or prescription drugs as a way to relieve emotional distress, "numbing" themselves to the effects of the sexual assault, or as a way to cope with symptoms of a mental health disorder resulting from the attack.

According to RAINN (2015), victims of rape are 13 times more likely to abuse alcohol and 26 times more likely to abuse drugs, demonstrating the significant connection between sexual violence and substance use. Furthermore, victims of child sexual assault are at a higher risk for addiction, which can lead to revictimization in adulthood, risk for incarceration, suicide risk, and comorbidity with mental health disorders (Asberg & Renk, 2013). Asberg and Renk (2013) reported that incarcerated female survivors of child sexual assault used more avoidant coping characterized by substance use in an effort to deal with these negative experiences. Daigre et al. (2015) conducted a study in which patients in an addictions treatment center were asked about abuse experiences within their lifetime. Almost 14% of the participants reported an instance of sexual abuse.

When working with clients who have been victims of sexual violence, the warning signs for addiction should be recognized when present. Victims dealing with addictions may present with depression or anxiety, disinterest in activities they once enjoyed, aggression or irrationality, or simply forgetfulness (SafeHelpline, 2016). According to the DSM-5 (APA, 2013), features of a substance use disorder include (1) relapse effects (e.g., intense craving for a substance); (2) rapid changes in behavior; (3) problems with impulse control; (4) engaging in risky behavior; (5) social impairment (e.g., failure to show up for work or other obligations); (6) increases in tolerance of a substance; or (7) withdrawal symptoms, which vary across substances. See Table 9.2 for additional resources for helping victims, perpetrators, and general information for counselors and individuals who work with sexual assault.

TABLE 9.2 Resources on Sexual Assault

Victim Support

Anti-Violence Project: www.avp.org

Childhelp USA: www.childhelpusa.org; hotline: 1-800-422-4453, 1-800-222-4453

Coalition to Abolish Slavery & Trafficking (CAST): www.castla.org

Male Survivor: www.malesurvivor.org

National Sexual Assault Telephone Hotline: 1-800-656-HOPE (4673)

National Sexual Violence Resource Center (NSVRC): www.nsvrc.org

Polaris Project: www.polarisproject.org/about

Rape, Abuse & Incest Alliance Network (RAINN): www.rainn.org

Substance Abuse Support

Free Substance Abuse Treatment Referral Helpline: 1-800-662-HELP (4357)

National Sexual Assault Telephone Hotline: 1-800-656-HOPE (4673)

Rape, Abuse & Incest National Network (RAINN): www.rainn.org

Safe Helpline Sexual Assault Support: www.safehelpline.org

Perpetrator Treatment and Management

Association for the Treatment of Sexual Abusers: www.atsa.com

Center for Sex Offender Management: www.csom.org

Men Can Stop Rape: www.mencanstoprape.org

STOP IT NOW!: www.stopitnow.org; hotline: 1-888-773-8368

Sex Offender Solutions & Education Network: sosen.org

Counseling Therapies and Training

Trauma-Focused Cognitive Behavioral Therapy Training (Medical University of South Carolina): tfcbt.musc.edu

Cognitive Processing Therapy Training (Medical University of South Carolina): cpt.musc.edu/

Cognitive Behavior Therapy (Beck Institute): www.beckinstitute.org

Cognitive Behavioral Therapy with Children and Adolescents Training: albertellis.org/professional-rebt-cbt/trainings/

National Center on Domestic and Sexual Violence: Training events around the country: www.ncdsv.org/ncd_upcomingtrainings.html

Office for Victims of Crime: Training and Technical Assistance Center—Sexual Assault Advocate/Counselor Training: www.ovcttac.gov/saact/

(continued)

TABLE 9.2 Resources on Sexual Assault (*continued*)

Additional Reading

Aymer, S. (2011). A case for including the "lived experience" of African American men in batterers' treatment. *Journal of African American Studies, 15,* 352–366. doi:10.1007/s12111-010-9150-1

Cunha, O., & Abrunhosa Gonçalves, R. (2013). Intimate partner violence offenders: Generating a data-based typology of batterers and implications for treatment. *European Journal of Psychology Applied to Legal Context, 5*(2), 9–17. doi:10.5093/ejpalc2013a2

Duane, Y., Carr, A., Cherry, J., McGrath, K., & O'Shea, D. (2002). Experiences of parents attending a programme for families of adolescent child sexual abuse perpetrators in Ireland. *Child Care in Practice, 8*(1), 46–57. doi:10.1080/13575270220140461

Guedes, A. (2012). Perpetrators of violence/batterers. Retrieved from http://www.endvawnow .org/en/articles/229-perpetrators-of-violence-batterers.html?next=230

Krahé, B., & Berger, A. (2013). Men and women as perpetrators and victims of sexual aggression in heterosexual and same-sex encounters: A study of first-year college students in Germany. *Aggressive Behavior, 39,* 391–404. doi:10.1002/ab.21482

Soloski, K. L., & Durtschi, J. A. (2013). Ethical issues regarding perpetrator involvement in the systemic treatment of incest. *Journal of Family Psychotherapy, 24,* 188–207. doi:10.1080/ 08975353.2013.817252

Wiggins, J., Hepburn, S., & Rossiter, R. (2013). Reducing harmful sexual behaviour in adolescents. *Learning Disability Practice, 16*(8), 16–23.

Victim versus Survivor

Before discussing interventions, it is important to address the terminology used by mental health professionals, advocates, law enforcement officers, and those in the legal system to describe persons who have experienced sexual trauma. While the term *victim* may be the more accurate term to define the person as a victim of a crime, *survivor* is a term that is used to define the person as having survived the crime and moving forward. Carol Mosley, Director of We End Violence, posits that both terms can be used (Mosley, 2013). The term *victim* is typically used by law enforcement, whereas *survivor* is typically used by mental health professionals and advocates working in the field. *Victim* indicates the feelings of powerlessness a person may feel after experiencing sexual violence; *survivor* indicates the reclaiming of power and focuses on healing. While the first part of this chapter addressed concepts related to victims, the rest of this chapter will focus more on survivors.

INTERVENTIONS WITH SURVIVORS OF SEXUAL VIOLENCE

Early evaluation and intervention are vital for survivors of sexual violence. Typically, two facilities provide intervention and evaluation services for victims. The first is the emergency room, where many victims of sexual violence first present themselves after having been physically injured during an attack. Once victims enter the health care system, they are treated for a variety of possible health concerns (e.g., pregnancy, STIs, HIV/AIDS, hepatitis B). The second treatment facility for survivors of sexual violence is a crisis center, which is typically in a different location from the emergency medical facility and can be a self-contained unit, providing all services on-site. The majority of these crisis centers have 24-hour crisis telephone services through which victims can make initial contact. Often, if victims of sexual violence present to a law enforcement facility, they will be taken to either an emergency room or a crisis center, depending on which facility typically handles these types of cases in the local community.

Services that are provided at emergency rooms or crisis centers may include (1) evidence collection, (2) medical interventions to treat possible health concerns, and (3) examinations by sexual assault nurse examiners (SANE nurses), who are specially trained to work with victims of sexual assault. The crisis center may use trained, on-call volunteers to assist survivors of sexual assault when victims present at the crisis center, police department, or emergency room. Counselors may participate in this volunteer program, often by providing the services during regular hours and by preparing, supporting, and supervising volunteer workers. The most important functions of these volunteers are to support survivors during the process of reporting and to help prepare them for future steps. Crisis counselors and volunteers help victims understand the medical examination and evidence collection process, anticipate legal requirements, and develop safety plans. The crisis center may also offer additional services, including short-term or long-term counseling, education, and legal assistance. Although these may be the two most prevalent places victims of sexual violence present or are taken, it is important for all counselors to have an understanding of the process and what may occur during medical examinations.

Medical examinations are a crucial crisis intervention strategy when dealing with sexual assault. The medical exam, however, can be both uncomfortable and overwhelming to a victim. Victims have experienced a violation that is both physically and psychologically intrusive, and many may fear that the medical exam required to collect evidence will lead to reliving the trauma they experienced.

It is important for counselors to become familiar with the medical exam process to help victims understand and prepare for the exam. By offering information about what to expect during the process, the counselor can allow the victim to gain some control. The U.S. Department of Justice's Office on Violence Against Women (2013) developed a national protocol for sexual assault forensic exams (SAFEs) to recognize the sensitive needs of victims of sexual violence and preserve evidence vital to the successful prosecution of offenders. Once a victim presents to an emergency room or crisis center, a SAFE is conducted by a trained medical professional, such as a SANE nurse. The SAFE typically takes about four hours to complete and involves collecting biological samples, including blood, urine, hair, and saliva, and obtaining oral, vaginal, and anal swabs and smears that may be used for DNA analysis and comparison. Urine samples help determine whether victims were drugged during the sexual assault. Clothing and any foreign materials on the body are collected, and many crisis centers provide donated clothing to victims once their clothing has been collected for evidence. For evidence preservation purposes, it is important for victims not to bathe, wash their hands, or brush their teeth; counselors should be knowledgeable about the need for collecting urine samples in case victims are unable to wait until the forensic examiner arrives. A final aspect of the medical exam involves treating any potential medical conditions that occur due to the sexual violence (e.g., pregnancy, STIs, HIV/AIDS, hepatitis B). These conditions are treated with oral medications during the exam. The CDC recommends follow-up testing for STIs 1 to 2 weeks after the assault and for syphilis and HIV testing 6, 12, and 24 weeks after the assault (U.S. Department of Justice, Office on Violence Against Women, 2013).

Because law enforcement may be an entry point for some victims of sexual violence, many law enforcement departments are offering specific training and specialized units for working with survivors of sexual violence. The first step for many departments is to train personnel to understand the dynamics of rape and sexual assault. This training may range from basic 1-day training to a more extensive course to help officers develop a deeper understanding of how to handle sexual violence. Training should include understanding the victims they will encounter, common reactions and responses victims may have, types of violence that may occur during assaults, and patterns of perpetrators. Officers need to be aware of services available to victims and how to help victims who have been sexually violated access those services.

Once the first responders have connected sexual violence victims to the health care system, the next step for law enforcement officials is the investigation, which may be handled by specialized units that are trained in investigating sexual violence, including procedures for interviewing survivors and collecting evidence. After the conclusion of the investigation, the case may be turned over to the local prosecutor's office, which may then develop a case to present to a judge and/or jury. Victims may be referred to a victims' assistance program to help deal with the personal impact of the trial. These programs can help victims understand their rights regarding the court case. In 2004, the Justice for All Act became law. Reauthorized in 2014, this law allows victims to write, submit, and/or present impact statements (U.S. Department of Justice, Office for Victims of Crime, 2006). Impact statements may be one of the first steps toward empowerment for victims of sexual violence. According to the National Center for Victims of Crime (2009), a victim impact statement allows the victim of a crime to share the effect(s) of the crime. Statements typically focus on the harm that the offense caused, including physical, emotional, and financial harm, as well as harm to family and other significant relationships. Statements are most often given in either written or oral form and can be used at sentencing. The Justice for All Reauthorization Act of 2013 includes the following crime victims' rights: (1) the right to be informed of a plea bargain or prosecution agreement in a timely manner, and (2) the right to be informed of one's eligibility to receive victims' rights and services. In addition, victims can receive services from the Victims' Rights Ombudsman of the Department of Justice (DOJ).

TREATMENT OF SURVIVORS OF SEXUAL VIOLENCE

As discussed earlier, rape trauma syndrome is an adaptation of PTSD used to understand symptoms experienced by survivors of sexual violence. Because there are significant similarities between rape trauma syndrome and PTSD, counselors should familiarize themselves with both. PTSD, ASD, and other related diagnoses were discussed in Chapter 1.

Short-Term/Immediate Interventions

Decker and Naugle (2009) stress the importance of victims determining their own needs and voicing them before any intervention begins. They found little empirical evidence for immediate intervention after sexual violence. After a thorough investigation of the literature, they found that psychological first aid (PFA)—a systematic set of skills known for working with victims of recent traumatic events—is the most favorable approach for immediate intervention with sexual violence victims. It is a practical set of actions that is meant to be used immediately, within 24 hours following a trauma. While PFA was originally intended for use following natural disasters, increasing evidence supports its use with victims following sexual violence. PFA can be used in a wide variety of settings, with a range of different clients, including children and clients from various multicultural backgrounds (Ruzek et al., 2007). PFA consists of eight essential measures referred to as "core actions," which are as follows: (1) contact and engagement, (2) safety and comfort, (3) stabilization, (4) information gathering, (5) practical assistance, (6) connection with social supports, (7) information on coping support, and (8) linkage with collaborative services. The benefits of PFA are that it can be used by mental health professionals who have been trained in the application of the core actions, and it promotes immediate support as well as long-term coping (Ruzek et al., 2007). Currently, there is a lack of PFA-qualified responders. Research shows that victims of sexual violence who do not get help immediately following an incident are at higher risk for mental health problems and increased risk of suicide (McCabe et al., 2014). Training in PFA is often offered by the American Red Cross and other health-conscious organizations. See Chapter 1 for more information on PFA.

CONDUCTING THE FIRST SESSION OR MEETING USING THE PSYCHOLOGICAL-FIRST-AID APPROACH   In PFA, the first assessment is about the safety of the survivor. Approach the victim gently and introduce yourself. Allow the victim to determine what role you will be in with him or her and respect these wishes. You can begin by explaining some of the supports you could offer—for example, comfort items such as a blanket—or your willingness to just sit quietly with the victim. Remember the factors that can impede the medical exam process (e.g., no brushing teeth, eating, drinking, showering, or changing clothes before the exam). While supporting the victim continually, assess his or her wish for your level of involvement. It is crucial to allow the victim to feel in control of this process. Offer to accompany the victim to the medical exam, if appropriate in your position. In some agencies, schools, and private practice settings, it may be more appropriate for support systems to be contacted to assist in this role. Ask the victim if she or he would like you to explain the exam process step by step. Let the victim lead the conversation; do not push or direct the dialogue, especially toward the incident. If the victim does wish to speak about the assault, it is crucial to be supportive; do not doubt or blame the victim. Use of active listening and empathic statements have the most impact at this stage. After the exam and any necessary protocol, such as speaking with law enforcement, assess the victim's need for safety. Determine the best place for the victim to go, the types of support necessary, and begin implementing those strategies.

Long-Term Interventions

After survivors have undergone the immediate procedures after the attack (e.g., medical interventions), long-term counseling services should be considered. Crisis counselors should perform a thorough evaluation to determine the most appropriate treatment plan. Several assessments exist that may be helpful when collecting information related to the assault, including the Clinician-Administered PTSD Scale for DSM-5—Child/Adolescent Version (CAPS-CA-5) (Pynoos et al., 2015), Clinician-Administered PTSD Scale for DSM-5 (CAPS-5; Weathers et al., 2013), The UCLA Child/Adolescent PTSD

Reaction Index for DSM-5 (Elhai et al., 2013), Assault Information and History Interview (AIHI; Foa & Rothbaum, 1998), and the PTSD Checklist for DSM-5 (PCL-5; Weathers et al., 2013). Self-report measures include the Impact of Event Scale–Revised (Weiss & Marmar, 1996) and the Rape Aftermath Symptom Test (Kilpatrick, 1988). As with any crisis situation, a risk assessment should be completed.

Another consideration is the length of the treatment program. Although some victims have already experienced short-term interventions (e.g., medical examinations, involvement with law enforcement), longer-term counseling may help them deal with the effects that occur long after the sexual violence. Foa and Rothbaum (1998) offer these suggestions to crisis counselors when working with survivors: (1) provide support to the survivor for other issues being dealt with (e.g., involvement in the legal system, family considerations, job stress); (2) take and maintain a nonjudgmental attitude; (3) show a level of comfort with the traumatic events described; (4) demonstrate competence with rape trauma syndrome; (5) feel confident about the treatments chosen; (6) focus on personal resources; and (7) normalize the response to the assault.

Parcesepe, Martin, Pollock, and Garcia-Moreno (2015) completed a systematic review to determine which mental health interventions were most effective for adult female sexual assault survivors. They reviewed articles from 1985 to 2012 that include studies pertaining to the treatment of adult female sexual assault survivors. They carefully selected articles that met the Downs and Black Checklist for Measuring Study Quality for inclusion in their review. Only nine articles met the study inclusion criteria. The results indicated that there are at least seven treatment modalities that are effective in treating adult female sexual assault survivors' symptoms and PTSD diagnosis, including assertion training, clinician-assisted emotional disclosure, cognitive processing therapy, eye movement desensitization and reprocessing (EMDR) therapy, prolonged exposure therapy, stress inoculation therapy, and supportive psychotherapy with information. Furthermore, they found that symptoms of depression related to the assault were best treated with cognitive processing therapy and EMDR therapy, while symptoms of anxiety were best treated with assertion training and supportive psychotherapy with information. Studies using cognitive processing therapy and prolonged exposure therapy reported long-term improvement for up to 6 years, whereas the other interventions studied did not offer follow-up data.

The sections that follow discuss techniques and approaches for long-term interventions with sexual assault survivors. They cover cognitive behavioral approaches, including trauma-focused cognitive behavioral therapy, cognitive processing therapy, prolonged exposure therapy, and EMDR therapy; anxiety management training programs, including stress inoculation training and relaxation training; and other approaches to trauma treatment, including psychoeducation and group counseling. Some of these techniques and approaches may require additional training and education.

Cognitive-Behavioral Approaches

Cognitive-behavioral approaches are well researched and have been shown to have positive results for survivors of sexual violence. Jaycox, Zoeller, and Foa (2002) outline a 12-session treatment plan using cognitive-behavioral therapy that includes (1) psychoeducation about trauma and the effects of trauma; (2) behavior techniques such as breathing retraining to reduce anxiety; (3) real-life and imaginal exposure; and (4) cognitive restructuring. Two of the most frequently used cognitive approaches are outlined below: trauma-focused cognitive behavioral therapy and cognitive processing therapy.

TRAUMA-FOCUSED COGNITIVE-BEHAVIORAL THERAPY   Created by Cohen, Mannarino, and Deblinger (2006), trauma-focused cognitive behavioral therapy (TF-CBT) is specifically geared toward working with children, adolescents, and their families. It consists of eight components characterized by the acronym PRACTICE: (1) **P**sychoeducation; (2) **R**elaxation and stress management skills; (3) **A**ffective expression and modulation; (4) **C**ognitive coping and processing; (5) **T**rauma narration; (6) **I**n vivo mastery of trauma; (7) **C**onjoint child-parent sessions; and (8) **E**nhancing future safety and development. TF-CBT can decrease the symptoms of PTSD, as well as other symptoms caused by assault. The treatment also provides relief for caregivers of the victim, providing a secondary gain for all those involved. Additional information can be found in the *How to Implement TF-CBT Manual* at www.nctsnet.org/nctsn_assets/pdfs/TF-CBT_Implementation_Manual.pdf (National Child Traumatic Stress Network, 2012).

COGNITIVE PROCESSING THERAPY   Cognitive processing therapy (CPT) is geared toward relieving PTSD symptoms by combining cognitive and exposure interventions. CPT is based on information processing theory, particularly related to how codes are stored and the ability to recall information, to influence how the trauma is perceived. Specifically, CPT focuses on the new information related to the trauma that does not match the victims' existing schema about themselves, the world, or the trauma. A schema is a generic guide to help victims deal with the overwhelming information that is processed daily, which influences coding, comprehending, and retrieving information. When an event happens that does not fit into a schema, the information must still be processed. Victims will either (1) alter the information or distort it in some way to fit into their existing schema, or (2) change the existing schema to accept the new information. When using CPT with survivors of sexual violence, assess the schema and determine where they are stuck, meaning where the new information of being victimized does not fit into an existing schema. The goal is to help survivors learn how to appropriately accommodate the new information instead of overaccommodating or distorting the information.

CPT is usually conducted in a one-and-a-half-hour group format over a 12-week period. However, it can also be used with individuals. The 12 sessions have the following themes: (1) introduction and education, (2) understanding the meaning of the event, (3) identifying thoughts and feelings, (4) remembering the incident, (5) identifying stuck points, (6) challenging questions, (7) identifying faulty thinking patterns, (8) discussing safety issues, (9) identifying trust issues, (10) identifying power and control issues, (11) identifying esteem issues, and (12) identifying intimacy issues and the meaning of the event. Resources and training for CPT can be found at cpt.musc.edu/resources. Read Voices from the Field 9.2.

PROLONGED EXPOSURE THERAPY   According to Foa and Rothbaum (1998), exposure therapy is considered one of the most appropriate treatments for PTSD symptoms related to sexual assault. It is a form of systematic desensitization that calls for repeated exposure to a traumatic event in order to reduce the fear, anxiety, and pathology associated with the event. During exposure therapy, clients, with eyes closed, are encouraged to recall the traumatic event in the safety of a counselor's office. These sessions are often

---

VOICES FROM THE FIELD 9.2
Using Cognitive Processing Therapy with Survivors of Sexual Violence

Amber Hiott

When I graduated from with my BA in psychology, I didn't have a clear idea of what I wanted to do. So, instead of pressuring myself, I started to volunteer at a local domestic violence and sexual assault center. Within 1 month of my volunteer work, I was offered a full-time position as a victim advocate. In this role, I was able to work directly with victims as a support and a resource. Working at this center inspired me to go back to school to become a mental health counselor; I wanted my life work to revolve around helping survivors of trauma. After receiving my M.Ed. in clinical mental health counseling, I began working at another sexual trauma center. At this center, I served as an individual and group counselor, and I had the privilege of working directly with both adolescents and adults. While each client was unique and had a distinct life story, client goals were often the same: "I want to get better." As their counselor, I would gently assist clients to concretely identify what "better" would look like for them, and once these goals were identified, the path to recovery and healing would begin.

One of the main tools I used when working with survivors is an evidence-based practice called cognitive processing therapy (CPT). This model suggests that after experiencing trauma, a person can be affected in five core areas: safety, trust, self-esteem, power and control, and intimacy. By using this model, I assisted clients in identifying their thoughts in each of the five core areas, and we worked together to shift these thoughts over the course of treatment. CPT also has an exposure component, which ultimately helps the survivor to "stop avoiding" and to account for the trauma in a safe and nonthreatening environment. This particular model provided enough structure to help clients feel secure, yet enough flexibility to offer personalized and individualized treatment.

Although CPT has proven to be extremely effective with the victims I work with, it is also important to evaluate individual needs and tailor the model accordingly. This approach has allowed me to help clients "get better," while also leaving me amazed and humbled by the resilience of every woman and man, adult and adolescent, I've had the honor of working with. I thank each of them for their testimony, their courage, their strength, and their survival.

---

recorded to allow the client to review at home in order to continue the repeated exposure to the memories, with the intent of continuing to lessen the fear and anxiety associated with the event. Although this treatment may be stressful, it is considered one of the most effective interventions for treating sexual assault survivors. Another form of exposure therapy, *in vivo* therapy, involves repeated exposure to real-life situations and/or places that remind the victim of the event in order to restore feelings of safety. It is important to note that exposure therapy has been criticized for being ineffective, dangerous, and increasing dropout rates, although few research findings support such claims (Foa, Zoellner, Feeny, Hembree, & Alvarez-Conrad, 2002).

EYE MOVEMENT DESENSITIZATION AND REPROCESSING THERAPY EMDR therapy attempts to help survivors process memories of their assault that cause psychological and psychosomatic symptoms that interfere with their daily living. EMDR therapy processes parts of the trauma and uses bilateral stimulation such as eye movement, tapping, or sounds to change the way the brain is processing a memory. EMDR therapy uses eight phases of treatment to identify and deal with the trauma that creates a person's current distress. These phases include (1) discussion of the client's history and treatment plan, (2) client preparation, (3) assessment of the target event, (4) desensitization, (5) installation, (6) body scan, (7) closure, and (8) re-evaluation.

Anxiety Management Training Programs

Several anxiety management training (AMT) programs are effective for treating PTSD symptoms following sexual violence. AMT programs are designed to help equip clients with tools to better handle anxiety. AMT treatments that have been found to be most successful working with sexual assault survivors include stress inoculation training and relaxation training.

STRESS INOCULATION TRAINING   Stress inoculation training (SIT) was developed by Meichenbaum (1996) as a treatment to help clients deal with a stressful event and to prevent or "inoculate" them against future stressors. According to Meichenbaum, SIT has three phases: (1) conceptualization, (2) skills acquisition and rehearsal, and (3) application and follow-through. In the conceptualization phase, the counseling relationship is developed, stressors are evaluated to determine severity, problem-solving methods are employed to determine stressors that can be changed, and goals are set. In the skills acquisition and rehearsal phase, coping skills are taught and rehearsed in the clinical setting so they can be applied in stressful situations. These coping skills include emotional regulation, self-soothing, relaxation training, problem-solving skills, communication tools, and social support networks. In the application and follow-through phase, the client applies the coping skills developed through modeling and role playing. In this final phase, ways to prevent relapse are discussed.

RELAXATION TRAINING   Relaxation techniques can be incorporated in any treatment plan when working with survivors of sexual violence. Survivors can learn how and when to use relaxation techniques and how to apply the techniques at times when they are triggered by the traumatic event causing dysfunction. These techniques include deep breathing, deep muscle relaxation, and cue-controlled relaxation, which involve teaching the client to recognize body tension, using it as a cue for employing relaxation techniques.

Other Approaches to Trauma Treatment

PSYCHOEDUCATION AND OTHER TREATMENTS   During the process of recovery, survivors must learn many things related to sexual violence, understand the myths that surround sexual violence, and develop awareness of negative thoughts they may experience, as well as any triggers associated with the assault. Several common reactions may occur: (1) fear and anxiety; (2) re-experiencing the trauma through nightmares or flashbacks; (3) increased arousal such as impatience or irritability; (4) avoidance of situations that remind the client of the assault; (5) numbness; (6) anger; (7) guilt and shame; (8) depression; (9) negative self-image; and (10) problems with intimate relationships, including issues with sexual pleasure.

GROUP COUNSELING   Group counseling is a common treatment modality for victims of sexual violence. Most rape crisis centers and abuse shelters offer some form of group counseling or therapy. The most common and most beneficial types of group counseling for victims of sexual violence are support or therapy groups. The group format allows survivors to share their stories with others in a supportive environment and gain an understanding of their symptoms and concerns. Group counseling encourages the feeling of belonging and facilitates the growth process. Jacobs, Masson, Harvill, and Schimmel (2012) recommend screening clients prior to having them enter a support or therapy group for sexual assault. They stress the importance of the client having had individual counseling and being at a point where the client is dedicated to moving forward in the treatment process. Jacobs et al. draw attention to the fact that many survivors early in the recovery process are still trying to make sense out of the assault and have not yet dealt with the guilt and shame that accompanies such abuse, and they are therefore not ready to enter into the group therapy process.

Read Voices from the Field 9.3 to gain an in-the-field perspective on working with clients who have experienced sexual assault.

VOICES FROM THE FIELD 9.3
Working with Victims of Sexual Assault in Mental Health Settings

Alissa Sawyer Beuerlein

After working in a variety of clinical settings, I have had my share of clients who are victims of sexual violence. I can recall that only a few weeks into my first "real job" in counseling at a community mental health center, I was both shocked and heartbroken at the overwhelming number of clients who reported being sexually violated. I have found since then that this is a global issue with far too little awareness. I have gone through various training programs in order to better treat these clients.

Common themes exist among many sexual assault victims. One such commonality is knowing who their abuser is prior to the sexual assault(s). I find this frequently among children, adolescents, and adults alike. There have been less than a handful of clients over the years who I have encountered who did not know the perpetrator prior to the sexual assault(s). A second commonality is repeated sexual assault by different people. This is a phenomenon I am still attempting to understand. The best way I can frame this in my own mind is that sexual assault victims lose a sense of self, self-respect, and self-esteem, and thus are more vulnerable to those who prey on others sexually than those who exude more confidence and self-respect.

A final common theme I have found among sexual assault victims is a willingness to "own" the responsibility for the assault(s). Attackers are very adept at making a victim feel responsible for the assault. They will fuse logic with lies to confuse the victim into believing that he or she is fully responsible for the attack. This is a pivotal issue to address in counseling, even if a client initially denies ownership of the attack.

One of the most important aspects of counseling sexual assault victims is helping them realize and accept that the assault was not their fault and that it was only the fault of their attacker. An equally important aspect of counseling with sexual assault victims is talking about the assault(s). Many victims are tired of discussing it and believe that if they could just "leave it behind" they would be able to "move on." However, this is far from reality. The more that victims of sexual violence attempt to repress memories and feelings about their assaults, the more their minds and bodies will remind them, and the more fearful they are likely to be. The best way I can describe this to my sexual assault clients is to compare their situation to a broken bone. If a child breaks his leg and allows it to heal on its own, it will heal improperly and will give the child incredible pain and lack of mobility. If the child then goes to the doctor, the doctor will have to first break the bone again in order to set it to heal properly. This is very similar to working with sexual assault victims. They must go back to the point of pain, look at it in truth and hurt again, now in a safe place, in order to best heal and move forward with their lives.

One of the approaches that I often use with sexual assault victims is eye movement desensitization and reprocessing (EMDR), an effective way for clients to reprocess past trauma so it is no longer in the forefront of their minds. Another approach I frequently use with sexual assault victims is trauma-focused cognitive-behavioral therapy (TF-CBT). I have found both EMDR and TF-CBT to be very effective tools for those who have suffered sexual assault, especially when owning too much responsibility for the assault(s).

SEXUAL VIOLENCE AND ASSAULT: ETHICAL AND LEGAL ISSUES

Ethical and legal issues regarding sexual violence include confidentiality, release of information, counselor competence, and personal values. When working with victims of sexual violence or assault, a counselor may experience ethical dilemmas related to confidentiality, which may conflict with personal values. It may be quite obvious to the counselor that reporting the assault may be in the best interest of the client. However, the counselor is both ethically and legally obligated to maintain confidentiality, even if it is counterintuitive to the client's needs. In addition, the counselor is ethically obligated to avoid imposing personal values on the client (American Counseling Association [ACA], 2014). The counselor must not persuade clients to report sexual assaults or endure forensic examinations against their will. Empowering clients to make decisions about what happens to their bodies is important, particularly after something as intrusive as a sexual assault.

According to the *ACA Code of Ethics* (ACA, 2014, p. 8), counselors "practice only within the boundaries of their competence, based on their education, training, supervised experience, state and national professional credentials, and appropriate professional experience." Although working with survivors of sexual violence is not considered a specialty area, counselors must develop knowledge and skills specific to dealing with victims to help these clients improve through counseling. Counselors should gain competence in treatment modalities applicable to sexual violence and assault issues (e.g., cognitive-behavioral approaches, exposure therapy, anxiety management programs) and develop skills related to rape trauma syndrome and PTSD prior to working with this population. Competence can be gained by attending workshops, seminars, or training sessions focused on how to work with sexual assault survivors. Counselors can choose to read literature about sexual assault or conduct conjoint counseling with another counselor who is experienced in working with sexual assault survivors.

Because many survivors are involved in the legal system, it is important to recognize that they may be particularly sensitive to having their information disclosed. Voluntary release of information forms should be in place to allow counselors of clients in crisis to share information with attorneys, medical personnel, and law enforcement. If a survivor chooses not to sign these documents, information cannot be revealed unless the counselor is legally required to do so (i.e., court order). Counselors should not assume that any subpoena received is "official" and would require disclosure. Many subpoenas have not been properly filed with the legal system and/or courts. Counselors should obtain consent from the client even in cases of subpoenas sent by the client's attorney. As a best practice, understanding what information the client agrees to share is crucial not only for ethical and legal purposes but also for the client–counselor relationship. Counselors are encouraged to seek legal counsel in any situation in which the legal system is involved. Legal representatives can help counselors prepare for possible court testimony and become familiar with state laws pertaining to sexual violence and crisis counseling.

Spirituality and Religious Issues Related to Sexual Violence and Assault

Integration of spirituality and religious beliefs in counseling has gained significant focus in recent years. Spirituality as a means to improved mental health has long been an accepted practice in dealing with substance abuse issues, as demonstrated by

Alcoholics Anonymous. According to Cashwell and Young (2011), the spiritual and/or religious life of clients can be crucial to their development, particularly when dealing with personal problems. Clients often create a spiritual existence that provides meaning, peace, and tranquility to their lives, which needs to be acknowledged and accepted by the counselor. Although research has been conducted to determine whether a person's spirituality and religious beliefs can be a way of coping with stressful events, particularly when dealing with trauma, the findings of these studies are inconsistent. More specifically, people may engage in positive or negative religious coping behaviors. Examples of positive coping behaviors include (1) using religion to find meaning, comfort, and support; (2) engaging in good deeds and helping others; and (3) involvement in church activities and/or attending religious services. Examples of negative coping behaviors include (1) using religion to avoid dealing with problems, (2) making bargains with God to make things better, and (3) feeling dissatisfied with religion after the assault (Ahrens, Abeling, Ahmand, & Hinman, 2010). Fallot and Heckman (2005) conducted research to examine the spirituality and religious coping behaviors used by women who had experienced personal traumas. According to their findings, participants in the study relied more on positive religious coping behaviors than the general population. However, one important finding in the study was that the more severe the trauma, the more participants engaged in negative religious coping behaviors. Ahrens et al. (2010) conducted a study of approximately 100 sexual assault survivors who reported a belief in God. According to their findings, sexual assault survivors who used positive religious coping behaviors experienced improved well-being and less depression than those who used negative religious coping behaviors. It is important to note that ethnicity played a significant part in the focus on religious coping behaviors. African American survivors tended to rely more heavily on their religious beliefs than White survivors.

In working with survivors of sexual violence who may have strong religious and/or spiritual beliefs, clients should be able to initiate a discussion of religion when they choose, and counselors should avoid imposing personal religious beliefs on the client. According to the *ACA Code of Ethics* (ACA, 2014), "Counselors are aware of their own values, attitudes, beliefs, and behaviors and avoid imposing values that are inconsistent with counseling goals. Counselors respect the diversity of clients, trainees, and research participants" (pp. 4–5).

When working with victims of sexual violence or assault who view their religious beliefs as a significant part of their lives, counselors should consider the following guidelines:

1. Do not ignore the strong spiritual/religious beliefs of clients. These beliefs are just as important as any other beliefs that clients may have. However, counselors should refrain from imposing their own religious beliefs onto clients.
2. Help clients see the benefits of their religious/spiritual beliefs to their wellness and recovery process.
3. If clients are experiencing negative religious coping skills (e.g., using religion to avoid dealing with problems, bargaining with God, feeling dissatisfied with religion), help them develop more positive religious coping skills (e.g., find meaning through their religious beliefs, helping others, becoming involved in religious activities).

The Association for Spiritual, Ethical, and Religious Values in Counseling (ASERVIC), a division of the ACA, developed *Competencies for Addressing Spiritual and Religious Issues in Counseling* to help counselors understand the skills and knowledge necessary to develop spiritual and religious sensitivity when working with clients (ASERVIC, 2016). A discussion of all the competencies can be found at the ASERVIC website: www.aservic.org/resources/spiritual-competencies/.

Multicultural Issues and Victims with Special Needs

According to the *ACA Code of Ethics* (ACA, 2014), counselors should be cognizant of the influence of individual differences based on "age, culture, disability, ethnicity, race, religion/spirituality, gender, gender identity, sexual orientation, marital status/partnership, language preference, socioeconomic status, or any basis proscribed by law" (p. 9). In addition, counselors are encouraged to use appropriate language that is clearly understandable by clients. When difficulty with a client's ability to understand occurs, counselors should "provide the necessary services (e.g., arranging for a qualified interpreter or translator)" to help clients comprehend information (ACA, 2014, p. 4). Addressing individual needs and services for victims of sexual assault who present with special needs is a crucial part of a crisis counselor's work.

According to the 2013 National Protocol for Sexual Assault Medical Forensic Examinations, counselors who work with victims of sexual assault should educate themselves about various populations in their communities in order to increase the quality of services provided to victims with special needs. Examples of special services may include (1) interpreters for hearing-impaired victims; (2) special equipment and supplies to perform a SAFE for victims with physical disabilities (e.g., a hydraulic-lift exam table); and (3) interpreters for non-English–speaking victims.

Other special services may include an understanding of the influence of cultural values on the response of victims to sexual violence. Examples include (1) cultural values that discourage a woman from disrobing in the presence of the opposite sex, particularly during any medical examinations; (2) the belief that the loss of virginity prior to marriage is disgraceful to the entire family and causes the victim to be undeserving of an honorable marriage; and (3) an awareness that certain cultures (e.g., Indian tribes) may have their own laws and regulations addressing sexual assault. In addition to understanding cultural beliefs, counselors need to be aware of victims' personal needs and beliefs that may be different from their overall cultural beliefs. For example, some victims may choose to have friends or family present during any services provided, but victims with disabilities may be reluctant to report a sexual assault due to their ability to remain independent being challenged by family members. Special populations such as male; lesbian, gay, bisexual, and transgender (LGBT); disabled; and vulnerable adult victims may present with unique reactions after sexual violence. It is important for counselors to treat clients as individuals and try to understand their unique needs. Confidentiality may need to be specifically emphasized with male victims who are fearful of the effect any public disclosures may have due to social stigmas associated with male sexual assault. Counselors should work to develop comprehensive services to meet the needs of male victims, including becoming visible in the male community. Counselors should honor a male victim's wishes to have a particular gender provide services. Male victims are often very reluctant to seek support from friends and families and should be encouraged to seek professional help when needed.

LGBTQ and Sexual Violence

The lesbian, gay, bisexual, transgender, and queer (and/or questioning) (LGBTQ) population who have experienced violence can present with unique challenges. The CDC's (2010) National Intimate Partner and Sexual Violence Survey found that the prevalence of sexual violence, stalking, and intimate partner violence for individuals who identify as lesbian, gay, or bisexual is similar to that for heterosexuals. However, bisexual women experience higher rates of sexual violence over their lifetime. According to the CDC report, 44% of women who identify as lesbian and 61% of women who identify as bisexual experience rape, physical violence, and/or stalking by a partner over their lifetime. Twenty-six percent of gay men and 37% of bisexual men experience rape, physical violence, and/or stalking by a partner over their lifetime. Approximately 22% of bisexual women have been raped by a partner over their lifetime. In addition, of bisexual women who have been raped, almost half (48%) experienced their first completed rape between the ages of 11 and 17 years.

Counselors should be aware that LGBTQ clients can experience discrimination when they attempt to access services after a sexual assault. Because of the possibility of being rejected, victims may be reluctant to seek help from crisis services, hospitals, shelters, or law enforcement. The LGBTQ population can experience hate-related sexual violence, which can lead LGBTQ individuals to feel unsafe in many settings. In addition, they may have to deal with stereotypes that present them as overly sexualized, which may lead them to being treated dismissively as overreacting to an incident of sexual violence. Due to the fact that the LGBTQ community may be small and tightly connected, victims may fear they will be betrayed by other members of the community if they accuse another member or fear they may be "outed" with friends and family if they access services. Providing a safe and supportive environment to deal with their concerns, including the sexual violence as well as other challenges, is crucial to helping them deal effectively with sexual violence. Counselors may also consider becoming a "SafeZone" to demonstrate their acceptance of working with the LGBTQ population. For more information about becoming a SafeZone, visit www.gayalliance.org/programs/education-safezone/safezone-programs/. See Case Study 9.4, which considers sexual assault in the LGBT population.

CASE STUDY 9.4

What Is Sexual Assault? Jane's Story

Imagine that you are a counselor in a private practice. Jane is a 45-year-old female computer programmer who has initiated services with you for problems associated with stress at work. Jane tells you she is having difficulty dealing with the extremely competitive environment. Jane identifies as lesbian and has recently come out to her adult children from a previous marriage, who want little contact after her disclosure. Jane looks disheveled and tired when she comes into the session, often telling you she is lonely. Jane has recently ended her first same-sex relationship since divorcing her husband several years ago.

During one session, Jane discloses that she gets angry easily. Upon further exploration, Jane reveals several incidents when she became very angry with her then girlfriend. After arguing for weeks, Jane recalls slamming her fists into the wall and threatening to hit her girlfriend. Jane graphically describes how the last time they fought, she was angry with her girlfriend for staying out all night and insisted that she was cheating on her. Jane goes on to describe how their last fight was when her girlfriend came home late. She shares that during the fight, Jane grabbed her girlfriend by the throat, pushed her down to the floor, ripped her shirt off, and bit her breasts, then she pulled down her girlfriend's pants and penetrated her with her fingers. Jane's girlfriend ran out of their apartment crying and has only returned to get her personal items. She will not respond to Jane's calls or texts. Jane is remorseful but still blames her girlfriend for provoking her by cheating. However, she wants to make amends with her girlfriend.

Discussion Questions

1. Would this incident meet the definition of sexual assault?
2. If this incident does meet the definition of sexual assault, what type is described in the scenario?
3. Considering legal and ethical issues, are there any steps you are required to take as a mandated reporter in this case?
4. Would you incorporate a DSM-5 diagnosis for this client? Explain.
5. What treatment modality would you use with this client?
6. Talk about what personal issues would come up for you while listening to the client's story.
7. With a peer, role-play implementation of the task model for crisis assessment and intervention featured in Chapter 1.

MOTIVATORS FOR RAPE

In 1979, Nicolas Groth wrote the classic book *Men Who Rape*, which defines different types of rape. The book has been published multiple times and continues to be the definitive source for understanding the dynamics of rapists. Groth (2001) defined *rape* as a "pseudosexual act, complex and multidetermined, but addressing issues of hostility (anger) and control (power) more than passion (sexuality)" (p. 2). Sex occurs during rape, but it is also the method by which aggression is expressed. Groth discovered three basic motivators of rape: (1) power, (2) anger, and (3) sadism. Power accounts for the majority of rapes committed (55%), while anger accounts for 40%, and sadism accounts for 5%. Understanding the types of rape is important for understanding treatment for victims and perpetrators.

Analyzing the Three Motivators Behind Rape

POWER   The power-motivated rape, the most common, is one in which "sexuality becomes an expression of conquest" (Groth, 2001, p. 13). Power is the ultimate form of gratification for the rapist. Victims are viewed as possessions that are obtained through sex. Having sexual intercourse with the victim is the goal rather than only achieving power and control. Unlike anger or sadistic rapists, the power rapist may use only the amount of force necessary to subdue his victim. Methods used to subdue the victim may include verbal threats (e.g., telling the victim that she will be hurt if she does not cooperate), intimidation using a weapon, and physical violence when the victim does not cooperate. Victims may often be kidnapped, held captive, and subjected to repeated assaults.

ANGER   In anger-motivated rape, the sexual encounter is considered a hostile act, often leading to physical brutality (Groth, 2001). The force used in the rape may exceed what is necessary to subdue the victim and achieve the goal of sexual penetration. The perpetrator attacks the victim, often exhibiting strong forms of violence (e.g., grabbing, hitting, beating, tearing clothes). This type of attack may take two forms: (1) a surprise attack, catching the victim off guard, or (2) a manipulated approach during which the perpetrator demonstrates a charisma and confidence to make the victim feel secure, only to change, suddenly becoming angry and aggressive. Anger-motivated rapes are typically brief, with the primary objectives of hurting, humiliating, and demeaning the victim.

SADISM   The sadistic rapist, the most brutal but least common of the types identified by Groth, commits an act in which anger and power are eroticized. This type of rape integrates sexuality and aggression to form a "single psychological experience known as sadism" (Groth, 2001, p. 44). The main goal of the sadistic rapist is to achieve sexual gratification through inflicting pain. The assault may be a bizarre encounter, often including bondage or types of ritualistic incidents such as body washing of the victim, dressing a certain way, burning, or biting. Parts of the victim's body, other than the sex organs, may become the focus of injury by the rapist, and foreign objects may be used to penetrate the victim. Homicide may be the end result of the encounter, even leading to necrophilia (i.e., sex with dead bodies). Victims' bodies may be mutilated either during the rape or after they are killed. Sadistically motivated rapes are typically premeditated, with the rapist often preying on victims regarded as promiscuous. Based on the current diagnostic criteria in the DSM-5 (APA, 2013), a rapist, regardless of motivational type, may be misdiagnosed as a sexual sadist. However, there is no support in the literature that suggests a sexual sadist is more likely to be a rapist.

PERPETRATORS OF SEXUAL VIOLENCE

When discussing sexual violence, it is important to consider treatment of not only the victims but also the perpetrators, in order to prevent future occurrences. In the sections that follow, the prevalence, characteristics, and treatment options regarding perpetrators of sexual violence are described.

Prevalence and Characteristics of Sexual Violence Perpetrators

The majority of sexual violence is perpetrated by males. According to the Bureau of Justice Statistics (2008), almost 98% of offenders are male, with only 2% being female. More than 40% of male offenders are over the age of 30 years. The vast majority (85%) of these perpetrators used no weapons during the assaults. In the assaults that used weapons, firearms were typically used. According to the Bureau of Justice Statistics, an examination of four datasets (i.e., arrests in the FBI's Uniform Crime Reports, state felony court convictions, prison admissions, and the National Crime Victimization Survey) revealed that sex offenders are older (over 30) and more likely to be White than are other violent offenders.

According to Groth (2001), several misconceptions exist about rapists: (1) rapists are sexually compulsive males who see women as provocative and malicious; (2) rapists are sexually frustrated males reacting to repressed stress; and (3) rapists are "demented sex-fiends" who harbor perverted desires. These misconceptions assume that the perpetrator's primary motivation is based on sexual needs and desires and that rape is the method for gratifying these desires. In reality, the rape of an adult is based on the nonsexual needs of the perpetrator, which include power and control, rather than sexual needs. The basic characteristics of perpetrators who commit power, anger, and sadistically motivated rapes are detailed below.

PERPETRATORS OF POWER-MOTIVATED RAPE   A power-motivated rapist may be attempting to validate strength and control in compensation for feelings of inadequacy. Like the perpetrator of anger rape, a power rapist finds little sexual gratification with the act; unlike the anger rape perpetrator, however, the power rapist may have fantasized about or planned the event. The fantasy may include a desire that the victim will not protest and will find the sexual prowess difficult to resist. When the victim does resist, the act is disappointing to the perpetrator because the fantasy does not come to fruition. At this point, the aggressor may feel the need to experience another rape in order to continue to pursue the fantasy. The power rape diverges from the anger rape in that the power rape may be premeditated, with the perpetrator often searching for victims or acting on opportunities. Victims of the power rape may be the same age as or younger than the perpetrator and are chosen based on availability, accessibility, and vulnerability. The power rapist may deny that the encounter was forced, often believing that the victim actually enjoyed the encounter. The rapist may attempt to make a kind gesture following the encounter as a way to discredit the victim.

PERPETRATORS OF ANGER-MOTIVATED RAPE   As described earlier, the purpose of an anger-motivated rape is to hurt, humiliate, or demean the victim. Methods employed by an anger rapist include both physical violence and verbal aggression. This rapist, however, finds that physical and verbal aggressions alone do not meet the desire and need for power and control, and sex becomes a weapon through which to release anger. Anger rape may also include other acts thought by the rapist to be particularly objectionable, such as sodomy or fellatio; or humiliating, such as urinating or ejaculating onto the victim. This rapist may have difficulties with an erection and may find little sexual gratification with the act. Anger-motivated rapes are typically brief, often unplanned by the rapists, and not a focus of the rapists' fantasies prior to the act.

PERPETRATORS OF SADISTICALLY MOTIVATED RAPE   The sadistically motivated rapist finds pleasure with the torment, anguish, suffering, and pain of the victim. The main goal of the sadistic rapist is to achieve sexual gratification through inflicting pain, even finding pleasure in the victim's futile resistance. The sadistically motivated rape is often premeditated, and the perpetrator goes to great lengths to avoid detection, often wearing gloves, wearing disguises, or blindfolding victims. A sadistically motivated rapist is frequently considered a psychopath, although the perpetrator is often married and employed and can appear personable and friendly.

Treatment of Sex Offenders

Because there is no evidence-based guidance about the most effective approaches to working with female sexual offenders (Center for Sex Offender Management, 2007), the primary focus of this treatment section will be on male offenders, with "sex offender" referring to a male unless specifically stated otherwise. When considering treatment for sex offenders, counselors should consider three aspects: (1) client dynamics, (2) treatment setting, and (3) treatment modality (Groth, 2001). First, client dynamics must be assessed through a comprehensive psychological evaluation that includes demographics, family background, medical history, education level, military history, interpersonal development (e.g., social, sexual, and marital information), occupational history, and criminal history. In addition, assessments should include behavioral observations, field investigations, medical examination, and psychometric examinations. The clinical assessment must obtain information about the perpetrator's sexual behavior, including premeditation, victim selection, style of attack, accompanying fantasies, role of aggression, sexual behavior (contact, duration, dysfunction), mood state, contributing factors (stressors), acceptance of responsibility, and recidivism and deterrence.

Second, appropriate treatment settings should be considered (Groth, 2001). Most offenders enter the mental health system through either the criminal justice or health care systems. The perpetrator may have been hospitalized for a mental illness or referred by the courts for treatment. Treatment facilities may typically specialize in the treatment of sex offenders and offer either inpatient or outpatient treatment. Group counseling may be the primary method of delivery of services in order to provide confrontation to a client population that may be prone to denial.

Lastly, there are specific treatment modalities that may be effective when treating sex offenders. However, it is important to recognize that no single treatment modality has been found to be the most effective treatment for sex offenders (Groth, 2001). Counselors should consider court requirements and the specific needs of each client to determine a course of treatment and possibly combine treatments in order to find a successful plan of action. Available treatment modalities include counseling, psychoeducation, behavior modification and cognitive-behavioral approaches, and incapacitation.

COUNSELING   Various methods of counseling are used to treat sex offenders. Individual counseling, group counseling, family counseling, and marital counseling are all used to help clients develop insight into their inappropriate behavior and choices, which are typically thought to be based on internal and emotional conflicts (Groth, 2001). Although counseling may be the most common treatment for sex offenders, it has several limitations. First, there is no clear evidence that this type of treatment works, particularly in isolation. Second, clients' intellectual functioning can affect their ability to develop insights related to their behavior; in addition, their ability to think abstractly, as well as their level of self-awareness, is crucial to the success of counseling. Third, the ability to develop a counseling relationship with clients is important. It is highly possible that this population is distrustful of any professional perceived as punitive. If clients have been required to attend counseling by a third party (e.g., by a judge), the challenge to developing a relationship increases.

PSYCHOEDUCATION   Life-skills training involves focusing on several areas where deficiencies may exist, such as sex education, social skills, empathy skills, and emotional regulation (Groth, 2001). Sex education can help the sex offender understand normal sexual functioning, as most experience sexuality in a dysfunctional way. Social skills training allows sex offenders to understand healthy relationships and develop improved interpersonal skills. Empathy-building skills help the sex offender develop sensitivity to people and recognize the needs of others. Possible techniques for inducing empathy include imitation, imagination (e.g., place yourself in someone else's shoes), or simple identification of emotions (e.g., I feel upset when someone else feels upset). What is important in a treatment program is that offenders *act* empathetic, rather than actually *feel* empathetic (Ward & Durrant, 2013). Emotional regulation is important for helping sex offenders cope with anger and aggression, which they typically release via a sexual assault. Relaxation techniques may also be used to address their feelings of frustration.

BEHAVIOR MODIFICATION AND COGNITIVE-BEHAVIORAL APPROACHES   Behavior modification for sex offenders primarily involves aversive conditioning in which a sexual response (such as an erection) is repeatedly paired with a noxious event, such as an electric shock or unpleasant smell (Groth, 2001). One behavior modification technique is to have an offender masturbate to ejaculation while fantasizing about an appropriate, nondeviant sexual encounter and partner; then, postorgasm, to have the offender continue to masturbate for an additional hour to a fantasy involving his preferred (and deviant) partner or sexual encounter, thus pairing the pleasurable experience with a socially appropriate partner and the uncomfortable experience with the behavior to be extinguished (Miller-Perrin & Perrin, 2007). Another behavior modification technique is covert sensitization in which guided imagery is used to help the client imagine his offense and then imagine a frightening or disgusting event. In both of the treatment modalities, repeating the techniques until the behavior is extinguished is the key to success. Although aversion therapy is commonly used, there is debate over whether it produces permanent results (Laws & Marshall, 2003).

CBT has also been used to treat offender populations, targeting cognitive distortions, deviant sexual practices and preferences, concurrent nonsexual behavioral and social challenges, and relapse prevention (Jennings & Deming, 2013). The Sex Offender Treatment and Evaluation Project (SOTEP) is a cognitive-behavioral treatment program for sex offenders in California (see Marques, Wiederanders, Day, Nelson, & van Ommeren, 2005) that has tracked participants longitudinally for 8 years. Results are mixed, with no statistical difference in rates of recidivism between participants and nonparticipants. However, the treatment has been associated with a significant reduction of reoffending in individuals who exhibit high levels of motivation and complete program goals, suggesting that there is potential for cognitive-behavioral approaches to reduce reoffending with at least some segment of sex offenders, those who are heavily motivated (D'Orazio, 2014).

Sex Offender-Specific (SOS) treatment groups should seek to support and reinforce prosocial behavior as well as facilitate healthy social interactions. According to Jennings and Deming (2013), cognitive behavioral techniques for such groups should effectively address the "behavioral" side of CBT. Behaviorally focused techniques include those that prompt group members to engage in self-disclosure, encourage members to identify problem behaviors, enhance members' self-esteem and empathy, and support members in managing deviant thoughts.

INCAPACITATION   Incapacitation for the sex offender can take several forms, including neurosurgery, surgical castration, and imprisonment/institutionalization. Neurosurgery involves removing parts of the hypothalamus, which decreases male hormone production and diminishes sexual arousal and impulsive behaviors. Surgical castration involves a sex offender losing the functions of his testes. Sex offenders may voluntarily undergo this procedure to help lessen sexual drives. Involuntary castration is extremely controversial, based on legal, moral, and ethical ambiguity. Imprisonment is the most common type of incapacitation (Groth, 2001), in which the confinement of the sex offender prevents commission of future acts.

See Case Study 9.5, which asks you to consider how to work with a perpetrator.

CASE STUDY 9.5

How Do You Work with a Perpetrator?

Refer back to Case Study 9.2, and now consider that James presents at the mental health center as your next appointment. Although he has not been charged with a sexual assault, he is disturbed by what he did to Sherry. After the incident, he was afraid Sherry would report him to the staff and that he would be asked to leave the rehab center. He knew he did not have any other place to go and would probably end up homeless if forced to leave. He asked the rehab center staff to make an appointment for him at the local mental health center. He reported the incident to you in detail. Although he can discuss the details of what he calls "the incident," he reports feeling as if he was outside of his body looking down at what was going on. He says he doesn't know why he did what he did to Sherry, who is someone he really cares about. He has tried to call Sherry, but she will not answer the phone. He would like to apologize to her but he is concerned she will never talk to him again. He is asking you to help him figure out what to do.

Discussion Questions

1. What additional information would you like to know about James through your initial interview?
2. What information would be helpful in understanding how you will work with James?
3. In this case, how would you proceed to work with James?
4. Discuss any ethical issues you need to consider when working with James.

TREATMENT FOR FEMALE OFFENDERS   Although there is little evidence-based guidance regarding treatment of female sex offenders, female perpetrators have higher rates and more severe experiences of sexual victimization than do male perpetrators (Center for Sex Offender Management, 2007). Treatment, therefore, may need to address the trauma that these female perpetrators (and male perpetrators who may have sustained similar sexual abuse) have encountered. Thus, while addressing victimization issues, it is important for clinicians to be empathetic regarding the abuse that perpetrators have sustained without minimizing or excusing the sexual offenses that they have committed. In treating any perpetrator of rape, the priority of treatment must be focused on the perpetrated act in the attempt to decrease the rate of recidivism.

Recidivism Rates of Adult Sex Offenders

As with any population, the overall recidivism rate for adult sex offenders is categorized by the type of sexual offense. Accurate recidivism rates are difficult to find because sexual crimes often go unreported to authorities. Thus, rates are based on arrest and re-arrest records of sexual offenders. Many studies have suggested that the older a victim is, the less likely the offense will be reported (U.S. Department of Justice, 2014b). While it would be easy to assume that sexual offenders have high rates of sexual recidivism, sex offenders are actually more likely to be charged with non–sex-related crimes later on. However, research also states that a former sex offender charged with a nonsexual crime may have been motivated by sexual pleasure (U.S. Department of Justice, 2014b). A Bureau of Justice Statistics study conducted by Langan, Schmitt, and Durose (2003) found that at a 3-year follow-up of 9,691 sex offenders released from prison, 5.3% were re-arrested for *sexual* crimes; 17.1% were re-arrested for violent crimes; and 43% were re-arrested for other crimes (U.S. Department of Justice, 2014b).

Studies show that treatment, specifically cognitive-behavioral and relapse-prevention approaches, show significant differences in sexual recidivism rates between treated and nontreated sex offenders. Oliver, Wong, and Nicholaichuk (2008) found that sex offenders who received treatment ($N = 472$) had sex-related recidivism rates of 11.1% at 3 years, 16.9% at 5 years, and 21.8% at 10 years; by contrast, nontreated sex offenders ($N = 265$) had sex-related recidivism rates of 17.7% at 3 years, 24.5% at 5 years, and 32.3% at 10 years (U.S. Department of Justice, 2014b). When interventions are used to treat this population, it is important to recognize that certain treatments are effective in reducing rates of sexual recidivism and some are not. Sex-related recidivism rates for some sex offenders who have received appropriate treatments are more likely to decrease compared with rates for sex offenders who have not received treatment.

Children and Adolescents as Sexual Perpetrators

When defining sexual problem behaviors in children and adolescents, professionals must consider the developmental level of the individual(s), the environment, and the context before prosecuting and treating the juvenile—sexual problem behaviors and consequences do not fit into a "one size fits all" model.

What is inappropriate sexual behavior for children and adolescents? There is no definitive answer to that question; however, the most accurate way to answer the question is to assess what is developmentally appropriate verbally, physically, and cognitively for the individual:

> When assessing these behaviors, professionals should pay attention to the context of the behaviors. Of particular importance is to determine whether the children engaged in the behaviors are of similar age, size, and developmental levels. If there are no power differentials between the children, and if the participation of the children is mutual and voluntary, it may be considered normative developmental behavior. (Russell, 2014, p. 1060)

To better understand and treat juvenile sex offenders (JSOs), it is important to be familiar with etiology as it relates to the "development, onset, and maintenance of sexually abusive behavior in this population" (U.S. Department of Justice, 2014b, p. 181). An excellent summary of etiology research on five areas that contribute to the increased likelihood of sexual offending behaviors is available on pp. 186–187 of the *Sex Offender Management Assessment and Planning Initiative* report (U.S. Department of Justice, 2014b): www.smart.gov/SOMAPI/pdfs/SOMAPI_Full%20Report.pdf.

Prior to creating a treatment plan, it is essential for counselors to assess whether the sexual behavior problems are secondary to a trauma or diagnostic disorder (e.g., conduct disorder). "Understanding maltreatment history, as well as the consequences of that history is an essential aspect of correct assessment and treatment of [J]SOs" (Pullman & Seto, 2012, p. 208). If the sexual behavior is secondary to abuse, treatment will focus on the behavior as a symptom. JSOs have more in common with nonsexual offending juvenile delinquents than with adult sex offenders (U.S. Department of Justice, 2014b).

Sex Offender Registry

In 2006, Congress passed the Adam Walsh Child Protection and Safety Act (AWA) "to protect children from sexual exploitation and violent crime, to prevent child abuse and child pornography, to promote Internet safety, and to honor the memory of Adam Walsh and other child crime victims." Title I of the AWA established the Sex Offender Registration and Notification Act (SORNA). SORNA allows the public to look up information on and track registered sex offenders for life. Information available to the public includes the offender's name, photograph, current and past address of residence, and the crime for which the individual was convicted (e.g., sexual act and sexual contact [any type or degree of genital, oral, or anal penetration, or any sexual touching of or contact with a person's body, either directly or through the clothing]; specified offenses against minors; possession, production, or distribution of child pornography).

As part of the SORNA requirements states must comply with, juveniles 14 years of age and older are adjudicated delinquent for certain sex offenses. However, it is up to the state to determine the age at which the juvenile will be eligible or mandated to register (some states do not require a minimum age). Moreover, certain states require the juvenile offender to remain on the registry for life, without eligibility for removal. That means that once the JSO turns 18 years of age, his or her information will be moved to the adult sexual offender (ASO) registry, where it will remain for life and be available for the public to view online. SORNA offenders include convicted juveniles who were tried as adults. Unlike adults convicted of a sexual offense, SORNA does not require all juveniles to be registered for *all* types of sexual offenses. Instead, SORNA requires registration "only for a defined class of older juveniles who are adjudicated delinquent for committing particularly serious sexually assaultive crimes (or attempts or conspiracies to commit such crimes)" (U.S. Department of Justice, 2014a, p. 20).

Originally, the juvenile court system had a goal of making decisions that were best for the child and to help guide the "juvenile offender toward life as a responsible, law abiding adult" (U.S. Department of Justice, Office of Sex Offender Sentencing, Monitoring, Apprehending, Registering, and Tracking [SMART], 2015, p. 2). However, through the years, the justice system has blurred the lines between what consequences are appropriate for juveniles offenders as compared with adult offenders.

Two factors determine whether an individual will be tried in court as an adult or juvenile: "(1) the age of the offender at the time of the offense, and (2) the specific offenses with which a juvenile is charged" (U.S. Department of Justice, SMART, 2015, p. 4). In addition, the severity and type of offense the juvenile is being charged with influences the prosecutor's decision. Because the age of the offender cannot be altered, ultimately it is the prosecutor's decision as to how the offender will be classified (adult or juvenile). How the offender is classified will affect the course of action through the entire judicial process with possible lifetime consequences. *However*, even if an offender is not the legal age of an adult (an age set by the state), 49 out of the 50 states have implemented at least one procedure that provides a way for a juvenile to be tried and charged as an adult for a serious sex offense (U.S. Department of Justice, SMART, 2015). The three methods states may use to try a juvenile as an adult are as follows:

- *Legislative Waiver:* States that use this method mandate that juveniles (of a certain age) charged with certain serious crimes *will be prosecuted* in adult criminal court.
- *Prosecutorial Waiver:* States that use this method provide the prosecutor with either full discretion in deciding whether to directly file in adult court, or, upon motion of a prosecutor (and sometimes the court *sua sponte*) in juvenile court, mandate that the case *will* be transferred from juvenile court for trial in adult criminal court.
- *Judicial Waiver:* This method is the most common. Upon motion of a prosecutor (and sometimes the court *sua sponte)*, a transfer hearing is conducted in juvenile court to determine whether the juvenile is amenable to further treatment and rehabilitation through the juvenile court system, and whether the juvenile should be transferred for trial in adult criminal court. Generally speaking, if the juvenile court finds that the juvenile is no longer amenable to treatment or rehabilitation in juvenile court, that juvenile will be transferred for trial as an adult (pp. 5–6).

A report by the Association for the Treatment of Sexual Abusers (ATSA, 2006) states, "policies placing children on public sex offender registries or segregating children with SB[P] may offer little or no actual community protection while subjecting children to potential stigma and social disadvantage" (p. 2). Emotions drive decisions, especially when considering the consequences for sex offenders. However, the long-term implications of allowing emotions to dictate laws are neither ethical nor effective. For example, JSOs have more in common with nonsexual offending juvenile delinquents than with adult sex offenders (U.S. Department of Justice, 2014b). Yet, the community and justice system continue to view JSOs and ASOs as equals in terms of legal consequences and treatment, even though research shows these are not effective for juveniles.

Treatment of Juvenile Sex Offenders

Targets of therapy for JSOs are to reduce problematic sexual behaviors and reduce the rates of recidivism. Previously, treatment for JSOs was similar to treatment for ASOs; however, through additional research and developments in the field, interventions individualized for JSOs were found to be effective. Meta-analysis not only suggests that treatment for JSOs reduces recidivism but also illustrates that treatment is cost-effective for taxpayers (U.S. Department of Justice, 2014b). Studies suggest that multisystemic therapy is effective in treating JSOs, and other treatments that include cognitive-behavioral interventions produce positive outcomes. Reitzel and Carbonell (2006) conducted a meta-analysis of nine studies on JSO treatment effectiveness with a sample size of 2,986 JSOs; the resulting average weighted effect size of 0.43 indicated that treatment has a statistically significant effect on recidivism. In another meta-analysis comparing seven recidivism studies, Winokur, Rozen, Batchelder, and Valentine (2006) found that JSOs who were treated had recidivism rates of 0 to 5%, while JSOs in the untreated comparison group had recidivism rates of 5 to 18%.

When sexual problem behaviors are identified early and treatment is introduced, the outcome can be very effective. Caregiver involvement in counseling is a core component, especially when treating JSOs who are 12 years old and younger. Counselors educate caregivers about providing supervision and creating a nonsexualized environment (e.g., change clothes with door closed, monitor what is on the television). "The enhancement of behavior management skills in parents may be far more important in the treatment of sexually abusive behaviors in children than traditional clinical approaches" (U.S. Department of Justice, 2014b, p. 249). Age-appropriate sex education should be a focus of treating sexual behavior problems with the child or adolescent. In a 20-year follow-up study, Worling, Littlejohn, and Bookalam (2009) found that *specialized* treatment for JSOs helps produce significant reductions in sexual and nonsexual reoffending. Multiple studies have shown that using more general treatments that are also used with other juvenile delinquent populations are more effective than the sex offender–specific treatments commonly used in the juvenile justice system.

MULTISYSTEMIC THERAPY   Multisystemic therapy (MST) is a comprehensive approach that simultaneously applies individualized interventions in four domains: individual, family, peer, school, and community. Treating JSOs with MST is similar to treating nonjuvenile sex offenders (Borduin, Shaeffer, & Heiblum, 2009). MST is often used with a variety of adolescent populations. MST treatment for JSOs differs from MST treatment for other delinquent populations in that the counselor links how the offender's sexual behaviors relate to each of the four domains. Various objectives are outlined in each domain. Studies have found that compared with community-based treatment services, MST treatment for JSOs significantly reduces rates of reoffending (sexual and nonsexual) after an average 8- to 9-year follow-up (Pullman & Seto, 2012). In the context of social skills training, it is worth noting that some JSOs do not lack social skills; however, the individuals do lack an understanding of how to use these skills in a socially acceptable manner.

COGNITIVE BEHAVIORAL THERAPY   Treating children and adolescents with sexual behavior problems using brief CBT significantly reduces the risk of sexual offending in the future (Pullman & Seto, 2012). Using CBT, counselors should focus on cognitive restructuring—"attacking" the antecedent and consequent (self-reinforcing) thought after engaging in the sexual offending behavior. Restructuring the antecedent will help the JSO refrain from engaging in the behavior. In addition, treatment should help alter the thoughts the individual may have after acting out on the behavior to create a "disconnect" between the self-reinforcing thoughts and sexually problematic behaviors.

RATIONAL EMOTIVE BEHAVIOR THERAPY   Rational emotive behavior therapy (REBT) is also effective with treating JSOs because it includes the emotional aspect in addition to the cognitions and behaviors—helping the individual challenge irrational thoughts, regulate emotions, and change behaviors. Adding the emotional aspect of REBT helps JSOs identify the feelings associated with the consequences of engaging in sexually problematic behaviors in relation to the juvenile's beliefs.

OVERVIEW OF THE ELEMENTS OF CRISIS INTERVENTION RELATED TO SEXUAL VIOLENCE

When dealing with crises related to sexual violence, it is important to recognize that victim reactions will vary and that no one reaction necessarily points to pathology. Victims of sexual violence may have many different reactions among the spectrum to their particular trauma; however, it is important to remain vigilant for symptoms of common disorders that may result from sexual violence, such as PTSD. Counselors may also pay close attention to the symptoms of rape trauma syndrome listed in Table 9.1 of this chapter.

Interventions employed during a crisis situation embody a range of theories and techniques, as well as a range of times from short-term preventive measures to long-term treatment measures. Counselors should be aware that when working with crisis and victims of traumatic situations, they may be opening themselves up to compassion fatigue, burnout, or even vicarious trauma. Counselors also should be mindful of their own reactions to and history of traumatic events and practice consistent self-care in order to avoid vicarious trauma with this population.

Summary

Sexual violence is a broad term used to describe an unwanted sexual act that is perpetrated on an individual via force or manipulation without the individual's consent. Sexual violence can take many forms, including rape, sexual harassment, intimate partner violence, and stalking. These crimes continue to be underreported despite emerging social and legal implications for perpetrators (e.g., the Violence Against Women Act, "shield laws"). According to the Rape, Abuse and Incest National Network (RAINN, 2015), a sexual assault occurs every 107 seconds in the United States. Victims of sexual violence are a significant proportion of society, with some reports estimating that at least 20% of women and up to 10% of men are sexually victimized in their lifetimes. The definitions of sexual violence vary from state to state, so it is important for counselors to be knowledgeable about legislation, resources, and best practices for working with survivors of sexual violence in their state and community.

Sexual assault is a type of sexual violence characterized by an attack or attempted attack involving unwanted sexual contact between the victim and the offender. It includes the use of force, but also verbal threats of an attack or threat of force. Rape is a type of sexual assault and is defined as forced sexual intercourse, which may take many forms.

Myths regarding rape still exist and should be debunked when working with victims of this crime. Those myths include the idea that a victim of rape was "asking for it" based on provocative dress or behavior, as well as the notion that only strangers in dark alleys commit sexual assaults.

Counselors should be knowledgeable about the three main motivators of rape: power, anger, and sadism. More recently, there have been growing concerns in the United States about sex trafficking, also discussed in this chapter. These are important concepts for both clinical counseling and school counseling.

The effects of sexual violence can manifest physically, behaviorally, emotionally/psychologically, or in combination. It is important to understand that not all victims of sexual violence will react the same way. While some may show immediate physical, cognitive-behavioral, or psychological problems, others may appear without symptoms. One responsibility of a crisis counselor is to provide support while keeping ethical and legal guidelines, and respecting a client's right to decide whether to report sexual violence. Counselors should also be aware of the possible increase in substance use following a sexual assault, as many victims use substances as a way of emotional "numbing," which can heighten the chance of developing a substance addiction following an attack. Primarily, clients need empathetic understanding, abuse-specific cognitive-behavioral strategies, and connection to resources in the community that best fit their needs.

Evidence-based treatments for victims of sexual violence include psychological first aid (PFA), trauma-focused cognitive-behavioral therapy (TF-CBT), cognitive processing therapy (CPT), prolonged exposure therapy, EMDR therapy, and stress inoculation therapy. Counselors should always take ethical and legal issues into account and consult the *ACA Code of Ethics* throughout treatment. Counselors should also pay close attention to any multicultural issues that may arise with special populations, such as LGBTQ clients and clients with disabilities.

Sexual offenders who perpetrate sexual violence are often perceived as a highly difficult population to treat. Offenders may be men, women, or children/adolescents. However, through education about the motivations of these individuals, counselors may be able to better implement treatment strategies or programs to rehabilitate sexual offenders. When working with perpetrators of sexual violence, the main goal is to reduce recidivism rates, or the chance of reoffending. For some offenders, it will be important to focus on trauma that the offender has experienced. Evidence-based treatments for perpetrators of sexual violence include counseling (individual, group, family, marital), psychoeducation, and CBT with a focus on behavior modification.

10 Child Sexual Abuse

Carrie Wachter Morris and Elizabeth Graves

PREVIEW

Child sexual abuse is one of the most underreported crimes, with survivors facing a number of potential physical, psychological, cognitive, behavioral, emotional, and spiritual consequences. Crisis counselors who intervene with victims of child sexual abuse need to be aware of the multitude of challenges these individuals face, best practices for treatment, and support services available in the local community. In this chapter, child sexual abuse will be defined, signs and symptoms described, and intervention strategies discussed. In addition, this chapter addresses perpetrators of child sexual abuse, their patterns of behavior, and common treatment options.

CHILD SEXUAL ABUSE

Child sexual abuse (CSA) affects children, families, and communities worldwide. Despite national efforts in the United States through the National Child Abuse and Neglect Data System (NCANDS) and the National Incidence System (NIS), exact statistics regarding the number of children and families affected by CSA are difficult to derive. Estimates of average annual CSA cases range from 60,956 (U.S. Department of Health and Human Services, Administration for Children and Families, Administration on Children, Youth and Families, Children's Bureau [U.S. Department of Health and Human Services], 2015) to 180,500 (Sedlak et al., 2010), and even these reports are thought to be underestimates. NCANDS data include only the reports of state Child Protective Services (CPS) workers, while the NIS contains data from CPS agencies and community professionals from nationally representative, randomly sampled counties. The NIS–4, which is considered the most comprehensive collection of child abuse and neglect data, does not include incidences of sexual abuse by perpetrators who are not in parental or caregiving roles. Although most of the sexual abuse cases that come to the attention of CPS involve intrafamilial relationships, it should be noted that most reported perpetrators of CSA are not immediate caregivers but non-family (extrafamilial) individuals known to the child or strangers (U.S. Department of Health and Human Services, 2015). Of the extrafamilial CSA incidences, only 20% are perpetrated by strangers, which means that the vast majority of extrafamilial CSA occurs at the hands of individual(s) whom the child or adolescent knows

(Hassan, Killion, Lewin, Totten, & Gary, 2015). Thus, many CSA cases would not fall into the definitions used for data collection of these national samples, leading to an underestimate of CSA incidents.

In addition to those victims who do not meet an agency definition, children who fail to come to the attention of these agencies and individuals are not included in estimates. Children and adolescents who have been sexually abused but have not disclosed the abuse, those who have disclosed the abuse but have not had that disclosure come to the attention of CPS, and those who have disclosed the abuse but have not had it substantiated are not included in the official count.

Recent studies have found that about 20% of females and less than 30% of males who reported being sexually abused as children ever disclosed the abuse to another person. When disclosures were made, 63% of females and 45% of males told friends their own age rather than parents, teachers, or mandated reporters (Priebe & Svedin, 2010). Thus, the incidence rates of CSA reported by government agencies are likely to be significantly lower than the actual incidence rates of CSA. Also, it should be noted that although the average percentage of substantiated child maltreatment cases that involved CSA was only 9.0% (U.S. Department of Health and Human Services, 2015), state reports of substantiated cases of CSA ranged from 2.7% to 62.5% of all substantiated child maltreatment cases. These data suggest a wide variability of substantiation among states and perhaps point to an underlying variability in the veracity with which these charges are pursued. In summary, there are considerable complications with determining incidence rates for CSA.

Determining lifetime prevalence rates for CSA is no easier task. Although more conservative agencies report that 20% of women and 10% of men are sexually victimized in their lifetime, modern researchers have found significantly higher numbers. For example, de Tychey, Laurent, Lighezzolo-Alnot, Garnier, and Vandelet (2015) estimated that one in three females experiences CSA; Young, Harford, Kinder, and Savell (2007) estimated that 42% of a sample of female public university students and 31% of a sample of male public university students were victims of CSA; and Stander, Olson, and Merrill (2002) reported CSA in 26% of males in a sample of Navy recruits. Decades ago, renowned CSA researcher David Finkelhor predicted that one day, as social barriers to males' CSA disclosure ameliorate, prevalence rates for CSA in males and females would match (Finkelhor, 1979). This prediction was radical at the time; today, it is becoming a reality. Complete Think About It 10.1.

THINK ABOUT IT 10.1

Think about the ramifications of CSA more deeply. If it is true that prevalence for sexual abuse in both male and female minor children is close to 1 in 3 in the United States, how might this pervasive, silenced history of abuse be affecting our culture? We might ask ourselves what remembered or repressed abuse memories linger in the conscious and unconscious minds of our nation's citizenry, and how those histories might impact the fears, thoughts, decisions, behaviors and experiences of those with whom we work—both as service providers and as colleagues. Specifically, how might our clients' thoughts, feelings, behaviors, and experiences stemming from childhood sexual abuse present subtly in counseling, independent of disclosure? How can we sensitize ourselves to those presentations?

Prevention of Child Sexual Abuse

Child advocates widely recognize that the best way to lower the staggering numbers of CSA is for those agencies, institutions, and individuals that serve children and families to focus their efforts and resources on preventing CSA. Schools and some community organizations across the United States have responded to this charge by offering annual group instruction to students in recognizing potentially dangerous adult behaviors, enforcing personal physical and psychological boundaries, getting away from those who violate those boundaries, and reporting odd adult behavior and boundary violations to caring and trusted adults. Although programs such as "Stranger Danger" and "Funny Tummy Feelings" have increased the number of after-the-fact disclosures of sexual abuse, it is unclear whether such programs are effective in preventing abuse. Still, those seeking to prevent sexual abuse in children should use prevention programs that involve children acting out for themselves and demonstrating for other children how to enforce personal boundaries with, get away from, and report such persons.

One recent and popular CSA prevention initiative places less emphasis upon the refusal skills of children and more upon the awareness and training of adults who work with children. Darkness to Light (2016) is an organization that seeks to educate multiple sectors of the community about CSA trends, prevalence, warning signs, child advocacy, prevention, and interventions under the presumption that it takes a whole community to keep children safe and protected from perpetrators. Using Darkness to Light's CSA prevention training program called "Stewards of Children," schools and community groups (e.g., club sports, youth groups, Scouts) across the United States are teaching school- and group-based CSA prevention facilitators to train employees to provide oversight of child safety procedures. More information is available at www.d2l.org.

Prevalence of Child Sexual Abuse by Gender, Age, Race, and Ability

Females appear to be the victims of CSA more often than males (see Aaron, 2012). This pattern has been consistent over time, with multiple iterations of the NIS reporting rates and retrospective studies underscoring this gender differential. One study found that about 40% of college undergraduate females and 31% of males reported a history of CSA (Young et al., 2007). Presently in the United States, approximately 1 in 3 females and 1 in 6 males have reportedly experienced sexual abuse as children (Hopper, 2010). When considering the gender of victims, however, it is also important to keep in mind that males are significantly less likely to disclose CSA than are females (Sorsoli, Kia-Keating, & Grossman, 2008). Therefore, the statistics available may not yet represent the true differential in the rates of male and female victimization.

The average age of victimization varies, with sources reporting the mean age of onset between 7 and 12 years of age (Trickett, 2006), but national statistics indicate higher rates of substantiated abuse at higher ages—e.g., 12 to 15 years of age (U.S. Department of Health & Human Services, 2015). Therefore, it appears that individuals may be substantially at risk for CSA across their childhood and adolescent years.

Unlike gender and (potentially) age, race does not appear to be a differentiating characteristic in occurrence of CSA, with consistent rates of CSA victimization in children of all races (U.S. Department of Health and Human Services, 2009). White children, however, had a slightly higher proportion of reported sexual abuse at the hands of biological parents than did children of other racial or ethnic backgrounds. This could be due to higher incidence rates, but it could also be linked to factors such as a greater distrust of the systems involved in child protection or a reliance on less formalized support systems to address issues of CSA. Reporting by this group may also be higher.

Finally, children with certain disabilities appear more likely to be sexually victimized than other children. Specifically, children who are at increased risk are those with blindness, deafness, and intellectual disabilities. These groups have an increased prevalence of abuse, may be perceived as having lower credibility in the eyes of adults (Mitra, Mouradian, & McKenna, 2013), or may lack the ability to disclose abuse.

DEFINING CHILD SEXUAL ABUSE AND RELATED TERMS

In addition to the difficulty in tracking actual numbers of children and adolescents who have been sexually abused, there is no single agreed-on definition of CSA. Further complicating the process of defining CSA is how to distinguish it from statutory rape. In the section that follows, CSA and statutory rape are defined, with an explanation of the distinction between statutory rape and CSA and how statutory rape may be handled differently.

Definitions of Child Sexual Abuse

Definitions of CSA vary across states and advocacy organizations. Broader definitions may include any sexual activity with a minor where consent cannot be or is not granted (see the review in Collin-Vézina, Daigneault, & Hébert, 2013). Definitions used by some states or research groups may be more detailed and include only specific sexual behaviors (e.g., penetration), specific perpetrator groups (e.g., intrafamilial), or specific ages or age differences (e.g., an age difference of 4 years). These narrower definitions place other sexual acts (e.g., showing pornography to a child, exposing one's genitalia to a child) or perpetrator groups (e.g., neighbors, acquaintances, strangers) in categories such as child exploitation, child molestation, or statutory rape. In the Child Abuse Prevention and Treatment Act (CAPTA, Public Law No. 93-247), child abuse and neglect are limited to "a parent or caretaker," and CSA is defined as

> the employment, use, persuasion, inducement, enticement, or coercion of any child to engage in, or assist any other person to engage in, any sexually explicit conduct or simulation of such conduct for the purpose of producing a visual depiction of such conduct; or . . . the rape, and in cases of caretaker or inter-familial relationships, statutory rape, molestation, prostitution, or other form of sexual exploitation of children, or incest with children (p. 44).

CAPTA specifies that "child" is specific to all individuals under the age of 18 years for sexual abuse.

Although CAPTA does give a definition of CSA, age of consent differs from state to state, and even within the same state, ages of consent may differ for heterosexual and homosexual relationships and for males and females. It is important for counselors working with children and adolescents to be aware of the most recent legislation for the state(s) within which they practice regarding CSA, age of consent, mandated reporting laws regarding sexual behaviors, and relationships involving individuals under the age of consent. For the purposes of this chapter, *child sexual abuse* is defined as any sexual contact, behavior, or exposure for the purposes of sexual gratification of another individual that involves a child who is unable or unwilling to give consent.

It should be noted that a state-sanctioned or researcher-operationalized definition of CSA may have little in common with CSA survivors' perceptions of their experiences. For example, one 15-year-old who has sexual contact with a 20-year-old may perceive the experience as abusive, while another 15-year-old having sexual contact with a 20-year-old may not regardless of age, gender, consent at the time of the contact, or the presence of injury. Although clients' perceptions of their experiences cannot necessarily influence the mandate of practitioners to report events that meet legal criteria for abuse, those perceptions are important to integrate into the therapeutic treatment. Research has shown that outcomes for sexual abuse survivors are determined in part by survivor perceptions of the experience as abusive or gratifying and that the narratives about the experience can change over time (Hunter, 2010). Therefore, it is important to explore clients' perceptions of their sexual contact/abuse experience as counselors and work with them to create resilience. Complete Think About It 10.2 and Activity 10.1 to further explore these complex and sometimes confusing concepts.

Statutory Rape

Complicating the definition of CSA further is the delineation between CSA and statutory rape. Legally, CSA usually includes only those individuals who are in parental or caretaking roles (e.g., babysitter, teacher, coach) with the child or adolescent. Statutory rape, however, refers primarily to a relationship "between a juvenile and an adult that

---

THINK ABOUT IT 10.2

Think about the case of an adolescent boy having sex with a much older woman. Imagine that an adolescent male client with whom you have been working for some time discloses to you in a boastful tone that when he turned 16, his best friend's 42-year-old mother offered to "rid him of his virginity." He shares with you that he believes this is why he "gets the girls," because she taught him how to please the ladies well. The laws in your state require you to report this to law enforcement, which you do. The perception this client has of his experience, however, is not one of "abuse." What approach might you choose as you go about working with this client in the aftermath of his disclosure?

ACTIVITY 10.1

Find the legislation for three different states (including the one you hope to practice in) on CSA, statutory rape, and the age of consent for opposite- and same-sex relationships. Note the key definitions in the laws and whom the laws identify as prosecutable perpetrators of CSA, statutory rape, and sexual victimization. Pay particular attention to issues of gender, age discrepancies, and legal guardianship/designated caretakers.

is illegal under the age of consent statutes, but that does not involve the degree of coercion or manipulation sufficient to qualify under criminal statutes as a forcible sex crime" (Hines & Finkelhor, 2007, p. 302). Just as age of consent statutes may vary from state to state, legal definitions and terminology for statutory rape also vary from one state to another. The Rape, Abuse, and Incest National Network (RAINN) keeps an up-to-date list of a variety of laws by state on its website, at www.rainn.org. The website also includes rape and sexual assault definitions by state.

THE CYCLE OF CHILD SEXUAL ABUSE

CSA typically develops through a cycle of behavior (Bennett & O'Donohue, 2014). This process begins when a perpetrator identifies a child who may be an easy target due to some sort of neediness, passivity, or suggestibility. In most cases, once a child has been identified, the perpetrator will begin "grooming" the child for sexual abuse by starting with nonsexual contact and behavior and progressing slowly to more sexual activity and behavior. By enticing the child though reinforcement (e.g., toys, candy, ice cream, attention, distorted acts of affection) and punishment (e.g., anger, threats against the child or the child's loved ones), a child can be coerced into a sexually abusive relationship.

CSA can lead to intergenerational abuse. Although it may seem that adults who were sexually abused as children should have a lower rate of CSA incidence in their own children due to increased vigilance and heightened awareness of the danger of victimization, the opposite appears to be true. As compared with the children of parents who were not subject to CSA in childhood, children whose parents have a history of CSA may experience a higher rate of sexual abuse. The reason for the higher rate is not necessarily that parents with a history of CSA, in turn, abuse their own children. In fact, only a fraction of victims of CSA experience sexual interest in children as adults; even fewer become CSA perpetrating adults (Underwood, 2015). Rather, several other reasons may explain this higher risk. First, since interfamilial CSA perpetrators tend to abuse children across several generations of family members, children in such families are often at greater risk for CSA (see the review in Thomas et al., 2013). Second, it may be that these parents, having had their own physical and psychological boundaries violated as children, may be less apt to know and teach appropriate boundaries to their own children, or to detect when their children are already caught in the grooming process (Wearick-Silva et al., 2014). Furthermore, because CSA can affect victims' ability to establish and maintain intimate bonds well into adulthood, those who experienced CSA as children sometimes may be less able to develop the parent–child bond than other parents (Kim, Trickett, & Putnam, 2010) and, therefore, may be less able to detect that something is amiss. Victims from one generation may have internalized responsibility for their sexual abuse or do not understand that perpetrators of CSA are most likely repeat offenders. Psychoeducation about CSA, even at the crisis level, may be needed to help decrease intergenerational cycles of abuse.

SIGNS AND SYMPTOMS OF CHILD SEXUAL ABUSE

Children and adolescents who have experienced CSA may respond and react in a variety of ways, ranging from nonresponse to more severe reactions, including post-traumatic stress disorder (PTSD) symptomology (Amado, Arce, & Herraiz, 2015).

Given this range of reaction, it is important to view children or adolescents in the context of developmentally appropriate behavior patterns, giving special attention to significant deviations from those norms and from typical developmental behaviors and milestones.

For example, a kindergarten-aged boy who touches his penis in class or a 4-year-old girl who lifts up her dress in a grocery store may be exhibiting developmentally normal behavior. If that kindergarten boy, however, accompanies the touching of his penis with moaning or thrusting behaviors or if the 4-year-old girl lifts up her dress and rubs up against another individual in a seductive manner, those behaviors are not developmentally appropriate and may signify that those children have witnessed sexual behaviors or been the victims of CSA.

Furthermore, researchers have suggested that an effective method of evaluating children's sexual behaviors as normal or concerning is to evaluate the motivation behind the behavior (Chaffin et al., 2008). If the motivation appears to be curiosity and the behavior falls within a developmentally appropriate range, there may be little to fear. However, if the motivation appears to be coercion or compulsion, or if it is accompanied by physical or psychological distress, there may be good cause for alarm (Kellogg, 2010). Table 10.1 provides summaries of cues that may indicate CSA.

One notably consistent symptom of CSA history across this body of research literature is substance use. In fact, researchers have found consistently high rates of sexual abuse survivors in substance use treatment centers (Banducci, Hoffman, Lejuez, & Koenen, 2014) and homeless adolescent populations (Rosario, Schrimshaw, & Hunter, 2012).

Although most research indicates that CSA outcomes and symptoms tend to be remarkably similar in boys and girls (Yuce et al., 2015), a fair amount of evidence also suggests otherwise. When gender differences present, they tend not to be in terms of severity or magnitude but rather in the manner in which they manifest. Specifically, boys tend to act out or externalize their symptoms, while girls tend to internalize their symptoms (Sigurdardottir, Halldorsdottir, & Bender, 2014). This means that boys who have experienced CSA may be more likely to engage in aggressive, violent, or risky behaviors, while girls who have experienced CSA may be more likely to present with depression, anxiety, or self-harming behaviors.

Finally, it is important to note that researchers have found that some children who were victims of CSA present without symptoms at the time of their evaluations (Trask, Walsh, & DiLillo, 2011). Reasons for these asymptomatic presentations may include narrowness of symptomology being studied, symptoms that have not yet manifested, or children's perceptions that the CSA was not intolerable, was not threatening, or did not exceed their normal functioning. Nevertheless, what researchers in this field call *sleeper effects*—the tendency of symptoms to present over time and across many phases of life-span development—tend to be the norm for children who are either symptomatic or asymptomatic for CSA. As a result, it is standard practice for counselors to provide sexually victimized children (regardless of symptom presentation) with psychoeducational treatment that helps them express their feelings and understand their feelings as normal, create a plan to prevent revictimization, and educate children's caregivers about CSA.

TABLE 10.1 Cues That May Indicate Child Sexual Abuse

Symptom Domain	Potential Signs of CSA	
Behavioral cues	Difficulty in walking or sitting	Talk about being damaged
	Frequent vomiting	Attempting to run away
	Sexually explicit drawings/writing	Cruelty to animals (especially those that would normally be pets)
	Sexual interaction with others	
	In-depth sexual play with peers	Fire setting
	Sexual interactions with animals/ toys	Eating-disordered behavior
		Self-injurious behavior
	Exceptionally secretive behavior	Use of sexual language inappropriate to developmental level
	Extreme compliance or withdrawal	
	Overt aggression	
	Extremely seductive behavior	Sexual victimization of others
	Sudden nonparticipation in school activities	Masturbation (if masturbation behaviors include masturbating to point of injury; masturbating repetitively or obsessively; being unable to stop masturbating; making groaning or moaning noises while masturbating; thrusting motions while masturbating)
	Crying without provocation	
	Regressive behaviors (e.g., thumb sucking, clinging, separation anxiety)	
	Sudden onset of wetting or soiling	
	Sudden phobic behavior	
	Suicide attempt	
Cognitive cues	Drop in school performance	
	Suicidal ideation	
	More sexual knowledge than is appropriate	
	Fear of males or fear of females	
Physical cues	Complaints of genital or anal itching, pain, or bleeding	
	Blood or discharge on undergarments	
	Frequent psychosomatic illnesses	
	Pregnancy at young age	
	Sexually transmitted infections at young age	
	Older, more sexualized appearance than peers	
	Sleep disturbances, nightmares, night terrors	
Psychological cues	Feelings of low self-worth	
	Depression	
	Anxiety	
	Guilt	
	Shame	
	Hostility	
	Flashbacks	
	Nightmares	

INTERVENTION STRATEGIES FOR VICTIMS OF CHILD SEXUAL ABUSE

When working with victims of CSA, it is important that counselors understand the dynamics of not only their own personal work with the client but also how the counseling process might affect the legal and social services processes and professionals that might also be working with the child and family. Counselors must understand how the crisis or therapeutic relationship will act in concert with other support services for the child from the initial interview through the reporting and counseling process. Without a thorough understanding, counselors may impede the progress of legal proceedings. In the sections that follow, intervention strategies are discussed; however, counselors must become familiar with the local legal and social services entities and professionals with whom they will be interacting to understand local procedures and laws regarding CSA.

Initial Disclosure and Interviewing for Child Sexual Abuse

When working with a child or adolescent who has recently disclosed CSA, it is critical to both the success of treatment and potential prosecution of the perpetrator that counselors respond to the disclosure with informed intention; that is, the intent to do no further psychological harm to the victim with statements that may be perceived as blaming. Informed intention is applied to the verbal and nonverbal responses made directly to survivors as well as the steps taken in the aftermath of the disclosure to respond appropriately. According to Whiffen and MacIntosh (2005), the worst long-term outcomes for clients with histories of CSA are consistently found in those children who met with unsupportive verbal or nonverbal responses following their disclosure of sexual abuse. All too often, common responses to such disclosures tend to be disbelief (e.g., "It is hard to believe that Coach would do such a thing—everyone knows he's so good with kids"), blame ("If it was so awful for you, then why did you go back to that house the next day?" or "Perhaps if you weren't so flirtatious with her, this wouldn't have happened"), shame ("That is disgusting—I can't believe you were involved in all that"), or catastrophizing ("You're damaged goods now—you'll never be the same again"). The result of such responses tends to be that the feelings of guilt, self-blame, and low self-worth initiated during the grooming process and reinforced in the abuse process are further deepened and internalized in the victim. Both short-term and long-term outcomes for those receiving responses like these are poor.

The same is true for nonverbal responses to disclosure. Looks of skepticism, rolling of eyes, or a disapproving shaking of the head communicate disbelief, blame, and disgust. Affirmative responses to a child's disclosure of CSA include attentive body posture, empathic facial expression, nodding head with belief, and refraining from expressions of alarm or shock. When children receive affirmative responses such as these, they sense that they have done the right thing in reporting the abuse, feel trust that the adult they told will respond appropriately, and have hope that the abuse will cease.

Similarly, it is important that the counselors receiving the disclosure follow appropriate procedural guidelines. Counselors should not ask leading questions regarding the veracity or nature of the abuse. There are specific protocols that CPS workers and law enforcement officers use when working with children and adolescents who have reported abuse, and members of those agencies should be responsible for the investigation of the alleged abuse. Many communities have child advocacy centers in which trained forensic interviewers work in concert with CPS, law enforcement, medical officials, and counselors to interview the child only once and document the interview.

When making a report regarding abuse, CPS will want to know the child's directory information, what other children are in the home, the nature and extent of the abuse that has occurred, and any other information that may be cause for protective intervention on behalf of the child (Mason, 2013). While each state's procedures on reporting abuse can vary, gathering this information, with as much detail and accuracy as possible, is crucial in aiding CPS with its report and, consequently, in getting the proper help and protection for the child. Therefore, while it may be appropriate to ask some general probing questions, crisis counselors should not suggest or make inferences that CSA has occurred. A question such as "It sounds like this was a difficult weekend for you, and you seem really upset. Is there some way I can help you?" is an appropriate prompt. Conversely, "Did someone sexually abuse you this weekend?" and "Sometimes daddies touch little girls and make them feel uncomfortable. Did that happen to you?" are inappropriate prompts.

It is important for counselors to be sensitive to the fear, emotional fragility, or flat affect of children and adolescents who are making a disclosure of CSA. Often children and adolescents may be afraid of making the disclosure because of the potential ramifications of the disclosure. These fears may be the result of a promise of retaliation by the perpetrator for the disclosure (e.g., a threat to harm the child or a family member); a belief that the perpetrator may go to jail; a fear that the victim will be blamed for the perpetrator's removal from the home; and feelings of loyalty, attachment, or love for the perpetrator. In addition, the child or adolescent may appear to have an inappropriately flat affect or a matter-of-fact attitude. Such presentations may indicate the belief that the abuse is normal (e.g., a form of sex education, a ritual to initiate one into manhood/womanhood) or reflect the preferred manner of coping with the abuse (dissociative responses).

It is important when working with a child or adolescent who is disclosing CSA to help maintain a sense of control of the information that he or she gives and understand the steps involved in the reporting process. This could include involving the child or adolescent, as appropriate, in making the report to CPS or describing the steps in the process as clearly as possible. It is very important not to make promises that cannot be guaranteed or kept. Counselors may find it helpful to involve appropriate individuals (e.g., CPS social worker, law enforcement officer, medical personnel) in helping lay out when the child can expect to be interviewed, any physical examination that might take place, what the potential consequences may be for the perpetrator of the abuse, and what sort of process will be involved if the child is, in fact, removed from the home. Equally important is reiterating, even multiple times, that the child is not at fault, not in trouble, and not to blame in any way. This can help the child maintain some sense of control and stability, even in an unfamiliar circumstance. See Case Study 10.1, which provides insight into what this reporting process might look like.

It should be noted that in Case Study 10.1, Justin had an established counselor–client relationship with Marcus, and so he was aware of some of the details that he would need to make a report to CPS. In some instances (i.e., when a child in crisis is seen for the first time by a counselor with no previous knowledge of the child), more time and attention may need to be given to gathering some of the basic information needed to make a CPS report.

CASE STUDY 10.1

Crisis Intake with a Child Sexual Abuse Client: Eliminating Blame

Eight-year-old Marcus has been seeing Justin, his clinical mental health counselor, for the past 3 months. Marcus was referred to Justin by the boy's mother, who expressed concern that her son began wetting his bed about 10 months ago, responding to the slightest criticism with emotions incongruent with the situation at hand, and refusing to play with other children at home or school. While routinely discussing his week at the start of the session, Marcus discloses to Justin that his stepfather "hurt my penis again." Although Justin is stunned, he remains outwardly calm and focuses on simply reflecting Marcus's words as a prompt for the child to continue.

MARCUS:	Yeah. All that happened last week. And then . . . my stepdad hurt my penis again.
JUSTIN:	Your stepfather sometimes hurts your penis. And he did it again last week . . .
MARCUS:	Yeah . . . (*Long silence ensues.*)
JUSTIN:	(*Says nothing, but inclines his head downward as if to scoop up Marcus's eyes, which are fixed on the floor.*)
MARCUS:	It really hurts when he does it. But I'm not allowed to talk about it or else he'll hurt me worse. And he said he'd tell mama what I've done to him if I tell anyone.
JUSTIN:	He has told you that, if you tell, bad things will happen to you— that your mama will blame you for it all.
MARCUS:	(*Suddenly raising fear-filled eyes to meet Justin's; he is nodding emphatically.*) She will, too. I get blamed for everything bad that happens even when it's not my fault.
JUSTIN:	You're afraid that your mama won't understand—that she'll get mad at you. (*Pause.*) Here's the thing, Marcus. You and I know that it's not your fault. It's your stepdad's fault because he is the adult who is supposed to take good care of you—not hurt you. It's never okay for people to do what he's been doing to you.
MARCUS:	Yeah, but he makes me do stuff. Stuff that makes me feel sick. It's really bad what he makes me do—and I have to do it. I have to do whatever he says. (*He drops his eyes to the floor.*)
JUSTIN:	You're really scared of your stepdad. You do whatever he tells you so he won't hurt you worse. That tells me that you sure mustered up a lot of courage when you decided to tell me this today—and that was the right thing to do. (*Short silence.*) Although I'm really sad that your stepdad has been hurting you, I also feel really glad that you told me because that tells me that you trust me to do the right things to keep you safe.

MARCUS: (*Nodding, but with some uncertainty in his eyes.*) Does that mean you're going to tell mama? (*His expression conveys a look of both anxiety and hopefulness.*)

JUSTIN: (*Nodding.*) Your mama needs to know this has been happening to you because it is her job to keep you safe. There are also some other people who need to know, too—people whose job it is to protect kids when adults do things like hurt little boys' penises and do stuff that's wrong. Sometimes it takes a few important people knowing this stuff for it to stop and stay stopped.

MARCUS: (*Lets out a soft but high-pitched whine and starts to shake and cry.*)

JUSTIN: (*Leaning forward.*) I know it seems pretty scary right now to think about your mom finding out that this has been going on. I also know that, together, we can figure out the best way for her to learn this news today. I'll be right here with you, Marcus.

MARCUS: (*Continues to cry quietly as Justin waits; after a minute or so, he nods and lifts his head.*)

JUSTIN: I wonder if it would help to stand up and take a deep breath so we can think clearly about how best to do this . . .

Justin and Marcus stand up and do some breathing exercises that Justin often does with his minor clients to help them calm and center themselves. Justin explains that kids have told him things like this in the past and asks Marcus if he'd like to know what typically happens after they do. Marcus indicates he would like to know. Justin explains that he has a friend named Joan in Child Protective Services (and/or law enforcement office) that he tells these things to, that she takes kids' stories like this very seriously, and that she sometimes helps moms understand that it's never the kid's fault.

Justin explains that both Marcus's mom and Justin's friend Joan need to hear his story and asks how he would like for them to find out (who should tell the story, who should find out first). Marcus decides that he wants Justin to tell his mom for him, but that he wants to be in the room while he does. He says he doesn't care who talks to Joan or when she is told. Because Justin is not sure about how Marcus's mother will react, Justin decides to tell Marcus that he thinks it is a good idea to tell Joan first because she might be able to come over either now or sometime soon and help. Justin calls the designated law enforcement officer with whom he has a relationship of trust while Marcus is in the room, telling her that there is a little boy with him right now who has told him something that worries him and that she needs to hear. The officer is available and agrees to come to Justin's office.

Justin explains that he needs to speak to Marcus's mother now. Justin reinforces that Marcus has done the right thing by telling him and that his job as Marcus's counselor is to make sure that Marcus's mother understands it is not her son's fault. Justin goes to the lobby to meet the mother. Together, Justin and Marcus tell the mother that Marcus's stepdad has been "hurting his penis." When her look of shock turns to anger and she demands to know details, Justin intervenes to help the mother understand that Marcus is very afraid that she will be mad at him and that part of why he hasn't told this in the past is that he is afraid of being blamed for this—that the stepdad has told Marcus that all this is the boy's fault. Justin tells the mother that, in accordance with a state mandate, he has called the local law enforcement authorities and that they will be on their way soon to come to the office to help Marcus and his mother get through the next few days.

It should be noted that Justin took pains to do several things correctly. First, when the boy was disclosing the abuse to him, he merely reflected the boy's own words, careful not to sabotage a potential prosecution by requiring the boy to tell his story in detail. In this case, the counselor gathered only enough information as was absolutely necessary to substantiate his own reasonable suspicions that the boy might have been sexually abused and then made the mandated report to the proper agency. He did not ask questions or pump the child for details about when, where, how often, etc., the abuse had occurred. Rather, with the amount of information that Marcus had already volunteered (that his stepfather had "hurt his penis again" and the most recent time was within the past week), when combined with information that he already had (e.g., the identity of the stepfather and the knowledge that the stepfather resided in the same home as Marcus and a younger sibling), he focused on the feelings the boy was having, validated those feelings, reinforced the boy's decision to disclose the abuse, supported him by letting him know that it was not his fault, and reassured him that he would help him through the process of telling and reporting.

Second, Justin did not use the word *abuse*. Knowing that this is a term that boys can sometimes find emasculating and disempowering, Justin chose only to use the boy's own words in very concrete (rather than euphemistic) terms such as "he hurt your penis."

Third, Justin remained calm and matter of fact, while communicating empathy with his tone and body language. The message this manner conveyed to the child was that adults can handle these things calmly without the response of blame or anger, which can be scary for children; that they care; and that they should be told in order to keep children safe.

Finally, Justin gave Marcus as many choices as he could. Some of those choices were who to tell first, who should do the telling, and where the telling should happen. This facilitated the child's sense of empowerment, restored to the child's confidence in his choices and, by proxy, reinforced his sense of self-worth.

In the weeks immediately following, Justin maintained consistent contact with Marcus's mom, the assigned CPS caseworker, law enforcement, and the local children's advocacy center. Although Justin agreed to see Marcus twice a week, the boy was very reluctant to talk about his abuse. Justin therefore decided that play therapy might be the best course of treatment. They undertook about 20 sessions of child-centered play therapy before Marcus's original presenting symptoms, and his later anxiety, depression, and anger dissipated.

Discussion Questions

1. What information do you need to collect for CPS?
2. How can you determine the safety of other family members?

Collecting Information for an Initial Report of Child Sexual Abuse

Counselors should be aware of not only the information they need to collect to report a case of CSA but also the CSA policies where they work in order to practice legally and ethically. Table 10.2 provides a list of questions related to the information and policies counselors should know about when reporting a case of CSA.

States have required mandated reporting forms that counselors, in any setting, should have on hand, since they will be required to submit them. Important information to include in a CSA report is presented in Table 10.3. When making an initial CSA

TABLE 10.2 Information and Policies to Know Regarding Child Sexual Abuse Reporting

- Whom do you notify?
- What specific information do you need to know in order to report?
- What other agency/school personnel should be involved?
- Who makes the report to CPS? How?
- Is there a time frame for making a verbal report followed by a written report?
- Who is responsible for monitoring or receiving feedback from CPS once the report is filed?
- What information should be included in the report? (This is dictated by state law and CPS policy.)
- What does the protocol indicate regarding confidentiality?
- Is the written report kept in a separate location from the client's normal file or cumulative folder?
- What follow-up is expected on reported cases?
- What role will you play in possible community or child protection teams?

TABLE 10.3 Information to Include in an Initial Report of Child Sexual Abuse

- Child's name
- Age
- Sex
- Address
- Parents' names and addresses
- Nature and extent of the condition observed
- Actions taken by the reporter (e.g., talking with the child)
- Identity of alleged perpetrator
- Type of abuse
- Timeframe of the abuse
- Where the act occurred
- Issues of potential risk for the child (e.g., Is the perpetrator in the home? Is there a threat of physical abuse for the child disclosing information? Might the child be kicked out of the home for reporting?)
- Are there other children who might be at risk from the alleged perpetrator?
- Reporter's name, location, and contact information

report to CPS, it is important for the mental health professional to document that the report was made, including to whom the report was made (both the agency and the name of the individual taking the report).

Each case of child abuse differs, and while some counselors may not want to scare a child by introducing what could be perceived as scary questions, it is possible to carefully ask follow-up questions on some of the basic and most crucial information that is often requested by CPS when filing a report. Depending on the unique situation and disposition of the child and the experience of the counselor, more information could be obtained (perpetrator name, place where alleged incident occurred, when the abuse took place, type of alleged abuse, knowledge of other children in the house) to provide CPS reviewers more information that may be needed for their processing and decision making on the case. Similarly, it is important for crisis counselors to weigh the safety of the child in determining whether family members should be contacted about the abuse.

Reporting Child Sexual Abuse

In the United States, every state has mandated reporting of CSA. Mandated reporters may differ by state but typically include mental health professionals, law enforcement officers, medical staff, and all personnel working in educational institutions who have contact with minor children (U.S. Department of Health and Human Services, 2015). The U.S. Department of Health and Human Services (HHS) maintains a website that allows counselors to search mandated reporting statutes by state to see who is a required mandated reporter in their region (see www.childwelfare.gov/topics/systemwide/laws-policies/state/?hasBeenRedirected=1). Despite the legal responsibility to report child abuse and neglect, there may be times when professionals choose not to report such information. This, however, can put the professional in conflict with legal and ethical guidelines, such as CAPTA (American Counseling Association, 2014), that require disclosure of suspicion of CSA. It is important for individuals serving children and adolescents to be knowledgeable of a counselor's legal and ethical responsibilities regarding CSA. This includes knowing not only the laws governing the reporting of CSA and the statutes of limitations for their particular state(s) but also the policies of the agency, organization, or school in which they practice. Many states have strong sanctions for mandated reporters who do not report suspected CSA cases. Complete the interviewing exercise in Activity 10.2.

The mandate for reporting suspicion of CSA can make it difficult to determine when steps should be taken, especially in cases where a child has not disclosed abuse but rather has exhibited some behaviors that seem to demonstrate a potential history of

---

ACTIVITY 10.2

Contact a member of Child Protective Services or a member of local law enforcement with experience in working with children and adolescents who have been sexually abused. Interview that individual about the process of making reports, including agency procedures when CSA has been reported, the process involved in interviewing and investigating CSA, and the timeline during which major events occur (e.g., initial interview of child, interview of family and/or alleged perpetrator, filing of legal charges, removal from home).

sexual abuse. While it is important to know your state(s) statutes regarding abuse, generally a report must be made within the first 48 hours after there is reasonable cause to believe or suspect a child is being subjected to abuse (U.S. Department of Health and Human Services, 2015). Although "reasonable cause" can feel vague, most state statutes hold personnel responsible for reporting when they can connect suspicions of abuse to observable evidence, such as statements made by a child, the child's appearance, or concerning behaviors (Mason, 2013). One way to help provide some clarification on when it is necessary to report is to develop professional relationships with contacts within the local CPS agency and local law enforcement, preferably prior to having a client who may be a victim of CSA. These contacts can help the counselor understand the process of local agencies and be individuals with whom that counselor can discuss hypothetical cases and appropriate action(s) or reporting procedures. These professional relationships can be especially helpful in cases where the line between CSA (and thus mandated reporting) and statutory rape (for which reporting is not typically mandated) is blurred.

CPS traditionally works with CSA cases involving parents or caregivers, especially those in the home. While CPS may be involved in other CSA cases, CPS's primary focus will typically be on parent/caregiver cases. Law enforcement agencies will typically handle extrafamilial cases or those that involve individuals who are not in a caretaking role.

CPS reports may be filed anonymously. Even if an anonymous report is made, however, counselors are mandated reporters and should document their reports. The documentation should include the report made, the date and time the report was made, and the name of the individual to whom the report was made. It should be cautioned that by reporting anonymously, the only record of mandated reporting is from the counselor's notes, since CPS will not have on file the identity of the reporter.

Reporting Past Incidents of Child Sexual Abuse

When working with adults who disclose past CSA, multiple factors must be taken into consideration. However, the most important consideration is one's state law on reporting past allegations of CSA. It is crucial for crisis counselors to understand when state law requires reporting past incidents of CSA. Duty to report statutes are also why the limits of confidentiality are an integral part of the counselor–client relationship. By reviewing the limits of confidentiality with clients, clients have the power and control in releasing information to the counselor that may also require a counselor to report past CSA.

Crisis counselors also need to consider adult clients in their own context regarding desired treatment outcomes (e.g., Is the client presenting with sexual dysfunction, relationship issues, difficulty in regulating mood, PTSD?), client abuse history (e.g., Who was the perpetrator? When did the abuse take place? What was the duration of the abuse?), as well as factors that might necessitate involving law enforcement or CPS (e.g., Is the abuser still alive? If so, does the abuser have access to children or adolescents who might also be victimized?).

Another factor to consider in treatment planning is whether adult clients have previously disclosed their abuse, and, if so, what the outcomes were of the disclosures. Is there documentation to substantiate a report being made? Crisis counselors should empower and respect the autonomy of the adult CSA survivor while also taking necessary steps to protect any children or adolescents who might be at risk as outlined by the laws of their practicing state.

Treatment of Survivors of Child Sexual Abuse

Although crisis counselors are often not part of the long-term clinical work with the client, they should be aware of professional counselors in the community who specialize in treating survivors of CSA as well as the various treatment options available.

A number of difficulties exist in identifying evidence-based practices for effectively treating survivors of CSA, based in part on the range of symptomology presented; the challenges that children have verbalizing their current mental, emotional, and physical states; and the reliance on parent and teacher reports, which may differ substantially both from each other and from the experience of the child (Benuto & O'Donohue, 2015). Although children and adolescents who have survived sexual abuse are usually served through a combination of individual and group counseling, the types of counseling offered can vary widely.

Cognitive-behavioral therapy (CBT) continues to be the most common approach used in working with CSA clients. CBT approaches have been the most widely used therapies in treating children and adolescents with post-traumatic symptomology (Benuto & O'Donohue, 2015), therefore, such strategies may be most beneficial to children and adolescents who are struggling specifically with post-traumatic stress, anxiety, or depression after being sexually abused. The most popular CBT treatment is trauma-focused cognitive-behavioral therapy, or TF-CBT (Cohen, Mannarino, & Deblinger, 2006); it employs eight components including psychoeducation, relaxation and stress management skills, cognitive coping and processing, and conjoint child–parent sessions (see Chapter 9). Any treatment using prolonged exposure therapy (or other forms of systematic desensitization) or cognitive restructuring must be careful to avoid interference with the child's story that could affect court testimony or the CPS investigation, and cause potential retraumatization of the sexual abuse (van der Kolk, 2015). It is important for crisis counselors to take advantage of training opportunities and continuing education on working with CSA survivors and seek specialized training in CBT-based therapies.

In their review of meta-analyses on the treatment outcomes for sexually abused children, Benuto and O'Donohue (2015) found CBT to be no more effective than any other treatment modality in working with this population. In response to this finding, one group of researchers has suggested that the type of treatment employed should depend on the developmental level and the presenting complaints displayed by the child (Hetzel-Riggin, Brausch, & Montgomery, 2007). For example, since CBT appears to be most successful with children who present with behavioral problems, group counseling appears to be most successful with those children with low self-concept or depression, and play therapies appear to be most successful with children who have deficits in social functioning, the modality should be tailored to the specific needs and characteristics of the child. Indeed, other meta-analytic studies have indicated that TF-CBTs are most successful when combined with play therapies and other similar psychodynamic interventions as well as with supportive therapies such as group therapy and parent-attachment therapies (Sánchez-Meca, Rosa-Alcázar, & López-Soler, 2011).

Play therapy has also been integrated in to the treatment of children who have experienced CSA (Singhal & Vahali, 2014). Although play therapy may lack the widespread acceptance of CBT, reviews of meta-analyses undertaken over the last few decades have consistently shown that play therapy significantly improved treatment outcomes in children across a diverse spectrum of issues (Bratton, Ray, Rhine, & Jones, 2005; Ray, Armstrong, Balkin, & Jayne, 2015). Many counselors with extensive experience in working with children prefer play therapy because the developmentally responsive nature of the therapy lends itself more naturally to children's innate communication style than does a therapy such as TF-CBT, which may rely on more advanced cognitive and verbal skills. In choosing a particular play therapy approach (e.g., child-centered, Jungian, Adlerian, Theraplay), the needs of both the child and family need to be considered.

Parent–child interaction therapy (PCIT) is another treatment approach that is becoming popular among counselors who treat CSA populations (Urquiza & Blacker, 2012). PCIT draws from play and operant therapy techniques and focuses on the psycho-education and training of parents in the use of play therapy–type strategies to increase the stability, trust, and communication in the parent–child relationship. As the relationship between parent and child strengthens across several counselor-directed play sessions, counselors and researchers have observed both significant decreases in the child's externalized behavioral problems and increases in the caregiver's parenting self-efficacy. These are two of the foremost presenting issues in families struggling to recover from abuse events (Cooley, Veldorale-Griffin, Petren, & Mullis, 2014). For this reason, PCIT may be appropriate for children demonstrating problematic externalized behaviors following abuse or who have suffered an attachment break with a primary caregiver as a result of the abuse events.

Finally, eye movement desensitization and reprocessing (EMDR) therapy has gained attention in recent decades for its effectiveness in treating children who are survivors of various forms of trauma, including sexual abuse (Chen et al., 2014; Ho & Lee, 2012; Rodenburg, Benjamin, de Roos, Meijer, & Stams, 2009). Trained counselors use a standardized protocol that accesses client memories of traumatic events in the past as well as triggers any symptoms in the present, and then work to install more adaptive coping processes for trauma triggers that may be experienced in the future. EMDR is a notable therapy for use with CSA populations because it has been shown to be effective both in the immediate aftermath (e.g., hours, days) of abuse as well as with adolescent and adult clients whose abuse is well in the past (Shapiro, 2012). Furthermore, recent studies have shown that EMDR has been more effective than TF-CBT in reducing depressive symptoms in trauma survivors (Ho & Lee, 2012) and may be a resilience-building therapy that serves to prevent further accumulation of traumatic recall, which can lead to later-developing disorders (Shapiro, 2012). Read Voices from the Field 10.1.

Child Sexual Abuse Coping Strategies and Their Impact on Treatment

A critical issue in the treatment and recovery of children who have experienced CSA is to determine the methods clients used to cope with the abuse. The worst outcomes are seen in those children and adolescents who chose avoidant coping strategies (Shapiro, Kaplow, Amaya-Jackson, & Dodge, 2012). Avoidant coping strategies can be characterized by

---

VOICES FROM THE FIELD 10.1

Protecting Shelby

Maegan Vick

Seven-year-old Shelby sat down with me as usual and traced the blisters she got on her palms from the monkey bars in our school's playground. By now, I was accustomed to Shelby asking to see me. We would talk about anything—from what she did at recess that day to how she was not getting along with her sister. However, I always felt she left something unsaid, something much bigger. During this session, she was really trying to convey to me that she did not want to go to her father's house for her usual weekend visit. She took a deep breath and finally said that her father had touched her bottom and that he got naked in front of her. She said she closed her eyes because she did not want to see. He made her get in the shower with him as well. I praised Shelby for being brave enough to share that information with me and promised I would get her some help, so her father would never do that again. She was apprehensive and worried her father would be in trouble. I eased her fear by saying that the people I would call would help him, because what he was doing was not OK. Our bodies belong to us and no one should ever touch us where our swimsuits cover our private areas. I contacted Child Protective Services and then referred Shelby to Owens's House, a nonprofit organization that helps children who are sexually abused and exploited.

---

verbal or psychic denial of the abuse, withdrawal from one's social network, dissociation, or dissociative forgetting of the abuse. Approach coping strategies can be characterized by reaching out to others for support, disclosing the abuse, or discussing the abuse with friends, family, and/or counselors.

Bessel van der Kolk, a scholar in the field of traumatic dissociation, hypothesized that the psychic stress resulting from various traumas may exceed a child's ability to cope. As a result, the child dissociates from the abuse for survival (van der Kolk, 2015). Therefore, if children have been traumatized by their abuse, counselors should allow for a period of stabilization, safety, and normal routines before attempting to facilitate treatment that directly addresses the abuse. Many scientist–practitioners who specialize in trauma treatment have addressed this dynamic by allowing for a period of safety-building and stabilization before addressing the sexual trauma (Rothschild, 2010).

See Case Study 10.2, which considers the role of a school counselor in reporting a case of CSA.

CASE STUDY 10.2

The Role of a School Counselor in the Disclosure of Child Sexual Abuse

Eleven-year-old Alicia arrives in her school counselor's office one day in tears. She is accompanied by a friend who holds her hand and speaks for her. The friend explains to Cherise, the school counselor, that something really bad is happening to Alicia and that it's got to stop because Alicia can't take it anymore. Cherise knows Alicia well from years of working with all students in classroom guidance and small groups, and she asks Alicia if she feels comfortable talking about what has happened with her alone. After the friend leaves, Alicia discloses that her grandfather has been sexually abusing her for at least the past year.

After making the proper reports to the authorities and helping Alicia tell her parents about the abuse, Cherise makes a referral for clinical mental health counseling. Several months go by with Cherise checking on Alicia and checking in with Alicia's teachers and family. All seems to be going well until one day, Alicia's mother calls Cherise asking her to see Alicia. Alicia's mother informs Cherise that Alicia refuses to speak about the abuse to anyone but Cherise.

Cherise agrees to see Alicia for six half-hour sessions over the next several weeks until the mother can find another clinical mental health counselor.

Alicia arrives after lunch one day for her session and says that she wants to write her story so she can finally get it out of her head. She reports that she wants to stop thinking about what happened because she is tired of feeling sick to her stomach all the time. Cherise affirms Alicia's courage to work on this goal, but she also expresses her concern that discussing the abuse may get in the way of Alicia's ability to focus on her schoolwork and be her usual self around her friends. Alicia dismisses this concern and starts decorating the front cover of her book. Over the next 6 weeks, Alicia and Cherise worked together to write Alicia's story. In keeping with tenets of some narrative therapies, Cherise suggested that Alicia write the ending to the story first. Alicia decides that she wants her story to end when she is 25 years old and has a family of her own, that her story has a happy ending, and that her dad (who also would eventually serve a jail sentence for taking indecent liberties with a minor) would one day love and accept her again and be able to look her in the eye with pride. At the end of their sessions together, Cherise agrees to invite Alicia's parents to school so that their daughter can read her story to them. The parents listen closely to Alicia's story, cry healing tears, and affirm their love for and pride in their daughter. Alicia's parents then get permission for their daughter to leave school to have a celebratory lunch together.

Alicia eventually saw a counselor the following year, after moving on to middle school. Her school performance didn't suffer the drop that her parents expected and doctors predicted. Throughout high school, Alicia's academic and social achievements thrived.

Discussion Questions

1. What are your state's laws regarding mandated reporting?
2. What are the primary treatment methods a counselor could use in this case?

PERPETRATORS OF CHILD SEXUAL ABUSE

When discussing CSA, it is important to consider not only the survivors but also the perpetrators. One issue that may be particularly challenging for some counselors who find themselves working with perpetrators of CSA is getting past their own negative reactions to the actions of their clients. Being able to provide perpetrators of CSA with the same unconditional positive regard as other client populations may be challenging. This population encounters societal issues including restrictions on movement and housing as well as a range of negative emotional and behavioral responses from family, friends, and members of the community. In the sections that follow, the prevalence of child sexual perpetration, the characteristics of perpetrators, and treatment options are outlined.

The Prevalence and Characteristics of Child Sexual Abuse Perpetrators

Perpetrators of CSA are both male and female, and they commit sex crimes against children for a variety of reasons. Some of these may be parallel to the reasons of sexual assault perpetrators, but some are distinctly different. In the following sections, male and female perpetrators of CSA are described, with a focus on the motivation that may drive behavior that is sexually abusive toward children or adolescents.

THE VICTIM–OFFENDER CYCLE   An important feature of CSA is that it often occurs in cycles. Although many researchers have investigated this relationship and found differing rates of the victim–perpetrator cycle, the ratio consistently fell within the 3:1 range. For example, recent research by Jennings, Zgoba, Maschi, and Reingle (2014) demonstrated that 40% of males with sexual assault or rape histories prior to 16 years of age later became offenders of sexual abuse themselves, while 60% did not. This is an important feature of CSA: although most offender treatment programs do not differentiate their interventions by personal abuse history of the perpetrator, it is possible that addressing the etiology of offending behaviors may hold insight to constructing more successful treatment programs in reducing recidivism rates. It is important for the crisis counselor to educate parents about signs, symptoms, and the cycle of perpetrated victimization.

MALE PERPETRATORS OF CHILD SEXUAL ABUSE   Like sexual assault perpetrators, individuals who sexually abuse children are predominantly male. Indeed, males are the perpetrators in 75 to 96% of reported child victimization cases (Lanning, 2010). Unlike sexual assault perpetrators, individuals who sexually abuse children fall along a continuum of motivation for committing the sexual abuse, ranging from manipulative to opportunist (Rebocho & Goncalves, 2012). Manipulative perpetrators are compulsive and driven by fantasies about their victims; they may participate in behaviors that groom their potential targets. Manipulative perpetrators are more likely than opportunist perpetrators to sexually abuse children or adolescents. By contrast, opportunist perpetrators commit sexual abuse because they are driven by basic sexual and nonsexual (e.g., power, anger) needs. In the case of opportunist offenders, the preferred sexual partner may or may not typically be a child. Thus, the child serves as a sexual substitute and may be part of a larger pattern of abusive behavior.

Based on a behavioral analysis of child molesters, Lanning (2010) describes a similar motivational continuum (situational to preferential) as well as a typology of perpetrators. These motivations and typology are not meant to be a basis for clinical treatment or diagnosis; instead, they are meant to help law enforcement officials recognize, identify, and gather relevant evidence about individuals who sexually abuse children.

Lanning (2010) identified three behavioral patterns of situational-type perpetrators (similar to opportunist perpetrators) of sexual abuse: (1) regressed, (2) morally indiscriminate, and (3) inadequate. Offenders who fit a regressed pattern are driven by a precipitating stressor and may find a readily available child to serve as a sexual substitute for a preferred adult partner. Offenders who fit a morally indiscriminate pattern abuse all or many types of individuals, so the sexual abuse of a child is less a specific preference for children than the result of a sociopathic level of indiscriminate abuse of people, regardless of their age or background. Finally, offenders who fit an inadequate pattern are typically perceived as nonmainstream, perhaps with preexisting mental or emotional problems, who may sexually abuse a child out of insecurity or curiosity about sexual behavior.

Individuals who are on the preferential side of the motivation continuum tend to sexually abuse children or adolescents either because children and/or adolescents are their preferred sexual partners or because children and/or adolescents are less threatening individuals with whom they can participate in sexual behaviors that are more bizarre or more shameful to the perpetrator. Not all preferential-type perpetrators, therefore, are pedophiles; many, however, have a paraphilia, which is defined in the *Diagnostic and Statistical Manual of Mental Disorders* (DSM-5) as a strong sexual preference for nonhuman objects, nonconsenting individuals, or the suffering and/or humiliation of themselves or their partners (American Psychiatric Association, 2013). Not all individuals who have a paraphilia (including pedophilia) commit CSA; therefore, it is important that counselors not assume that all, most, or even many individuals who have a paraphilia will sexually abuse children.

The four behavioral patterns of preferential-type perpetrators of sexual abuse are as follows: (1) seduction, (2) introverted, (3) diverse, and (4) sadistic (Lanning, 2010). Offenders who fit the seduction pattern form the largest group of acquaintance child molesters. They are able to identify with children and engage in grooming potential victims. When grooming children, the perpetrator will give potential victims gifts and positive attention, making them feel loved and understood to the point where they may willingly participate in sexual acts. Unlike those who fit the seduction pattern, offenders who fit the introverted pattern lack the verbal and social skills to seduce children and may resort to the traditionally stereotypical behaviors of lurking around playgrounds or abducting children with whom they have no prior relationship. This pattern parallels the inadequate pattern of situational-type offenders, but with a specific preference for children. Offenders who fit the diverse pattern are interested in sexual experimentation, and they choose a child target because of the novelty or taboo, or because the child is a more vulnerable partner with whom sexual experimentation can take place. Finally, offenders who fit the sadistic pattern represent a small percentage of perpetrators, but they are the most likely to abduct or kill their victims. Sadistic perpetrators are aroused by the infliction of pain, humiliation, and suffering in victims.

FEMALE PERPETRATORS OF CHILD SEXUAL ABUSE   Recent statistics collected by Child Protective Services agencies across the United States show that between 15 and 20% of reported CSA cases are perpetrated by women (McLeod, 2015). Thus, female perpetrators of sexual abuse appear to be fewer in number than their male counterparts. However, the perception of female perpetrators of CSA is distinct from that of male perpetrators. For example, there is more of a social media acceptance of older females seducing younger males (e.g., the *American Pie* series of movies, the songs "Stacy's Mom" and "That Summer") than there is of similar relationships between older males and adolescent females (e.g., *Lolita*). Moreover, males themselves often fail to see sexual behavior toward them that is initiated by significantly older women as abuse, even though it more than meets the legal criteria (Deering & Mellor, 2011). Therefore, law enforcement officers, criminal justice personnel, and mental health providers must be aware of their own biases and stereotypes about the demographic characteristics of sex offenders to understand the severity of abuse for the victim and properly treat the female perpetrator.

Due to the relatively smaller numbers of female perpetrators, the literature on female perpetrators is still sparse compared with that on male perpetrators. In ground-breaking research, Mathews, Matthews, and Speltz (1989) clustered female offenders into three subtypes: (1) male-coerced, (2) predisposed, and (3) teacher/lover. Male-coerced female offenders tend to abuse children in concert with a dominant male partner, and they may grant access to children out of a fear of abandonment by a dominant male partner. Predisposed female offenders typically act alone in victimizing their own children or other easily accessible young children. They are typically survivors of incestuous relationships with continued psychological problems and deviant or paraphilic sexual fantasies. Teacher/lover female offenders have a more regressed pattern of behavior, have strained peer relationships, and perceive themselves as being in romantic relationships or as sexually mentoring their victims, therefore resisting the idea that their actions might be criminal in nature.

Since then, Vandiver and Kercher (2004) and Sandover and Freeman (2007) analyzed larger samples of female sex offenders in Texas and reported finding six clusters of female offenders, differing on characteristics that included offender age, victim age, victim gender, total number of arrests, any drug arrest, any incarceration term, and whether the offender was rearrested after the arrest for a sexual offense. Although the two studies had some differences in identified clusters, in both the average female sex offender was a Caucasian in her early 30s, and the average victim age was just under 12 years old. In the Sandover and Freeman study, all six clusters targeted victims under 18 years old. It is important to note, however, that these clusters are inclusive only of women who had been arrested for sex offenses and labeled as sex offenders, and thus may not be inclusive of female perpetrators of CSA who have not been arrested or identified.

Treatment of Adult Sex Offenders

Because there is no evidence-based guidance about the most effective approaches to working with female sexual offenders (Gannon & Cortoni, 2010), the primary focus of this treatment section will be on male offenders, with "sex offender" referring to males unless specifically stated otherwise.

When considering treatment for sex offenders, crisis counselors should structure their work to target the following: (1) matching interventions to meet the level of risk posed by the offender, (2) targeting the specific remedial needs of the offender, and (3) tailoring approaches to the offender in a culturally responsive way (Yates, 2013). By following these risk, need, and responsivity (RNR) principles (Hanson, Bourgon, Helmus, & Hodgson, 2009), those treating sexual offenders can optimize treatment and reduce rates of recidivism. This approach represents a shift from viewing sex offenders in a problem-oriented way that tries to fit them into neat categories with one-size-fits-all solutions toward viewing them as whole people whose treatment should be individually tailored to address their specific needs and strengths (D'Orazio, 2014)—much like how we might approach counseling with a nonoffending population.

Within the RNR framework, it is imperative that intensity of interventions be specifically matched based on the "risk principle," or the risk of recidivism by the identified offender. Doing so is a more effective use of sometimes limited resources. Moreover, evidence exists that recidivism rates increase when the intensity of intervention does not match the risk presented by the offender. This is the case not only for higher risk offenders who receive less intensive intervention, but also for low-risk offenders who receive a higher intensity intervention (Andrews & Bonta, 2010; Yates, 2013). In fact, some researchers recommend no specialized treatment for those at the lowest end of the risk spectrum, 100 to 200 hours of treatment for offenders with moderate risk, and at least 300 hours for offenders who present at the top 10 to 20% of the risk spectrum (Hanson & Yates, 2013; Hanson, Lloyd, Helmus, & Thornton, 2012).

Because of the variations among perpetrators of sexual abuse, no single assessment has emerged as the standard for predicting recidivism, although actuarial assessments are currently thought to be the best predictors (Association for the Treatment of Sexual Abusers, 2012). Common examples of actuarial assessments are the Static-99 (Hanson & Thornton, 2000; Helmus, Thornton, Hanson, & Babchishin, 2012), the level of service/case management inventory (LS/CMI) (Andrews, Bonta, & Wormith, 2004), and the sex offender risk appraisal guide (SORAG) (Quinsey, Harris, Rice, & Cormier, 2006). Although actuarial assessments are the current benchmark, there is some support for using structured guides, which combine standardized aspects and actuarial assessments with clinical judgment. Some examples of structured guides include the sexual violence risk-20 (SVR-20) (Boer, Hart, Kropp, & Webster, 1997) and the risk of sexual violence protocol (RSVP) (Hart et al., 2003). The estimate of risk of adolescent sexual offense recidivism (ERASOR) (Worling & Curwen, 2001) is a structured guide for adolescent risk assessment.

Second, the needs principle means targeting individual factors that increase likelihood of recidivism (particularly those that can be changed) for intervention. Some examples of these include lack of positive role models and influences, issues with both overall self-regulation and sexual self-regulation, attitudes that support sexual assault, issues with intimacy, and problems cooperating with supervision (Hanson, Harris, Scott, & Helmus, 2007; Yates, 2013). These factors need to be assessed prior to beginning treatment and used to tailor an individual treatment plan (Yates, 2013).

Third, treatment should be delivered in a way that is culturally responsive and individualized for the preferences and characteristics of the individual. While a cognitive-behavioral approach is often preferred, learning style, cognitive ability, personality, language, culture, and anxiety level are all factors that should be taken into account when delivering treatment. With this culturally responsive approach, the hope is to increase engagement and reduce recidivism (Yates, 2013).

D'Orazio (2014) recommends five ways of improving sex offender treatment within the RNR framework. First, focus on assessing the client in totality, including examining and treating past trauma. Childhood trauma in sex offenders is significantly higher than in the general population, and without attending to healing some of those long-ago wounds, the remainder of treatment is likely to fall short. This step includes empathetic validation of those wounds (although not the offender's behaviors). Much like with other client populations, this ability to meet the client where he is and receive him as a fellow human being is key to establishing a therapeutic alliance that will benefit the remainder of treatment.

Second, attend to the affective aspects of the offender (D'Orazio, 2014). Many treatment programs focus on cognitions and behaviors, but by ignoring the emotion, we ignore a main component of the offender's world that may drive the behaviors that we are trying to decrease. Allow room for present affective responses to the people in his life as well as his experience of treatment and interactions with the treatment provider. This may also include attention to modeling facilitative communication skills and appropriate self-disclosure by the counselor of her or his own feelings.

Third, cultivate empathy for the offender as a way to facilitate the change process (D'Orazio, 2014). She reminds us that these men, too, are people who need our empathy in order to see themselves as capable of or deserving of change. Particularly when working with this population, reminding ourselves of Rogers's (1961) core conditions and using accurate empathy to help them feel understood and cared for can further open them up to the treatment process.

Fourth, embrace the "mystery of wholeness" (D'Orazio, 2014, p. 6) and resist the pull to standardize all treatment processes. This is a reminder that the offender is more than just the sum of his parts and needs to be seen as an individual. It relates specifically back to the responsivity principle and allows for us to tailor our work specifically to the needs of each individual. With this step, D'Orazio urges us to be fully present in the moment with these clients and to be attentive to verbal and nonverbal responses, and also include attention to creative, holistic, and multimodal treatment approaches for additional ways to work with the whole client, rather than just specific aspects of his experience or existence.

Finally, take care of the therapist (D'Orazio, 2014). Vicarious traumatization and burnout are two factors that counselors battle when working with any clients who have experienced trauma, and this population is no different. Self-care and prioritizing our own health and well-being as a vehicle for provision of effective treatment for others is vital.

FAMILY SYSTEMS COUNSELING   In the case of incestuous CSA, a family systems approach to treatment may be taken (e.g., the Child Sexual Abuse Treatment Program; see Mohl, 2010). This systems-oriented counseling may involve individual counseling for the child, the nonoffending parent(s), and the perpetrator; marital therapy; counseling with the nonoffending parent(s) and child; counseling with the offender and the child; group counseling; and family therapy with the purpose of retaining or reunifying the family (Mohl, 2010). It should be noted that family counseling with the offender and the child would need to be undertaken with great care.

FEMALE OFFENDERS   Virtually no current evidence-based guidance regarding treatment of female CSA offenders exists in the literature. Most modes of treatment for male offenders have been applied to female offenders, taking into account the unique issues leading a female to offend in CSA situations. If the female offender was also a victim of CSA, a portion of the treatment may need to address the trauma that she encountered. While addressing victimization issues, it is important for counselors to be empathetic regarding the abuse that perpetrators have sustained without minimizing or excusing the sexual offenses that they have committed. For any perpetrator of CSA, the priority of treatment must first be focused on the perpetrated act in an attempt to decrease the rate of recidivism, secondly on the perpetrator as victim.

Treatment of Adolescent Sex Offenders

As more research has been done on adolescent sexual offenders, it has become clear that there are extensive differences between adolescent and adult sexual offenders. As such, juvenile sexual offenders should be seen as a distinct population from adult offenders, and treatment of juvenile sexual offenders should, thus, look different from the treatment of adult sexual offenders. For example, juvenile sexual offenders as a group appear to have more similarities to juvenile nonsexual offenders than they do to adult sexual offenders (U.S. Department of Justice, 2014b). Even without treatment, adolescents are far less likely to re-offend than adult sexual offenders.

That said, research on treatment for adolescent sexual offenders is emerging that suggests that multisystemic therapy and cognitive-behavioral treatments are particularly promising (U.S. Department of Justice, 2014b). Treatment services for adolescent sexual offenders also need to be tailored to the contexts of the individuals, however, and there is some indication that the family, peer, and environmental contexts of the youth are relevant and important to increasing the effectiveness of treatment of juvenile sexual offenders (Letourneau & Bourduin, 2008; U.S. Department of Justice, 2014b). Read Voices from the Field 10.2.

VOICES FROM THE FIELD 10.2
The Troubled Family

Sherdene Simpson

As I entered the lobby of my office building, I heard the sound of the phone ringing and noticed an array of people sitting around talking. Even though the environment appeared normal, I noticed that there was a man and woman sitting stoically in the corner of the waiting room. I noticed that the woman had two little girls sitting next to her. Two boys stood near the man; both stood motionless. As I walked by, I offered an enthusiastic, "Good morning." The parents looked up with tears in their eyes and said "hello." The children in an almost rehearsed manner waved and looked away. I entered my office and stood still for a moment. Something about my interaction with them had felt uncomfortable. The phone rang; it was a call from the office manager calling to say that there was a family in the lobby who needed to be seen immediately. She shared that the man expressed that they were not leaving until they met with me. I told her that I would see them, and instructed her to give them the intake paperwork. At first, I did not find the situation to be that unusual. I work on a church staff, so it is not uncommon for parishioners to stop into our counseling center and request to see me without a scheduled appointment.

After they completed the paperwork, I invited the family into my office. The parents stood up to come with me, and all four children remained positioned on the sofa like mini-figurines. I looked back several times as the parents and I left the waiting area, but the children remained motionless. I was taken aback because even the youngest child, who appeared to be about 3 years old, sat perfectly still.

I intended to facilitate my usual routine of conducting a thorough clinical assessment, but the father dominated the next few minutes by explaining that he wanted help for his family but was afraid to share with me. The mother said that she did not want anyone "to go to jail." The father interrupted his wife, saying that he was angry and did not know what to do. I immediately felt that they had experienced a tragedy. My thoughts starting running as I considered the word "jail" and all that word could imply.

I quickly stopped them both from sharing and reviewed in great detail my informed consent procedures and the limits to confidentiality. When I stopped

(continued)

talking, I felt that they stopped breathing. The room felt thick with silence and I could hear every movement in the hallway. It felt like we sat in silence for days. In a harsh voice, the man uttered, "I thought we were safe coming to our church." As I began to talk, a scream came from the chair across from me that changed the entire climate of the room. The woman, gripping her chair, yelled, "I'm not leaving here. We're getting help or else." The husband sat back with streams of tears falling from his eyes. He began to share their story.

He explained that his 10-year-old daughter was being sexually abused by her brother, aged 12. As he spoke, his voice faded in and out. He shared his confusion, frustration, and feelings of failure. He continued to report the anger and disdain that he felt toward his son. The wife chimed in and expressed her feelings of grief and numbness. Sadly, in graduate school, no one had taught me what to do when emotionally charged crisis situations like this emerge. As a grief recovery specialist, I knew that this family needed a heart with ears. So, I listened, and I listened, and I listened.

I invited the 10-year-girl into my office and heard the stories of sexual abuse that she had endured over the past 2 years. She was very candid in her emotions and shared the anger and disappointment she felt for her brother. She also said that she forgave him for his "sinful" behavior and was hopeful that God would heal her heart. The resilience that this child possessed left me in awe. After she left the room, I continued to hear her small voice saying, "I know that God will heal my heart."

Afterward, I invited the 12-year-old brother into my office; he appeared overwhelmed with fear and nervousness. I told him quickly that I was a counselor, not a police officer. He settled in and shared with me stories of his journey through pornography and

masturbation and ultimately described the sexual urges that led him to abuse his sister. He appeared remorseful and said that he never meant to hurt his sister and that he is hopeful that she will forgive his behavior. He said in an almost adult manner, "I need to be healed from my sexual desires."

Nothing could have prepared me for the stories that I was exposed to by this family. The graphic depiction of the sexual abuse and the emotional devastation of this family will ring in my memories for years to come. What do you do when the victim and the perpetrator are siblings? How do you manage having such a close connection to all of the players involved in a situation such as this?

The emotionally drained father looked at me and asked, "Will my family ever be healed?" This was the first time in years of practicing as a counselor that I was utterly speechless. Because we were in a church setting and their resource as a family was their religion and faith, I pulled on this source of strength and reinforced their belief that their faith, combined with counseling, would glue their family back together.

The layered complexity of the situation and its immediacy was affecting me on multiple levels. In the midst of all these emotions, as a counselor, I knew that legally and ethically I had to report this case. Emotionally, I empathized with their pain. Professionally, I needed to explore support services for this family. Cognitively, I was perplexed. There were layers of presenting concerns that emerged in the stories of sexual abuse.

This situation, while overwhelming, taught me the importance of being calm in crisis situations. It also taught me that clients find a sense of stability in counselors' comportment and composure in crisis situations. Finally, it taught me the importance of building upon clients' strengths and resources in times of crisis.

OVERVIEW OF THE ELEMENTS OF CRISIS INTERVENTION RELATED TO CHILD SEXUAL ABUSE

Safety

In the immediate aftermath of disclosure, it is important to ensure minor clients' physical and emotional safety. Responsibility for the child's physical safety is often transferred to law enforcement or other agencies once the investigation begins, although safety should not be promised by the counselor. If the primary caregiver is not the reported perpetrator, then the counselor should work with the caregiver to ensure that no further interaction between the child and perpetrator takes place until law enforcement or the court can put the needed child safety plans into place. If the perpetrator is a custodial caregiver, then the counselor should report this to CPS or, in some instances, to law enforcement immediately. Guaranteeing the child's emotional safety can be more abstract and, therefore, sometimes more challenging. Safety of any kind can only be assured while the child is in the office. False promises of safety should not be made to victims.

Diagnostic Considerations during a Crisis

Counselors working with children who have a history of CSA should be aware that reactions to sexual abuse are very specific to the individual. Some individuals may present with symptoms mimicking anxiety or mood disorders, dissociative disorders, sleep or other physical disorders, and even personality disorders. Those suffering particularly traumatic abuse can present with post-traumatic symptoms consistent with PTSD and other stress disorders. Furthermore, because sexual abuse is an interpersonal crime often perpetrated by family members, family friends, and other known and trusted adults, symptoms can present in ways consistent with what may look like a child's disordered attachment to his or her caregivers. It is important, therefore, that counselors are careful not to pathologize presenting behaviors when it is clear that situational stressors like sexual abuse may be operative forces.

In a crisis, most victims of CSA are reacting normally to an abnormal event. Therefore, providing a diagnosis during a crisis is usually not appropriate. It is important for the counselor to know whether the client has a preexisting mental health or medical issue to be able to undertake a thorough assessment. How a child reacts may be complicated by an existing mental health or medical issue, and knowing about any such issues allows the crisis counselor to make appropriate referrals. The counselor should conduct a thorough developmental history of minor clients and remain sensitive to indicators of potential abuse or disordered attachment styles over the entire course of treatment. It is not uncommon for children to disclose their sexual abuse history to their counselor in the termination session. Both being aware of one's own intuition about potential abuse and being sensitive to more concrete indicators of abuse can place the counselor in a better position to address abuse, regardless of abuse history disclosure.

Essential Child Sexual Abuse–Specific Crisis Intervention Skills

Skills essential to providing crisis intervention counseling to children with sexual abuse histories are the same skills that are activated when working with clients experiencing other types of crises. Being able to skillfully reflect both the affect and content of the child's words without imbuing them with added meaning is key to helping them unfold the story. Crisis counselors must be comfortable in asking questions about sexual interactions in order to gather information to make an appropriate decision on mandated reporting and also for referrals to long-term counseling. Counselor disposition is equally, if not more, important during intervention. The ability to remain calm and unruffled, warm and open, reassuring and nonjudgmental is essential to maintaining a therapeutic relationship that can help minor clients weather the storm of what has happened and what may come. Table 10.4 provides additional resources on CSA.

TABLE 10.4 Resources on Child Sexual Abuse

Prevention of Child Sexual Abuse

Darkness to Light: Stewards of Children Training: www.d2l.org

American Psychological Association. (2016). Understanding and preventing child abuse and neglect. Retrieved from www.apa.org/pi/families/resources/child-sexual-abuse.aspx

Scholes, L., Jones, C., & Nagel, M. (2014). Boys and CSA prevention: Issues surrounding gender and approaches for prevention. *Australian Journal of Teacher Education, 39*(11), 1–16.

Wurtele, S. K., & Kenny, M. C. (2010). Preventing online sexual victimization of youth. *Journal of Behavior Analysis of Offender and Victim Treatment and Prevention, 2*(1), 63–73. doi:10.1037/h0100468

Treatment of Child Sexual Abuse

1in6 (support and treatment of males who have experienced CSA): 1in6.org

National Children's Advocacy Center: www.nationalcac.org

Terry, K. J., & Tallon, J. (2004). Child sexual abuse: A review of the literature. Retrieved from www.usccb.org/issues-and-action/child-and-youth-protection/upload/child-sexual-abuse-literature-review-john-jay-college-2004.pdf [the review covers perpetrators of sexual abuse (criminal typologies)]

Summary

Child sexual abuse continues to be a pervasive, yet elusive, social phenomenon. Although survivors of CSA may comprise a small percentage of society, it is important to keep in mind that all authoritative CSA data-collection agencies openly acknowledge that reported CSA prevalence and incidence rates are underestimated. Therefore, much progress is needed in the way of both preventing CSA and creating support systems for all children such that they have a safe adult to whom they can disclose shame-provoking abuse experiences and receive help. Recent prevention programs such as Darkness to Light's "Stewards of Children" raise social awareness of CSA, help adults involved in children's lives protect the safety of those children, and help foster trusting child–adult relationships wherein children may be more likely to disclose their abuse and get help. However, there is still much ground to gain in educating parents and primary caregivers about society's hidden dangers and in training children in personal safety planning and adult refusal skills. As technology continues to change and expand, so too will such programs, as law enforcement agencies consistently find that those who seek

to sexually victimize children are often at the forefront of pushing the envelope of emerging technologies' capacities (Wolak, Finkelhor, & Mitchell, 2012). In summary, there is much to be done both to keep children safe now and to keep abreast of maintaining children's safety well into the future.

Crisis counselors may be the first professionals to whom abuse is disclosed and should understand mandated reporting, appropriate assessment tools for screening CSA, and the process for making appropriate long-term referrals. Treatment for children in the aftermath of sexual abuse continues to evolve as well. Attachment-based therapies (such as child-centered play therapy or parent–child interaction therapy) appear to work well for children who have been abused by close family members or family friends or for those whose primary attachment figures were unavailable when the abuse occurred. Body-based therapies (such as EMDR therapy) seem to work well with children whose abuse experiences meet criteria for a traumatic experience. Researchers and therapists continue to grapple with therapies that work best for those who have not storied their sexual abuse as "abuse," but who nevertheless suffer similar detrimental outcomes of CSA. Getting survivors of CSA help in storying and assimilating their abuse experiences is important for the sake of their own life trajectories, but also for the sake of generations to come. As researchers continue to learn more about trauma-induced DNA-structure changes that are passed down through generations of offspring, it is becoming apparent just how critical effective clinical practice with this population really is. Certainly, greater research is needed to establish more and varied evidence-based therapies that can help survivors find their way to recovery and resilience.

Although much may still be unknown about CSA prevalence and the neuroscience of trauma, a good deal *is* known about how a counselor can best help a child in the immediate aftermath of disclosure. First and foremost, it is critical that the counselor believe the child, receive his or her disclosure with both professionalism (competence and composure) and empathy, and report the abuse to the proper state agency or authorities. Concretely speaking, empathic reflection of the child's experience should be the primary skill employed during the session. Keep in mind that repeated questions can feel like interrogations or investigations, overuse of content reflections can communicate practitioner fear, and silence can feel judgmental. Some children may want to story their experience, a process that helps them make meaning from the abuse and even, eventually, perhaps find benefits from it (i.e., "this was a terrible thing, but it has allowed me to reach out to other

kids who have had this happen, too—and it has made me a stronger person"). Other children may not want to discuss their abuse experiences for a long time or at all. Finding therapeutic interventions to accommodate the varying needs and developmental levels of minor clients is as much art as it is science.

Regardless of the therapy chosen, the strength and quality of the therapeutic relationship and how it is maintained are critical. Counselors need to build a relationship with their minor clients that is strong enough to help them trust another adult again, trust themselves, and venture out into the world with confidence. It is important to remember that no two victims of sexual abuse react in the same way. While some may show immediate physical, cognitive-behavioral, or psychological signs, others may present without any apparent symptoms. Parents, teachers, caregivers, and all involved in the child's treatment plan need to be educated about such responses so that the child's experience after disclosure is one of support rather than judgment. As a critical player in facilitating that network of support, counselors should remember to always act ethically, in accordance with laws, and with supervision and/or peer consultation in order that the therapeutic relationship sustains recovery from abuse and fosters growth in the aftermath.

Treating CSA can be complex and both personally and professionally challenging. Self-care is always an important ethic to maintain, but particularly so in working with victims or perpetrators of CSA.

11 Military and First Responders

Seth C. W. Hayden and Lisa R. Jackson-Cherry*

PREVIEW

This chapter focuses on the unique needs of and crisis intervention with military personnel accept and first responders. The first part of this chapter will explore the challenges and needs of military personnel and their families. Whether they provide services in a community agency, a K–12 or postsecondary school setting, or in a rehabilitation context, crisis counselors will likely encounter military personnel and/or families in need of assistance. Military families are a significant part of our communities, with two thirds residing in the larger civilian community and the remainder on military bases (Clever & Segal, 2013). The mental health needs of military personnel and their family members and the increasing demand by this population for access to counseling services requires that counselors understand military culture and effective methods for supporting this population. This chapter provides an in-depth discussion of the military experience and offers various approaches to assist military service members and their families.

The second part of this chapter explores the unique issues encountered by first responders and what crisis counselors should be aware of when working with this population. First responders are the individuals who are the first on a scene to emergency calls involving protection of the community and medical and other emergency situations, such as injuries and fatalities, criminal/civil wrongdoings, accidents, and a multitude of other crisis situations. First responders mainly comprise law enforcement officers (LEOs), emergency medical services (EMS) professionals, and firefighters. First responders and their family members experience unique needs that differ from those of mainstream society. Exposure to daily life-threatening situations, witnessing violent and often fatal atrocities against individuals, while focusing on concern for safety of the community, self, and family members can have an effect on first responders.

MILITARY PERSONNEL AND THEIR FAMILIES

Military personnel and their families comprise a significant segment of the U.S. population. As of January 2016, more than 1.3 million Americans were on active duty in the military (U.S. Department of Defense, 2016). An additional 810,800 service members

*We are grateful for the research assistance of Ana Rivera and Manar Al-Garni, M.A. students in the Clinical Mental Health Counseling program at Marymount University.

comprise the National Guard and the Reserve service (U.S. Department of Defense, Office of the Assistant Secretary of Defense for Readiness and Force Management, 2014). The impact of serving in combat and the effects of deployment on our military and their family members has been the focus of the media and research since the Authorization for Use of Military Force Against Iraq Resolution was passed in 2002 and Operation Iraqi Freedom (OIF) began on March 20, 2003. Statistics on fatalities and physical injuries are staggering and continue to rise, even with decisions made for troop withdrawal. As of November 2015, according to the U.S. Department of Defense (see www.defense.gov/releases/default.aspx) there were 4,409 total fatalities (including soldiers killed in action and nonhostile action) and 31,928 wounded in action (WIA). Of the total reports of fatalities, 98% were male; 91% noncommissioned officers; 82% active duty; 11% National Guard; 74% Caucasian; 9% African American; 11% Latino; 54% under the age of 25 years; and 72% from the U.S. Army. Of the total number of wounded troops reported, 20% include serious brain or spinal injuries. This total of wounded troops excludes psychological injuries.

When considering that 55% of those deployed to Operation Enduring Freedom (OEF) and OIF are married, millions of spouses and children in military families comprise an additional segment significantly affected by the military experience. Within military service, deployment affects a large portion of service members and their families; 55.2% of active duty military members are married, and 37.8% of active duty military members are married with children. The largest group of children is aged between birth and 5 years (495,156) (Office of the Deputy Under Secretary of Defense, 2013), which indicates that many married service members have young children.

Since 2001, over 1.9 million U.S. military personnel have been deployed in conjunction with OIF and OEF (Institute of Medicine, 2010). This ever-expanding community of people associated with the military experience demonstrates the need for counselors to understand the unique needs of this population as it relates to wellness and healthy functioning.

THE RELEVANCE OF THE MILITARY POPULATION TO COUNSELORS

While counselors have a long history of working with military men and women and their families in various capacities, the current and anticipated need has necessitated military systems such as the Veterans Health Administration to formally incorporate licensed mental health counselors into the treatment mechanism of the organization. The Veterans Benefits, Healthcare, and Information Technology Act of 2006 established explicit recognition of both mental health counselors and marriage and family therapists within the Veterans Health Administration (Public Law 109-461). While this development provided the needed emphasis for counselors to operate within the military mental health apparatus, an occupational code to allow the Veterans Health Administration to hire counselors was not created until late 2008. Creation of the new occupational code has since been addressed, which means that positions for licensed mental health counselors are now posted within the federal government for the purposes of providing direct counseling services to military personnel and their families.

Counseling is a resource that is frequently used by military personnel. A survey by the Iraq and Afghanistan Veterans of America (2014) found that 73% of its members who reported a mental health injury have sought counseling services. The level of access and use of services means that counselors must have an understanding of various aspects of the military experience to provide competent assistance to service members and their families.

Military Culture

The military has a culture consisting of shared values that significantly affects service members and their families, and (to a lesser and more variable degree) veterans and their families; that is, once enculturated, the shared values tend to persist beyond active duty. According to the U.S. Department of Veterans Affairs National Center for Veterans Analysis and Statistics (2014), the projected veteran population for September 2014 was approximately 22,000,000, or roughly 7% of the population of the United States. Central themes within military culture are loyalty, teamwork, leadership, obedience, and hierarchy (Green, Buckman, Dandeker, & Greenberg, 2010). Additional values, philosophies, and traditions of military culture include military time, acronyms, and language. These elements are connected to concepts such as discipline, patriotism, subordination, ceremony, and cohesion (Hsu, 2010). This culture is the unique context in which military service members and families function, and it can significantly affect the work of counselors.

CULTURAL DIFFERENCES IN THE MILITARY   When discussing military culture, it is important to consider the within-group differences as opposed to viewing the military as a monolithic entity. There are cultural differences among branches (i.e., Army, Navy, Air Force, Marines, and Coast Guard), and each branch has its own operational structure and procedures, which can present issues during joint operational missions (Green et al., 2010). Counselors who encounter a service member or service family member would benefit from learning the specific organization, common language, hierarchy, and unique characteristics of the person's affiliated branch of the military. The different branches of the military also have their own subcultures based on the type of unit, primary mission, distinct values, and hierarchical structure. Across all branches, officers and enlisted members have cultural differences, expectations, and experiences due to their status and rank.

RESERVISTS AND NATIONAL GUARD VERSUS CAREER ACTIVE DUTY MILITARY   Cultural differences also exist between active duty service members and National Guard/reservists. The recent conflicts in Iraq and Afghanistan have called reservists to active duty in unprecedented numbers, requiring them to maintain a balance of civilian life and active duty deployment. Sudden changes in cultural context can be difficult for reservists and their families. The military culture tends to favor total immersion, creating the potential for reservists to feel more isolated from active military despite serving in the same mission. Counselors who encounter reservists would benefit from assessing the degree to which reservists' issues may be related to and distinct from this cultural dynamic.

Apart from the cultural dynamic, reservists experience significant concerns in comparison to their active duty counterparts. Deployed U.S. reservists experienced higher rates of suicidal ideation and attempts than did active duty personnel who had been deployed. Deployed U.S. reservists also displayed higher rates of post-traumatic stress disorder (PTSD) symptomatology than did active duty personnel and reservists who had not been deployed. A significant concern is the fact that the highest rates of suicidal ideation and attempts were among reservists who had served in theaters other than Iraq and Afghanistan (Riviere, Kendall-Robbins, McGurk, Castro, & Hoge, 2011). Counselors working with National Guard and reservists and their families should be aware of the unique aspects of this population's experience within the military to properly address their needs. Reservists may receive less support and possibly decreased benefits after the deployment ends.

Mental Health and Military Stigmatization

Perceived stigma for receiving mental health intervention may prevent an individual from seeking counseling services. Research has found that veterans of the OEF and OIF who met screening criteria for a psychiatric disorder were more likely than veterans who did not meet these criteria to perceive increased stigma and barriers to mental health care. In addition, negative beliefs about mental health care, particularly psychotherapy, and decreased perceptions of unit support were associated with increased stigma and barriers to care, and negative beliefs about mental health care were associated with decreased likelihood of mental health counseling and medication (Pietrzak, Johnson, Goldstien, Malley, & Southwick, 2009).

Not only is the service member influenced by this stigma, but also the service member's family may avoid accessing services because of the stigma associated with seeking mental health assistance. Service members often report believing that career advancement can be detrimentally affected by the behavior of their family members (Laser & Stephens, 2011). The stigma attached to receiving services can be a challenge for counselors working with service members and their families.

MENTAL HEALTH CHALLENGES   Significant mental health concerns have arisen in military veterans, especially those who have participated in the most recent engagements. Fifty-three percent of respondents in a recent survey indicated some kind of mental health injury; of those respondents, 18% were diagnosed with traumatic brain injury (TBI), and 44% were diagnosed with PTSD (Iraq and Afghanistan Veterans of America, 2014). In addition, 31% of respondents had considered taking their own life since joining the military.

Finally, it is important to consider the relational quality of the military couple. Divorce rates of service members have been on a continual rise since 2001. The annual divorce rate in 2001 was 2.65% and rose to 3.7% in 2011 (Bushatz, 2011), reflecting a steady and consistent increase in marital issues. A counselor working with a military family should evaluate the relational satisfaction within the marriage or determine ways to enhance relational bonds prior to prolonged periods of separation.

The Cycle of Deployment

Deployment is an experience not shared by other segments of our population. Although this experience may not rise to the level of a crisis, the unique aspects of deployment can be significantly stressful for military service members, potentially exacerbating combat-related stress responses. However, preplanning for deployment may decrease crisis situations. The length of deployment, which was once fairly predictable, has been uncertain in the face of frequent deployment extensions and multiple deployments in a short period of time to Afghanistan and Iraq. The deployment cycle does not solely cover the service members' time in theater, since military members are also involved in predeployment and postdeployment processing requirements (Erbes, Polusny, MacDermid, & Compton, 2008). Logan (1987) first conceptualized deployment as a cycle as opposed to a singular event (Lincoln, Swift, & Shorteno-Fraser, 2008). More recently, Pincus, House, Christensen, and Adler (2005) developed this idea further and divided the cycle into five distinct phases: (1) predeployment (from notification to departure), (2) deployment (from departure to return), (3) sustainment, (4) redeployment, and (5) postdeployment. Each phase can affect both service members and their families.

During predeployment, partners prepare to rely on alternative sources of social support (Erbes et al., 2008) and form new roles and norms for the household. Children within the family require significant logistical arrangements as the nondeployed caregiver likely will function as a lone parent for an extended period of time. There also exists the potential that the serving member may not return on time, requiring additional preparation and coping by the family.

During deployment, it is typical for both partners to worry about the safety and well-being of family members in addition to their concern for maintaining the relational bond (Erbes et al., 2008). Safety concerns occur with both war-zone deployments and nonwar-zone deployments, although these concerns are certainly stronger in war-zone activities. Current technology allows for unprecedented communication between service members and family members, but these interactions do not always prevent stress. Issues experienced by both the deployed service member and the nondeployed partner still occur apart from each other without full engagement in problem solving due to distance. Children in the family may also struggle with the absence of a caregiver. Celebrations and milestones are often missed by the deployed member, which may cause a sense of isolation and disconnect within the family and resentment by family members.

Postdeployment (or reintegration) presents the potential for a wide range of concerns regarding the adjustment of having the service member return to the family (Erbes et al., 2008), such as adapting to new roles and rules in the family, reinforcing one's authority in the house, and coping with internal or external feelings of blame or guilt for the absence. The reintegration period requires that the service member and partner reconstruct their relationship and roles at home, as both have inevitably changed as a result of the deployment. The family must also adjust to the resumption of roles of partner or parent (Lincoln et al., 2008) and changes in caretaking roles, discipline, and other familial functions. Complete Think About It 11.1.

This cycle of deployment presents significant elements to consider when assisting military personnel and families. The majority of families possess the skills to successfully cope with deployment, but some do struggle with the stress and experience negative consequences (Chandra, Martin, Hawkins, & Richardson, 2010). Deployment, when conceptualized as a cycle, provides a more accurate framework within which to consider the challenges of service members and their families related to their time in the military.

THINK ABOUT IT 11.1

Think about working with a family seeking counseling prior to the deployment of a family member. You may have only one session to work with the family. What would you discuss to prepare the family for the separation? What questions would be important to ask?

THE PHYSICAL AND EMOTIONAL EFFECTS OF WAR-ZONE DEPLOYMENT

For the first time in history, the number of psychological casualties related to combat far outstrips the number of physical injuries or deaths (Sammons & Batten, 2008). Some projections of the current rate of psychological issues resulting from active service estimate that over 30% of combatants will develop symptoms consistent with a mental health diagnosis. Currently, 40% of veterans who were deployed to OEF (Afghanistan) and OIF have accessed or are currently accessing services at the U.S. Department of Veterans Affairs Medical Center for mental health concerns, including PTSD, anxiety, and depression. These numbers illustrate the high volume of negative mental outcomes related to active duty military in Iraq and Afghanistan.

Apart from the high prevalence of mental health issues, TBI is especially significant in recent military conflicts. This type of injury has become known as a "signature wound" of OEF and OIF veterans, with the incidence of TBIs reported as being far higher in these conflicts than in previous conflicts (Bagalman, 2011). In 2010, a full 45,606 service members were diagnosed with TBI-related conditions at Veterans Affairs medical facilities. Within U.S. Department of Defense health care systems, 30,703 service members sustained TBI and an estimated 20% of OEF and OIF veterans have suffered some form of a TBI (Tanielian & Jaycox, 2008). The prevalence of TBI within our military population increases the likelihood a counselor will encounter this issue when working with service members. Crisis counselors should be aware of this rate and inquire as to the experiences during war-zone deployments that may have increased a veteran's chances of developing a TBI. Appropriate referrals should be made to medical professionals to ensure the treatment of the whole person. While injuries and mental health issues may manifest over time, there is also an indication that symptoms of combat-related mild traumatic brain injury (MTBI) or PTSD may disappear or be significantly reduced after returning from combat. A counselor encountering these issues would benefit from determining both the symptomatology related to PTSD and MTBI, the time frame associated with the injury, and the past and current treatment implemented to address these issues.

Other physical injuries may also be present at the same time as mental health and other medical issues. Advances in life-saving medical procedures and medical technologies mean that counselors may be working with military personnel with many physical and mental health issues. Many service members may return with polytraumatic injuries, including TBI, injuries to several body systems (e.g., skin/soft tissue, eye injuries), complex pain syndromes, and PTSD (Collins & Kennedy, 2008). This reality presents a special clinical situation in which counselors may need to work closely with other providers who are serving military members and their families to address complex issues of mental and physical injuries related to their experiences during deployment.

SEPARATION FROM THE MILITARY AND MENTAL HEALTH ISSUES

There has been conflicting information on suicide rates and the military population involved in recent war-zone deployments. For example, a recent media report indicated that the rate of suicide was growing among active duty personnel (Roan, 2012). A research study reported a significantly higher rate of suicide in veteran men compared with nonveteran men (Kaplan, McFarland, Huguet, & Newsom, 2012). *Military Times*, which conducted the largest study to date exploring suicide rates of military members, found no link between combat deployment and suicide (Kime, 2015). This study consisted of 3.9 million service members either in active or reserve duty from 2001 to 2009. The study reported that a total of 31,962 deaths, including 5,041 suicides, took place during that time. It found that the suicide rates were not higher for military personnel deployed to Iraq, Afghanistan, or other war-zone countries. Of the 5,041 total suicides, 1,162 involved military personnel who had deployed and 3,879 involved military personnel who had never deployed. The study found the suicide rate for the military was 17.78 per 100,000 person-years (a statistical measure) compared with 18.1 per 100,000 person-years in the general population. The suicide rate increased slightly to 19.92 per 100,000 person-years for those who experienced multiple deployments. However, a much higher suicide rate of 26.48 per 100,000 person-years was associated with those who had early separation with deployment. Another important finding was that the suicide rate for those in the Army who had experienced early separation and no deployment was 28.1 per 100,000 person-years. Similarly, the suicide rate for Marines who had experienced early separation and no deployment was 32.6 per 100,000 person-years.

Based on the *Military Times* study (Kime, 2015), separation from the military appears to be a determining factor when evaluating increased suicide risk in the military: 26.06 per 100,000 person-years after separating from military service compared with 15.12 per 100,000 person-years for those who did not separate from the military. It is possible that many military members who separate from the military may have had preexisting mental health or medical risk factors that may have contributed to their separation, leading to a "less than honorable" or "dishonorable" discharge. In the military, the connection of meaning, purpose, and identification to one's career may be another reason the link between separation from the military and higher suicide rates was discovered. Likewise, the support and connection while in the military is considered a strong support mechanism. Separation from this support may increase suicide rates, in particular when some sense of humiliation is felt due to the type of military discharge. This study's findings provide critical information to crisis counselors and the field of counseling. When working with military personnel, asking about military separation is crucial. See Case Study 11.1, which considers how to provide counseling to a client who experiences TBI and PTSD and separation from the military.

CASE STUDY 11.1

Dealing with Traumatic Brain Injury and Post-Traumatic Stress Disorder

Raul is a recently transitioned male of Hispanic descent who provided 12 years of quality service as a marine prior to suffering a TBI. In addition to his TBI, Raul experiences PTSD and is not able to serve with his unit. He indicated, "I feel like a failure due to my not being there for them." Raul indicates the stress of his injury and the sense of isolation he has been experiencing due to his issues relate to not returning to combat with his unit.

Discussion Questions

1. What unique stressors does Raul present based on your understanding of PTSD and separation from the military?
2. What specific questions would you want to ask Raul to better understand the impact of his situation based on the information you have been given?
3. What referrals and resources would be helpful to offer Raul?

MILITARY WOMEN   After women return from deployments, they tend to present with similar mental health problems as their male counterparts: PTSD, depression, relationship difficulties, and increased substance use. The cause for some of these mental health diagnoses may differ for men and women. The impact of combat on women is just becoming evident, and it will take some time to understand the full impact as more data are collected. Since the start of the Iraq and Afghanistan wars, over 26,000 female veterans have been diagnosed with some sort of mental disorder. As of 2009, 11,713 female military service members diagnosed with PTSD reported sexual assault as a main cause of distress (Robbins, 2010). As of 2009, over 3,200 sexual assaults were reported in the military, an increase of 11% from 2008, and Veterans Affairs hospitals reported an estimated 22% of women experienced some aspect of sexual trauma during their military career (Robbins, 2010).

ISSUES FOR MILITARY FAMILIES RELATED TO DEPLOYMENT

It is important to recognize that many military families display a high level of resilience regarding the stress of deployment. Although many successfully manage the situation, military families often experience problems meeting the challenges. The following section discusses the ways in which military families may struggle with the deployment experience.

Familial Stress Associated with Deployment

Given the high rate of veterans who are married and have children, it is important to consider the influences deployments have on family members. Previous studies indicated that deployment was associated with increased stress among nondeployed parents (Chandra, Lara-Cinisomo et al., 2010). Factors such as length of parental deployment and poorer nondeployed caregiver mental health were significantly associated with a greater number of challenges for children both during deployment and deployed-parent reintegration. There is evidence of higher rates of separation and divorce as well as incidents of domestic violence with OEF/OIF combat veterans (Sayers, Farrow, Ross, & Oslin, 2009).

Extensions in deployment and multiple deployments because of extended conflicts in Iraq and Afghanistan have affected nondeployed spouses and deployed spouses and partners. SteelFisher, Zaslavsky, and Blendon (2008) found that spouses who experienced deployment extensions reported higher rates of mental health issues and evaluated the Army more negatively than previous spouses who did not experience extensions. A counselor who assists families experiencing multiple deployments may encounter high levels of stress and frustration within the family and expressions of frustration with the military structure related to the prolonged deployments.

In families with children, research indicates that child maltreatment and neglect occur at higher rates during deployment (Gibbs, Martin, Kupper, & Johnson, 2007). Deployment exacerbates a parent's struggle to fulfill children's needs. While the caregivers' interactions with their children may be affected by deployment, the mental health of the children is also a concern. Barker and Berry (2009) found that children unable to cope with a deployed parent often demonstrated increased behavioral problems at deployment and attachment problems at reunion compared with children whose parents had not recently deployed. Research indicates that the mental health of children and adolescents is influenced by the stress of a parent's deployment (Lincoln et al., 2008). Dealing with the unavailability of a parent for an extended period of time, along with the heightened stress within the family, can contribute to emotional issues that manifest in children of deployed service members. Family members may also worry about the physical and mental well-being of the returning service member and a potential subsequent deployment (Chandra, Lara-Cinisomo et al., 2010; Chandra, Martin et al., 2010; Chandra et al., 2011).

Reunification

In addition to the time apart, challenges exist during the reunification of the service member with the nondeployed spouse and family. Previous research regarding reunification has indicated potential struggles within the family (Chandra, Lara-Cinisomo et al., 2010; Chandra, Martin et al., 2010; Chandra et al., 2011). There may be conflict associated with familial roles and boundaries that require renegotiation. There may be conflict over ways the house was managed and the loss of the spouse's newfound independence. Military family members may also struggle with adjusting to new relationships that were developed during deployment. Feelings of abandonment during the prolonged separation may also exist. Unresolved issues may also reemerge and occur simultaneously with new issues related to readjustment to the new familial dynamic. Family members may also struggle with negotiating a balance between the support networks formed during deployment and independence. Children within the family may reject, show apathy toward, or have anxiety around the returning family member. Children may also display loyalty toward the nondeployed parent while also being resistant to the disciplining of the returning parent. Complete Think About It 11.2.

THINK ABOUT IT 11.2

Think about what it would be like to provide marriage counseling to a couple, one of whom is in the military. The husband says that he has just come home from his second deployment; each deployment lasted 13 months. The presenting issue is centered on the husband not feeling involved in the family and the kids not listening to his authority. During the session, the husband states that he feels restless and has difficulty sleeping, is unable to concentrate, has headaches, and sometimes feels dizzy. What are your primary and secondary priorities?

COUNSELOR INTERVENTION WITH MILITARY SERVICE MEMBERS

The U.S. Department of Defense and the Veterans Health Administration provide myriad services designed to support military personnel and families. While these organizations strive to support service members and their families, there is recognition of the need for quality interventions from community-based organizations and personnel to address the ongoing needs of this population (Burnam, Meredith, Tanielian, & Jaycox, 2009). Despite the counselor's setting or primary focus, there is a strong possibility of encountering service members and veterans in one's counseling practice.

The discussion of interventions that follows will largely focus on systemic interventions as opposed to viewing an issue in isolation. In addition, this section will provide specific strategies to address common issues among military personnel, such as PTSD, TBI, suicide, and family issues. Collaboration between civilian and military counselors and integration of support services by military family service providers is useful when assisting families (Hayden, 2011).

The approaches reviewed below are by no means an exhaustive list of ways to support military personnel and families. This discussion is intended to provide tangible means to intervene in crisis situations. Collaboration and service integration are key, but clinical expertise and experience will be a preeminent resource for assisting this population as you consider their unique needs. Crisis counselors should be aware of the issues outlined in this chapter and gather information from the military service member and family in order to make a referral to the appropriate treatment provider. Crisis counselors should have knowledge of various treatments in order to appropriately make a referral to the next level.

Interventions for Post-Traumatic Stress Disorder

When addressing PTSD, collaborating with other service providers is a critical component of effective intervention. A counselor addressing various issues associated with PTSD would benefit from considering the previously mentioned aspects of the military context in which military members and their families operate. Doing so involves acquiring general knowledge of the cultural realities of this population via education, training, and supervision. Lack of awareness of military culture can be a therapeutic barrier in counseling. Learning about the context within which military personnel and families function will enhance the counselor's ability to engage with service members in counseling. The interventions that follow were chosen because of empirical evidence that supports their use. The goal is to provide the reader with some tangible interventions to address common issues within this population.

RESILIENCE RELATED TO POST-TRAUMATIC STRESS DISORDER   Military mental health has focused on building preventive resilience to PTSD prior to exposure to traumatic events. Evidence for this approach is ample when focusing on psychoeducational discussions of resilience, enhancing awareness of emotional and physical experiences, and attention to positive emotional experiences and social bonds (Kent, Davis, Stark, & Stewart, 2011). Working with service members to develop resilience when it is apparent they are likely to be exposed to traumatic events provides a preventive approach as opposed to a reactive approach in addressing PTSD. Prevention is an important aspect in crisis intervention. Education and counseling prior to a deployment can assist in decreasing crises, in this case PTSD.

TRAUMA-FOCUSED COGNITIVE-BEHAVIORAL THERAPY   One intervention often used to address PTSD is trauma-focused cognitive-behavioral therapy (TF-CBT), an approach endorsed in clinical practice guidelines by the Veterans Health Administration, Department of Defense (2010). These guidelines provide evidence-based practices related to commonly encountered mental health issues within the military population. TF-CBT involves confronting the memories of the traumatic events and the feared and avoided external situations that remind clients of the events (Creamer, Wade, Fletcher, & Forbes, 2011). The maladaptive interpretations and beliefs associated with the events interfere with adaptation and recovery (Forbes et al., 2007). This cognitive-behavioral approach offers a framework within which to address PTSD (see Chapter 10).

Some TF-CBT approaches have evidence of effectiveness. Prolonged exposure techniques, where the service member is subjected to the avoided or feared event *in vivo*, have demonstrated effectiveness in the treatment of PTSD (Powers, Halpern, Ferenschak, Gillihan, & Foa, 2010). There has been support for the use of TF-CBT in adults (Bisson, Roberts, Andrew, Cooper, & Lewis, 2013) and specifically with veterans (Goodson, Helstrom, Halpern, Ferenschak, & Gillihan, 2011). Crisis counselors implementing this intervention are cautioned to ensure that they are competently trained in this technique due to the intensity and affective elements associated with exposure to traumatic stimulus.

COGNITIVE PROCESSING THERAPY   Cognitive processing therapy has shown positive effects for addressing PTSD. Cognitive processing therapy focuses on the range of emotions, in addition to anxiety, that may result from traumatization (e.g., shame, sadness, anger). A benefit of this approach to PTSD is that cognitive processing therapy can be generalized to comorbid mental health conditions and day-to-day problems, and it is in a manualized format that allows for widespread dissemination (Monson et al., 2006). Cognitive processing therapy can be implemented using a 12-session, manualized approach (Resick, 2001) focused primarily on cognitive interventions. The following brief overview of this approach will assist with providing an understanding of how to implement this intervention. Crisis counselors should know who is able to provide these services (i.e., to be able to make a referral) if the services cannot be provided during a limited exposure to the military client.

A counselor begins cognitive processing therapy by offering psychoeducational information related to the symptoms of PTSD, keeping in mind the cognitive and information processing aspects of the condition (Monson et al., 2006). After the initial session, the client is asked to write an "impact statement" in which he or she details the meaning of the traumatic event, including beliefs about why the event happened. This statement is then discussed in subsequent sessions with the counselor, evaluating various problematic beliefs and cognitions. The client is then taught to identify the connection between events, thoughts, and feelings with homework assignments related to understanding the relationship among these elements. The counselor then follows up with the client on the homework. Various activities, such as having the client consider current stressful events and gradually processing these events, are aspects through which the counselor guides the client through a reprocessing of various experiences. The counselor challenges problematic beliefs and cognitions when clinically appropriate. Typical homework assignments involve worksheets in which the service member processes his or her day-to-day life to enable analysis and modification of various maladaptive beliefs and cognitions. Counseling concludes with the consolidation of treatment gains.

EYE MOVEMENT DESENSITIZATION AND REPROCESSING   Eye movement desensitization and reprocessing (EMDR) is a one-on-one form of psychotherapy designed to reduce trauma-related stress, anxiety, and depressive symptoms of PTSD (Substance Abuse and Mental Health Services Administration [SAMHSA], 2010). Steps in this approach include first reviewing the client's history and assessing for readiness for this intervention followed by the preparation phase of having the client identify a positive memory associated with feelings of safety or calm that can be used if psychological distress associated with the traumatic memory is triggered. The counselor then works with the client to elicit the target traumatic memory, with attention on the image, negative belief, and body sensations. EMDR includes repetitive dual attention exercises, combining motor task and traumatic memory, then processing the negative thought, associations, and/or body sensations. A common motor task is a side-to-side eye movement to follow a counselor's finger. Other potential dual-attention tasks include hand tapping or auditory tones. This activity is repeated until the client reports no distress. Client progress is reviewed as scenarios and positive sense of self when recalling the target trauma are discussed. Ongoing supportive activities include journaling, noting any material related to the traumatic memory and focusing on the previously identified positive, safe, or calm memory whenever distress with the target trauma is activated.

This approach has been endorsed as an effective treatment for PTSD within the Veterans Health Administration, Department of Defense (2010), although there are indications of a lack of extensive quality research to support using EMDR in the treatment of PTSD for military service members (Verstrael, van der Wurff, & Vermetten, 2013). This means it is important for the counselor to determine the appropriate situation in which to implement this approach in addition to determining if a referral for EMDR is warranted. Additional research studies into the use of EMDR with veterans that consists of larger sample sizes would be useful.

MINDFULNESS-BASED STRESS REDUCTION FOR MENTAL HEALTH ISSUES   While cognitive-based approaches such as the prolonged exposure technique have shown utility in stress reduction, a trial of cognitive processing therapy for military-related PTSD found that 30 to 50% of veterans who participated in prolonged exposure or cognitive processing therapy did not exhibit clinically significant improvements (Forbes et al., 2012). In addition, the dropout rate for these treatments appears to be high (Kehle-Forbes, Meis, Spoont, & Polusny, 2015), indicating the need to develop alternative techniques to address PTSD.

Polusny et al. (2015) found that a mindfulness-based group intervention was effective in reducing the severity of PTSD symptoms. The intervention involved focusing on the present moment (i.e., immediate emotional and physical states, including discomfort) in a nonjudgmental and accepting way. The sessions included didactic training and formal practice of three meditation techniques (i.e., body scan, sitting meditation, and mindful yoga). These sessions, coupled with a day-long silent retreat, allowed for a prolonged practice of these techniques. Participants were also encouraged to practice these techniques at home. Cultivating present-moment awareness in ordinary daily activities was an additional element of this approach. This approach can be useful when considering alternative forms of treatment due to the apparent lack of effectiveness in previous treatments such as prolonged exposure, or when a client either already engages in mindfulness-based activities or prefers an alternative approach. This approach can also be used for a variety of mental health issues, including anxiety and depression.

Traumatic Brain Injury

The severity of TBI injuries ranges from mild—involving a brief change in mental status and consciousness—to severe—involving an extended period of unconsciousness or amnesia after the injury (Centers for Disease Control and Prevention, 2006). Due to the potential for TBIs being undiagnosed or misdiagnosed, a clinician should inquire about any sort of head trauma when working with service members who may come to counseling for other issues, such as PTSD, anxiety, or depression (Landau & Hissett, 2008). The most frequent unmet needs of this population are improving memory and problem solving, managing stress and emotional upsets, controlling anger, and improving job skills. Several of these issues fall within the realm of counseling, heightening the likelihood of counselor involvement in treatment. Asking about direct or indirect exposure to improvised explosive devices (IEDs) is crucial to treat the whole person and make appropriate referrals to medical professionals.

Suicide Risk Assessment

Suicide risk assessment should always be the focus of crisis counselors. Equally important in this assessment, although less evident, is the risk of harm to others. Assessing for the potential to harm oneself and assessing for indications of isolation are critical to ensure the safety of the client. It is important for crisis counselors to ask questions about separation from the military, current relationship issues, psychological and physical injuries, and unresolved memories when assessing for suicide or homicidal ideation and behaviors.

Joiner's interpersonal-psychological theory of suicide (Monteith, Menefee, Pettit, Leopoulos, & Vincent, 2013) has relevance to this population. Joiner's theory holds that people who die by suicide may perceive themselves as a burden to others, have a thwarted sense of belonging, and have the capability to engage in a lethal act as a result of experiences that caused pain and fear (Joiner, 2005). A study of U.S. Air Force suicides has shown that these three elements collectively differentiated a sample of living Air Force personnel from a sample of Air Force personnel who died by suicide (Nademin et al., 2008). This differentiation is also an indication that perceived burdensomeness and its interaction with belongingness are significant predictors of suicidal ideation (Monteith et al., 2013). Exploring or helping to develop a new sense of meaning after a deployment may also be an essential aspect in decreasing lethality.

Supporting Military Families

Military families may be affected by deployment and by the potential physical and mental health issues service members develop related to their combat experiences. This highlights the need to continually consider the family when working with service members. It is essential for civilian and military providers to collaborate with each other to ensure that the family's needs are being effectively addressed (Hoshmand & Hoshmand, 2007).

Hayden (2011) surveyed service providers in U.S. Army Family Centers and found frequent collaboration between military and civilian providers. Military family support professionals indicated collaboration enhanced their awareness of services, increased access to services for family members, and enhanced continuity of care. Continuity of care is critical given the frequent mobility of this population. Service

ACTIVITY 11.1

Over the next week, investigate the clinical mental health, rehabilitative, religious/spiritual, and medical resources available for military members and family members in your community to develop your understanding of community resources for potential referrals.

providers also indicated collaboration could be expanded through outreach between civilian and military providers in addition to reorganizing support services to lower barriers among branches of the military. Since the family system within the military is continually experiencing change, professional intervention should be systems-oriented and multilayered (Huebner, Mancini, Wilcox, Grass, & Grass, 2007). Complete Activity 11.1 to enhance your knowledge of community resources for referrals.

An additional intervention is to develop programs that integrate education and training for families of injured service members who are being followed throughout the military medical services or Veterans Affairs hospitals. Acting in collaboration with military medical services and Veterans Affairs hospitals, specific community mental health specialists with specific training and expertise in treating children and families of military personnel is important. Lincoln et al. (2008) have also suggested building interdisciplinary trainings for community-based mental health professionals with the goal of normalizing expectations regarding psychological reactions to deployments, clinical problems associated with all phases of deployment, interventions, and resources available to children and families of service members. A counselor is uniquely positioned to be a critical asset to military service members and families by addressing healthy adaptation, resilience, and additional issues when they arise.

THE SPIRITUAL AND RELIGIOUS NEEDS OF DEPLOYED MILITARY SERVICE MEMBERS

An area receiving even less attention in the literature has been how spiritual and religious practices may affect mental health during predeployment, deployment, and reintegration. Of Americans, 69% reported being very or moderately religious and 40% reported attending religious services on a regular basis (Newport, 2012). In a study conducted with approximately 300 deployed military service members in Iraq, Sterner and Jackson-Cherry (2015) found religious and spiritual practices to be reflective of the general population and a strong support for many military service members while deployed. In fact, many of those who were surveyed stressed the importance of their practices to work through many of the existential and relationship struggles they encountered while deployed. In taking a preventive approach, it would seem essential to evaluate effective and positive coping mechanisms that have been helpful in noncombat situations and make those strategies available while in combat.

The wellness approach proposes that a "well" person is one who has balanced essential dimensions, such as intellectual, emotional, physical, social, occupational, and spiritual components. Indeed, spiritual and religious beliefs and practices have been viewed as influencing worldviews and behaviors, and are relied upon by many as a coping mechanism through religious ceremonies and services (Biema, 2001). Prayer, meaning, and positive faith have been linked to reduced symptoms of post-traumatic stress in those service members directly and indirectly exposed to the trauma. Gerber, Boals, and Schuettler (2011) found positive religious coping practices were directly related to post-traumatic growth and inversely related to post-traumatic stress. In a study of deployed military personnel, Harris et al. (2011) found that individuals who perceived their spirituality as a source of validation and acceptance were more likely to find healthy meaning in their deployment and recover from trauma. Sterner and Jackson-Cherry (2015) found that having a sense of purpose, maintaining healthy relationships or supports during deployment, and integrating religious and/or spiritual practices can be essential to decreasing symptoms of anxiety and depression while deployed. Read Voices from the Field 11.1 and 11.2 to gain further insights about military service members.

VOICES FROM THE FIELD 11.1
Anonymous Responses from Deployed Military in Combat

- **What makes you feel at peace?**

"After praying and talking to my younger children and seeing them happy and innocent brings peace."

"Knowing that in my mind God or a higher power is there with me and he will only give me what I can handle."

- **What events tested your faith/spirituality?**

"When I knew soldiers who were killed in combat, and some of them were Christians and others were not. It's just conflicting for me personally when thinking about someone I know who was a good person and a good soldier and wondering whether or not he's in Heaven."

"Death of soldiers, close call with husband, marriage issues all had me questioning 'why' but it wasn't for long that I got my answer from His word (the Bible)."

"When the bridge was blown up, it made me thank God as soon as we got a second to stop and think."

VOICES FROM THE FIELD 11.2
A Warrior's Story

Tracy Roberts

Working as a rehabilitation counselor with a U.S. Marine Corps veteran of Iraq recently provided me with the opportunity to hear about his combat experience and blast injuries and learn about what it is like for him to live with MTBI, PTSD, chronic pain, and vision impairment. Our work together came to focus on identifying his goals for his post-injury civilian life and creating strategies together, ultimately implementing them while integrating recommendations from our entire team of treating medical professionals and discipline-specific specialists, such as occupational, physical, and speech therapists. Re-entering civilian life as a food ministry volunteer worker was one of his goals. To accomplish it, we implemented systematic desensitization as one treatment for his PTSD, first driving by the facility, next visiting it while it was empty, then again for a short period of time when operational, and ultimately returning weekly to volunteer on a regular basis. We identified and used cognitive interventions for MTBI like written instructions, pain management tools such as a special portable stool, and visual aids such as specially filtered sunglasses for photosensitivity. All the while, my client and I processed his grief over significant loss and his awareness of the challenges and rewards specific to finding the strength, courage, and spirit to continue to engage life as fully as possible.

TABLE 11.1 Resources on Counseling Military Personnel and Veterans

Online Resources

SAMHSA's National Registry of Evidence-Based Programs and Practices—Eye

Movement Desensitization and Reprocessing: legacy.nreppadmin.net/ViewIntervention
.aspx?id=199

U.S. Department of Veterans Affairs Suicide Prevention website: www.mentalhealth.va.gov/
suicide_prevention/

Veterans Crisis Line: www.veteranscrisisline.net

Veterans Self-Check Quiz: www.vetselfcheck.org

Articles and Reports

Bisson, J. I., Roberts, N. P., Andrew, M., Cooper, R., & Lewis, C. (2013). Psychological therapies
for chronic post-traumatic stress disorder (PTSD) in adults (Review). *Cochrane Database
System Review, 12,* CD003388.

Goodson, J., Helstrom, A., Halpern, J. M., Ferenschak, M. P., Gillihan, S. J., & Powers, M. B.
(2011). Treatment of posttraumatic stress disorder in U.S. combat veterans: A meta-analytic
review. *Psychological Reports, 109,* 573–599.

Kehle-Forbes, S. M., Meis, L. A., Spoont, M. R., & Polusny, M. A. (2015). Treatment initiation and
dropout from prolonged exposure and cognitive processing therapy in a VA outpatient
clinic. *Psychological Trauma: Theory, Research, Practice, and Policy.* doi:10.1037/tra0000065.

Monteith, L. L., Menefee, D. S., Pettit, J. W., Leopoulos, W. L., & Vincent, J. P. (2013). Examining
the interpersonal-psychological theory of suicide in an inpatient veteran sample. *Suicide
and Life-Threatening Behavior, 43,* 418–428.

Polusny, M. A., Erbes, C. R., Thuras, P., Moran, A., Lamberty, G. J., Collins, R. C . . . Lim, K. O.
(2015). Mindfulness-based stress reduction for posttraumatic stress disorder among
veterans: A randomized clinical trial. *JAMA, 314*(5), 456–465.

Verstrael, S., van der Wurff, P., & Vermetten, E. (2013). Eye movement desensitization and
reprocessing (EMDR) as treatment for combat-related PTSD: A meta-analysis. *Military
Behavioral Health, 1*(2), 68–73.

Veterans Health Administration, Department of Defense. (2010). *Clinical practice guideline for
management of post-traumatic stress.* Version 2.0. Washington, DC: Veterans Health
Administration, Department of Defense.

Table 11.1 above provides additional resources for working with military personnel and veterans.

CRISIS INTERVENTION AND FIRST RESPONDERS

A limited number of jobs involve facing dangerous and life-threatening situations on a regular basis; two prime examples are military combat service members and first responders. Indeed, retired or inactive military often choose second careers as civilian first responders. First responders consist primarily of the following professions: law enforcement officers (LEOs), emergency medical services (EMS) professionals, and firefighters (Public Safety and Homeland Security Bureau, 2010). By their nature and profession, first responders are those professionals, either volunteer or paid, who, because of their occupational responsibilities and sworn duties, are the first to respond

THINK ABOUT IT 11.3

Think about what it must be like to be a first responder to the scene of a crisis or disaster. Before reading the information that follows on stressors experienced by first responders, list the types of common calls experienced by first responders and the types of trauma to which they are exposed.

in a variety of emergency calls from citizens and often to potentially life-threatening situations. In the broadest of definitions, the goal of first responders is to safeguard the health and safety of victims, all while maintaining their own personal safety.

First responders are deployed into dangerous situations daily. They are the forgotten professionals who witness horrifying acts of violence, witness the consequences of criminal and violent acts, observe deaths, and intervene with victims of every age. First responders are among the most scrutinized of all professions, often the least respected, receive little recognition for their actions, have work schedules that conflict with normal family and personal functioning, are underpaid, and experience assaults on their own lives by the citizens they are sworn to protect. First responders are exposed to traumatic experiences, making them vulnerable to a variety of mental health issues; however, first responders are often among the least inclined to seek mental health services. Complete Think About It 11.3.

LAW ENFORCEMENT OFFICERS

According to the National Law Enforcement Officers Memorial Fund (2016), there are more than 900,000 sworn LEOs in the United States. LEOs include state and local police officers, sheriff's deputies, federal law enforcement agents, and correctional officers. LEOs are employed in local communities; local, state, and national parks; college campuses; airports; transit systems; natural resource areas (such as waterways, hunting and gaming areas); drug and alcohol enforcement agencies; and correctional facilities.

LEOs are most often the first responders on the scene. It is a misconception that the main task of LEOs is to fight crime; most emergency calls for law enforcement intervention tend to focus on maintaining peace and solving problems caused by citizens (Olivia, Morgan, & Compton, 2010). The general public tends to contact law enforcement when all options and personal resources have failed, after a crime has been committed, or with the expectation that police will solve problems even if a crime has not been committed. The public perceives law enforcement to be available 24/7, although often police are contacted to respond to situations that are not within the scope of law enforcement. Subsequently, citizens become frustrated when no action is taken regarding their call. Family issues (excluding those calls that meet the threshold for legal intervention, such as domestic violence), mental illnesses (excluding risk issues), substance use, and parenting issues are just a few examples of matters that law enforcement may be called to intervene in, but which are outside the scope of law enforcement concern. Calls must include some potential infraction of a law in order for a police officer to follow through with any action.

Crisis counselors should be aware of the roles of LEOs and the factors that affect their decisions when called to intervene in a situation. Law enforcement interventions are controlled by the policies and procedures of a department and the law. The underlying priority is to protect the community and the officers. For example, during an involuntary hospitalization for a minor, LEOs who provide transportation to the hospital will follow common protocol and handcuff the patient and place him or her in the back seat. This protocol is followed in many departments for safety purposes. It is important to inform the patient and loved ones that the protocol is standard so that the patient and loved ones do not think the patient did something wrong. Counselors may view this protocol as inappropriate, since we view the patient as someone who is in emotional pain. However, a person in pain may react in various ways, such as fight or flight. While officers are transporting a patient, safety of both the patient and officers must be secured.

According to the Bureau of Justice Statistics ("Training/Academy Life," 2016), the median duration of basic officer recruit training is 18 weeks, which is in addition to the field training component following academy training. Across the majority of training topics in the United States, the following components are integrated into the basic training curriculum and are listed from least to greatest attention during training: firearms skills, basic first aid/cardiopulmonary resuscitation (CPR), emergency vehicle operations, self-defense, criminal law, domestic violence, ethics and integrity, investigations, patrol procedures/techniques, juvenile law and procedures, constitutional law, cultural diversity, health and fitness, officer civil/criminal liability, human relations, use of nonlethal weapons, community policing, stress prevention/management, hate crimes/bias crimes, mediation skills/conflict management, domestic preparedness, problem solving, computers/information, basic foreign language (e.g., survival Spanish) (see www.bjs.gov/index.cfm?ty=tp&tid=77).

Stressors of Law Enforcement Officers

Many of the same stressors that affect other first responders also impact the law enforcement community. Shift work, missing family functions, disrupted sleep patterns, poor eating habits leading to health issues, relationship issues, and exposure to traumatic situations that could increase PTSD symptoms and depression are consistent across many first responder professionals. The following sections describe stressors experienced on a more regular basis by LEOs than other first responders.

DEATHS AND ASSAULTS ON LAW ENFORCEMENT OFFICERS   Recent media attention has focused on LEO response to criminal activities in communities. In comparison, limited attention has focused on injuries of and attacks on police officers. More than 20,000 LEOs have been killed in the line of duty in the United States, with 1,466 LEOs killed in the line of duty during the past 10 years. This is an average of 1 death every 60 hours, or 146 deaths per year. Data compiled by the National Law Enforcement Officers Memorial Fund reports 124 LEOs died in the line of duty in 2015, a 4% increase from 2014, when 119 officers were killed. Line-of-duty deaths receive more attention than other work-related injuries, however, the number of assaults and injuries on officers is alarming. In 2014, a full 48,315 LEOs were assaulted in the line of duty, and 28.3% of these assaults resulted in injuries (Federal Bureau of Investigation, 2013a). Injuries can lead to early retirement, which can affect an individual's sense of purpose and meaning, and separate individuals from their social support system.

STRESS AND SUICIDE Larned (2010) compared common factors that contribute to suicide between the general population and the law enforcement community. In the general population, common factors leading individuals to attempt suicide include loss of a spouse or child through divorce or death, legal issues, loneliness, sexual accusations, loss of employment, and retirement. Although LEOs are influenced by many of the same factors that influence the general population, they are also affected by occupational factors unique to the law enforcement community that may increase suicidal behaviors through increased stress. Violanti, Mnatsakanova, and Andrew (2013b) reported that LEOs are four times more likely than the general population to display suicide ideation, behaviors, and PTSD symptoms due to increased exposure to trauma. They also suggested that due to the increased exposure to trauma, LEOs are four times more likely to engage in substance use. However, this information is based on the general population and does not take into account officer resilience, training, internal debriefing, their call to the profession, and their understanding of these risks. Chronic exposure to trauma does not automatically equate with the development of PTSD symptoms or increased suicide behaviors.

O'Hara, Violanti, Levenson, and Clark (2013) reported that suicide is not discussed in law enforcement communities or among officers because LEO suicide is viewed as a dishonorable act that is stigmatizing to the profession. However, other research on PTSD linked an increase of suicidal behavior of LEOs to an increased level of PTSD (Chae & Boyle, 2013). O'Hara et al. (2013) reviewed rates of LEO suicide for 2008 (141 suicides), 2009 (143 suicides), and 2012 (126 suicides). Their study discovered common indicators based on the LEO profiles that allowed the investigators to develop a suicide prevention program. The study's data on police suicide indicated the following: officers who had an average of 16 years of service had a higher rate of suicide; male officers committed the majority of suicides (91%); the age group most at risk for suicide was 40 to 44 year olds; 63% were single; 11% were military veterans; firearms were used in 91.5% of suicide deaths; personal problems were prevalent prior to the suicide in 83% of the suicides; and 11% had legal problems pending.

The following are common warning signs an LEO may be contemplating suicide. Understanding the warning signs and including a common profile of those at higher risk can allow departments to develop suicide prevention programs for LEOs. Critical warning signs include

- Talking about suicide or death, and even glorifying death
- Direct verbal cues such as "I wish I were dead" and "I am going to end it all."
- Less direct verbal cues, such as "What's the point of living?" or "Soon you won't have to worry about me," or "Who cares if I'm dead, anyway?"
- Change from involvement to self-isolating
- Expressions that life is meaningless or hopeless
- Giving away possessions
- Sudden improvement in mood after being depressed. *This is a critical warning sign indicating one has come to terms with his/her own death and may be relieved*
- Increased annoyance that others are going to ruin his or her reputation or career
- Change to neglecting his or her appearance and hygiene and not caring
- Expressions of feeling out of control

- Changes in behaviors that include hostility, blaming, and being argumentative and insubordinate; or a change in behavior to passive, defeated, and hopeless
- Expressed interest in suicide or homicide
- Expression of being overwhelmed and unable to develop solutions to problems
- Requesting another officer to keep weapons
- Displaying weapon unnecessarily or in an unsafe manner
- Being more reckless or increasing risks taken on the job
- Deteriorating job performance
- Increased issues with alcohol and/or drugs (Chae & Boyle, 2013)

OCCUPATIONAL STRESSORS   LEOs experience constant occupational stress that permeates all aspects of the job and can affect their families. LEOs are constantly scrutinized by the community more than any other first responders due to the "us versus them" mentality. Lawsuits and complaints to internal affairs by citizens are common. LEOs are exposed to homicide, horrific sexual crimes, personal endangerment, threats to self or family members, inconsistent work hours, outward disrespect by the community, inconsistent shift work which affects family life, disruptive sleep patterns, lack of social interactions due to schedules, increased personal safety issues, and recent intentional harm to and assaults on law enforcement. Police are expected to make life-changing decisions within seconds and may not have time to process and weigh the consequences. There are usually no second chances. Rarely do LEOs intervene with individuals displaying positive behaviors. Even with victims, the potential for vicarious trauma and job dissatisfaction increase due to not having closure, not knowing if their intervention made a difference, and constant exposure to the negative behaviors of society. These stressors bleed into family life, and can increase isolation and substance use.

Complete Activity 11.2 to better understand how LEOs are perceived in the media.

RETIREMENT   There are conflicting data on retirement and suicide within the LEO community. Violanti et al. (2011) discovered suicide rates were 8.4 times higher in working LEOs compared with those who were separated from the police force or retired. However, officers whose retirements were the result of a disability that occurred in the line of duty displayed increased suicide rates. Lack of a sense of purpose and meaning may be one factor leading to increased suicidal behaviors, as well as no longer having the social support of fellow officers. The information provided in the previous section on military and separation may also be important to review and assess for LEOs. Severing supports with the law enforcement community, having limited supports to turn to, having little access to mental health intervention, and a humiliating separation may increase depression and suicidal behaviors. Read Voices from the Field 11.3.

ACTIVITY 11.2

Over the next week, observe the media's portrayals of LEOs. Are they positive or negative? How do you think these reactions and the "us versus them" mentality affect first responders? Visit the Officer Down Memorial Page (www.odmp.org) and read about line-of-duty deaths. Read the comments from the community and first responders to increase your understanding of how the deaths impact the police and the community as a whole.

VOICES FROM THE FIELD 11.3
Stories from a Career in Law Enforcement

Stephen R. Band

The following are some "true stories" that took place over the course of my law enforcement career as a director of the FBI Behavioral Science Unit and an LEO.

Tempting as it was for me to turn the townhouse doorknob and enter to determine whether the reportedly suicidal occupant was incapacitated, I stepped back. My inner voice resonated, "just because the hair stands up on the back of your neck doesn't mean that nothing is wrong . . . something is wrong (or not right)." Hours later it was determined the "suicidal *and* homicidal" man sat on the stairs behind the door with a shotgun. He decided to "cut in half" whoever dared to enter. Was it the phenomenon of intuition or an inner voice that guided my emotions and actions to live another day?

It was a day like any other on patrol many years ago. The cruiser was moving through the center of the city—a shopping district where folks shopped on streets of our city and primarily moved about with public transportation. There at the bus stop stood a 4-year-old girl holding her mom's hand waiting for the bus to arrive. As the bus pulled up, her hand broke away from her mom's. She then stumbled from the high curb to the street just as the bus pulled up, fell under the huge bus tires, and was instantly crushed to death. The horror and screaming was immense as I stepped from the cruiser. My thoughts raced: "Who knew something like this could ever happen?" (I did; I've been exposed to real-life horror before); "Who cares?" (I did and do, but not to the extent I would ever freeze like a deer in

the headlights); "No problem" (I've got this, my inner voice affirmed). After all, who was I going to call, the police? I WAS the police. A familiar cognitive process constructively detached my perspective into objectivity and the actions that followed.

I'd always found autopsies to be quite disturbing compared with actual law enforcement assignments. Remaining objective seemed to be the key to overcoming the sights, sounds, and smells. One day, a medical examiner asked jokingly if I was going to be OK during the procedure. I informed him that it was not my favorite duty. He was about to enhance my repertoire of coping strategies. Intellectualization is the key, he informed me; do not personalize the experience. Instead, be scientifically objective—be focused and amazed regarding the science of the human body and how it will reveal secrets and you won't be otherwise sickened by the experience. He was so right, and I've used "intellectualization" to adjust thoughts that would only serve as an impasse to potentially incapacitating emotions.

Our inner voice or cognitive process can serve us well in the face of many challenges, or take us to places we'd prefer not to be. People, circumstances, and things cannot upset you. Rather, you upset yourself by the belief they can upset you. Thoughts are, in fact, a creation of the mind, not facts. Is the "roller coaster ride" scary or exciting? Understand this illusion and you will do well on the journey to your preferred future; perhaps a preferred future in responding professionally to critical incidents.

FAMILY MEMBERS OF LAW ENFORCEMENT OFFICERS   Due to the exposure to various traumatic calls, law enforcement families may have increased levels of chronic fear of safety for self and their LEO family member(s). Family members do not witness the atrocities committed in society, nor are they personally involved with traumatic accident scenes, suicides, homicides, abuse to vulnerable populations, or the consequences of violent acts. Families do not personally hear or witness the constant traumatic stories of victims that are often ingrained into the memories of LEOs. However, many officers come home to share their experiences and stories with their family members. The repetition of stories and themes can create fear, anxiety, and depression among family members. Children may be at a higher risk of distress due to their developmental levels when processing the information.

Vicarious trauma and vicarious stress have been studied in detail in mental health workers, crisis workers, and even court workers who hear stories of those experiencing

When I was little, I always loved when people asked me what my father did because I would get to tell them that he was a police officer. I was proud to be his daughter, and he was like a superhero to me. I remember looking out my window when he would drive away for his midnight shift, the shift he was on most of my life. I called him every night while he was at work, and then I would cry because I was worried he might not come back. We knew some police officers did not come home to their families. It was the worst feeling I ever experienced. Even now, in my freshman year in college, I find myself constantly checking my surroundings and being less trusting of people I do not know. I am a more cautious person now because of the stories I would hear from him, which gave me a glimpse into a very scary world that most people could not imagine. I am saddened at how the media portrays police officers and the negative comments I hear from others about the police.~*Gabrielle Cherry (age 18)*

As a child of a police officer, I am constantly worried about my dad when he leaves for work. All I ever hear on the news is "an officer was killed today." It happens almost every day. My dad always puts the lives of people he does not know before his own because he is a caring man; even if it means losing his own life and us not having our father anymore. This scares me more than I have told anyone, and I do not want my dad to think I am scared so I keep it to myself. My dad has friends, family, and coworkers who have been killed because they were helping others. That's why every chance I get, I say "I love you," because I never know if it could be the last time I see him.~*Alexandra Cherry (age 13)*

trauma. If vicarious trauma and vicarious stress can result from repeated exposure to traumatic experiences or hearing the firsthand trauma experiences of another (Famili, Kirschner, & Gamez, 2014), it is not a big stretch to believe that vicarious trauma or vicarious stress can also be experienced by law enforcement family members. A crisis counselor should be aware of the effects on families and know signs of vicarious stress or vicarious trauma, such as preoccupation with the LEO family member being injured or killed in the line of duty. Additionally, hearing only stories of crimes committed may increase stress and preoccupation with becoming victimized, may impact the ability of family members to build trust in others, or increase family members' level of suspicion. In addition, selected media attention on the minority of negative LEO behaviors can also create an "us versus them" mentality, placing family members in a situation where they will most often be loyal to their LEO family and potentially decrease other social supports.

Read Voices from the Field 11.4.

EMERGENCY MEDICAL SERVICES PROFESSIONALS

According to the National Association of Emergency Medical Technicians (2015), there were 840,669 U.S. EMS professionals in 2014; including emergency medical responders (EMRs), emergency medical technicians (EMTs), advanced emergency medical technicians (AEMTs), and paramedics. This number includes approximately 150,000 full-time professionals and 500,000 to 830,000 volunteer and part-time professionals.

EMS professionals range in training and skills and are permitted to offer medical services according to their provider level. EMRs provide basic emergency skills for critical patients. They can perform medical interventions while awaiting additional medical providers. They may serve on a transport team, but most likely will not be the primary

EMS provider. EMTs provide basic, noninvasive interventions to reduce the mortality of acute emergency responses; they can perform all of the duties of EMRs and have additional skills for patient transport. EMTs provide the majority of emergency care and, in some locales, are the highest level of patient care and transport available. AEMTs are trained to perform all the duties of the EMR and EMT and can also conduct limited advanced and pharmacological interventions. Paramedics are allied health professionals who are trained in advanced assessment to formulate a field impression and provide invasive and pharmacological interventions. Paramedics have advanced training and skills and may perform a broad range of interventions for critical and emergency patients.

Stressors of Emergency Medical Services Professionals

Although the skills and training among the various EMS professionals may be different, they share similar stressors and witness the same emergency situations. Additionally, the stressors of EMS professionals appear to be consistent across many studied cultures (Erich, 2014; Minnie, Goodman, & Wallis, 2015). For example, a Toronto study reported that 87% of EMS professionals, when questioned 24 hours following an emergency call, reported some form of stress related to the emergency call (Ward, Lombard, & Gwebushe, 2006). It is estimated that 16 to 24% of Canada's EMS professionals will be diagnosed with PTSD; 16% of South African paramedic trainees meet the criteria for PTSD; and 22% of EMS professionals in the United Kingdom have developed symptoms of PTSD. According to the Centers for Disease Control and Prevention (2012), EMS professionals in the United States experience PTSD and suicide ideation 10 times greater than the 3.6% national average for the general public reported by the American Psychiatric Association (2013).

According to EMS professionals, the calls that cause the most stress are those that involve children, the serious injury or death of a colleague, and the death of a patient while in the EMS professional's care. Calls involving violent crime victims, burn patients, multiple casualties, suicides, and road traffic accidents are also traumatic. Any of these calls should warrant attention for a crisis counselor; however, a significant death, injury to a vulnerable person such as a child, and a line-of-duty death or injury should involve some intervention or screening process after the fact. In addition, injury rates at work are high for EMS professionals. Twenty-five percent of all EMS professionals reported a line-of-duty injury, usually due to transport (Heick, Young, & Peek-Asa, 2009).

As reported above, suicide ideation for EMS professionals is higher than it is in the general population. Newland, Barber, Rose, and Young (2015) found a variety of factors that may increase suicide ideation with EMS providers including the following: sleep deprivation, feeling underappreciated, poor nutrition, limited exercise, long shifts, high call volume, and low pay. American Addictions Centers (2015) confirms the existence of the above stressors and adds the following: lack of administrative support; competitiveness of the profession; and an overall 30% increase in nonemergency calls leading to stress, burnout, high rate of depression, and PTSD. Even less severe injuries can contribute to anxiety, poor health, family problems, abuse of alcohol and drugs, withdrawal, depression, and burnout. Guilt is frequently experienced by EMS providers, and not knowing the outcome of a patient can exacerbate the inability to gain closure and know whether actions taken actually saved a person's life. Read Voices from the Field 11.5.

Jason Stubbs

As a paramedic, we are trained to handle calls of all natures and illnesses. We transport patients with symptoms of minor pain, serious traumatic injuries, and death. I have been an EMS provider for 23 years and have encountered calls of all types. You hope, when your shift starts, that the day will be uneventful. Not for your sake, but for the citizens you are serving. One Monday afternoon in September, my partner and I were finishing up our reports from an earlier call when the alarm sounded. "Medical Box 6-1, Paramedic 600 respond for a fall. You are responding to a 16-month-old suffering from a fall. There is a language barrier and limited information." In my experience, most "fall" injuries are minor in nature and 16-month-olds tend to fall often. This would just be another "run of the mill" call.

As we arrived on the scene, my partner decided that he would go in the house and begin assessing the patient while I parked the vehicle and prepared equipment. As I finished backing in the driveway and put the ambulance in park, I looked in the mirror to see my partner running out of the house with a limp, lifeless child in his arms. This was no "fall" after all. We immediately began working on the child. The family was Hispanic and spoke little to no English and we were unable to determine what events led to the child going into cardiac arrest, as there were no signs of injury that would lead us to suspect a fall or any other traumatic injury. The child was pulseless and apneic. We began

CPR and I placed the child on the cardiac monitor, which revealed no cardiac activity. I intubated the child and we worked vigorously to revive this child as the local hospital was 15 minutes away. Upon arrival in the emergency room, we worked with physicians for over an hour to try to revive him to no avail.

As we were cleaning up our unit, and the adrenalin was subsiding, I began to reflect on this call. Then it hit me, my daughter is the same age as this child. This could have been my child lying on that hospital bed. I started personal questioning: Did I do everything that I could have to save this child? Did I do everything that I would have done to save MY child? There was still 14 hours left to go on my shift before I could hold my child again. On the way back to the station, I called home to talk to my daughter. Hearing her voice hit me hard. All I could think about was the parents of the child I had just tried to save, but I could only watch them as they stood by the bed and mourned their loss.

We are taught that we cannot save every patient. We learn how to distance ourselves from our patients and always be ready for the next one. There have been many calls over the years, and even though we try to compartmentalize them, they have long-term effects on us. We occasionally compare our calls to our everyday lives. I have seen several outstanding paramedic careers end due to PTSD. Without our Critical Incident Stress Management Team, our providers' careers would not last very long.

FIREFIGHTER PROFESSIONALS

The National Fire Protection Association (Haynes & Stein, 2016) estimates that 1,134,400 firefighters were accounted for in the 2014 census, with 31% serving as career firefighters and 69% as volunteer firefighters. Approximately 45.5% of all fire departments in the United States also provide EMS, and 15.5% provide EMS and advanced life-support services. In 2014, there were 64 firefighter deaths, with 22 of those deaths occurring at the scene of the call. As was consistent from previous years among firefighters, most line-of-duty fatalities were attributed to sudden cardiac death (36 deaths, or 56%). As with LEOs, firefighters are more vulnerable to injuries but not assault. In 2013, there were 65,880 line-of-duty firefighter injuries. Due to the unique nature of the profession, many firefighters are also certified and have dual roles as EMS professionals. Therefore, it is important to refer back to the section on EMS professionals because many who serve in this dual profession may experience various types of stressors.

Stressors of Firefighter Professionals

Research on the unique stressors of firefighters is limited compared with that for other first responders. However, it is suspected that many of the stressors that affect EMS professionals and LEOs extend to firefighters and may also lead firefighters to experience burnout and increased stress. Similar to other first responders, firefighters often respond to calls that involve life-threatening and emergency situations and then are expected to return back to work for another call (Cacciatore, Carlson, Michaelis, Klimek, & Staffan, 2011). This expectation and the fact that firefighters often face public scrutiny can lead to compassion fatigue and job dissatisfaction.

The suicide rates for firefighters are unknown, and no nationally accepted agency collects such statistics on firefighters (Wilmoth, 2014). Death certificates do not always include career data, which makes the collection of the suicide rates for firefighters difficult. Because the majority of firefighters are volunteers (69%), affiliation with a fire department would not likely be mentioned on a death certificate. Similarly, the death certificate for a retired firefighter does not necessarily include occupation information. The most recognized credible resource for the suicide rates of firefighters is Jeff Dill, a firefighter and licensed counselor who specializes in behavioral mental health issues in relation to firefighters (Wilmoth, 2014). He gathers information from suicide reports on the website of the Firefighter Behavioral Health Alliance (FFBHA), a nonprofit organization he founded in 2011. He reports that 360 confirmed firefighter suicides occurred between 2000 and 2013, with the highest rates being in recent years; 57 in each of 2012 and 2013. Another recent study was conducted by the National Volunteer Fire Council (NVFC, 2014) and included 800 firefighters to determine levels of suicidal behaviors. Results indicated that one in four professional firefighters and one in five volunteer firefighters considered suicide during their firefighter career.

Fire departments around the country have increased attention on behavioral health problems, specifically alcohol and drug use, depression, and PTSD. Although empirical studies and data on behavioral health are as limited as those on suicide rates, it is estimated that PTSD symptoms may be experienced by as many as 37% of firefighters (Wilmoth, 2014). As with other first responders, acknowledgment and requests for assistance to address mental health concerns continue to be perceived as a weakness and negatively by commanding officers.

CRISIS INTERVENTION WITH FIRST RESPONDERS

Exposure to traumatic calls does not mean that first responders will necessarily develop PTSD, depression, anxiety, or other mental health issues. It is plausible to assume that the majority of first responders, like military service members, chose their career because they are able to adapt to trauma, handle trauma better than others in the community due to personality and resilience, apply training to deter the effects of any trauma, distance themselves from trauma, and enjoy aspects of the job that counter the trauma. Moreover, they were likely drawn to their career due to the unpredictability and dangers of crisis calls. As well, they typically have strong support systems and coping skills.

Most first responders can handle the effects of traumatic calls without any issues that affect their functioning and ability to deliver services. However, any action to decrease or limit the chances of a call turning into a traumatic event, or to combat the high level of suicide ideation and completion is imperative and should be understood by crisis counse-lors. Although there are some unique stressors among LEOs, EMS, and firefighters, first responders share many similar stressors. Common interventions that have been used with first responders include Psychological First Aid (PFA) and Critical Incident Stress Management (CISM). PFA and CISM will be explained in detail in Chapter 12 in relation to working with victims of disaster situations. This section will focus on these and other interventions with first responders. Although the stages and phases may be similar, the goals may differ from disaster victim to first responder. Complete Think About It 11.4.

Psychological First Aid

PFA has been endorsed as a practice model by the Institute of Medicine and is viewed as emotional first aid for first responders (Castellano & Plionis, 2006). The goals of PFA, when applied to first responders, are to (1) provide education and information, (2) pro-vide comfort and enable peer support, (3) increase recovery, (4) promote positive mental health and resilience, and (5) provide access to continued care if needed. PFA was adapted its use in from other emergency situations and initially formally applied to LEOs working during the terrorist attacks on the United States on September 11, 2001, and again follow-ing Hurricane Katrina. PFA has become a best practice model, since the intervention pro-vided during these large-scale emergency responses was found to be effective.

PFA identifies five imperative phases to be integrated with first responders: (1) assessment phase, (2) stabilization phase, (3) triage phase, (4) communication phase, and (5) hotline phase.

The *assessment phase* was designed to provide immediate access to mental health services for those first responders at high risk for emotional reactions due to the crisis event. During the terrorist attacks on 9/11, mental health tents were placed directly at recovery and rescue areas for immediate care. The tents were staffed 24/7 with peers and clinical staff trained to work with first responders during disaster incidents. Most first responders, like military personnel, were dedicated to completing their mission and staying with other first responders. Removing a first responder from the disaster site could cause more traumatic experiences and mental health issues as well as increased guilt in relation to leaving coworkers. It was essential for the assessment phase to take place in a visible location so that first responders could be assessed, receive any needed assistance, and then continue their mission. The *stabilization phase* includes three main priorities: (1) mandatory medical checkups every 12 hours; (2) visible spiritual leadership to sustain morale; and (3) information from media outlets, which, during 9/11, included access to televisions for updated information from outside the disaster zones. During the *triage phase*, performance is assessed hourly and opportunities are provided for regrouping and peer stress intervention. The group cohesion of this phase promotes resilience and a supportive environment. The goal of the *communication phase* is to provide information and education on perceived stressors and anticipated stressors, as well as information on critical incident stress referrals. The *hotline phase* includes intense follow-up with first responders to maintain contact and provide assessments and referrals if needed. In relation to 9/11, the hotline phase provided services for family members for several years after the event.

Critical Incident Stress Management

Many LEO, EMS, and firefighter departments continue to use Critical Incident Stress Debriefing (CISD), which is a component of CISM and is the most common intervention used to provide psychological debriefings to decrease the level of stress resulting from emergency calls. Recently, PFA has been the preferred crisis intervention approach in many mental health agencies. Most researchers do not believe the CISM model to be flawed. However, they do believe that CISM groups should be conducted by mental health providers instead of untrained first responder peers. Wee, Mills, & Koehler (1999) found that EMS professionals who received CISD from mental health providers within 3 months following a civil disturbance (e.g., riots, protests) showed fewer stress-related concerns and decreased symptoms of depression and anxiety. Although the original core elements of CISM were developed by Everly and Mitchell (1999), various other organizations have created and enacted variations of CISM/CISD in their disaster relief efforts (e.g., American Red Cross, National Organization for Victims Assistance, the Salvation Army).

An alternative intervention to CISM/CISD is MANERS psychological first aid, developed by an Australian health agency. MANERS comprises the following components: *m*inimize exposure; *a*cknowledge the event; *n*ormalize the experience; *e*ducate as required; *r*estore or *r*efer to professional help; and *s*elf-care. With the high rate of mental health concerns resulting from witnessing emergency critical incidences and subsequent inaction related to self-referral for mental health services due to stigmas, CISM and MANERS programs should be facilitated by trained mental health providers and not peers.

See Case Study 11.2, which considers interventions for first responders at the scene of a hostage taking.

CASE STUDY 11.2

Responding to a Hostage Situation

Once a recent 14-hour hostage standoff finally ended, a mother and young child were killed by the hostage taker (the estranged father), one LEO was killed in the gun fire exchange, and two other LEOs sustained non–life-threatening gunshot injuries. One officer, who was shot in the back, is expected to be paralyzed. EMS professionals were on the scene since the beginning of the police intervention, anticipating transport of any injured persons to the hospital. As part of the CISM team connected with the police department, describe your action plan for intervening in this situation.

Discussion Questions

1. What groups would you assess as being a priority and how would you proceed?
2. If the timeframe for the standoff lasted longer than expected, how would the intervention change and how would you implement PFA, CISM, or MANERS during the standoff?
3. What unique stressors would the injured officers or family members of the officers experience that may need to be addressed? What resources would you think are important to have available for them?
4. What intervention would you integrate if, during a debriefing, a first responder terminated prior to you getting a comprehensive assessment?

Other Crisis Interventions

The majority of literature on first responders focuses on the professional training and crisis intervention provided by first responders to the community. Other research emphasizes stressors and trauma experienced by first responders. With all the reported stressors, limited research exists on other counseling interventions to address stressors, outside of PFA and CISM. The support first responders find in one another and in the first responder community should not be underemphasized because it is an important part of effective crisis intervention. First responders often believe they will be criticized by their peers for seeking mental health services, although they are often the first to provide needed intervention resources to victims. Many first responders believe their career will be negatively affected if they reach out for mental health services.

FIRST RESPONSE RESILIENCY PROGRAM   Debriefing with peers continues to be the most common form of intervention used to decrease burnout and the stress of the job. Due to the high rate of peer debriefing, a former paramedic and a firefighter developed an extensive resilience-based program that was first implemented to assist in the management of stress and facilitate academic success for military members deployed to Iraq and Afghanistan who were transitioning to civilian life and entering college. The program was successful and the developers were asked to adapt the program for emergency personnel, which resulted in the First Response Resiliency Program (FRP). The FRP focuses on increasing resilience skills and building a strong social support system to decrease or prevent mental health issues (Gunderson, Grill, Callahan, & Marks, 2014). The FRP includes a curriculum of 12 resiliency skills: setting goals; optimizing nutrition; exercising; getting adequate sleep; engaging in relaxation techniques; identifying ABCs (i.e., *activating* events, *beliefs*, and *consequences*); reviewing perspectives; managing self-defeating thoughts; enhancing empathy; weighing wins and losses; reaching out; and developing social support.

PSYCHOEDUCATION PROGRAMS   Due to the common stressors among first responders, stress reduction programs should include psychoeducation programs on healthy ways to combat stress: exercise, healthy eating habits, developing social groups within and outside the department, and talking to family members about stress. Providing information to family members early on can assist the family in understanding expectations and how to find supports. As noted in the stressors among firefighters, cardiac-related line-of-duty fatalities are high for firefighters. In response to this specific issue, improvements in medical screenings and adoption of fitness and wellness programs for firefighters are essential.

SUPPORT FROM ORGANIZATIONAL LEADERSHIP   Organizational supervisors should monitor workload and high-risk assignments. The severity of vicarious traumatization was connected to increased time spent with traumatized clients, large caseloads, and long work hours (Cornille & Meyers, 1999). Research by Cornille and Meyers (1999) also showed that having a more diverse caseload is linked with decreased vicarious traumatization. High-risk assignments such as child homicides and abuse cases that involve torture or cases of incest should be distributed among investigators who possess the necessary skills to deal with their personal emotions. Allowing first responders to attend workshops and training in other areas can help them learn different topics and take a break from their stressful cases.

INTERVENTION WITH FAMILIES OF FIRST RESPONDERS   Intervention and psychoeducation with children of LEOs can help normalize the unique issues only they encounter as children of LEO(s). Concerns of Police Officers (COPS) is an organization that assists family members of LEO(s) who died in the line of duty. Concerns of Police Officers-Kids (COPS-Kids) is a component of COPS that focuses directly on the needs of children and step-children of LEOs who died in the line of duty. Various camps are available year-round as well as group counseling during National Law Enforcement Officers Memorial Week every year in May, allowing children to connect with others in similar situations. Similar counseling groups and camps are also available for parents, spouses, siblings, in-laws, and other individuals connected to LEOs. Crisis counselors and school counselors should be aware of the unique issues children of LEOs may encounter that may complicate grief over another death.

RETIREMENT PROGRAMS   Retired officers can be a great asset in training activities that are beneficial to the retiree and new recruits. Retirement for the general population can affect a person's sense of meaning and purpose. Additionally, retirees encounter a multitude of mental health and medical issues. Violanti et al. (2013a) found an increased risk of medical disease and death connected to retirement of LEOs, mainly liver and colon conditions. They report the average life expectancy for male LEOs to be 66 years of age and predict that the average male LEO will live 10.6 years after retirement. By comparison, the average age of death for males in the general population is 76 years of age. This negative aspect of retirement can be amplified with first responders when their identity is connected to their career and the "us versus them" social support has diminished upon retirement. This group of retired LEOs is in need of an intervention program in any department, including psychoeducation and support groups. Individuals who experience a disability-related retirement have additional stressors, risks, and potential mental health and medical concerns that require special focus.

Summary

Serving the needs of military personnel and their families presents unique challenges for counselors working in a variety of settings. The chance of providing counseling to a military member who has been deployed or working with family members during deployment continues to rise. Many military members will take advantage of services provided in their military communities. More are seeking counseling with civilian counselors because over two thirds of service members live in civilian neighborhoods. More reservists, who make up a large segment of the individuals deployed, are also seeking counseling. Since 2001, the number of women service members exposed to trauma in the military who are being seen for mental health concerns has risen. These mental health concerns may be consistent with those of their male counterparts; however, the root of the mental health diagnosis may be different. An overwhelming number of women report experiencing sexual assault while in the military.

Understanding military cultural norms and expectations is essential to treating the whole person. Deployments offer a unique experience not known to civilians never deployed or exposed to deployments. Many deployed military service members may encounter physical or mental health issues requiring collaboration and services from counselors. Families left behind during deployment also may experience mental health concerns requiring professional counseling services. Predeployment, deployment, and postdeployment each bring about changes and require adjustments. Most service members and their families make adjustments and do not encounter individual or family crises. Others may require some additional assistance to deal with the deployment or reintegration back into the family and culture. In taking a preventive approach, counselors who are working with military prior to deployment may find it helpful to the service member to treat the whole person and explore all the aspects on the wellness wheel (Myers, Sweeney, & Witmer, 2000), including spirituality and religious practices. This chapter offered an overview of the common problems encountered by military personnel and their families and strategies to assist with mental health issues.

In addition to military combat service members, first responders, who mainly comprise LEOs, EMS professionals, and firefighters, are the first to respond to a variety of emergency calls from the community. First responders, as a group, are exposed to a multitude of traumatic situations and experiences on a daily basis. They witness violence, horrendous deaths, victims, and criminal acts by citizens of the community. An alarming number of first responders report depression, anxiety, and PTSD symptoms and present with a higher rate of suicide ideation and behaviors than the general population. The stress associated with the occupation, shift work, poor eating habits, disrupted sleep patterns, and missing family functions due to work often permeate into family life and other relationships. LEOs have additional stressors of increased line-of-duty deaths, assaults by citizens, and line-of-duty injuries than other first responders. Retirement and separation from the first responder community appear to have a negative impact on the health and well-being of most first responders.

Although mental health services are accessible to first responders, as they are for military personnel, most first responders can be hesitant to access mental health services due to the perceived effect on their career. The support first responders provide to one another should not be overlooked. It appears to be an effective coping mechanism for many first responders. PFA and CISM approaches appear to be the most predominant formal interventions with first responders. Crisis counselors should be aware of the unique issues experienced by first responders and their family members when intervening with this population.

12 Emergency Preparedness and Response in the Community and Workplace

Jason M. McGlothlin

PREVIEW

Emergency preparedness and effective responses by crisis counselors are reviewed in this chapter. Given the emphasis that the Council for Accreditation of Counseling and Related Educational Programs (CACREP) has placed on training counselors to work with crises, trauma, disasters, and emergencies, this chapter will focus on crisis intervention models and the clinical implications of natural disasters, terrorism, riots, and hostage situations, as well as the role of the counselor in relation to the community and workplace. The content of this chapter infuses information found in previous chapters to allow readers to synthesize what they have previously read.

STANDARDS FOR CRISIS COUNSELING PREPARATION

Given recent terrorist attacks, national disasters, and crisis situations, the notion of crisis intervention and emergency response has become ingrained in counselor training standards. The most recent curriculum standards of CACREP (Council for Accreditation of Counseling and Related Educational Programs, 2016) place a heavy emphasis on the training of counselors in crisis intervention, trauma-informed practices, and emergency response. For example, all master's level training programs must have curriculum pertaining to the "effects of crisis, disasters, and trauma on diverse individuals across the lifespan (2.F.3.g.)" and "crisis intervention, trauma-informed, and community-based strategies such as Psychological First Aid (2.F.5.m)." Also, all master's-level CACREP specialty areas must have knowledge of the impact of crisis and trauma on clients. Crisis intervention, trauma counseling, and disaster counseling have become integrated in CACREP standards, and they are expected to continue to be part of accreditation requirements for the foreseeable future.

LEADERSHIP ROLES IN A MULTIDISCIPLINARY CRISIS RESPONSE TEAM

Multidisciplinary crisis response teams (MCRTs) have various names, including first responder teams, primary and emergency health care teams, school response teams, and community emergency response teams (CERTs). The hallmark of MCRTs is that they comprise multiple individuals from different professions, each serving a specific function, who collaborate to provide different perspectives on the crisis or disaster. A similar concept that counselors are familiar with is a multidisciplinary treatment team, in which counselors, social workers, vocational workers, psychiatrists, and nurses, work to treat a client, couple, or family. In the case of MCRTs, the client is in crisis. Members of an MCRT work jointly with individuals, families, and groups in a variety of different roles not only to help individuals but also to help reduce the impact of the crisis or disaster on the community.

The role of leadership is essential in managing a crisis or disaster. A variety of leadership roles may be involved, depending on the nature of the event, to respond effectively and to mitigate the effects of the crisis or disaster. If the crisis or disaster is large scale, the Federal Emergency Management Agency (FEMA) or Red Cross may play a significant role in the leadership of managing the situation. They may even coordinate all or at least most efforts. Police, firefighters, and Special Weapons and Tactics (SWAT) members provide leadership in instilling safety and rescue. Medical personnel (e.g., physicians, nurses, emergency medical technicians [EMTs]) lead the effort to treat physical trauma. Mental health clinicians (e.g., counselors, social workers, psychiatrists, psychologists) provide crisis intervention and emotional support to victims of disaster or first responders. Counselors on an MCRT may also be designated to fulfill any of the following leadership roles:

- *Media liaison:* A team member who effectively communicates with the media and other inquiring bodies (e.g., the government, FEMA, families, loved ones).
- *Mortality liaison:* In some crises or disasters, the loss of life is so great or impactful that a member of the MCRT must be designated to accurately convey loss of life to families (see Chapter 5 for information on death notification procedures).
- *The MCRT leader:* In every MCRT, a leader is designated to oversee how the team responds to the crisis or disaster, delegate who is responsible for what, and evaluate the effectiveness of the response.

Read Voices from the Field 12.1.

VOICES FROM THE FIELD 12.1
Crises in the Workplace

Scott Baker

During my time as a crisis counselor on an MCRT, it was not unusual to encounter workplace emergencies. In a large city in the Southwest, the mobile crisis counseling teams had been specially trained by the local fire department to assist with disaster situations. One afternoon, we were called upon by the fire department to assist with such a scenario.

Upon arrival, we were informed that a young man had jumped from a high-rise building. Despite the fire department's best efforts, there was no way to hide the gruesome scene. Our first intervention was for ourselves, taking deep breaths and focusing on the job at hand, reminding ourselves of our training and creating a mental checklist of the steps that we would follow. The first step was to coordinate with other responding teams to identify clients and responsibilities.

The person in charge of the crisis response informed us that our job was to assist the employees who had been working in the high rise. Those employees had evacuated the building when the young man

(continued)

accessed the roof, setting off the fire alarms throughout the building. Thinking the alarm was a test or the result of some minor incident, the employees were certainly not prepared for what they witnessed as they evacuated the building. The young man was falling and screaming, "Get out of the way!" He hit the ground, surrounded by those who had been working inside.

As is common in workplace crises, the situation was more complicated than it seemed. In this case, the employees working inside the building were managers of the large company that owned the building. There had been a labor dispute, and the regular workers were striking. In response, the company had sent managers to staff the building. This added to the horror of the employees, as a rumor quickly spread that the suicidal man was a displaced worker, causing many to feel extreme guilt. It became very important to stop the spread of this rumor, and, once the information became available, to inform the employees that the suicide was unrelated to the labor dispute.

Each crisis team was assigned to conduct a group intervention with 8 to 10 employees. While one team member encouraged the employees to discuss what they had experienced, the other monitored for individual needs. My role was the latter, and I quickly identified my client, a large, middle-aged man who looked very pale, but otherwise unaffected. I spoke with him individually. He proceeded to explain that he was one of the first people outside, and he described, in horrific detail and with very little emotion, what he had seen. After purging his traumatic memory, he looked directly at me and matter-of-factly said, "Well, I guess I'd better get back to work." He started to stand up, but he seemed unsteady on his feet and about to fall over.

I directed him to sit down, explained that he would not be returning to work, and attended to his basic needs. I alerted an EMT, who monitored my client's shock response. We made a list of the things he had to do for the rest of the day, including taking his medication, eating dinner, and avoiding use of alcohol. We made a second list of what symptoms he might expect, how he might cope with each, and what he should do if coping was not working. We identified who would take him home, who would help him through the evening, and where he would go for continued assistance.

When the response was over and all immediate needs met, we returned to the office. Though our shift was over, we stayed and engaged in Critical Incident Stress Debriefing. Even with careful attention to this postcrisis intervention, it was several weeks before I stopped driving past that high rise on my way home from work.

Although natural disasters, terrorism, riots, and hostage situations are all crisis events, a victim's response to a particular event often varies depending on the event and the perception of it by the victim. Crisis counselors should be aware of the unique responses by victims to an event in order to effectively intervene.

NATURAL DISASTERS

Broadly defined, natural disasters are events caused by forces of nature. The consequences of natural disasters come in many forms, ranging from power outages resulting from high winds to mass casualties and staggering death tolls resulting from a tsunami. In a natural disaster, people may blame God or a higher power or rationalize why it would occur. However, if it appears that human negligence was associated with the natural disaster, placing blame on human error is a common reaction by those who experienced the disaster. For example, Hurricane Katrina was a natural disaster, but the destruction was more catastrophic due to human error: the levee failure and delayed action by local government due to poor crisis planning and response.

Many crisis intervention strategies such as Psychological First Aid (PFA), Critical Incident Stress Management (CISM), and Crisis Counseling Program (CCP) can be used to intervene with humans involved in crisis events. However, when responding to a natural disaster, counselors must be aware of the dynamics of the specific disaster to be better prepared for what to expect from their clients and the environment in the aftermath of the disaster.

In Chapter 2, emphasis was placed on safety concerns and precautions for crisis counselors in crisis situations. Safety and self-care are especially critical when responding to a natural disaster. In a natural disaster, counselors who are at the disaster site may see death and dismemberment, experience remarkable emotional reactions to the crisis, and be exposed to harmful situations. Chapter 2 discussed proactive approaches that a counselor could take when working with clients in crisis. When reading the remainder of this section, reflect back on Chapter 2 and relate what you learned to natural disasters. The following list presents considerations counselors should keep in mind in relation to specific natural disasters:

- *Winter storms:* When counselors work in such conditions, they should be mindful of taking care of their own needs to stay warm and hydrated. They should not stay outdoors for long periods of time; when outdoors, they should make sure all body parts are covered, especially the neck and wrist areas; and they should eat and drink on a regular basis to conserve energy and warmth. Lastly, crisis counselors should be aware of the local resources to counter the effects of a winter storm.
- *Earthquakes:* Counselors need to be mindful not only of the environment during an earthquake situation but also of their clients and themselves. They need to make sure that steps are taken to protect themselves and their clients from future aftershocks, check for injuries, and inquire with clients about the location of family members who may be trapped or removed due to the earthquake.
- *Floods:* When responding to victims of flooding, counselors need to be prepared for additional flash floods. If flash floods occur, get to higher ground, never walk or drive through floodwaters, and stay away from flood-prone areas such as ditches, storm drains, and low-lying areas. The most distinguishing aspect of floods is the psychological effect it has on victims. In the wake of fires, earthquakes, tornados, and other disasters, many of the victim's belongings are completely destroyed and disintegrated—gone—and any that remain are not intact. Victims of these natural disasters may have a sense of finality or closure with the notion that "my things are gone and I need to get new things." However, the psychological toll is different for flood victims in that they can see their belongings and how they have been damaged by the flood. Their belongings are not disintegrated and gone, although they are destroyed. Counselors need to pay close attention to how flood victims respond emotionally to revisiting their homes and rebuilding their lives.
- *Hurricanes:* Crisis counselors may be called on to respond to large-scale hurricane sites, such as Katrina. It is important for counselors to follow up with their clients and connect them with long-standing mental health treatment. Crisis counselors also need to know that, because of the intense damage that hurricanes create, dangerous situations can persist after the initial impact of the hurricane. Therefore, in order to stay safe, they should work only in areas that officials have declared as being safe, not approach or be around downed power lines, and not get separated from others.
- *Tornados:* Crisis counselors must be cautious of working near a site at which a tornado touched down because it can be a dangerous environment. Broken glass, rubble, sharp objects, jagged metal, and unstable structures could be present.

When working with a client who has suffered loss due to a tornado, uncertainty about the future and physical heath are the issues of most concern. However, those living in tornado-prone areas (typically known as "tornado alleys") could have existential concerns about when a tornado is going to happen again and why this destruction is happening to them.

• *Wildfires:* Counselors need to keep safe by staying abreast of how the fire is progressing. Some fires move very quickly, and crisis counselors need to make sure they are staying away from the fire's path. Crisis counselors need to be aware of a client's perception of actual and perceived loss. In other words, some clients might know that their home or community was destroyed by the fire (actual loss). Other clients may have been evacuated before the fire came to their community, so they may not know whether their home is gone but they anticipate its loss (perceived loss). This actual or perceived loss includes not only material possessions but also loved ones, pets, and the like. For more information on loss, refer to Chapter 5.

Responses to Natural Disasters

With any natural disaster, there are periods of transition, displacement, relocation, and rebuilding. The psychological toll that natural disasters take on victims is monumental, and counselors need to be aware of all the developmentally appropriate consequences of such events (Baggerly & Exum, 2008). For example, in the aftermath of Hurricane Katrina, job sites were gone, colleges and schools were gone, grocery stores were gone, homes were gone, and victims had to face many questions: Where will I live? Where will I go to school? How will I finish my college degree? Where will I work? How will I get food? A critical task for counselors is to work with clients to become more aware of available resources, prioritize what is important, and help clients triage short-term necessities from long-term wants.

Besides natural disasters, counselors may be called on to respond to disastrous events that are the result of human factors, for example, house fires or structural fires, chemical spills, nuclear disasters or nuclear meltdowns, contagion, and natural gas explosions. As with natural disasters, counselors need to ensure their own safety while they attend to the needs of clients in crisis. James and Gilliland (2017) provided a timeline of responses and interventions for natural disasters, as illustrated in Table 12.1. Read Voices from the Field 12.2.

TABLE 12.1 Timeline for Intervening in a Disaster

Time	Possible Response	Intervention Needed
Initial disaster strikes	• Shock • Fear/panic • Self-preservation • Family preservation • Helplessness/hopelessness • Denial/disbelief • Confusion/disorientation	• Evidence of resources available • Evidence of chaos reduction

(continued)

TABLE 12.1 Timeline for Intervening in a Disaster (*continued*)

Time	Possible Response	Intervention Needed
Hours after disaster	• Same as above • Anger • Grief • Energy/emotion • Action without efficiency • Rumination of disaster	• Evidence of resources available • Evidence of chaos reduction • Organization/control • Ventilation • Problem solving • Connection with loved ones
Days after disaster	• Fear • Denial/disbelief • Anger • Emotion • Rumination of disaster • Cohesion of community • Optimism • Thoughts of predisaster life • That which does not kill me makes me stronger!	• Gathering information about loved ones, neighborhoods, etc. • Crisis intervention therapies • Financial/government support
First month after disaster	• Stopping talking about disaster • Rumination of disaster • Resilience • Possible setbacks	• Prevention of acute stress disorder and possibly post-traumatic stress disorder • Promotion of wellness model • Life viewed as different but goes on
Months after disaster	• Disappointment • Physical and emotional fatigue • Possible onset of panic disorder, anxiety disorder, suicide, depression, etc. • Moving on!	• Psychotherapy • Resources • Continual support from loved ones
One year after disaster	• Significance of anniversary • Family disputes if family members are not on the same level of recovery from disaster • Move on!	• "Life will go on" focus of counseling • Family therapy
Reflection of disaster	• Move on! • Literally move and rebuild? • Grow and build life	• Support • Validation of safety

Source: Compiled from James, R. K., & Gilliland, B. (2017). *Crisis intervention strategies* (8th ed.). Boston, MA: Cengage Advantage Books.

VOICES FROM THE FIELD 12.2

Volunteering as a Disaster Mental Health Counselor

Jason M. McGlothlin

I have been a volunteer disaster mental health counselor for the Red Cross for about two decades. This experience has been one of the most personally and professionally rewarding experiences in my career. I have been exposed to disasters that help me grow and expand my skills, gain experience that allows me to contextualize my teaching and work with clients, and become a more insightful counselor. I highly recommend that all counselors go through the Red Cross disaster mental health counselor training! It provides you with experiences that you would not get otherwise.

Initially, when a disaster strikes, people experience feelings of shock, fear, panic, confusion, and, possibly, disorientation. Statements such as "I can't believe this is happening" and "This can't be happening" are typical. Almost immediately after the disaster occurs, people transition into preservation mode. Thoughts quickly enter the mind regarding the safety of self and family. During this initial time of the disaster, people need to know or be assured that basic survival resources (e.g., safety, food, water) are available. People also need to know that the chaos created by the disaster (e.g., physical or material destruction, community-wide or group-wide panic) will subside. At this point in the disaster, first responders must be visible to increase a sense of hope and reduce feelings of helplessness.

Hours after a disaster strikes, the same emotions and reactions that occurred at the onset of the disaster may continue, although these reactions would likely be decreased, even if the decrease is minimal. Feelings of anger and grief may continue, and people may experience an inability to stop thinking about the disaster. Powerful emotions typically prevent victims from organizing an effective response. Likewise, if the crisis turns to chaos, people may not be able to either provide or receive help.

Hours after the disaster first responders should help people regain a sense of safety in their lives. First responders can be of substantial help by providing basic problem-solving strategies. Individuals may not be able to solve large or complex problems until personal safety needs have been met. Providing resources is crucial, such as connecting people with family members and providing them with resources to meet basic needs such as shelter and safety.

After a few days, people may still experience thoughts of fear, denial, disbelief, anger, heightened emotions, and continual rumination over the disaster. However, some people may begin to see optimism in getting past the disaster and moving on with life. Community-wide efforts may start to emerge to address disaster-related issues. Community efforts instill hope in moving past the disaster and even getting back to a predisaster life (e.g., going back to work, buying groceries). First responders should continue to help people gather information about loved ones, neighbors, pets, and others that victims are concerned about. At this point, first responders can use specific crisis intervention counseling strategies with a focus on rebuilding life to a predisaster state. Also, financial and government support is needed by victims within days after the disaster.

Months after the disaster, people may stop talking about the disaster as life begins to mirror how life was before the disaster occurred. Resilience is a positive sign of healthy adjustment. However, some people continue to ruminate over the disaster.

Rumination can be a precursor to post-traumatic stress disorder (PTSD) or acute stress disorder. Setbacks to resilience can occur because some factors are still out of the control of many people (e.g., government assistance does not occur in a timely fashion).

Helping people a month after a disaster requires transition from the role of a first responder to that of a crisis counselor or other mental health clinician. Clinicians at this point should assess for and intervene to address acute stress disorder and prevent PTSD. Clinicians should promote a wellness philosophy that helps people reestablish physical, emotional, and spiritual health and reinforces the perspective that life can continue, although somewhat differently since the disaster.

The months that follow a disaster represent a time when people can either thrive or become stagnant. People who thrive are those who learned from the events surrounding the disaster and feel as if they are stronger because they survived. These individuals do not perceive the disaster as uncontrollable, often possess effective coping skills, and have a good support system. People who become stagnant at this point can experience physical, emotional, and spiritual exhaustion. If this exhaustion persists, it can lead to thoughts of suicide or to symptoms of depression or intense anxiety, especially if life has not returned to a predisaster state.

Whether people are thriving or stagnating several months after the disaster, it is critical that family and other loved ones show continual support for those who experienced the disaster and that resources are available to help them move on with their lives. Also at this point, people may need to begin formal individual or group psychotherapy in order to prevent or manage symptoms of PTSD, suicide, depression, panic disorder, anxiety disorder, or other feelings that may impair their functioning.

At the 1-year anniversary of the disaster, some victims may have moved on with their lives. However, family disputes may occur when a family member continues to focus on the disaster and continually talks about the events surrounding it, while other family members have moved on with their lives. Because such conflicts can create distance between some family members, family counseling, or individual counseling that focuses on wellness, symptom reduction, and the finding of meaning in life may be warranted.

One year after the disaster, most individuals will have moved on with life. However, those who were significantly devastated by the disaster may need to relocate their residence in order to either distance themselves from the daily reminder of the disaster or rebuild their lives. With these individuals, counselors need to focus on support, validation of safety issues, and possibly continued care connections to counselors in the area where these individuals may relocate.

Overall, the results of a disaster can have short- and long-term consequences for people that may be perfectly normal. In classic works, Everly and Mitchell (1999), along with Alexander (2005), summarized the typical responses to disaster:

- *Cognitive reactions:* blaming, uncertainty, poor troubleshooting abilities, poor concentration, disorientation, lessened self-esteem, intrusive thoughts of or rumination on the disaster, hypersensitivity, confusion, nightmares, blaming others, and difficulty with memory.
- *Physical reactions:* increased heart rate, tremors, dizziness, weakness, chills, fainting, reduced libido, headaches, vomiting, shock, fatigue, sweating, and rapid breathing.
- *Emotional reactions:* apathy, feelings of being overwhelmed, depression, irritability, anxiety, agitation, panic, helplessness, hopelessness, anger, grief, fear, guilt, loss of emotional control, and denial.

- *Behavioral reactions:* difficulty eating and/or sleeping, restlessness, conflicts with others, withdrawal from others, lack of interest in social activities, and increased drug/alcohol use.

Those who work over a period of time with people who have experienced a disaster need to be able to recognize when "normal reactions" to disaster become substantially debilitating. In order to prevent those normal reactions from becoming debilitating, an immediate response to those exposed to a disaster is critical. The goal of such a response is also to reduce panic and chaos.

Everly and Mitchell (1999) proposed that three essential elements need to take place in order to prevent panic and chaos immediately following a disaster. First, a command post needs to be established in order to help people locate and recognize one centralized location of leadership and organization in a time of chaos and disarray. Second, connections need to be made between those exposed to the disaster and needed resources. Third, it is essential to communicate with those in need and create an atmosphere in which feelings of helplessness are extinguished.

The previous information is purposely intended to be general in nature. However, counselors need to consider that everyone experiences natural disasters differently. For example, individuals with some physical disabilities may experience increased frustration due to their difficulty with mobility and lack of transportation after a natural disaster. Children may experience differing levels of age-appropriate fear and thoughts of losing their parents. Older adults may experience heightened physical problems. Individuals from different cultural or spiritual backgrounds may experience increased safety concerns if their cultural or spiritual group is seen as being responsible for acts of terrorism. The basic concept that counselors must remember is that even in times of crisis, an individual's multicultural background and the demographic variables that make him or her unique play an integral part in how that individual experiences, perceives, reacts to, and recovers from the crisis. See Case Studies 12.1 and 12.2, which focus on real-life community crisis situations.

CASE STUDY 12.1

Dealing with a Flood

Anton, a 50-year-old Brazilian man, lives in rural Missouri. He has lived alone for the past 30 years, working in his home as a graphic designer. Anton does not have any family left and rarely talks to anyone except his clients. Two years ago, his hearing began to diminish, and now he has no hearing in his left ear and only 15% of normal hearing capacity in his right ear.

For the past 6 days, torrential rains have plagued his town. The local news and emergency broadcast system warned of flooding and urged residents to evacuate. Rather than evacuate, Anton began to place sandbags around his home to keep the water out. Unfortunately, the water rose too quickly and spilled over the sandbags. Now Anton's home and home office are 7 feet under water. He was rescued by the local fire and rescue unit yesterday evening.

As a crisis counselor, you are meeting Anton for the first time, just 22 hours after he was rescued. You are meeting him in a school gymnasium that has been converted into a shelter for flood victims.

Discussion Questions

1. As a crisis counselor, what would be your priority with Anton?
2. What might be Anton's thoughts, feelings, and behaviors?
3. What resources do you think Anton needs to be connected with?
4. What might be some multicultural considerations for Anton, located in rural Missouri?
5. What might be some long-term effects of this flood on Anton's professional and personal life?
6. What might be some barriers to his recovery?
7. What would be some key counseling skills to use with this client? See Chapter 4 for information on crisis intervention skills.
8. Referring back to Chapter 6, assess this client's potential suicidality. Could Anton be suicidal? If so, at what level of lethality do you think he might present? Discuss various ways to assess Anton for suicide, and think of follow-up strategies to keep Anton safe.
9. With a peer, role-play implementation of the task model of crisis assessment and intervention presented in Table 1.1.

CASE STUDY 12.2

Dealing with a Residential Fire

The Zhang family—Kane, the 32-year-old father; Miya, the 28-year-old mother; Asa, the 7-year-old daughter; and Kenji, the 3-month-old son—lives on the sixth floor of a 9-story apartment building in a major metropolitan area. Last week there was an electrical fire in their neighbor's apartment. As a result, their entire floor caught fire, as did parts of the floors above and below them. The majority of the building experienced significant smoke damage. The Zhang family was awakened at 2:30 a.m. by fire alarms and the smell of smoke. They barely escaped the fire; Kane and Asa both got second-degree burns and Miya got third-degree burns on 10% of her body. All four family members also experienced significant smoke inhalation.

After the fire was extinguished, the tenants were taken to the hospital and treated. The building was declared to be unsafe, and the Zhang family and the rest of the tenants were told that they could not move back into the building.

As a crisis counselor, you are meeting with the entire Zhang family for the first time 3 weeks after the fire. They are living with family nearly 40 miles away from their previous home and did not recover any of their belongings from the fire.

Shortly after the fire, Kane started to drink heavily (a minimum of 8 beers a day and a maximum of a fifth of bourbon a day). You are meeting them in a group room in a local mental health clinic.

Discussion Questions

1. As a crisis counselor, what would be your priority with the Zhang family?
2. What might be some of their thoughts, feelings, and behaviors?

3. Consider the appropriateness of individual, group, or family counseling for this family. How might each be conducted if found to be appropriate?
4. How might you facilitate growth in this family?
5. What might be some developmental concerns for each of the family members?
6. What might be some multicultural considerations for the family?
7. What physical concerns might you have for each of the family members?
8. Consider the reaction and consequence of Kane's recent drinking.
9. With a peer, role-play implementation of the task model of crisis assessment and intervention presented in Table 1.1.

In Case Studies 12.1 and 12.2, no one died, but there was a tremendous amount of loss. What might be some emotions related to loss and grief in each of the case studies? Even though there was no loss of life, could the individuals in the case studies progress through different stages of grief and loss? Complete Activity 12.1.

ACTIVITY 12.1

Research your city and state emergency management plan. Make note of how this plan would directly affect you and your family. Also, make note of how it would affect you as a counselor.

TERRORISM

Broadly defined, terrorism involves acts of violence or threats of violence intended to create terror. However, the Federal Bureau of Investigation (2015) distinguishes between two types of terrorism: international terrorism and domestic terrorism.

International terrorism activities have the following three characteristics:

1. They involve violent acts or acts dangerous to human life that violate federal or state law.
2. They appear to be intended (a) to intimidate or coerce a civilian population; (b) to influence the policy of a government by intimidation or coercion; or (c) to affect the conduct of a government by mass destruction, assassination, or kidnapping.
3. They occur primarily outside the territorial jurisdiction of the United States, or transcend national boundaries in terms of the means by which they are accomplished, the persons they appear intended to intimidate or coerce, or the locale in which their perpetrators operate or seek asylum.

Domestic terrorism activities have the following two characteristics:

1. They involve acts dangerous to human life that violate federal or state law.
2. They appear to be intended (a) to intimidate or coerce a civilian population; (b) to influence the policy of a government by intimidation or coercion; or (c) to affect the conduct of a government by mass destruction, assassination, or kidnapping; and occur primarily within the territorial jurisdiction of the United States.

More specifically, Post, McGinnis, and Moody (2014) suggested that it is not one's psychological makeup or issues of psychopathology that differentiates a terrorist from an average civilian. What makes a person become a terrorist is one's identification with a group and the group dynamics of that group. For example, groups like the Weather Underground and the Red Army Faction in Germany Perpetrate terrorist acts because they believe they are rebelling against their parents' loyalties to a specific government group. By contrast, groups like the Irish Republican Army (IRA) (i.e., nationalist-separatist groups) are continuing in their parents' footsteps in a resistance to a governmental group. Additionally, fundamentalist groups (i.e., Al-Qaeda or ISIS) primarily have a religious "group think" in which they are carrying out the will of God or a higher power.

While most terrorists are what Post et al. (2014) described as abiding to a group-think mentality, over the past several years the notion of the lone-wolf (and lone-homegrown) terrorist has emerged. The lone-wolf terrorist dispenses acts of terror separate from others and, in many situations, in a response to the philosophy of a larger terrorist organization. The lone wolf may or may not be part of a larger terrorist network or cell and is typically seen as seeking recognition or glory alone, and has a clear vision of what the world should be like.

The September 11, 2001, attacks on the World Trade Center, the Pentagon, and United Airlines Flight 93 outside of Shanksville, Pennsylvania, are certainly considered acts of terrorism; specifically domestic terrorism. The current atrocities committed by ISIS throughout the world are examples of international terrorism. However, the broad definition of *terrorism* could also include a coworker entering the workplace with a weapon threatening to kill people. While any example of terrorism is tragic and may fit into the above broad definitions, each act can be very different and have different results on human victims and communities. Clearly, 9/11 fits under the schema of terrorism, but many would consider the example of a coworker with a weapon more an act of violence than terrorism.

An elevated level of stress is a natural response to a crisis, whether it is a natural disaster, an act of terrorism, or mass destruction. In fact, most of the psychological reactions to natural disasters are the same as the psychological reactions to acts of terrorism. The key difference between natural disasters and terrorism is that with acts of terrorism, there is someone to blame. Pure acts of terrorism create feelings of actual blame toward a person or group of people.

Reactions to a natural disaster, riots, or terrorism create two distinct forms of trauma. Individual trauma affects a person's mental and emotional states and requires the person to react to the event in some compensatory manner. On the other hand, collective trauma occurs on a community-wide level whereby communities either join together and prevail, or fragment and possibly create isolation and further conflict. With this information as context, complete Think About It 12.1.

THINK ABOUT IT 12.1

Think about September 11, 2001, when the World Trade Centers and the Pentagon were attacked (or some other disaster you have experienced personally or vicariously). Reflect on the information presented in Table 12.1, especially the "Possible Response" column. Think about your own responses to 9/11 at the different time intervals presented in the table (between 10 a.m. and noon on September 11, later that evening, a few days later, a month later, a few months later, a year later, and now). How did your emotions, thoughts, and behaviors change? Would your responses differ with a natural disaster? If yes, how? What plan would you put into place to gain some control over a similar situation that is not under your control. Explain.

INTERVENTIONS AFTER A DISASTER OR ACT OF TERRORISM

Little literature exists on the types of therapeutic strategies that are most effective when working with victims of a disaster. Regardless of the modality of intervention, the essential crisis intervention microskills (presented in Chapter 4) are critical to building a therapeutic foundation with clients in crisis. Some argue that cognitive behavioral therapy (CBT) can be highly effective due to the positive outcomes for adult clients with PTSD (Lonergan, 2014). Sories, Maier, Beer, and Thomas (2015) state that play therapy is the most beneficial approach with children because it allows children to express the trauma. In contrast, one could contend that meeting a child's basic human needs should be the main concern. Perhaps the most appropriate intervention could be developmental, such as responding initially with a Rogerian approach to allow the client to feel accepted and heard, followed by an existential approach to help the client establish or redefine meaning in his or her life. No matter what type of intervention is implemented, most agree that early interventions increase personal recovery from a disaster (Lopes, Macedo, Coutinho, Figueira, & Ventura, 2014).

Fortunately, the literature does provide insight into some models for intervening in times of disaster. PFA, CISM, and the CCP have appeared in the literature as models that have been successfully implemented in recent disasters such as the terrorist attacks on September 11, 2001, and Hurricane Katrina. A discussion of these models follows.

Psychological First Aid

PFA is grounded in evidenced-based research and provides mental health clinicians with tools to help reduce the beginning stress and trauma caused by a crisis or disaster. The underpinnings of PFA are rooted in the notion that individuals are resilient to some degree and that severe trauma does not necessarily develop into long-term mental health problems. PFA is a practical approach that emphasizes the treatment of individuals experiencing a variety of emotional, psychological, behavioral, spiritual, and physical reactions to a crisis or disaster. PFA has been shown to work with individuals of all ages as well as in group settings.

According to the National Child Traumatic Stress Network (2012), the basic guidelines of PFA are as follows:

- Be compassionate and provide emotional comfort.
- Connect with individuals in a nonintrusive and non-threatening manner.
- Recognize that the relationship between the individual and the clinician is important.
- Empower individuals to believe in the notion that they are safe and that they will continue to be safe.
- Encourage individuals to be specific in their immediate.
- Focus on heightened emotional states with individuals and attempt to reduce feelings of being overwhelmed and hopeless.
- Help individuals reduce feelings of isolation by connecting them to their family and friends as soon as possible.

- Be aware of cultural and spiritual differences, as they may play a large role in reaction to and coping with trauma.
- Provide individuals with realistic resources and the practicalities of such resources (i.e., when and where they are available).

When delivering PFA, begin by observing the situation; do not approach individuals until you observe how they are behaving in the moment. Once that is accomplished and you believe that your presence would not be too intrusive, ask the person in crisis how you could be helpful and about their immediate needs (e.g., something to eat, medical attention). At this point, individuals in crisis will run the gamut of responses from acting shy and avoiding you to bombarding you with information. Remain calm with the client and speak slowly. Be empathetic and take your time. If individuals want to talk, then simply listen and try to pick up on the subtle resources they might need.

At this early point in the conversation, you want to focus on the positive accomplishments that have kept them alive, safe, etc. Because PFA focuses on immediacy, try to keep the conversation on what the individual wants to accomplish in the moment and in the immediate future (i.e., the next hour or day). Although it may be easy to get the individual to recount the events of the trauma and it is okay for some of this dialogue to occur, PFA would stress that you focus less on the traumatic event and more on the recovery from the event. The goal of this interaction is to reduce stress, provide resources, empower with hope, and promote positive functioning.

In an attempt to provide an overview of PFA, Everly and Flynn (2005) reported that PFA begins with helping those in need to meet their basic physical needs (e.g., safety, food, water, shelter). After those physical needs are met, or are about to be met, a crisis counselor practicing PFA attempts to help meet the client's psychological needs (e.g., emotional and behavioral support, empathy, consolation). Next, connecting the client with friends, family, and other loved ones must take place. In addition, measures to decrease a victim's isolation must occur. Lastly, clinicians practicing PFA should provide avenues for follow-up care. The above steps were successfully used by direct responders after the 9/11 terrorist attack in New York City.

PFA has developed into the hallmark of crisis response. Compared with other types of crisis response, PFA is a gentler approach that allows for open communication, immediate support, focus on the positive, and empowerment. While some other approaches of debriefing are seen as intrusive or dictating that individuals need help, PFA is offered to people inquiring how help can be provided.

Everly, Phillips, Kane, and Feldman (2006) stated that PFA "is emerging as the crisis intervention of choice in the wake of critical incidents such as trauma and mass disaster" (p. 130). According to Ruzek et al. (2007), PFA is

> a systematic set of helping actions aimed at reducing initial post-trauma distress and supporting short- and long-term adaptive functioning. Designed as an initial component of a comprehensive disaster/trauma response, PFA is constructed around eight core actions: contact and engagement, safety and comfort, stabilization, information gathering, practical assistance, connection with social supports, information on coping support, and linkage with collaborative services. (p. 17)

PFA is typically an individual approach to treatment; however, Everly et al. (2006) have suggested that group approaches can also be beneficial to those experiencing crisis. Overall, the goals of PFA are to provide resources, education, and information to those in need; promote help-seeking behaviors (especially mental health services); provide empathy and support during the crisis; and aid in moving those in immediate crisis to a precrisis state of adjustment (Everly & Flynn, 2005).

PFA has been employed in the field of counseling and mental health for over 60 years, and various elements of PFA have been around even longer (Eifling & Moy, 2015). However, insufficient scholarly research and literature exists to show the true effectiveness of PFA and to create specific guidelines and competencies of practice (Dieltjens, Moonens, van Praet, De Buck, & Vanderkerckhove, 2014). McCabe et al. (2014) suggested that this insufficient research is largely due to the fact that PFA training varies so much that many advanced skills are not standardized. McCabe et al. (2014) established a consensus on what PFA training should include. The following six competencies are a result of their work:

- *Competency 1—Initial contact, rapport building, and stabilization:* It requires knowledge and skill in active listening, empathy, and establishing rapport.
- *Competency 2—Brief assessment and triage:* It requires knowledge and skill in helping to screen, assess, and identify functional and dysfunctional behaviors.
- *Competency 3—Intervention:* It requires knowledge and skill in the techniques used to decrease distress and increase coping.
- *Competency 4—Triage:* It requires knowledge and skill in how to triage people who are in need of immediate help versus delayed help.
- *Competency 5—Referral, liaison, and advocacy:* It requires knowledge and skill in "demonstrating timeliness and persistence in referring persons requiring more intensive care to appropriate postevent care providers and programs" (p. 623).
- *Competency 6—Self-awareness and self-care:* It requires knowledge and skill in identifying and addressing signs of burnout, stress, and vicarious trauma.

Critical Incident Stress Management

The fundamental components of CISM are set out in the foundational work of Everly and Mitchell (1999). This model begins with choosing potentiating pairings—specific crisis interventions (e.g., venting, debriefing) to best meet the needs of each client. Once such interventions are identified, the crisis counselor specifically chooses catalytic sequences—the order in which to use the potentiating pairings. Lastly, the polythetic nature of the situation emerges—how one implements the potentiating pairings and the catalytic sequences based on the individual needs of each situation or disaster. Essentially, CISM is an eclectic approach to crisis intervention that takes into consideration the client's individual needs, the interventions available, and the nature of the situation.

The hallmark of CISM is the Critical Incident Stress Debriefing (CISD) model, which is the primary crisis intervention tool used within CISM (Pack, 2013). The purpose of CISD is to reduce the initial stressors and distressful emotions and behaviors along with attempting to prevent further onset of more severe mental and emotional responses (i.e., PTSD symptoms). According to Everly and Mitchell (1999), it is structured in its delivery and has the following seven phases:

1. *Introduction phase:* The counselor sets the rules and tone of the discussion.
2. *Facts phase:* Clients discuss what happened during the crisis from each person's perspective.
3. *Thoughts phase:* Clients discuss the main emotion and cognition they experienced while going through the crisis.
4. *Reactions phase:* Clients discuss the worst part of the crisis.
5. *Symptoms phase:* Clients describe their symptoms of distress during and after the crisis.
6. *Teaching phase:* The counselor teaches ways to reduce stressors and the impact of stress.
7. *Reentry phase:* The counselor answers questions and summarizes comments.

Furthermore, it helps to triage those who might need more or more intensive help and to assist people to anticipate possible problematic events in the future. The ultimate goal of CISM (along with CISD) is to help clients normalize their reactions to the crisis by allowing them to vent, obtain feedback in a supportive setting, and process emotions.

According to Castellano and Plionis (2006), CISM was successfully implemented during 9/11 to augment established individual counseling through the following six components:

- *Component 1—Acute crisis counseling provided by peer counselors:* Crisis counselors and law enforcement officers with crisis intervention skills provided crisis intervention to law enforcement officers who initially responded to the 9/11 terrorist attack in New York. Component 1 lasted 3 months after the attack and consisted of traditional crisis intervention techniques.
- *Component 2—Executive leadership program:* Because so many senior/superior police officers saw their lower-ranked colleagues die or become devastated by the 9/11 terrorist attack, specific crisis intervention services and educational seminars were developed and delivered to this population.
- *Component 3—The multidisciplinary team:* A multidisciplinary team delivered trainings around the clock for everyone working at the site of the 9/11 terrorist attack. Crisis intervention seminars and counseling sessions were called "trainings" at the time because they would be better received and attended by those who may have stereotypes about mental health services.
- *Component 4—Acute traumatic stress group training sessions:* For the large number of those in need of crisis intervention, 2-day psychoeducational group sessions helped to decrease isolation, normalize emotions and reactions to the attack, decrease guilt, and increase coping mechanisms.
- *Component 5—Hotline:* Telephone crisis hotlines were highly emphasized and used to help those who responded to the 9/11 terrorist attack. Hotlines are seen as a 24/7 resource that can provide support and information in times when others may not be available. Hotlines are necessary in many crisis intervention plans.
- *Component 6—Reentry program:* 9/11 responders who directly witnessed death, carnage, and destruction were deemed to be at high risk and identified as

individuals who would have difficulty going back to their jobs and families. The reentry program focused on such high-risk responders to help them get back to their "normal" life.

Crisis Counseling Program

According to Castellano and Plionis (2006), the CCP is frequently used for responses to natural disasters. The CCP model consists of the following components:

- *Assess strengths:* The crisis counselor must identify not only what the problems are (e.g., stranded people, postdisaster crime) but also what human and material resources are available.
- *Restore predisaster functioning:* The key to restoring life to what it was before the disaster (especially emotional status) is to attempt to reduce the chaos of the disaster.
- *Accept the face value:* Crisis counselors must help clients reorganize life to accommodate for the impact of the disaster (e.g., "Your home was completely destroyed by the hurricane; now how can you move on?").
- *Provide validation:* The provision of unconditional positive regard, acceptance, and validation is critical to the growth of disaster victims.
- *Provide a psychoeducational focus:* The provision of psychoeducation (on both a group and an individual level) regarding the normal (and abnormal) reactions to disaster can play a central role in helping disaster victims monitor their own recovery.

RIOTS

Riots have taken place on numerous occasions in the United States and across the world. A *riot* is defined as a "disturbance of the peace by several persons, assembled and acting with a common intent in executing a lawful or unlawful enterprise in a violent and turbulent manner" ("Riot," 2016). In the United States, race riots occurred during the 1960s, the Kent State University riots and shootings happened in 1973, riots took place in Los Angeles in 1992, and, more recently, riots occurred in Ferguson, Missouri, and Baltimore, Maryland in 2015. When riots occur, the following question is always raised: Why do people riot? Well, the answer is complex. To simplify matters, consider that there are primarily two different forms of riots: sporting or celebratory riots and riots as a reaction to a perceived wrongdoing.

Sporting or celebratory riots occasionally occur after a sports team wins a significant game (e.g., the baseball World Series, NBA Championship, World Cup championship soccer). Sporting or celebratory riots are sometimes difficult to comprehend because they happen after something apparently good has occurred. But consider that you have seen people yell at referees, cheer loudly, and even scream in celebration at sporting events. Now add alcohol consumption and a crowd celebration that gets "out of control," and the result is a group-think occurrence in which all are cheering for their particular team. Primal urges and adrenaline flare, and a mob forms and acts aggressively.

Contrary to sporting or celebratory riots, riots that occur as a result of a perceived wrongdoing are fundamentally different. Little is known in the mental health scholarly literature about exactly why people riot as a result of a perceived wrongdoing. However, one could speculate that people feel disrespected, have little power in society, and are frequently seen as "less than" by society. Riots give them power and show the media and society that they can make a statement that is impactful.

During a riot, authorities attempt to provide security and safety to the public. Three levels of police actions could take place. The first and least responsive would be to provide a local police presence to deal with crowd control, minor disorderly issues, etc. Second, additional local police and special police units (e.g., SWAT) can be used to handle larger scale crowd control, acts of vandalism, and acts of aggression to the community. Third, the National Guard could provide the highest level of support during a riot.

National Guard personnel, aircraft, vehicles, and other equipment can be dispatched in times of natural disasters (i.e., earthquakes, floods) and human-made emergencies such as riots, civil unrest, and terrorist attacks. In such times, the state's governor can enact the National Guard and the "mission" of the National Guard is determined by the governor and the adjutant general. Most recently, the National Guard has been tasked with providing homeland security measures during a riot by using aerial drone surveillance (Lowenberg, 2016).

During a riot, there are many players: (1) the people who riot; (2) the police, fire department, and other first responders who try to protect others from the riot; and (3) the victims of the riot who either are hurt physically or financially (e.g., a business owner whose business is vandalized). In a broader sense, riots also influence and are influenced by the surrounding community, the media, and society at large. Researchers concur that the closer one is to a riot (either physically or emotionally), the more likely PTSD symptoms will occur (Stiles et al., 2015). Other symptoms that can arise include a reduced sense of safety manifesting in anxiety and somatic reactions, helplessness, hopelessness, a sense that life is overwhelming, and difficulties performing daily tasks.

Certainly each riot has different circumstances and players. However, Bowenkamp (1995), writing about civil unrest in Los Angeles, California, in the 1990s, observed that those who directly experienced a riot go through the following phases: (1) the victims work together to recover; (2) the victims feel supported as governmental and private agencies help with recovery; (3) the victims become angry, frustrated, and generally confused by the systemic red tape of agencies and delays in recovery; and (4) the victims eventually enter the official "recovery phase," which is distinguished by a coordinated effort by the community to rebuild.

Beyond treating and helping clients adjust to these phases, counselors need to pay specific attention to how children perceive and are affected by riots. Stiles et al. (2015) studied children after the Ferguson, Missouri, riots in 2015, and found that they best "recover" from a riot if school personnel (e.g., teachers, school counselors), families, caregivers, and community members use the riot as an age-appropriate learning opportunity to discuss related issues (e.g., feeling safe, appropriate ways to express feelings, community building, racism [in the specific case of the riots in Ferguson, Missouri]).

The key to working with children and adults during the aftermath of a riot is to instill hope for the future and that the community will rebuild. As stated above, the

THINK ABOUT IT 12.2

Think about how you would respond during a riot. Imagine that a riot broke out in your town as a result of a man not being sentenced for murder when most people in your town believed that he was guilty. The media has been present for the past 2 months, covering the trial. The riot began yesterday, after the verdict was read. Businesses have been looted, fires have been started, and mobs of people are threatening to march in the streets and become violent. What emotions would you feel? What would be your safety concerns? How would you protect yourself? Would you join the rioting group? Which people in your life would you be most concerned about? What do you think the media should do? Who are the groups of victims needing intervention? Could you work with a group in need of intervention even if your views differed from theirs?

final phase of working with a post-riot community is the recovery phase, which emphasizes the rebuilding of the community. It is important to keep in mind that instilling hope for the future and that a sense of community will return should not take place in the final recovery phase only. From the first interaction, counselors must empathize with clients and emphasize these core ideas to help facilitate the therapeutic relationship. While doing so, counselors should highlight that the community will work together to rebuild what was once known, a sense of safety, the vitality of the community, and the overall sense of community. Complete Think About It 12.2.

HOSTAGE SITUATIONS

Hostage situations are rare in the United States; however, there are specific ramifications of such situations that mental health practitioners need to consider, given that a substantial portion of hostage takers have a mental or emotional disorder (Grubb, 2010). Literature on hostage negotiation is vast, and a thorough discussion of specific negotiation strategies is beyond the scope of this chapter. However, a brief discussion of hostage situations may allow crisis counselors and other mental health practitioners to gain some insight into the experiences of hostages and hostage takers, and better prepare counselors to work with victims and perpetrators of these crisis circumstances.

There are essentially five stages of a hostage situation: (1) alarm, (2) crisis, (3) uncertainty, (4) accommodation, and (5) resolution, as shown in Table 12.2. The alarm stage occurs at the initial onset of the hostage situation and is typically the most volatile and dangerous period of time. Hostage takers believe that terror must be instilled in the hostages in order to keep them under control, and any hint of panic by hostages creates extreme overreactions by hostage takers. During this stage, hostage takers are highly emotional, aggressive, irrational, and abusive.

During the alarm stage, hostages are confused by the sudden turn of events and feel victimized. They suddenly feel like there is no escape from the situation and become paralyzed not only due to threats of physical harm but also due to the severe shock resulting from aggressive actions by the hostage takers. Similar to the experiences of disaster victims, hostages during this stage express denials such as "I can't believe this is happening." As a result of the events that take place during the alarm stage, survivors

TABLE 12.2 Stages of Typical Hostage Situations

Stage	Characteristics of Hostage Takers	Characteristics of Hostages
Alarm	• Volatile • Dangerous • Highly emotional • Highly aggressive • Highly irrational • Abusive to others • Signs of panic create overreactions	• Most traumatized • Confused • Victimized • Shock • Helpless/defenseless • Denial • Paralyzed
Crisis	• Initial reason • Volatility • Danger • Grandiose/ridiculous demands • Rants • Securing the area and hostages • Fear of authorities/paranoia • Need for attention • Verbal abuse followed by violence	• Relationship with hostage taker is central to outcome • Denial • Increased fear if hostage taker is unpredictable • Fugue episodes • Claustrophobia • Reliance on hostage takers • Hopelessness
Uncertainty	• Ambiguity of outcome • Confusion • Fight or flight	• Ambiguity of outcome • Confusion • Fight or flight
Accommodation	• Long-lasting time period • Fatigue • Increased control of hostages	• Time stands still • Boredom • Brief feelings of terror • Fatigue • Passivity • Possible Stockholm syndrome
Resolution	• Fatigue • Realization of lost expectations • Contemplation of outcome • Suicide becomes possible outcome	• Fatigue • Seeing closure

of hostage situations share similar characteristics with abused children, abused women, and concentration camp survivors.

As the alarm stage ends, the crisis stage begins. During this time, hostage takers begin to realize the magnitude of the situation and continue to be highly dangerous and volatile, but also realize that they must secure their surroundings from authorities and attempts by hostages to escape. The crisis stage also begins the hostage takers' interactions with the authorities, with the hostage takers frequently making grandiose or ridiculous demands with the expectation that the authorities will meet such demands. Hostage takers during this stage need attention, which they use as a means to show that they are in power. Typically, this showing of power begins with yelling at or verbal abuse of the hostages but can quickly escalate to violence.

During the crisis stage, hostages begin to develop a relationship with the hostage takers. They rely on them for everything—from food and water to permission to use the restroom. Hostages soon learn that the more cooperative they are, the less violent the hostage takers will be toward them. If a hostage shows panic or contradicts a hostage taker, then violence may occur. Hostages still experience hopelessness, denial, and fear, although fear drastically increases if hostage takers are unpredictable or appear disorganized. Occasionally, hostages will experience a significant loss of time or go into a fugue state as a defense mechanism to cope with the trauma. They may also experience a sense of claustrophobia and may feel the need to get out of their situation even though they know there could be dangerous consequences if they do take such action.

The third stage (uncertainty) has parallel characteristics among the hostage takers, the hostages themselves, and even the hostage negotiators (Van den Heuvel & Alison, 2014). During this stage, the crisis stage has either escalated or de-escalated, but the situation is not yet under control. Thoughts of hopelessness (as evident in the crisis stage) are subsiding, but no one knows the outcome of the situation.

The fourth stage of a hostage situation is the accommodation stage, which is marked by time standing still and fatigue for both the hostages and the hostage takers. Overall, this stage is somewhat peaceful because dominance over the hostages is established and acts of violence may not be deemed necessary by the hostage takers. Hostages become passive and bored. They may even experience Stockholm syndrome, a situation in which hostages develop positive feelings for the hostage takers and negative feelings for the authorities, while hostage takers gain concern and positive feelings for the hostages. Crisis counselors need to assess for injuries to any of the hostages during this time, or any of the stages, by the hostage taker. In these cases, when a person may have experienced Stockholm syndrome and another person is harmed, guilt or self-blame may be experienced by the hostage. Everyone is emotionally and physically exhausted. Typically, this is the longest of the five stages of a hostage situation.

The resolution stage is the last stage in a hostage situation. Hostage takers and hostages alike are weary and see that a resolution (whether good or bad) is nearing. Both realize that this situation will not last forever. Hostage takers begin to realize that their demands, or their initial expectations, are not going to be met. The hostage takers contemplate suicide, killing the hostages and themselves, or ending the situation peacefully. No matter what the outcome, the hostage takers and the hostages typically know that the situation is ending.

Once the hostage situation is over, significant de-escalation, ventilation, and self-preservation issues need to be addressed through crisis intervention strategies provided to the hostages and possibly to the hostage takers. Long-term individual and group counseling may need to be implemented to provide preventative measures for PTSD to the hostages. See Case Studies 12.3 and 12.4, which provide additional insights into the dynamics of hostage situations and the resulting treatment needs of hostages. Also complete Activity 12.2 to find out more about crisis procedures on your campus or nearby K–12 school.

CASE STUDY 12.3

A Commercial Hostage Situation

In a small convenience store located in an Appalachian town, two men wearing masks, attempt to rob the store. Both men have guns. Besides the two gunmen, the people in the store are the owner, who is behind the checkout counter, and six customers, located in different aisles in the store. The gunmen ask for money from the cash register, but the owner denies their request. While the gunmen and the owner are arguing, one of the customers calls the police from his cell phone, and within 4 minutes, a police car pulls up in front of the store. One of the gunmen locks the store's front door, and the robbery has quickly turned into a hostage situation. The hostage situation lasts for 7 hours. Given the information presented earlier, imagine what goes on during those 7 hours.

Discussion Questions

1. Discuss how the hostage takers and the hostages think, feel, and act during the different stages of the situation.
2. What would be some follow-up resources for the hostages?
3. What might be some multicultural considerations for the hostages?
4. What would be some key counseling skills to use with the hostages? See Chapter 4 for information on such skills.

CASE STUDY 12.4

A Family Hostage Situation

Martin is a 38-year-old construction worker who has been married four times and has four children. He has one child (Pat, aged 20 years) with his first wife, and three boys (Ben, aged 10 years; Todd, aged 6 years; and Sig, aged 4 years) with his current wife, Michelle. Within the past 3 weeks, Martin broke his wrist while working, he lost his job because of his anger outbursts and his pushing one of his coworkers after an argument, and he was notified that he needs to pay $22,000 in back taxes to the Internal Revenue Service. Earlier today, Michelle told him that she was leaving him and that she was taking the children with her. During this conversation, the police were called because neighbors were concerned about the yelling they heard. When the police arrived, Martin did not answer the door and told the police that he had a gun and "no one is coming out unless they are in a body bag."

Martin kept Michelle and her three children at gunpoint for 3½ hours. During this time, he yelled, talked as if he was on a rant, cried uncontrollably, put his gun to Michelle's head and threatened to pull the trigger, and slapped Michelle and Ben in the face. After talking to a police negotiator on and off for over 2 hours, Martin shot himself in the head in front of Michelle and his children.

When the police and the hostage negotiator entered the house, they found Michelle holding her husband's hand, while he lay dead on the floor. Two of her children were sitting on the couch, still afraid to move, while Ben ran out the door into the hands of the police. Michelle and her children spent the next 4 hours debriefing with the hostage negotiator and other support staff. Later, Michelle saw a counselor twice a week for 8 months, then once a week for 4 months, and then once a month thereafter.

Discussion Questions

1. Overall, what do you think Michelle experienced during this situation? What about her children?
2. How do you think Michelle and the children experienced each stage of the hostage situation as described above?
3. What would be some of the emotions, behaviors, and thoughts felt by this family immediately after the hostage situation ended?
4. How should Martin's son Pat (from his first marriage) be informed of this situation? What should be said?
5. What would be the crisis counselor's initial treatment goals with Michelle and her children?
6. How might treatment differ for Michelle, Ben, and the other two children taken hostage?
7. What do you think was the reason Michelle was able to decrease treatment over time?
8. With a peer, role-play implementation of the task model of crisis assessment and intervention presented in Table 1.1.

ACTIVITY 12.2

Many colleges/universities and K–12 schools have lockdown procedures in case there is an active shooter on campus or a hostage situation. Locate the crisis, lockdown, and active shooter procedures on your campus or nearby K–12 school. Reflect on what you need to do in these situations. If you cannot find the information you are looking for, what does that mean?

OVERVIEW OF THE ELEMENTS OF CRISIS INTERVENTION RELATED TO EMERGENCY PREPAREDNESS AND RESPONSE IN THE COMMUNITY AND WORKPLACE

This chapter discussed the importance of crisis intervention during the training of counselors; how multidisciplinary crisis responses work; different aspects of natural disasters, terrorism, riots, and hostage situations; and different models of crisis intervention. Two critical concepts need to be considered when contextualizing all of this material. First, it is critical that counselors keep their clients safe. In all of the devastating crisis situations discussed in this chapter, counselors need to take measures to protect their clients not only from immediate threats of danger or emotional strife but also from potential physical, emotional, and cognitive difficulties. While the care of clients is critical, counselors need to pay close attention to their own safety and the potential for burnout and vicarious trauma. Think about what steps you can take on a continual basis to take care of yourself!

TABLE 12.3 Resources on Coping and Intervening in Community and Workplace Crises
American Red Cross: www.redcross.org
Disaster Assistance.gov—Access to Disaster Help and Resources: www.disasterassistance.org
Federal Emergency Management Agency: www.fema.gov
National Child Traumatic Stress Network: www.nctsn.org

Second, this chapter did not present much information on diagnoses and other mental health concerns. Think about the unique symptoms of the different mental health diagnoses that would contribute to the process and progress people make during a disaster. How might someone with a mood disorder, schizophrenia, substance use issues, suicidality, etc. experience a crisis? How might the crisis intervention models presented in this chapter and in Chapter 1 need to be altered? It is important to understand that individuals who go through an extreme crisis do not always develop PTSD or another mental or emotional disorder. It is important to remember this point because you do not want to pathologize individuals who go through situational crises. Table 12.3 provides additional resources for further exploration of how to cope with and intervene in community and workplace crises.

Summary

This chapter began by discussing the necessity to train counselors in emergency preparedness, trauma counseling, and a multitude of crises and that this training has become a mainstay in counselor education standards. As a result, this chapter focused on critical areas that counselors who may work in a variety of crisis situations should know about. MCRTs were described, and the function and utility of these teams were presented. Most importantly, the notion of the interdisciplinary and collegial nature of these teams were highlighted.

A significant portion of this chapter helped to provide a knowledge base on different types of situations in which emergency preparedness would be required. For example, differing types of natural disasters were presented (i.e., winter storms, earthquakes, floods, hurricanes, tornados, and wildfires). It is important to note that a major difference between natural disasters and other, human-made, disasters is that with natural disasters, clients could easily blame God or a higher power rather than a specific person or group. To help provide insight into how blame plays a role in the aftermath of a natural disaster, a timeline was provided that shows the possible responses of survivors of a natural disaster along with the interventions needed to help such survivors, starting at the point immediately after the disaster happens and continuing to years after the disaster occurred. Ending the discussion of natural disasters, the typical cognitive, physical, emotional, and behavioral reactions to disasters were presented.

After a thorough discussion of natural disasters, the notion of terrorism was discussed. Terrorism and different types of terrorism were defined and some reasons why an individual might become a terrorist were given. Acts of terrorism create unique challenges for counselors because there are individuals (or groups of individuals) to blame. Strategies to work with communities to help regain a sense of safety were presented.

Various models of crisis intervention were discussed in this chapter, including PFA, CISM, and CCP. All of these interventions have merit, and the common thread that runs through these models is the idea that the key to treating those who have experienced a crisis (all forms) is early intervention. The sooner crisis counselors respond, reduce panic or chaos, create a sense of hope and support, and establish connections between those in need and appropriate resources, the better.

Riots and types of riots were defined and key reasons why riots occur were discussed. An emphasis was placed on how counselors need to establish a sense of hope for the future and that the community that experienced the riot will rebuild.

The final topic presented in this chapter was hostage situations. This chapter highlighted the stages of a typical hostage situation along with some common characteristics of hostages and hostage takers. As with disasters, there are many systematic factors and evolutionary components of a hostage situation. Although hostage situations are relatively rare, those providing mental health services should be aware of the unique characteristics of those who have experienced a hostage situation because it could influence the approach to treatment.

All crises evolve through different stages—and then end. Those who experience crisis, disaster, or trauma also evolve in that they, hopefully, resolve or at least experience a lessened impact of the situation. Crises affect lives in systemic ways; every aspect of a person's life can be affected by a crisis.

13 Emergency Preparedness and Response in Schools and Universities

Bradley T. Erford*

PREVIEW

Emergency preparedness and effective responses by counselors in schools and universities are reviewed in this chapter. Mitigation and prevention strategies are emphasized as critical elements in the school environment. Crisis preparedness, response, recovery, and debriefing procedures are applied to school and university settings. Special emphasis is given to strategies for how to help students and parents during and after a crisis event. Finally, several case studies are provided to help prepare counselors-in-training for potential crisis situations encountered in academic environments. As in Chapter 12, the content of this chapter infuses information found in previous chapters to allow readers to synthesize what they have previously read.

CHARACTERISTICS OF AND RESPONSES TO SCHOOL AND UNIVERSITY CRISES

Schools and universities are called upon to respond to a variety of crises both on a local and national level. As these crises occur, it becomes the responsibility of the school or university community to respond in a timely manner so that accurate information is provided, while helping students, teachers, administrators, parents, and communities cope with the crisis. Kerr (2009) defines a school crisis as a "temporary event or condition that affects a school, causing individuals to experience fear, helplessness, shock, and/or horror [and] requires extraordinary actions to restore a sense of psychological and physical security" (p. 9). This definition also applies to the university campus. Crises do not need to occur on school or university property to have a devastating effect on the academic community.

A school or university crisis brings chaos that affects perceptions of safety and stability for an entire academic community. It exposes students and staff to loss and undermines personal security and safety routines. School is a place where students, families, and school staff expect stability and safety. When a crisis occurs, it is understood that personnel will react in a professional manner to make certain that information, support, and counseling services are provided. Everyone in the school community

---

*Special thanks go to Michele Garofalo for her contributions to the first two editions of this chapter.

needs to feel informed, supported, and safe. Personnel play a vital role in managing crises and providing coping strategies to restore a stable and safe environment. The approach must be organized and sensitive to the needs of diverse students, teachers, parents, administrators, and other community members.

Crises affecting schools and universities can happen on a continuum with a wide range—from the individual level to national and international levels. On the individual level, for example, 1 in 7 youths in the United States seriously consider suicide each year. Of all deaths occurring in 2014 in the 15- to 24-year-old age bracket, about 14% were suicides (Centers for Disease Control and Prevention, 2017). Furthermore, one youth dies of suicide every 2 hours, and six youths survive a suicide attempt every 2 hours. Whether a crisis occurs at the national level (e.g., September 11, 2001, Hurricane Katrina) or the local level (e.g., the death of a student or a teacher as a result of an automobile accident, illness, or suicide), it will certainly have an impact on the school or university community. The response must be planned, organized, and coordinated effectively in order to provide the necessary support and services. A secondary goal is to prevent additional crises stemming from the initial crisis. For example, if there has been a suicide, personnel need to address the immediate impact of the suicide, but they must also attempt to reduce the possibility of any related suicide attempts.

A couple of precautions are important to consider at this point, also. First, professional counselors should always act with safety protocols in mind and be sensitive to the possibility of secondary trauma. In addition, professional counselors should not interfere at places of work unless invited to do so. For example, a university or school shooting is a tragic event, but administrative protocols must be followed and coordinated. Help from counselors, faculty, and students may very well be welcomed, but should be coordinated by the on-site crisis team in conjunction with emergency first responders.

The Office of Safe and Drug-Free Schools in the U.S. Department of Education (2017) identified four phases of a comprehensive school crisis plan: (1) mitigation and prevention, which addresses what schools can do to reduce or eliminate risk to life and property; (2) preparedness, which refers to the process of planning for a crisis; (3) response, which refers to the actions taken during the crisis; and (4) recovery, which refers to restoring the school environment after a crisis. Each of these phases will be addressed in turn, and this process is applicable to public and private K–12 schools, community colleges, and public and private colleges and universities.

Mitigation and Prevention

Mitigation is any sustained action taken to reduce or eliminate long-term risk to life and property from a hazard event. Mitigation encourages long-term reduction of hazard vulnerability (Federal Emergency Management Agency, 2014). Mitigation and prevention involve assessing the dangers in a school and community and identifying strategies to prevent and reduce injury and property damage. Both the school and community must work together in preventing crises. The Federal Emergency Management Agency (FEMA) has done extensive work to help communities with their mitigation planning. Mitigation procedures strive to decrease the need for subsequent responses rather than simply increasing response capability. FEMA has outlined five action steps for mitigation and prevention in schools and universities:

1. *Know the school building.* Regular safety audits of the physical plant must be carried out along with an assessment of any potential hazards on campus. Parking lots, playgrounds, driveways, outside structures, and fencing should be examined. The information collected is then used for mitigation and prevention planning.

2. *Know the community.* It is necessary to work with local emergency management officials to assess hazards in the community. The probability of natural disasters (e.g., hurricanes, tornadoes, earthquakes, floods) and industrial and chemical accidents (e.g., fuel spill, water contamination) must be considered. Potential hazards related to terrorism should also be carefully assessed (e.g., geographic location, government buildings).

3. *Bring together regional, local, and school leaders.* Schools and universities must work collaboratively with state and local governments to ensure support of their mitigation efforts.

4. *Make regular school and university safety and security efforts part of the mitigation/prevention practices.* Schools and universities must conduct needs assessments regularly to identify common types of incidents and continually refine the safety plan.

5. *Establish clear lines of communication.* Communication among stakeholders is critical as agencies and schools work together. It is necessary for families and the community to understand that schools, universities, and local governments are working together to ensure the safety of the academic community and the larger community. Schools and universities must keep students and families informed about the safety measures being developed.

Preventive efforts begin with an awareness of all activities occurring in the school or university environment, as well as the emotional climate. Personnel must be aware of what is occurring in the hallways, restrooms, cafeteria, etc. in order to assess any risk that may be present (e.g., bullying, gang activity, talk of intended violence or harm). Steps should be taken to secure the building from outside intruders—for example, by employing public safety or school resource officers, implementing a sign-in procedure for visitors, supervision in all parts of the building (including the playground and playing fields), surveillance cameras, keeping entrances to the building locked, and in some instances metal detectors. It would be wise for schools and universities to work in conjunction with local law enforcement agencies to consult on additional ways to maintain safety and security.

All prevention efforts must also include education for everyone in the academic community. Training of faculty and staff to develop knowledge, attitudes, and skills is an effective component of any crisis intervention program. Prevention programs on the topics of bullying, substance use/abuse, suicide, drinking and driving, depression, intimate partner violence, stress management, and conflict resolution should be carried out for students at a developmentally appropriate level. School counselors are instrumental in delivering classroom guidance presentations and small-group counseling sessions on these topics. Character education programs also are in place in most schools and help to foster a positive school climate. Active shooter response and other emergency drills have become a necessity in both schools and universities, and administrators should ensure students are prepared to follow institutional guidelines for emergency evacuation or "shelter-in-place."

Attention to building a positive school climate is critical in prevention efforts. The University of South Florida (2012) proposed that *school climate* refers to the physical, aesthetic, and psychological qualities within a school or university community. Personnel can help foster a positive climate by facilitating connectedness, participation, academic success, and safety as well as through training, policies, and positive concern for all participants in the educational process. Schools and universities should provide extracurricular activities (e.g., clubs, activities, organizations), involve students in school decisions, promote safety and cleanliness of the facilities, promote high academic standards, reduce bullying, and equivalently enforce disciplinary standards. In other words, a positive climate aimed at preventing crises is respectful, caring, and supportive of all stakeholders in the academic community.

Training programs for personnel (including coaches, bus drivers, cafeteria workers, and janitors) must be implemented to make all employees aware of warning signs and symptoms (risk factors) and appropriate methods for intervention. Prevention-based curricula generally promote awareness but should also train gatekeepers (all faculty and staff) on the signs of suicide or threat, as well as how to screen those students who present as high risk. While much has been written about risk factors contributing to suicide and other threats, from a strengths-based perspective it is important to consider and promote protective factors, including family cohesion, support from adults, connectedness to the school, stable living environment, responsibilities for others (e.g., siblings, pets), participation in sports and other extracurricular activities, and positive peer and adult relationships (University of South Florida, 2012).

Preparedness and Advance Planning

Preparedness and advance planning has a positive impact on crisis response. When planning for a crisis, policies and procedures must always be considered. Kerr (2009) defined a policy as a "brief written expression of guiding ideas, derived from regulations, mandates, or an organization's philosophy" (p. 17). A crisis policy provides guidance to those responding to the crisis and authorizes a course of action. In contrast, procedures provide detailed implementation protocols or step-by-step crisis plans.

PLANNING FOR A CRISIS   Every school or university should have a crisis plan in place that is shared with all faculty, administrators, and staff prior to any crisis event, implemented quickly in a crisis, reviewed annually and after a crisis event, and updated as needed. National data from the *School Survey on Crime and Safety* (U.S. Department of Education, National Center for Education Statistics, 2016) indicated that the majority of schools have written crisis plans. Many times schools and universities are faced with responding to crises as they are unfolding (e.g., intruder in the school building, terrorist attack, natural disaster). During the planning phase, it is important to predict and describe the types of crises the plan will address in the school or university based on needs and vulnerabilities.

ESTABLISHING A CRISIS TEAM   The first step in crisis planning is to establish a crisis team. This team should include a team leader (usually the principal in K–12 schools or a vice-president in universities), professional counselors, faculty, and other mental health support personnel (e.g., school social worker, psychologist, security officer, nurse, custodian or building manager, staff members, and communications coordinator). The team should also include individuals who have specialized training in crisis intervention and grief/loss counseling as well as professional counselors, social workers, psychologists, and psychiatrists from the community.

Kerr (2009) suggested that responsibilities be shared among the following team members whether in schools or universities:

1. *Crisis team leader:* usually the principal or another administrator.
2. *Crisis team leader designee:* a person who takes over if the team leader is absent.
3. *Off-site manager:* a senior staff member without direct student responsibilities who can prepare in-shelter facilities in the event of an evacuation
4. *Security coordinator:* a school resource officer, security guard, or other staff member who can work with others to secure the school until law enforcement arrives.
5. *Medical responder:* usually the school nurse or a staff member with medical training.
6. *Communications coordinator:* someone who manages the communications until the designated spokesperson takes over. This person may need to work with additional individuals who can translate information to be relayed in to all languages represented in the school community.
7. *Mental health specialist:* a school counselor, psychologist, or social worker who is responsible for providing counseling support and services.
8. *Facilities manager:* a custodian or building manager who can address utility needs, direct traffic, and provide floor plans to public safety responders.
9. *Other staff members, including teachers* (pp. 36–37).

During times of crisis, the role of the professional counselor is critical. Counselors are expected to provide counseling for students, coordinate all counseling activities, communicate with faculty and parents, seek support from the crisis team, and contact neighboring schools. Counselors provide direct counseling services during intervention and postvention phases of the crisis. They are also expected to serve students and personnel during times of crisis by providing individual and group interventions; to consult with administrators, faculty, parents, and professionals; and to coordinate services with the school and the community (American School Counselor Association, 2012).

The crisis team should be provided with extensive training that occurs on an ongoing basis. The crisis team should meet at the beginning of each academic year to review procedures and receive training. In addition, it should meet several times during the academic year to receive additional training and discuss case scenarios and appropriate responses. Contact information should be updated at these training sessions so that team members can be reached quickly and easily in the event of a crisis. These training sessions provide an opportunity for team members to become acquainted and share strategies to be implemented if a crisis occurs. These sessions are also a time to assign specific responsibilities to each team member and to reassign responsibilities, if necessary. For success, it is critical that the crisis team have the full support of the administration. Complete Think About It 13.1.

THINK ABOUT IT 13.1

Think about how a crisis team could develop and implement an optimal crisis plan. What steps would they take?

TAKING STEPS TO PREPARE FOR A CRISIS   The Center for Mental Health in Schools at UCLA (2008) recommends steps that could be taken in preparation for a crisis:

- Post on the wall of each classroom an outline of emergency procedures and crisis team information.
- At the beginning of each academic year, distribute updated information to all personnel explaining the crisis plan and responsibilities of the crisis team.
- Provide in-service training for all staff at the beginning and midpoint of the school year.
- Perform disaster/crisis drills (e.g., lockdown, shelter-in-place, evacuation, hurricane, tornado, intruder on campus).

While full-scale disaster drills may be difficult to carry out, a practical method and alternative to a full-scale drill is the tabletop exercise, which is designed so that crisis teams, first responders, and other community partners come to the table to evaluate whether written plans would work in an actual emergency. In this exercise, a hypothetical scenario is discussed to assess how school and community partners would respond to the situation. Based upon the results of the tabletop exercise, revisions to the crisis plan may be made (Trump, 2009).

When preparing for drills, it is important to contact representatives from local school systems or universities, law enforcement, and emergency response agencies. Inquire about kinds of crisis situations that have happened or are likely to happen in your area so that you may consider them as you are developing your drill. It would be extremely important for the crisis team to present an in-service training to all personnel, including bus drivers, administrative assistants, custodians, food services staff, and anyone employed by the school or university. Professionals from the local community who have expertise in crisis counseling should also be invited to participate in the training.

CREATING TRAUMA-SENSITIVE SCHOOLS   The Trauma and Learning Policy Initiative (2016) provides a systemic model for change to make academic environments more sensitive to individuals and families coping with trauma: Trauma Lens and the Flexible Framework. A focus of the framework is to identify local priorities and develop sensitive solutions embedded in the educational context. This initiative, which is a collaboration of Massachusetts Advocates for Children and Harvard Law School, also works for legislative changes that integrate often discordant child advocacy programs and lead to proactive changes. The following publications are free for download at the initiative's website: *Helping Traumatized Children Learn*, Volumes 1 and 2 (see traumasensitiveschools.org/tlpi-publications/).

IMPLEMENTING THE WRITTEN CRISIS PLAN   The crisis team is responsible for implementing a written crisis plan that outlines the response to crises. This plan should detail exact steps to be taken in the event of a crisis situation. Although most school districts will have a general plan, each school would need to adapt the plan to its needs. Often, schools and universities are called upon to respond to crises as they are unfolding (e.g., intruder on campus, violent event in the building, natural disaster, terrorist attack). Each school or university should have a plan for responding to such situations, and each faculty member should know how to implement the plan. This plan should be shared with everyone in the academic community so that they are aware of response procedures. This information must be translated in to all languages represented in the academic community. Parents/guardians must be informed of the plan prior to any crisis. A letter or brochure (written in all languages spoken by families) should be developed and sent to parents/guardians explaining this plan so everyone will understand what will occur during a crisis situation (e.g., lockdown, shelter-in-place, evacuation). While the letter or brochure should not describe specific actions or locations in detail in case a parent/guardian might be the intruder, it should provide a general overview so that parents/guardians are secure in the knowledge that their children are safe. Parents/guardians must be informed so that they understand that the school or university has planned for crises and to reassure them that a plan exists to keep all students safe.

FEMA (2014) recommends the following action steps in developing the crisis plan: (1) identify and involve stakeholders; (2) consider existing efforts; (3) determine what the crisis plan will address; (4) define roles and responsibilities; and (5) develop methods for communicating with the staff, students, families, and the media. Decisions need to be made regarding how the school or university will communicate with individuals who are directly or indirectly involved in the crisis. Because crisis team members and staff will need to have several means of communication (e.g., walkie-talkies, cell phones, intercom), it is important to obtain necessary equipment and supplies ahead of time. Staff must also be given the necessary equipment to respond in a crisis, such as emergency response guide, phones, radios, contact information for families, student rosters, first-aid supplies, food, and water. Universities should have updated contact information for students, in particular commuter students, in case of emergencies.

When a crisis occurs, it is imperative to determine as quickly as possible whether students and staff need to be evacuated from the building, returned to the building, or locked down in the building. Evacuation requires all students and staff to leave the building. The evacuation plan should include backup buildings to serve as emergency shelters (e.g., religious institutions, community centers, businesses, or other schools). Agreements for using these spaces should be confirmed prior to the beginning of each school year. Evacuation plans should also include contingencies for weather conditions as well as transportation methods for students.

Sometimes an incident may occur while students are outside, and they will need to return to the building. Once inside the building, the situation may call for a lockdown. Lockdowns are appropriate when a crisis occurs outside of the school and an evacuation would be dangerous. A lockdown may also be necessary when there is a crisis within the school, such as an intruder or shooter. In a lockdown, all exterior doors are locked and students and staff stay in their classrooms. Windows may need to be covered and classroom doors locked to prevent an intruder from gaining access to potential victims. Alternatively, "shelter-in-place" may need to be used when there is not time to evacuate or when it may be harmful to leave the building (because of hazardous material spills, hurricane, flooding, violent intruders, etc.).

In the event of a crisis, emergency responders need to know exact locations of everything in a school. Site maps should include information about classrooms, hallways, and stairwells, location of utility shutoffs, and potential staging sites. Emergency responders should have copies of this information in advance. In addition to maps, it is essential to designate locations for emergency responders to organize, for medical personnel to treat the injured, for the public information officer to brief the media, and for families to be reunited with students.

During a crisis, it is imperative to account for all students, staff, and visitors. Before a crisis occurs, families should be informed of release procedures. Finally, drills and crisis exercises for staff, students, and emergency responders must be carried out frequently whether in large scale or using tabletop exercises.

A key consideration in any crisis intervention plan is the method for communicating with students, staff, families, and the media. FEMA (2014) recommends that one of the first steps in planning for communication is to develop a mechanism to notify students and staff that an incident is occurring and to instruct them on what to do. This communication should cover the methods available to reunite students with their families as quickly as possible and to provide factual information for the academic community. The crisis plan should indicate what information will be shared and who is responsible for conveying the information (U.S. Department of Education, Office of Safe and Drug-Free Schools, 2017).

When sharing information, it is necessary to consider and provide for language and cultural differences. Information should be shared in all languages represented at the school. In addition, there should be individuals available who speak these languages to respond to parents' questions. Information may be shared by activating emergency response messages to phones via text, voice message, e-mail, website, telephone tree, or letter. In addition, a crisis plan should address how to implement these services:

- Return the academic environment to its normal routines.
- Provide physical and emotional support to all those affected by the crisis.
- Identify and refer those at risk for unhealthy behaviors and reactions.
- Provide care for the crisis team. One strategy to help prevent burnout would be to assign crisis team members on a rotating basis (Knox & Roberts, 2005).
- Evaluate responses to refine and improve future responses.

Specific crisis plans should be developed for a variety of crisis situations, as each crisis may require different responses. Plans should be developed for the following, at a minimum:

- Natural disasters (weather)
- Intruder in the building
- Emergency in neighborhood
- Facilities issues (electrical outage, heating, plumbing)
- Individual accidents and illnesses
- Hostage situations
- Death of student, faculty member, or other personnel
- Terrorist attack
- Suicide

- Bomb threat
- Events outside school that affect the school community (students/staff witnessing an accident, crime, etc.)

Response

According to Trump (2009), the terms *emergency* and *crisis* are often used interchangeably. However, the two terms have different meanings. An *emergency* refers to actions taken immediately to manage an event that may threaten the safety of all parties with the goal of stopping or minimizing the event. Emergency guidelines would be implemented when there is an event that threatens the safety of the academic community (e.g., intruder in the building, shooting in the building, natural disaster, fire, bomb). A crisis involves actions taken after an emergency situation is under control to deal with the emotional needs of all parties affected by the event. By separating these concepts, schools and universities are able to create concise and clear guidelines to use as references.

According to FEMA (2014), in the event of an emergency, personnel should take the following steps:

- Assess the situation and choose the appropriate response.
- Notify the appropriate emergency responders and then the crisis team and administration.
- Decide whether to evacuate or lock down the school or specific campus buildings.
- Provide emergency first aid to those in need.
- Keep supplies needed to aid in crisis management and support nearby and organized at all times.
- Trust leadership of the crisis team and emergency responders. This trust will help to minimize the chaos that occurs during a crisis.
- Communicate accurate and appropriate information to stakeholders and the media.
- Activate the student release system.
- Allow for flexibility in implementing the crisis plan.
- Document steps taken. Write down every action taken during the response to provide a record of appropriate implementation of the crisis plan.

At times, a crisis affects a large number of students and personnel, and a systematic response from the school or university is required (American School Counselor Association, 2013). Examples of crises that may dictate a systemic response include student homicide or suicide, unexpected death, and natural disasters. Although crises are, unfortunately, an uncontrollable aspect of school life, the manner in which professional counselors respond to a crisis can be controlled. Professional counselors often play leadership roles in helping schools and universities develop and implement a systemic crisis plan, which is comprehensive and well planned, mobilizes resources, and operates quickly (Erford, 2016).

Crisis response plans should exist both on a district level and on an individual school or university level. Professional counselors may be members of the district critical response teams or solely members of the school-level university response team. In either case, the professional counselor takes a leadership role in the prevention, intervention, and post-incident support of critical responses (American School Counselor Association, 2013). In this role, professional counselors provide individual and group counseling; consult with administrators, teachers, parents, and professionals; and coordinate services within the school and the community.

Crisis plans need to be put in place before a crisis occurs. Crisis response planning committees and crisis response teams (CRTs) are instrumental in planning for, coordinating, and implementing a systemic crisis response. Local businesses and agencies in the area should also be informed of active practice drills. James and Gilliland (2017) recommended the following minimum requirements for a crisis plan:

- *Physical requirements:* Identify locations for temporary counseling offices. An operations/communications center should be identified where crisis intervention procedures are monitored, needs are assessed, and information for the media is disseminated. Other suggestions include a break room, a first-aid room, and an information center designed to handle media personnel and to facilitate parent communication.
- *Logistics:* Address specific areas that need consideration as an intervention plan is implemented. For example, attention needs to be given to the manner in which on-site and off-site communication will take place. Other logistics that need attention include providing (1) procedural checklists to ensure that the intervention plan is being followed, (2) building plans for emergency personnel, and (3) food and drink for crisis personnel.
- *Crisis response:* Prepare a sequential plan for crisis response that includes gathering and verifying the facts, assessing the impact of the crisis to determine what assistance is needed, providing triage assessment to determine who is most in need of immediate attention, providing psychological first aid as a first-order response, having a model in place, providing crisis intervention, and following through by briefing, debriefing, and demobilizing.

In response to a crisis, team members should first strive to ensure student safety and simultaneously send for help from support personnel (inside or outside of the school as appropriate). Crisis counselors should listen actively, be direct and honest, know their limits, help keep the students informed at each intervention step, and inform parents as soon as possible. They should not panic, rush or lose patience with students, act shocked, judge, underreact, or preach (University of South Florida, 2012).

In response to a crisis that the University of South Florida faced (in this instance, the death by suicide of a student on campus), the following steps, which can be modified for other types of crises, were suggested:

1. An administrator should contact the police or medical examiner in order to verify the death and get the facts surrounding the death.
2. Inform the university president or superintendent of the school district of the death.
3. Prepare and activate procedures for responding to the media.
4. Notify and activate the crisis response team.
5. Contact the family of the deceased.
6. Schedule a time and place to notify faculty members and all other staff.
7. Contact community support services.

8. Arrange a meeting for parents/caregivers.
9. Meet with all students in small groups.
10. Provide additional survivor support services, such as suicide bereavement support groups.
11. Members of the crisis team should have knowledge of the victim's classes to gauge which students and teachers may need intervention.
12. Establish support stations or counseling rooms.
13. Debrief staff.
14. Reschedule any immediate stressful academic exercises.
15. In the case of a suicide, avoid flying the school flag at half-mast in order to avoid glamorizing the death.
16. During any memorialization, focus on prevention, education, and living.
17. Collaborate with students to utilize social media effectively to disseminate information and promote suicide prevention efforts.
18. Inform local crisis telephone lines and local mental health agencies about the death.
19. Provide information about visiting hours and funeral arrangements to staff, students, parents, and community members.
20. Encourage the family of the deceased to schedule the funeral after school hours.
21. Arrange for students, faculty, and staff to be excused from school to attend the funeral.
22. Follow up with students who are identified as at risk (University of South Florida, 2012).

Read Voices from the Field 13.1.

VOICES FROM THE FIELD 13.1
On Call

Tricia Uppercue

It is Sunday evening, and I'm relaxing before the start of a new week when the phone rings. It is the supervisor of school counseling, who informs me that a high school student in the county died over the weekend. He drowned in a local swimming area, surrounded by friends who tried to save him. She asks me to report on Monday morning to the high school that the student attended to provide counseling to the students, staff, and faculty as part of the county crisis team.

On Monday morning, I arrive at the school. The mood is somber and I see many students crying in the hallways. All of the appropriate personnel are assembled in the library, the designated area for students and staff to report to if they are upset and need support. Chairs are arranged in groups in the main library and in a small room next to the library to accommodate students who

need one-on-one counseling as well as those who may want to be in a group setting with others.

Many students make their way to the library. Most are friends of the victim, some were at the scene where he died; others students knew of the victim, and some may not have known the victim but the tragedy of his death reminds them of a personal trauma they have experienced. They are shaken and saddened by the loss of their classmate. I become part of a group of students who are concerned about their friends who were at the scene of the drowning. Feelings of anger, sorrow, and guilt are evident as they discuss the details of the drowning, death of loved ones, and memories of their deceased friend.

Everyone grieves differently, and members of the crisis team are prepared to deal with individual needs. Some students stay home to be with family members,

(continued)

and others come to school to be surrounded by friends. Being with loved ones is a necessary part of the grieving process. Others may want to be involved in an activity, such as making cards for the victim's loved ones. Most, I found, may need time with a counselor, either individually or in a group, to process their thoughts and feelings.

As a counselor, being a part of the crisis team is an important role. I am able to provide support, and allow students to work through the grieving process and express their thoughts and feelings. I have learned that whether I am involved in a crisis within the school in which I work or if I am called to another school where the students may not know me, many students just need someone to listen to and support them, and they are grateful to have that opportunity within the school setting.

WHAT SHOULD YOU DO IF . . . ?   If there is no written crisis plan, facilitate the development of a written plan. Then follow it. Ordinarily, there are two things that can put a professional counselor and school or university at risk for legal action: (1) not having a written plan for dealing with crises, and (2) not following an existing written plan. It is essential for professional counselors to be familiar with their district, school, or university crisis response plans. If no such plan is in place, counselors should work with administrators and other personnel to create and implement a plan to respond to crises. They should also work collaboratively with administration to develop a policy and procedure manual; many school districts, private schools, and universities have written plans and are very willing to share them. A sample crisis plan from the Los Angeles Unified School District is presented in Figure 13.1.

Likewise, if there is no established crisis team, professional counselors should facilitate convening and training one using available community resources. Professional counselors can be instrumental in leading workshops in the academic community to communicate the plan to others. A helpful resource that provides information and guidance for crisis planning is *School Crisis Guide: Help and Healing in a Time of Crisis*, produced by the National Education Association (2017). The University of South Florida (2012) also provides sound suggestions for how to respond to and work with the media during crises. Documenting what has been done to develop a written plan and train a crisis team is the best way to prepare professionals for community crisis events and protecting professionals and systems from adverse legal ramifications.

When law enforcement officers arrive on the scene, they are in control until the safety of all is secured. Crisis team members should coordinate with law enforcement officers, and it is good practice to have a law enforcement liaison on the crisis team. Total cooperation with law enforcement is crucial to return the environment to normal as quickly as possible.

Recovery

The goal of recovery is to return to a stable, precrisis environment and return students to learning as quickly as possible. However, FEMA (2014) cautions that healing and recovery may take months or even years, depending on the traumatic event. Personnel need to understand that healing is a process that will take time. It is necessary to plan for recovery during the preparedness phase so that roles and responsibilities of everyone who will participate in the recovery process are defined. There are different models for implementing services and support during the recovery process. Many school systems will have a system-wide crisis intervention team that will go to the school where the crisis has occurred and provide counseling and support for days or weeks

I. ASSESSMENT

___A. Identify problem and determine degree of impact on school.
___B. Take steps to secure the safety and security of the site as needed.
___C. Make incident report to district administrator.
___D. Determine if additional support is needed.
    ___1. Call school police and/or city police.
    ___2. Call Cluster Crisis Team.
    ___3. Call other district crisis personnel.
___E. Alter daily/weekly schedule as needed.

II. INTERVENTION: COMMUNICATION

___A. Set up a Command Center.
___B. Establish Sign-In Procedures at ALL campus entry sites*
___C. Administrator/designee/crisis manager should:
    ___1. Review facts/determine what information should be shared.
    ___2. Consider police investigation parameters.
    ___3. Notify family with sensitivity and dispatch. (Consider a personal family contact.)
___D. Develop and disseminate a bilingual fact sheet (written bulletin).
    ___1. Faculty
    ___2. Students
    ___3. Parents/community
___E. Begin media interactions.
    ___1. Identify a media spokesperson. (Office of Communications may be utilized.)
    ___2. Designate a location for media representatives*
___F. Contact neighboring schools.
___G. Contact schools of affected students' siblings.
___H. Organize other communication activities.
    ___1. Classroom presentations/discussions
    ___2. Parent/community meetings
    ___3. School staff meeting
___I. Provide for rumor control.
    ___1. Keep a TV set or radio tuned to a news station.
    ___2. Verify ALL facts heard.
    ___3. Update fact sheet as needed.
    ___4. Utilize student leaders
        (a) as sources knowledgeable of rumors among students.
        (b) as peer leaders to convey factual information.
        (c) as runners (written bulletins should be sealed when necessary).

III. INTERVENTION: FIRST AID AND EMERGENCY RELEASE PLAN

___A. Initiate First Aid Team procedures.
___B. Designate Emergency Health Office location*
___C. Initiate Emergency Release Plan procedures.
___D. Designate student check-out location*

IV. INTERVENTION: PSYCHOLOGICAL FIRST AID/COUNSELING

___A. Logistics: Designate rooms/locations/areas**
    ___1. Individual counseling—location: _____ **
    ___2. Group counseling—location: _____ **
    ___3. Parents—location: _____ **

FIGURE 13.1 A sample crisis plan developed by the Los Angeles Unified School District.

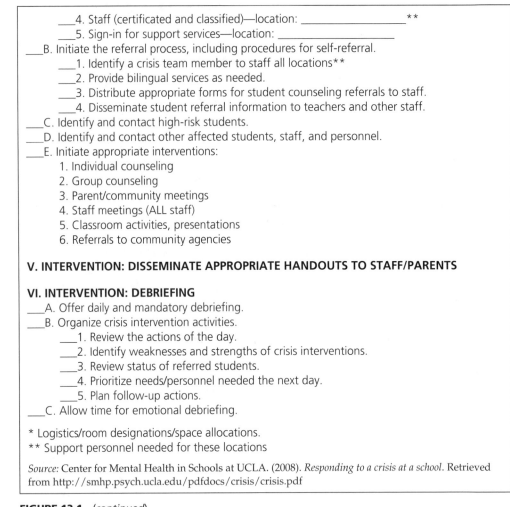

___4. Staff (certificated and classified)—location: _____ **

___5. Sign-in for support services—location: _____

___B. Initiate the referral process, including procedures for self-referral.

    ___1. Identify a crisis team member to staff all locations**

    ___2. Provide bilingual services as needed.

    ___3. Distribute appropriate forms for student counseling referrals to staff.

    ___4. Disseminate student referral information to teachers and other staff.

___C. Identify and contact high-risk students.

___D. Identify and contact other affected students, staff, and personnel.

___E. Initiate appropriate interventions:

    1. Individual counseling

    2. Group counseling

    3. Parent/community meetings

    4. Staff meetings (ALL staff)

    5. Classroom activities, presentations

    6. Referrals to community agencies

V. INTERVENTION: DISSEMINATE APPROPRIATE HANDOUTS TO STAFF/PARENTS

VI. INTERVENTION: DEBRIEFING

___A. Offer daily and mandatory debriefing.

___B. Organize crisis intervention activities.

    ___1. Review the actions of the day.

    ___2. Identify weaknesses and strengths of crisis interventions.

    ___3. Review status of referred students.

    ___4. Prioritize needs/personnel needed the next day.

    ___5. Plan follow-up actions.

___C. Allow time for emotional debriefing.

* Logistics/room designations/space allocations.

** Support personnel needed for these locations

Source: Center for Mental Health in Schools at UCLA. (2008). *Responding to a crisis at a school.* Retrieved from http://smhp.psych.ucla.edu/pdfdocs/crisis/crisis.pdf

FIGURE 13.1   *(continued)*

following the crisis. Other schools or universities may have the crisis team provide counseling and services for the academic community.

During the recovery phase, personnel need to keep students, families, and the media informed. It is imperative to clearly state what steps have been implemented to provide for student safety. In addition, families and community members need to be informed about services being provided for students and families at school and in the community. Cultural differences should be considered when composing letters or announcements to students and parents. It may be necessary to translate letters and other forms of communication into the representative languages.

While in the recovery phase, remember to focus on the building as well as the people. There may be damage to the building that needs to be repaired. FEMA (2014) recommends conducting safety audits to assess the building and develop plans for repairs. In addition to assessing the damage to the building, it is critical to continue to assess the emotional needs of all students and staff to determine who will need the services of the professional counselor, social worker, school psychologist, or other mental health professional. Specific suggestions for interventions with students, staff, and families will be discussed later in this chapter.

Debriefing

Debriefing is a time for the crisis team members to gather and share their unique experiences of the crisis in a private and safe environment. It is extremely important to allow some time for the crisis team members to share their thoughts and feelings. Team members may have been the faculty, counselors, and mentors of the victims. Or the event may have triggered some other unresolved crisis in their lives. Hence, support for the crisis team is critical. It is important for the team leader to invite team members to share what happened, what the experience was like, what memory stands out in their mind that is hard to erase, and what each can do to take care of themselves during and after the crisis. Turner (2010) offered the following suggestions for self-care after a crisis:

- Debrief with partner, team members, or supervisor.
- Attend regular support meetings.
- Find ways to relax such as music, exercise, meditation, hobbies, reading, or sports.
- Maintain a healthy balance in life and separate work from leisure time.
- Acknowledge personal feelings.
- Spend quality time with family and friends who are not connected with your crisis work.
- Visit a place that is peaceful such as a church, synagogue, park, or art gallery. Write in a journal.

See Chapter 14 for additional counselor self-care strategies and suggestions.

Evaluation of the crisis response and recovery efforts is a necessary part of the crisis plan. FEMA (2014) suggests conducting interviews with the crisis team, emergency responders, families, faculty, students, and staff in order to determine what efforts were successful along with changes that are necessary. The following are examples of questions to ask:

- Which classroom-based interventions proved most successful and why?
- Which assessment and referral strategies were the most successful and why?
- What were the most positive aspects of staff debriefings and why?
- Which recovery strategies would you change and why?
- Do other professionals need to be tapped to help with future crises?
- What additional training is necessary to enable the school and the community at large to prepare for future crises?
- What additional equipment is needed to support recovery efforts?
- What other planning actions will facilitate future recovery efforts? (FEMA, 2014, pp. 5–6)

Helping Students during and after Crises

Students will need to talk about what they have experienced during the crisis and it is important to offer a variety of counseling services for students so that they feel supported and receive needed help. Individual counseling and small-group counseling give students an opportunity to express their feelings and receive support. Classroom guidance lessons and class meetings may also be extremely helpful and can provide a forum for students to express emotions, obtain accurate information, and ask questions in both K–12 and university settings. These sessions should focus on providing facts and dispelling rumors, sharing stories, sharing reactions, empowering students, and providing closure. Younger children may not be able to articulate their feelings but will benefit from opportunities to draw, paint, or participate in other creative activities. Adolescents and young adults should be encouraged to talk about their feelings in small-group discussions or through writing about their experiences. It is also essential to consider how substance use intersects with crisis issues in schools and universities (see Chapter 7).

Finally, integration of services is critical not only in the aftermath of a crisis but for longer term follow-up weeks and months later. Thus, links between the crisis team and community agencies, college counseling centers, and student services is essential. Importantly, these links should be established during the planning phase of crisis team activities so that seamless integration can occur.

Read Voices from the Field 13.2.

VOICES FROM THE FIELD 13.2
Dealing with the Death of a Student by Suicide

Nicole Adamson

As part of a class assignment during my first semester as a school counseling master's student, I enthusiastically decided to shadow the high school counselor in my hometown. My connections with the members of my rural community run deep, and many of the students at the school were younger siblings of my high school friends. Many Friday nights were spent caring for these students when their parents went out to celebrate their anniversaries or birthdays. Needless to say, I was truly excited to return to the high school and experience the culture from a different vantage point.

As I walked into the building, I immediately sensed something was wrong; the tension was palpable. I approached the school counselor's office only to find several sobbing students. When the school counselor saw that I had come to shadow her, she met with me privately and informed me that she was dealing with a crisis situation. A male student had died the previous evening as a result of suicide.

To further complicate the situation, I knew the student personally, as his family lived next door to one of my closest friends. This news greatly affected me and I was torn between a desire to mourn and a desire to help the young students who knew and loved this student. The minimal training I'd had at that point had not prepared me to handle a situation such as this.

I did not know how to integrate my personal reactions with my emerging professional role.

The school counselor handled the situation with confidence. First, she called a local agency to assist in meeting with students who needed individual assistance. She then continued to meet with students until the external agency's counselors arrived. When these counselors came and met individually with students, I had an opportunity to learn from these observations.

Later that day, as I processed these events, I gained an awareness of the complexities of a school counselor's job. I had previously understood the classroom guidance, student planning, and system support aspects of the school counselor's responsibilities, but on that day I gained an understanding of school counselors' important role in managing responsive services. I learned that my own emotions were natural and could help me empathize with the thoughts and feelings of students in a crisis. I also learned that counselors must sometimes set aside their own needs in order to best help others.

Although that day was filled with pain and struggle, it informed and colored my experience as an emerging counselor. I gained an acute understanding of the complexities of the school counseling profession, and I learned the value of crisis response preparedness. I also learned from an excellent school counselor how to identify and use resources in order to respond appropriately and effectively to a crisis.

Helping Parents/Guardians during and after a School Crisis

When there is a crisis, parents/guardians must receive accurate information along with appropriate suggestions for assisting students. It is very helpful to send a letter to parents/guardians that includes accurate information, symptoms, common and uncommon reactions they might observe in their children, and suggestions to help those who are experiencing distress as a result of the crisis. Figure 13.2 presents a sample letter to parents/guardians related to the death of a student. These letters should be developed before a crisis so that, when a crisis occurs, they can be quickly adapted to the uniqueness of the existing crisis and then copied and distributed. These letters can be sent home and put on the school or university website; however, the website should never be the only means of communication, since there are many families without this technological resource. The letters should be written in all languages that are represented in the academic community.

Dear Parents/Guardians:

   I regret to inform you of the death of one of our students. Laurie Jones, a fifth grader, died on January 15 of leukemia. I know that you join me in my concern and sympathy for the family.

   The students were told of Laurie's death today by their classroom teachers. Crisis counselors visited each class and provided an opportunity for students to talk, ask questions, and share their feelings. Those children who were most upset met privately with counselors for additional counseling and support. Counseling services will continue to be made available to students this week and in the future as needed.

   Notes and cards may be sent to the family at the following address: Mr. and Mrs. Jackson Jones XXX Elm Street, Arlington, VA 222XX. A memorial service will be held at St. John's Church on Monday, January 19 at 9:00 a.m. The church is located at 1500 Main Street, Arlington, VA 22207. In lieu of flowers, the family requests that donations be made to the Leukemia and Lymphoma Society.

   Your children may experience a wide range of emotions as a result of Laurie's death. The following suggestions may be useful as you help your children cope with their grief:

- Encourage your children to talk about their feelings or to draw pictures to express their emotions.
- Offer support and let your children know that you are available to talk with them and answer questions.
- Allow your children to be sad and to cry.
- Reassure your children that they are healthy, and discuss fears they may have about their own death or the death of a family member.
- Explain the ritual of funerals and memorial services. If children express a desire to attend the memorial service, it is recommended that you accompany them.
- Monitor your child's emotional state and behavior. If you notice prolonged sadness, withdrawal from social contact, changes in eating or sleeping habits, or other behavior unusual for your child, please contact Ms. Brown, our professional school counselor, who will be available to offer support and resources to you and your child. She can be reached at XXX-555-3607 or Jaclyn.Brown@xxx.k-12

If you have questions or concerns, please don't hesitate to contact me.
Sincerely,
Mrs. Helen Smith, Principal
XXX-555-2438, Helen.Smith@xxx.k-12

FIGURE 13.2   A sample letter to parents/guardians.

Depending on the nature of the crisis, it may be necessary to invite parents/guardians to a group meeting at school so that they can receive accurate information, share feelings and questions, and learn ways to support their children during and following the crisis. The goals of the family/community meeting are to impart information and to assist the family and community members in processing their reactions to the crisis. At this meeting, the crisis team can offer support and suggestions, while also passing along information about services that are available in the community (American School Counselor Association, 2013). Regarding universities, protocols for contacting parents may vary from e-mail to text alerts. The important thing is for universities and schools to have a contact strategy before a crisis occurs. This will allow immediate notification of parents to reduce undue worrying and later complaints of non-notice or misinformation.

The National Association of School Psychologists (NASP, 2015) offers the following guidelines to help faculty, parents, and other caregivers support students who have experienced loss:

- Give students the opportunity to tell their story and be a good listener.
- Recognize that all students are different and their views of the world are unique and shaped by different experiences.
- Understand that grieving is a process, not an event. Allow adequate time for each student to grieve in whatever way chosen. Also, remember that encouraging students to resume normal activities without the opportunity to deal with their emotional pain may cause negative reactions.
- Provide honest information about the tragic event in developmentally appropriate ways.
- Encourage students to ask questions about loss and death.

Notifying Students of a Death, Accident, or Event

In addition to guidelines in the crisis plan, the following steps should be followed for situations where students are notified of a death, accident, or event.

- Gather the crisis team members for a planning meeting. The team members should obtain and verify the facts of the incident and designate the person who will continue to gather factual information. At this time, the team should decide on the format for conveying the information to faculty, students, staff, parents (e.g., large-group meetings, classroom meetings, emergency alert/texts/e-mails/letters to parents).
- Conduct a meeting for faculty and staff before the academic day begins to inform them of the situation and to give them information about how the crisis plan will be implemented.
- Form teams that can announce the crisis event via individual classroom sessions, meetings of smaller groups of students, general assemblies, or announcements to larger groups. Keep in mind that meeting with smaller groups and holding general assemblies are the preferred methods for passing along the information. The public address system should be used only if absolutely necessary.
- Have the leader of the crisis team determine the assignments for crisis team members, taking into account team member strengths and comfort levels. Possible roles for team members include direct contact with groups of students, individual counseling sessions, and administrative tasks. Crisis intervention should never be done

alone. Team members should always work in pairs. Two crisis team members should observe the class and look for high-risk students. Having two team members working together allows one team member to escort a distressed child out of the room for private counseling, while the other team member continues working with the group. Team members who are experiencing the same intervention are able to debrief each other and can monitor each other's stress levels and react accordingly.

- Introduce crisis team members to the students. Even if students know the staff, faculty, counselors, and administrators from other interactions, students must be made aware that these people are also crisis team members and be apprised of the team members' roles during the crisis event.
- Ask students if any of them have heard about the event. Allow students to tell what they know or have heard about the event. This will not only allow the sharing of information but will also allow any rumors to be discussed in the group so the team can verify or deny them publicly.
- Deliver the facts of the event in developmentally appropriate terms, and clarify any rumors or incorrect information. Allow enough time for students to ask questions.
- When appropriate, allow children to tell their stories about this experience or similar ones. List all the feelings voiced on the blackboard and spend some time talking about the normalcy of these feelings.
- In crises that may involve another student, allow students to talk about memories each has of the absent student.
- If the event involves a student who may be able to return to classes, discuss what they may encounter when the student returns and how they can help the student.
- If the event involves the death of a student, keep in mind the additional issues to address—for example, what to do with the empty desk. Often, the desk will be left vacant for a period of time; however, a time limit should be established and shared with the other students so they understand that the desk eventually will be removed. It is crucial to involve the students in this process.
- If developmentally appropriate, share information regarding the funeral, including the type of funeral and cultural rituals.
- Provide information regarding the resources that are available at the school or university and in the community and provide additional handout materials that can be helpful to the students in working through the crisis.

Differences in strategies may exist between and among K–12 schools and university settings because of embedded cultures or uniqueness of communities or settings. What is essential is that crisis teams have a priori strategies for dissemination of information to parents, residents, commuters, and graduate students.

Complete Activity 13.1, which asks you how you would feel and react in a crisis situation. Also complete Think About It 13.2.

ACTIVITY 13.1

In your own imagination, put yourself in a crisis situation of your choosing. If you were the counselor, discuss how you would feel and react. What steps would you take to ensure the safety of the academic community? Discuss how the crisis team would be involved and how the crisis plan would be implemented.

THINK ABOUT IT 13.2

Think about the best ways to intervene with the students, faculty, staff, parents/guardians, and community in schools or universities with which you have been associated. What would they be?

RESPONSES TO NATIONAL CRISES BY SCHOOLS AND UNIVERSITIES

Many crises occur miles away from our schools and universities or even in other states or countries (e.g., hurricanes, earthquakes, terrorist attacks, school shootings, war). However, such crises may have a tremendous impact on our students throughout the nation. Personnel must always respond in a way that reassures students, faculty, staff, and parents/guardians. It is important that they follow these guidelines:

- Present accurate information in developmentally appropriate ways.
- Give students opportunities to express feelings and ask questions.
- Provide information for teachers and parents/guardians so that they can help students.
- Organize service activities so that students and all members of the school community can provide assistance to victims (e.g., collect money/clothing for victims, organize fund-raisers, correspond with children who were affected).

Table 13.1 provides a listing of resources and websites with additional helpful information on dealing with crises on school and university campuses. Case Studies 13.1 through 13.3 apply the skills learned thus far in the chapter. Also read Voices from the Field 13.3.

TABLE 13.1 Resources on Emergency Preparedness and Response in Schools and Universities

American Hospice Foundation—Information and activities for children and adolescents coping with loss/disaster/crisis: www.americanhospice.org

American Red Cross: www.redcross.org

American School Counselor Association—Resource section offers articles/activities that can be used to assist schools in responding to crisis and the needs of the school community: www.schoolcounselor.org

Center for Mental Health Services—Tips for talking about disaster: www.mentalhealth.org/cmhs/emergencyservices/after.aps

Emergency Response and Crisis Management (ERCM) Technical Assistance Center: www.ercm.org

FEMA for Kids: FEMA website for children to help them understand and prepare for disaster: www.fema.gov/kids/

National Association of School Psychologists—Information on helping children, youth, parents, teachers, and schools cope with crisis: www.nasponline.org

National Education Association—NEA Health Information Network www.nea.org/crisis/bihome.html#response

TABLE 13.1 Resources on Emergency Preparedness and Response in Schools and Universities (*continued*)

Responding to Crisis at a School: UCLA Resource Aid Packet http://smhp.psych.ucla.edu/pdfdocs/crisis/crisis.pdf

UCLA Center for Mental Health in Schools—Basic information on responding to crisis in schools: smhp.psych.ucla.edu

U.S. Department of Education—Tips for helping students recover from traumatic events: www.ed.gov/parent/academic/help/recovering

U.S. Department of Education, Office of Safe and Drug-Free Schools—Information on crisis planning to create drug-free schools: www.ed.gov/admins/lead/safety/crisisplanning.html

U.S. Department of Education, Office of Safe and Drug-Free Schools—*Practical Information on Crisis Planning: A Guide for Schools and Communities:* www2.ed.gov/admins/lead/safety/emergencyplan/crisisplanning.pdf

CASE STUDY 13.1

A Student with a Terminal Illness

Laurie was a Grade 5 student diagnosed with leukemia within the past year. During this time, she was absent from school while receiving chemotherapy treatment for her cancer and had lost her hair. The students were aware of her condition. Her parents just called the school and reported that Laurie died. The principal asks you to call a meeting of the crisis team, teachers, and appropriate staff to discuss how to best approach the other students about Laurie's death. As the leader of this team, consider the following questions.

Discussion Questions

1. Who needs to be contacted before offering any news? What do you need to know?
2. How do you decide what groups are the priority to receive intervention?
3. Who are some typical groups?
4. What questions would you expect to have from students?

CASE STUDY 13.2

School Shooting

A young male enters the dining area, takes out a gun, and begins shooting at students seated at tables. Eight students are hit before the gunman runs out of the building. You are a crisis team member and come into the dining area just after the shooting has occurred.

Discussion Questions

1. What immediate steps should be taken to ensure the safety of everyone on campus?
2. Discuss how the crisis team would be involved and how the crisis plan would be implemented.

3. How should the team intervene with students, faculty, staff, parents, and community?

4. With a peer as a student in this situation, role-play implementation of the task model of crisis assessment and intervention presented in Table 1.1.

CASE STUDY 13.3

Death of a Teacher

It is 8:00 a.m. and the administrator calls you to the office to say that a faculty member died suddenly last evening.

Discussion Questions

1. Discuss how you might react to this situation.
2. What steps should be taken to inform the faculty, staff, students, and parents?
3. Discuss how the crisis team would be involved and how the crisis plan would be implemented.
4. How should the school/university intervene with students, faculty, staff, and parents?

VOICES FROM THE FIELD 13.3
My Last Day

Tori Stone

It was the last day of school. I was wrapped up in last-day-of-school thoughts: saying good-bye to my Grade 8 students; the adaptation of *A Midsummer Night's Dream* the Grade 8 students were presenting; the faculty luncheon that afternoon. I remember sending the girls who would take the class passes to the main office on that errand, but they returned because they wanted me to give them stickers. That stands out in my mind: the innocence of the girls returning for the stickers. I was handing them the stickers when the principal came running through, yelling "Lock it down, lock it down, lock it down!" I can still remember the sound of his voice. It was clear that something was very wrong.

I pushed the girls into my office, closed the door, and turned off the lights. I had the girls crawl under my desk and hide themselves in the corner farthest from the door. I pulled the phone onto the floor and called my guidance director to find out what was going on. She told me there was a student with several rifles and ammunition in the office. I remember thinking to myself, "I can't call these parents and tell them that their children are dead. If someone has to die, it will have to be me." This sounds heroic, but it wasn't. I was more scared than I had ever been in my life. It occurred to me that I didn't want to die; that I might want to have children; that wooden doors are not bullet proof. When one of the girls started to panic, I talked to her calmly about other things. I gave her tissues and patted her back. I told the girls I would protect them. This statement still has the weight of a lie in my head. I knew there was little I could do to protect them.

Time passed, but I'm still not sure how long exactly. Finally, someone pounded on the door and yelled, "SWAT police, come out with your hands up!" The girls cried; I was scared as well. When we opened the door there were SWAT team members in riot gear surrounding my office. They pointed guns at our heads

(continued)

and yelled at us to run. I was afraid, the girls were crying, and I felt angry. I yelled at the SWAT team to stop yelling at the children. They did not stop yelling. They told us to "Shut up and run!" We ran. There were kids in costumes because of the play. I remember seeing little girls dressed like fairies with bare feet. The juxtaposition of SWAT members pointing guns at children in tutus will stay with me forever.

Things I learned: stay calm; follow procedure; act like you are okay in front of the students, even if you are not. Schools should conduct lockdown drills more than once per school year. It should be second nature to staff members to secure their classrooms. Once a building is evacuated for a gunman incident, the building is a crime scene. You cannot reenter. We had 1,100 children outside for more than 4 hours on a 95 degree day; we had no water and very little shelter from the sun. Some children were overcome by fear, others by the heat. If you work in a small district, ask questions about where students will be moved to in the event of an emergency. Getting to another large venue where kids can have access to water and restrooms, and where parents can pick them up, is essential.

The next day we returned to school and everything was eerily just as we left it. The stickers were still on my desk, balls stood in place on the gymnasium floor, there were shoes in the hallways because kids literally ran out of their shoes. Initially, parents were kind and supportive, but eventually, in search of a reason that could resurrect their sense of security, they wanted to place blame. As a staff we faced many questions—from "Why are there no metal detectors?" to "Why wasn't there water and sunscreen buried someplace on the campus in case of this kind of event?" Parents were scared, and their fear turned quickly to anger; anger that an incident such as this could happen and because we could not promise that it would not happen again. I think back to myself as young and naïve, and never expected the anger and the blame, so I wasn't prepared for it. The truth is, a barricaded hostage event, or worse, a school shooting, could happen at any time, at any school in the country. As counselors, we are trained to handle critical incidents, and that training is invaluable, but it does not make us impenetrable to random acts of violence. That may very well be the most valuable lesson I learned from this event.

RESPONDING TO CRISES IN UNIVERSITY SETTINGS

Colleges and universities strive to keep campuses safe so that students may grow intellectually and personally. However, this is a constant challenge because the structures of universities can be complex. The purpose of this section is to provide more specific guidance on methods and procedures for counselors working in higher education. All higher education settings must prepare for crises and have plans in place to ensure the safety and well-being of all students, faculty, and staff.

The four phases identified by the U.S. Department of Education's Office of Safe and Drug-Free Schools (2017) also serve as a model for crisis planning at the college/ university level. Discussed earlier in this chapter, they include: mitigation/prevention, preparedness, response, and recovery. Indeed, most of the information presented in this chapter and throughout this book can be applied to university campuses with appropriate modifications. But additional attention is given to universities here because of widespread variations in size, number of students, location expanse, and administrative complexity.

Colleges and universities must be prepared to respond to the death of any member of the campus community (student or faculty); decompensation of a student as a result of a prior mental health diagnosis; natural disasters; terrorist attacks; bomb threats; fire; and other acts of violence. A response for each of these events should be developed and a crisis plan should be prepared and practiced. Everyone who is a member of the campus community (including parents) should be aware of emergency procedures and crisis plans. These procedures and plans should be described on the website and should be discussed with students, faculty, and staff. All campuses should have an alert system (e.g., text, e-mail, website, phone message notification) in place whereby the students, faculty, staff and parents can be alerted to potential emergencies on campus.

Shelter-in-Place

Shelter-in-place means selecting a "small, interior room, with no or few windows, and taking refuge there" (National Terror Alert Response Center, 2017). In schools and universities, typically students shelter-in-place because of active shooter or weather-related events.

ACTIVE SHOOTER SHELTER-IN-PLACE   FEMA (2013) provided excellent advice on responding to an active shooter situation in its *Guide for Developing High-Quality School Emergency Operations Plans*:

- Train staff to overcome denial and to respond immediately, including fulfilling their responsibilities toward individuals in their charge. For example, train staff to recognize the sounds of danger, act, and forcefully communicate the danger and necessary action (e.g., "Gun! Get out!") to those in their charge. In addition, those closest to the public address or other communications system, or otherwise able to alert others, should communicate the danger and necessary action.
- Upon recognizing the danger, as soon as it is safe to do so, staff or others must alert first responders by contacting 911 with as clear and accurate information as possible.
- Run: If it is safe to do so for yourself and those in your care, the first course of action that should be taken is to run out of the building and far away until you are in a safe location. Students and staff should be trained to
  - Leave personal belongings behind;
  - Visualize possible escape routes, including physically accessible routes for students and staff with disabilities as well as persons with access and functional needs;
  - Avoid escalators and elevators;
  - Take others with them, but not to stay behind because others will not go;
  - Call 911 when safe to do so; and
  - Let a responsible adult know where they are.
- Hide: If running is not a safe option, hide in as safe a place as possible. Students and staff should be trained to hide in a location where the walls might be thicker and have fewer windows. In addition:
  - Lock the doors;
  - Barricade the doors with heavy furniture;
  - Close and lock windows and close blinds or cover windows;
  - Turn off lights;
  - Silence all electronic devices;
  - Remain silent;
  - Hide along the wall closest to the exit but out of view from the hallway (allowing for an ambush of the shooter and for possible escape if the shooter enters the room);

- Use strategies to silently communicate with first responders if possible, for example, in rooms with exterior windows make signs to silently signal law enforcement officers and emergency responders to indicate the status of the room's occupants; and
  - Remain in place until given an all clear by identifiable law enforcement officers.
- Fight: If neither running nor hiding is a safe option, as a last resort when confronted by the shooter, adults in immediate danger should consider trying to disrupt or incapacitate the shooter by using aggressive force and items in their environment, such as fire extinguishers, and chairs. (pp. 64–65)

"In a study of 41 active shooter events that ended before law enforcement officers arrived, the potential victims stopped the attacker themselves in 16 instances. In 13 of those cases they physically subdued the attacker" (FEMA, 2013, p. 66).

STORM SHELTER-IN-PLACE   FEMA (2011) published *Storm Safe: Sheltering in Place*, which provides the following helpful tips for a number of storm-related crises:

- Heat Wave
  - Stay indoors as much as possible and limit exposure to the sun.
  - Stay on the lowest floor out of the sunshine if air conditioning is not available.
- Thunderstorm and Lightning
  - Stand or sit away from doors and windows that lead outside.
  - Stand away from concrete walls, and avoid lying on concrete floors.
  - Close doors and windows to the outside to prevent wind damage and injuries.
- Hurricane
  - Listen to local watches and warnings about evacuating.
  - If you live in a high-rise building, hurricane winds are stronger at higher elevations or floors.
  - If you are unable to evacuate, go to your wind-safe room.
  - If you don't have a wind-safe room, take refuge in a small interior room, closet, or hallway on the lowest level.
  - Lie on the floor under a table or another sturdy object.
- Tornado
  - Go to a pre-designated shelter area such as a safe room, basement, storm cellar, or the lowest building level.
  - If there is no basement, go to the center of an interior room on the lowest level (closet, interior hallway) away from corners, windows, doors, and outside walls.
  - Put as many walls as possible between you and the outside. Get under a sturdy table and use pillows, blankets, or other "cushions" to protect your head and neck. As a last resort, use your arms to protect your head and neck.
- Winter Storm
  - Select a location where heat can best be conserved, such as the side of the house that receives the most sunlight and is away from cold winds.
  - Interior rooms are probably the best option.
  - A basement may be a good location.
  - If necessary, seal off rooms that are not being used by shutting doors, closing window coverings, etc. (p. 3)

Threat Assessment Teams

In an effort to prevent acts of violence, many institutions of higher education have created threat assessment teams. These teams are usually composed of representatives from various departments, including academic affairs, student affairs, legal counsel, mental health services, and public safety. Threat assessment teams evaluate persons of concern who may pose a potential risk of violence. Drysdale, Modzeleski, and Simons (2010) defined a three-step process in threat assessment: (1) identify individuals whose behavior causes concern or disruption on or off campus affecting students, faculty, or staff; (2) assess whether the identified individual possesses the intent and ability to carry out an attack against the community, and if the individual has taken steps to prepare for the attack; and (3) manage the threat posed by the individual, to include disrupting potential plans of attack, mitigating the risk, and implementing strategies to facilitate long-term resolution (p. 27). Apply the skills and knowledge learned in this chapter to university-specific Case Studies 13.4 and 13.5. Also read Voices from the Field 13.4.

CASE STUDY 13.4

Shooting of Students in a Dormitory

The Dean of Students at a large university has just been informed that two students have been shot in a dormitory and have been taken to the hospital. The gunman has not been identified or captured.

Discussion Questions

1. If you were the Dean of Students, how would you feel and react?
2. What steps should be taken to ensure the safety of everyone on campus?
3. What steps should the university take to inform and protect students, faculty, staff, and other campus employees?
4. How should parents be informed?
5. What should occur in the hours and weeks after the event has occurred?

CASE STUDY 13.5

A Flood on Campus

Recent storms have caused local rivers to overflow, and the entire town (including the college campus) is experiencing extreme flooding. Students are unable to leave their dormitories, libraries, or classrooms.

Discussion Questions

1. What steps should be taken to ensure the safety of everyone on campus?
2. What steps should the university take to inform and protect students, faculty, staff, and other campus employees?
3. How should parents be informed?
4. What should occur in the hours and weeks after the event has occurred?

VOICES FROM THE FIELD 13.4
Collaboration in the Midst of a Campus Crisis

Kyoung Mi Choi

Because most of the students had returned home for Thanksgiving break, the campus seemed very quiet. Just as I finished my Thanksgiving dinner with friends and was ready to relax, I received a phone call from my supervisor at the Center for International Student Services. With some trepidation, I answered the phone: "Hi, there's been a really bad car accident, and four international students were involved. I'm not sure of the exact situation yet, but would you be able to accompany the DPS [Department of Public Safety] officers to the hospital? They need someone who can speak Korean and communicate with the survivors and their families in Korea. I'll update you with more detailed information later." My heart stopped; I knew something was seriously wrong.

Instead of DPS officers, the Vice President of Student Affairs came to my apartment gate. I briefly greeted him and followed him to the car. As we arrived at the hospital, we were directed to the emergency area. There were two students lying on the beds in two small separate rooms. I was wondering about what happened to the other two students.

Shortly after, I found out that the driver and one of the passengers were the only survivors and the other students were killed in the car accident. One survivor could not even say a word; tears were rolling down her cheeks. These two students were there—by themselves—wondering about their friends' safety.

Because of the traumatic incident, the students had difficulty communicating in English, a nonnative language for them. I tried to comfort them in Korean while simultaneously translating between the students and the DPS officers, the Victim Protective Services, and the hospital staff. What was even more difficult was that I also had to call the students' parents in Korea; delivering this information to parents who were halfway around the world from their children was difficult.

As a counselor on a college campus, I have worked with international students as a peer mentor, consultant, and educator for international students. Working with international students requires much collaboration and relationship building within all of the functional areas in Student Affairs. Especially when a crisis happens, the first person contacted is often not the student's parents, but college staff, oftentimes counselors.

At last, the four students' parents were contacted, flights were arranged, and the families arrived on campus. The community, especially ethnic churches and organizations, were actively involved in the funeral preparations and services. The Korean Student Association also set up meetings to support the survivors and the deceased students' families. The campus counseling services provided the survivors and other students who were affected by this incident with individual and group counseling sessions. The Residence Life staff also assisted the deceased students' parents in collecting their children's belongings. The whole campus worked together to support the survivors, mourn the losses, and educate students about safety.

Some Final Issues

It is essential to remember that crises subject generally normal functioning people to extreme circumstances that outstrip their abilities to cope. Therefore, it is important for counselors to not pathologize normal reactions to crisis situations. Diagnostic considerations during crises must be given the special consideration due. Likewise, it is important to consider the intersection of alcohol or drug use on high school or university campuses and how these behaviors may contribute to or occur in response to crisis situations. Chapter 7 provided more information on the interplay of substance use and crises. Finally, professional counselors employed by schools and universities have special responsibilities for the safety of the students and to engage in substantial self-care activities to optimize their availability to these populations of vulnerable students. The next and final chapter (Chapter 14) provides an expanded discussion of counselor self-care. Complete Activity 13.2, which asks you to bring together the information you have learned in this chapter.

ACTIVITY 13.2

In small groups, construct a scenario of a crisis situation in an academic setting. What immediate steps should be taken to ensure the safety of everyone in the area? Discuss how the crisis team would be involved and how the crisis plan would be implemented. How should the crisis team intervene with students, teachers, staff, parents, and the community?

Summary

This chapter provided a detailed overview of crises in schools and universities and how to respond to such crises. An emphasis was placed on how to create a network of support because educational systems have so many stakeholders to address (e.g., students, parents, faculty, staff, administrators). The components of a comprehensive crisis plan include determining the composition of the crisis team, gathering the crisis team members for a planning meeting, deciding how to announce the event and discuss or review classroom activities, and holding a team debriefing. The four phases of a crisis plan are mitigation and prevention; preparedness; response; and recovery, which includes debriefing strategies. Numerous case studies were provided to allow counselors to apply knowledge and skills gained. All crises evolve through different stages—and then end. Those who experience crisis, disaster, or trauma also evolve in that they, hopefully, resolve or at least experience a lessened impact of the situation. Crises affect lives in systemic ways; every aspect of one's life can be affected by a crisis.

CHAPTER

14 Counselor Self-Care
in Crisis Situations

James Jackson, Latofia Parker, and Judith Harrington

PREVIEW

This culminating chapter explores the relevance of self-care for professional counselors providing crisis- and trauma-related services and identifies strategies by which counselors might incorporate self-care as an intentional element of counselor professional practice.

COUNSELOR SELF-CARE IS ESSENTIAL

Self-care is recognized as an essential aspect of the professional functioning of counselors (Corey & Corey, 2015; Erford, 2018). Counselor self-care has been identified as a potential protective factor against the development of counselor deficits in internal resources that negatively impact personal and professional functioning through pathways such as burnout (Puig et al., 2012), impairment (Lawson, Venart, Hazler, & Kottler, 2007), and compassion fatigue (Christopher & Maris, 2010). Additionally, multiple benefits of self-care exist for students in counselor training programs (Christopher & Maris, 2010; Roach & Young, 2007; Schure, Christopher, & Christopher, 2008). Research concerning self-care for counseling students has suggested benefits for the promotion of counselor professional development, such as enhanced empathy skills (Shapiro, Brown, & Biegel, 2007) and improved client treatment outcomes (Grepmair et al., 2007).

The importance of counselor self-care is further underscored by the inclusion of self-care and related terms such as *wellness, impairment,* and *effectiveness* in the ethical codes of the American Counseling Association (ACA, 2014), the American Mental Health Counselors Association (AMHCA, 2010), Association for Counselor Education and Supervision (ACES, 2011), and the American School Counselor Association (ASCA, 2010), as well as past and current standards of the Council for Accreditation of Counseling and Related Educational Programs (CACREP, 2016). Thus, a growing body of research, counselor training standards, and ethical codes identify self-care as an important component of counselor professional functioning. Likewise, counselor educators and counseling supervisors are encouraged to incorporate self-care as an intentional component of the counselor development process.

Counselor Ongoing Self-Assessment

A major component of ethical practice is the ability of the counselor to monitor her or his own mental health and engage in self-care. Welfel (2016) points out that counselors face emotional challenges both in the workplace and at home. Counselors have lives, family responsibilities, community obligations, and stressors and/or crises that affect their personal functioning. In addition, counselors are not immune from mental disorders, substance use, previous traumatic experiences, and painful narratives. In order to provide ethical best practice, counselors must nurture self-awareness and actively engage in self-care, and this is particularly important for counselors working in crisis situations.

Self-assessment is the process by which counselors self-monitor and maintain self-awareness of their reactions, behaviors, feelings, and thoughts, thereby recognizing how these internal processes affect their sense of self and their functioning as helping professionals. Self-assessment is crucial to providing effective crisis intervention services, particularly when counselors are called upon to engage in long-term responses to disaster-related destruction while also juggling the work demands associated with responding to the needs of others. A counselor who is unable to attend to his or her internal state is unlikely to be of much help in a crisis situation; thus, self-awareness and self-care are fundamentally important to best practice. In addition to inner-awareness when serving in a disaster context, it is important that counselors also monitor their own crisis-related needs. For example, while providing disaster care to crisis victims, counselors should be mindful to also attend to their own basic needs of food, water, safe shelter, and provisions for their own families. In essence, crisis counselors should have a plan in place for their personal well-being. Read Voices from the Field 14.1, which provides a personal reflection on the power of counselor supervision in self-care.

VOICES FROM THE FIELD 14.1
Counselors Living and Working in Dangerous Settings

James Jackson

The weekly counseling supervision group members were just settling into their seats as one of the members who had missed the previous group session said, "Sorry I wasn't able to be here for supervision last week. I was helping my family deal with a crisis; my nephew was kidnapped and I had to help get him back." The concerned expressions and supportive statements from the other group members were accompanied by heads nodding knowingly; this was not the first time the life of a group member had been impacted by the kidnapping of a loved one. Indeed, war-related violence had touched each member of the group to the point that many had seemingly grown accustomed to living in the shadow of the threat of

injury or death. I was aware of the ongoing violence, and that nearby buildings as well as vehicles in surrounding parking lots had twice been struck by gunfire in recent months while sounds of heavy weapons fire thundered in the distance. I was aware, too, that many in the supervision group had personal experiences of violence to share, although the details provided were often limited out of concern for sharing information that might increase the risk of danger for those sharing as well as others in the group.

As the supervision group continued, it became a kind of holding vessel as the member processed her experience, including her relief at the safe return of her family member. The other group members supported her first through careful listening and acknowledging

(continued)

her experience, then by sharing from the gifts of their own experiences. As they continued, the members soon began providing examples of their own practical self-care and safety strategies they had developed for minimizing risk. I was struck by how these counselors met such daily threats and injustices with amazing faith, resilience, and courage, and by how the powerful support the supervision group members provided for one another was a resource for their effective, ongoing therapeutic work with clients living with many of these same dangers.

Self-Assessment of the Counselor during Crises

Self-assessment and intentional self-care, while important for all counselors, are of particular importance to counselors who work with crisis-affected and traumatized clients. Crises can take an emotional, cognitive, physical, and spiritual toll on counselors. Counselors should debrief with colleagues and supervisors and periodically do self-check-ins to monitor for indications of reduced functioning and job dissatisfaction, which can lead to burnout and have a negative effect on clients. Since a lack of well-being on the part of counselors can hardly foster wellness in clients, counselors have a responsibility to monitor their own mental health and seek supervision, counseling, and other resources when needed. This is especially critical during crisis intervention circumstances when emotions are running high, the environment is charged with anxiety, basic goods and services may be curtailed or limited, and clients are suffering and in distress. In such contexts, commitment to assessment and maintenance of a healthy mind, body, and spirit are essential in the preservation of wellness and best practice.

In our culturally diverse society, it is important to remember that self-assessment also includes regular evaluation of counselor values, which affect the care counselors provide. Counselors are obligated to learn and consistently assess how their own cultural, ethnic, and racial identities affect their values and beliefs about the work they do and the ways they conceptualize their role as helpers. The way in which counselors perceive themselves and their own cultural context, as well as the cultural context of the clients they serve, can also affect their maintenance of a healthy mind and spirit. Additionally, the wear and tear of repeated exposure to the traumatic narratives from which clients seek relief can alter a counselor's assumptive beliefs about the world and can disregulate multicultural competencies that are expected of clinicians. For example, a mental health professional who works with women victimized by male batterers may find her assumptive beliefs about the goodness of all men altered, which would be a threat to the standards that the field expects of counselors.

The importance of self-care for practitioners working with clients in crisis is emphasized by Lambert and Lawson (2013), who studied the professional resilience and post-traumatic growth of counselors who had worked with survivors of hurricanes Katrina and Rita. These authors examined how providing trauma services affected counselors who were *survivor volunteers* (themselves survivors of these events) as well as counselors who were *responder volunteers* (those serving as external volunteers). Post-traumatic growth, as measured in the areas of personal strength, relating to others, appreciation of life, spiritual change, and new possibilities, was significantly greater among survivor volunteers than among responder volunteers. Additionally, counselors who engaged in self-care practices indicated higher levels of compassion satisfaction and lower levels of burnout. Lambert and Lawson (2013) found that "the level of self-care following exposure to vicarious trauma affects whether counselors will have positive or negative outcomes in their personal and professional lives" (p. 267).

Welfel (2016) highlights specific recommendations regarding self-awareness for best practice. Counselors should be mindful of the risks associated with practice and also celebrate the rewards associated with helping others; should set clear limits and not overextend themselves; should engage in self-care; should recognize when they are emotionally exhausted and seek support, including counseling; and should avoid emotional isolation. In short, all counselors have an ethical obligation to be mindful of their own health and well-being and to engage in restorative practices. Failure to self-assess and attend to restoration can lead to countertransference, burnout, compassion fatigue, and vicarious trauma—and, ultimately, to counselor impairment. The circumstances that lead to countertransference, burnout, compassion fatigue, and vicarious trauma are further discussed in the following sections. The concept of vicarious resiliency is also discussed.

Countertransference

Countertransference occurs when counselors ascribe characteristics of significant people and events in their past to their clients. Client emotions, behaviors, and issues may stir up unresolved or buried emotions within a counselor, who might then identify too closely with the client and use the counseling relationship to fulfill unmet needs. Dealing with one's own "stuff" is a vital aspect of good practice and healthy self-assessment. Exploring personal issues and increasing self-awareness underpin healthy practice and should be an ongoing part of counselor self-care and work. It is important for counselors to examine their internal reactions to clients.

In cases that evoke unresolved issues, counselors should seek consultation, supervision, and personal counseling. A self-aware counselor will be cognizant of times when a client's issues strike close to home and interfere with the counselor's ability to be objective. Welfel (2016) recommends that counselors check in with their professional support system to examine each counselor's interpretations of a case and to determine when a case that strongly triggers a counselor's issues should be referred. In cases of referrals, counselors should seek supervision and possibly personal counseling. See Case Study 14.1, which examines one counselor's experience of countertransference.

CASE STUDY 14.1

A Counselor's Countertransference Experience

Rachel is a licensed professional counselor (LPC) in private practice. She went through a messy divorce 3 years ago and feels she has healed from that experience. Today she has a new couple coming in to see her. They are seeking counseling and state that they want to try to save their marriage. During the intake session, Rachel is struck by how similar the husband is to her former husband. His angry tone of voice and some of the emotionally charged statements he makes to his wife remind Rachel of difficult encounters in her own marriage. Rachel feels herself wanting to protect the wife. She thoroughly dislikes the husband.

Discussion Questions

1. Should Rachel continue to see the couple? Explain.
2. If Rachel decides to continue, what can she do to ensure best practice?
3. If Rachel decides not to continue, what should she do regarding her own self-care?

Burnout

Leiter and Maslach (2009) define *burnout* as "a psychological syndrome that involves a prolonged response to chronic interpersonal stressors on the job" (p. 332). Some elements of job satisfaction include but may not be limited to satisfaction with compensation and the types of work duties performed and satisfaction as reflected through steady attendance at work, punctuality, devotion to the job, morale, and productivity. Maslach (2003) identified three dimensions of burnout—cynicism, a sense of inefficacy, and exhaustion—and noted that the strain of burnout results from a lack of fit between the person and the job. Working conditions associated with burnout include social conflict, work overload, and a lack of time and other necessary resources. Lawson and Myers (2011) noted that the demands associated with such a lack of resources can ultimately result in counselors becoming ineffective practitioners.

Burnout occurs when counselors become exhausted both physically and emotionally through overwork, lack of support or overdemands from the agency, and an inability to engage in self-care strategies. Burnout can result in a sense of emotional numbness and detachment from clients. Obviously, counselors who experience burnout face lowered job satisfaction and increased absenteeism. Health problems can develop, thus complicating the possibility for a return to functioning. Counselors and other mental health professionals who provide crisis services are at increased risk for burnout due to the emotionally intense nature of their jobs. Burnout is a cumulative process; over time, emotional exhaustion builds and may result in a sense of detachment and cynicism that leads to a diminished capacity to provide effective services (Newell & MacNeil, 2010).

Empathy, the quality that lies at the core of counselor efficacy, can also be the very factor that leads to counselor burnout (Clark, 2014). Through empathy, a counselor comprehends a client's circumstances and emotional responses. Empathic counselors communicate understanding and create a therapeutic environment for client healing. Most counselors enter the profession because they naturally possess empathic qualities and care about others; however, daily exposure to client trauma and pain can overwhelm a counselor and lead to burnout. Sadly, burnout ultimately damages a counselor's capacity to experience empathy and function as a helper.

Lee, Cho, Kissinger, and Ogle (2010) used the Counselor Burnout Inventory (CBI) to examine counselor burnout. The CBI scales are Exhaustion, Incompetence, Negative Work Environment, Devaluing Client, and Deterioration in Personal Life. The study identified three types of counselors facing burnout: (1) well-adjusted counselors, who indicated the highest levels of job satisfaction and positive self-esteem; (2) persevering counselors, who, while having burnout symptoms such as exhaustion, were able to respond appropriately to client needs and had positive self-esteem; and (3) disconnected counselors, who had high levels of client devaluation (which can be connected to compassion fatigue) and low self-esteem. The study also found that persevering counselors had higher incomes than well-adjusted counselors, with disconnected counselors having the lowest income. Job satisfaction and self-esteem seemed to be the differentiating elements between the burnout types. The use of burnout assessments such as the CBI could foster more targeted intervention and support, thereby addressing burnout more effectively. Additionally, the Professional Quality of Life (ProQOL) scale is a measure of compassion satisfaction and fatigue developed by Stamm (2009) that provides the counselor with a score for compassion satisfaction, burnout, and secondary traumatic stress. Persons interested in using this measure, which is available in many languages, can do so for free while giving credit to Stamm. The scale is available at www.proqol.org.

Compassion Fatigue

Counselor exposure to client pain and suffering can lead to a sense of being overwhelmed by client stories; this goes beyond burnout to a condition called compassion fatigue. Erford (2018) notes that compassion fatigue differs from burnout in that burnout is a state of exhaustion caused by the emotional nature of the counseling profession and overwork, whereas compassion fatigue is a preoccupation with traumatic client cases and personal identification with this trauma. Overidentification with trauma creates symptoms within the counselor that are comparable to the symptoms of post-traumatic stress disorder. Fortunately, self-care can be used to combat the exhaustion of mental and physical resources, the generalized stress of burnout, and the emotional exhaustion of compassion fatigue. Conversely, the concept of compassion satisfaction describes the satisfaction of helping others and being an effectual mental health professional (Lawson & Myers, 2011). Wellness and self-care are factors in fostering compassion satisfaction for counselors.

Related to compassion fatigue is the concept of secondary traumatic stress. Although these terms are often used interchangeably (Newell & MacNeil, 2010), *secondary traumatic stress* refers specifically to behaviors and emotions resulting from exposure to traumatic stories. Essentially, the empathic exposure to another person's trauma experience affects a counselor's behavior and reactions. For example, a counselor experiencing secondary traumatic stress might become more irritable or hypervigilant. Being aware of these signs can help counselors recognize their need to access support.

Vicarious Trauma

Counselors who work with traumatized clients may experience vicarious trauma, which differs from burnout, compassion fatigue, and secondary traumatic stress. While all are similar constructs and all generate secondary trauma reactions, vicarious trauma additionally affects a counselor's worldview and sense of self (Trippany, White Kress, & Wilcoxon, 2004). Vicarious trauma reactions result from indirect exposure to trauma, such as through extreme or repeated exposure to details of traumatic events. Examples of vicarious experiences that meet the *Diagnostic and Statistical Manual of Mental Disorders* (DSM-5) (American Psychiatric Association [APA], 2013) criteria include (1) witnessing the event in person, (2) learning of a traumatic, fatal (or potentially fatal) event that happened to a close family member or friend, and (3) repeated first-hand or extreme exposure to event details that are aversive in nature, including work-related exposure through pictures, movies, television, or other media. The inclusion of recurring trauma exposure as a new diagnostic criterion in the DSM-5 (APA, 2013) is a step forward in recognizing and de-stigmatizing the treatment needs among first responders experiencing post-traumatic stress due to vicarious trauma (Royle, Keenan, & Farrell, 2009) and serves to emphasize the importance of self-care for counseling professionals with whom clients share their personal stories of trauma.

It stands to reason, then, that counselors who work with trauma clients are at a higher risk for vicarious trauma than are counselors working in other settings. While burnout is a response to occupational stress, vicarious trauma involves a personal cognitive reaction within the counselor to a client's experience (Erford, 2018). Essentially, exposure to the trauma stories of the client can trigger pervasive alterations in a counselor's cognitive schema, resulting in disruptions to the counselor's sense of safety, trust, esteem, control, and intimacy. In effect, the boundary between the client's trauma experience and the counselor's worldview is blurred, as the counselor's beliefs and thinking begin to shift in response to exposure to client trauma (Newell & MacNeil, 2010).

An awareness of the impact of vicarious trauma on clinicians has led to the development of prevention strategies that can be implemented at the organizational level (Sansbury, Graves, & Scott, 2015). Trippany et al. (2004) developed the following guidelines for vicarious trauma prevention: (1) case management specifically limiting the number of trauma clients per week as much as possible; (2) peer supervision, which provides an avenue for debriefing and consultation; (3) agencies assuming responsibility to provide supervision, consultation, staffing, continuing education, and employee benefits, including personal counseling; (4) training and education on trauma work; (5) personal coping mechanisms, which include leisure activities and creative endeavors; and (6) spirituality to facilitate connection and meaning.

Sansbury et al. (2015) identify similar prevention strategies that address vicarious traumatization: ensuring clinicians have appropriate training in providing trauma services; focusing on trauma recovery concepts such as empowerment, collaboration, and trust; educating staff on concepts such as burnout, vicarious trauma, and compassion fatigue and regular engagement in self-assessments concerning these concepts; managing clinician caseloads; and providing mindfulness, awareness, and stress-reduction training to clinicians. While all counselors must be alert to signs of vicarious trauma, it is particularly important for counselors working with trauma clients to be intentional about self-care and self-awareness in their professional and personal lives.

Vicarious Resiliency

An emerging concept in mental health is *vicarious resiliency* (Hernandez, Engstrom, & Gangsei, 2010; Ling, Hunter, & Maple, 2014). While counselors can be affected adversely by trauma work, they can also experience affirmative thoughts, feelings, and beliefs through hearing their clients' stories of resiliency—adaptation to difficulties in a positive and empowered manner. According to Hernandez, Gangsei, and Engstrom (2007), "therapists may find their ability to reframe negative events and coping skills enhanced through work with trauma survivors" (p. 240). The capability of clients to deal with trauma and restore their lives was found to be empowering to counselors. Vicarious resiliency can lead to increased hope in one's ability to cope with problems as well as an increased belief in human empowerment. Hernandez et al. (2010) noted that it is possible for vicarious trauma and vicarious resiliency to co-occur.

Ling et al. (2014) studied the qualitative experiences of counselors engaged in trauma work and identified themes of resiliency these counselors experienced toward mitigating the potential impact of vicarious trauma. Counselors who thrived in trauma work were those who had a sense of purpose and perceived empowerment. These counselors described a process of "navigating the empathic journey" (p. 303), which involved developing and implementing proactive strategies for managing reactions to indirect trauma exposure. Awareness of personal reactions to traumatic stories and maintaining boundaries were expressed in terms of empathic stamina and self-reflexivity leading to personal and professional balance and well-being. Finally, counselors successful in sustaining interest and commitment to trauma work valued professional development, career path flexibility, and a work environment that promoted a sense of support, value, and autonomy. Read Case Study 14.2 to deepen your understanding of vicarious resiliency.

CASE STUDY 14.2

Vicarious Resiliency after a House Fire

Two years ago, Jennifer and her husband, Ryan, lost their house in a fire. They were able to escape with their two children and the family dog without harm, but the family lost everything in the fire. Jennifer worked through this crisis with Ann, her counselor until 6 months ago, when she moved into a new home in another city. She has come back in to see Ann for a follow-up appointment.

ANN:	It's so good to see you, Jennifer. I appreciated you e-mailing me the pictures of your lovely new house. It's been a long journey.
JENNIFER:	Yes, I appreciate you being there for me through this. So much of what we worked on has helped me cope. I see things differently now.
ANN:	How so?
JENNIFER:	Well . . . life, life is what really matters. I mean, at first I was in shock and I couldn't believe it. I questioned God, I had so many mixed emotions.
ANN:	Yes, I remember how difficult it was for you to accept and cope with this tragedy at first. But I also remember your courage in seeing things through, not only in the nuts and bolts details of insurance and moving, but also in your resolve to face feelings and place this event into your life story as a challenge met and an opportunity to learn and grow.
JENNIFER:	I guess that's what I want to focus on today with you. I'm different because of the fire. Of course, I wish it hadn't happened, but I believe I'm a better person because of it and I wouldn't want to trade that growth and knowledge about what I can accomplish and also about what really matters.
ANN:	The fire helped you discover the resiliency you had within you all along.

JENNIFER: Yes, I appreciate my husband and children more. I know that life, relationships, and loved ones are what really matter. I don't care about material things anymore. I no longer mourn the possessions I lost in the fire because I know the emotions connected to them were because of the people they reminded me of. A fire can never take away my memories of my grandmother and mother. The memories are real. The antiques were things that can be replaced, but I haven't lost my memories. I feel very free and joyful. I appreciate every day and every person in my life.

ANN: You're living life with more awareness of love and relationships. How wonderful to fully realize the depth and importance of the people in your life.

JENNIFER: I think back to how I was before the fire, I was so distracted and busy and I often took my family for granted. Now I'm thankful every day for life and the people I love.

Discussion Questions

1. What has Jennifer learned through her crisis event?
2. What might the counselor learn from Jennifer's story?
3. How do stories like Jennifer's foster vicarious resiliency?

SELF-CARE STRATEGIES

It is imperative for mental health professionals providing crisis services to engage in restorative activities in order to regroup, revitalize, and prevent the effects of burnout, compassion fatigue, and vicarious trauma. Counselor well-being is dependent on intentional choices to manage time, nurture personal and professional relationships, and grow as a professional. Erford (2018) proposed that leisure activities, social support through connection with friends and family, spirituality, and time in nature were important elements that served to counterbalance the effects of burnout in the mental health field. The following sections will explore the importance of integrating self-care into counseling training curricula and into counseling supervision, especially during moments of crisis. Read Voices from the Field 14.2.

VOICES FROM THE FIELD 14.2
A Personal Reflection on Self-Care

Charlotte Daughhetee

Since I have been writing about self-care, I decided to do a completely unscientific survey. I asked my friends how they relax and rejuvenate. Here are some of the answers I got: riding a bike 100 miles, reading a book, fishing, gardening, yoga, attending NASCAR races, lying in a hammock taking a nap, having a beer with friends, cooking, watching NCAA basketball, walking the dog, quilting, fencing, and playing a harp.

(continued)

As you can see, relaxation comes in many forms. A meaningful authentic self-care plan should be tailor-made for each individual. All mental health professionals need to be intentional about integrating personalized enjoyable activities into unique self-care plans that come from personal experiences. Ask yourself, "When did I feel relaxed and renewed, and what was I doing?" Take what you were doing and do more of it! Follow a solution-focused approach to self-care.

Clients can also benefit from exploring their own distinctive methods of revitalization and restoration. Instead of recommending standard stress-relief activities, encourage clients to create their own program, something that truly reflects the activities they love, by having them explore the life-enhancing activities that have worked for them in the past. Once clients have identified their self-care activities, have them plan those activities into their week.

So, as I head into a new week, what activities are included in my self-care plan? Walking, lunch with friends, a movie with my husband, reading a new book about Tudor England, and bird-watching in the state park. How about you? What will you do this week to refresh yourself and enhance your wellness?

Emphasizing Self-Care in Counselor Training Programs

Students enrolled in graduate counselor preparation programs can attest that considerable demands are placed upon students in terms of both personal and professional development.

Developmental experiences, assignments, and course experiences frequently invite students to examine personal values in the context of the role of the professional counselor as they work toward developing a cohesive counselor identity. For example, the ethical mandate in the *ACA Code of Ethics* (ACA, 2014) against making a professional referral based on a counselor's personal values implies that the counselor has, at some point, developed an awareness of her or his personal values. With such an expectation, counselor training programs might conceivably engage counseling students in course experiences that include an element of an examination of personal values; such an examination might well involve feelings of discomfort for the student. Counselor education programs might appropriately encourage student self-care by providing referral resources for students to access to assist with both personal and professional concerns that arise as a by-product of engaging in course experiences.

Indeed, self-care strategies implemented as part of the graduate training of counselors have shown significant benefits for participants. Shapiro et al. (2007) examined the impact of an 8-week mindfulness-based stress reduction (MBSR) intervention on the mental health and capacity for mindfulness among therapists in training. The MBSR intervention included 2-hour weekly sessions during which students practiced sitting meditation, body scanning, yoga, guided meditation, and informal strategies for incorporating mindfulness into daily life. This study found that participants in MBSR reported significant decreases in stress, anxiety, negative affect, and rumination, and significant increases in both positive affect and self-compassion.

While focusing on individual student needs regarding self-care might appear the most direct path to addressing self-care, Wolf, Thompson, and Smith-Adcock (2012) noted that systemic barriers to wellness often exist within counselor education programs. Awareness of contextual factors impacting student wellness efforts suggests the use of a systemic approach grounded in the values of the counseling profession and infused throughout the curriculum.

One potentially useful framework counselor training programs might consider as a context for addressing the systemic self-care needs of students is the wheel of wellness model (Myers, Sweeney, & Witmer, 2000). This holistic model of wellness is grounded in Adlerian theory and focuses on the five life tasks of spirituality, friendship, love, self-direction, and work and leisure. Wolf et al. (2012) suggested holistic strategies stemming from this model that counseling programs might implement to promote student wellness. These holistic strategies might include faculty modeling self-care by engaging in self-care practices; providing opportunities for student participation in support groups; including wellness activities in course requirements for students; and encouraging students to develop and implement their own unique self-care plans. Such an expectation on the part of counselor training programs that all counselor trainees engage in self-care might effectively address the tendency for counselors to overlook self-care needs in favor of helping others (Skovholt & Trotter-Mathison, 2014).

Counselor education programs have a gatekeeping responsibility to promote wellness within their programs. In the same manner that informed consent is an ongoing process in the counseling relationship, wellness should be an ongoing theme throughout a student's training program. From the moment that students enter counseling training programs until the time they exit, promotion of wellness should be ingrained into their overall professional identity.

Roach and Young (2007) suggest that it is advantageous for counselor education programs to develop comprehensive plans that help students address all components of personal development. They suggest that helping students develop a greater sense of wellness has both short-term and long-term benefits. By incorporating wellness into their lifestyles, counseling students have the potential to improve their personal awareness, experience more satisfaction, and consequently become more competent to meet the demands of graduate training and future work roles by dealing more effectively with stress and anxiety, therefore reducing impairment and burnout.

Similar research has indicated that supervised experiences in counseling training programs that include self-care have potential benefits that extend beyond promoting personal wellness and protective factors against impairment. For example, in a summary of qualitative research conducted over 9 years, Christopher and Maris (2010) described the positive outcomes of a graduate course in mindfulness on the counseling students enrolled in the course. The course, entitled "Mind-Body Medicine and the Art of Self-Care," was a 15-week class that met for 2½ hours, twice per week. The dual goals of the class were to instruct students in self-care strategies to implement in graduate school and beyond; and to teach students how mindfulness practices were being used in counseling and behavioral medicine. Course objectives addressed both personal and professional growth and were intended to (1) provide students with self-care skills and techniques; (2) promote understanding of Eastern and Western traditions of contemplative practice; (3) increase awareness of contemporary efforts to apply contemplative interventions to health care; (4) instruct students concerning the effectiveness of contemplative applications in behavioral medicine; (5) increase awareness of ethical considerations related to the mind/body interventions; and (6) promote awareness of how culture and cultural perspectives on wellness impact the therapeutic process. A significant course requirement was a reflective journal in which students described and processed personal reactions to course content and experiential activities.

The qualitative themes that emerged from the data indicated that students received personal and professional benefits from participating in the course. Personal benefits described included (1) increased awareness, relaxation, and ability to focus; (2) enhanced mental, emotional, and physical health; and (3) increased self-acceptance and improved interpersonal relationships. Significantly, students described additional benefits that affected their professional work with clients, including the following: more attention to the process of counseling and increased comfort with silence; increased awareness and acceptance of clients and self-identity as a counselor; and a positive impact on the therapeutic relationship, the development of theoretical orientation, and case conceptualization.

Similarly, in a study of the impact of personal meditation on the treatment efficacy of counselors in training, Grepmair et al. (2007) found that clients of meditating psychotherapy trainees reported significantly higher global functioning, decreased symptoms, and more security about socializing. These clients further reported decreased symptom problems in the areas of obsessiveness, anxiety, anger, and phobias, and indicated better understanding of the process of counseling and developmental goals as well as more optimism about their own progress. Such research suggests that counseling students and supervisees who attend to their self-care needs may ultimately benefit not only personally but also professionally through increased capacity for effectiveness with clients.

Supervision and Self-Care

Counselors working with crisis situations require ongoing supervision to help them process the complexity of crisis clinical situations. The inability to receive supervisory support and oversight has the potential of having a deleterious impact on crisis counselors' personal and professional development (Dupre, Echterling, Meixner, Anderson, & Kielty, 2014).

Crisis supervision has been described as a tool for enhancing both the counselor's crisis management skills and overall professional development (Dupre et al., 2014). In Dupre et al.'s study evaluating counselors' perceptions of crisis supervision, participants reported that supervision was absolutely important for successful resolution of the crisis and stated that effective supervision includes "immediate and specific feedback, clear guidance for navigating the crisis, opportunities for timely debriefing, and focused discussion on countertransference reactions" (p. 90).

Counselors working in crisis situations, especially those in the postlicensure stage of professional development, share a desire for ongoing supervision (Dupre et al., 2014). These counselors, who often work in isolation, depend on clinical supervision and peer support to help them balance countertransference reactions with the need to maintain a level of empathic distance. The clinical supervisor in a crisis situation has the potential to facilitate post-traumatic growth of supervisees by ensuring that supervisees have the space needed to make meaning out of the crisis situation. Participants in the Dupre et al. study suggested that effective supervisors believe in counseling, believe in the sacredness of supervision time, protect supervisees, are willing to hold supervisees' stuff, help supervisees regulate powerful emotions, and are committed to helping supervisees grow through the crisis.

Savic-Jabrow (2010) found that sole practitioners identified supervision as their primary form of support and self-care. Trainees and beginning counselors are supervised as part of their professional evolution, but it is important for counselors to seek out peer support through supervision and consultation throughout their careers. This type of ongoing support is an essential part of continuing competency and best practice (Daughhetee, Puleo, & Thrower, 2010).

Self-care is a critical component of the supervision of all counselors, and supervisors should be prepared to assist supervisees to address their unique self-care needs in relation to the challenges of providing services to specific populations. For example, Chassman, Kottler, and Madison (2010) noted that counselors who provide services related to sexual concerns are required to be immersed in their clients' internal sexual worlds. In the course of working with either victims of sexual abuse or sexual perpetrators, counselors are "exposed to sexual information and often to vivid images of deviant sexual behavior" (p. 269). Self-monitoring and self-care are necessities for counselors who work with adolescents with sexual behavior problems; supervision is a resource that helps counselors normalize feelings, maintain personal and professional boundaries, and separate work from personal experiences. Chassman et al. noted the difficulties that supervisees often face in exploring their personal reactions to their work, which can make supervisees reluctant to access supervision as a self-care resource.

In light of the vast benefits associated with receiving ongoing supervision, it is unfortunate when supervisees experience reluctance in seeking help from supervisors for fear of appearing less "expert" or perhaps even impaired professionally. Figley (2002) noted the isomorphism of the "conspiracy of silence" (p. 1440) surrounding the topic of compassion fatigue, and suggested one primary step counselors might take is to model an open discussion of struggles concerning compassion fatigue and compassion stress. Supervisors might promote such transparency through modeling and openly discussing self-care strategies with supervisees. Sixbey and Daniels (2008) developed a crisis-oriented approach for clinical supervision that mirrors the Stoltenberg model of counselor development. Their work evolved in the aftermath of the year when their region was impacted by multiple hurricanes in a narrow time frame, and counselors, supervisors, and crisis workers were called to serve while also managing the devastation to their own personal lives and property. Erford (2018) advocated for providing counselors with opportunities for increasing awareness of levels of personal wellness by completing wellness assessments.

Supervisors have a variety of strategies available to assist supervisees in developing and maintaining personalized self-care. Examples of such strategies are as follows:

- *Supervision orientation:* Including development of self-care strategies as a component of an initial orientation to the supervision relationship communicates to supervisees that self-care is a valued aspect of professional counselor development and that the well-being of supervisees is important.
- *SMART goals:* Self-care plans that demonstrate intentionality and accountability in the form of measurable goals are more likely to be implemented. Self-care strategies in the context of the SMART framework might be developed into goals that are *S*pecific, *M*easurable, *A*ttainable, *R*ealistic, and *T*imely.
- *Portfolios:* Supervisors might require students and licensure-seeking counselors to develop and maintain a professional development portfolio to include self-care strategies.
- *Success stories:* Supervision activities that include an accountability piece are more likely to invite supervisee compliance. Self-care activities might be regularly

included as required supervision assignments, and students might share their success stories as a means of demonstrating accountability in the supervision process.

- *Bibliotherapy:* O'Halloran and Linton (2000) identified several domain-specific book titles as potential self-care resources for counseling practitioners. For example, a potential resource identified for addressing self-care in the emotional domain is *Counseling as an Art: The Creative Arts in Counseling* by Samuel Gladding (2014). Supervisors might include such resources as assigned reading in formal supervision contracts. The addition of a reflective component to the assignment might increase the impact of the content, serve to personalize the material for the supervisee, introduce a measure of accountability, and further increase the likelihood that supervisees will follow through with self-care strategies.

- *Ongoing training:* One method for preventing burnout and secondary traumatic stress can be the "work smarter" strategy. Continuing education may be a more serious self-care approach than leisure-types self-care strategies, conventional wisdom would suggest that learning, staying abreast of the field and its evolving best practices, and having one's knowledge and skills sharpened continually can be a powerful prevention tool to the depletion of energy when under-trained. Covey's (2013) motivational and performance-improving models included that of "sharpening the saw." This habit (number seven) engendered all things self-care-related. Working smart with ample training and practicing within one's scope of competence while assisting clients in crisis can be an efficiency-enhancing strategy.

It is clear that counselors have a personal and professional responsibility to engage in self-care. Newell and MacNeil (2010) emphasize the need for self-care as a best practice and stress the need for burnout assessment, peer support, continuing education, training on early warning signs, and self-care practices. Monitoring one's own mental, physical, and spiritual health; managing time; nurturing relationships; and fostering professional growth are vital elements of self-care and best practice.

No matter where you are in your process of counselor professional development, you can resolve to start—or continue—to make self-care a priority. An excellent resource for wellness and self-care information came from the ACA's Task Force on Counselor Wellness and Impairment. For information on the task force and additional wellness strategies, visit the ACA website at www.counseling.org/wellness_taskforce/index.htm. Read Voices from the Field 14.3 through 14.5, which provide personal reflections on the importance of counselor self-care. Also see Case Study 14.3, which challenges you to consider essential supervision issues related to counselor wellness and self-care.

VOICES FROM THE FIELD 14.3

Taking Care of Myself

Hayden Belisle

I vividly remember my professors and internship supervisors explaining the importance of self-care and the value of supervision throughout graduate school. I also recall thinking that I would get around to that "one day." On particularly difficult days during my internship and during the first couple of years that I was practicing as a school counselor, I sought solace in "retail therapy." I could be overwhelmed by a very troubling case, and it was amazing how much better I would feel

(continued)

after a good trip to the mall. Well, as you might imagine, the relief from the stress was fleeting . . . and not covered by insurance! I share that, not to make light of a very important issue, but to be honest about the fact that I didn't take caring for myself as seriously as I should have at the very beginning of my career.

By my second or third year as a school counselor, I was beginning to feel somewhat burned out. I questioned whether I had made the right career choice. I know that feeling burned out when your career has barely even started seems crazy, but it happens. I had extremely challenging cases and many students and situations that absolutely broke my heart. All of this was very difficult for me to deal with, and although I have an incredible support system outside of work, I was not participating in peer consultation or supervision of any type.

Believing that my calling in life is to be a counselor, I knew that I had to make some changes, not only for myself but also for the children and families I was working with. I began seeking opportunities to consult with other counselors and tried to be intentional about taking better care of myself. This helped tremendously.

Knowing that I had a network of colleagues who were just a phone call away if I needed help on a case or simply someone to listen to and support me was a great relief. After putting it off for several years, I finally began the process to become an LPC. Although it may sound dramatic, after my first session of supervision, it felt as though a huge boulder had been lifted from my shoulders. Having the opportunity to discuss cases and get feedback from someone that I highly respect and trust as a professional has been invaluable. I have found that it has greatly enhanced my confidence as a professional and it has challenged me to continue growing and improving. I can honestly say that I have felt far less overwhelmed and emotionally drained since I started meeting with my supervisor. My only regret is that I did not start sooner!

I would encourage anyone who is entering the counseling profession to develop a strong support system that includes other counselors and a plan for self-care. It is extremely easy to get burned out when you are not intentional about taking good care of yourself. When we don't care for ourselves, we cannot give our clients the care that they deserve.

VOICES FROM THE FIELD 14.4
Figuring Out What Works for You

Maegan Vick

Worn out? Tired? Typing papers while attempting to watch your favorite show? Working late to help clients who have long left your office? These are all the signs of an overworked individual. They are also signs of a passionate and dedicated counselor. It is hard sometimes to put that book down, turn off the computer, or even allow your mind to temporarily forget one of the many clients and coworkers you are dedicated to helping. But you have to draw that line somewhere. Otherwise you face counselor burnout and a decline in your own happiness and effectiveness. Self-care has to be placed at the forefront for counselors. If you are not good to yourself, you cannot possibly be any good to others. It took some tears, sleepless nights, and pure fatigue for me to understand this point clearly.

Everyone has to figure out what works for them. What works for me includes truly looking at the children I work with and stopping for a few moments to

enjoy them, rather than worrying over how to fix their situations. It is me driving to that old barn and watching the horses graze in the sunset. It is me pulling off the side of the road to buy some pumpkins from children selling them for Halloween and me picking wildflowers in a nearby field. It is me spending time with my family and friends. It is also me saying "no" to people, and knowing that doesn't mean I don't care to help them. It simply means I care enough to take care of me. It is also scheduling that appointment with my counselor when I see the need. It is me listening to my body, soul, and mind and knowing when boundaries need to be set, knowing when I need "me time." In the world of counseling, it is very easy to get stuck in that rut of giving away your time to everyone else and leaving none for yourself. New and veteran counselors, a word to the wise: Do not get stuck in that rut. Ongoing supervision and effective self-care strategies are important for crisis counselors. It is essential for

(continued)

counselors to include self-reflection as part of self-care questions such as the following:

1. Do you listen to yourself and realize you need to set boundaries and schedule some "me time"? What signs tell you that you are in need of self-care?

2. What activities, people, etc., in your life help you refuel? How could you integrate these into your life more consistently?

VOICES FROM THE FIELD 14.5
Self-Care and Working with Suicidal Clients

Rachel M. Hoffman

I clearly remember my first experience working with a suicidal client. I was working in an inpatient setting, and although I had expected to encounter suicidal clients, I wasn't quite prepared to encounter suicidal clients who did not appear, at least initially, to want to change. Working with someone with a complete disregard for his or her own life challenged my personal belief system and, although I had been prepared as a counselor, I still found myself wanting to fall back on convincing the client of reasons to live. Thankfully, I had the support of a strong clinical supervisor and, through his guidance, I was able to bracket my own feelings related to death in order to be helpful to the client.

It is important to have realistic expectations for change and to recognize that the process of suicidality is not one that is quickly resolved. Understanding the function of assessment, intervention, and follow-up is important for working successfully with suicidal clients. I believe that it is important for counselors to understand that part of being helpful with suicidal clients is understanding that change may be a slow process. However, it is necessary for counselors to remember that clients are not only capable of change but also possess the skills to make those changes.

I believe that self-care is of the utmost importance when working in crisis situations, especially those dealing with suicidal clients. Debriefing with a supervisor or peer can be helpful in the immediate aftermath of a suicidal crisis. Making time daily to engage in self-care is an essential consideration for counselors who work in stressful situations. Personally, I've found that taking a "5-minute mindfulness break" each day can help me reconnect and regroup in a healthy way.

CASE STUDY 14.3
Supervision in Crisis Counseling

Kurt, a recent graduate of a counseling program, has a job in an agency that provides services to low-income individuals, couples, and families. State budget cuts and an economic downturn have increased the client load beyond capacity. Kurt is pursuing his LPC credentials and receives supervision from an approved counselor outside of his agency. This arrangement has proven to be a good thing because the director of his agency is too stressed and overwhelmed to provide supervision. Everyone at the agency is overwhelmed.

Although Kurt is thankful for all the client contact hours he is receiving, he is beginning to wonder how he will maintain his current pace. He keeps up with all of his case notes but has noticed that some of the other counselors put off doing case notes and paperwork and that they seem cynical about their clients. He feels like he is barely keeping his head above water and that the job is very hard on him. His LPC supervisor has expressed concern about his caseload and the effect it might have on him and his ability to provide appropriate care, but Kurt has assured her that he's doing fine.

A major stressor at the agency has been the behavior of the director. While at times the director is jovial and supportive, he sometimes flies off the handle for no reason and becomes enraged. Kurt has not been on the receiving end of these rages yet, but everyone on the staff seems to walk on eggshells and dreads that they will be the next target. They are all thankful for those days when the director is in a good mood, but as time passes the staff is beginning to sense that the director is becoming increasingly stressed, and they dread the inevitable outbursts of rage.

Kurt has not addressed the director's behavior with his LPC supervisor. He doesn't want her to think poorly of the director, and he also wonders if maybe it's not as bad as it seems. One day the director is in a particularly bad mood, and the staff is tense and nervous. Kurt hears the director screaming at the receptionist and calling her names in front of a waiting room full of clients. That evening, Kurt comes clean with his supervisor about how bad things are at the agency. His supervisor says, "What you're describing is the cycle of abuse." Kurt is stunned and realizes that the entire staff at the agency has been caught up in an abuse cycle.

Discussion Questions

1. Why do you think Kurt has avoided telling his supervisor the truth about his workplace?
2. Do you believe the director is impaired? Is client care at risk?
3. What effect does the director's behavior have on staff? On clients?
4. What, if anything, should the supervisor do with this information?
5. What should Kurt do?

OVERVIEW OF THE ELEMENTS OF CRISIS INTERVENTION RELATED TO SELF-CARE

Self-care is recognized as an essential aspect of professional functioning in counseling ethical codes and training standards, and by professional counseling associations. While counselors who provide crisis intervention services are particularly at risk for secondary trauma, potential long-term effects such as compassion fatigue, impairment, burnout, and secondary traumatic stress may be mitigated or avoided by regularly engaging in appropriate self-care strategies.

Developing self-awareness is an important part of maintaining counselor wellness. Counselors who are committed to self-assessment and maintenance of a healthy mind, body, and spirit are better prepared for the stressors associated with crisis work. Furthermore, ethical best practice requires counselors to engage in self-monitoring and to appropriately seek supervision and personal counseling, as needed.

Counselor training programs and counseling supervisors can promote professional resilience by emphasizing the importance of counselor self-care as an aspect of professional functioning. Counselor educators can foster a culture of wellness through modeling self-care, providing program and course opportunities for students to experience self-care activities, and inviting students to take the initiative in developing and implementing their own self-care plans. Counseling supervisors can also promote a trusting supervisory relationship in which supervisees feel supported in sharing their countertransference and other personal reactions in providing crisis and trauma services and are able to ask for help without fearing the supervisor's judgment. Students and supervisees who regularly engage in self-care benefit from increased effectiveness in their personal lives as well as in their professional work with clients.

Table 14.1 provides a number of online and print resources on counselor self-care.

TABLE 14.1 Resources on Counselor Self-Care

Online Resources

ACA Task Force on Counselor Wellness and Impairment: www.counseling.org

ACA Traumatology Interest Network: www.counseling.org

Clinician Survivor Task Force—Clinicians as Survivors: After a Suicide Loss: mypage.iu.edu/~jmcintos/therapists_mainpg.htm

Disaster Mental Health Graduate Certificate (University of South Dakota): catalog.usd.edu/preview_program.php?catoid=20&poid=3012

Gift from Within—PTSD Resources for Survivors and Caregivers: giftfromwithin.org/html/articles-on-ptsd.html

Substance Abuse and Mental Health Services Administration: www.samhsa.gov

Substance Abuse and Mental Health Services Administration—self-care for homeless service providers: www.samhsa.gov/homelessness-programs-resources/hpr-resources/self-care

The Trauma Stewardship Institute: www.traumastewardship.com

Print Resources

Altman, D. (2011). *One minute mindfulness: Fifty simple ways to find peace, clarity, and new possibilities in a stressed out world*. Novato, CA: New World Library.

Borysenko, J. (2003). *Inner peace for busy people: 52 simple strategies for transforming your life*. Carlsbad, CA: Hay House.

Kottler, J. A. (2011). *The therapist's workbook: Self-assessment, self-care, and self-improvement exercises for mental health professionals* (2nd ed.). Hoboken, NJ: Wiley.

Louden, J. (2012). *The woman's retreat book: A guide to restoring, rediscovering, and reawakening your true self in a moment, an hour, a day, or a weekend*. New York, NY: HarperOne.

O'Hanlon, B. (2000). *Do one thing different: 10 simple ways to change your life*. New York, NY: William Morrow.

Rothschild, B. (2006). *The psychophysiology of compassion fatigue and vicarious trauma help for the helper: Self-care strategies for managing burnout and stress*. New York, NY: Norton.

Skovholt, T. M., & Trotter-Mathison, M. J. (2010). *The resilient practitioner: Burnout prevention and self-care strategies for counselors, therapists, teachers, and health professionals* (2nd ed.). New York, NY: Routledge.

Teater, M., & Ludgate, J. (2014). *Overcoming compassion fatigue*. Eau Claire, WI: PESI.

Van Dernoot Lipsky, L., & Burk, C. (2009). *Trauma stewardship: An everyday guide to caring for self while caring for others*. San Francisco, CA: Berrett-Koehler.

Weiss, L. (2004). *Therapist's guide to self-care*. New York, NY: Routledge.

Wicks, R. J. (2008). *The resilient clinician*. London, UK: Oxford University Press.

Wolin, S., & Wolin, S. (1993). *The resilient self*. New York, NY: Villard Books.

Summary

Counselor self-assessment and self-care are critical for maintaining optimal professional functioning, particularly for counselors who provide services for clients experiencing crisis and trauma. The unique demands of crisis and trauma work can take a substantial toll on the personal and professional well-being of counselors, who may experience countertransference, burnout, compassion fatigue, and vicarious trauma. Failure to recognize the emerging signs of these conditions can lead to compromising both counselor personal wellness and professional effectiveness.

Burnout, compassion fatigue, and vicarious trauma are common terms describing reactions to job-related stress including mental and physical exhaustion, cynicism, feelings of ineffectiveness, detachment from clients, and emotional numbness. Counselors who experience work overload, lack of resources (including time), social conflict, and a lack of fit with their job are at risk for developing symptoms of burnout that, if not addressed through self-care, can negatively impact client treatment outcomes. Intentionally allocating and protecting time for self-care strategies, staying involved with social support systems, attending to spiritual needs, and maintaining connection with nature are strategies counselors can use to promote personal and professional development while counterbalancing the potential for burnout.

While burnout has long been recognized as a potential risk for counseling practitioners engaged in crisis work, an emerging awareness of the potential for personal and professional growth is captured through the concept of vicarious resiliency. Clients' stories of resiliency can empower counselors in ways that enhance coping skills, promote positive beliefs, increase hopefulness, and instill confidence in clients' abilities to restore their lives. Counselors are better positioned to promote and sustain their own resiliency when they are aware of common reactions associated with engaging in work with clients who have experienced trauma, remain vigilant regarding appropriate professional boundaries, engage in professional development opportunities, and balance their awareness of the risks of burnout with recognition of signs of post-traumatic growth.

The importance of self-care for maintaining ethical practice is recognized in professional counseling ethical codes, such as the *ACA Code of Ethics* (ACA, 2014), which requires that counselors regularly monitor their personal mental health and engage in ongoing self-care. Such continuous self-assessment involves maintaining awareness of thoughts, feelings, and behaviors as indicators of professional functioning. Awareness of internal reactions to client work, such as countertransference reactions, is an important aspect of self-care because the work clients do in session can evoke in counselors unrecognized or unresolved issues that might interfere with the therapy. Counselors who fail to identify their own reactions to client experiences might unintentionally use the counseling relationship to address personal needs.

Ongoing supervision is important for maintaining counselor awareness. Supportive supervisors and colleagues are invaluable resources to assist in monitoring for signs of decreased effectiveness and potential burnout. The support provided through supervision can foster a sense of community for practitioners who would otherwise feel professionally isolated, and also serves as a collaborative context for exploring and processing reactions to crisis work. Counselors who have the benefit of supportive supervision are better positioned to create meaningful narratives that foster post-traumatic growth.

Counselor education programs routinely require students to engage in curricular activities that promote personal development as an aspect of professional training. Course activities that invite personal reflection, examination of values, and consideration of interpersonal and family dynamics place unique demands on students; thus, counselor training programs have a responsibility to balance these requirements through integrating self-care and wellness strategies into the curriculum. Such an integrated approach might reasonably involve promoting self-care among both counseling faculty and students, providing access to resources such as counseling services, and designing curricular experiences targeting student wellness. The potential benefits for students who engage in curricular experiences that focus specifically on self-care include increased mental focus and relaxation, self-acceptance, improved overall health, as well as enhanced development of clinical skills.

Counselors should keep in mind the following key practices regarding counselor self-care:

- In addition to aligning with ethical practice, counselors who regularly monitor their personal mental health and engage in ongoing self-care are potentially enhancing their effectiveness.
- Counselors should understand concepts such as countertransference, burnout, compassion fatigue, and vicarious trauma and be aware of emerging signs of these conditions.
- Counselors should also be aware of vicarious resiliency and compassion satisfaction as positive aspects of working with crisis and trauma clients.

- Consultation and supportive supervision are necessary components of effective crisis intervention work.
- Organizations should support clinical staff through mindfulness training, limiting caseloads, and providing an environment that supports clinician engagement in ongoing self-care.
- Counselor education programs and counseling supervisors should promote self-care as a component of counselor professional identity by supporting student and supervisee development and the implementation of self-care plans.

Intentionally attending to these key practices at the start of the training process and establishing them as non-negotiable components of one's professional counselor identity can help counselors maintain professional and ethical boundaries, best practices, and life–work balance throughout their careers.

REFERENCES

Aaron, M. (2012). The pathways of problematic sexual behavior: A literature review of factors affecting adult sexual behavior in survivors of childhood sexual abuse. *Sexual Addiction & Compulsivity, 19*, 199–218. doi:10.1080/10720162.2012.690678

Adam Walsh Child Protection and Safety Act, 42 U.S.C. § 16911 et seq. (2006).

Ahrens, C. E., Abeling, S., Ahmad, S., & Hinman, J. (2010). Spirituality and well-being: The relationship between religious coping and recovery from sexual assault. *Journal of Interpersonal Violence, 25,* 1242–1263. doi:10.1177/0886260509340533

Ainsworth, M. (1969). Object relations, dependency and attachment: A theoretical review of the infant-mother relationship. *Child Development, 40*, 969–1025.

Alexander, D. A. (2005). Early mental health intervention after disasters. *Advances in Psychiatric Treatment, 11*, 12–18. doi:10.1192/apt.11.1.12

Almond, L., & Budden, M. (2012). The use of text messages within a crisis negotiation: Help or hindrance? *Journal of Police Crisis Negotiations, 12*(1), 1–27. doi:10.1080/15332586.2011.593343

Amado, B. G., Arce, R., & Herraiz, A. (2015). Psychological injury in victims of child sexual abuse: A meta-analytic review. *Psychosocial Intervention, 24*(1), 49–62. doi:10.1016/j.psi.2015.03.002

American Addictions Centers. (2015). EMS responders: The stress is killing us. Retrieved from http://americanaddictioncenters.org/blog/ems-responders-the-stress-is-killing-us/

American Association of Suicidology. (2006a). *Assessing and managing suicide risk.* Washington, DC: Author.

American Association of Suicidology. (2006b). IS PATH WARM. Retrieved from https://store.samhsa.gov/shin/content/SVP06-0153/SVP06-0153.pdf

American Association of Suicidology. (2012). Suicide in the USA fact sheet. Retrieved from http://www.suicidology.org/Portals/14/docs/Resources/FactSheets/USA2012.pdf

American Counseling Association. (2011). Task force on counselor wellness and impairment. Retrieved from http://www.counseling.org/wellness_taskforce/index.htm

American Counseling Association. (2014). *ACA Code of Ethics.* Alexandria, VA: Author.

American Mental Health Counselors Association. (2010). *AMHCA code of ethics.* Alexandria, VA: Author.

American Mental Health Foundation. (2015). Psychiatric patient assaults on healthcare staff: A worldwide perspective. Retrieved from http://americanmentalhealthfoundation.org/2015/01/psychiatric-patient-assaults-on-healthcare-staff-a-worldwide-perspective/

American Pet Products Association. (2016). 2015–2016 APPA national pet owners survey. Retrieved from http://www.americanpetproducts.org/press_industrytrends.asp

American Psychiatric Association. (2003). Practice guidelines for the assessment and treatment of patients with suicidal behaviors. Retrieved from http://www.psych.org/psych_pract/treatg/pg/pg_suicidalbehaviors.pdf

American Psychiatric Association. (2004). Committee on Psychiatric Dimensions of Disaster: Disaster psychiatry handbook. Retrieved from http://www.psych.org/Resources/DisasterPsychiatry/APADisasterPsychiatryResources/DisasterPsychiatryHandbook.aspx

American Psychiatric Association. (2013). *Diagnostic and statistical manual of mental disorders* (5th ed.). Washington, DC: Author.

American Psychiatric Association. (2016). What is psychiatry? Retrieved from http://www.psychiatry.org/patients-families/what-is-psychiatry

American Red Cross. (2013). *Foundations of disaster mental health participants workbook.* Washington, DC: Author.

American School Counselor Association. (2008). The role of the professional school counselor. Retrieved from http://www.schoolcounselor.org/content.asp?pl=325&sl=133&contentid=240

American School Counselor Association. (2010). *Ethical standards for school counselors.* Alexandria, VA: Author.

American School Counselor Association. (2012). *The ASCA National Model: A framework for school counseling programs* (3rd ed.). Alexandria, VA: Author.

American School Counselor Association. (2013). Position statement: The school counselor and safe schools and crisis response. Retrieved from https://www.schoolcounselor.org/asca/media/asca/PositionStatements/PS_SafeSchools.pdf

American Society for Addiction Medicine. (2013). *The ASAM criteria: Treatment criteria for addictive, substance-related, and co-occurring conditions* (3rd ed.). Chevy Chase, MD: Author.

Andrews, D., & Bonta, J. (2010). *The psychology of criminal conduct* (4th ed.). New York, NY: Routledge.

Andrews, D. A., Bonta, J., & Wormith, S. J. (2004). *The Level of Service/Case Management Inventory* (LS/CMI). Toronto, ON: Multi-Health Systems.

Andriessen, K. (2009). Can postvention be prevention? *Crisis, 30*(1), 43–47. doi:10.1027/0227-5910.30.1.43

Ard, K. L., & Makadon, H. J. (2011). Addressing intimate partner violence in lesbian, gay, bisexual, and transgender patients. *Journal of General Internal Medicine, 26*, 930–933. doi:10.1007/s11606-011-1697-6

Asaro, M. R. (2001). Working with adult homicide survivors: Part II: Helping family members cope with murder. *Psychiatric Care, 37*(4), 115–126. doi:10.1111/j.1744-6163.2001.tb00643.x

Asberg, K., & Renk, K. (2013). Comparing incarcerated and college student women with histories of childhood sexual abuse: The roles of abuse severity, support, and substance use. *Psychological Trauma: Theory, Research, Practice, and Policy, 5*(2), 167–175. doi:10.1037/a0027162

Association for Counselor Education and Supervision. (2011). *Best practices in clinical supervision ACES task force report.* Alexandria, VA: Author.

Association for Spiritual, Ethical, and Religious Values in Counseling. (2016). Competencies for addressing spiritual and religious issues in counseling. Retrieved from http://www.aservic.org/resources/spiritual-competencies/

Association for the Treatment of Sexual Abusers. (2006). Report of the task force on children with sexual behavior problems. Retrieved from http://www.atsa.com/research

Association for the Treatment of Sexual Abusers. (2012). Sex offender risk assessment. Retrieved from https://www.atsa.com/pdfs/SexOffenderRiskAssessmentBriefWithBibliography2012.pdf

Australian Academy of Medicine. (2016). Bereavement, known as sorry business, is a very important part of Aboriginal culture. Retrieved from http://www.aams.org.au/mark_sheldon/ch7/ch7_sensitive_areas.htm

Babor, T. F., Higgins-Biddle, J. C., Saunders, J. B., Monteiro, M. G., & World Health Organization (2001). *AUDIT The Alcohol Use Disorders Identification Test: Guidelines for use in primary care* (2nd ed.). Geneva, Switzerland: World Health Organization.

Bagalman, E. (2011). *Traumatic brain injuries among veterans* (Report No. R40941). Washington, DC: Congressional Research Service. Retrieved from http://www.nashia.org/pdf/tbi_among_veterans_may_2011.pdf

Baggerly, J., & Exum, H. (2008). Counseling children after natural disasters: Guidance for family therapists. *American Journal of Family Therapy, 36*(1), 79–93. doi:10.1080/01926180601057598

Banducci, A. N., Hoffman, E. M., Lejuez, C. W., & Koenen, K. C. (2014). The impact of childhood abuse on inpatient substance users: Specific links with risky sex, aggression, and emotion dysregulation. *Child Abuse & Neglect, 38*, 928–938. doi:10.1016/j.chiabu.2013.12.007

Bandura, A. (1977). *Social learning theory.* New York, NY: General Learning Press.

Barboza, S., Epps, S., Bylington, R., & Keene, S. (2010). HIPAA goes to school: Clarifying privacy laws in the education environment. *Internet Journal of Law, Healthcare and Ethics, 6*(2). Retrieved from http://www.ispub.com/journal/the-internet-journal-of-law-healthcare-and-ethics/volume-6-number-2/hipaa-goes-to-school-clarifying-privacy-laws-in-the-education-environment.html

Barker, L. H., & Berry, K. D. (2009). Developmental issues impacting military families with young children during single and multiple deployments. *Military Medicine, 174*, 1033–1040. doi:10.7205/MILMED-D-04-1108

Bartlett, M. L., & Forbes, L. L. (2015). Legal and ethical considerations when treating suicidal clients. *The South Carolina Counseling Forum, 1*(1), 26–45.

Beck, A. T., Steer, R. A., & Brown, G. K. (1996). *Manual for the Beck Depression Inventory–II.* San Antonio, TX: Psychological Corporation.

Bedera, N., & Nordmeyer, K. (2015). "Never go out alone": An analysis of college rape prevention tips. *Sexuality & Culture, 19*, 533–542. doi:10.1007/s12119-015-9274-5

Bedi, R. P. (2006). Concept mapping the client's perspective on counseling alliance formation. *Journal of Counseling Psychology, 53*, 26–35. doi:10.1037/0022-0167.53.1.26

Bennett, L., & Williams, O. (2011). Controversies and recent studies of batterer intervention program effectiveness. Retrieved from http://www.vawnet.org/applied-research-papers/print-document.php?doc_id=373

Bennett, N., & O'Donohue, W. (2014). The construct of grooming in child sexual abuse: Conceptual and measurement issues. *Journal of Child Sexual Abuse: Research, Treatment, & Program Innovations for Victims, Survivors, & Offenders, 23*, 957–976. doi:10.1080/10538712.2014.960632

Bennice, J. A., & Resick, P. A. (2003). Marital rape history, research, and practice. *Trauma Violence Abuse, 4*, 228–246. doi:10.1177/1524838003004003003

Benuto, L. T., & O'Donohue, W. (2015). Treatment of the sexually abused child: Review and synthesis of recent meta-analyses. *Children and Youth Services Review, 56*, 52–60. doi:10.1016/j.childyouth.2015.06.009

Berzoff, J. N., & Silverman, P. R. (Eds.). (2010). *Living with dying: A handbook for end-of-life healthcare practitioners.* Irving, NY: Columbia University Press.

Biema, D. V. (2001, October 8). Faith after the fall. *Time, 158*, 76.

Bisson, J. I., Roberts, N. P., Andrew, M., Cooper, R., & Lewis, C. (2013). Psychological therapies for chronic post-traumatic stress disorder (PTSD) in adults (Review). *Cochrane Database System Review, 12*, CD003388.

Bland, D. (1994). *The experiences of suicide survivors 1989–June 1994.* Baton Rouge, LA: Baton Rouge Crisis Intervention Center.

Blauner, S. R. (2002). *How I stayed alive when my brain was trying to kill me—One person's guide to suicide prevention*. New York, NY: HarperCollins.

Blow, F. C., Brower, K. J., Schulenberg, J. E., Demo-Dananberg, L. M., Young, J. P., & Beresford, T. P. (1992). The Michigan Alcoholism Screening Test-Geriatric Version (MAST-G): A new elderly-specific screening instrument. *Alcoholism: Clinical and Experimental Research, 16*, 372.

Boelen, P. A., de Keijser, J., van den Hout, M. A., & van den Bout, J. (2007). Treatment of complicated grief: A comparison between cognitive-behavioral therapy and supportive counseling. *Journal of Consulting and Clinical Psychology, 75*, 277–284. doi:10.1037/0022-006X.75.2.277

Boer, D. P., Hart, S. D., Kropp, P. R., & Webster, C. D. (1997). *Manual for the Sexual Violence Risk-20: Professional guidelines for assessing risk of sexual violence*. Vancouver, BC: The Mental Health, Law, & Policy Institute.

Bonanno, G. A., Neria, Y., Mancini, A., Coifman, K. G., Litz, B., & Insel, B. (2007). Is there more to complicated grief than depression and post-traumatic stress disorder? A test of incremental validity. *Journal of Abnormal Psychology, 116*, 342–351. doi:10.1037/0021-843X.116.2.342

Bond, T., & Mitchels, B. (2014). *Confidentiality & record keeping in counselling & psychotherapy* (2nd ed.). London, UK: Sage.

Bonomi, A. E., Anderson, M. L., Cannon, E. A., Slesnick, N., & Rodriguez, M. A. (2009). Intimate partner violence in Latina and Non-Latina women. *American Journal of Preventive Medicine, 36*, 43–48. doi:10.1016/j.amepre.2008.09.027

Borduin, C., Schaeffer, C., & Heiblum, N. (2009). A randomized clinical trial of multisystemic therapy with juvenile sexual offenders: Effects on youth social ecology and criminal activity. *Consult Clinical Psychology, 77*, 26–37. doi:10.1037/a0013035

Borneman, T., Ferrell, B., & Pulchaski, C. M. (2010). Evaluation of the FICA tool for spiritual assessment. *Journal of Pain and Symptom Management, 40*, 163–173. doi:10.1016/j.jpainsymman.2009.12.019

Boss, P. G. (2002). *Family stress management: A contextual approach* (2nd ed.). Thousand Oaks, CA: Sage.

Boss, P. G. (2006). *Loss, trauma, and resilience: Therapeutic work with ambiguous loss*. New York, NY: Norton.

Bowenkamp, C. (1995). The Los Angeles civil unrest: Implications for future mental health counseling interventions. *Journal of Mental Health Counseling, 17*(3), 301–311.

Bowlby, J. (1960). *Attachment and loss: Attachment* (Vol. I). New York, NY: Basic Books.

Bowlby, J. (1971). *Attachment and Loss, Vol. 1. Attachment* (Pelican ed.). London, UK: Penguin Books.

Bowlby, J. (1973). *Attachment and loss: Separation, anxiety, and anger* (Vol. II). New York, NY: Basic Books.

Bowlby, J. (1980). *Attachment and loss: Loss, sadness and depression* (Vol. III). New York, NY: Basic Books.

Bratton, S., Ray, D., Rhine, T., & Jones, L. (2005). The efficacy of play therapy with children: A meta-analytic review of treatment outcomes. *Professional Psychology: Research and Practice, 36*, 376–390. doi:10.1037/0735-7028.36.4.376

Breiding, M. J., Basile, K. C., Smith, S. G., Black, M. C., & Mahendra, R. (2015). Intimate partner violence surveillance uniform definitions and recommended data elements. Version 2.0. Retrieved from http://www.cdc.gov/violenceprevention/pdf/intimatepartnerviolence.pdf

Breiding, M. J., Smith, S. G., Basile, K. C., Walters, M. L., Chen, J., & Merrick, M. T. (2014, September 5). Prevalence and characteristics of sexual violence, stalking, and intimate partner violence victimization—National Intimate Partner and Sexual Violence Survey, United States, 2011. *Morbidity and Mortality Weekly Report, 63*, 1–18. Retrieved from http://www.cdc.gov/mmwr/preview/mmwrhtml/ss6308a1.htm?s_cid=ss6308a1_e

Brems, C. (2000). *Dealing with challenges in psychotherapy and counseling*. Belmont, CA: Wadsworth/Thompson Learning.

Brock, S. E. (2013). Preparing for the school crisis response. In J. Sandoval (Ed.), *Crisis counseling, intervention and prevention in the schools* (3rd ed., pp. 19–30). New York, NY: Routledge.

Brownmiller, S. (1975). *Against our will*. New York, NY: Ballantine Books.

Brownridge, D. A., Chan, K. L., Hiebert-Murphy, D., Ristock, J., Tiwan, A., Leung, W., & Santos, S. C. (2008). The elevated risk for non-lethal post-separation violence in Canada: A comparison of separated, divorced, and married women. *Journal of Interpersonal Violence, 23*, 117–135. doi:10.1177/0886260507307914

Bryant, C. D. (Ed.). (2003). *Handbook of death and dying* (Vol. 1). Thousand Oaks, CA: Sage.

Bureau of Justice Statistics. (2008). Definitions. Retrieved from http://www.ojp.usdoj.gov/bjs/abstract/cvus/definitions.htm#rape_sexual_assault

Bureau of Justice Statistics. (2012). Special report: Stalking victims in the United States-revised. Retrieved from http://www.bjs.gov/content/pub/pdf/svus_rev.pdf

Bureau of Justice Statistics. (2016a). Domestic violence. Retrieved from http://www.bjs.gov/index.cfm?ty=tp&tid=235

Bureau of Justice Statistics. (2016b). Rape and sexual assault. Retrieved from http://www.bjs.gov/index.cfm?ty=tp&tid=317

Burgess, A. W. (Ed.). (1985). *Rape and sexual assault: A research handbook*. New York, NY: Garland.

Burgess, A. W., & Holmstrom, L. L. (1974). Rape trauma syndrome. *American Journal of Psychiatry, 131*, 981–986.

Burnam, M., Meredith, L., Tanielian, T., & Jaycox, L. (2009). Mental health care for Iraq and Afghanistan war veterans. *Health Affairs, 28,* 771–782. doi:10.1377/hlthaff.28.3.771

Bushatz, A. (2011, December 11). Military divorce rates continue steady climb. Retrieved from http://www.military.com /news/article/military-divorce-rates-continue-steady-climb. html

Butler, R. N. (1963). The life review: An interpretation of reminiscence in the aged. *Psychiatry, 26,* 65–76.

Buttell, F. P. (2001). Moral development among court-ordered batterers: Evaluating the impact of treatment. *Research on Social Work Practice, 11*(1), 93–107. doi:10.1177/104973150101100106

Byock, I. (1997). *Dying well: Peace and possibilities at the end of life.* New York, NY: Berkley Publishing Group.

Cacciatore, J., Carlson, B., Michaelis, E., Klimek, B., & Staffan, S. (2011). Crisis intervention by social workers in fire departments: An innovative role for social workers. *National Association of Social Workers, 56*(1), 81–88.

Campbell, F. (2005). *Intention style and survival outcome.* Baton Rouge, LA: ASIST Trainers.

Campbell, J. C. (2001). Danger assessment. Retrieved from http://www.ncdsv.org/images/dangerassessment.pdf

Caplan, G. (1961). *An approach to community mental health.* New York, NY: Grune and Stratton.

Caplan, G. (1964). *Principles of preventive psychiatry.* New York, NY: Basic Books.

Capuzzi, D., & Stauffer, M. D. (2012). History and etiological models of addiction. In D. Capuzzi & M. D. Stauffer (Eds.), *Foundations of addiction counseling* (2nd ed., pp. 1–15). Upper Saddle River, NJ: Pearson.

Carnelley, K. B., Wortman, C. B., Bolger, N., & Burke, C. T. (2006). The time course of grief reactions to spousal loss: Evidence from a national probability sample. *Journal of Personality and Social Psychology, 91,* 476–492. doi:10.1037 /0022-3514.91.3.476

Carr, J. L. (2005). *American College Health Association campus violence white paper.* Baltimore, MD: American College Health Association.

Carroll, A., Lyall, M., & Forrester, A. (2004). Clinical hopes and public fears in forensic mental health. *Journal of Forensic Psychiatry and Psychology, 15,* 407–425. doi:10.1080 /14789940410001703282

Cashwell, C., & Young, J. (2011). *Integrating spirituality and religion into counseling: A guide to competent practice* (2nd ed.). Alexandria, VA: American Counseling Association.

Castellano, C., & Plionis, E. (2006). Comparative analysis of three crisis intervention models applied to law enforcement first responders during 9/11 and Hurricane Katrina. *Brief Treatment and Crisis Intervention, 6,* 326–336. doi:10.1093 /brief-treatment/mhl008

Catalano, S. (2013, November). Intimate partner violence: Attributes of victimization 1993–2011 (Special Report No. NCJ243300). Retrieved from http://www.bjs.gov/content /pub/pdf/ipvav9311.pdf

Cavaiola, A. A., & Colford, J. E. (2006). *A practical guide to crisis intervention.* Boston, MA: Lahaska.

Center for Mental Health in Schools at UCLA. (2008). Responding to a crisis at a school. Retrieved from http:// smhp.psych.ucla.edu/pdfdocs/crisis/crisis.pdf

Center for Sex Offender Management. (2007). Female sex offenders. Retrieved from http://www.csom.org/pubs/female _sex_offenders_brief.pdf

Center for Substance Abuse Treatment. (2009). *Addressing suicidal thoughts and behaviors in substance abuse treatment* (Treatment Improvement Protocol Series 50. HHS Publication No. [SMA] 09-4381). Rockville, MD: Substance Abuse and Mental Health Services Administration.

Centers for Disease Control and Prevention. (2006). Fact sheet on traumatic brain injury. Retrieved from http://www.cdc .gov/ncipc/tbi/factsheets/facts_about_tbi.pdf

Centers for Disease Control and Prevention. (2010). National intimate partner and sexual violence survey: An overview of 2010 findings on victimization by sexual orientation. Retrieved from http://www.gov/violenceprevention/pdf /cdc_nisvs_victimization_final-a.pdf

Centers for Disease Control and Prevention. (2011a). National Intimate Partner and Sexual Violence Survey. Retrieved from http://www.cdc.gov/ViolencePrevention/pdf/NISVS _Report2010-a.pdf

Centers for Disease Control and Prevention. (2011b). Self-directed violence surveillance: Uniform definitions and recommended data elements. Retrieved from http:// www.cdc.gov/violenceprevention/pdf/self-directed -violence-a.pdf

Centers for Disease Control and Prevention. (2012). QuickStats: Prevalence of current depression among persons aged ≥ 12 years, by age group and sex—United States, national health and nutrition examination survey, 2007–2010. Retrieved from http://www.cdc.gov/mmwr/preview /mmwrhtml/mm6051a7.htm

Centers for Disease Control and Prevention. (2014a). Mortality data. Retrieved from http://www.cdc.gov/nchs/deaths.htm

Centers for Disease Control and Prevention. (2014b). *Sexual violence surveillance: Uniform definitions and recommended data elements.* Atlanta, GA: Author.

Centers for Disease Control and Prevention. (2014c). Understanding teen dating violence fact sheet. Retrieved from http://www.cdc.gov/violenceprevention/pdf/teen-dating -violence-factsheet-a.pdf

Centers for Disease Control and Prevention. (2015a). 10 leading causes of death by age group, United States—2013.

http://www.cdc.gov/injury/images/lc-charts/leading_causes_of_death_by_age_group_2013-a.gif

Centers for Disease Control and Prevention. (2015b). Deaths: Leading causes for 2012. Retrieved from http://www.cdc.gov/nchs/data/nvsr/nvsr64/nvsr64_10.pdf

Centers for Disease Control and Prevention. (2015c). Sexual violence: Consequences. Retrieved from http://www.cdc.gov/ViolencePrevention/sexualviolence/consequences.html

Centers for Disease Control and Prevention. (2015d). Suicide fact sheet. Retrieved from http://www.cdc.gov/violenceprevention/pdf/suicide_factsheet-a.pdf

Centers for Disease Control and Prevention. (2015e). Understanding youth violence. Retrieved from http://www.cdc.gov/violenceprevention/pdf/yv-factsheet-a.pdf

Centers for Disease Control and Prevention. (2017). Vital statistics data available online. Retrieved from http://www.cdc.gov/nchs/data_access/vitalstatsonline.htm

Cerel, J., & Campbell, F. (2008). Suicide survivors seeking mental health services: A preliminary examination of the role of an active postvention model. *Suicide and Life Threatening Behavior, 38*(1), 30–34. doi:10.1521/suli.2008.38.1.30

Chae, M. H., & Boyle, D. J. (2013). Police suicide: Prevalence, risk, and protective factors. *Policing, 36*(1), 91–118. doi:10.1108/13639511311302498

Chaffin, M., Berliner, L., Block, R., Johnson, T. C., Friedrich, W., Louis, D., . . . Silovsky, J. (2008). Report of the ATSA Task Force on Children with Sexual Behavior Problems. *Child Maltreatment, 18*, 199–218. doi:10.1177/1077559507306718

Chandra, A., Lara-Cinisomo, S., Jaycox, L. H., Tanielian, T., Burns, R. M., Ruder, T., & Han, B. (2010). Children on the homefront: The experience of children from military families. *Pediatrics, 125*, 16–25. doi:10.1542/peds.2009-1180

Chandra, A., Lara-Cinisomo, S., Jaycox, L. H., Tanielian, T., Han, B., Burns, R. M., & Ruder, T. (2011). *Views from the homefront: The experiences of youth and spouses from military families.* Santa Monica, CA: RAND Corporation.

Chandra, A., Martin, L., Hawkins, S., & Richardson, A. (2010). The impact of parental deployment on child social and emotional functioning: Perspectives of school staff. *Journal of Adolescent Health, 46*, 218–226. doi:10.1016/j.jadohealth.2009.10.009

Chang, J. C., Decker, M. R., Moracco, K. E., Martin, S. L., Petersen, R., & Frasier, P. Y. (2005). Asking about intimate partner violence: Advice from female survivors to healthcare providers. *Patient Education and Counseling, 59*, 141–147. doi:10.1016/j.pec.2004.10.008

Charles, D. R., & Charles, M. (2006). Sibling loss and attachment style. *Psychoanalytic Psychology, 23*, 72–90. doi:10.1037/0736-9735.23.1.72

Chassman, L., Kottler, J., & Madison, J. (2010). An exploration of counselor experiences of adolescents with sexual behavior problems. *Journal of Counseling & Development, 88*, 269–276. doi:10.1002/j.1556-6678.2010.tb00022.x

Chen, J., Chen, T., Vertinsky, I., Yumagulov, L., & Park, C. (2013). Public-private partnerships for the development of disaster resilient communities. *Journal of Contingencies and Crisis Management, 21*, 130–143. doi:10.1111/1468-5973.12021

Chen, Y., Hung, K., Tsai, J., Chu, H., Chung, M., Chen, S., . . . Chou, K. (2014). Efficacy of eye-movement desensitization and reprocessing for patients with posttraumatic stress disorder: A meta-analysis of randomized controlled trials. *Plos ONE, 9*(8), 1–17. doi:10.1371/journal.pone.0103676

Child Abuse Prevention and Treatment Act, 42 U.S.C. § 5101 et seq. (2010).

Childress, S. (2013). A meta-summary of qualitative findings on the lived experiences among culturally diverse domestic violence survivors. *Issues in Mental Health Nursing, 34*, 693–705. doi:10.3109/01612840.2013.791735

Chiles, J. A., & Strosahl, K. D. (1995). *The suicidal patient: Principles of assessment, treatment, and case management.* Washington, DC: American Psychiatric Press.

Cho, H., & Kim, W. (2012). Intimate partner violence among Asian Americans and their use of mental health services: Comparisons with White, Black, and Latino victims. *Journal of Immigrant and Minority Health, 14*, 809–815. doi:10.1007/s10903-012-9625-3

Christopher, J. C., & Maris, J. A. (2010). Integrating mindfulness as self-care into counselling and psychotherapy training. *Counselling & Psychotherapy Research, 10*, 114–125. doi:10.1080/14733141003750285

Clark, A. J. (2014). *Empathy in counseling and psychotherapy: Perspectives and practices.* New York, NY: Routledge.

Clever, M., & Segal, D. R. (2013). The demographics of military children and families. *The Future of Children, 23*(2), 13–39.

Cohen, J. A., Mannarino, A. P., & Deblinger, E. (2006). *Treating trauma and traumatic grief in children and adolescents.* New York, NY: Guilford Press.

Collin-Vézina, D., Daigneault, I., & Hébert, M. (2013). Lessons learned from child sexual abuse research: Prevalence, outcomes, and preventive strategies. *Child & Adolescent Psychiatry & Mental Health, 7*(1), 1–9. doi:10.1186/1753-2000-7-22

Collins, B. G., & Collins, T. M. (2005). *Crisis and trauma developmental-ecological intervention.* Boston, MA: Houghton Mifflin/Lahaska Press.

Collins, R. C., & Kennedy, M. C. (2008). Serving families who have served: Providing family therapy and support in interdisciplinary polytrauma rehabilitation. *Journal of Clinical Psychology: In Session, 64*, 993–1003. doi:10.1002/jclp.20515

Connors, G. J., DiClemente, C. C., Velasquez, M. M., & Donovan, D. M. (2013). *Substance abuse treatment and the stages of change: Selecting and planning interventions* (2nd ed.). New York, NY: Guilford Press.

Cooley, M. E., Veldorale-Griffin, A., Petren, R. E., & Mullis, A. K. (2014). Parent–child interaction therapy: A meta-analysis of child behavior outcomes and parent stress. *Journal of Family Social Work, 17*(3), 191–208. doi:10.1080/10522158.2014.888696

Coombs, D., Harrington, J. A., & Talbott, L. L. (2010). Youth suicides in Alabama: A focus on gun safety. *Alabama State Association for Health, Physical Education, Recreation, and Dance Journal, 31*(1), 31–35.

Corey, G., Corey, M., Corey, C., & Callanan, P. (2014). *Issues and ethics in the helping professions* (9th ed.). Boston, MA: Brooks Cole.

Corey, M., & Corey, G. (2015). *Becoming a helper* (7th ed.). Boston, MA: Cengage Learning.

Cornell, D. G. (2007, May 15). Best practices for making college campuses safe (statement before the U.S. House Committee on Education and Labor). Retrieved from http://www.youthviolence.edschool.virginia.edu/prevention/congress/testimony%202007.htm

Cornille, T., & Meyers, T. (1999). Secondary traumatic stress among child protective service workers: Prevalence, severity, and predictive factors. *Traumatology, 5*(1), 15–31. doi:10.1177/153476569900500105

Corr, C. A., & Balk, D. E. (2011). *Children's encounters with death, bereavement, and coping.* New York, NY: Springer.

Corr, C. A., Nabe, C. M., & Corr, D. M. (2012). *Death and dying: Life and living* (7th ed.). Belmont, CA: Wadsworth/Thomson Learning.

Costello, E. J., Erkanli, A., Keeler, G., & Angold, A. (2004). Distant trauma: A prospective study of the effects of September 11th on young adults in North Carolina. *Applied Developmental Science, 8*, 211–220. doi:10.1207/s1532480xads0804_4

Coulter, M., & VandeWeerd, C. (2009). Reducing domestic violence and other criminal recidivism: Effectiveness of a multi-level batterer's intervention program. *Violence and Victims, 24*, 139–152. doi:10.1891/0886-6708.24.2.139

Council for Accreditation of Counseling and Related Educational Programs. (2016). *2016 CACREP standards.* Alexandria, VA: Author.

Covey, S. R. (2013). *The 7 habits of highly effective people: Powerful lessons in personal change.* New York, NY: Simon & Schuster.

Craig, R. J. (2004). *Counseling the alcohol and drug dependent client: A practical approach.* Boston, MA: Pearson.

Creamer, M., Wade, D., Fletcher, S., & Forbes, D. (2011). PTSD among military personnel. *International Review of Psychiatry, 23*, 160–165. doi:10.3109/09540261.2011.559456

Cronholm, P. F., Fogarty, C. T., Ambuel, B., & Harrison, S. L. (2011). Intimate partner violence. *American Family Physician, 83*, 1165–1172.

Crosby, A. E., Ortega, L., & Melanson, C. (2011). *Self-directed violence and surveillance: Uniform definitions and recommended data elements,* version 1.0. Atlanta, GA: Centers for Disease Control and Prevention, National Center for Injury Prevention and Control.

Cui, M., Gordon, M., Ueno, K., & Fincham, F. D. (2013). The continuation of intimate partner violence from adolescence to young adulthood. *Journal of Marriage and Family, 75*, 300–313. doi:10.1111/jomf.12016

Currier, J. M., Holland, J. M., & Neimeyer, R. A. (2006). Sense-making, grief and the experience of violent loss: Toward a meditational model. *Death Studies, 30*, 403–428. doi:10.1080/07481180600614351

Daigre, C., Rodrigues-Cintas, L., Tarifa, N., Rodriguez-Martos, L., Grau-Lopez, L., Berenguer, M., Casas, M., . . . Roncero, C. (2015). History of sexual emotional or physical abuse and psychiatric comorbidity in substance-dependent patients. *Psychiatry Research, 229*, 743–749. doi:10.1016/j.psychres.2015.08.008

Dank, M., Lachman, P., Zweig, J. M., & Yahner, J. (2014). Dating violence experiences of lesbian, gay, bisexual, and transgender youth. *Journal of Youth Adolescence, 43*, 846–857. doi:10.1007/s10964-013-9975-8

Darby, P. J., Allan, W. D., Kashani, J. H., Hartke, K. L., & Reid, J. C. (1998). Analysis of 112 juveniles who committed homicide: Characteristics and a closer look at family abuse. *Journal of Family Violence, 13*, 365–375. doi:10.1023/A:1022823219276

Darke, S. (2009). Substance use and violent death: A case for the "too hard" basket. *Society of the Study of Addiction, 104*, 1063–1064. doi:10.1111/j.1360-0443.2009.02562.x

Darkness to Light. (2016). Child sexual abuse prevention programs. Retrieved from http://www.d2l.org/site/c.4dICIJOkGcISE/b.6069275/k.31EB/Prevention.htm

Daughhetee, C., Puleo, S., & Thrower, E. (2010). Scaffolding of continuing competency as an essential element of professionalism. *Alabama Counseling Association Journal, 36*(1), 15–22.

Davidson, R. J., Kabat-Zinn, J., Schumacher, J., Rosenkranz, M., Muller, D., Santorelli, S. F., . . . Sheridan, J. F. (2003). Alterations in brain and immune function produced by mindfulness meditation. *Psychosomatic Medicine, 65*, 564–570. doi:10.1097/01.PSY.0000077505.67574.E3

Dawgert, S. (2009). Substance use and sexual violence. Building prevention and intervention responses: A guide for counselors and advocates. Retrieved from http://www.pcar.org/sites/default/files/pages-pdf/substance_use_and_sexual_violence.pdf

Decker, S., & Naugle, A. (2009). Immediate intervention for sexual assault: A review with recommendations and implications for practitioners. *Journal of Aggression, Maltreatment, and Trauma, 18*, 419–441. doi:10.1080/10926770902901485

Deering, R., & Mellor, D. (2011). An exploratory qualitative study of the self-reported impact of female-perpetrated childhood sexual abuse. *Journal of Child Sexual Abuse, 20*(1), 58–76. doi:10.1080/10538712.2011.539964

Dennis, M. L., Foss, M. A., & Scott, C. K. (2007). An eight-year perspective on the relationship between the duration of abstinence and other aspects of recovery, *Evaluation Review, 31*, 585–612. doi:10.1177/0193841X07307771

Despenser, S. (2007). Risk assessment: The personal safety of the counselor. *Therapy Today, 18*(2), 12–17.

de Tychey, C., Laurent, M., Lighezzolo-Alnot, J., Garnier, S., & Vandelet, E. (2015). Prevalence of sexual abuse in childhood: Some critical methodological reflections. *Journal of Child Sexual Abuse: Research, Treatment, & Program Innovations for Victims, Survivors, & Offenders, 24*(4), 401–411. doi:10.1080/10538712.2015.1029105

Dieltjens, T., Moonens, I., Van Praet, K., De Buck, E., & Vanderkerckhove, P. (2014). A systematic literature search on psychological first aid: Lack of evidence to develop guidelines. *PLoS ONE, 9*(12), 1–13. doi:10.1371/journal.pone.0114714

Diem, C., & Pizarro, J. M. (2010). Social structure and family homicides. *Journal of Family Violence, 25*, 521–532. doi:10.1007/s10896-010-9313-9

DiMaggio, C., Galea, S., & Li, G. (2009). Substance use and misuse in the aftermath of terrorism. A Bayesian meta-analysis. *Addiction, 104*, 894–904. doi:10.1111/j.1360-0443.2009.02526.x

Dodgen, C. E., & Shea, W. M. (2000). *Substance use disorders: Assessment and treatment.* San Diego, CA: Academic Press.

Doka, K. J. (Ed.). (2002). *Disenfranchised grief: New directions, challenges, and strategies for practice.* San Francisco, CA: Jossey-Bass.

Doka, K. J. (2005, May). New perspectives on grief. *Counseling Today*, 56–57.

Domestic Abuse Intervention Programs. (2013). *Creating a process of change for men who batter: The Duluth Curriculum.* Minneapolis, MN: Author.

D'Orazio, D. M. (2014). Lessons learned from history and experience: Five simple ways to improve the efficacy of sexual offender treatment. *International Journal of Behavioral Consultation and Therapy, 8*(3–4), 2–7. doi:10.1037/h0100975

Douglas, E. M., Hines, D. A., & McCarthy, S. C. (2012). Men who sustain female-to-male partner violence: Factors associated with where they seek help and how they rate those resources. *Violence and Victims, 27*, 871–894. doi:10.1891/0886-6708.27.6.871

Dragisic, T., Dickov, A., Dickov, V., & Milatovic, V. (2015). Drug addiction as risk for suicide attempts. *Materia Sociomedica, 27*, 188–191. doi:10.5455/msm.2015.27.188-191

Drake, R. E., Mueser, K. T., Brunette, M. F., & McHugo, G. J. (2004). A review of treatments for people with severe mental illnesses and co-occurring substance use disorders. *Psychiatric Rehabilitation Journal, 27*, 360–374. doi:10.2975/27.2004.360.374

Drapeau, C. W., & McIntosh, J. L. (2015). U.S.A. suicide: 2013 official final data. Retrieved from http://www.floridasuicideprevention.org/PDF/2013%20US%20Suicide%20Official%20Final%20Data%20AAS.pdf

Draucker, C. B., & Martsolf, D. S. (2010). The role of electronic communication technology in adolescent dating violence. *Journal of Child and Adolescent Psychiatric Nursing, 23*, 133–142. doi:10.1111/j.1744-6171.2010.00235.x

Driessen, M., Schulte, S., Luedecke, C., Schaefer, I., Sutmann, F., Ohlmeier, M., . . . Havemann-Reinicke, U. (2008). Trauma and PTSD in patients with alcohol, drug, or dual dependence: A multi-center study. *Alcoholism: Clinical & Experimental Research, 32*, 481–488. doi:10.1111/j.1530-0277.2007.00591.x

Drysdale, D., Modzeleski, W., & Simons, A. (2010). *Campus attacks: Targeted violence affecting institutions of higher education.* Washington, DC: U.S. Secret Service, U.S. Department of Homeland Security, Office of Safe and Drug-Free Schools, U.S. Department of Education, and Federal Bureau of Investigation, and U.S. Department of Justice.

Duplechain, R., & Morris, R. (2014). School violence: Reported school shootings and making schools safer. *Education, 135*, 145–150.

Dupre, M., Echterling, L. G., Meixner, C., Anderson, R., & Kielty, M. (2014). Supervision experiences of professional counselors providing crisis counseling. *Counselor Education and Supervision, 53*, 82–96. doi:10.1002/j.1556-6978.2014.00050.x

Durborow, N., Lizdas, K., Flaherty, A., Marjavi, A., & Family Violence Prevention Fund. (2010). Compendium of state statutes and policies on domestic violence and health care. Retrieved from http://www.futureswithoutviolence.org/userfiles/file/HealthCare/Compendium%20Final.pdf

Dutton, D., & Sonkin, D. J. (Eds.). (2013). *Intimate violence: Contemporary treatment innovations.* New York, NY: The Haworth Press.

Earley, P. (2007). *Crazy: A father's search through America's mental health madness.* New York, NY: Penguin Group.

Eckhardt, C., Holtzworth-Munroe, A., Norlander, B., Sibley, A., & Cahill, M. (2008). Readiness to change, partner violence subtypes, and treatment outcomes among men in treatment for partner assault. *Violence and Victims, 23*, 446–476. doi:10.1891/0886-6708.23.4.446

Edwards, K. M., Murphy, M. J., Tansill, E. C., Myrick, C., Probst, D. R., Corsa, R., . . . Gidycz, C. A. (2012). A qualitative analysis of college women's leaving processes in abusive relationships. *Journal of American College Health, 60*, 204–210. doi:10.1080/07448481.2011.586387

Egan, G. (2013). *The skilled helper: A problem-management and opportunity-development approach to helping* (10th ed.). Pacific Grove, CA: Brooks/Cole.

Eifling, K., & Moy, P. (2015). Evidenced-based EMS: Psychological first aid during disaster response. What's the best we can do for those who are suffering mentally? *EMS World, 44*(7), 32–34.

Eisenberg, D., Hunt, J., & Spear, N. (2015). Help-seeking for mental health on college campuses: Review of evidence and next steps for research and practice. *Harvard Review of Psychiatric Practice, 20*, 222–232. doi:10.3109/10673229.2012.712839

Elhai, J. D., Layne, C. M., Steinberg, A. S., Brymer, M. J., Briggs, E. C., Ostrowski, S. A., & Pynoos, R. S. (2013). Psychometric properties of the UCLA PTSD Reaction Index. Part II: Investigating factor structure findings in a national clinic-referred youth sample. *Journal of Traumatic Stress, 26*, 10–18. doi:10.1002/jts.21755

Elliott, T. L., Fatemi, D., & Wasan, S. (2014). Student privacy rights: History, Owasso, and FERPA. *Journal of Higher Education Theory and Practice, 14*(4). Retrieved from http://www.na-businesspress.com/JHETP/ElliotTL_Web14_4_.pdf

Ellis, A. (1962). *Reason and emotion in psychotherapy*. New York, NY: Lyle Stuart.

Ells, G. T., & Rockland-Miller, H. S. (2010). Assessing and responding to disturbed and disturbing students: Understanding the role of administrative teams and institutions of higher education. *Journal of College Student Psychotherapy, 25*(1), 8–23. doi:10.1080/87658225.2011.532470

Erbes, C. R., Polusny, M. A., MacDermid, S., & Compton, J. A. (2008). Couple therapy with combat veterans and their partners. *Journal of Clinical Psychology: In Session, 64*, 972–983. doi:10.1002/jclp.20521

Erford, B. T. (2013). *Assessment for counselors* (2nd ed.). Belmont, CA: Cengage Wadsworth.

Erford, B. T. (2016a). *A lifespan odyssey for counseling professionals*. Boston, MA: Cengage.

Erford, B. T. (Ed.). (2016b). *Professional school counseling: A handbook of theories, programs, and practices* (3rd ed.). Austin, TX: Pro-ed.

Erford, B. T. (Ed.). (2018). *Orientation to the counseling profession* (3rd ed.). Columbus, OH: Pearson Merrill.

Erford, B. T., Lee, V. V., & Rock, E. (2015). Systematic approaches to counseling students experiencing complex and specialized problems. In B. T. Erford (Ed.), *Transforming the school counseling profession* (4th ed., pp. 288–313). Columbus, OH: Pearson Merrill.

Erich, J. (2014). Earlier than too late: Stopping stress and suicide among emergency personnel. Retrieved from http://www.emsworld.com/article/12009260/suicide-stress-and-ptsd-among-emergency-personnel

Erikson, E. H. (1997). *The life cycle completed*. New York, NY: Norton.

Eronen, M., Angermeyer, M. C., & Schulze, B. (1998). The psychiatric epidemiology of violent behavior. *Social Psychiatry and Psychiatric Epidemiology, 33* (Suppl.), 13–23.

Evans, D. R., Hearn, M. T., Uhlemann, M. R., & Ivey, A. E. (2011). *Essential interviewing: A programmed approach to effective communication* (8th ed.). Belmont, CA: Brooks/Cole.

Everly, G. S., & Flynn, B. W. (2005). Principles and practices of acute psychological first aid after disasters. In G. S. Everly & C. L. Parker (Eds.), *Mental health aspects of disasters: Public health preparedness and response* (Rev. ed., pp. 79–89). Baltimore, MD: Johns Hopkins Center for Public Health Preparedness.

Everly, G. S., & Mitchell, J. (1999). *Critical incident stress management* (2nd ed.). Ellicott City, MD: Chevron.

Everly, G. S., Phillips, S. B., Kane, D., & Feldman, D. (2006). Introduction to and overview of group psychological first aid. *Brief Treatment & Crisis Intervention, 6*, 130–136. doi:10.1093/brief-treatment/mhj009

Ewing v. Goldstein, 120 Cal. App. 4th 807 (2004).

Ewing, J. A. (1984). Detecting alcoholism: The CAGE questionnaire. *Journal of the American Medical Association, 252*, 1905–1907. doi:10.1001/jama.1984.03350140051025

Executive Office of the Department of Health and Human Services in Massachusetts. (2015). Does batterer intervention work? Retrieved from http://www.mass.gov/eohhs/gov/departments/dph/programs/communityhealth/dvip/violence/batter-intervention/does-batterer-intervention-work.html

Fallot, R. D., & Heckman, J. P. (2005). Religious/spiritual coping among women trauma survivors with mental health and substance use disorders. *Journal of Behavioral Health Services and Research, 32*, 215–226. doi:10.1007/BF02287268

Famili, A., Kirschner, M., & Gamez, A. (2014). Vicarious traumatization: A guide for managing the silent stressor. *The Police Chief*. Retrieved from http://www.policechiefmagazine.org/magazine/index.cfm?fuseaction=display_arch&article_id=3489&issue_id=92014

Family Educational Rights and Privacy Act, 20 U.S.C. § 1232g; 34 CFR Part 99.

Farmer, T. W., Farmer, E. M. Z., Estell, D. B., & Hutchins, B. C. (2007). The developmental dynamics of aggression and the prevention of school violence. *Journal of Emotional & Behavioral Disorders, 15*, 197–208. doi:10.1177/10634266070150040201

Farrow, T. L. (2002). Owning their expertise: Why nurses use no suicide contracts rather than their own assessments. *International Journal of Mental Health Nursing, 11*, 214–219. doi:10.1046/j.1440-0979.2002.00251.x

Fauteux, K. (2010). De-escalating angry and violent clients. *American Journal of Psychotherapy, 64*, 195–213.

Federal Bureau of Investigation. (2013a). 2013 law enforcement officers killed and assaulted. Retrieved from https://www.fbi.gov/about-us/cjis/ucr/leoka/2013/officers-assaulted/assaults_topic_page_-2013

Federal Bureau of Investigation. (2013b). Crime in the United States. Retrieved from https://www.fbi.gov/about-us/cjis/ucr/crime-in-the.u.s/2013/crime-in-the-u.s.-2013/offenses-known-to-law-enforcement/expanded-homicide/expanded_homicide_data_table_1_murder_victims_by_race_and_sex_2013.xls

Federal Bureau of Investigation. (2013c). A study of active shooter incidents in the United States between 2000 and 2013. Retrieved from https://www.fbi.gov/news/stories/2014/september/fbi-releases-study-on-active-shooter-incidents/pdfs/a-study-of-active-shooter-incidents-in-the-u.s.-between-2000-and-2013

Federal Bureau of Investigation. (2015). Definition of terrorism in the U.S. code. Retrieved from https://www.fbi.gov/about-us/investigate/terrorism/terrorism-definition

Federal Bureau of Investigation, National Center for the Analysis of Violent Crime. (2001). Workplace violence: Issues in response. Retrieved from http://www.fbi.gov/publications/violence.pdf

Federal Emergency Management Agency. (2011). Storm safe: Sheltering in place. Retrieved from https://emilms.fema.gov/is909/assets/05_shelteringinplace.pdf

Federal Emergency Management Agency. (2013). Guide for developing high quality school emergency operations plans. Retrieved from https://www.fbi.gov/about-us/office-of-partner-engagement/active-shooter-incidents/emergency-plans-for-schools

Federal Emergency Management Agency. (2014). National preparedness guidelines. Retrieved from http://www.fema.gov/media-library-data/20130726-1718-25045-3265/npg.pdf

Figley, C. R. (2002). Compassion fatigue: Psychotherapists' chronic lack of self-care. *Journal of Clinical Psychology, 58*, 1433–1441. doi:10.1002/jclp.10090

Finkelhor, D. (1979). *Sexually victimized children.* New York, NY: Free Press.

Flannery, R. B., LeVitre, V., Rego, S., & Walker, A. (2011). Characteristics of staff victims of psychiatric patient assaults: 20-year analysis of the Assaulted Staff Action Program. *Psychiatry Quarterly, 18*, 11–21. doi:10.1007/s11126-010-9153-z

Fleming, M. F. (2003). Screening for at-risk, problem, and dependent alcohol use. In R. K. Hester & W. R. Miller (Eds.), *Handbook of alcoholism treatment approaches: Effective alternatives* (3rd ed.) (pp. 64–77). Boston, MA: Allyn and Bacon.

Foa, E. B., & Rothbaum, B. O. (1998). *Treating the trauma of rape: Cognitive behavioral therapy for PTSD.* New York, NY: Guilford Press.

Foa, E. B., Zoellner, L., Feeny, N., Hembree, E., & Alvarez-Conrad, J. (2002). Does imaginal exposure exacerbate PTSD symptoms? *Journal of Counseling and Clinical Psychology, 70*, 1022–1028. doi:10.1037/0022-006X.70.4.1022

Foden-Vencil, K. (Writer). (2015, March 9). College rape case shows a key limit to medical privacy law. *All Things Considered* [Radio series episode]. Retrieved from http://www.npr.org/sections/health-shots/2015/03/09/391876192/college-rape-case-shows-a-key-limit-to-medical-privacy-law

Forbes, D., Creamer, M., Phelps, A., Bryant, R., McFarlane, A., Devilly, G., . . . Newton, S. (2007). Australian guidelines for the treatment of adults with acute stress disorder and posttraumatic stress disorder. *Australian and New Zealand Journal of Psychiatry, 43*, 637–648. doi:10.1080/00048670701449161

Forbes, D., Lloyd, D., Nixon, R. D. V., Elliott, P., Varker, T., Perry, D., . . . Creamer, M. (2012). A multisite randomized controlled effectiveness trial of cognitive processing therapy for military-related posttraumatic stress disorder. *Journal of Anxiety Disorders, 26*, 442–452. doi:10.1016/j.janxdis.2012.01.006

Forester-Miller, H., & Davis, T. (1996). *A practitioner's guide to ethical decision making.* Alexandria, VA: American Counseling Association.

Fowler, J. W. (1981). *Stages of faith.* New York, NY: Harper Collins.

Frankl, V. (1959). *Man's search for meaning.* Boston, MA: Beacon Press.

Franz, S., & Borum, R. (2011). Crisis intervention teams may prevent arrests of people with mental illness. *Police Practice and Research, 12*, 265–272. doi:10.1080/15614263.2010.497664

Freeman, J., & Sugai, G. (2013). Recent changes in state policies and legislation regarding restraint or seclusion. *Exceptional Children, 74*, 427–438.

Freud, S. (1917). *Mourning and melancholia.* London, UK: Hogarth Press.

Freud, S., & Breuer, J. (2004) *Studies in hysteria* (N. Luckhurst, Trans.). London, UK: Penguin Books.

Furber, G., Jones, G. M., Healey, D., & Bidargaddi, N. (2014). A comparison between phone-based psychotherapy with and without text messaging support in between sessions for crisis patients. *Journal of Medical Internet Research, 16*(10). doi:10.2196/jmir.3096

Furukawa, M. F. (2011). Electronic medical records and the efficiency of hospital emergency departments. *Medical Care Research and Review, 68*(1), 75–95. doi:10.1177/1077558710372108

Gannon, T. A., & Cortoni, F. (2010). *Female sexual offenders: Theory, assessment, and practice.* Chichester, UK: Wiley-Blackwell.

Garrido, E. F., Culhane, S. E., Petrenko, C. L. M., & Taussig, H. N. (2011). Psychosocial consequences of intimate partner violence (IPV) exposure in maltreated adolescents: Assessing more than IPV occurrence. *Journal of Family Violence, 26*, 511–518. doi:10.1007/s10896-011-9386-0

Gary, J. M. (2010). A mouse click away: Internet resources for students in crisis in geographically isolated or self-sequestered communities. *Journal of School Counseling, 8*(1).

Gerber, M. M., Boals, A., & Schuettler, D. (2011). The unique contributions of positive and negative religious coping to post traumatic growth and posttraumatic stress disorder. *Psychology of Religion and Spirituality, 3*, 298–307. doi:10.1037/a0023016

Gibbs, D. A., Martin, S. L., Kupper, L. L., & Johnson, R. E. (2007). Child maltreatment in enlisted soldiers' families during combat-related deployments. *Journal of the American Medical Association, 298*, 528–535. doi:10.1001/jama.298.5.528

Gibbs, D. A., Walters, J. L. H., Lutnick, A., Miller, S., & Kluckman, M. (2015). Services to domestic minor victims of sex trafficking: Opportunities for engagement and support. *Children and Youth Services Review, 54*, 1–7. doi:10.1016/j.childyouth.2015.04.003

Gidycz, C. A., Loh, C., Lobo, T., Rich, C., Lynn, S. J., & Pashdag, J. (2007). Reciprocal relationships among alcohol use, risk perceptions, and sexual victimization: A prospective analysis. *Journal of American College Health, 56*(1), 5–14. doi:10.3200/jach.56.1.5-14

Gladding, S. T. (2010). *The counseling dictionary: Concise definitions of frequently used terms* (5th ed.). Upper Saddle River, NJ: Pearson.

Gladding, S. T. (2014). *Creative arts in counseling* (4th ed.). Alexandria, VA: American Counseling Association.

Glass, N., Clough, A., Case, J., Hanson, G., Barnes-Hoyt, J., Waterbury, A., . . . Perrin, N. (2015). A safety app to respond to dating violence for college women and their friends: The MyPlan study randomized controlled trial protocol. *BMC Public Health, 15*, 871. doi:10.1186/s12889-015-2191-6

Glasgow, R. E., Kaplan, R. M., Ockene, J. K., Fisher, E. B., & Emmons, K. M. (2012). Patient-reported measures of psychosocial issues and health behavior should be added to electronic health records. *Health Affairs, 31*, 497–504. doi:10.1377/hlthaff.2010.1295

Glasser, W. (1965). *Reality therapy: A new approach to psychiatry.* New York, NY: Harper and Row.

Goddard, C., & Bedi, G. (2010). Intimate partner violence and child abuse: A child-centered perspective. *Child Abuse Review, 19*, 5–20. doi:10.1002/car.1084

Goodson, J., Helstrom, A., Halpern, J. M., Ferenschak, M. P., Gillihan, S. J., & Powers, M. B. (2011). Treatment of posttraumatic stress disorder in US combat veterans: A meta-analytic review. *Psychological Reports, 109*, 573–599. doi:10.2466/02.09.15.16.PR0.109.5.573-599

Gould, M. S. (2010). Schools and suicide: Latest and best school-based strategies. Webinar hosted by WellAware and the Wyoming Department of Health.

Graham-Kevan, N., & Archer, J. (2003). Physical aggression and control in heterosexual relationships: The effects of sampling. *Violence and Victims, 18*, 181–196. doi:10.1891/vivi.2003.18.2.181

Granello, D. H., & Granello, P. F. (2007a). *Suicide: An essential guide for helping professionals and educators.* Boston, MA: Allyn & Bacon.

Granello D. H., & Granello P. F. (2007b). Suicide assessment: Strategies for determining risk. *Counselling, Psychotherapy, and Health, 3*(1), 42–51.

Green, T., Buckman, J., Dandeker, C., & Greenberg, N. (2010). The impact of culture clash on deployed troops. *Military Medicine, 175*, 958–963. doi:10.7205/MILMED-D-10-00146

Greenberg, L. S., & Pascual-Leone, A. (2006). Emotion in psychotherapy: a practice-friendly research review. *Journal of Clinical Psychology: In Session, 62*, 611–630. doi:10.1002/jclp.20252

Greenstone, J. L., & Leviton, L. C. (2011). *Elements of crisis intervention: Crisis and how to respond to them* (3rd ed.). Pacific Grove, CA: Brooks/Cole.

Grepmair, L., Mitterlehner, F., Loew, T., Bachler, E., Rother, W., & Nickel, M. (2007). Promoting mindfulness in psychotherapists in training influences the treatment results of their patients: A randomized, double-blind, controlled study. *Psychotherapy and Psychosomatics, 76*, 332–338. doi:10.1159/000107560

Groth, A. N. (2001). *Men and rape: The psychology of the offender.* New York, NY: Basic Books.

Grubb, A. (2010). Modern day hostage (crisis) negotiation: The evolution of an art form within the policing arena. *Aggression & Violent Behavior, 15*(5), 341–348. doi:10.1016/j.avb.2010.06.002

Guldin, M., O'Connor, M., Sokolowski, I., Jensen, A. B., & Vedsted, P. (2011). Identifying bereaved subjects at risk of complicated grief: Predictive value of questionnaire items in a cohort study. *BMC Palliative Care, 9*, 1–9. doi:10.1186/1472-684X-10-9

Gunderson, J., Grill, M., Callahan, P., & Marks, M. (2014, March). Evidence-based program improves & sustains first-responder behavioral health. *Journal of Emergency Medical Services.*

Halifax, J. (2011). *Being with dying: Cultivating compassion and fearlessness in the presence of death.* Boston: MA: Shambhala.

Hammersly, R. (2014). Constraint theory: A cognitive, motivational theory of dependence. *Addiction Research and Theory, 22*(1), 1–14. doi:10.3109/16066359.2013.779678

Hanson, R. K., Bourgon, G., Helmus, L., & Hodgson, S. (2009). The principles of effective correctional treatment also apply to sexual offenders: A meta-analysis. *Criminal Justice and Behavior, 36*, 865–891. doi:10.1177/0093854809338545

Hanson, R. K., Harris, A. J. R, Scott, T.-L., & Helmus, L. (2007). Assessing the risk of sexual offenders on community supervision: The dynamic supervision project. Retrieved from http://www.publicsafety.gc.ca/res/cor/rep/_fl/crp2007-05-en.pdf

Hanson, R. K., Lloyd, C. D., Helmus, L., & Thornton, D. (2012). Developing non-arbitrary metrics for risk communication: Percentile ranks for the Static-99/R and Static-2002/R sexual offender risk tools. *International Journal of Forensic Mental Health, 11*, 9–23. doi:10.1080/14999013.2012.667511

Hanson, R. K., & Thornton, D. (2000). Improving risk assessments for sex offenders: A comparison of three actuarial scales. *Law and Human Behavior, 24*, 119–136. doi:10.1023/A:1005482921333

Hanson, R. K., & Yates, P. M. (2013). Psychological treatment of sex offenders. *Current Psychiatry Reports, 15*, 1–8.

Hard, P. F. (2012, April). *In the eye of recovery: Disaster interventions and considerations with sexual minorities.* Presented at Auburn University Research Week, Auburn, AL.

Harrington, J. A. (2007, March). Obstacles in effective suicide intervention in suicide: Responding to the emergency. Training workshop for Chilton Shelby Mental Health Center, Birmingham, AL.

Harrington, J. A. (2011, September). Safety plan design with notes for mental health professionals. Suicide training session with Gateway Family Services, Birmingham, AL.

Harris, J. I., Erbes, C. R., Engdahl, B. E., Thuras, P., Murray-Swank, N., Grace, D., . . . Le, T. V. (2011). The effectiveness of a trauma-focused spiritually integrated intervention for veterans exposed to trauma. *Journal of Clinical Psychology, 67*, 425–438. doi:10.1002/jclp.20777

Hart, S. D., Kropp, P. R., Laws, D. R., Klaver, J., Logan, C., & Watt, K. A. (2003). *The Risk for Sexual Violence Protocol (RSVP): Structured professional guidelines for assessing risk of sexual violence.* Burnaby, BC: Mental Health, Law, and Policy Institute, Simon Fraser University.

Hassan, M., Killion, C., Lewin, L., Totten, V., & Gary, F. (2015). Gender-related sexual abuse experiences reported by children who were examined in an emergency department. *Archives of Psychiatric Nursing, 29*(3), 148–154. doi:10.1016/j.apnu.2015.01.006

Hatton, R. (2003). Homicide bereavement counseling: A survey of providers. *Death Studies, 27*, 427–448. doi:10.1080/07481180302878

Hayden, S. (2011). Addressing needs of military families during deployment: Military service providers' perceptions of integrating support services. University of Virginia. ProQuest Dissertation and Thesis Abstracts (UMI No. 3485316).

Haynes, H., & Stein, G. (2016). U.S. fire department profile 2014. Retrieved from www.nfpa.org/news-and-research/fire-statistics-and-reports/fire-statistics/the-fire-service/administration/us-fire-department-profile

Hays, D. G., & Erford, B. T. (2018). *Developing multicultural counseling competence* (3rd ed.). Columbus, OH: Pearson Merrill.

Healey, L., Humphreys, C., & Howe, K. (2013). Inclusive domestic violence standards: Strategies to improve interventions for women with disabilities? *Violence and Victims, 28*, 50–68. doi:10.1891/0886-6708.28.1.50

Health Insurance Portability and Accountability Act of 1996. 42 U.S.C. § 1320d-9 (2011).

Healthcare Providers Service Organization. (2014). Documentation: An important step in avoiding malpractice. Retrieved from http://www.hpso.com/risk-education/individuals/articles/Documentation-An-important-step-in-avoiding-malpractice

Healthcare Providers Service Organization. (2015). Documentation do's and dont's. Retrieved from http://www.hpso.com/risk-education/individuals/articles/Documentation-Dos-and-Donts

Healthcare Providers Service Organization. (2016). Good documentation brings peace of mind. Retrieved from http://www.hpso.com/risk-education/individuals/articles/Good-Documentation-Brings-Peace-of-Mind

Healthcare Providers Service Organization. (2017). When to disclose confidential information. Retrieved from http://www.hpso.com/risk-education/individuals/articles/When-to-Disclose-Confidential-Information-Counselor-Version.

Hebda, T., & Czar, P. (2013). *Handbook of informatics for nurses & healthcare professionals* (5th ed.). Boston, MA: Pearson.

Hedlund, J., & Vieweg, B. (1984). The Michigan Alcoholism Screening Test (MAST): A comprehensive review. *Journal of Operational Psychiatry, 15*, 55–64.

Heick, R., Young, T., & Peek-Asa, C. (2009). Occupational injuries among emergency medical service providers in the United States. *Journal of Occupational and Environmental Medicine, 51*(B), 963–968. doi:10.1097/JOM.0b013e3181af6b76

Helmus, L., Thornton, D., Hanson, R. K., & Babchishin, K. M. (2012). Improving the predictive accuracy of Static-99 and Static-2002 with older sex offenders: Revised age weights. *Sex Abuse, 24*, 64–101. doi:10.1177/1079063211409951

Hernandez, P., Engstrom, D., & Gangsei, D. (2010). Exploring the impact of trauma on therapists: Vicarious resilience and related concepts in training. *Journal of Systemic Therapies, 29*(1), 67–83. doi:10.1521/jsyt.2010.29.1.67

Hernandez, P., Gansei, D., & Engstrom, D. (2007). Vicarious resilience: A new concept in work with those who survive trauma. *Family Process, 46*, 229–241. doi:10.1111/j.1545-5300.2007.00206.x

Hernandez, G., Hamdani, S., Rajabi, H., Conover, K., Stewart, J., Arvanitogiannis, A., . . . Shizgal, P. (2006). Prolonged rewarding stimulation of the rat medial forebrain bundle: Neurochemical and behavioral consequences. *Behavioral Neuroscience, 120*, 888–904. doi:10.1037/0735-7044.120.4.888

Hetzel-Riggin, M. D., Brausch, A. M., & Montgomery, B. S. (2007). A meta-analytic investigation of therapy modality outcomes for sexually abused children and adolescents: An exploratory study. *Child Abuse and Neglect, 31*, 125–141. doi:10.1016/j.chiabu.2006.10.007

Hien, D., & Ruglass, L. (2009). Interpersonal partner violence and women in the United States: An overview of prevalence rates, psychiatric correlates and consequences and barriers to help seeking. *International Journal of Law and Psychiatry, 32*, 48–55. doi:10.1016/j.iljp.2008.11.003

Hill, R. (1949). *Families under stress*. Westport, CT: Greenwood Press.

Hill, R. (1958). Social stresses on the family: Generic features of families under stress. *Social Casework, 39*, 139–150.

Hillbrand, M. (2001). Homicide-suicide and other forms of co-occurring aggression against self and others. *Professional Psychology: Research and Practice, 32*, 626–635. doi:10.1037/0735-7028.32.6.626

Hines, D. A., & Finkelhor, D. (2007). Statutory sex crime relationships between juveniles and adults: A review of social scientific research. *Aggression and Violent Behavior, 12*, 300–314. doi:10.1016/j.avb.2006.10.001

Ho, M. K., & Lee, C. W. (2012). Cognitive behaviour therapy versus eye movement desensitization and reprocessing for post-traumatic disorder—Is it all in the homework then? *European Review of Applied Psychology, 62*(4), 253–260. doi:10.1016/j.erap.2012.08.001

Holtzworth-Munroe, A., Bates, L., Smultzer, N., & Sandin, E. (2007). A brief review of the research on husband violence. *Aggression and Violent Behavior, 2*, 65–99.

Hooyman, N. R., & Kramer, J. (2008). *Living through loss: Interventions across the lifespan*. New York, NY: Columbia University Press.

Hopper, J. (2010). Sexual abuse of males: Prevalence, possible lasting effects, and resources. Retrieved from http://www.jimhopper.com/male-ab/

Horne, C. (2003). Families of homicide victims: Utilization patterns of extra- and intrafamilial homicide survivors. *Journal of Family Violence, 18*(2), 75–82. doi:10.1023/A:1022831530134

Horvath, A. O., Del Re, A. C., Fluckiger, C., & Symonds, D. (2012). Alliance in individual psychotherapy. In J. C. Norcross (Ed.), *Psychotherapy relationships that work: Therapist contributions and responsiveness to patients* (2nd ed., pp. 37–69). New York, NY: Oxford University Press.

Horwitz, A. V., & Wakefield, J. C. (2012). *The loss of sadness: How psychiatry transformed normal sorrow into depressive disorder* (Reprint ed.). New York, NY: Oxford University Press.

Hoshmand, L. T., & Hoshmand, A. (2007). Support for military families and communities. *Journal of Community Psychology, 35*, 171–180. doi:10.1002/jcop.20141

Houser, R. A., & Thoma, S. (2012). *Ethics in counseling and therapy: Developing an ethical identity*. Thousand Oaks, CA: Sage.

Hsu, J. (2014). Overview of military culture. Retrieved from https://www.apa.org/about/gr/issues/military/military-culture.pdf

Huebner, A. J., Mancini, J. A., Wilcox, R. M., Grass, S. R., & Grass, G. A. (2007). Parental deployment and youth in military families: Exploring uncertainty and ambiguous loss. *Family Relations, 56*, 112–122. doi:10.1111/j.1741-3729.2007.00445.x

Hughes, A., & Gilmour, N. (2010). Attitudes and perceptions of work safety among community mental health workers. *North American Journal of Psychology, 12*, 129–144.

Humphrey, K. M. (2009). *Counseling strategies for loss and grief*. Alexandria, VA: American Counseling Association.

Humphreys, C., & Thiara, R. K. (2003). Neither justice nor protection: Women's experiences of post-separation violence. *Journal of Social Welfare and Family Law, 25*, 195–214. doi:10.1080/0964906032000145948

Hunter, S. V. (2010). Evolving narratives about childhood sexual abuse: Challenging the dominance of the victim and survivor paradigm. *Australian & New Zealand Journal of Family Therapy, 31*(2), 176–190. doi:10.1375/anft.31.2.176

Hyman, I., Forte, T., DuMont, J., Romans, S., & Cohen, M. M. (2009). Help-seeking behavior for intimate partner violence among racial minority women in Canada. *Women's Health Issues, 19*, 101–108. doi:10.1016/j.whi.2008.10.002

Institute of Medicine. (IOM). (2010). *Returning home from Iraq and Afghanistan: Preliminary assessment of readjustment needs of veterans, service members, and their families*. Washington, DC: National Academies Press. Retrieved from http://books.nap.edu/openbook.php?record_id=12812&page=R1

International Association for Suicide Prevention. (2000). Guidelines for suicide prevention. Retrieved from http://www.med.uio.no/iasp/english/guidelines.html

International Labor Organization. (2012). Global estimate of forced labour: Executive summary. Retrieved from http://www.ilo.org/wcmsp5/groups/public/declaration/documents/publication/wcms_181953.pdf

Iraq and Afghanistan Veterans of America. (2014). 2014 IAVA member survey: Perceptions and views from Iraq and Afghanistan combat veterans on the challenges and successes of the new greatest generation of veterans. Retrieved from http://media.iava.org/IAVA_Member_Survey_2014.pdf

Ivey, A. E., Ivey, M. B., & Zalaquett, C. P. (2014). *Intentional interviewing and counseling* (8th ed.). Stamford, CT: Cengage Learning.

Jackson-Cherry, L. (2009). *The importance of counselor awareness and training in the death notification process: A new role for professional counselors*. Alexandria, VA: American Counseling Association.

Jacobs, D. G. (Ed.). (1999). *The Harvard Medical School guide to suicide assessment and intervention*. San Francisco, CA: Jossey-Bass.

Jacobs, E., Masson, R., Harvill, R., & Schimmel, C. (2012). *Group counseling: Strategies and skills* (7th ed.). Belmont, CA: Brooks/Cole Cengage Learning.

James, R., & Gilliland, B. (2017). *Crisis intervention strategies* (8th ed.). Boston, MA: Cengage.

James, S. (2009). Romeo and Juliet were sex offenders: An analysis of the age of consent and a call for reform. *UMKC Law Review, 1*, 241–262.

Jaycox, L., Zoellner, L., & Foa, E. (2002). Cognitive-behavior therapy for PTSD in rape survivors. *Psychotherapy in Practice, 58*, 891–906. doi:10.1002/jclp.10065

Jellinek, E. M. (1960). *The disease concept of alcoholism.* New Brunswick, NJ: Hillhouse Press.

Jennings, J. L., & Deming, A. (2013). Effectively utilizing the "behavioral" in cognitive-behavioral group therapy of sex offenders. *International Journal of Behavioral Consultation and Therapy, 8*(2), 7–13. doi:10.1037/h0100968

Jennings, W. G., Zgoba, K. M., Maschi, T., & Reingle, J. M. (2014). An empirical assessment of the overlap between sexual victimization and sex offending. *International Journal of Offender Therapy & Comparative Criminology, 58*, 1466–1480. doi:10.1177/0306624X13496544

Jobes, D. A. (2008). Collaborative assessment and management of suicidality. Training seminar hosted by Health Education, Birmingham, AL.

Jobes, D. A. (2016). *Managing suicidal risk second edition: A collaborative approach.* New York, NY: Guilford Press.

Jobes, D. A., & O'Connor, S. (2016). Managing suicide risk collaboratively: The CAMS framework. Retrieved from http://www.empathos.resources.com

Johnson, B. (2012). Aftercare for survivors of human trafficking. *Social Work and Christianity, 39*(4), 370–389.

Johnson, D. (2015). *PLAID PALS: Dave's suicide risk assessment* [Kindle]. Retrieved from http://www.amazon.com/kindle/dp/B00VS6L7NO/ref=rdr_kindle_ext_eos_detail

Johnson, R., Persad, G., & Sisti, D. (2014). The Tarasoff rule: The implications of interstate variation and gaps in professional training. *The Journal of the American Academy of Psychiatry and the Law, 42*, 469–477.

Joiner, T. E. (2005). *Why people die by suicide.* Cambridge, MA: Harvard University Press.

Jongsma, A. E. (2014). *The crisis counseling and traumatic events treatment planner* (2nd ed.). Hoboken, NJ: John Wiley & Sons.

Jordan, J. R. (2006). Suicide survivors defining needs and interventions. Retrieved from http://www.med.navy.mil/sites/nmcphc/Documents/health-promotion-wellness/psychological-emotional-wellbeing/suicide-survivors.pdf

Juhnke, G. A., Vacc, N. A., Curtis, R. C., Coll, K. M., & Paredes, D. M. (2003). Assessment instruments used by addictions counselors. *Journal of Addictions and Offender Counseling, 23*, 66–72. doi:10.1002/j.2161-1874.2003.tb00171.x

Juodis, A., Starzomski, A., & Porter, S. (2014). A comparison of domestic and non-domestic homicides: Further evidence for distinct dynamics and heterogeneity of domestic homicide perpetrators. *Journal of Family Violence, 29*, 299–313. doi:10.1007/s10896-014-9583-8

Juodis, M., Starzomski, A., Porter, S., & Woodworth, M. (2014). What can be done about high-risk perpetrators of domestic violence? *Journal of Family Violence, 29*, 381–390. doi:10.1007/s10896-014-9597-2

Jussab, F., & Murphy, H. (2015). "I just can't" "I'm frightened for my safety. I don't know how to work with her": Practitioners' experiences of client violence and recommendations for future practice. *Professional Psychology Research and Practice, 46*, 287–297. doi:10.1037/pro0000035

Kalafat, J., Gould, M. S., & Munfakh, J. L. H. (2005). Final progress report: Hotline Evaluation and Linkage Project Category II. Washington, DC: Substance Abuse and Mental Health Services Administration.

Kanable, R. (2010). Death notifications: The toughest job in law enforcement. *Police and Security News, 26*(2), 1–4.

Kanan, L. M. (2010). When students make threats. *Tech Directions, 70*(5), 31–35.

Kaplan, M., McFarland, H., Huguet, N., & Newsom, J. (2012). Estimating the risk of suicide among U.S. veterans: How should we proceed from here? *American Journal of Public Health, 102*(S1), S21–S23. doi:10.2105/AJPH.2011.300611

Kaplan, W. A., & Lee, B. A. (2013). *The law of higher education* (5th ed.). San Francisco, CA: Josey Bass.

Kehle-Forbes, S. M., Meis, L. A., Spoont, M. R., & Polusny, M. A. (2015). Treatment initiation and dropout from prolonged exposure and cognitive processing therapy in a VA outpatient clinic. *Psychological Trauma: Theory, Research, Practice, and Policy.* doi:10.1037/tra0000065

Kellogg, N. D. (2010). Sexual behaviors in children: Evaluation and management. *American Family Physician, 82*, 1233–1238.

Kent, M., Davis, M., Stark, S., & Stewart, L. (2011). A resilience-oriented treatment of posttraumatic stress disorder: Results of a preliminary randomized clinical trial. *Journal of Traumatic Stress, 34*, 591–595. doi:10.1002/jts.20685

Kerr, M. M. (2009). *School crisis prevention and intervention.* Columbus, OH: Pearson Merrill Prentice Hall.

Khawaja, M., Linos, N., & El-Roueiheb, Z. (2008). Attitudes of men and women towards wife beating: Findings from Palestinian refugee camps in Jordan. *Journal of Family Violence, 23*, 21–218. doi:10.1007/s10896-007-9146-3

Kilpatrick, D. G. (1988). Rape aftermath symptom test. In M. Hersen & A. S. Bellack (Eds.), *Dictionary of behavioral assessment techniques* (pp. 366–367). New York, NY: Pergamon Press.

Kim, K., Trickett, P. K., & Putnam, F. W. (2010). Childhood experiences of sexual abuse and later parenting practices among non-offending mothers of sexually abused and comparison girls. *Child Abuse & Neglect, 34*, 610–622. doi:10.1016/j.chiabu.2010.01.007

Kime, P. (2015, April 1). Study: No link between combat deployment and suicides. *Military Times*. Retrieved from http://www.militarytimes.com/story/military/benefits/health-care/2015/04/01/suicide-troops-veterans-combat-study-says-no-link-between-combat-deployment-suicides/70771276/

Kinch, M. S., Haynesworth, A., Kinch, S. L., & Hoyer, D. (2014). An overview of FDA-approved new molecular entities: 1827–2013. *Drug Discovery Today, 19*, 1033–1039. doi:10.1016/j.drudis. 2014.03.018

Kistenmacher, B. R., & Weiss, R. L. (2008). Motivational interviewing as a mechanism for change in men who batter: A randomized control trial. *Violence and Victims, 23*, 558–570. doi:10.1891/0886-6708.23.5.558

Kivisto, A. J., Berman, A., Watson, M., Gruber, D., & Paul, H. (2015). North American psychologists' experiences of stalking, threatening, and harassing behavior. A survey of ABPP Diplomates. *Professional Psychology: Research and Practice, 46*, 277–286. doi:10.1037/pro0000025

Kleespies, P. M. (1998). *Emergencies in mental health practice*. New York, NY: Guilford Press.

Klott, J., & Jongsma, A. E. Jr. (2015). *The suicide and risk assessment and prevention treatment planner with DSM-5 updates*. Hoboken, NJ: Wiley & Sons.

Knapp, S. J., & VandeCreek, L. D. (2012). *Practical ethics for psychologists: A positive approach* (2nd ed.). Washington, DC: American Psychological Association.

Knox, K. S., & Roberts, A. R. (2005). Crisis intervention and crisis team models in schools. *Children and Schools, 27*(2), 93–100. doi:10.1093/cs/27.2.93

Kohlberg, L. (1976). Moral stages and moralization: The cognitive-developmental approach. In T. Lickona (Ed.), *Moral development and behavior: Theory, research, and social issues* (pp. 41–59). New York, NY: Holt, Rinehart, and Winston.

Kohlberg, L. (1984). *The psychology of moral development: The nature and validity of moral stages (Essays on Moral Development, Volume 2)*. San Francisco, CA: Harper & Row.

Koss, M. P. (1993). Detecting the scope of rape: A review of prevalence research methods. *Journal of Interpersonal Violence, 8*, 198–222. doi:10.1177/088626093008002004

Kress, V. E., Protivnak, J. J., & Sadlak, L. (2008). Counseling clients involved with violent intimate partners: The mental health counselor's role in promoting client safety. *Journal of Mental Health Counseling, 30*, 200–210. doi:10.17744/mehc.30.3.e0r8773472l6016

Kübler-Ross, E. (1969). *On death and dying*. New York, NY: Collier Books.

Kübler-Ross, E. (1972). *Questions and answers on death and dying*. New York, NY: Simon and Schuster/Touchstone.

Kübler-Ross, E. (1975). *Death: The final stage of growth*. Englewood Cliffs, NJ: Prentice-Hall.

Kübler-Ross, E., & Kessler, D. (2005). *On grief and grieving*. New York, NY: Scribner.

Laajasalo, T., & Hakkanen, H. (2004). Background characteristics of mentally ill homicide offenders: A comparison of five diagnostic groups. *Journal of Forensic Psychiatry and Psychology, 15*, 451–474. doi:10.1080/1478994042000226750

Lambert, S. F., & Lawson, G. (2013). Resilience of professional counselors following Hurricanes Katrina and Rita. *Journal of Counseling & Development, 91*, 261–268. doi:10.1002/j.1556-6676.2013.00094.x

Landau, J., & Hissett, J. (2008). Mild traumatic brain injury: Impact on identity and ambiguous loss in the family. *Families, Systems, and Health, 1*, 69–85. doi:10.1037/1091-7527.26.1.69

Langan, P. A., Schmitt, E. L., & Durose, M. R. (2003). *Recidivism of sex offenders released from prison in 1994*. Retrieved from http://www.bjs.gov/content/pub/pdf/rsorp94.pdf

Langdon, S., Armour, C., & Stringer, M. (2014). Adult experience of mental health outcomes as a result of intimate partner violence victimisation: A systematic review. *European Journal of Psychotraumatology, 5*, 247–294. doi:10.3402/ejpt.v5.24794

Lanning, K. V. (2010). *Child molesters: A behavioral analysis for professionals investigating the sexual exploitation of children*. Alexandria, VA: National Center for Missing and Exploited Children.

Large, M. M., Ryan, C. J., Singh, S. P., Paton, M. B., & Nielssen, O. B. (2011). The predictive value of risk categorization in schizophrenia. *Harvard Review of Psychiatry, 19*(1), 25–33. doi:10.3109/10673229.2011.549770

Largen, M. A. (1985). The anti-rape movement—Past and present. In A. W. Burgess (Ed.), *Rape and sexual assault: A research handbook* (pp. 1–13). New York, NY: Garland.

Larned, J. G. (2010). Understanding police suicide. *Forensic Examiner, 19*(3), 64–71, 125.

Larson, D. R., & Hoyt, W. T. (2007). What has become of grief counseling? An evaluation of the empirical foundations of the new pessimism. *Professional Psychology: Research and Practice, 38*, 347–355. doi:10.1037/0735-7028.38.4.347

Laser, J. A., & Stephens, P. M. (2011). Working with military families through deployment and beyond. *Clinical Social Work Journal, 39*(1), 28–38. doi:10.1007/s10615-010-0310-5

Laux, J. M. (2002). A primer on suicidology: Implications for counselors. *Journal of Counseling & Development, 80*, 380–384.

Laws, D. R., & Marshall, W. L. (2003). A brief history of behavioral and cognitive behavioral approaches to sexual offenders: Part 1. Early developments. *Sexual Abuse: A Journal of Research and Treatment, 15*, 75–92. doi:10.1023/A:1022325231175

Lawson, G., & Myers, J. E. (2011). Wellness, professional quality of life, and career sustaining behaviors: What keeps us well? *Journal of Counseling & Development, 89*, 163–171.

Lawson, G., & Venart, B. (2005). Preventing counselor impairment: Vulnerability, wellness, and resilience. In G. R. Walz & R. K. Yep (Eds.), *VISTAS: Compelling perspectives on counseling 2005* (pp. 243–246). Alexandria, VA: American Counseling Association.

Lawson, G., Venart, E., Hazler, R. J., & Kottler, J. A. (2007). Toward a culture of counselor wellness. *Journal of Humanistic Counseling, Education & Development, 46*(1), 5–19.

Lee, R., Caruso, M., Goins, S., & Southerland, J. (2003). Addressing sexual assault on college campuses: Guidelines for a prevention/awareness week. *Journal of College Counseling, 6*(1), 14. doi:10.1002/j.2161-1882.2003.tb00223.x

Lee, S. M., Cho, S. H., Kissinger, D., & Ogle, N. T. (2010). A typology of burnout in professional counselors. *Journal of Counseling & Development, 88*, 131–138. doi:10.1002/j.1556-6678.2010.tb00001.x

Leiter, M. P., & Maslach, C. (2009). Nurse turnover: The mediating role of burnout. *Journal of Nursing Management, 17*, 331–339. doi:10.1111/j.1365-2834.2009.01004.x

Letourneau, E. J., & Borduin, C. M. (2008). The effective treatment of juveniles who sexually offend: An ethical imperative. *Ethics and Behavior, 18*, 286–306. doi:10.1080/10508420802066940

Lewis, J. A., Dana, R. Q., & Blevins, G. A. (2002). *Substance abuse counseling* (3rd ed.). Pacific Grove, CA: Brooks/Cole.

Li, C., Inman, A., & Alvarez, A. (2018). Individuals and families of Asian descent. In D. G. Hays & B. T. Erford (Eds.), *Developing multicultural counseling competence: A systems approach* (3rd ed., pp. 246–276). Boston, MA: Pearson.

Lies, M. A., & Simonsen, C. B. (2015). Workplace violence: Putting employers on the horns of a dilemma. *Professional Safety, 60*(6), 25–27.

Lincoln, A., Swift, E., & Shorteno-Fraser, M. (2008). Psychological adjustment and treatment of children and families with parents deployed in military combat. *Journal of Clinical Psychology: In Session, 64*, 984–992. doi:10.1002/jclp.20520

Lindemann, E. (1944). Symptomatology and management of acute grief. *American Journal of Psychiatry, 101*, 141–148. doi:10.1176/ajp.101.2.141

Ling, J., Hunter, S. V., & Maple, M. (2014). Navigating the challenges of trauma counselling: How counsellors thrive and sustain their engagement. *Australian Social Work, 67*, 297–310. doi:10.1080/0312407X.2013.837188

Linley, P., & Joseph, S. (2004). Positive change following trauma and adversity: A review. *Journal of Traumatic Stress, 17*, 11–21. doi:10.1023/B:JOTS.0000014671.27856.7e

Lipsky, S., Caetano, R., & Roy-Byrne, P. (2009). Racial and ethnic disparities in police-reported intimate partner violence and risk of hospitalization among women. *Women's Health Issues, 19*, 109–118. doi:10.1016/j.whi.2008.09.005

Lisak, D., Gardinier, L., Nicksa, S. C., & Cote, A. M. (2010). False allegations of sexual assault: An analysis of ten years of reported cases. *Violence Against Women, 16*, 1318–1334. doi:10.1177/1077801210387747

Loeber, R., & Farrington, D. P. (2011). *Young homicide offenders and victims: Development, risk factors and prediction from childhood.* New York, NY: Springer.

Logan, K. V. (1987). The emotional cycle of deployment. *U.S. Naval Institute Proceedings, 113*, 43–47.

Logan, T. K., Walker, R., & Shannon, L. (2008). Factors associated with separation and ongoing violence among women with civil protective orders. *Journal of Family Violence, 23*, 377–385. doi:10.1007/s10896-008-9164-9

Lonergarn, M. (2014). Cognitive behavioral therapy for PTSD: The role of complex PTDS on treatment outcome. *Journal of Aggression, Maltreatment & Trauma, 23*, 494–512. doi:10.1080/10926771.2014.904467

Lonsway, K. A., Archambault, J., & Lisak, D. (2009). False reports: Moving beyond the issue to successfully investigate and prosecute non-stranger sexual assault. *The Voice, 3*(1), 1–11. Retrieved from http://ndaa.org/pdf/the_voice_vol_3_no_1_2009.pdf

Lopes, A. P., Macedo, T. F., Coutinho, E., Figueira, I., & Ventura, P. R. (2014). Systematic review of efficacy of cognitive-behavior therapy related to treatments for victims of natural disasters: A worldwide problem. *PLoS ONE, 9*(10), 1–11.

Lowenberg, T. J. (2016). The role of the national guard in national defense and homeland security. Retrieved from http://www.ngaus.org/sites/default/files/pdf/primer%20fin.pdf

Luepker, E. (2012). *Record keeping in psychotherapy and counseling: Protecting confidentiality and the professional relationship* (2nd ed.). New York, NY: Routledge.

Luthar, S. S. (2006) Resilience in development: A synthesis of research across five decades. In D. Cicchetti & D. J. Cohen (Eds.), *Developmental psychopathology. Volume 3. Risk, disorder, and adaptation* (2nd ed., pp. 739–795). New York, NY: Wiley.

Mahoney, A. (2010). Religion in families—1999–2009: A relational spirituality framework. *Journal of Marriage and Family, 72*, 805–827. doi:10.1111/j.1741-3737.2010.00732.x

Mann, J. J., Apter, A., Bertolote, J., Beautrais, A., Currier, D., Haas, A., . . . Hendin, H. (2005). Suicide prevention strategies: A systematic review. *Journal of the American Medical Association, 294*, 2064–2074. doi:10.1001/jama.294.16.2064

Maris, R. W. (1992). Overview of the study of suicide assessment and prediction. In R. W. Maris, A. L. Berman, J. T. Maltsberger, & R. I. Yufit (Eds.), *The assessment and prediction of suicide* (pp. 3–22). New York, NY: Guilford Press.

Maris, R. W., Berman, A. L., & Silverman, M. M. (2000). *Comprehensive textbook of suicidology*. New York, NY: Guilford Press.

Marlatt, G. A. (Ed.). (1998). *Harm reduction: Pragmatic strategies for managing high-risk behaviors*. New York, NY: Guilford Press.

Marques, J. K., Wiederanders, M., Day, D. M., Nelson, C., & van Ommeren, A. (2005). Effects of a relapse prevention program on sexual recidivism: Final results from California's Sex Offender Treatment and Evaluation Project (SOTEP). *Sexual Abuse: A Journal of Research and Treatment, 17*, 79–107.

Martin, J. (2015, January 9). Student sues University of Oregon coach over alleged gang-rape [Television series episode]. Retrieved from http://www.cnn.com/2015/01/09/justice/university-of-oregon-title-ix-lawsuit/

Maslach, C. (2003). Job burnout: New directions in research and intervention. *Current Directions in Psychological Science, 12*, 189–192. doi:10.1111/1467-8721.01258

Mason, J. (2013). *Reporting child abuse and neglect in North Carolina.* (3rd ed.). Chapel Hill, NC: UNC School of Government.

Masten, A. S., & Obradovic, J. (2008). Disaster preparation and recovery: Lessons from research on resilience in human development. *Ecology and Society, 13*(1), 9.

Mathews, R., Matthews, J. K., & Speltz, K. (1989). *Female sexual offenders: An exploratory study*. Orwell, VT: Safer Society Press.

Mayo Clinic. (2016). Complicated grief. Retrieved from http://www.mayoclinic.com/health/complicated-grief/DS01023/DSECTION=2

McCabe, O. L., Everly Jr., G. S., Brown, L. M., Wendelboe, A. M., Hamad, N. H. A., Tallchief, V. L., . . . Links, J. M. (2014). Psychological first aid: A consensus-derived, empirically supported, competency-based training model. *American Journal of Public Health, 104*, 621–628. doi:10.2105/AJPH.2013.301219

McCubbin, H. I., & Patterson, J. M. (1982). Family adaptation to crisis. In H. I. McCubbin, A. E. Cauble, & J. M. Patterson (Eds.), *Family stress, coping, and social support* (pp. 26–47). Springfield, IL: Charles C. Thomas.

McGothlin, J. (2008). *Developing clinical skills in suicide assessment, prevention, and treatment*. Alexandria, VA: American Counseling Association.

McKenry, P. C., & Price, S. J. (2005). *Families and change: Coping with stressful events and transitions* (3rd ed.). Thousand Oaks, CA: Sage.

McLeod, A. L., Hays, D. G., & Chang, C. Y. (2010). Experiences of female intimate partner violence survivors: Accessing personal and community resources. *Journal of Counseling & Development, 88*, 303–310. doi:10.1002/j.1556-6678.2010.tb00026.x

McLeod, D. (2015). Female offenders in child sexual abuse cases: A national picture. *Journal of Child Sexual Abuse, 24*(1), 97–113. doi:10.1080/10538712.2015.978925

McLeod, S. A. (2013). Kohlberg. Retrieved from http://www.simplypsychology.org/kohlberg.html

Mee-Lee, D. (2013). How to really use the new edition of the ASAM criteria: What to do and what not to do. Retrieved from http://www.counselormagazine.com/2013/Nov-Dec/ASAM_Criteria/

Meichenbaum, D. H. (1996). Stress inoculation training for coping with stressors. *The Clinical Psychologist, 49*, 4–7.

Meloy, J. R., Hoffiman, J., Guldimann, M. A., & James, D. (2011). The role of warning behaviors in threat assessment: An exploration and suggested typology. *Behavioral Sciences and the Law, 30*, 256–279. doi:10.1002/bsl.999

Meloy, J. R., & O'Toole, M. E. (2011). The concept of leakage in threat assessment. *Behavioral Sciences and the Law, 29*, 513–527. doi:10.1002/bsl.986

Miller, G. A. (1999). *The SASSI Manual Substance Abuse Measures* (2nd ed.). Springfield, IL: SASSI Institute.

Miller, T., Clayton, R., Miller, J. M., Bilyeu, J., Hunter, J., & Kraus, R. F. (2000). Violence in the schools: Clinical issues and case analysis for high-risk children. *Child Psychiatry and Human Development, 30*, 255–272. doi:10.1023/B:CHUD.0000037153.18246.70

Miller, W. R., & Hester, R. K. (2003). Treating alcohol problems: Toward an informed eclecticism. In R. K. Hester & W. R. Miller (Eds.), *Handbook of alcoholism treatment approaches: Effective alternatives* (3rd ed.) (pp. 1–12). Boston, MA: Allyn and Bacon.

Miller, W. R., & Rollnick, S. (2013). *Motivational interviewing: Helping people change* (3rd ed.). New York, NY: Guilford Press.

Miller, W. R., Wilbourne, P. L., & Hettema, J. E. (2003). What works? A summary of alcohol treatment outcome research. In R. K. Hester & W. R. Miller (Eds.), *Handbook of alcoholism treatment approaches: Effective alternatives* (3rd ed., pp. 13–63). Boston, MA: Allyn and Bacon.

Miller-Perrin, C. L., & Perrin, R. D. (2007). *Child maltreatment: An introduction* (2nd ed.). Thousand Oaks, CA: Sage.

Minnie, L., Goodman, S., & Wallis, Z. (2015). Exposure to daily trauma: The experiences and coping mechanism of emergency medical personnel. A cross-sectional study. *African Journal of Emergency Medicine, 5*(1), 12–18. doi:10.1016/j.afjem.2014.10.010

Mitra, M., Mouradian, V. E., & McKenna, M. (2013). Dating violence and associated health risks among high school students with disabilities. *Maternal and Child Health Journal, 17*, 1088–1094. doi:10.1007/s10995-012-1091-y

Mohl, A. (2010). Sexual abuse of the child: A treatment model for the incestuous family. *The Journal of Psychohistory, 38*, 168–181.

Monson, C. M., Schnurr, P. P., Resick, P. A., Friedman, M. J., Young-Xu, Y., & Stevens, S. P. (2006). Cognitive processing therapy for veterans with military-related posttraumatic stress disorder. *Journal of Consulting and Clinical Psychology, 74*, 898–907. doi:10.1037/0022-006X.74.5.898

Monteith, L. L., Menefee, D. S., Pettit, J. W., Leopoulos, W. L., & Vincent, J. P. (2013). Examining the interpersonal–psychological theory of suicide in an inpatient veteran sample. *Suicide and Life-Threatening Behavior, 43*, 418–428. doi:10.1111/sltb.12027

Montgomery County Emergency Service, Inc. (2006). After a suicide: A postvention primer for providers. *MCES Quest Comprehensive Behavioral Health Services, 5*(2), 1–11.

Mosley, C. (2013). The language we use: Victim and survivor. Retrieved from http://www.weendviolence.com/blog/2013/06/04/the-language-we-use-victim-and-survivor/

Moss, R., & Cook, C. C. H. (2012). Maintenance and relapse prevention. In D. Capuzzi, & M. D. Stauffer (Eds.), *Foundations of addictions counseling* (2nd ed., pp. 260–277). Upper Saddle River, NJ: Pearson.

Mueller, S., & Tschan, F. (2011). Consequences of client initiated workplace violence: The role of fear and perceived prevention. *Journal of Occupational Health Psychology, 16*, 217–229. doi:10.1037a0021723

Muldoon, J. P., & Gary, J. (2011). Motivating factors to enhance treatment compliance for male batterers: Getting them "in the door" and staying "in the room." *Journal of Mental Health Counseling, 33*, 144–160.

Murphy, C. M., & Ting, L. A. (2010). The effects of treatment for substance use problems on intimate partner violence: A review of empirical data. *Aggression and Violent Behavior, 15*, 325–333.

Murphy, G. (2010). *Following up with individuals at high risk for suicide: Developing a model for crisis hotline and emergency department collaboration.* New York, NY: National Suicide Prevention Lifeline.

Myers, J. E., Sweeney, T. J., & Witmer, J. M. (2000). The wheel of wellness counseling for wellness: A holistic model for treatment planning. *Journal of Counseling & Development, 78*, 251–266.

Nademin, E., Jobes, D. A., Pflanz, S. E., Jacoby, A. M., Ghahramanlou-Holloway, M., Campise, R., . . . Johnson, L. (2008). An investigation of interpersonal-psychological variables in Air Force suicides: A controlled-comparison study. *Archives of Suicide Research, 12*, 309–326. doi:10.1080/13811110802324847

Nason-Clark, N. (2009). Christianity and the experience of domestic violence: What does faith have to do with it? *Social Work and Christianity, 36*, 379–393.

National Action Alliance for Suicide Prevention, Suicide Attempt Survivors Task Force. (2014). *The way forward: Pathways to hope, recovery, and wellness with insights from lived experience.* Washington, DC: Author.

National Alliance of Mental Illness. (2016). Dual diagnosis and integrated treatment of mental illness and substance abuse disorder. Retrieved from https//www.nami.org/Learn-More/Mental-Health-Conditions/related-Conditions/Dual-Diagnosis

National Association of Emergency Medical Technicians. (2015). About us. Retrieved from http://www.naemt.org/about_ems.aspx

National Association of School Psychologists. (2015). Addressing grief. Retrieved from https://www.nasponline.org/resources-and-publications/resources/school-safety-and-crisis/addressing-grief

National Association of Social Workers. (2017). Verbal de-escalation techniques. Retrieved from http://www.naswma.org/?page=520

National Center for Victims of Crime. (2005). *Lethality risk assessment.* Washington, DC: Author.

National Center for Victims of Crime. (2009). Victim impact statements. Retrieved from http://www.ncvc.org/ncvc/main.aspx?dbName=DocumentViewer&DocumentID=32515

National Center for Victims of Crime. (2015). Workplace violence. Retrieved from http://victimsofcrime.org/docs/default-source/ncvrw2015/2015ncvrw_stats_workplace.pdf?sfvrsn=2

National Center on Elder Abuse. (2015). Elder abuse and prevalence. Retrieved from http://www.ncea.aoa.gov/nceroom/Main_Site/pdf/Publication/final Statis-tics050331.pdf

National Child Traumatic Stress Network. (2012). TF-CBT implementation manual. Retrieved from http://www.nctsnet.org/nctsn_assets/pdfs/TF-CBT_Implementation_Manual.pdf

National Coalition of Anti-Violence Programs. (2007). *Lesbian, gay, bisexual and transgender domestic violence in the United States in 2006.* Retrieved from http://www.ncavp.org/common/document_files/Reports/2006NationalDVReport(Final).pdf

National Conference of State Legislatures. (2015). Mental health professionals duty to warn. Retrieved from http://www.ncsl.org/research/health/mental-health-professionals-duty-to-warn.aspx

National Eating Disorder Association. (2012). Trauma and eating disorders. Retrieved from https://www.nationaleatingdisorders.org/sites/default/files/ResourceHandouts/TraumaandEatingDisorders.pdf

National Education Association. (2017). School crisis guide: Help and healing in a time of crisis. Retrieved from http://neahealthyfutures.org/wp-content/uploads/2015/05/schoolcrisisguide.pdf

National Institute of Justice. (2008). Drug-facilitated rape on campus. Retrieved from http://www.nij.gov/topics/crime/rape-sexual-violence/campus/pages/drug-facilitated.aspx

National Institute of Justice. (2009). *Practical implications of current domestic violence research: For law enforcement, prosecutors and judges*. Washington, DC: U.S. Department of Justice.

National Institute on Drug Abuse. (1980). *Theories on drug abuse: Selected contemporary perspectives* (NIDA Research Monograph 30). Washington, DC: U.S. Department of Health and Human Services.

National Law Enforcement Officer Memorial Fund. (2016). Law enforcement facts. Retrieved from http://www.nleomf.org/facts/enforcement/

National Resource Center on Domestic Violence. (2011). Lethality assessment tools: A critical analysis. Retrieved from http://www.vawnet.org/applied-research-papers/print-document.php?doc_id=387

National Suicide Prevention Lifeline. (2007). Lifeline suicide risk assessment policy: Lifeline suicide risk assessment standards. Retrieved from https://www.suicidepreventionlifeline.org/media/5388/Suicide-Risk-Assessment-Standards.pdf

National Terror Alert Response Center. (2017). Shelter in place: Know where, know how. Retrieved from http://www.nationalterroralert.com/shelterinplace/

National Volunteer Fire Council. (NVFC). (2014). Suicide in the fire and emergency services: Adopting a proactive approach to behavioral health awareness and suicide prevention. Retrieved from http://www.nvfc.org/files/documents/ff_suicide_report.pdf

Neimeyer, R. A. (2001). *Meaning reconstruction and the experience of loss*. Washington, DC: American Psychological Association.

New York State. (2015, July 7). Governor Cuomo signs "Enough is Enough" legislation to combat sexual assault on college and university campuses. Retrieved from http://www.governor.ny.gov/news/governor-cuomo-signs-enough-enough-legislation-combat-sexual-assault-college-and-university

Newell, J. M., & MacNeil, G. A. (2010). Professional burnout, vicarious trauma secondary traumatic stress and compassion fatigue: A review of theoretical terms, risk factors and prevention methods for clinicians and researchers. *Best Practices in Mental Health, 6*(2), 57–68.

Newland, C., Barber, E., Rose, M., & Young, A. (2015). *Survey reveals alarming rates of EMS provider stress and thoughts of suicide*. Retrieved from http://www.jems.com/articles/print/volume-40/issue-10/features/survey-reveals-alarming-rates-of-ems-provider-stress-and-thoughts-of-suicide.html

Newman, C. (2012). Back from the brink: Using CBT to help suicidal patient to choose to live. Seminar for Canterbury Methodist Church training. Birmingham, AL.

Newport, F. (2012). Seven in 10 Americans are moderately or very religious. Retrieved from http://www.gallup.com/poll/159050/seven-americans-moderately-religious.aspx?utm

Newsome, D. W., & Gladding, S. T. (2013). *Clinical mental health counseling in community and agency settings* (4th ed.). Columbus, OH: Pearson Merrill.

Norcross, J. C., Krebs, P. M., & Prochaska, J. O. (2011). Stages of change. *Journal of Clinical Psychology, 67*, 143–154. doi:10.1002/jclp.20758

Nordstrom, A., Dahlgren, L., & Kullgren, G. (2006). Victims' relations and factors triggering homicides committed by offenders with Schizophrenia. *Journal of Forensic Psychiatry and Psychology, 12*, 192–203. doi:10.1080/14789940600631522

Nordstrom, K., & Allen, M. H. (2007). Managing the acutely agitated and psychotic patient. *CNS Spectrum, 12*, 5–11.

Norris, H., & Rosen, C. S. (2009). Innovations in disaster mental health services and evaluation: National, state, and local responses to Hurricane Katrina (Introduction to the special issue). *Administrative Policy Mental Health, 36*, 159–164. doi:10.1007/s10488-009-0218-y

North, C. S. (2010). A tale of two studies of two disasters: Comparing psychosocial responses to disaster among Oklahoma City bombing survivors and Hurricane Katrina evacuees. *Rehabilitation Psychology, 55*, 241–246. doi:10.1037/a0020119

Occupational Safety and Health Administration. (2015). Guidelines for preventing workplace violence for healthcare and social service workers. Retrieved from https://www.osha.gov/Publications/osha3148.pdf

O'Farrell, T. J., & Fals-Stewart, W. (2003). Marital and family therapy. In R. K. Hester & W. R. Miller (Eds.), *Handbook of alcoholism treatment approaches: Effective alternatives* (3rd ed., pp. 188–212). Boston, MA: Allyn and Bacon.

Office of the Deputy Under Secretary of Defense. (2013). 2013 demographics report. Retrieved from http://download.militaryonesource.mil/12038/MOS/Reports/2013-Demographics-Report.pdf

Office of National Drug Control Policy. (2004). *The economic costs of drug abuse in the United States, 1992–2002*. Washington, DC: Executive Office of the President.

O'Halloran, T. M., & Linton, J. M. (2000). Stress on the job: Self-care resources for counsellors. *Journal of Mental Health Counseling, 22*, 354–364.

O'Hara, A. F., Violanti, J. M., Levenson Jr., R. L., & Clark, Sr., R. G. (2013). National police suicide estimates: Web surveillance study III. *International Journal of Emergency Mental Health and Human Resilience, 15*(1), 31–38.

Okie, S. (2001, October 14). Use of anti-anxiety drugs jumps in US: Number of new prescriptions increases sharply in Washington and New York. *Washington Post*, p. A8.

Oliver, M., Wong, S., & Nicholaichuk, T. P. (2008). Outcome evaluation of a high-intensity inpatient sex offender treatment program. *Journal of Interpersonal Violence, 24*, 522–536.

Olivia, J., Morgan, R., & Compton, M. (2010). A practical view of de-escalation skills in law enforcement: Helping individuals in crisis while reducing police liability and injury. *Journal of Police Crisis Negotiations, 10*(1–2), 15–29. doi:10.1080/15332581003785421

Oppel, R. A. (2011, May 23). Steady decline in major crimes baffles experts. *New York Times.* Retrieved from http://www.nytimes.com/2011/05/24/us/24crime.html

O'Toole, M. E. (2000). The school shooter: A threat assessment perspective. Retrieved from http://www.fbi.gov/publications/school/school2

O'Toole, M. E. (2014). The mission-oriented shooter: A new type of mass killer. *Journal of Violence and Gender, 1*(1), 9–10. doi:10.1089/vio.2013.1502

Pabian, Y. L., Wefel, E., & Beebe, R. S. (2009). Psychologists' knowledge of their states' laws pertaining to Tarasoff-type situations. *Professional Psychology: Research and Practice, 40*(1), 8–14. doi:10.1037/a0014784

Pack, M. J. (2013). Critical incident stress management: A review of the literature with implications for social work. *International Social Work, 56,* 608–627. doi:10.1177/0020872811435371

Page, D. (2008). Death notifications: Breaking the bad news. Retrieved from http://www.officer.com/article/10249064/death-notification-breaking-the-bad-news

Parcesepe, A., Martin S., Pollock, M., & Garcia-Moreno, C. (2015). The effectiveness of mental health interventions for adult female survivors of sexual assault: A systematic review. *Aggression and Violent Behavior, 25,* 15–25. doi:10.1016/j.avb.2015.0.004

Pargament, K. (2011). *Spiritually integrated psychotherapy: Understanding and addressing the sacred.* New York, NY: Guilford Press.

Park, C. L., Cohen, C. H., & Murch, R. L. (1996). Assessment and prediction of stress-related growth. *Journal of Personality, 64,* 71–105. doi:10.1111/j.1467-6494.1996.tb00815.x

Parker, S. (2011). Spirituality in counseling: A faith development perspective. *Journal of Counseling & Development, 89,* 112–119. doi:10.1002/j.1556-6678.2011.tb00067.x

Parkes, C. M., & Prigerson, H. G. (2009). *Bereavement: Studies of grief in adult life* (4th ed.). New York, NY: Routledge.

Patterson, W. M., Dohn, H. H., Bird, J., & Patterson, G. A. (1983). Evaluation of suicidal patients: The SAD PERSONS Scale. *Psychosomatics, 24,* 343–349. doi:10.1016/S0033-3182(83)73213-5

Payne, S., & Delbert, E. (2011). Safe2tell. *New Directions for Youth Development, 129,* 103–111.

Pearlman, L. A., & MacIan, P. S. (1995). Vicarious traumatization: An empirical study of the effects of trauma work on trauma therapists. *Professional Psychology: Research and Practice, 26,* 558–565. doi:10.1037/0735-7028.26.6.558

Pedersen, P. B. (1991). Multiculturalism as a generic approach to counseling. *Journal of Counseling & Development, 70,* 6–12.

Peled, E., Eisikovits, Z., Enosh, G., & Winstok, Z. (2000). Choice and empowerment for battered women who stay: Toward a constructivist model. *Social Work, 45*(1), 9–25.

Pietrzak, R. H., Johnson, D. C., Goldstein, M. B., Malley, J. C., & Southwick, S. M. (2009). Perceived stigma and barriers to mental health care utilization among OEF-OIF veterans. *Psychiatric Services, 60*(8), 1118–1122. doi:10.1176/ps.2009.60.8.1118

Pincus, S. H., House, R., Christensen, J., & Adler, L. E. (2005). The emotional cycle of deployment: A military family perspective. Retrieved from http://www.hooah4health.com/deployment/familymatters/emotionalcycle.htm

Piper, W. E., Ogrodniczuk, J. S., McCollum, M., & Rosie, J. S. (2002). Relationships among affect, work and outcome in group therapy for patients with complicated grief. *American Journal of Psychotherapy, 56,* 347–362.

Polaris Project. (2014). The facts. Retrieved from https://polarisproject.org/facts

Polivy, J., & Herman, C. P. (2002). If at first you don't succeed. *American Psychologist, 57,* 677–689. doi:10.1037/0003-066X.57.9.677

Polusny, M. A., Erbes, C. R., Thuras, P., Moran, A., Lamberty, G. J., Collins, R. C., . . . Lim, K. O. (2015). Mindfulness-based stress reduction for posttraumatic stress disorder among veterans: A randomized clinical trial. *Journal of the American Medical Association, 314,* 456–465. doi:10.1001/jama.2015.8361

Post, J. M., McGinnis, C., & Moody, K. (2014). The changing face of terrorism in the 21st century: The communications revolution and the virtual community of hatred. *Behavioral Sciences & the Law, 32,* 306–334. doi:10.1002/bsl.2123

Powers, M., Halpern, J., Ferenschack, M., Gillihan, S., & Foa, E. (2010). A meta-analytic review of prolonged exposure for posttraumatic stress disorder. *Clinical Psychology Review, 30,* 635–641. doi:10.1016/j.cpr.2010.04.007

Pozgar, G. D. (2016). *Legal aspects of healthcare administration* (12th ed.). Burlington, MA: Jones & Bartlett Learning.

Priebe, G., & Svedin, C. G. (2010). Child sexual abuse is largely hidden from the adult society: An epidemiological study of adolescents' disclosures. *Child Abuse & Neglect, 32,* 1095–1108. doi:10.1016/j.chiabu.2008.04.001

Prochaska, J. O., & DiClemente, C. C. (1992). Stages of change in the modification of problem behaviors. In M. Hersen, R. M. Eisler & P. M. Miller (Eds.), *Progress in behavior modification* (Vol. 28, pp. 183–218). Sycamore, IL: Sycamore.

Prospero, M., & Vohra-Gupta, S. (2008). The use of mental health services among victims of partner violence on college campuses. *Journal of Aggression, Maltreatment, and Trauma, 16,* 376–390. doi:10.1080/10926770801926450

Public Safety and Homeland Security Bureau. (2010). Mission. Retrieved from http://transition.fcc.gov/pshs/

Puig, A., Baggs, A., Mixon, K., Park, Y. M., Kim, B. Y., & Lee, S. M. (2012). Relationship between job burnout and personal wellness in mental health professionals. *Journal of Employment Counseling, 49*(3), 98–109. doi:10.1002/j.2161-1920.2012.00010.x

Pullman L., & Seto M. (2012). Assessment and treatment of adolescent sexual offenders: Implications of recent research on generalist versus specialist explanations. *Child Abuse & Neglect, 36,* 203–209. doi:10.1016/j.chiabu.2011.11.003

Purcell, R., Powell, M. B., & Mullen, P. C. (2005). Clients who stalk psychologists: Prevalence, methods, motives. *Professional Psychology: Research and Practice, 36,* 531–543. doi:10.1037/0735-7028.36.5.537

Pynoos, R. S., Weathers, F. W., Steinberg, A. M., Marx, B. P., Layne, C. M., Kaloupek, D. G., . . . Kriegler, J. A. (2015). Clinician-administered PTSD scale for DSM-5—child/adolescent version. Retrieved from http://www.ptsd.va.gov

Quinnett, P. (2012). What is QPR? Retrieved from http://www.qprinstitute.com/about.html

Quinsey, V. L., Harris, A. J., Rice, M. E., & Cormier, C. (2006). *Violent offenders: Appraising and managing risk.* (2nd ed.). Washington, DC: American Psychological Association.

Ramachandran, D. V., Covarrubias, L., Watson, C., & Decker, M. R. (2013). How you screen is as important as whether you screen: A qualitative analysis of violence screening practices in reproductive health clinics. *Journal of Community Health, 38,* 856–863. doi:10.1007/s10900-013-9690-0

Range, L. M., Campbell, C., Kovac, S. H., Marion-Jones, M., Aldridge, H., Kogas, S., . . . Crump, S. (2002). No suicide contracts: An overview and recommendations. *Death Studies, 26,* 51–74. doi:10.1080/07481180210147

Rape, Abuse and Incest National Network. (RAINN). (2015). The nation's largest anti-sexual assault organization. Retrieved from https://www.rainn.org

Raphael, B. (2000). Promoting the mental health and wellbeing of children and young people. Retrieved from http://www.health.gov.au/internet/main/publishing.nsf/content/48F5C63B02F2CE07CA2572450013F488/$File/promdisc.pdf

Ratts, M. J., Singh, A. A., Nassar-McMillan, S., Butler, S. K., & McCullough, J. R. (2015). Multicultural and social justice counseling competencies. Retrieved from http://www.multiculturalcounseling.org/index.php?option=com_content&view=article&id=205:amcd-endorses-multicultural-and-social-justice-counseling-competencies&catid=1:latest&Itemid=123

Ray, D. C., Armstrong, S. A., Balkin, R. S., & Jayne, K. M. (2015). Child-centered play therapy in the schools: Review and meta-analysis. *Psychology in the Schools, 52*(2), 107–123. doi:10.1002/pits.21798

Rebocho, M. F., & Goncalves, R. A. (2012). Sexual predators and prey: A comparative study of the hunting behavior of rapists and child molesters. *Journal of Interpersonal Violence, 27,* 2770–2789. doi:10.1177/0886260512438280

Reid, J. A., & Jones, S. (2011). Exploited vulnerability: Legal and psychological perspectives on child sex trafficking victims. *Victims and Offenders, 6,* 207–231. doi:10.1080/15564886.2011.557327

Reitzel, L. R., & Carbonell, J. L. (2006). The effectiveness of sexual offender treatment for juveniles as measured by recidivism: A meta-analysis. *Sexual Abuse: A Journal of Research and Treatment, 18,* 401–421.

Remley, T. P., & Herlihy, B. (2014). *Ethical, legal, and professional issues in counseling* (4th ed.). Upper Saddle River, NJ: Pearson.

Renzenbrink, I. (2011). *Caregiver stress and staff support in illness, dying, and bereavement.* New York, NY: Oxford University Press.

Resick, P. A. (2001). *Cognitive processing therapy: Generic version.* St. Louis, MO: University of Missouri–St. Louis.

Richards, D., & Vigano, N. (2013). Online counseling: A narrative and critical review of the literature. *Journal of Clinical Psychology, 69,* 994–1011. doi:10.1002/jclp.21974

Richman, J. A., Wislar, J. S., Flaherty, J. A., Fendrich, M., & Rospenda, K. M. (2004). Effects on alcohol use and anxiety of the September 11, 2001, attacks and chronic work stressors: A longitudinal cohort study. *American Journal of Public Health, 94,* 2010–2015.

Richmond, J. S., Berlin, J. S., Fishkind, A. B., Holloman, Jr., G. H., Zeller, S. L., Wilson, M. P., . . . Ng, A. T. (2012). Verbal de-escalation of the agitated patient: Consensus statement of the American Association for Emergency Psychiatry Project BETA De-escalation Workgroup. *Western Journal of Emergency Medicine, 13,* 17–25. doi:10.5811/westjem.2011.9.6864

Riot. (2016). In *Thefreedictionary.com*. Retrieved from http://legal-dictionary.thefreedictionary.com/Riot

Riviere, L. A., Kendall-Robbins, A., McGurk, D., Castro, C. A., & Hoge, C. W. (2011). Coming home may hurt: Risk factors for mental ill health in U.S. reservists after deployment in Iraq. *The British Journal of Psychiatry, 198*(2), 136–142. doi:10.1192/bjp.bp.110.084863

Rizo, C. F., & Macy, R. J. (2011). Help seeking and barriers of Hispanic partner violence survivors: A systematic review of the literature. *Aggression and Violent Behavior, 15,* 250–264. doi:10.1016/j.avb.2011.03.004

Roach, L. F., & Young, M. E. (2007). Do counselor education programs promote wellness in their students? *Counselor Education & Supervision, 47*(1), 29–45. doi:10.1002/j.1556-6978.2007.tb00036.x

Roan, S. (2012, March 8). Suicides among army personnel up 80% in four years. *Los Angeles Times.* Retrieved from http://www.latimes.com/health/boostershots/la-heb-armysuicide-20120308,0,7002109.story

Robbins, S. (2010, July 31). VA, military facing challenges of women's health care. *Stars and Stripes*. Retrieved from http://www.stripes.com/news/europe/va-military-facing-challenges-of-women-s-health-care-1.112971

Rock, M., & Rock, J. (2006). *Widowhood: The death of a spouse*. Victoria, BC: Trafford.

Rodenburg, R., Benjamin, A., de Roos, C., Meijer, A. M., & Stams, G. J. (2009). Efficacy of EMDR in children: A meta-analysis. *Clinical Psychology Review, 29*, 599–606. doi:10.1016/j.cpr.2009.06.008

Roe, K. J. (2004). The Violence Against Women Act and its impact on sexual violence public policy: Looking back and looking forward. Retrieved from http://www.nrcdv.org/docs/Mailings/2004/NRCDVNovVAWA.pdf

Roe-Sepowitz, D. (2007). Adolescent female murderers: Characteristics and treatment implications. *American Journal of Orthopsychiatry, 77*, 489–496. doi:10.1037/0002-9432.77.3.489

Rogers, C. R. (1961). *On becoming a person: A therapist's view of psychotherapy*. New York, NY: Houghton-Mifflin.

Rolling, E., & Brosi, M. (2010). A multi-leveled and integrated approach to assessment and intervention of intimate partner violence. *Journal of Family Violence, 25*, 229–236. doi:10.1007/s10896-009-9286-8

Rosario, M., Schrimshaw, E. W., & Hunter, J. (2012). Homelessness among lesbian, gay, and bisexual youth: Implications for subsequent internalizing and externalizing symptoms. *Journal of Youth and Adolescence, 41*, 544–560. doi:10.1007/s10964-011-9681-3

Rosenberg, J. (2014). Mass shootings and mental health policy. *Journal of Sociology and Social Work, 41*(1), 107–121.

Rosenberg, M. S. (2003). Voices from the group: Domestic violence offenders' experience of intervention. *Journal of Aggression, Maltreatment, and Trauma, 7*, 305–317. doi:10.1300/J146v07n01_13

Rosenblatt, P. C., Walsh, R. P., & Jackson, D. A. (1976). *Grief and mourning in cross-cultural perspective*. New Haven, CT: Human Relations Area Files Press.

Ross, J. (2011). Personality and situational correlates of self-reported reasons for intimate partner violence among women verses men referred for batterers intervention. *Behavioral Science Law, 29*, 711–727. doi:10.1002/bsl.1004

Rothschild, B. (2010). *Eight keys to safe trauma recovery*. New York, NY: Norton.

Rothstein, M. A. (2014). Tarasoff duties after Newtown. *Journal of Law, Medicine and Ethics, 42*(1), 104–109. doi:10.1111/jlme.12123

Rowe, C. L., La Greca, A. M., & Alexandersson, A. (2010). Family and individual factors associated with substance involvement and PTS symptoms among adolescents in greater New Orleans after Hurricane Katrina. *Journal of Consulting and Clinical Psychology, 78*, 806–817. doi:10.1037/a0020808

Royle, L., Keenan, P., & Farrell, D. (2009). Issues of stigma for first responders accessing support for post-traumatic stress. *International Journal of Emergency Mental Health, 11*(2), 79–85.

Rudd, M. D. (2006). *The assessment and management of suicidality*. Sarasota, FL: Professional Resource Exchange.

Rudd, M. D., Joiner, T. E., & Rajab, M. H. (2004). *Treating suicidal behavior: An effective, time-limited approach*. New York, NY: Guilford Press.

Russell, A. (2014). Multidisciplinary response to youth with sexual behavior problems. *William Mitchell Law Review, 40*, 1058–1082.

Ruzek, J. L., Brymer, M. J., Jacobs, A. K., Layne, C. M., Vernberg, E. M., & Watson, P. J. (2007). Psychological first aid. *Journal of Mental Health Counseling, 29*(1), 17–27. doi:10.17744/mehc.29.1.5racqxjueafabgwp

Rynearson, E. K. (2012). The narrative dynamic of grief after homicide. *Omega, 65*, 507–510. doi:10.2190/OM.65.3.f

SafeHelpline. (2016). About us. Retrieved from https://safehelpline.org/effects-of-sexual-assault/substance-abuse

Saindon, C., Rheingold, A. A., Baddeley, J., Wallace, M. M., Brown, C., & Rynearson, E. K. (2014). Restorative retelling for violent loss: An open clinical trial. *Death Studies, 38*, 251–258. doi:10.1080/07481187.2013.783654

Sammons, M. T., & Batten, S. V. (2008). Psychological service for returning veterans and their families: Evolving conceptualization of the sequelae of war-zone experiences. *Journal of Clinical Psychology: In Session, 64*, 921–927. doi:10.1002/jclp.20519

Sánchez-Meca, J., Rosa-Alcázar, A. I., & López-Soler, C. (2011). The psychological treatment of sexual abuse in children and adolescents: A meta-analysis: Erratum. *International Journal of Clinical and Health Psychology, 11*(2), 67–93.

Sandover, J. C., & Freeman, N. J. (2007). Typology of female sex offenders: A test of Vandiver and Kercher. *Sexual Abuse: A Journal of Research and Treatment, 19*, 73–89.

Sankaranarayanan, A. (2007). Suicide risk made easy. *The Internet Journal of Mental Health, 5*.

Sansbury, B. S., Graves, K., & Scott, W. (2015). Managing traumatic stress responses among clinicians: Individual and organizational tools for self-care. *Trauma, 17*(2), 114–122. doi:10.1177/1460408614551978

Saunders, J. B., Aasland, O. G., Babor, T. F., de la Fuente, J. R., & Grant, M. (1993). Development of the Alcohol Use Disorders Identification Test (AUDIT): WHO collaborative project on early detection of persons with harmful alcohol consumption. *Addiction, 88*, 791–804.

Savic-Jabrow, P. C. (2010). Where do counsellors in private practice receive their support? A pilot study. *Counselling and Psychotherapy Research, 10*, 229–232. doi:10.1080/14733140903469889

Sayers, S. L., Farrow, V. A., Ross, J., & Oslin, D. W. (2009). Family problems among recently returned military veterans referred for a mental health evaluation. *Journal of Clinical Psychiatry, 70,* 163–170. doi:10.4088/JCP.07m03863

Schmidt, M. C., Kolodinsky, J. M., Carsten, G., Schmidt, F. E., Larson, M., & MacLachlan, C. (2007). Short term change in attitude and motivating factors to change abusive behavior of male batterers after participating in a group intervention program based on the pro-feminist and cognitive-behavioral approach. *Journal of Family Violence, 22,* 91–100. doi:10.1007/s10896-007-9064-4

Schneider, B. (2009). Substance use disorders and risk for completed suicide. *Archives of Suicide Research, 13,* 303–316. doi:10.1080/13811110903263191

Schure, M. B., Christopher, J., & Christopher, S. (2008). Mind-body medicine and the art of self-care: Teaching mindfulness to counseling students through yoga, meditation, and Qigong. *Journal of Counseling & Development, 86,* 47–56.

Scott, C. L., & Resnick, P. J. (2012). Patient suicide and litigation. In R. I. Simon, & R. E. Hales (Eds.), *Suicide assessment and management* (2nd ed., pp. 539–552). Washington, DC: American Psychological Association.

Sedlak, A. J., Mettenburg, J., Basena, M., Petta, I., McPherson, K., Greene, A., . . . Li, S. (2010). *Fourth National Incidence Study of Child Abuse and Neglect (NIS–4): Report to Congress.* Washington, DC: U.S. Department of Health and Human Services, Administration for Children and Families.

Seligman, L., & Reichenberg, L. (2011). *Selecting effective treatments: A comprehensive, systematic guide for treating mental disorders.* New York, NY: Wiley.

Seligman, M. E. (1975). *Helplessness: On depression, development and death.* San Francisco, CA: Freeman.

Selye, H. (1956). *The stress of life.* New York, NY: McGraw Hill.

Selzer, M. L. (1971). The Michigan Alcoholism Screening Test: The quest for a new diagnostic instrument. *American Journal of Psychiatry, 127,* 1653–1658. doi:10.1176/ajp.127.12.1653

Selzer, M. L., Vinokur, A., & Van Rooijen, L. J. (1975). A self-administered Short Michigan Alcohol Screening Test (SMAST). *Studies on Alcohol, 36,* 117–126.

Sethi, S., & Uppal, S. (2006). Attitudes of clinicians in emergency room towards suicide. *International Journal of Psychiatry in Clinical Practice, 10*(3), 182–185. doi:10.1080/13651500600633543

Shapiro, D. N., Kaplow, J. B., Amaya-Jackson, L., & Dodge, K. A. (2012). Behavioral markers of coping and psychiatric symptoms among sexually abused children. *Journal of Traumatic Stress, 25*(2), 157–163. doi:10.1002/jts.21674

Shapiro, E. (2012). EMDR and early psychological intervention following trauma. *European Review of Applied Psychology, 62*(4), 241–251. doi:10.1016/j.erap.2012.09.003

Shapiro, S. L., Brown, K. W., & Biegel, G. M. (2007). Teaching self-care to caregivers: Effects of mindfulness-based stress reduction on the mental health of therapists in training. *Training & Education In Professional Psychology, 1*(2), 105–115. doi:10.1037/1931-3918.1.2.105

Shared Hope International. (2015). The problem. Retrieved from http://sharedhope.org/theproblem/what-is-sex-trafficking/

Shea, S. C. (2011). *The practical art of suicide assessment: A guide for mental health professionals and substance abuse counselors.* Hoboken, NJ: Wiley.

Shear, M. K., McLaughlin, K. A., Ghesquiere, A., Gruber, M. J., Sampson, N. A., & Kessler, R. C. (2011). Complicated grief associated with Hurricane Katrina. *Depression and Anxiety, 28,* 648–657. doi:10.1002/da.20865

Shepard, M. F., & Campbell, J. A. (1992). The Abusive Behavior Inventory: A measure of physchological and physical abuse. *Journal of Interpersonal Violence, 7*(3), 291–305. doi:10.1177/088626092007003001

Sheperis, D. S., & Sheperis, C. J. (2015). *Clinical mental health counseling: Fundamentals of applied practice.* Upper Saddle River, NJ: Pearson.

Shorey, R. C., Tirone, V., & Stuart, G. L. (2014). Coordinated community response components for victims of intimate partner violence: A review of the literature. *Aggression and Violent Behavior, 19,* 363–371.

Sigurdardottir, S., Halldorsdottir, S., & Bender, S. S. (2014). Consequences of childhood sexual abuse for health and well-being: Gender similarities and differences. *Scandinavian Journal of Public Health, 42*(3), 278–286. doi:10.1177/1403494813514645

Simon, R. I. (2004). *Suicide risk: Guidelines for clinically based risk management.* Washington, DC: American Psychiatric Publishing.

Simon, R. I. (2011). Patient violence against health care professionals: Safety assessment and management. *Psychiatric Times, 28*(2), 16–21.

Simon, R. I. (2012). *Patient safety and freedom of movement: Coping with uncertainty.* In R. I. Simon & R. E. Hales (Eds.), *Suicide assessment and management* (2nd ed., pp. 539–552). Washington, DC: American Psychological Association.

Singhal, M., & Vahali, H. O. (2014). Building broken sandcastles: Explorations in play therapy with a sexually abused child. *Journal of Indian Association for Child & Adolescent Mental Health, 10*(2), 132–144.

Sinozich, S, & Langton, L. (2014). *Special report: Rape and sexual assault victimization among college-age females, 1995–2013.* Washington, DC: Bureau of Justice Statistics of the U.S. Department of Justice.

Sixbey, M. B., & Daniels, H. (2008). Supervisors aiding in exploring therapist perceptions of crisis experiences based on level of experience. Presented at Southern Association of Counselor Education and Supervision, Houston, TX.

Skovholt, T. M., & Trotter-Mathison, M. J. (2014). *The resilient practitioner: Burnout prevention and self-care strategies for counselors, therapists, teachers, and health professionals.* New York, NY: Routledge.

Smith, B. L., & Kercher, G. A. (2011). Adolescent sexual behavior and the law. Retrieved from http://www.crimevictimsinstitute.org/documents/Adolescent_Behavior_3.1.11.pdf

Smith, D. L. (2008). Disability, gender, and intimate partner violence: Relationships from the behavioral risk factor surveillance system. *Sexuality and Disability, 26*, 15–28. doi:10.1007/s11195-007-9064-6

Smith, D. W., Christiansen, E. H., Vincent, R., & Hann, N. E. (1999). Population effects of the bombing of Oklahoma City. *Journal of the Oklahoma State Medical Association, 92*, 193–198.

Snyder, C. M. J., & Anderson, S. A. (2009). An examination of mandated versus voluntary referral as a determinant of clinical outcome. *Journal of Marital and Family Therapy, 35*, 278–292. doi:10.1111/j.1752-0606.2009.00118.x

Sories, F., Maier, C., Beer, A., & Thomas, V. (2015). Addressing the needs of military children through family-based play therapy. *Contemporary Family Therapy: An International Journal, 37*, 209–220. doi:10.1007/s10591-015-9342.x

Sorsoli, L., Kia-Keating, M., & Grossman, F. (2008). "I keep that hush-hush": Male survivors of sexual abuse and the challenges of disclosure. *Journal of Counseling Psychology, 55*, 333–345. doi:10.1037/0022-0167.55.3.333

Sperry, L., & Shafranske, E. (Eds.) (2005). *Spiritually oriented psychotherapy.* Washington, DC: American Psychological Association.

Stalking Resource Center. (2012). *Stalking fact sheet.* Washington, DC: National Center for Victims of Crime.

Stamm, B. H. (2009). *Professional quality of life: Compassion satisfaction and fatigue version 5.* Retrieved from proqol.org/ProQol_Test.html

Stander, V. A., Olson, C. B., & Merrill, L. L. (2002). Self-definition as a survivor of childhood sexual abuse among Navy recruits. *Journal of Consulting and Clinical Psychology, 70*, 369–377.

Stanley, B., & Brown, G. (2009). Safety planning guide. Retrieved from http://www.sprc.org/sites/sprc.org/files/SafetyPlanningGuide%20Quick%20Guide%20for%20Clinicians.pdf

Stauffer, M. D., Capuzzi, D., & Tanigoshi, H. (2008). Assessment: An overview. In D. Capuzzi & M. D. Stauffer (Eds.), *Foundations of addictions counseling* (pp. 76–100). Boston, MA: Allyn and Bacon.

SteelFisher, G. K., Zaslavsky, A. M., & Blendon, R. J. (2008). Health-related impact of deployment extensions on spouses of active duty army personnel. *Military Medicine, 173*, 221–229. doi:10.7205/MILMED.173.3.221

Sterner, W., & Jackson-Cherry, L. R. (2015). The influence of spirituality and religion on coping for combat-deployed military personnel. *Journal of Counseling and Values, 60*(1), 48–66. doi:10.1002/j.2161-007X.2015.00060.x

Stickney, D., & Nordstrom, R. H. (2010). *Water bugs and dragonflies: Explaining death to young children.* Cleveland, OH: Pilgrim Press.

Stiles, D. A., Moyer, J. M., Brewer, S., Klaus, L. M., Falconer, J., & Moss, L. (2015). Practicing psychology in challenging times: School and the Ferguson crisis. *Educational and Child Psychology, 32*(4), 21–38.

Straus, M. A., Hamby, S. L., Boney-McCoy, S., & Sugarman, D. B. (1996). Revised Conflict Tactics Scale (CTS2): Development and preliminary psychometric data. *Journal of Family Issues, 17*(3), 283–316. doi:10.1177/019251396017003001

Streed, T. (2011). A template for the investigation of suicidal behavior and subject precipitated homicide. *Investigative Sciences Journal, 3*(1), 1–32.

Substance Abuse and Mental Health Service Administration. (2010). Eye movement desensitization and reprocessing. Retrieved from http://nrepp.samhsa.gov/ViewIntervention.aspx?id=199

Substance Abuse and Mental Health Services Administration. (2014). Results from the 2013 *National Survey on Drug Use and Health: Summary of national findings* (NSDUH Series H-48, HHS Publication No. [SMA] 14-4863). Rockville, MD: Author.

Substance Abuse and Mental Health Services Administration. (2015). Trauma informed approach and trauma specific interventions. Retrieved from http://www.samhsa.gov/nctic/trauma-interventions

Substance Abuse and Mental Health Services Administration. (2016). Co-occurring disorders. Retrieved from http://www.samhsa.gov/co-occurring

Substance Abuse and Mental Health Services Administration. (2017). National registry of evidence-based programs and practices. Retrieved from http://www.nrepp.samhsa.gov

Sude, M. E. (2013). Text messaging and private practice: Ethical challenges and guidelines for developing personal best practices. *Journal of Mental Health Counseling, 35*, 211–227. doi:10.17744/mehc.35.3.q37l2236up62l713

Suicide Prevention Resource Center. (2009). The role of faith communities in preventing suicide: A report of an interfaith suicide prevention dialogue. Retrieved from http://www.sprc.org/sites/sprc.org/files/library/faith_dialogue.pdf

Suicide Prevention Resource Center. (2012). Best practices registry. Retrieved from http://www.sprc.org/bpr

Suicide Prevention Resource Center. (2016). Assessing and managing suicide risk: Core competencies for mental health professionals. Retrieved from http://www.sprc.org/training-institute/workshops-and-toolkits

Survivors of Loved Ones' Suicides, Inc. (2006). The suicide paradigm. Retrieved from http://www.adph.org/suicideprevention/assets/SuicideParadigm.pdf

Taft, C. T., Bryant-Davis, T., Woodward, H. E., Tillman, S., & Torres, S. E. (2009). Intimate partner violence against African American women: An examination of the socio-cultural context. *Aggression and Violent Behavior, 14*, 50–58. doi:10.1016/j.avb.2008.10.001

Tanielian, T., & Jaycox, L. (Eds.). (2008). *Invisible wounds of war: Psychological and cognitive injuries, their consequences and services to assist recovery.* Santa Monica, CA: RAND Corporation.

Tarasoff v. Regents of the University of California, 529 P.2d. 553, 118 Cal. Rptr. 129 (1974), *vacated*, 17 Cal. 3d 425, 551 P.2d 334, 131 Cal. Rptr. 14 (1976).

Tcherni, M. (2011). Structural determinants of homicide: The big three. *Journal of Quantitative Criminology, 27*, 475–496. doi:10.1007/s10940-011-9134.x

Tedeschi, R. G., & Calhoun, L. G. (2004). A clinical approach to post-traumatic growth. In P. A. Linley & S. Joseph (Eds.), *Positive psychology in practice* (pp. 405–419). Hoboken, NJ: Wiley.

Teitelbaum, J. B., & Wilensky, S. E. (2013). *Essentials of health policy and law* (2nd ed.). Boston, MA: Jones & Bartlett.

Texas Association of Hostage Negotiators. (2003). Suicide lethality checklist. Retrieved from http://www.tahn.org

Thomas, M. D., Bennett, L. W., & Stoops, C. (2012). The treatment needs of substance abusing batterers: A comparison of men who batter their female partners. *Journal of Family Violence, 28*, 121–129. doi:10.1007/s10896-012-9479-4

Thomas, S. P., Phillips, K., Carlson, K., Shieh, E., Kirkwood, E., Cabage, L., . . . Worley, J. (2013). Childhood experiences of perpetrators of child sexual abuse. *Perspectives in Psychiatric Care, 49*(3), 187–201. doi:10.1111/j.1744-6163.2012.00349.x

Thyer, B. A., Dulmus, C. N., & Sowers, K. M. (Eds.). (2012). *Human behavior in the social environment: Theories for social work practice.* New York, NY: John Wiley & Sons.

Tishler, C. L., Gordon, L. B., & Landry-Meyer, L. (2000). Managing the violent patient: A guide for psychologists and other mental health professionals. *Professional Psychology: Research and Practice, 31*(1), 34–41. doi:10.1037/0735-7028.31.1.34

Todahl, J., & Walters, E. (2011). Universal screening for intimate partner violence: A systematic review. *Journal of Marriage and Family Therapy, 37*, 355–369. doi:10.1111/j.1752-0606.2009.00179x

Toray, T. (2004). The human-animal bond and loss: Providing support for grieving clients. *Journal of Mental Health Counseling, 26*, 244–259. doi:10.17744/mehc.26.3.udj040fw2gj75lqp

Tower, L. E. (2006). Barriers in screening women for domestic violence: A survey of social workers, family practitioners, and obstetrician-gynecologists. *Journal of Family Violence, 21*, 245–257. doi:10.1007/s10896-006-9024-4

Tower, M. (2007). Intimate partner violence and the health care response: A postmodern critique. *Health Care for Women International, 28*, 438–452. doi:10.1080/07399330701226404

Training/academy life. (2016). Retrieved from http://discoverpolicing.org/what_does_take/?fa=training_academy_life

Trask, E. V., Walsh, K., & DiLillo, D. (2011). Treatment effects for common outcomes of child sexual abuse: A current meta-analysis. *Aggression and Violent Behavior, 16*, 6–19.

Trauma and Learning Policy Initiative. (2016). Our model of change. Retrieved from http://traumasensitiveschools.org/about-tlpi/successes/

Trickett, P. K. (2006). Defining child sexual abuse. In M. M. Feerick, J. F. Knutson, P. K. Trickett, & S. M. Flanzer (Eds.), *Child abuse and neglect: Definitions, classifications, and a framework for research* (pp. 123–150). Baltimore, MD: Brookes.

Trippany, R. L., White Kress, V. E., & Wilcoxon, A. S. (2004). Preventing vicarious trauma: What counselors should know when working with trauma survivors. *Journal of Counseling and Development, 82*(1), 31–37.

Trump, K. S. (2009). School emergency planning: Back to basics. *Student Assistance Journal, 1*, 13–17.

Turner, R. J. (2010). Understanding health disparities: The promise of the stress process model. In W. R. Avison, C. S. Aneshensel, S. Schieman, & B. Wheaton (Eds.), *Advances in the conceptualization and study of the stress process: Essays in honor of Leonard I. Pearlin* (pp. 3–21). New York, NY: Springer.

Underwood, E. (2015). Measuring child abuse's legacy. *Science, 347*(6229), 1408. doi:10.1126/science.347.6229.1408

University of South Florida. (2012). Youth suicide school-based prevention guide. Retrieved from http://theguide.fmhi.usf.edu/

Urquiza, A. J., & Blacker, D. (2012). Parent-child interaction therapy for sexually abused children. In P. Goodyear-Brown & P. Goodyear-Brown (Eds.), *Handbook of child sexual abuse: Identification, assessment, and treatment* (pp. 279–296). Hoboken, NJ: John Wiley & Sons Inc.

U.S. Bureau of Labor Statistics. (2015). Occupational outlook handbook: Rehabilitation counsellors. Retrieved from http://www.bls.gov/ooh/community-and-social-service/rehabilitation-counselors.htm

U.S. Department of Defense. (2016). U.S. Armed Forces current numbers. Retrieved from file:///C:/Users/haydensc/Downloads/ms0_1601.pdf

U.S. Department of Defense, Office of the Assistant Secretary of Defense for Readiness and Force Management. (2014). Total force planning and requirements directorate, Defense manpower requirements report, fiscal year 2015. Retrieved from http://prhome.defense.gov/Portals/52/Documents/RFM/TFPRQ/docs/F15%20DMRR.pdf

U.S. Department of Education. (2007). Safe schools & FERPA: FERPA guidance on emergency management. Retrieved from http://www2.ed.gov/policy/gen/guid/fpco/ferpa/safeschools/index.html

U.S. Department of Education. (2008). Family Educational Rights and Privacy Act. Retrieved from http://www2.ed.gov/policy/gen/guid/fpco/ferpa/index.html

U.S. Department of Education, National Center for Education Statistics. (2016). Indicators of school crime and safety: 2014. Retrieved from https://nces.ed.gov/pubsearch/pubsinfo.asp?pubid=2015072

U.S. Department of Education, Office for Civil Rights. (2011). Know your rights: Title IX prohibits sexual harassment and sexual violence where you go to school. Retrieved from http://www2.ed.gov/about/offices/list/ocr/docs/title-ix-rights-201104.pdf

U.S. Department of Education, Office of Safe and Drug-Free Schools. (2017). *Practical information on crisis planning: A guide for schools and communities.* Retrieved from http://www2.ed.gov/admins/lead/safety/emergencyplan/crisisplanning.pdf

U.S. Department of Health and Human Services. (2002). Standards for privacy of individually identifiable health information; Final rule. Retrieved from http://www.hhs.gov/ocr/privacy/hipaa/news/2002/combinedregtext02.pdf

U.S. Department of Health and Human Services. (2005). Health information privacy: When does the Privacy Rule allow covered entities to disclose protected health information to law enforcement officials? Retrieved from http://www.hhs.gov/ocr/privacy/hipaa/faq/disclosures_for_law_enforcement_purposes/505.html

U.S. Department of Health and Human Services. (2006). Health information privacy: Can health care information be shared in a severe disaster? Retrieved from http://www.hhs.gov/ocr/privacy/hipaa/faq/disclosures_in_emergency_situations/960.html

U.S. Department of Health and Human Services. (2008). Hurricane Katrina bulletin: HIPAA privacy and disclosures in emergency situations. Retrieved from https://www.hhs.gov/sites/default/files/katrinanhipaa.pdf

U.S. Department of Health and Human Services. (2009). Mandatory reporters of child abuse and neglect: State statutes series. Retrieved from http://www.childwelfare.gov/systemwide/laws_policies/statutes/manda.cfm

U.S. Department of Health and Human Services. (2017). Health information privacy: Is the HIPAA Privacy Rule suspended during a national or public emergency. Retrieved from http://www.hhs.gov/ocr/privacy/hipaa/faq/disclosures_in_emergency_situations/1068.html

U.S. Department of Health and Human Services, Administration for Children and Families, Administration on Children, Youth and Families, Children's Bureau. (2015). Child maltreatment 2013. Retrieved from http://www.acf.hhs.gov/programs/cb/research-data-technology/statistics-research/child-maltreatment

U.S. Department of Justice. (2011). *The economic impact of illicit drug use on American society* (Product No. 2011-Q0317-002). Washington, DC: Author.

U.S. Department of Justice. (2012). Sexual assault. Retrieved from http://www.ovw.usdoj.gov/sexassault.htm

U.S. Department of Justice (2013). Data collection: National Crime Victimization Study. Retrieved from http://www.bjs.gov/index.cfm?ty=dcdetail&iid=245

U.S. Department of Justice. (2014a). Frequently asked questions: The Sex Offender Registration and Notification Act (SORNA) final guidelines. Retrieved from http://ojp.gov/smart/pdfs/faq_sorna_guidelines.pdf

U.S. Department of Justice. (2014b). *Sex offender management assessment and planning initiative* (Grant Report 2010-DB-BX-K086). Washington, DC: National Criminal Justice Association. Retrieved from http://www.smart.gov/SOMAPI/pdfs/SOMAPI_Full%20Report.pdf

U.S. Department of Justice, Office for Victims of Crime. (2006). OVC fact sheets: The Justice for All Act. Retrieved from http://www.ojp.usdoj.gov/ovc/publications/factshts/justforall/welcome.html

U.S. Department of Justice, Office of Sex Offender Sentencing, Monitoring, Apprehending, Registering, and Tracking. (2015). SMART summary: Prosecution, transfer, and registration of serious juvenile sex offenders. Retrieved from http://www.smart.gov/pdfs/SMARTSummary.pdf

U.S. Department of Justice, Office on Violence Against Women. (2013). *A national protocol for sexual assault medical forensic examinations: Adults/adolescents* (2nd ed.). Retrieved from https://www.ncjrs.gov/pdffiles1/ovw/241903.pdf

U.S. Department of State. (2013). Definitions and methodology: Trafficking in persons report 2013 (Face of Modern Day Slavery). Retrieved from http://www.state.gov/j/tip/rls/tiprpt/2013/210543.htm

U.S. Department of Veterans Affairs, National Center for Veterans Analysis and Statistics. (2014). Projected veteran population 2013–2043. Retrieved from http://www.va.gov/vetdata/docs/quickfacts/population_slideshow.pdf

U.S. Equal Employment Opportunity Commission. (2016). Facts about sexual harassment. Retrieved from http://www.eeoc.gov/eeoc/publications/fs-sex.cfm

U.S. Secret Service. (2010). National Threat Assessment Center: Secret Service school initiative. Retrieved from http://www.secretservice.gov/NTAC_ssi.shtml

Van Brunt, B. (2015). *Harm to others: The assessment and treatment of dangerousness.* Alexandria, VA: American Counseling Association.

Van den Heuvel, C., & Alison, L. (2014). Coping with uncertainty: Police strategies for resilient decision-making and action implementation. *Cognition, Technology & Work, 16*(1), 25–45. doi:10.1007/s10111-012-0241-8

van der Kolk, B. A. (2015). *The body keeps the score: Brain, mind, and the body in the healing of trauma.* New York, NY: Penguin.

Vandiver, D., & Kercher, G. (2004). Offender and victim characteristics of registered female sexual offenders in Texas: A proposed typology of female sexual offenders. *Sexual Abuse: A Journal of Research and Treatment, 16*, 121–137. doi:10.1023/B:SEBU.0000023061.77061.17

Varma, S., Gillespie, S., McCracken, C., & Greenbaum, V. J. (2015). Characteristics of child commercial sexual exploitation and sex trafficking victims presenting for medical care in the United States. *Child Abuse & Neglect, 44*, 98–105. doi:10.1016/j.chiabu.2015.04.004

Verstrael, S., van der Wurff, P., & Vermetten, E. (2013). Eye movement desensitization and reprocessing (EMDR) as treatment for combat-related PTSD: A meta-analysis. *Military Behavioral Health, 1*(2), 68–73. doi:10.1080/21635781.2013.827088

Veterans Health Administration, Department of Defense. (2010). *Clinical practice guideline for management of post-traumatic stress* (Version 2.0). Washington, DC: Author.

Villalba, J. (2018). Individuals and families of Latin descent. In D. G. Hays & B. T. Erford (Eds.), *Developing multicultural counseling competence: A systems approach* (3rd ed., pp. 277–300). Boston, MA: Pearson.

Violanti, J. M., Gu, J. K., Charles, L. E., Fekedulegn, D., Andrew, M. E., & Burchfiel, C. M. (2011). Is suicide higher among separated/retired police officers? An epidemiological investigation. *International Journal of Emergency Mental Health, 13*(4), 221–228.

Violanti, J. M., Hartley, T. A., Gu, J. K., Fekedulegn, D., Andrew, M. E., & Burchfiel, C. M. (2013a). Life expectancy in police officers: A comparison with the U.S. general population. *International Journal of Emergency Mental Health, 15*(4), 217–228.

Violanti, J., Mnatsakanova, A., & Andrew, M. (2013b). Suicidal ideation in police officers: Exploring an additional measure. *Suicidology Online, 4*, 31–44.

Vlahov, D., Galea, S., Ahern, J., Rudenstine, S., Resnick, H., Kilpatrick, D., . . . Crum, R. M. (2006). Alcohol drinking problems among New York City residents after the September 11 terrorist attacks. *Substance Use and Misuse, 41*, 1295–1311. doi:10.1080/10826080600754900

Vlahov, D., Galea, S., Resnick, H., Ahern, J., Boscarino, J. A., Bucuvalas, M., . . . Kilpatrick, D. (2002). Increased consumption of cigarettes, alcohol, and marijuana among Manhattan residents after the September 11 terrorist attacks. *American Journal of Epidemiology, 155*, 988–996.

von Feigenblat, O. F., Dominguez, C. D., & Valles, J. E. G. (2015). The Family Educational Rights and Privacy Act: FERPA. *Journal of Alternative Perspectives in the Social Sciences, 6*, 229–335.

Walfish, S., Barnett, J. E., Marlyere, K., & Zielke, R. (2010). "Doc, there's something I have to tell you": Patient disclosure to their psychotherapist of unprosecuted murder and other violence. *Ethics and Behavior, 20*, 311–323. doi:10.1080/10508422.2010.491743

Walker, J. K. (2015). Investigating trans people's vulnerabilities to intimate partner violence/abuse. *Partner Abuse, 6*, 107–125. doi:10.1891/1946-6560.6.1.107

Walker, L. E. (1979). *The battered woman.* New York, NY: Harper and Row.

Walsh, F. (2012). *Normal family processes: Growing diversity and complexity* (4th ed.). New York, NY: Guilford Press.

Walsh, F., & McGoldrick, M. (Eds.). (2004). *Living beyond loss: Death in the family* (2nd ed.). New York, NY: Norton.

Walters, M. L., Chen, J., & Breiding, M. J. (2013). The National Intimate Partner and Sexual Violence Survey (NISVS): 2010 findings on victimization by sexual orientation. Retrieved from http://www.cdc.gov/violenceprevention/pdf/nisvs_sofindings.pdf

Wang, C. C. (2007). Person-centered therapy with a bereaved father. *Person-Centered Journal, 14*, 73–97.

Ward, C. L., Lombard, C. J., & Gwebushe, N. (2006). Critical incident exposure in South African emergency services personnel: Prevalence and associated mental health issues. *Emergency Medicine Journal, 23*, 226–231. doi:10.1136/emj.2005.025908

Ward, T., & Durrant, R. (2013). Altruism, empathy, and sex offender treatment. *International Journal of Behavioral Consultation and Therapy, 8*(3–4), 66–71. doi:10.1037/h0100986

Warren, L. J., Mullen, P. E., & Ogloff, J. R. P. (2011). A clinical study of those who utter threats to kill. *Behavioral Sciences and the Law, 29*, 141–154. doi:10.1002/bsl.974

Warshaw, R. (1988). *I never called it rape: The Ms. report on recognizing, fighting and surviving date and acquaintance rape.* New York, NY: Harper and Row.

Watlington, C. G., & Murphy, C. M. (2006). The roles of religion and spirituality among African American survivors of domestic violence. *Journal of Clinical Psychology, 62*, 837–857.

Wearick-Silva, L. E., Tractenberg, S. G., Levandowski, M. L., Viola, T. W., Pires, J. A., & Grassi-Oliveira, R. (2014). Mothers who were sexually abused during childhood are more likely to have a child victim of sexual violence. *Trends in Psychiatry and Psychotherapy, 36*(2), 119–122. doi:10.1590/2237-6089-2013-0054

Weathers, F. W., Blake, D. D., Schnurr, P. P., Kaloupek, D. G., Marx, B. P., & Keane, T. M. (2013). The Clinician-administered PTSD scale for *DSM-5* (CAPS-5). Retrieved from http://www.ptsd.va.gov

Wee, D. F., Mills, D. M., & Koehler, G. (1999). The effects of Critical Incident Stress Debriefing. *Journal of Emergency Mental Health, 1*(1), 33–37

Weiss, D. S., & Marmar, C. R. (1996). The impact of event scale—revised. In J. Wilson, & T. M. Keane (Eds.), *Assessing psychological trauma and PTSD* (pp. 399–411). New York, NY: Guilford Press.

Welfel, E. R. (2016). *Ethics in counseling and psychotherapy* (4th ed.). Belmont, CA: Brooks/Cole.

Werner-Wilson, R. J., Zimmerman, T. S., & Whalen, D. (2000). Resilient response to battering. *Contemporary Family Therapy, 22*, 161–188. doi:10.1023/A:1007777702757

Whiffen, V. E., & MacIntosh, H. B. (2005). Mediators of the link between childhood sexual abuse and emotional distress. *Journal of Trauma, Violence, & Abuse, 6*, 24–39. doi:10.1177/1524838004272543

The White House, United States Government. (2014). Fact sheet: Launch of the "It's On Us" public awareness campaign to help prevent campus sexual assault. Retrieved from http://www.whitehouse.gov/the-press-office/2014/09/19/fact-sheet-launch-it-s-us-public-awareness-campaign-help-prevent-campus-

Whitehead, S. (2012). Suicide evaluation: The DEAD PIMP assessment. Retrieved from http://theemtspot.com/2012/03/14/suicidal-evaluation-the-dead-pimp-assessment/

Wilcox, H. C., Rria, A. M., Calderia, K. M., Vincent, K. B., Pinchevsky, G. M., & O'Grady, K. E. (2010). Prevalence and predictors of persistent suicide ideations, plans, and attempts during college. *Journal of Affective Disorders, 27*(1–3), 287–294. doi:10.1016/j.jad.2010.04.017

Wilcox, N. (2015). The importance of mental health training in law enforcement. Retrieved from https://leb.fbi.gov/2015/july/the-importance-of-mental-health-training-in-law-enforcement

Williams, R., & Vinson, D. C. (2001). Validation of a single screening question for problem drinking. *Journal of Family Practice, 50*, 307–312.

Wilmoth, J. (2014). Trouble in mind. Retrieved from http://www.nfpa.org/newsandpublications/nfpa-journal/2014/may-june-2014/features/special-report-firefighter-behavioral-health

Winokur, M., Rozen, D., Batchelder, K., & Valentine, D. (2006). Juvenile sexual offender treatment: A systematic review of evidence-based research. Retrieved from http://www.ssw.chhs.colostate.edu/research/swrc/files/jsotsystematicreview.pdf

Wise, R. A., King, A. R., Miller, J. C., & Pearce, M. W. (2011). When HIPAA and FERPA apply to university training clinics. *Training and Education in Professional Psychology, 5*(1), 48–56. doi:10.103/a0022857

Wolak, J., Finkelhor, D., & Mitchell, K. (2012). *Trends in law enforcement responses to technology-facilitated child sexual exploitation crimes: The Third National Juvenile Online Victimization Study.* Durham, NH: Crimes Against Children Research Center.

Wolf, C. P., Thompson, I. A., & Smith-Adcock, S. (2012). Wellness in counselor preparation: Promoting individual well-being. *Journal of Individual Psychology, 68*, 164–181.

Womenshealth.gov. (2012). Date rape drugs fact sheet. Retrieved from http://www.womenshealth.gov/publications/our-publications/fact-sheet/date-rape-drugs.pdf

Wong, J., & Mellor, D. (2014). Intimate partner violence and women's health and wellbeing: Impacts, risk factors, and responses. *Contemporary Nurse: A Journal for the Australian Nursing Profession, 46*, 170–179. doi:10.5172/conu.2014.46.2.170

Worden, J. W. (2001). *Children and grief: When a parent dies.* New York, NY: Guilford Press.

Worden, J. W. (2009). *Grief counseling and grief therapy: A handbook for the mental health practitioner* (4th ed.). New York, NY: Springer.

World Health Organization. (2013). Global and regional estimates of violence against women. Retrieved from http://apps.who.int/iris/bitstream/10665/85239/1/9789241564625_eng.pdf

Worling, J., Litteljohn, A., & Bookalam, D. (2009). 20-year prospective follow-up study of specialized treatment for adolescents who offended sexually. *Behavioral Sciences and the Law, 28*(1), 46–57. doi:10.1002/bsl.912

Worling, J. R., & Curwen, T. (2001). Estimate of risk of adolescent sexual offense recidivism (Version 2.0: The "ERASOR"). In M. C. Calder (Ed.), *Juveniles and children who sexually abuse: Frameworks for assessment* (pp. 372–397). Lyme Regis, UK: Russell House Publishing.

Yates, P. (2013). Treatment of sexual offenders: Research, best practices, and emerging models. *International Journal of Behavioral Consultation and Therapy, 8*(3), 89–95. doi:10.1037/h0100989

Yechezkel, R., & Ayalon, L. (2013). Social workers' attitudes towards intimate partner abuse in younger vs. older women. *Journal of Family Violence, 28*, 381–391. doi:10.1007/s10896-013-9506-0

Yoshihama, M., Dabby, C., & Asian and Pacific Islander Institute on Domestic Violence. (2015). Facts & stats report: Domestic violence in Asian & Pacific Islander homes. Retrieved from http://www.api-gbv.org/files/Facts.Stats-APIIDV-2015.pdf

Young, M. E. (2013). *Learning the art of helping: Building blocks and techniques* (5th ed.). Upper Saddle River: NJ: Pearson Education.

Young, M. S., Harford, K. L., Kinder, B., & Savell, J. K. (2007). The relationship between childhood sexual abuse and adult mental health among undergraduates: Victim gender doesn't matter. *Journal of Interpersonal Violence, 22*, 1315–1331. doi:10.1177/0886260507304552

Yuce, M., Karabekiroglu, K., Yildirim, Z., Şahin, S., Sapmaz, D., Babadagi, Z., . . . Aydin, B. (2015). The psychiatric consequences of child and adolescent sexual abuse. *Archives of Neuropsychiatry, 52,* 393–399. doi:10.5152/npa.2015.7472

Zalaquett, C., Carrión, I., & Exum, H. (2009). Counseling survivors of national disasters: Issues and strategies for a diverse society. In J. Webber (Ed.), *Terrorism, trauma, and tragedies: A counselor's guide to preparing and responding.* Alexandria, VA: American Counseling Association.

Zeoli, A. M., Grady, S., Pizarro, J. M., & Melde, C. (2015). Modeling the movement of homicide by type to inform public health prevention efforts. *American Journal of Public Health, 105,* 2035–2041. doi:10.2105/AJPH.2015.302732

Zhang, N., & Parsons, R. D. (2016). *Field experience: Transitioning from student to professional.* Thousand Oaks, CA: Sage.

Zinzow, H. M., Resnick, H. S., Amstadter, A. B., McCauley, J. L., Ruggiero, K. J., & Kilpatrick, D. G. (2010). Drug-or alcohol-facilitated, incapacitated, and forcible rape in relationship to mental health among a national sample of women. *Journal of Interpersonal Violence, 25,* 2217–2236. doi:10.1177/0886260509354887

INDEX

A

AA. *See* Alcoholics Anonymous (AA)
AAS. *See* American Association of Suicidology (AAS)
ABCDE assessment approach, 8–9
ABC-X model of crisis, 15–16, 179
Abeling, S., 304
Ability, and CSA, 321–322
Absenteeism, 437
Abuse. *See* Child sexual abuse (CSA); Substance abuse
ACA. *See* American Counseling Association (ACA)
ACA Code of Ethics, 56–57, 64, 68, 70, 71, 72, 73, 75, 76, 77, 78, 302, 304, 305
Accelerated Rehabilitative Disposition (ARD), 214
Acceptance, as stage in death, 110
Accountability, for IPV, 262–263, 264. *See also* Health Insurance Portability and Accountability Act
Acquaintance rape, 278
ACSA. *See* American School Counselor Association (ACSA)
Active listening, 88–89
Acute battering incident, of cycle of violence theory, 238
Acute grief, 4
Acute risks, for suicide, 158, 160–161
Acute Stress Disorder (ASD), 4, 23, 292
diagnostic criteria for, 23–24
Acute stressors, 17–19
Adamson, Nicole, 281, 420
Adam Walsh Child Protection and Safety Act (AWA), 314
Adaptation
concept of, 15
defined, 25
by families, 25
Adaptational theory, 5
Addiction, 202, 203–204. *See also* Substance abuse; Substance dependence
sexual violence and, 292–293
Adolescent(s)
dating violence among, 252–253
sex offenders, treatment of, 344
as sexual perpetrators, 313–314
Adult(s)
dating violence among, 252–253
sex offenders, treatment of, 341–343
sex offenders, recidivism rates of, 313
Adversity, 25
Affect, assessment of, 8
Affirmative consent, 279

Afghanistan Veterans of America, 350
African Americans
eye contact in counseling, 85
IPV prevalence, 246–247
AFSP. *See* American Foundation for Suicide Prevention (AFSP)
Against Our Will (Brownmiller), 275
Age, and CSA, 321–322
Aggression, irritable, 102–103
Ahern, J., 201
Ahmad, S., 304
Ahrens, C. E., 304
Ainsworth, M., 113
Alabama Suicide Prevention and Resources Coalition (ASPARC), 161
Al-ANON, 225
Alcázar, A. I., 335
Alcohol, sexual assault and, 282
Alcohol and other drug (AOD) addiction, 203–204, 270
Alcohol/drug-facilitated penetration, 277
Alcoholics Anonymous (AA), 225, 304
Alcoholism. *See also* Substance abuse; Substance dependence
Jellinek view of, 203
Alcohol Use Disorders Identification Test (AUDIT), 206–207
Aldridge, H., 151
Alexander, D. A., 386
Alexandersson, A., 201
Alison, L., 399
Allan, W. D., 183
Allen, M. H., 101
Almond, L., 36
Alvarez, A., 248
Amado, B. G., 324
Amaya-Jackson, L., 336
Ambuel, B., 242, 255, 257
Amelioration of grief, 129
American Addictions Centers, 371
American Association of Suicidology (AAS), 67, 150, 153, 157, 161, 162, 170, 179
American Counseling Association (ACA), 27, 56, 57, 271, 302, 305, 433
Code of Ethics, 56–57, 64, 68, 70, 71, 72, 73, 75, 76, 77, 78, 302, 304, 305
American Foundation for Suicide Prevention (AFSP), 153, 197
American Mental Health Counselors Association (AMHCA), 433
American Mental Health Foundation (AMHF), 48
American Pet Products Association, 121

American Psychiatric Association (APA), 4, 22, 23, 30, 108, 114, 123, 124, 171, 196, 211, 239, 291, 292, 308, 371, 438
American Red Cross, 30, 60, 74, 76, 80, 81, 297
American School Counselor Association (ACSA), 29, 193, 409, 413, 414, 422
American Society of Addiction Medicine (ASAM), 213–215
AMHCA. *See* American Mental Health Counselors Association (AMHCA)
AMHF. *See* American Mental Health Foundation (AMHF)
AMSR. *See* Assessing and Managing Suicide Risk (AMSR)
Amstadler, A. B., 230
AMT. *See* Anxiety management training (AMT) programs
Anderson, M. L., 246
Anderson, R., 444
Andrew, M., 359, 377
Andrew, M. E., 367
Andrews, D., 342
Andriessen, K., 153
Anger
chronic, 102
externalized, 113
grief and, 113–114
Angermeyer, M. C., 190
Anger-motivated rape, 308
perpetrators of, 309
Angold, A., 201
Anxiety management training (AMT) programs, 301
APA. *See* American Psychiatric Association (APA)
Applied Suicide Intervention Skills Training (ASIST), 154
Approach coping, 337
Apter, A., 153, 173
Arce, R., 324
Archambault, J., 284
Archer, J., 270
ARD. *See* Accelerated Rehabilitative Disposition (ARD)
Ard, K. L., 250, 251
Armour, C., 260
Armstrong, S. A., 336
Arvanitogiannis, A., 203
ASAM. *See* American Society of Addiction Medicine (ASAM)
Asaro, M. R., 194
Asberg, K., 292
ASD. *See* Acute Stress Disorder (ASD)